*D Jali*

*Sept. 98*

**thomson com**

changing the way the world learns

To get extra value from this book for no additional cost, go to:

# http://www.thomson.com/wadsworth.html

*thomson.com* is the World Wide Web site for Wadsworth/ITP and is your direct source to dozens of on-line resources. *thomson.com* helps you find out about supplements, experiment with demonstration software, search for a job, and send e-mail to many of our authors. You can even preview new publications and exciting new technologies.

**thomson.com:** *It's where you'll find us in the future.*

## From the Wadsworth Series in Communication Studies

Milly S. Barranger, *Theatre: A Way of Seeing*, 4E

Karlyn Kohrs Campbell, *The Rhetorical Act*, 2E

Karlyn Kohrs Campbell and Thomas Burkholder, *Critiques of Contemporary Rhetoric*, 2E

Kenneth C. Crannell, *Voice and Articulation*, 3E

Austin J. Freeley, *Argumentation and Debate: Critical Thinking for Reasoned Decision Making*, 9E

Cheryl Hamilton, *Successful Public Speaking*

Cheryl Hamilton with Cordell Parker, *Communicating for Results: A Guide for Business and the Professions*, 5E

Kathleen Hall Jamieson and Karlyn Kohrs Campbell, *The Interplay of Influence: News, Advertising, Politics, and the Mass Media*, 4E

Clella Jaffe, *Public Speaking: A Cultural Perspective*

Charles U. Larson, *Persuasion: Reception and Responsibility*, 7E

Stephen Littlejohn, *Theories of Human Communication*, 5E

Gay Lumsden and Donald Lumsden, *Communicating with Credibility and Confidence*

Gay Lumsden and Donald Lumsden, *Communicating in Groups and Teams: Sharing Leadership*, 2E

Katherine Miller, *Organizational Communication: Approaches and Processes*

Rebecca Rubin, Alan Rubin, and Linda Piele, *Communication Research: Strategies and Sources*, 4E

Larry A. Samovar and Richard E. Porter, *Communication Between Cultures*, 2E

Larry A. Samovar and Richard E. Porter, *Intercultural Communication: A Reader*, 8E

Sarah Trenholm and Arthur Jensen, *Interpersonal Communication*, 3E

Julia T. Wood, *Communication in Our Lives*

Julia T. Wood, *Communication Theories in Action: An Introduction*

Julia T. Wood, *Everyday Encounters: An Introduction to Interpersonal Communication*

Julia T. Wood, *Gendered Lives: Communication, Gender, and Culture*, 2E

Julia T. Wood, *Relational Communication: Continuity and Change in Personal Relationships*

Rudolph Verderber, *The Challenge of Effective Speaking*, 10E

Rudolph Verderber, *Communicate!*, 8E

Rudolph Verderber and Kathleen Verderber, *Inter-Act: Using Interpersonal Communication Skills*, 7E

# Intercultural Communication

## A Reader

### Eighth Edition

**Larry A. Samovar**
San Diego State University

**Richard E. Porter**
California State University, Long Beach
Emeritus

Wadsworth Publishing Company
I⬤P® An International Thomson Publishing Company

Belmont • Albany • Bonn • Boston • Cincinnati • Detroit • London • Madrid • Melbourne
Mexico City • New York • Paris • San Francisco • Singapore • Tokyo • Toronto • Washington

Communication Studies Editor: Todd R. Armstrong
Assistant Editor: Lewis DeSimone
Editorial Assistant: Michael Gillespie
Production: Mary Douglas, Rogue Valley Publications
Composition: ColorType
Print Buyer: Barbara Britton
Interior Design: Harry Voigt
Cover Design: Harry Voigt
Cover Photo: Magnified crystals of vitamin C. Spike Walker/
 Tony Stone Images
Printer: Quebecor/Fairfield

*This book is printed on
acid-free recycled paper.*

**Library of Congress Cataloging-in-Publication Data**

Intercultural communication : a reader / [edited by] Larry
 A. Samovar, Richard E. Porter. — 8th ed.
   p. cm.
   Includes bibliographical references and index.
   ISBN 0-534-51573-8
   1. Intercultural communication.   I. Samovar, Larry A.
II. Porter, Richard E.
HM258.I52   1996
303.48'2 — dc20                              96-11911

**For more information, contact
Wadsworth Publishing Company**

Wadsworth Publishing Company
10 Davis Drive
Belmont, California 94002, USA

International Thomson Publishing Europe
Berkshire House 168-173
High Holborn
London, WC1V 7AA, England

Thomas Nelson Australia
102 Dodds Street
South Melbourne 3205
Victoria, Australia

Nelson Canada
1120 Birchmount Road
Scarborough, Ontario
Canada M1K 5G4

International Thomson Editores
Campos Eliseos 385, Piso 7
Col. Polanco
11560 México D.F. México

International Thomson Publishing GmbH
Königswinterer Strasse 418
53227 Bonn, Germany

International Thomson Publishing Asia
221 Henderson Road
#05-10 Henderson Building
Singapore 0315

International Thomson Publishing Japan
Hirakawacho Kyowa Building, 3F
2-2-1 Hirakawacho
Chiyoda-ku, Tokyo 102, Japan

# Table of Contents

Preface    ix

**Part One**
**Intercultural Communication: An Introduction    1**

**Chapter 1    Approaches: Understanding Intercultural Communication    3**

An Introduction to Intercultural Communication, *Richard E. Porter and Larry A. Samovar*    5

Communication in a Global Village, *Dean C. Barnlund*    27

Cultural Identity and Intercultural Communication, *Mary Jane Collier*    36

Context and Meaning, *Edward T. Hall*    45

Understanding Whiteness in the United States, *Judith N. Martin*    54

Five Paradigms of Ethnic Relations, *Rod Janzen*    63

**Part Two**
**Sociocultural Backgrounds:**
**What We Bring to Intercultural Communication    73**

**Chapter 2    International Cultures: Understanding Diversity    75**

The Impact of Confucianism on Interpersonal Relationships and Communication Patterns in East Asia, *June Ock Yum*    78

Dominant Cultural Patterns of Hindus in India, *Nemi C. Jain and Ellen D. Kussman*    89

A Comparison of Arab and American Conceptions of "Effective" Persuasion, *Janice Walker Anderson*    98

Cultural Patterns of the Maasai, *Lisa Skow and Larry A. Samovar*    107

Palevome: Foundations of Struggle and Conflict in Greek Interpersonal Communication, *Benjamin J. Broome*  116

Irish Conversations, *Martin J. Gannon*  125

**Chapter 3**   **Co-Cultures: Living in Two Cultures**  135

Who's Got the Room at the Top? Issues of Dominance and Nondominance in Intracultural Communication, *Edith A. Folb*  138

An African American Communication Perspective, *Sidney A. Ribeau, John R. Baldwin, and Michael L. Hecht*  147

Understanding Communication of Persons with Disabilities as Cultural Communication, *Dawn O. Braithwaite and Charles A. Braithwaite*  154

Gender, Communication, and Culture, *Julia T. Wood*  164

Understanding the Co-Culture of the Elderly, *Valery C. McKay*  174

**Part Three**
**Intercultural Interaction:**
**Taking Part in Intercultural Communication**  183

**Chapter 4**   **Verbal Processes: Thinking and Speaking**  187

Culture, Problem Solving, and Pedagogical Style, *Devorah A. Lieberman*  191

The Crossroads of Language and Culture, *Mary Fong*  207

That's Greek to Me: Between a Rock and a Hard Place in Intercultural Encounters, *Wen-Shu Lee*  213

Finnish and American Linguistic Patterns: A Cultural Comparison, *Donal Carbaugh*  221

Utilizing an Inductive Approach to Studying African American Male Communications, *Mark P. Orbe*  227

Language as a Mirror of Reality: Mexican American Proverbs, *Shelly M. Zormeier and Larry A. Samovar*  235

**Chapter 5**   **Nonverbal Interaction: Action, Sound, and Silence**  241

Cues of Culture: The Basis of Intercultural Differences in Nonverbal Communication, *Peter Andersen*  244

Nonverbal Communication: A Reflection of Cultural Themes, *Edwin R. McDaniel* 256

Variables in the Use of Personal Space in Intercultural Transactions, *Carol Zinner Dolphin* 266

Monochronic and Polychronic Time, *Edward T. Hall* 277

**Chapter 6    Cultural Contexts: The Influence of the Setting    285**

Cultural Influences on Communication in Multinational Organizations: The Maquiladora, *Edwin R. McDaniel and Larry A. Samovar* 289

Contrasts in Discussion Behaviors of German and American Managers, *Robert A. Friday* 297

Culture and Its Impact on Negotiation, *Lisa A. Stefani, Larry A. Samovar, and Susan A. Hellweg* 307

The "Five Asian Dragons": Management Behaviors and Organizational Communication, *Guo-Ming Chen and Jensen Chung* 317

The Group: A Japanese Context, *Dolores Cathcart and Robert Cathcart* 329

Negotiating Cultural Understanding in Health Care Communication, *Patricia Geist* 340

The Influence of Culture on Classroom Communication, *Lisa A. Stefani* 349

**Part Four**
**Intercultural Communication: Seeking Improvement    365**

**Chapter 7    Communicating Interculturally: Becoming Competent    367**

Stumbling Blocks in Intercultural Communication, *LaRay M. Barna* 370

A Model of Intercultural Communication Competence, *Brian H. Spitzberg* 379

Managing Intercultural Conflicts Effectively, *Stella Ting-Toomey* 392

Adapting to a New Culture, *Young Yun Kim* 404

Aesthetics as a Bridge to Multicultural Understanding, *James Steven Sauceda* 417

Chapter 8    Ethical Considerations: Prospects for the Future   428

The Limits to Cultural Diversity, *Harlan Cleveland*   431

Intercultural Personhood: An Integration of Eastern and Western Perspectives, *Young Yun Kim*   434

Peace as an Ethic for Intercultural Communication, *David W. Kale*   448

Epilogue   454

Index   459

# Preface

The occasion of this eighth edition of our book continues to be one of excitement. The fact that we have been received with the popularity to warrant a new edition is exciting and obviously pleasing. Yet, as we proceeded, we wanted to be cautious enough to preserve the basic framework and philosophy that has sustained us through the seven previous editions. It would have been improvident of us to abandon an orientation to intercultural communication that has found wide acceptance for over two decades. The field as well as the authors, however, have continued to evolve. We knew, therefore, that some reshaping would be necessary.

This new edition grants us the opportunity to combine two complementary positions. First, it reflects our continued belief that the basic core of the field should not be changed for the sake of simply being novel. Such change would pilfer the book of those concepts that have been infused into all the other editions. Second, it reflects our belief that as our intercultural contacts change in number and intensity, there is a need to present essays that mirror that change. We have perceived each new edition as an opportunity to examine that change and to stake out new territory for the field — territory that takes into account the complexities of communicating in the 1990s.

As the field of intercultural communication has grown, we have attempted in each new edition to grow with the field and to fuse the old with the new. In 1972, the first edition contained 34 articles and essays. The seventh edition contained 42; now we include 46 articles in our collection of readings. Some have appeared in all previous editions. In this eighth edition, we have 20 new essays, 17 of which were prepared especially for this volume.

## Approach

The basic energizing motive for this book has remained the same since both authors became interested in the topic of intercultural communication nearly 30 years ago. It is our sincere belief that the ability to communicate effectively with people from diverse cultures and co-cultures benefits each of us as individuals and has potential to benefit the other 5.5 billion people with whom we share this planet. We have intentionally selected materials that will assist you in understanding those intercultural communication principles that are instrumental to the achievement of success when interacting with people from diverse cultures.

Fundamental to our approach is the conviction that communication is a social activity; it is something people do with and to each other. While the activity might begin in our heads, it is manifested in our behaviors — be they verbal or nonverbal. In both explicit and implicit ways, the information and the advice contained in this book is usable; the ideas presented can be translated into action.

## Use

As in the past, we intend this anthology to be for the general reader. We have, consequently, selected materials that are broadly based, comprehensive, and suitable for both undergraduate and graduate students. Although the level of difficulty varies from article to article, we have not gone beyond the level found in most textbooks aimed at college and university students.

*Intercultural Communication: A Reader* is designed to meet three specific needs. The first comes from a canon which maintains that successful intercultural communication is a matter of highest importance if humankind and society are to survive. Events during the last 30 years have created a world that sees us linked together in a multitude of ways. From pollution to economics to health care, what happens to one culture has the potential to happen to all cultures. This book, then, is designed to serve as a *basic anthology* for courses concerned with the issues associated with human interaction. Our intention is to make this book theoretical and practical so that the issues associated with intercultural communication can be first understood and then acted upon.

Second, the book may be used as a *supplemental text* to existing service and basic communication skills courses and interpersonal communication courses. The rationale is a simple one: Understanding other cultures is indispensable in this age of cross-cultural contact. It matters very little if that contact is face to face or on the public platform.

Third, the book provides *resource material* for courses in communication theory, small group communication, organizational and business communication, and mass communication, as well as for courses in anthropology, sociology, social psychology, social welfare, social policy, business, and international relations. The long list of possible uses only serves to underscore the increased level of intercultural interaction that is characteristic of what is often called the "global village."

## Organization

The book is organized into four closely related parts. In Part One, "Intercultural Communication: An Introduction," our purpose is twofold: We hope to acquaint you with the basic concepts of intercultural communication while at the same time arousing your interest in the topic. Hence, the essays in this part are both theoretical and philosophical. The selections explain what intercultural communication is and why it is important.

Part Two, "Socio-Cultural Backgrounds: What We Bring to Intercultural Communication," has two chapters that both serve the same goal: They seek to examine the influence of socio-cultural forces on human interaction. Chapter Two deals with how these forces direct the communication patterns of people from international cultures. To make this point, we have selected cultures from the Arab world, East Asia, India, and Greece. While many cultures have been left out, you will still be able to gain an appreciation of the link between culture and behavior.

Chapter Three moves us from the international arena to co-cultures that operate within the United States. Here again, space constraints have limited the total number of co-cultures we could include. Yet, we believe that by having selected groups such as Latinos, African Americans, the disabled, gays and lesbians, women, and the elderly, you will get an image of the cultural diversity found in those groups with whom most of you come in contact on a regular basis. Many of these same co-cultures, and others, are so very important to the study of intercultural communication that we return to them in later chapters.

In Part Three, "Intercultural Interaction: Taking Part in Intercultural Communication," our analysis focuses on the verbal and nonverbal symbols used in intercultural communication as well as the context in which they occur. In Chapter Four, we offer readings that will introduce you to some of the difficulties you might encounter when your intercultural partner employs a different language system. We will look at how these verbal idiosyncrasies and distinctions influence problem-solving, speaking, perception, translation, interpreting, and understanding.

Chapter Five, which is also concerned with symbols, explains some of the ways in which cultural diversity in nonverbal messages can influence the entire transaction. Differences in movement, facial expressions, eye contact, silence, space, time, and the like are detailed so that you might have a better appreciation of how culture and communication work in tandem.

Chapter Six continues with the theme of how culture modifies interaction. This time, however, the interaction is examined in a specific context. The assumption is that there are culturally diverse rules that influence how members of a culture behave in certain settings. To clarify this important issue we have selected seven "places" where cultures often follow rules that differ from those found in North America. More specifically, we look at settings related to business, groups, negotiations, counseling, education, and health care.

Part Four, "Intercultural Communication: Seeking Improvement," contains two chapters concerned with improving intercultural communication. The readings offered in Chapter Seven are intended to provide you with knowledge and suggestions for improving intercultural communication. Each essay presents some type of practical recommendations.

The eighth and final chapter probes the ethical and future dimensions of intercultural communication. Essays that deal with moral issues and the future directions and challenges of intercultural communication are at the center of this chapter. It is the intent of this chapter to ask you not to conclude your study of intercultural communication with the reading of a single book or the completion of one course. We believe that the study of intercultural communication should be a lifetime endeavor. Each time we want to share an idea or feeling with someone from another culture we face a new and exhilarating learning experience. We urge everyone to seek out as many of these experiences as possible. A philosopher once wrote, "Tomorrow, when I know more, I'll recall that piece of knowledge and use it better."

## Assistance

As in the past, a number of people have helped us rethink and reshape this project. We express appreciation to our editor Todd Armstrong. And, of course, to Rebecca Hayden, who had enough courage and insight some 25 years ago to decide that intercultural communication should and would become a viable discipline. Both of these editors were stern enough to keep us in check while at the same time allowing us the flexibility to move in new directions.

In a culture that values change, this collection would not have survived for more than 25 years if we had not been fortunate enough to have so many scholars willing to contribute original essays to each of the editions. Here in the eighth edition we acknowledge the work of June Ock Yum, Nemi C. Jain, Judith N. Martin, Ellen D. Kussman, Lisa Skow, Edith A. Folb, Dawn O. Braithwaite, Charles A. Braithwaite, Julia T. Wood, Valery C. McKay, Shelly M. Zormeier, Susan A. Hellweg, Devorah A. Lieberman, Mary Fong, Mark Orbe, Edwin R. McDaniel, Lisa Stefani, Peter Andersen, LaRay M. Barna, Brian H. Spitzberg, Young Yun Kim, David W. Kale, Mary Jane Collier, Dolores Cathcart, Robert Cathcart, Stella Ting-Toomey, Sidney Ribeau, John Baldwin, Michael Hecht, Patricia Geist, James Sauceda, Tom Bruneau, and Wen-Shu Lee. We thank all of you for letting us expose your work to thousands of other people who share your commitment to intercultural matters.

Finally we express our gratitude to the countless users of prior editions who have allowed us to "talk to them" about intercultural communication. While it may have been a rather intangible connection, we have greatly appreciated it.

*Larry A. Samovar*
*Richard E. Porter*

# Part One

## Intercultural Communication: An Introduction

*Precision of communication is important, more important than ever, in our era of hair-trigger balances, when a false or misunderstood word may create as much disaster as a sudden thoughtless act.*
*— James Thurber*

Intercultural communication, as we might rightly suspect, is not new; it has existed as long as people from different cultures have been encountering one another. What is new, however, is the systematic study of exactly what happens in intercultural contacts and interactions when the communication process involves culturally diverse people.

Perhaps the initial impetus for the study of intercultural communication was the knowledge that technology has produced the means of our own self-destruction. Historically, intercultural communication, more often than not, has employed a rhetoric of force rather than reason. But, with the agents of change sweeping the world, perhaps we are now seeking forms of communication other than traditional force. The reason for this new study is also pragmatic. Our mobility, increased contact among cultures, a global economy and marketplace, and the emergence of multicultural organizations and workforces require that we develop communication skills and abilities appropriate to a multicultural society and to life in a global village.

Traditionally, intercultural communication took place only among an extremely small proportion of the world's populace. Ministers of state and government, certain merchants, missionaries, explorers, and a few tourists were primarily the travelers and visitors to foreign lands. Until rather recently, we Americans had little contact with other cultures, even within our own country. Members of nonwhite races were segregated. Only in recent years have laws changed to foster integrated schools, workforces, and, to some extent, neighborhoods. In addition, those who made up the vast white middle Euro-America remained at home, rarely leaving their own country. This situation, of course, has changed markedly; we are now a mobile society among ever increasing mobile societies.

This increased contact with other cultures and domestic co-cultures makes it imperative for us to make a concerted effort to understand and to

1

get along with people who may be vastly different from us. The ability, through increased awareness and understanding, to coexist peacefully with people who do not necessarily share our background, views, beliefs, values, customs, habits, or lifestyles can benefit us in our own neighborhoods and also can be a decisive factor in forestalling international conflict.

Before we begin our inquiry, we need to specify the nature of intercultural communication and to recognize that people holding various viewpoints see it somewhat differently. From what we have already said, you should suspect that the topic of intercultural communication can be explored in a variety of ways. Scholars who look at intercultural communication from a mass media point of view are concerned with such issues as international broadcasting, worldwide freedom of expression, Western domination of information, and the use of modern electronic technologies for instantaneous worldwide transmission of information. Other groups investigate international communication, with this emphasis on communication between nations and between governments. It is the communication of diplomacy and propaganda. Still others are interested in the communication inherent in international business, which includes such diverse concerns as negotiations and communication within multicultural organizations.

Our concern is with the more personal aspects of communication — what happens when people from different cultures interact face to face. Hence, we identify our approach as one that examines the interpersonal dimensions of intercultural communication as it occurs in a variety of contexts. We have selected articles for this collection because they focus on those variables of both culture and communication that come into play *during the communication encounter* — that time when participants from different cultures are trying to share ideas, information, and feelings.

Inquiry into the nature of intercultural communication has raised many questions, but it has produced few theories and far fewer answers. Most of the inquiry has been associated with fields other than communication, primarily anthropology, international relations, social psychology, and socio- and psycholinguistics. Although the direction of research has been diverse, the knowledge has not been coordinated. Much that has emerged has been more a reaction to current socio-racial-ethnic concerns than an attempt to define and explain intercultural communication. But it is quite clear that knowledge of intercultural communication can aid in solving communication problems before they arise. School counselors who understand some of the reasons why the poor perceive school as they do might be better able to treat young truants. Those who know that Native Americans and Latinos use eye contact in ways that differ from other Americans may be able to avert misunderstanding. And, perhaps, those who realize that some people treat illness as a curse may be better able to deliver necessary health care. In essence, we are saying that many problems can be avoided by understanding the components of intercultural communication.

# 1

## Approaches: Understanding Intercultural Communication

This exploration of intercultural communication begins with a series of diverse articles that (1) introduce the philosophy underlying our concept of intercultural communication, (2) provide a general orientation and overview of intercultural communication, (3) theorize about the analysis of intercultural transactions, (4) provide insight into cultural differences, and (5) demonstrate the relationships between culture and perception. Our purpose at this point is to give you a sufficient introduction to the many wide and diverse dimensions of intercultural communication so that you will be able to approach the remainder of this volume with an appropriate frame of reference to make your further inquiry interesting, informative, and useful.

We begin with "An Introduction to Intercultural Communication" in order to introduce some of the specific topics and issues associated with the study of intercultural communication and to present in rather broad terms what it involves. We start by defining and explaining the role of human communication. We then turn our attention to the specific areas of culture and communication and show how they interrelate to form the field of intercultural communication. By examining the major variables that affect intercultural communication, we better understand how it operates. By knowing at the outset of the book what the study of intercultural communication entails, you should have a greater appreciation for the selections that follow.

Dean C. Barnlund, in "Communication in a Global Village," traces communication and transportation developments that have led to the apparent figurative shrinking of the contemporary world and the emergence of the global community. He points out the ramifications of the global village in terms of the forms and kinds of interactions that necessarily accompany such a new community of people. Barnlund considers problems of meaning associated with cultural differences, interpersonal encounters, intercultural encounters, and the role of the "collective unconscious" in intercultural interactions.

We then turn our attention to how people come to identify with the various general and specific cultures in which they have membership. In "Cultural Identity and Intercultural Communication," Mary Jane Collier begins with an introduction to the notion of culture by considering symbols and meanings, cultural norms, cultural history, types of cultures based on national and ethnic considerations as well as gender, profession, geographic location, organizations, and physical ability or disability. She shows how each of these factors contributes to the identification of culture across a general–specific dimension. After having shown the range of cultures available to individuals, Collier discusses cultural identification, showing the diverse mechanisms by which individuals come to the particular cultural identification they hold.

Edward T. Hall, in "Context and Meaning," discusses the grand connection between culture and human communicative behavior by demonstrating how culture provides a highly selective screen between people and their outside worlds. This cultural filter effectively designates what people attend to as well as what they choose to ignore. This link between culture and behavior is further illustrated through Hall's discussion of high- and low-context communication, in which he shows how people from different cultural backgrounds learn to concentrate on the unique aspects of their environments.

With the relationship between culture and communication firmly established, we turn next to two essays that deal with the notion of ethnicity. In the first, Judith N. Martin discusses the topic of white ethnicity. In "Understanding Whiteness in the United States," she answers the question of what it means to be a white person in the United States. She provides an insight into how ethnic identities — including that of a white European American — are negotiated, co-created, reinforced, and challenged through communication. By making comparisons to other ethnic co-culture identities, Martin is able to reveal the distinctness of the white ethnic identity in order to better help us understand both the notion and uniqueness of ethnic identity.

In the second article about identity, Rod Janzen provides us with the notion that there are a number of ways in which we might conceptualize ethnic relations and ethnic identity in the United States. In "Five Paradigms of Ethnic Relations," he traces the history of ethnic identity in the United States and provides us with a set of five possible ways of conceptualizing ethnicity as our society moves into the twenty-first century. His development of the five paradigms, or categories, of ethnicity is based upon the elements of language, religion, culture, race, and political tradition.

# An Introduction to Intercultural Communication

RICHARD E. PORTER
LARRY A. SAMOVAR

"The times, they are a changin'," proclaimed Bob Dylan in his popular folk song of the 1960s. Dylan was right; the times were changing. And, as we move into the final half decade of the twentieth century, the times still "are a changin'." Numerous events have caused major changes to occur, both worldwide and locally. These changes have transformed the world into the global village forecast by Marshall McLuhan in the 1960s. From an intercultural communication perspective, four of the events leading to the development of the global village are crucial: (1) improvements in transportation technology, (2) developments in communication technology, (3) globalization of the economy, and (4) changes in immigration patterns. These events have produced major transformations in both worldwide and local patterns of communication and interaction and are of primary concern to the study of intercultural communication.

*Improvements in transportation technology* have helped to shrink the earth to a figurative global village by creating the means for people to travel almost anywhere in the world within less than a day's time. Aircraft now in the design stage will increase travel speeds so that the travel time between China and the United States, for instance, will

come to be measured in durations of minutes. Also in development are single-state-to-orbit (SSTO) rocket vehicles that will provide near-earth-orbit capabilities to an increased number of nations and cultures.

*Developments in communication technology* paralleled those in travel technology and prompted further movement toward the global village. It is now possible for people to have instantaneous vocal, graphic, and textual communication with most parts of the world. Indeed, with a few hundred dollars' worth of battery-powered equipment in the form of a facsimile machine and a cellular telephone, it is possible to be in instant oral and print communication with others in almost any place in the world while driving interstate highways in the United States. In addition, the development of the Internet and the World Wide Web have provided a means for people everywhere to interact with one another and to transmit, store, and retrieve information about nearly any topic virtually anywhere in the world.

Although these improvements in communication technology have produced many effects, three are significant to intercultural communication. First, new communication technology has created an almost free flow of news and information throughout the world and has become so important in the everyday conduct of commerce and government that it cannot be set aside. These changes have made it virtually impossible to keep communication capabilities out of the hands of common citizens. Government attempts to censor the free flow of ideas, opinions, and information have been frustrated. In China, for instance, during the Tiananmen Square demonstrations of mid-1983, the Chinese government attempted to ban foreign correspondents from reporting observed incidents, cutting their access to telephone and television broadcast facilities. American television viewers, however, were informed of many incidents by reporters using their cellular telephones to call the United States via a communications satellite. By the time the Chinese government reacted to this technology, the story and all information had long

This original essay first appeared in print in the seventh edition. This updated version appears here for the first time. All rights reserved. Permission to reprint must be obtained from the authors and the publisher. Richard E. Porter is Professor Emeritus at California State University, Long Beach, and Larry A. Samovar teaches at San Diego State University.

since been disseminated to the world. In other parts of the world, similar incidents have occurred; for example, the widespread and multiple changes that took place in the former Soviet Union are due in part to the availability of news and information. And, because of today's communication technology, events in Bosnia, as well as in Somalia and Haiti, cannot escape world scrutiny.

Second, communication technology also has dissolved our isolation. Not more than a half century ago it was virtually impossible for the average citizen to have an informed awareness of what was happening outside her or his city, let alone be informed about the world. People had to wait for reports to arrive by mail or appear in newspapers, where the news could be up to several months old. Although transcontinental and transoceanic telegraph and telephone services and the development of radio permitted essentially instantaneous contact, those channels of communication were quite easy to control in terms of who might use them and what information they might contain. The situation today is quite different. With existing communication technology we can sit in our living rooms and watch events anywhere on earth, or, indeed, in space, as these events are actually happening. Only a scant few years ago we had to wait hours, days, and even weeks to learn who won gold medals in the Olympic Games. Today, we can witness these events in our living rooms as they occur.

Third, the immediacy of this new communication technology has impacted us in another manner: In the past when news and information reception was delayed and we learned of events days, perhaps weeks, after they occurred, it was difficult to develop strong feelings about what might have happened thousands of miles away. But, consider how different is the impact of reading in a newspaper that the police have beaten someone while making an arrest from that of actually watching the videotape of the Rodney King beating. Similarly, television coverage of the Reginald Denny beating as it occurred at the outset of the 1992 riots in Los Angeles could not help but move us. The ability to deny the cruelty of these acts is virtually reduced to zero. And it hardly seems nec-

essary to mention the worldwide impact of the televised O. J. Simpson trial.

*Globalization of the economy* has further brought people together. At the end of World War II, the United States was the only military and economic superpower. Most of the rest of the world's economy was in disarray. Most industries had been destroyed, and few banks were functioning.

Because the United States escaped World War II with its industry and its banking system intact, it was the dominant economic force in the world. Only 5 percent of American businesses faced international competition. In the 1990s, however, 75 percent of American industries face international competition. This leads to interdependence among national economies and to intercultural contact in arenas of both politics and business.

As the economy has internationalized, the U.S. presence overseas has increased dramatically. Today, over 8,000 U.S. companies have international operations in foreign countries. American holdings total over $309 billion, with some $3.5 billion committed to more than 600 joint ventures with China. American companies also are engaging in joint ventures with other Asian countries. IBM, for instance, has worked with Japan to build a plant there to produce advanced versions of computer memory chips. The Allied Signal Corporation of Morristown, New Jersey, "expects to complete plans for at least 10 joint ventures or wholly owned operations in China in the next two years."[1] And a $92 million venture involving Hoa Binh Limited of Vietnam and such American companies as General Instrument, ITS, and Standard Communications is being planned to broadcast local and international television programs in the cities of Hanoi, Ho Chi Minh City, Danang, and Can Tho.[2] Additionally, young Americans are finding jobs abroad. Fourteen percent of the Stanford University business school class of 1994 elected to seek jobs abroad, compared with 6 percent in 1989. At New York University's Stern School of Business, the number of American students taking overseas jobs jumped 20 percent in 1994 compared to 1993. Student applications for the University of Michigan's overseas-study programs in 20 countries have increased 70 percent since 1992.[3] In addition, 1 million Americans apply for business passports each year, with more than 2.5 million Americans now working abroad.

Simultaneously, foreign presence in the United States has increased; over 8,000 foreign firms operate in the United States. Foreigners have invested more than $300 billion and own nearly $1.5 trillion in U.S. assets, a 200 percent increase since 1980. In 1990, overseas concerns controlled over 13 percent of American industrial assets, causing companies such as AT&T to prepare thousands of its annual stockholder reports in foreign languages. Foreign investors own more than 1 million acres of U.S. farmland and 64 percent of the commercial property in downtown Los Angeles.

The interconnectedness of the global economy seems to become more apparent on a daily basis. This was evidenced recently when key stock markets in Mexico City, Buenos Aires, Tokyo, Taipei, Hong Kong, New York, and London fell due in part to the collapse of Barings Investment Bank in London.[4] It is obvious that the strength of our economy depends on communication with and among other cultures such as those of Japan, Germany, Great Britain, the Netherlands, Korea, Italy, France, Canada, Saudi Arabia, and many smaller nations.

*Changes in immigration patterns* have also contributed to the development of the global village. Although transportation improvements, communication technology, and globalization of the economy have figuratively shrunk the world, the world's population has continued to increase and shift. In 1974, the world numbered approximately 3.9 billion people and was growing by nearly 80 million a year. Since 1974, the world's population has expanded by nearly 1.7 billion and now increases by nearly 90 million annually. This has a severe impact on ecosystems, and fresh-water supplies continue to shrink. Experts question whether the world can adequately feed and shelter the 5 billion mouths that will be added during the next 50 years. Refugees produced by population pressures in Africa and Asia already threaten to destabilize nations.[5]

Recent immigration patterns have physically shifted segments of the world population. Legal migration to North America – the United States and Canada – is nearly double what it was in the decade of the 1960s. In the 1980s, 872,704 legal immigrants entered North America from many parts of the world including sub-Saharan Africa, North Africa and western Asia, south Asia, eastern and Southeast Asia, Latin America, and the Caribbean.[6]

As a result of population growth and immigration, contacts with new cultures or with cultures that previously appeared unfamiliar, alien, and at times mysterious are becoming a normal part of our day-to-day routine. People from Vietnam, Cambodia, Laos, Cuba, Haiti, Colombia, Nicaragua, El Salvador, and Ecuador, among others, have entered the United States to become our neighbors and add to the cultural diversity of our society. As these people adjust to this culture, we will have increasing intercultural contacts in our daily lives. Adaptation to this new cultural diversity by American businesses was demonstrated recently when some telephone companies advertised in the Chinese language to remind the Chinese community to call home during the Chinese New Year holiday.

While this global phenomenon involving transportation, communication, an international economy, and migration was taking place, change was also taking place within our own boundaries. Domestic events made us focus our attention on often-demanding co-cultures. African Americans, Asians, Latinos, Native Americans, women, homosexuals, the poor, the disabled, the homeless, and countless other groups became visible and vocal as they cried out for recognition and their rightful place in our community.

This attention on co-cultures made us realize that although intercultural contact is inevitable, it is not always successful. The communicative behavior of the co-cultures frequently disturbed many of us. Their behavior seemed strange and, at times, perhaps bizarre; frequently it failed to meet our normal expectations. We discovered, in short, that intercultural communication is difficult. Even when the natural barrier of a foreign language is dissolved, we can still fail to understand and to be understood.

These communication difficulties, both in the international arena and on the domestic scene, give rise to a major premise: *The difficulty with being thrust into a global village is that we do not yet know how to live like global villagers; there are too many of us who do not want to live with "them."* Ours is a culture in which racism and ethnocentrism run deep. Although there has been a lessening of overt racial violence since the 1960s, the enduring racist-ethnocentric belief system has not been appreciably affected.

For centuries, not only Americans, but most other groups of people as well have classified themselves and their neighbors by the color of their skin. Belief in the reality of race is at the heart of how people traditionally perceive differences in those around them; it is how they define themselves. And, until recently, it was a basis used by many scientists to describe the evolution of humanity.[7] Today, an ever growing number of anthropologists and geneticists are convinced that the biological concept of race has become an antiquated approach to self and group description and identity. Recent genetic research has indicated that "people can be divided just as usefully into different groups based on the size of their teeth, or their ability to digest milk or resist malaria."[8] These characteristics are easily identified as hereditary characteristics shared by large numbers of people, and they are no more useful nor less significant than use of skin colors to delineate race. Scientists do not claim that all humans are the same, but race does not lend assistance in understanding how people are different.[9]

In many respects, racism and ethnocentrism have become institutionalized and are practiced unconsciously. The result is a structured domination of people of color by the white European American power structure. Perhaps it would behoove us to adopt the concept of race advanced by Viktor Frankl, who asserts that there are but two races of humankind: **the decent and the indecent.**[10] Both are found everywhere, and they penetrate into all groups – transcending ethnicity, national origin, religion, gender, and sexual preference. With such an approach we may be able to eliminate, or at least lessen significantly, this deep-seated antagonism and be able to assume our proper place in a global village community.

Our incapacity to yet behave as good citizens in the global village is cause for major concern because we have not learned to respect and accept one another. We must come to recognize, as Israeli Prime Minister Shimon Peres has so clearly stated: **All people have the right to be equal and the equal right to be different.** If we can recognize and operate from this assumption, we can learn to communicate with one another effectively, to learn to understand one another, even if our cultures are different. Then, when we have a strong desire to communicate, we can face and attempt to conquer the difficulties imposed upon us by cultural diversity and its impact on the communication process.

Concern with the difficulties cultural diversity poses for effective communication has given rise to the marriage of culture and communication and to the recognition of intercultural communication as a field of study. Inherent in this fusion is the idea that *intercultural communication entails the investigation of those elements of culture that most influence interaction when members of two different cultures come together in an interpersonal setting.*

To help us understand what is involved in intercultural communication we will begin with a fundamental definition: **Intercultural communication** occurs whenever a message produced in one culture must be processed in another culture. The rest of this essay will deal with intercultural communication and point out the relationships between communication, culture, intercultural communication, and cultural context.

## Communication

To understand intercultural interaction, we must first understand human communication. Understanding human communication means knowing something about what happens when people interact, why it happens, the effects of what happens, and finally what we can do to influence and maximize the results of a particular communication event.

## Understanding and Defining Communication

We begin with the basic assumption that communication is a form of human behavior derived from a need to connect and interact with other human beings. Almost everyone desires social contact with other people, and this need is met through the act of communication, which unites otherwise isolated individuals. Our behaviors become messages to which other people may respond. When we talk, we are obviously behaving; but when we wave, smile, frown, walk, shake our heads, or gesture, we also are behaving. These behaviors frequently become messages; they communicate something to someone else.

Before behaviors can become messages, however, they must meet two requirements: (1) they must be observed by someone, and (2) they must elicit a response. In other words, any behavior that elicits a response is a *message*. If we examine this last statement, we can see several implications.

First, the word *any* tells us that both verbal and nonverbal behaviors may function as messages. Verbal messages consist of spoken or written words (speaking and writing are word-producing behaviors), while nonverbal messages consist of the entire remaining behavior repertory.

Second, behavior may be either conscious or unconscious. We frequently do things without being aware of them. This is especially true when nonverbal behavior involves such habits as fingernail biting, toe tapping, leg jiggling, head shaking, staring, and smiling. Even such things as slouching in a chair, chewing gum, or adjusting glasses may be unconscious behaviors. Since a message consists of behaviors to which people may respond, we must thus acknowledge the possibility of producing messages unknowingly.

Third, we frequently behave unintentionally, in some cases uncontrollably. For instance, if we are embarrassed, we may blush or speak with vocal disfluencies; we do not intend to blush or stammer, but we do so anyway. Again, these unintentional behaviors can become messages if someone perceives them and responds to them.

This concept of conscious-unconscious, intentional-unintentional behavioral relationships gives us a basis to formulate a clearer definition of communication. **Communication** may be defined as *that which happens whenever someone responds to the behavior or the residue of the behavior of another person.* When someone perceives our behavior or its residue and attributes meaning to it, communication has taken place regardless of whether our behavior was conscious or unconscious, intentional or unintentional. If we think about this for a moment, we must realize that it is impossible for us not to behave. Being necessitates behavior. If behavior has communication potential, then it is also impossible for us not to communicate. In other words, we cannot *not* communicate.

Behavioral **residue** (just mentioned in our definition) refers to those things that remain as a record of our actions. For instance, this essay that you are reading is a behavioral residue — it resulted from certain behaviors. As the authors, we had to engage in a number of behaviors; we had to research, think, and use our word processors. Another example of behavioral residue might be the odor of cigar smoke lingering in an elevator after the cigar smoker has departed. Smoking the cigar in the elevator was the behavior; the odor is the residue. The response you have to that odor is a reflection of your past experiences and attitudes toward cigars, smoking, smoking in public places, and, perhaps, people who smoke cigars.

Our approach to communication has focused on the behavior of one individual causing or provoking a response from another by the attribution of meaning to behavior. **Attribution** means that we draw upon our past experiences and give meaning to the behavior that we observe. We might imagine that somewhere in each of our brains is a meaning reservoir in which are stored all of the experience-derived meanings we possess. These various meanings have developed throughout our lifetime as a result of our culture acting upon us as well as the result of our individual experiences within that culture. Meaning is relative to each of us because each of us is a unique human being with a unique background and a unique set of experiences. When we encounter a behavior in our environment, each of us dips into our individual, unique meaning reservoirs and selects the meaning we believe is most likely to be appropriate for the behavior encountered and the social context in which it occurred.

If someone walks up to us and says, "If you've got a few minutes, let's get a cup of coffee," we observe this behavior and respond to it by giving it meaning. The meaning we give it is drawn from our experience with language and word meaning and also from our experience with this person and the social context. Our response could vary significantly depending upon prior experiences and the circumstances. If the person is a friend, we may interpret the behavior as an invitation to sit and chat for a few minutes. On the other hand, if the behavior comes from someone with whom we have had differences, we might respond by attributing conciliatory goodwill to the message and seeing an invitation to try to settle past differences. Yet another example could be a situation in which the person is someone you have seen in a class but do not know. Then your ability to respond is diminished because you may not be able to infer fully the other person's intention. Perhaps this is someone who wants to talk about the class; perhaps it is someone who only wants companionship until the next class; or if gender differences are involved, it is perhaps someone attempting to "hit" on you. Your response to the observed behavior is dependent upon knowledge, experience, and social context.

Usually this works quite well, but at other times it fails and we misinterpret a message; we attribute the wrong meaning to the behavior we have observed. This may be brought about by inappropriate behavior when someone does or says something not intended. Or it could occur when the experiential backgrounds of people are sufficiently different that behavior is misinterpreted.

## The Ingredients of Communication

Next, we examine the *ingredients* of communication, the various components that fit together to form what we call communication. Since our purpose in studying intercultural communication is to develop communication skills to apply with conscious intent, our working definition of communi-

cation will specify intentional communication. We further define *communication* as *a dynamic transactional behavior-affecting process in which people behave intentionally to induce or elicit a particular response from another person.* Communication is complete only when the intended behavior is perceived by the intended receiver and that person responds to and is affected by the behavior. These transactions must include all conscious or unconscious, intentional or unintentional, verbal, nonverbal, and contextual stimuli that act as cues about the quality and credibility of the message. The cues must be clear to both the behavioral source of the transaction and the processor of that behavior.

This definition allows us to identify eight specific ingredients of communication within the framework of intentional communication. First is a *behavioral source.* This is a person with both a need and a desire to communicate. The need may be a social desire to be recognized as an individual, to share information with others, or to influence the attitudes and behaviors of one or more others. The source's wish to communicate indicates a desire to share his or her internal state of being with another human being. Communication, then, is really concerned with the connecting of individuals and the sharing of internal states with varying degrees of intention to influence the information, attitudes, and behaviors of others.

Internal states of being cannot be shared directly; we must rely on symbolic representations of our internal states. This brings us to the second ingredient, *encoding.* **Encoding** is an internal activity in which verbal and nonverbal behaviors are selected and arranged to create a message in accordance with the contextual rules that govern the interaction and the rules of grammar and syntax applicable to the language being used.

The result of encoding is expressive behavior that serves as a *message,* the third ingredient, to represent the internal state that is to be shared. A **message** is a set of verbal and/or nonverbal symbols that represent a person's particular state of being at a particular moment in time and space. Although encoding is an internal act that produces a message, a message is external to the source; it is the behavior or behavioral residue that must connect a source and a responder across time and space.

Messages must have a means by which they move from source to responder, so the fourth communication ingredient is the *channel,* which provides a connection between a source and a responder. A **channel** is the physical means by which a message moves between people.

The fifth ingredient is the *responder.* **Responders** observe a source's behavior or its residue and, as a consequence, become linked to the message source. Responders may be those intended by the source to receive the message, or they may be others who, by whatever circumstance, intercept and perceive the behavior once it has entered a channel. Responders have problems with messages, not unlike the problems sources have with internal states of being. Messages usually impinge on people in the form of light or sound energy, although they may be in forms that stimulate any of the senses. Whatever the form of sensory stimulation, people must convert these energies into meaningful experiences.

Converting external energies into a meaningful experience is called **decoding**, the sixth ingredient of communication. Decoding is akin to a source's act of encoding, because it also is an internal activity. Through this internal processing of a message, meaning is attributed to those behaviors that represents a source's internal state of being.

**Response**—what a person decides to do about a message — is the seventh ingredient. Responses may vary from an unconscious decision to do nothing to a conscious, immediate overt physical act of violence. If communication has been somewhat successful, the response of the message recipient will resemble to some degree that desired by the source who created the response-eliciting behavior.

The final ingredient of communication is *feedback,* information available to a source that permits her or him to make qualitative judgments about communication effectiveness. Through the interpretation of feedback, one may adjust and adapt behavior to an ongoing situation. Although feedback and response are not the same thing, they are clearly related. Response is what a person decides

to do about a message, and feedback is information about the effectiveness of communication. They are related because a message recipient's behavior is the normal source of feedback.

These eight ingredients of communication make up only a partial list of the factors that function during a communication event. In addition to these elements, when we conceive of communication as a process, several characteristics help us understand how communication actually works.

First, communication is *dynamic:* It is an ongoing, ever changing activity. As participants in communication, we constantly are affected by each other's messages and, as a consequence, we undergo continual change. Each of us in our daily lives meets and interacts with people who exert some influence over us. Each time we are influenced, we are changed in some way, which means that as we go through life we do so as continually changing, or dynamic, individuals.

A second characteristic of communication is that it is *interactive.* Communication must take place between people. This implies two or more people who bring to a communication event their own unique backgrounds and experiences that serve as a backdrop for communicative interaction. Interaction also implies a reciprocal situation in which each party attempts to influence the other — that is, each party simultaneously creates messages designed to elicit specific responses from the other.

Third, communication is *irreversible.* Once we have said something and someone has received and decoded the message, we cannot retrieve it. This circumstance sometimes results in what is called "putting your foot in your mouth." The source may send other messages in attempts to modify the effect, but it cannot be eliminated. This is frequently a problem when we unconsciously or unintentionally send a message to someone. We may affect them adversely and not even know it; then during future interactions we may wonder why that person is reacting to us in what we perceive to be an unusual manner.

Fourth, communication takes place in a *physical* and a *social context;* both establish the rules that govern the interaction. When we interact with someone, it is not in isolation but within specific physical surroundings and under a set of specific social dynamics. Physical surroundings include specific physical objects such as furniture, window coverings, floor coverings, lighting, vegetation, or the presence or absence of physical clutter; noise levels; and acoustics — as well as competing messages. Many aspects of the physical environment can and do affect communication: The comfort or discomfort of a chair, the color of the walls, or the total atmosphere of a room are but a few.

The symbolic meaning behind physical surroundings, a kind of nonverbal communication, also governs communication. Social context defines the social relationships that exist between people as well as the rules that govern the interaction. In our culture in the United States, we tend to be somewhat cavalier toward social hierarchies and to pay much less attention to them than do people in other cultures. Nevertheless, relationships such as teacher-student, employer-employee, parent-child, admiral-seaman, senator-citizen, physician-patient, and judge-attorney establish rules that specify expected behavior and thus affect the communication process.

Quite frequently, physical surroundings actually define the social context. An employer may sit behind a desk while an employee stands before the desk to receive an admonition. In a courtroom, the judge sits elevated facing the courtroom, jurors, and attorneys, indicating the social superiority of the judge to the other officers of the court. Attorneys sit side by side, indicating a social equality between accuser and accused until such time as the jury of peers renders a verdict. No matter what the social context, it will have some effect on communication. The form of language used, the respect or lack of respect shown one another, the time of day, personal moods, who speaks to whom and in what order, and the degree of nervousness or confidence people express are but a few of the ways in which the social context can affect communication.

At this point, we should see clearly that human communication does not take place in a social vacuum. Rather, communication is an intricate matrix of social acts taking place in a complex social environment that reflects the way people live and how they come to interact with and get along in their world. This social environment is culture, and if we truly are to understand communication, we must also understand culture.

## Culture

### The Basic Function of Culture

Culture is a complex, abstract, and pervasive matrix of social elements that functions as an all-encompassing form or pattern for living by laying out a predictable world in which an individual is firmly oriented. Culture enables us to make sense of our surroundings, aiding the transition from the womb to this new life.

From the instant of birth, a child is formally and informally taught how to behave. Children, regardless of their culture, quickly learn how to behave in a manner that is acceptable to adults. Within each culture, therefore, there is no need to expend energy deciding what an event means or how to respond to it. The assumption is that people who share a common culture can usually be counted on to behave "correctly" and predictably. Hence, culture reduces the chances of surprise by shielding people from the unknown. Try to imagine a single day in your life without access to the guidelines your culture provides. Without the rules that govern your actions, you would soon feel helpless. From how to greet strangers to how to spend our time, culture provides us with structure. To lack culture is to lack structure. We might even go so far as to say that "our primary mode of biological adaptation is culture, not anatomy."[11]

### Definition of Culture

We have already indicated that culture is a complex matrix of interacting elements. Culture is ubiquitous, multidimensional, complex, and all-pervasive. Because it is so broad, there is not a single definition or central theory of what it is. Definitions of culture run the gamut from "an all-encompassing phenomenon" to descriptions listing nearly all human activity. For our purposes, we define **culture** as the deposit of knowledge, experience, beliefs, values, attitudes, meanings, hierarchies, religion, notions of time, roles, spatial relations, concepts of the universe, and material objects and possessions acquired by a group of people in the course of generations through individual and group striving.

## The Ingredients of Culture

Although scholars may lack a definitive ingredient list for culture, most agree that any description should include the three categories submitted by Almaney and Alwan. They contend that

*cultures may be classified by three large categories of elements: artifacts (which include items ranging from arrowheads to hydrogen bombs, magic charms to antibiotics, torches to electric lights, and chariots to jet planes); concepts (which include such beliefs or value systems as right or wrong, God and man, ethics, and the general meaning of life); and behaviors (which refer to the actual practice of concepts or beliefs).* [12]

These authors provide an excellent example of how these three aspects might be reflected within a culture: "Whereas money is considered an artifact, the value placed upon it is a concept, but the actual spending and saving of money is behavior."[13]

Other inventories provide additional listings of the content of culture. Some of these additional ingredients of particular interest to intercultural communication include cultural history, cultural personality, material culture, role relationships, art, language, cultural stability, cultural beliefs, ethnocentrism, nonverbal behavior, spatial relations, time, recognition and reward, and thought patterns.[14]

## The Characteristics of Culture

Six characteristics of culture are of special importance to intercultural communication: (1) *culture is learned,* (2) *culture is transmissible,* (3) *culture is dynamic,* (4) *culture is selective,* (5) *the facets of culture are interrelated,* and (6) *culture is ethnocentric.*

**Culture Is Not Innate; It Is Learned** From infancy on, members of a culture learn their patterns of behavior and ways of thinking until they have become internalized. The power and influence of these behaviors and perceptions can be seen in the ways in which we acquire culture. Our culture learning proceeds through interaction, observation, and imitation. A little boy in North America whose father tells him to shake hands when he is introduced to a friend of the family is learning culture. The Arab baby who is read the Koran when he or she is one day old is learning culture. The Hindu child who lives in a home where the women eat after the men is learning culture. The Jewish child who helps conduct the Passover celebration is learning culture.

All of this learning occurs as conscious or unconscious conditioning that leads one toward competence in a particular culture.[15] This activity is frequently called **enculturation,** denoting the total activity of learning one's culture.

**Culture Is Transmissible** The symbols of a culture enable us to pass on the content and patterns of a culture. We can spread our culture through the spoken word as when the recorded voice of radio actor Brace Beemer brings us the voice of the Lone Ranger from the 1940s or when the recorded voice of President Franklin Roosevelt tells us that the date December 7, 1941, will live on "in infamy." We can use the written word as a symbol and let others learn our history by reading about the War of Independence, learn about Abraham Lincoln through reading the Gettysburg Address, or even learn cultural strategies of persuasion by reading Aristotle's *Rhetoric.*

We also can use nonverbal actions as symbols— for example, showing others that we usually shake hands to greet one another. National flags symbolize our claim to territory or demonstrate our loyalty. Rolls Royce automobiles and Rolex watches are evidence of our success and status. A cross speaks of our love for God. The use of symbols is at the core of culture.

The portability of symbols allows us to package and store them as well as transmit them. The mind, books, pictures, films, videos, and the like enable a culture to preserve what it deems to be important and worthy of transmission. Each individual, regardless of his or her generation, is heir to a massive "library" of information that has been collected in anticipation of his or her entry into the culture.

**Culture Is Dynamic** As with communication, culture is ongoing and subject to fluctuation; cultures seldom remain constant. As ideas and products evolve within a culture, they can produce change through the mechanisms of invention and diffusion.

**Invention** is usually defined as the discovery of new practices, tools, or concepts that most members of the culture eventually accept. In North America, the civil rights movement and the invention of television are two good examples of how ideas and products reshaped a culture.

Change also occurs through **diffusion,** or borrowing from another culture. The assimilation of what is borrowed accelerates as cultures come into direct contact with each other. For example, as Japan and North America share more commerce, we see Americans assimilating Japanese business management practices and the Japanese incorporating American marketing tactics.

In addition to invention and diffusion, other factors foster cultural change. The concept of *cultural calamity* illustrates how cultures change. Consider for a moment the effects of war or revolution. The calamity of Vietnam brought changes to both Vietnam and the United States. Not only did it create a new population of refugees, but it also forced us to reevaluate some cultural assumptions concerning global influence and military power. Currently, many cultural changes are taking place in Eastern Europe and the former Soviet Union. The elimination of the Berlin Wall, the unification of East and West Germany, the dissolution of the Soviet Union into numerous smaller states, and the problems of adjustment to new economies and governments are producing enormous changes in the affected cultures.

Although cultures do change, most change affects only the surface structure of the culture. The deep structure resists major alterations. While visible changes in dress, food, transportation, housing, and the like are simply attached to the existing cultural value system. Elements associated with the deep structure of a culture — such as values, ethics and morals, work and leisure, definitions of freedom, the importance of the past, religious prac-

tices, the pace of life, and attitudes toward gender and age — are so very deep in the structure of a culture that they tend to persist generation after generation. Even the demands for more liberal governments in China and Russia have their roots in the histories of those countries. In the United States, studies conducted on American values show that most of the central values of the 1990s are similar to the values of the past 200 years. When analyzing cultural change we cannot let ourselves be fooled just because downtown Tokyo looks much like Paris, London, or New York. Most of what is important in a culture is below the surface. It is like the moon — we observe the front, which appears flat and one-dimensional, but there is another side and dimensions that we cannot see.

**Culture Is Selective** Every culture represents a limited choice of behavior patterns from the infinite patterns of human experience. This selection, whether it be what shoes to wear or how to reach God, is made according to the basic assumptions and values that are meaningful to each culture. Because each individual has only these limited cultural experiences, what we know is but an abstraction of what there is to know. In other words, culture also defines the *boundaries* of different groups.[16]

This characteristic is important to all students of intercultural communication for two reasons. First, it reminds us that what a culture selects to tell each succeeding generation is a reflection of what that culture deems important. In the United States, for example, being healthy is highly valued, and therefore messages related to that idea are selected. Second, the notion of selectivity also suggests that cultures tend to separate one group from another. If one culture selects work as an end (Japan), while another emphasizes work as a means to an end (Mexico), we have a cultural separation.

**Facets of Culture Are Interrelated** This characteristic serves to inform us that culture is like a complex system. As Hall clearly states, "You touch a culture in one place and everything else is affected."[17] The women's movement in the United States may serve as an example of this. "Women's movement" may be but two simple words, but the phenomenon has been like a large stone cast into a pond. The movement has brought about changes in gender roles, sexual practices, educational opportunities, the legal system, career opportunities, and even female-male interaction.

**Culture Is Ethnocentric** The characteristic of **ethnocentrism,** being centered on one's own group, might well relate most directly to intercultural communication. The important tie between ethnocentrism and communication can be seen in the definition of the word itself. Keesing notes that ethnocentrism is a "universal tendency for any people to put its own culture and society in a central position of priority and worth."[18] Ethnocentrism, therefore, becomes the perceptual window through which a culture interprets and judges all other cultures. Ethnocentrism leads to a subjective evaluation of how another culture conducts its daily business. That this evaluation can only be negative is clear if you realize that a logical extension of ethnocentrism is the position that "our way is the right way." Most discussions of ethnocentrism even enlarge the concept to include feelings of superiority. Keesing notes, "Nearly always the folklore of a people includes myths of origin which give priority to themselves, and place the stamp of supernatural approval on their particular customs."[19]

As we have seen, culture is extremely complex and influences every aspect of our lives. There are, however, specific aspects of culture that are of particular interest in the study of intercultural communication. For the sake of simplicity and to put some limitation on our discussion, we will examine three major elements: *perceptual processes, verbal processes,* and *nonverbal processes.*

These three interacting cultural elements are the constituent elements of intercultural communication. When we combine them, as we do when we communicate, they are like the components of a quadraphonic stereo system — each one relates to and needs the other to function properly. In our discussion, we separate these elements to identify and discuss them, but in actuality they do not exist in isolation nor do they function alone.

## Perception

In its simplest sense, **perception** is the internal process by which we select, evaluate, and organize stimuli from the external environment. In other words, perception is the conversion of the physical energies of our environment into meaningful experience. A number of corollary issues arising out of this definition help explain the relationship between perception and culture. A basic belief is that people behave as they do because of the ways in which they perceive the world and that these behaviors are learned as part of their cultural experience. Whether in judging beauty or describing snow, we respond to stimuli as we do primarily because our culture has taught us to do so. We tend to notice, reflect on, and respond to those elements in our environment that are important to us. We in the United States might respond principally to a thing's size and cost, while in Japan color might be the important criterion.

**Social Perception** Social perception is the process by which we construct our unique social realities by attributing meaning to the social objects and events we encounter in our environments. It is an extremely important aspect of communication. Culture conditions and structures our perceptual processes so that we develop culturally inspired perceptual sets. These sets not only help determine which external stimuli reach our awareness but, more important, they also significantly influence the social aspect of perception — the social construction of reality — by the attribution of meaning to these stimuli. The difficulties in communication caused by this perceptual variability can best be overcome or minimized by knowing about and understanding the cultural elements that are subject to diversity, coupled with an honest and sincere desire to communicate successfully across cultural boundaries.

There are three major sociocultural elements that have a direct and major influence on the meanings we develop for our perceptions. These elements are our *belief/value/attitude systems, world view,* and *social organization.* When these three elements influence our perceptions and the meanings we develop for them, they affect our individual, subjective aspects of meanings. We all may see the same social entity and agree upon what it is in objective terms, but what the object or event means to us individually may differ considerably. Both an American and a Chinese might agree in an objective sense that a particular object is a young dog, but they might disagree completely in their interpretation of the dog. The American might see it as a cute, fluffy, loving, protective pet. The Chinese, on the other hand, might see the dog as something especially fit for the Sunday barbecue. You see, it is an American's cultural background that interprets the dog as a pet, and it is the Chinese cultural background that regards dog meat as a delicacy.

*Belief/Value/Attitude Systems* In a general sense, **beliefs** can be viewed as individually held subjective probabilities that some object or event possesses certain characteristics. A belief involves a link between the belief object and the characteristics that distinguish it. The degree to which we believe that an event or an object possesses certain characteristics reflects the level of our subjective probability and, consequently, the depth or intensity of our belief. That is, the more certain we are in a belief, the greater is the intensity of that belief.

Culture plays an important role in belief formation. Whether we accept the *New York Times,* the Bible, the entrails of a goat, tea leaves, the visions induced by peyote, or the changes specified in the Taoist *I Ching* as sources of knowledge and belief depends on our cultural backgrounds and experiences. In matters of intercultural communication, there are no rights or wrongs as far as beliefs are concerned. If someone believes that voices in the wind can guide one's behavior along the proper path, we cannot throw up our hands and declare the belief wrong (even if we believe it to be wrong); we must be able to recognize and to deal with that belief if we wish to obtain satisfactory and successful communication.

**Values** are the valuative aspect of our belief/value/attitude systems. Valuative dimensions include qualities such as usefulness, goodness, aesthetics, need satisfaction, and pleasure. Although each of us has a unique set of personal values,

other, cultural values also tend to permeate a culture. **Cultural values** are a set of organized rules for making choices, reducing uncertainty, and reducing conflicts within a given society. They are usually derived from the larger philosophical issues inherent in a culture. These values are generally normative in that they inform a member of a culture what is good and bad, right and wrong, true and false, positive and negative, and so on. Cultural values define what is worth dying for, what is worth protecting, what frightens people, what are considered to be proper subjects for study or ridicule, and what types of events lead individuals to group solidarity. Cultural values also specify which behaviors are important and which should be avoided within a culture.

Values express themselves within a culture as rules that prescribe the behaviors that members of the culture are expected to perform. These are called **normative** values. Thus, Catholics are supposed to attend Mass, motorists are supposed to stop at stop signs, and workers in our culture are supposed to arrive at work at the designated time. Most people follow normative behaviors; a few do not. Failure to do so may be met with either informal or codified sanctions. The Catholic who avoids Mass may receive a visit from a priest; the driver who runs a stop sign may pay a fine; and the employee who is tardy too frequently may be discharged.

Normative values also extend into everyday communicative behavior by specifying how people are to behave in specific communication contexts. This extension acts as a guide to individual and group behavior that minimizes or prevents harm to individual sensitivities within cultures.

Beliefs and values contribute to the development and content of *attitudes*. An **attitude** may be defined formally as a learned tendency to respond in a consistent manner to a given object of orientation. This means that we tend to avoid those things we dislike and to embrace those we like. Attitudes are learned within a cultural context. Whatever cultural environment surrounds us helps shape and form our attitudes – our readiness to respond – and ultimately our behavior.

*World View* This cultural element, though somewhat abstract, is one of the most important elements found in the perceptual aspects of intercultural communication. World view deals with a culture's orientation toward such philosophical issues as God, humanity, nature, the universe, and others that are concerned with the concept of being. In short, our world view helps us locate our place and rank in the universe. Because world view is so complex, it is often difficult to isolate during an intercultural interaction. In this examination, we seek to understand its substance and its elusiveness.

World view issues are timeless and represent the most fundamental bases of a culture. A Catholic's world view differs from that of a Moslem, Hindu, Jew, Taoist, or atheist. The way in which Native Americans view the individual's place in nature differs sharply from the Euro-American's view. Native Americans see themselves as one with nature; they perceive a balanced relationship between humankind and the environment, a partnership of equality and respect. Euro-Americans, on the other hand, see a human-centered world in which humans are supreme and are apart from nature. They may treat the universe as theirs—a place to carry out their desires and wishes through the power of science and technology.

World view influences a culture at very profound levels. Its effects are often quite subtle and not revealed in such obvious and often superficial ways as dress, gestures, and vocabulary. We can think of a world view as analogous to a pebble tossed into a pond. Just as the pebble causes ripples that spread and reverberate over the entire surface of the pond, world view likewise spreads itself over a culture and permeates every facet of it. World view influences beliefs, values, attitudes, uses of time, and many other aspects of culture. In its subtle way, it is a powerful influence in intercultural communication because, as a member of a culture, each communicator's world view is so deeply imbedded in the psyche that it is taken for granted; and each communicator tends to assume automatically that everyone else views the world as he or she does.

*Social Organization* The manner in which a culture organizes itself and its institutions also affects how members of the culture perceive the world and how they communicate. It might be helpful to look directly at two of the dominant social units found in a culture.

The *family*, although it is the smallest social organization in a culture, is one of the most influential. The family sets the stage for a child's development during the formative periods of life, presents the child with a wide range of cultural influences that affect almost everything from his or her first attitudes to the selection of toys, and guides the child's acquisition of language and the amount of emphasis placed on it. Skills from vocabulary building to developing dialects are the purview of the family. The family also offers and withholds approval, support, rewards, and punishments, having a marked effect on the values children develop and the goals they pursue. If, for example, children learn by observation and communication that silence is paramount in their culture, as Japanese children do, they will reflect that aspect of culture in their behavior and bring it to intercultural settings.

The *school* is another social organization that is important. By definition and history, schools are endowed with major portion of the responsibility for passing on and maintaining a culture. They are a community's basic link with its past as well as its taskmaster for the future. Schools maintain culture by relating to new members what has happened, what is important, and what one as a member of the culture must know. Schools may teach geography or wood carving, mathematics or nature lore; they may stress revolution based on peace or predicated on violence, or they may relate a particular culturally accepted version of history. But whatever is taught in a school is determined by the culture in which that school exists.

## Verbal Processes

Verbal processes include not only how we talk to each other but also the internal activities of thinking and developing meaning for the words we use. These processes, verbal language and patterns of thought, are vitally related to perception and the attachment and expression of meaning.

**Verbal Language** Any discussion of language in intercultural settings must include an investigation of language issues in general before dealing with specific problems of foreign language, language translation, and the argot and vernacular of cocultures. Here, in our introduction to the various dimensions of culture, we will look at verbal language as it relates to our understanding of culture.

In the most basic sense, **language** is an organized, generally agreed upon, learned symbol system used to represent human experiences within a geographic or cultural community. Each culture places its own individual imprint on word symbols. Objects, events, experiences, and feelings have a particular label or name solely because a community of people has arbitrarily decided to so name them. Thus, because language is an inexact system of symbolically representing reality, the meanings for words are subject to a wide variety of interpretations.

Language is the primary vehicle by which a culture transmits its beliefs, values, norms, and world view. Language gives people a means of connecting and interacting with other members of their culture and a means of thinking. Language thus serves as a mechanism for communication and as a guide to social reality. Language influences perceptions, transmits meaning, and helps mold patterns of thought.

**Patterns of Thought** The mental processes, forms of reasoning, and approaches to problem solving prevalent in a community make up another major component of culture. Unless they have had experiences with people from other cultures who follow different patterns of thought, most people assume everyone thinks and solves problems in much the same way. We must be aware, however, that there are cultural differences in aspects of thinking and knowing. This diversity can be clarified and related to intercultural communication by making a general comparison between European and Asian patterns of thought. In most European thought there is an assumption of a direct relationship between mental concepts and the concrete world of reality. This orientation places great stock in logical considerations and rationality. There is a belief that truth is out there somewhere and that it can be discovered by following correct logical sequences – one need only turn over the right rocks in the right order and truth will be there. The Asian view, best illustrated by Taoist thought, holds that problems are solved quite differently. To begin with, people are not granted instant rationality; truth is not found by active searching and the application of Aristotelian modes of reasoning. On the contrary, individuals must prepare themselves to receive truth and then wait. If truth is to be known, it will make itself apparent. The major difference in these two views is in the area of activity. To the Western mind, human activity is paramount and ultimately will lead to the discovery of truth; in the Taoist tradition, truth is the active agent, and if it is to be known, it will make itself apparent.

A culture's thought patterns affect the way individuals in that culture communicate, which in turn affects the way each person responds to individuals from another culture. We cannot expect everyone to employ the same patterns of thinking, but understanding that many patterns exist and learning to accommodate them will facilitate our intercultural communication.

## Nonverbal Processes

Verbal processes are the primary means for the exchange of thoughts and ideas, but closely related nonverbal processes often can overshadow them. Most authorities agree that the realm of nonverbal processes comprises the following topics: gestures, facial expressions, eye contact and gaze, posture and movement, touching, dress, objects and artifacts, silence, space, time, and paralanguage. As we turn to the cultural nonverbal processes relevant to intercultural communication, we will consider three aspects: *nonverbal behavior* that functions as a silent form of language, the *concept of time,* and *the use and organization of space.*

**Nonverbal Behavior** It would be foolish for us to try to examine all of the elements that constitute nonverbal behavior because of the tremendous range of activity included in this form of human activity. An example or two will enable us to visualize how nonverbal issues fit into the overall scheme of intercultural understanding. For example, touch can demonstrate how nonverbal communication is a product of culture. German women as well as men shake hands at the outset of every social encounter; in the United States, women are less likely to shake hands. Vietnamese men do not shake hands with women or elders unless the woman or the elder offers the hand first. In Thailand, people do not touch in public, and to touch someone on the head is a major social transgression. You can imagine the problems that would arise if one did not understand some of these differences.

Another example of nonverbal communication is eye contact. In the United States we are encouraged to maintain good eye contact when we communicate. In Japan and other Asian countries, however, eye contact often is not important; and among Native Americans, children are taught that eye contact with an adult is a sign of disrespect.

The eyes can also be used to express feelings. For instance, widening the eyes may note surprise for an Anglo, but the feelings denoted by eye widening are culturally diverse. Widened eyes may also indicate anger by a Chinese, a request for help or assistance by a Latino, the issuance of a challenge by a French person, and a rhetorical or persuasive effect by an African American.

As a component of culture, nonverbal expression has much in common with language: Both are coding systems that we learn and pass on as part of the cultural experience. Just as we learn that the word *stop* can mean "to halt or cease," we also learn that an arm held up in the air with the palm facing another person frequently means the same thing. Because most nonverbal communication is culturally based, what it symbolizes often is a case of what a culture has transmitted to its members. The nonverbal symbol for suicide, for example, varies among cultures. In the United States it is usually a finger pointed at the temple or drawn across the throat. In Japan, it is a hand thrust onto the stomach, and in New Guinea it is a hand placed on the neck. Both nonverbal symbols and the responses they generate are part of cultural experience, what is passed from

generation to generation. Every symbol takes on significance because of one's past experience with it. Even such simple acts as waving the hand can produce culturally diverse responses. In the United States, we tend to wave good-bye by placing the hand out with the palm down and moving the hand up and down; in India and in parts of Africa and South America, this is a beckoning gesture. We should also be aware that what may be a polite or friendly gesture in one culture may be an impolite and obscene gesture in another. Culture influences and directs those experiences and is, therefore, a major contributor to how we send, receive, and respond to nonverbal symbols.

**The Concept of Time** A culture's concept of time is its philosophy toward the past, present, and future and the importance or lack of importance it places on time. Most Western cultures think of time in lineal-spatial terms; we are time-bound and well aware of the past, present, and future. In contrast, the Hopi Indians pay very little attention to time. They believe that each object — whether a person, plant, or animal — has its own time system. Even within the dominant mainstream of American culture, we find groups that perceive time in ways that appear strange to many outsiders. Latinos frequently refer to Mexican or Latino time when their timing differs from the predominant Anglo concept, and African Americans often use what is referred to as "hang loose" time — a concept of time that gives priority to what is happening at that instant.

**Use of Space** The way in which people use space as a part of interpersonal communication is called **proxemics.** It involves not only the distance between people engaged in conversation but also their physical orientation. Arabs and Latinos, for example, tend to be physically closer when they interact than are North American Anglos. It is important to realize that people of different cultures have different ways in which they relate to one another spatially. When talking to someone from another culture, therefore, we must realize that what would be a violation of our personal space in our culture is not so intended by the other person. We may experience feelings that are difficult to handle; we may believe that the other person is overbearing, boorish, or even making inappropriate, unacceptable sexual advances when indeed the other person's movements are only manifestations of his or her cultural learning about how to use space.

Physical orientation is also culturally influenced, and it helps to define social relationships. North Americans prefer to sit where they are face to face or at right angles to one another. We seldom seek side-by-side arrangements. Chinese, on the other hand, often prefer a side-by-side arrangement and may feel uncomfortable when placed in a face-to-face situation.

We also tend to define social hierarchies through our nonverbal use of space. Sitting behind a desk while speaking with someone who is standing is usually a sign of a superior-subordinate relationship, with the socially superior person seated. Misunderstandings can easily occur in intercultural settings when two people, each acting according to the dictates of his or her culture, violate each other's expectations. If we were to remain seated when expected to rise, for example, we could easily violate a cultural norm and unknowingly insult our host or guest.

Room furnishings and size can also be an indication of social status. In corporate America, status within the corporation is often measured by desk size, office size, and the presence of carpet on the office floor (and whether the carpet is wall-to-wall or a mere rug).

How we organize space also is a function of our culture. Our homes, for instance, preserve nonverbally our cultural beliefs and values. In South America, house designs preserve privacy with only one door opening onto the street and everything else behind walls. North Americans are used to large unwalled front yards with windows looking into the house, allowing passers-by to see what goes on inside. In South America, a North American is liable to feel excluded and wonder what goes on behind all those closed doors.

## Intercultural Communication

The link between culture and communication is crucial to understanding intercultural communication because it is through the influence of culture that people learn to communicate. A Korean, an Egyptian, or an American learns to communicate like other Koreans, Egyptians, or Americans. Their behavior conveys meaning because it is learned and shared; it is cultural. People view their world through categories, concepts, and labels that are products of their culture.

Cultural similarity in perception makes the sharing of meaning possible. The ways in which we communicate, the circumstances of our communication, the language and language style we use, and our nonverbal behaviors are primarily all a response to and a function of our culture. And, as cultures differ from one another, the communication practices and behaviors of individuals reared in those cultures will also be different.

Our contention is that intercultural communication can best be understood as cultural diversity in the perception of social objects and events. A central tenet of this position is that minor communication problems are often exaggerated by perceptual diversity. To understand others' worlds and actions, we must try to understand their perceptual frames of reference; we must learn to understand how they perceive the world. In the ideal intercultural encounter, we would hope for many overlapping experiences and a commonalty of perceptions. Cultural diversity, however, tends to introduce us to dissimilar experiences and, hence, to varied and frequently strange and unfamiliar perceptions of the external world.

In all respects, everything so far said about communication and culture applies to intercultural communication. The functions and relationships between the components of communication obviously apply, but what especially characterizes intercultural communication is that sources and responders come from different cultures. This alone is sufficient to identify a unique form of communicative interaction that must take into account the role and function of culture in the communication process.

In this section, intercultural communication will first be defined and then discussed through the perspective of a model. Finally, its various forms will be shown.

## Intercultural Communication Model

**Intercultural communication** occurs whenever a message that must be understood is produced by a member of one culture for consumption by a member of another culture. This circumstance can be problematic because, as we have already seen, culture forges and shapes the individual communicator. Culture is largely responsible for the construction of our individual social realities and for our individual repertoires of communicative behaviors and meanings. The communication repertoires people possess can vary significantly from culture to culture, leading to all sorts of difficulties. Through the study and understanding of intercultural communication, however, these difficulties can at least be reduced and at best nearly eliminated.

Cultural influence on individuals and the problems inherent in the production and interpretation of messages between cultures are illustrated in Figure 1. Here, three cultures are represented by three distinct geometric shapes. Cultures A and B are purposefully similar to each other and are represented by a square and an irregular octagon that resembles a square. Culture C is intended to be quite different from Cultures A and B. It is represented both by its circular shape and its physical distance from Cultures A and B. Within each represented culture is another form similar to the shape of the influencing parent culture. This form represents a person who has been molded by his or her culture. The shape representing the person, however, is somewhat different from that of the parent culture. This difference suggests two things: First, there are other influences besides culture that affect and help mold the individual; and, second, although culture is the dominant shaping force on an individual, people vary to some extent from one another within any culture.

Message production, transmission, and interpretation across cultures is illustrated by the series of triangles connecting them. When a message leaves the culture in which it was encoded, it carries the content intended by its producer. This is represented

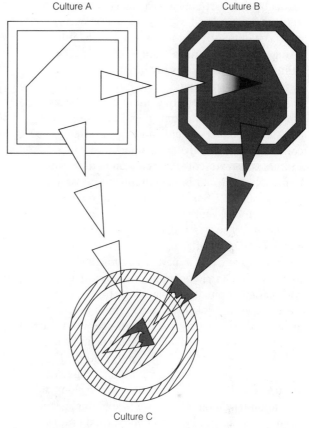

Culture A          Culture B

Culture C

**Figure 1** Model of intercultural communication.

by the triangles leaving a culture having the same pattern as that within the message producer. When a message reaches the culture where it is to be interpreted, it undergoes a transformation because the culture in which the message is decoded influences the message interpretation and hence its meaning. The content of the original message changes during that interpretation phase of intercultural communication because the culturally different repertoires of social reality, communicative behaviors, and meanings possessed by the interpreter do not coincide with those possessed by the message producer.

The degree of influence culture has on intercultural communication is a function of the dissimilarity between the cultures. This also is indicated in the model by the degree of pattern change that occurs in the message triangles. The change that occurs between Cultures A and B is much less than the change between Cultures A and C and between Cultures B and C. This is because there is greater similarity between Cultures A and B. Hence, the repertories of social reality, communicative behaviors, and meanings are similar; and the interpretation effort produces results more nearly like the content intended in the original message. Since Culture C is represented as being quite different from Cultures A and B, the interpreted message is considerably different and more nearly represents the pattern of Culture C.

The model suggests that there can be wide variability in cultural differences during intercultural communication, due in part to circumstances or forms. Intercultural communication occurs in a wide variety of situations that range from interactions between people for whom cultural differences are extreme to interactions between people who are members of the same dominant culture and whose differences are reflected in the values and perceptions of co-cultures existing within the dominant culture. If we imagine differences varying along a minimum-maximum dimension (see Figure 2), the degree of difference between two cultural groups depends on their relative social uniqueness. Although this scale is unrefined, it allows us to examine intercultural communication acts and gain insight into the effect cultural differences have on communication. To see how this dimensional scale helps us understand intercultural communication, we can look at some examples of cultural differences positioned along the scale.

The first example represents a case of maximum differences – those found between Asian and Western cultures. This may be typified as an interaction between two farmers, one who works on a communal farm on the outskirts of Beijing in China and the other who operates a large mechanized and automated soybean, corn, and dairy farm in Michigan. In this situation, we would expect to find the greatest number of diverse cultural factors. Physical appearance, religion, philosophy, economic systems, social attitudes, language, heritage, basic conceptu-

**Figure 2** Arrangement of compared cultures, subcultures, and subgroups along a scale of minimum to maximum sociocultural differences.

alizations of self and the universe, and degree of technological development are cultural factors that differ sharply. We must recognize, however, that these two farmers also share the commonalty of farming, with its rural lifestyle and love of land. In some respects, they may be more closely related than they are to members of their own cultures who live in large urban settings. In other words, across some cultural dimensions, the Michigan farmer may have more in common with the Chinese farmer than with a Wall Street securities broker.

Another example nearer the center of the scale is the difference between American culture and

German culture. Less variation is found: Physical characteristics are similar, and the English language is derived in part from German and its ancestor languages. The roots of both German and American philosophy are found in ancient Greece, and most Americans and Germans share some form of the Judeo-Christian tradition. Yet there are some significant differences. Germans have political and economic systems that are different from those found in the United States. German society tends toward formality while in the United States we tend toward informality. Germans have memories of local warfare and the destruction of their cities and economy, of having been a defeated nation on more than one occasion. The United States has never lost a war on its own territory.

Examples near the minimal end of the dimension can be characterized in two ways. First are variations found between members of separate but similar cultures — for instance, between U.S. Americans and English-Canadians. The differences are less than those found between American and German cultures, between American and Greek cultures, between American and British cultures, or even between American and French-Canadian cultures, but greater than generally found within a single culture. Second, minimal differences also may be seen in the variation between co-cultures within the same dominant culture. Sociocultural differences may be found between members of the Catholic church and the Baptist church; environmentalists and those who advocate further development of Alaskan oil resources; middle-class Americans and the urban poor; mainstream Americans and the gay and lesbian community; the able and the disabled; or male-dominance advocates and female-equality advocates.

In both of these categorizations, members of each cultural group have much more in common than do the examples found in the middle or at the maximum end of the scale. They probably speak the same language, share the same general religion, attend the same schools, and live in the same neighborhoods. Yet, these groups to some extent are culturally different; they do not fully share their experiences, nor do they share their perceptions. They see their worlds differently.

## Communication Context

Any communicative interaction takes place within some social and physical context. When people are communicating within their culture, they are usually aware of the context and it does little to hinder the communication. When people are engaged in intercultural communication, however, the context in which that communication takes place can have a strong impact. Unless both parties to intercultural communication are aware of how their culture affects the contextual element of communication, they can be in for some surprising communication difficulty.

## Context and Communication

We begin with the assumption that communicative behavior is governed by **rules**, principles or regulations that govern conduct and procedure. Communication rules act as a system of expected behavior patterns that organize interaction between individuals. Communication rules are both culturally and contextually bound. Although the social setting and situation may determine the type of rule that is appropriate, the culture determines the rules. In Iraq, for instance, a contextual rule prohibits females from having unfamiliar males visit them at home; in the United States, however, it is not considered socially inappropriate for unknown males to visit females at home. Rules dictate behavior by establishing appropriate responses to stimuli for a particular communication context.

Communication rules include both verbal and nonverbal components; the rules determine not only what should be said but also how it should be said. Nonverbal rules apply to proper gestures, facial expressions, eye contact, proxemics, vocal tone, and body movements. Unless we are prepared to function in the contextual environment of another culture, we may be in for a disappointing experience. The intercultural situation can be one of high stress, both physically and mentally. The effects of this stress are called *culture shock.* In order to avoid culture shock, we need to have a full understanding of communication context and how it differs culturally. We must remember that cultural

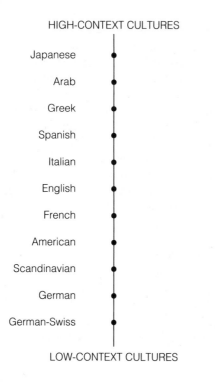

HIGH-CONTEXT CULTURES

Japanese

Arab

Greek

Spanish

Italian

English

French

American

Scandinavian

German

German-Swiss

LOW-CONTEXT CULTURES

**Figure 3** High- and low-context cultures.[11]

contexts are neither right nor wrong, better nor worse; they are just different.

Having determined that cultures develop rules that govern human interaction in specific contexts, we now need to gain some insight into a general concept of context. Anthropologist Edward T. Hall has written extensively about context.[20] Although he categorizes cultures as being either high-context or low-context, context really is a cultural dimension that ranges from high to low. Figure 3 places various cultures along that dimension.[21]

In high-context cultures most of the information is in the physical context or is internalized in the people who are a part of the interaction. Very little information is actually coded in the verbal message. In low-context cultures, however, most of the information is contained in the verbal message, and very little is embedded in the context or within the participants. In high-context cultures such as those of Japan, Korea, and Taiwan, people tend to be more

aware of their surroundings and their environment and do not rely on verbal communication as their main information source. The Korean language contains the word *nunchi,* which literally means "being able to communicate through your eyes." In high-context cultures, so much information is available in the environment that it is unnecessary to state verbally what is obvious. Oral statements of affection, for instance, are very rare; when the context says "I love you," it is not necessary to state it orally.

There are four major differences in how high- and low-context cultures affect the setting. First, verbal messages are extremely important in low-context cultures. It is in the verbal message that the information to be shared is coded; it is not readily available from the environment because people in low-context cultures tend not to learn how to perceive information from the environment. Second, low-context people who rely primarily on verbal messages for information are perceived as less attractive and less credible by people in high-context cultures. Third, people in high-context cultures are more adept at reading nonverbal behavior and the environment. Fourth, people in high-context cultures have an expectation that others are also able to understand the unarticulated communication; hence, they do not speak as much as people from low-context cultures.

## Summary

In many respects the relationship between culture and communication is reciprocal; each affects and influences the other. What we talk about, how we talk about it; what we see, attend to, or ignore; how we think; and what we think about are influenced by our culture. In turn, what we talk about, how we talk about it, and what we see help shape, define, and perpetuate our culture. Culture cannot exist without communication; one cannot change without causing change in the other.

We suggested that the chief problem associated with intercultural communication is error in social perception brought about by the cultural diversity that affects the perceptual process. The attribution of meaning to messages is in many respects influenced by the culture of the person responding to the message behavior. When the message being interpreted is encoded in another culture, the cultural influences and experiences that produced the message may have been entirely different from the cultural influences and experiences that are being drawn on to interpret and respond to the message. Consequently, unintended errors in meaning attribution may arise because people with entirely different backgrounds are unable to understand one another accurately.

We discussed several sociocultural variables that are major sources of communication difficulty. Although they were discussed in isolation, we cannot permit ourselves to conclude that they are unrelated; they are all related in a matrix of cultural complexities. For successful intercultural communication, we must be aware of these cultural factors affecting communication in both our own culture and the culture of the other party. We need to understand not only cultural differences, which will help us determine sources of potential problems, but also cultural similarities, which will help us become closer to one another.

The approach we have taken is also based on a fundamental assumption: *The parties to intercultural communication must have an honest and sincere desire to communicate and to seek mutual understanding.* This assumption requires favorable attitudes about intercultural communication and an elimination of superior-inferior relationships based on membership in particular cultures, races, religions, or ethnic groups. Unless this basic assumption has been satisfied, our theory of cultural diversity in social perception will not produce improvement in intercultural communication.

At the beginning of this article we mentioned how changes in transportation and communication technology have brought us to the brink of the global village. We also suggested that we, as a people, do not yet know how to live as global villagers. We want to return to this point as we finish and leave you with some thoughts about it.

The prevailing direction in the United States today seems to be toward a pluralistic, multicultural society. An underlying assumption of this position, one that is seldom expressed or perhaps seldom realized, is that this requires that we as a society be accepting of the views, values, and behaviors of other cultures. This means that we must be willing to "live and let live." We do not seem able or willing to do this, however, nor are we sure that it is proper to do so in all circumstances. But if we are to get along with one another, we must develop toleration for others' culturally diverse customs and behaviors — a task that will be difficult.

Even within the dominant mainstream culture, we are unable to accept diversity; for example, we find ourselves deeply divided over such issues as right to life versus freedom of choice. When we must cope with the diversity of customs, values, views, and behaviors inherent in a multicultural society, we find ourselves in much greater states of frustration and peril. Three closely timed events covered extensively in the news media serve as examples of our difficulty. Cable News Network (CNN) carried a story on March 2, 1990, about fundamentalist Christians in a southern community who were demanding the removal of a statue of Buddha from the front of an Asian restaurant because "it is the idol of a false god; it's in the New Testament." Also, news media carried a story about a judge who dismissed wife-beating charges against an Asian man because this behavior was appropriate and acceptable in the man's culture. The action by the judge was immediately assailed by the feminist movement even though the judge had admonished the man that he could not persist in this behavior in the future because it is not acceptable in this society and further charges would not be dropped. The final event was a series of news reports in the Los Angeles print media relating to the disappearance of young dogs and puppies in portions of the Los Angeles area where there had been an influx of Southeast Asian immigrants. The speculation was that these animals were ending up on barbecue spits, since dog meat is considered a delicacy by these immigrants.

These events have led us to conclude that there are some major obstacles we must overcome if we are to become proper members of the global village. Perhaps the greatest challenge is in determining what rules will govern the global village and, perhaps more importantly, who will generate those rules. We want to raise this issue here because it is important and worthy of much consideration. We do not have the answers, but we can formulate the questions and provide some guidelines for thinking about the answers.

We believe it is necessary to start from an assumptive position: *Cultural diversity is desirable and we elect to embrace and become a multicultural society*. We realize that our question about who writes the rules has a pragmatic answer: the dominant culture. But ours is an axiological concern: What ought to be the rules that govern interaction in a culturally diverse, truly multicultural society? And, who ought to be determining these rules?

What we may really be asking is, How much cultural diversity in the major aspects of social behavior can we permit and still remain cohesive as a society? Ought we to or can we permit wife beating among co-cultures if wife beating is a part of a co-culture's heritage? When we go out on our patios on Sunday afternoon and place a piece of dead steer on our barbecue, ought we to or can we permit our Southeast Asian neighbor to place a dead puppy on his or her barbecue spit if eating dog meat is a part of that cultural heritage? Ought we to or can we permit Samoan adults to discipline their children by harsh beatings if that behavior is a part of the Samoan cultural tradition? Ought we to or can we permit Asian parents to treat their children's illnesses by coining, where the child is rubbed with a coin that leaves long bruises on the back and arms in order to drive out the evil that is causing the child to be sick?

As our society continues to accept immigrants and refugees, we will find a continuing increase in cultural diversity. If we continue to assert actively the value of cultural diversity and claim to embrace and accept a multicultural global village orientation, we must be prepared to accept and tolerate the inherent diversity. A culturally diverse society can exist if and only if diversity is permitted to flourish.

We cannot solve the problem here, but we hope that you will continue to think about these issues because the time is upon us when we must adapt ourselves to the multicultural society that goes with the global village. And the manner in which we can adapt to the changing population will in large mea-sure determine how these problems are solved. We hope that your thinking about these issues now will better prepare you for life in the global village.

## Notes

1. "Pacific Watch," Los Angeles *Times*, July 3, 1995, p. D4.

2. "Pacific Watch," Los Angeles *Times*, January 30, 1995, p. D5.

3. *Time*, September 19, 1994, p. 44.

4. Los Angeles *Times*, February, 28, 1995, p. D1.

5. *Time*, June 20, 1994, p. 74.

6. Los Angeles *Times*, July 12, 1994, p. H6.

7. Robert Lee Holz, "Is Concept of Race a Relic?" Los Angeles *Times*, April 15, 1995, p. A1.

8. Ibid.

9. Ibid.

10. Viktor Frankl, *Man's Search for Meaning* (Boston: Beacon Press, 1962), pp. 86–87.

11. Marvin Harris, *Cows, Pigs, Wars, and Witches: The Riddles of Culture* (New York: Random House, 1974), p. 84.

12. A. J. Almaney and A. J. Alwan, *Communicating with the Arabs* (Prospect Heights, Ill.: Waveland Press, 1982), p. 5.

13. Ibid., p. 5.

14. Carley H. Dodd, *Dynamics of Intercultural Communication*, 2d ed. (Dubuque: Wm. C. Brown, 1987), pp. 40–49.

15. E. Adamson Hoebel and Everett L. Frost, *Cultural and Social Anthropology* (McGraw-Hill, 1974), p. 58.

16. Edward T. Hall, *Beyond Culture* (Garden City, N.Y.: Anchor, 1977), pp. 13–14.

17. Ibid.

18. Felix M. Keesing, *Cultural Anthropology: The Science of Custom* (New York: Holt, Rinehart and Winston, 1965), p. 46.

19. Ibid.

20. Hall, *Beyond Culture*.

21. L. Copeland and L. Griggs, *Going International: How to Make Friends and Deal Effectively in the Global Marketplace* (New York: Random House, 1985).

# Communication in a Global Village

## DEAN C. BARNLUND

*Nearing Autumn's close.*
*My neighbor—*
*How does he live, I wonder?*
— Bashō

These lines, written by one of the most cherished of *haiku* poets, express a timeless and universal curiosity in one's fellow man. When they were written, nearly three hundred years ago, the word "neighbor" referred to people very much like one's self—similar in dress, in diet, in custom, in language—who happened to live next door. Today relatively few people are surrounded by neighbors who are cultural replicas of themselves. Tomorrow we can expect to spend most of our lives in the company of neighbors who will speak in a different tongue, seek different values, move at a different pace, and interact according to a different script. Within no longer than a decade or two the probability of spending part of one's life in a foreign culture will exceed the probability a hundred years ago of ever leaving the town in which one was born. As our world is transformed our neighbors increasingly will be people whose life styles contrast sharply with our own.

The technological feasibility of such a global village is no longer in doubt. Only the precise date of its attainment is uncertain. The means already exist: in telecommunication systems linking the world by satellite, in aircraft capable of moving people faster than the speed of sound, in computers which can disgorge facts more rapidly than men can formulate their questions. The methods for bringing people closer physically and electronically are clearly at hand. What is in doubt is whether the erosion of cultural boundaries through technology will bring the realization of a dream or a nightmare. Will a global village be a mere collection or a true community of men? Will its residents be neighbors capable of respecting and utilizing their differences, or clusters of strangers living in ghettos and united only in their antipathies for others?

Can we generate the new cultural attitudes required by our technological virtuosity? History is not very reassuring here. It has taken centuries to learn how to live harmoniously in the family, the tribe, the city, state, and the nation. Each new stretching of human sensitivity and loyalty has taken generations to become firmly assimilated in the human psyche. And now we are forced into a quantum leap from the mutual suspicion and hostility that have marked the past relations between peoples into a world in which mutual respect and comprehension are requisite.

Even events of recent decades provide little basis for optimism. Increasing physical proximity has brought no millennium in human relations. If anything, it has appeared to intensify the divisions among people rather than to create a broader intimacy. Every new reduction in physical distance has made us more painfully aware of the psychic distance that divides people and has increased alarm over real or imagined differences. If today people occasionally choke on what seem to be indigestible differences between rich and poor, male and female, specialist and nonspecialist within cultures, what will happen tomorrow when people must assimilate and cope with still greater contrasts in life styles? Wider access to more people will be a doubtful victory if human beings find they have nothing to say to one another or cannot stand to listen to each other.

Time and space have long cushioned intercultural encounters, confining them to touristic exchanges. But this insulation is rapidly wearing thin. In the world of tomorrow we can expect to live— not merely vacation—in societies which seek different values and abide by different codes. There we

From Dean C. Barnlund. *Public and Private Self in Japan and the United States* (Tokyo: Simul Press, Inc., 1975), pp. 3-24. Reprinted by permission of the publisher. Professor Barnlund taught at San Francisco State University. Footnotes deleted.

will be surrounded by foreigners for long periods of time, working with others in the closest possible relationships. If people currently show little tolerance or talent for encounters with alien cultures, how can they learn to deal with constant and inescapable coexistence?

The temptation is to retreat to some pious hope or talismanic formula to carry us into the new age. "Meanwhile," as Edwin Reischauer reminds us, "we fail to do what we ourselves must do if 'one world' is ever to be achieved, and that is to develop the education, the skills and the attitudes that men must have if they are to build and maintain such a world. The time is short, and the needs are great. The task faces all men. But it is on the shoulders of people living in the strong countries of the world, such as Japan and the United States, that this burden falls with special weight and urgency."

Anyone who has truly struggled to comprehend another person — even those closest and most like himself — will appreciate the immensity of the challenge of intercultural communication. A greater exchange of people between nations, needed as that may be, carries with it no guarantee of increased cultural empathy; experience in other lands often does little but aggravate existing prejudices. Studying guidebooks or memorizing polite phrases similarly fails to explain differences in cultural perspectives. Programs of cultural enrichment, while they contribute to curiosity about other ways of life, do not cultivate the skills to function effectively in the cultures studied. Even concentrated exposure to a foreign language, valuable as it is, provides access to only one of the many codes that regulate daily affairs; human understanding is by no means guaranteed because conversants share the same dictionary. (Within the United States, where people inhabit a common territory and possess a common language, mutuality of meaning among Mexican-Americans, White Americans, Black-Americans, Indian-Americans — to say nothing of old and young, poor and rich, pro-establishment and anti-establishment cultures — is a sporadic and unreliable occurrence.) Useful as all these measures are for enlarging appreciation of diverse cultures, they fall short of what is needed for a global village to survive.

What seems most critical is to find ways of gaining entrance into the assumptive world of another culture, to identify the norms that govern face-to-face relations, and to equip people to function within a social system that is foreign but no longer incomprehensible. Without this kind of insight people are condemned to remain outsiders no matter how long they live in another country. Its institutions and its customs will be interpreted inevitably from the premises and through the medium of their own culture. Whether they notice something or overlook it, respect or ridicule it, express or conceal their reaction will be dictated by the logic of their own rather than the alien culture.

There are, of course, shelves and shelves of books on the cultures of the world. They cover the history, religion, political thought, music, sculpture, and industry of many nations. And they make fascinating and provocative reading. But only in the vaguest way do they suggest what it is that really distinguishes the behavior of a Samoan, a Congolese, a Japanese, or an American. Rarely do the descriptions of a political structure or religious faith explain precisely when and why certain topics are avoided or why specific gestures carry such radically different meanings according to the context in which they appear.

When former President Nixon and former Premier Sato met to discuss a growing problem concerning trade in textiles between Japan and the United States, Premier Sato announced that since they were on such good terms with each other the deliberations would be "three parts talk and seven parts 'haragei.'" Translated literally, "haragei" means to communicate through the belly, that is to feel out intuitively rather than verbally state the precise position of each person.

Subscribing to this strategy — one that governs many interpersonal exchanges in his culture — Premier Sato conveyed without verbal elaboration his comprehension of the plight of American textile firms threatened by accelerating exports of Japanese fabrics to the United States. President Nixon — similarly abiding by norms that govern interaction within his culture — took this comprehension of the American position to mean that new export quotas would be forthcoming shortly.

During the next few weeks both were shocked at the consequences of their meeting: Nixon was infuriated to learn that the new policies he expected were not forthcoming, and Sato was upset to find that he had unwittingly triggered a new wave of hostility toward his country. If prominent officials, surrounded by foreign advisers, can commit such grievous communicative blunders, the plight of the ordinary citizen may be suggested. Such intercultural collisions, forced upon the public consciousness by the grave consequences they carry and the extensive publicity they receive, only hint at the wider and more frequent confusions and hostilities that disrupt the negotiations of lesser officials, business executives, professionals and even visitors in foreign countries.

Every culture expresses its purpose and conducts its affairs through the medium of communication. Cultures exist primarily to create and preserve common systems of symbols by which their members can assign and exchange meanings. Unhappily, the distinctive rules that govern these symbol systems are far from obvious. About some of these codes, such as language, we have extensive knowledge. About others, such as gestures and facial codes, we have only rudimentary knowledge. On many others — rules governing topical appropriateness, customs regulating physical contact, time and space codes, strategies for the management of conflict — we have almost no systematic knowledge. To crash another culture with only the vaguest notion of its underlying dynamics reflects not only a provincial naïvete but a dangerous form of cultural arrogance.

It is differences in meaning, far more than mere differences in vocabulary, that isolate cultures, and that cause them to regard each other as strange or even barbaric. It is not too surprising that many cultures refer to themselves as "The People," relegating all other human beings to a subhuman form of life. To the person who drinks blood, the eating of meat is repulsive. Someone who conveys respect by standing is upset by someone who conveys it by sitting down; both may regard kneeling as absurd. Burying the dead may prompt tears in one society, smiles in another, and dancing in a third. If spitting on the street makes sense to some, it will ap-

pear bizarre that others carry their spit in their pocket; neither may quite appreciate someone who spits to express gratitude. The bullfight that constitutes an almost religious ritual for some seems a cruel and inhumane way of destroying a defenseless animal to others. Although staring is acceptable social behavior in some cultures, in others it is a thoughtless invasion of privacy. Privacy, itself, is without universal meaning.

Note that none of these acts involves an insurmountable linguistic challenge. The words that describe these acts — eating, spitting, showing respect, fighting, burying, and staring — are quite translatable into most languages. The issue is more conceptual than linguistic; each society places events in its own cultural frame and it is these frames that bestow the unique meaning and differentiated response they produce.

As we move or are driven toward a global village and increasingly frequent cultural contact, we need more than simply greater factual knowledge of each other. We need, more specifically, to identify what might be called the "rulebooks of meaning" that distinguish one culture from another. For to grasp the way in which other cultures perceive the world, and the assumptions and values that are the foundation of these perceptions, is to gain access to the experience of other human beings. Access to the world view and the communicative style of other cultures may not only enlarge our own way of experiencing the world but enable us to maintain constructive relationships with societies that operate according to a different logic than our own.

## Sources of Meaning

To survive, psychologically as well as physically, human beings must inhabit a world that is relatively free of ambiguity and is reasonably predictable. Some sort of structure must be placed upon the endless profusion of incoming signals. The infant, born into a world of flashing, hissing, moving images, soon learns to adapt by resolving this chaos into toys and tables, dogs and parents. Even adults who have had their vision or hearing restored through surgery describe the world as a frightening and sometimes unbearable experience; only after days of effort are they able to transform blurs and noises into meaningful and therefore manageable experiences.

It is commonplace to talk as if the world "has" meaning, to ask what "is" the meaning of a phrase, a gesture, a painting, a contract. Yet when thought about, it is clear that events are devoid of meaning until someone assigns it to them. There is no appropriate response to a bow or a handshake, a shout or a whisper, until it is interpreted. A drop of water and the color red have no meaning, they simply exist. The aim of human perception is to make the world intelligible so that it can be managed successfully; the attribution of meaning is a prerequisite to and preparation for action.

People are never passive receivers, merely absorbing events of obvious significance, but are active in assigning meaning to sensation. What any event acquires in the way of meaning appears to reflect a transaction between what is there to be seen or heard, and what the interpreter brings to it in the way of past experience and prevailing motive. Thus the attribution of meanings is always a creative process by which the raw data of sensation are transformed to fit the aims of the observer.

The diversity of reactions that can be triggered by a single experience — meeting a stranger, negotiating a contract, attending a textile conference — is immense. Each observer is forced to see it through his own eyes, interpret it in the light of his own values, fit it to the requirements of his own circumstances. As a consequence, every object and message is seen by every observer from a somewhat different perspective. Each person will note some features and neglect others. Each will accept some relations among the facts and deny others. Each will arrive at some conclusion, tentative or certain, as the sounds and forms resolve into a "temple" or "barn," a "compliment" or "insult."

Provide a group of people with a set of photographs, even quite simple and ordinary photographs, and note how diverse are the meanings they provoke. Afterward they will recall and forget different pictures, they will also assign quite distinctive meanings to those they do remember. Some will recall the mood of a picture, others the actions; some the appearance and others the attitudes of persons portrayed. Often the observers cannot agree upon even the most "objective" details — the number of people, the precise location and identity of simple objects. A difference in frame of mind — fatigue, hunger, excitement, anger — will change dramatically what they report they have "seen."

It should not be surprising that people raised in different families, exposed to different events, praised and punished for different reasons, should come to view the world so differently. As George Kelly has noted, people see the world through templates which force them to construe events in unique ways. These patterns or grids which we fit over the realities of the world are cut from our own experience and values, and they predispose us to certain interpretations. Industrialist and farmer do not see the "same" land; husband and wife do not plan for the "same" child; doctor and patient do not discuss the "same" disease; borrower and creditor do not negotiate the "same" mortgage; daughter and daughter-in-law do not react to the "same" mother.

The world each person creates for himself is a distinctive world, not the same world others occupy. Each fashions from every incident whatever meanings fit his own private biases. These biases, taken together, constitute what has been called the "assumptive world of the individual." The world each person gets inside his head is the only world he knows. And it is this symbolic world, not the real world, that he talks about, argues about, laughs about, fights about.

## Interpersonal Encounters

Every communication, interpersonal or intercultural, is a transaction between these private worlds. As people talk they search for symbols that will enable them to share their experience and converge upon a common meaning. This process, often long and sometimes painful, makes it possible finally to reconcile apparent or real differences between them. Various words are used to describe this moment. When it involves an integration of facts or ideas, it is usually called an "agreement"; when it involves sharing a mood or feeling, it is referred to as "empathy" or "rapport." But "understanding" is a broad enough term to cover both possibilities; in either case it identifies the achievement of a common meaning.

If understanding is a measure of communicative success, a simple formula – which might be called the *Interpersonal Equation* – may clarify the major factors that contribute to its achievement.

*Interpersonal Understanding = f (Similarity of Perceptual Orientations, Similarity of Belief Systems, Similarity of Communicative Styles)*

That is, "Interpersonal Understanding" is a function of or dependent upon the degree of "Similarity of Perceptual Orientations," "Similarity of Systems of Belief," and "Similarity of Communicative Styles." Each of these terms requires some elaboration.

"Similarity in Perceptual Orientations" refers to a person's prevailing approach to reality and the degree of flexibility he manifests in organizing it. Some people can scan the world broadly, searching for diversity of experience, preferring the novel and unpredictable. They may be drawn to new foods, new music, new ways of thinking. Others seem to scan the world more narrowly, searching to confirm past experience, preferring the known and predictable. They secure satisfaction from old friends, traditional art forms, familiar life styles. The former have a high tolerance for novelty; the latter a low tolerance for novelty.

It is a balance between these tendencies, of course, that characterizes most people. Within the same person attraction to the unfamiliar and the familiar coexist. Which prevails at any given moment is at least partly a matter of circumstance: when secure, people may widen their perceptual field, accommodate new ideas or actions; when they feel insecure they may narrow their perceptual field to protect existing assumptions from the threat of new beliefs or life styles. The balance may be struck in still other ways: some people like to live in a stable physical setting with everything in its proper place, but welcome new emotional or intellectual challenges; others enjoy living in a chaotic and disordered environment but would rather avoid exposing themselves to novel or challenging ideas.

People differ also in the degree to which their perceptions are flexible or rigid. Some react with curiosity and delight to unpredictable and uncategorizable events. Others are disturbed or uncomfortable in the presence of the confusing and complex. There are people who show a high degree of tolerance for ambiguity; others manifest a low tolerance for ambiguity. When confronted with the complications and confusions that surround many daily events, the former tend to avoid immediate closure and delay judgment while the latter seek immediate closure and evaluation. Those with little tolerance for ambiguity tend to respond categorically, that is, by reference to the class names for things (businessmen, radicals, hippies, foreigners) rather than to their unique and differentiating features.

It would be reasonable to expect that individuals who approach reality similarly might understand each other easily, and laboratory research confirms this conclusion: people with similar perceptual styles attract one another, understand each other better, work more efficiently together and with greater satisfaction than those whose perceptual orientations differ.

"Similarity in Systems of Belief" refers not to the way people view the world, but to the conclusions they draw from their experience. Everyone develops a variety of opinions toward divorce, poverty, religion, television, sex, and social customs. When belief and disbelief systems coincide, people are likely to understand and appreciate each other better. Research done by Donn Byrne and replicated by the author demonstrates how powerfully human beings are drawn to those who hold the same beliefs and how sharply they are repelled by those who do not.

Subjects in these experiments were given questionnaires requesting their opinions on twenty-six topics. After completing the forms, each was asked to rank the thirteen most important and least important topics. Later each person was given four forms, ostensibly filled out by people in another group but actually filled out to show varying degrees of agreement with their own answers, and invited to choose among them with regard to their attractiveness as associates. The results were clear: people most preferred to talk with those whose attitudes duplicated their own exactly, next chose those who agreed with them on all important issues, next chose those with similar views on unimportant issues, and finally and reluctantly chose those who disagreed with them completely. It appears that most people most of the time find satisfying relationships easiest to achieve with someone who shares their own hierarchy of beliefs. This, of course, converts many human encounters into rituals of ratification, each person looking to the other only to obtain endorsement and applause for his own beliefs. It is, however, what is often meant by "interpersonal understanding."

Does the same principle hold true for "Similarity of Communicative Styles"? To a large extent, yes. But not completely. By "communicative style" is meant the topics people prefer to discuss, their favorite forms of interaction – ritual, repartee, argument, self-disclosure – and the depth of involvement they demand of each other. It includes the extent to which communicants rely upon the same channels – vocal, verbal, physical – for conveying information, and the extent to which they are tuned to the same level of meaning, that is, to the factual or emotional content of messages. The use of a common vocabulary and even preference for similar metaphors may help people to understand each other.

But some complementarity in conversational style may also help. Talkative people may prefer quiet partners, the more aggressive may enjoy the less aggressive, those who seek affection may be drawn to the more affection-giving, simply because both can find the greatest mutual satisfaction when interpersonal styles mesh. Even this sort of complementarity, however, may reflect a case of similarity in definitions of each other's conversational role.

This hypothesis, too, has drawn the interest of communicologists. One investigator found that people paired to work on common tasks were much more effective if their communicative styles were similar than if they were dissimilar. Another social scientist found that teachers tended to give higher grades on tests to students whose verbal styles matched their own than to students who gave equally valid answers but did not phrase them as their instructors might. To establish common

meanings seems to require that conversants share a common vocabulary and compatible ways of expressing ideas and feelings.

It must be emphasized that perceptual orientations, systems of belief, and communicative styles do not exist or operate independently. They overlap and affect each other. They combine in complex ways to determine behavior. What a person says is influenced by what he believes and what he believes, in turn, by what he sees. His perceptions and beliefs are themselves partly a product of his manner of communicating with others. The terms that compose the Interpersonal Equation constitute not three isolated but three interdependent variables. They provide three perspectives to use in the analysis of communicative acts.

The Interpersonal Equation suggests there is an underlying narcissistic bias in human societies that draws similar people together. Each seeks to find in the other a reflection of himself, someone who views the world as he does, who interprets it as he does, and who expresses himself in a similar way. It is not surprising, then, that artists should be drawn to artists, radicals to radicals, Jews to Jews – or Japanese to Japanese and Americans to Americans.

The opposite seems equally true: people tend to avoid those who challenge their assumptions, who dismiss their beliefs, and who communicate in strange and unintelligible ways. When one reviews history, whether he examines crises within or between cultures, he finds people have consistently shielded themselves, segregated themselves, even fortified themselves, against wide differences in modes of perception or expression (in many cases, indeed, have persecuted and conquered the infidel and afterwards substituted their own cultural ways for the offending ones). Intercultural defensiveness appears to be only a counterpart of interpersonal defensiveness in the face of uncomprehended or incomprehensible differences.

## Intercultural Encounters

Every culture attempts to create a "universe of discourse" for its members, a way in which people can interpret their experience and convey it to one another. Without a common system of codifying sensations, life would be absurd and all efforts to share meanings doomed to failure. This universe of discourse — one of the most precious of all cultural legacies — is transmitted to each generation in part consciously and in part unconsciously. Parents and teachers give explicit instruction in it by praising or criticizing certain ways of dressing, of thinking, of gesturing, of responding to the acts of others. But the most significant aspect of any cultural code may be conveyed implicitly, not by rule or lesson but through modelling behavior. The child is surrounded by others who, through the mere consistency of their actions as males and females, mothers and fathers, salesclerks and policemen, display what is appropriate behavior. Thus the grammar of any culture is sent and received largely unconsciously, making one's own cultural assumptions and biases difficult to recognize. They seem so obviously right that they require no explanation.

In *The Open and Closed Mind,* Milton Rokeach poses the problem of cultural understanding in its simplest form, but one that can readily demonstrate the complications of communication between cultures. It is called the "Denny Doodlebug Problem." Readers are given all the rules that govern his culture: Denny is an animal that always faces North, and can move only by jumping; he can jump large distances or small distances, but can change direction only after jumping four times in any direction; he can jump North, South, East or West, but not diagonally. Upon concluding a jump his master places some food three feet directly West of him. Surveying the situation, Denny concludes he must jump four times to reach the food. No more or less. And he is right. All the reader has to do is explain the circumstances that make his conclusion correct.

The large majority of people who attempt this problem fail to solve it, despite the fact that they are given all the rules that control behavior in this culture. If there is difficulty in getting inside the simplistic world of Denny Doodlebug — where the cultural code has already been broken and handed to us — imagine the complexity of comprehending behavior in societies where codes have not yet been deciphered. And where even those who obey these codes are only vaguely aware and can rarely describe the underlying sources of their own actions.

If two people, both of whom spring from a single culture, must often shout to be heard across the void that separates their private worlds, one can begin to appreciate the distance to be overcome when people of different cultural identities attempt to talk. Even with the most patient dedication to seeking a common terminology, it is surprising that people of alien cultures are able to hear each other at all. And the peoples of Japan and the United States would appear to constitute a particularly dramatic test of the ability to cross an intercultural divide. Consider the disparity between them.

Here is Japan, a tiny isolated nation with a minimum of resources, buffeted by periodic disasters, overcrowded with people, isolated by physical fact and cultural choice, nurtured in Shinto and Buddhist religions, permeated by a deep respect for nature, nonmaterialist in philosophy, intuitive in thought, hierarchical in social structure. Eschewing the explicit, the monumental, the bold and boisterous, it expresses its sensuality in the form of impeccable gardens, simple rural temples, asymmetrical flower arrangements, a theater unparalleled for containment of feeling, an art and literature remarkable for their delicacy, and crafts noted for their honest and earthy character. Its people, among the most homogeneous of men, are modest and apologetic in manner, communicate in an ambiguous and evocative language, are engrossed in interpersonal rituals and prefer inner serenity to influencing others. They occupy unpretentious buildings of wood and paper and live in cities laid out as casually as farm villages. Suddenly from these rice paddies emerges an industrial giant, surpassing rival nations with decades of industrial experience, greater resources, and a larger reserve of technicians. Its labor, working longer, harder and more frantically than any in the world, builds the earth's largest city, constructs some of its ugliest buildings, promotes the most garish and insistent advertising anywhere, and pollutes its air and water beyond the imagination.

And here is the United States, an immense country, sparsely settled, richly endowed, tied through waves of immigrants to the heritage of Europe, yet forced to subdue nature and find fresh solutions to the problems of survival. Steeped in the Judeo-Christian tradition, schooled in European abstract and analytic thought, it is materialist and experimental in outlook, philosophically pragmatic, politically equalitarian, economically competitive, its raw individualism sometimes tempered by a humanitarian concern for others. Its cities are studies in geometry along whose avenues rise shafts of steel and glass subdivided into separate cubicles for separate activities and separate people. Its popular arts are characterized by the hugeness of Cinemascope, the spontaneity of jazz, the earthy loudness of rock; in its fine arts the experimental, striking, and monumental often stifle the more subtle revelation. The people, a smorgasbord of races, religions, dialects, and nationalities, are turned expressively outward, impatient with rituals and rules, casual and flippant, gifted in logic and argument, approachable and direct yet given to flamboyant and exaggerated assertion. They are curious about one another, open and helpful, yet display a missionary zeal for changing one another. Suddenly this nation whose power and confidence have placed it in a dominant position in the world intellectually and politically, whose style of life has permeated the planet, finds itself uncertain of its direction, doubts its own premises and values, questions its motives and materialism, and engages in an orgy of self criticism.

It is when people nurtured in such different psychological worlds meet that differences in cultural perspectives and communicative codes may sabotage efforts to understand one another. Repeated collisions between a foreigner and the members of a contrasting culture often produce what is called "culture shock." It is a feeling of helplessness, even of terror or anger, that accompanies working in an alien society. One feels trapped in an absurd and indecipherable nightmare.

It is as if some hostile leprechaun had gotten into the works as a cosmic caper rewired the connections that hold society together. Not only do the actions of others no longer make sense, but it is impossible even to express one's own intentions clearly. "Yes" comes out meaning "No." A wave of the hand means "come," or it may mean "go." Formality may be regarded as childish, or as a devious

form of flattery. Statements of fact may be heard as statements of conceit. Arriving early, or arriving late, embarrasses or impresses. "Suggestions" may be treated as "ultimatums," or precisely the opposite. Failure to stand at the proper moment, or failure to sit, may be insulting. The compliment intended to express gratitude instead conveys a sense of distance. A smile signifies disappointment rather than pleasure.

If the crises that follow such intercultural encounters are sufficiently dramatic or the communicants unusually sensitive, they may recognize the source of their trouble. If there is patience and constructive intention the confusion can sometimes be clarified. But more often the foreigner, without knowing it, leaves behind him a trail of frustration, mistrust, and even hatred *of which he is totally unaware*. Neither he nor his associates recognize that their difficulty springs from sources deep within the rhetoric of their own societies. Each sees himself as acting in ways that are thoroughly sensible, honest and considerate. And – given the rules governing his own universe of discourse – each is. Unfortunately, there are few cultural universals, and the degree of overlap in communicative codes is always less than perfect. Experience can be transmitted with fidelity only when the unique properties of each code are recognized and respected, or where the motivation and means exist to bring them into some sort of alignment.

## The Collective Unconscious

Among the greatest insights of this modern age are two that bear a curious affinity to each other. The first, evolving from the efforts of psychologists, particularly Sigmund Freud, revealed the existence of an "individual unconscious." The acts of human beings were found to spring from motives of which they were often vaguely or completely unaware. Their unique perceptions of events arose not from the facts outside their skins but from unrecognized assumptions inside them. When, through intensive analysis, they obtained some insight into these assumptions, they became free to develop other ways of seeing and acting which contributed to their greater flexibility in coping with reality.

The second of these generative ideas, flowing from the work of anthropologists, particularly Margaret Mead and Ruth Benedict, postulated a parallel idea in the existence of a "cultural unconscious." Students of primitive cultures began to see that there was nothing divine or absolute about cultural norms. Every society had its own way of viewing the universe, and each developed from its premises a coherent set of rules of behavior. Each tended to be blindly committed to its own style of life and regarded all others as evil. The fortunate person who was able to master the art of living in foreign cultures often learned that his own mode of life was only one among many. With this insight he became free to choose from among cultural values those that seemed to best fit his peculiar circumstances.

Cultural norms so completely surround people, so permeate thought and action, that few ever recognize the assumptions on which their lives and their sanity rest. As one observer put it, if birds were suddenly endowed with scientific curiosity they might examine many things, but the sky itself would be overlooked as a suitable subject; if fish were to become curious about the world, it would never occur to them to begin by investigating water. For birds and fish would take the sky and sea for granted, unaware of their profound influence because they comprise the medium for every act. Human beings, in a similar way, occupy a symbolic universe governed by codes that are unconsciously acquired and automatically employed. So much so that they rarely notice that the ways they interpret and talk about events are distinctively different from the ways people conduct their affairs in other cultures.

As long as people remain blind to the sources of their meanings, they are imprisoned within them. These cultural frames of reference are no less confining simply because they cannot be seen or touched. Whether it is an individual neurosis that keeps an individual out of contact with his neighbors, or a collective neurosis that separates neighbors of different cultures, both are forms of blindness that limit what can be experienced and what can be learned from others.

It would seem that everywhere people would desire to break out of the boundaries of their own experiential worlds. Their ability to react sensitively to a wider spectrum of events and peoples requires an overcoming of such cultural parochialism. But, in fact, few attain this broader vision. Some, of course, have little opportunity for wider cultural experience, though this condition should change as the movement of people accelerates. Others do not try to widen their experience because they prefer the old and familiar, seek from their affairs only further confirmation of the correctness of their own values. Still others recoil from such experiences because they feel it dangerous to probe too deeply into the personal or cultural unconscious. Exposure may reveal how tenuous and arbitrary many cultural norms are; such exposure might force people to acquire new bases for interpreting events. And even for the many who do seek actively to enlarge the variety of human beings with whom they are capable of communicating there are still difficulties.

Cultural myopia persists not merely because of inertia and habit, but chiefly because it is so difficult to overcome. One acquires a personality and a culture in childhood, long before he is capable of comprehending either of them. To survive, each person masters the perceptual orientations, cognitive biases, and communicative habits of his own culture. But once mastered, objective assessment of these same processes is awkward since the same mechanisms that are being evaluated must be used in making the evaluations. Once a child learns Japanese or English or Navaho, the categories and grammar of each language predispose him to perceive and think in certain ways, and discourage him from doing so in other ways. When he attempts to discover why he sees or thinks as he does, he uses the same techniques he is trying to identify. Once one becomes an Indian, an Ibo, or a Frenchman — or even a priest or scientist — it is difficult to extricate oneself from that mooring long enough to find out what one truly is or wants.

Fortunately, there may be a way around this paradox. Or promise of a way around it. It is to expose the culturally distinctive ways various peoples construe events and seek to identify the conventions that connect what is seen with what is thought with what is said. Once this cultural grammar is assimilated and the rules that govern the exchange of meanings are known, they can be shared and learned by those who choose to work and live in alien cultures.

When people within a culture face an insurmountable problem they turn to friends, neighbors, associates, for help. To them they explain their predicament, often in distinctive personal ways. Through talking it out, however, there often emerge new ways of looking at the problem, fresh incentive to attack it, and alternative solutions to it. This sort of interpersonal exploration is often successful within a culture for people share at least the same communicative style even if they do not agree completely in their perceptions or beliefs.

When people communicate between cultures, where communicative rules as well as the substance of experience differs, the problems multiply. But so, too, do the number of interpretations and alternatives. If it is true that the more people differ the harder it is for them to understand each other, it is equally true that the more they differ the more they have to teach and learn from each other. To do so, of course, there must be mutual respect and sufficient curiosity to overcome the frustrations that occur as they flounder from one misunderstanding to another. Yet the task of coming to grips with differences in communicative styles – between or within cultures – is prerequisite to all other types of mutuality.

# Cultural Identity and Intercultural Communication

## MARY JANE COLLIER

Several useful approaches that can help you understand and improve the quality of your intercultural communication encounters are included in this book. One option you have for understanding why you and others behave in particular ways and learning what you can do to increase the appropriateness and effectiveness of your communication is to view communication from the perspective of cultural identity enactment.

This article presents an approach to culture that focuses on how individuals enact or take on one or more cultural identities. Questions that are answered here include the following: (1) What is a cultural identity? (2) How are multiple cultural identities created and negotiated with others? (3) How can knowledge of the cultural identity approach help you become more competent when dealing with persons who are taking on an identity different from yours? (4) What are the benefits of such an approach to intercultural communication research, training, and practice?

## Culture

We approach culture here in a very specific way. **Culture** is defined as a historically transmitted system of symbols, meanings, and norms (Collier & Thomas, 1988; Geertz, 1983; and Schneider, 1976). Notice the emphasis placed on the communication process in the definition. Notice also, that culture

---

This original essay first appeared in the seventh edition. All rights reserved. Permission to reprint must be obtained from the publisher and the author. Mary Jane Collier teaches at Oregon State University.

is *systemic,* meaning it comprises many complex components that are interdependent and related; they form a type of permeable boundary.

## Symbols and Meanings

The components of the system are the patterned symbols such as verbal messages, nonverbal cues, emblems, and icons, as well as their interpretations or assigned meanings. Culture is what groups of people say and do and think and feel. Culture is not the people but the communication that links them together. Culture is not only speaking a language and using symbols but interpreting those symbols consistently; for example, traffic lights in South Africa are called "robots" and in England elevators are called "lifts." In urban areas, gang members change the items of clothing that denote gang membership periodically so that only in-group members know who is "in" and who is "out."

## Norms

Another major component of the system of culture is normative conduct. **Norms** here are patterns of appropriate ways of communicating. It is important not only to speak with symbols that are understood, or to use nonverbal gestures or modes of dress so that the cues will be understood consistently, but also to use the symbols at acceptable times, with the appropriate people, with the fitting intensity. Japanese Americans may send their children to Japanese school and speak Japanese at home, but they may speak English at work and use direct and assertive forms of communication in business or educational settings. Malay women may wear traditional Muslim dress and show respectful silence to elders in the family, but they may be assertive and use a louder tone of voice among women in social settings.

## History

The cultural system of communication is historically transmitted and handed down to new members of the group. Groups with histories include corporations, support groups, national groups, or civil rights groups. History is handed down when new employees are trained, "ground rules" are explained to new members of groups such as Alcoholics Anonymous, or dominant beliefs and the value of democracy are taught to U.S. American children in school.

We learn to become members of groups by learning about past members of the group, heroes, important precepts, rituals, values, and expectations for conduct. We are taught how to follow the norms of the group. In this way we perpetuate the cultural system. When a person becomes a college professor and joins a particular academic institution, she or he is taught about the mission of the institution, past academic heroes (faculty who have won awards, published prestigious works), the importance of "publish or perish" versus the importance placed on effective instruction, the role of sports or liberal arts in the institution, commitment to multiculturalism, and so on. The symbols and norms change over the life of the system, but there is enough consistency in what is handed down to be able to define the boundaries between systems (universities) and distinguish cultural members of one system from members of another.

## Types of Cultures

Many groups (though not all) form cultural systems. Examples of many types of groups have already been included. In some cases, shared history or geography provides commonality of world view or life style which helps create and reinforce a cultural system of communication.

To create a culture groups must first define themselves as a group. This definition may be made on the basis of nationality, ethnicity, gender, profession, geography, organization, physical ability or disability, community, or type of relationship, among others. We will discuss many of these groups later.

Once the group defines itself as a unit, a cultural system may develop. For instance, U.S. Americans define themselves as a group based on use of English as a shared code; reinforcement of democracy through political discussion and action; individual rights and freedoms of speech, press, religion, and assembly being explicitly described in the Bill of Rights and enforced in the courts; and so forth. Attorneys or sales clerks or homemakers may be linked by similarities in daily activities and standard of living. Friends may see their group as including persons who like the same activities and support one another.

**National and Ethnic Cultures** To better understand the many different types of cultures, we can categorize them from the more general and more common, to those that are more specific. National and ethnic cultures are fairly general. These kinds of groups base membership on heritage and history that has been handed down among several generations. Their history is based on traditions, rituals, codes of language, and norms.

Persons who share the same nationality were born in a particular country and spent a significant number of years and a period of socialization in that country. Such socialization promotes and reinforces particular values, beliefs, and norms. Because many people contribute to the creation of a national culture's symbols, meanings, and norms, "national culture" is fairly abstract so predictions about language use and what symbols mean can only be generalized. Japanese national culture, for instance, has been described as collectivistic, high context, high on power distance, and other-face oriented (Gudykunst & Ting-Toomey, 1988). Yet, not all Japanese people follow these norms in every situation. But, when comparing Japanese to Germans, the Japanese, as a group, are more group oriented and emphasize status hierarchies more than the Germans as an overall group (Hofstede, 1980).

**Ethnicity** is a bit different – ethnic groups share a sense of heritage and history, and origin from an area outside of or preceding the creation of their present nation-state of residence (Banks, 1984). Ethnic groups, in most but not all cases, share racial characteristics and many have a specific history of having experienced discrimination. In the United States, ethnic group members include African Americans, Asian Americans (Japanese Americans, Chinese Americans, Vietnamese Americans, Korean Americans, and so on), Mexican Americans, Polish Americans, Irish Americans, Native American Indians, and Jewish Americans, just to name a few examples.

Remember that national and ethnic cultures are the *communication systems* that are created by persons who share the same nationality or ethnicity. From this perspective, culture is the process of creating a perceived commonality and community of thought and action. Culture is based on what people say and do and think and feel *as a result* of their common history and origins.

**Gender** Many subcategories of gender cultures exist. Groups create, reinforce, and teach what is interpreted as feminine or masculine. Groups also reinforce what is appropriate or inappropriate for a good husband, wife, feminist, chauvinist, heterosexual, gay, or lesbian. Mothers and fathers, religious leaders, teachers, and the media all provide information about how to be a member of a particular gender culture.

**Profession** Politicians, physicians, field workers, sales personnel, maintenance crews, bankers, and consultants share common ways of spending time, earning money, communicating with others, and learning norms about how to be a member of their profession. Health care professionals probably share a commitment to health, to helping others, and to improving others' quality of life. They also share educational background, knowledge about their aspect of health care, and standards of practicing their profession.

**Geographical Area** Geographical area sometimes acts as a boundary, contributing to the formulation of a cultural group. In South Africa, the area surrounding Cape Town has its own version of spoken Afrikaans, has a higher population of Coloreds (those of mixed race), and is viewed by many as the most cosmopolitan area in South Africa. The South in the United States has its own traditions, historical orientation, and southern drawl. Rural communities sometimes differ from urban communities in political views, values, life styles, and norms.

**Organization** Large corporations such as IBM, Nike, or Xerox create the most common type of organizational culture. In this culture members are taught the corporate symbols, myths, heroes, and legends, and what it means to be an employee. The proper chain of command, procedures and policies, and schedules are also taught. Finally, they learn the norms in the corporation – who to talk to, about what, at which particular moment. Some corporations value "team players" while others value "individual initiative." Some corporations have mottos like "Never say no to an assignment" or "Never be afraid to speak up if you don't have what you need."

Support groups have their own version of organizational culture. Alcoholics Anonymous, Overeaters Anonymous, and therapy and support groups, among others, form their own sets of symbols, interpretations, and norms. "Let go and let God" is an important requirement in the Anonymous groups; relinquishing individual control to a higher power is a tool in managing one's addictions. Social living groups, such as sororities and fraternities, international dormitories, and the like, often create their own cultures as well.

**Physical Ability or Disability** Groups form a culture based upon shared physical ability or disability. Professional athletic teams teach rookies how to behave and what to do to be an accepted member of the team. Persons who have physical handicaps share critical life experiences and groups teach them how to accept and overcome their disability, as well as how to communicate more effectively with those who do not have the disability (Braithwaite, 1991).

## Cultural Identification as a Process

Each individual, then, has a range of cultures to which she or he belongs in a constantly changing environment. Everyone may concurrently or simultaneously participate in several different cultural systems each day, week, and year. All cultures that are created are influenced by a host of social, psychological, and environmental factors as well as institutions and context.

Consider African Americans in the United States. In the last 30 years, myriad factors have all affected what it means to be African American in the United States including: civil rights marches, leaders such

as Martin Luther King, Jr., affirmative action, racism, the resurgence of the Ku Klux Klan, television shows such as *Roots* and *Cosby,* films by Spike Lee, Anita Hill's testimony in the hearing of Supreme Court nominee Clarence Thomas, and the riots among African Americans and Hispanics in South Central Los Angeles following the Rodney King verdict.

Cultures are affected not only by changing socioeconomic and environmental conditions, but by other cultures as well. A person who is a member of a support group for single mothers in her community is influenced by other cultural groups such as feminists, conservative religious groups, or the Republican party members who made family values and two-parent families an important issue in the 1992 presidential campaign. The important questions from a cultural identity approach may be things like, "What does it mean to be a single mother who is Euro-American, Catholic, out of work, and living in a large city in the Midwest? How does that identity come to be and how is it communicated to others? How does it change across different contexts and relationships?"

## Cultural Identity

Diverse groups can create a cultural system of symbols used, meanings assigned to the symbols, and ideas of what is considered appropriate and inappropriate. When the groups also have a history and begin to hand down the symbols and norms to new members, then the groups take on a *cultural identity.* **Cultural identity** is the particular character of the group communication system that emerges in the particular situation.

## A Communication Perspective

Cultural identities are negotiated, co-created, reinforced, and challenged through communication; therefore we approach identity from a communication perspective. *Social psychological perspectives* view identity as a characteristic of the person and personality, and self as centered in social roles and social practices. A *communication perspective* views identity as something that emerges when messages are exchanged between persons. Thus, **identity** is defined as an enactment of cultural communication (Hecht, Collier, & Ribeau, 1993).

Identities are *emergent;* they come to be in communication contexts. Since you are being asked to emphasize a communication perspective, what you study and try to describe and explain are identity patterns as they occur among persons in contact with one another. Although we have noted that such factors as media, literature, and art influence identity, our focus is directed at the interaction between people. Identities are co-created in relationship to others. Who we are and how we are differs and emerges depending upon who we are with, the cultural identities that are important to us and the others, the context, the topic of conversation, and our interpretations and attributions.

## Properties of Cultural Identity

As students are researchers in intercultural communication, we can apply our knowledge about how cultural identities are enacted and developed in order to explain and improve our understanding of others' conduct. We outline the properties or characteristics of cultural identities and then compare the properties across different cultural groups. These comparisons ultimately help us build theories of cultural and intercultural identity communication.

The first property we outlined is self-perception; this addresses both avowal by the individual and ascription by others. Second, we note modes of expressing identity. Identities are expressed through core symbols, labels, and norms. The third property focuses on the scope of the identity, and whether the identity takes an individual, a relational, or a communal form. A fourth property examines the enduring, yet dynamic, quality of cultural identity. Fifth, affective, cognitive, and behavioral components of identity provide us with a means of contrasting what groups think, feel, say, and do. Sixth, we describe the content and relationship levels of interpretation in messages revealing cultural identity. Content and relationship

interpretations allow us to understand when power and control issues contribute to conflict or when friendships and trust can be developed. Seventh, salience and variations in intensities characterize identity in new or unusual settings. Being the one who stands out in an otherwise homogeneous group causes us to be conscious of and perhaps alter the intensity with which we claim our identity.

**Avowal and Ascription Processes** Each individual may enact various cultural identities over the course of a lifetime as well as over the course of a day. Identities are enacted in interpersonal contexts through avowal and ascription processes. **Avowal** is the self an individual portrays, analogous to the fact or image she or he shows to others. Avowal is the individual saying, "This is who I am."

**Ascription** is the process by which others attribute identities to an individual. Stereotypes and attributions communicated are examples of ascriptions. In part, identity is shaped by others' communicated views of us. For example, a black Zulu female's cultural identities in South Africa are not only shaped by her definition and image of what it means to be a black Zulu female but also by the white Afrikaners for whom she works, her Zulu family and relatives, the township in which she lives in poverty, her white teachers who speak Afrikaans and English, and so forth.

Another way of thinking about this is to say that cultural identities have both subjective and ascribed meanings. In Japan, a philosophy and practice known as *amae* is common. **Amae** signifies an other-orientation or group-orientation, and a sense of obligation to the group. An individual is expected to sacrifice individual needs and give to others; others are expected to reciprocate, thereby maintaining the harmony and cohesiveness of the group (Doi, 1989; Goldman, 1992).

**Amae** represents the interdependence of subjective and ascribed meanings in relationships. The meanings may not be shared across cultural groups, however. To many Japanese, such a complex, long-term, obligatory relationship with members of in-groups is a functional and revered system of relational maintenance. To U.S. Americans, such rules and obligations to others may appear to be unnecessary, threaten individuality and choice, and therefore be unacceptable.

Information about avowal and ascription can be useful in understanding the role others play in developing your own cultural identities. If a particular group has low self-esteem or a high need for status, those aspects of identity may be influenced by the stereotypes or conceptions held and communicated by other groups.

**Modes of Expression: Core Symbols, Labels, and Norms** Cultural identities are expressed in core symbols, labels, and norms. **Core symbols** tell us about the definitions, premises, and propositions regarding the universe and the place of humans in the universe that are held by members of the cultural group. They are expressions of cultural beliefs about the management of nature and technology and such institutions as marriage, education, and politics. The symbols point us to the central ideas and concepts and the everyday behaviors that characterize membership in that cultural group.

Sometimes these core symbols can be summarized into a set of fundamental beliefs; sometimes a particular mode of dress, gesture, or phrase captures the essence of a cultural identity. Carbaugh (1989) analyzed transcripts of the popular television talk show, *Donahue*. After doing a content analysis of the comments made by audience members, he proposed *self-expression* as a core symbol of mainstream U.S. identity.

Authenticity, powerlessness, and expressiveness were identified as three core symbols among African Americans (Hecht, Ribeau, & Alberts, 1989; Hecht, Larkey, Johnson, & Reinard, 1991). These core symbols were posited after African Americans were asked to describe recent satisfying and dissatisfying conversations with other African Americans and with Euro-Americans, and to describe strategies for conversational improvement. African Americans talked about the need for persons to be authentic, honest, and real, described the negative impact of feeling powerless, and outlined a need to be expressive in their conduct.

*Labels* are a category of core symbols. The same label may vary widely in its interpretation. The term *American* is perceived as acceptable and common

by many residents of the United States and as ethnocentric and self-centered by residents of Central America and Canada, and is associated with a group that is privileged, wealthy, and powerful by some countries that are not industrialized. *Hispanic* is a general term many social scientists use to describe "persons of Mexican, Puerto Rican, Cuban, Central or South American, or other Spanish culture of origin, regardless of race" (Marin & Marin, 1991, p. 23).

Persons may choose to describe their own ethnicity with a much more specific label such as *Mexican American* or *Chicano* or *Chicana*. Chicano and Chicana individuals may have their own ideas about what it means to be a member of that culture. Whether the label was created by members of the group or members of another group provides useful information about what the label means and how it is interpreted.

Cultural groups create and reinforce standards for "performing the culture" appropriately and effectively. Norms for conduct are based upon core symbols and *how they are interpreted*. Defining who you are tells you what you should be doing. Norms of appropriate and acceptable behavior, moral standards, expectations for conduct, and criteria to decide to what degree another is behaving in a competent manner form the prescriptive or evaluative aspect of cultural identity. An individual is successful at enacting identity when one is accepted as a competent member of the group. Immigrants, for example, are judged to be competent and accepted by members of the U.S. American culture when they speak English, use appropriate greetings, demonstrate respect for the individual rights of their neighbors to privacy, and so forth.

Attention to the property of shared norms gives us the ability to determine what is appropriate from the point of view of the group members. Comparing norms of conduct across groups and identifying norms in intercultural conversations is helpful in figuring out how to improve our own individual effectiveness as a communicator. Finally, identification of norms in this way provides valid information for trainers, teachers, and practitioners as they develop their training programs.

## Individual, Relational, and Communal Forms of Identity

Identities have individual, relational, and communal properties. As researchers of culture, we can study culture from the point of view of individuals. Each person has individual interpretations of what it means to be U.S. American or Austrian or Indian, and each person enacts his or her cultural identities slightly differently. If we want to understand why an individual behaves in a particular way, we can ask him or her to talk about that cultural identity and experience as a group member.

When we study culture from a relational point of view we observe the interaction between people, friends, coworkers, or family members, who identify themselves as members of the same or different groups. Then we can identify the themes in their talk such as trust or power.

Collier (1989) found that Mexican American friends emphasized the importance of their relationship by meeting frequently and spending a significant portion of time together. They also described the most important characteristics of friendship as support, trust, intimacy, and commitment to the relationship. In contrast, when Mexican Americans and Anglo-Americans talked about their friendships with one another, they described common activities, goals, and respect for family.

When we study culture in terms of its communal properties we observe the public communication contexts and activities in communities and neighborhoods that establish cultural identity. Rituals, rites of passage, and holiday celebrations are other sources of information about how persons use cultural membership to establish community with one another.

## Enduring and Changing Property of Identity

Cultural identities are both enduring and changing. As already mentioned, cultures have a history that is transmitted to new members over time. Cultural identities change because of economic, political, social, psychological, and contextual factors, not to mention the influence of other cultural identities.

Enacting the cultural identity of being gay or lesbian in the 1990s has certain things in common with being gay in the 1980s and 1970s. Individuals who "come out of the closet" encounter similar stereotypes and ascriptions to those in earlier centuries. However, the political climate in some areas of the country in which ballot initiatives were proposed to limit the rights of gays or link gays with other groups such as sadomasochists, affect the cultural identity of the group. Sometimes context changes how one manifests identity and how intensely one avows an identity. Announcing your affiliation and pride as a member of the Right to Life, anti-abortion coalition, at a rally of pro-abortion supporters is different from attending a Right to Life meeting and avowing your identity in that context.

## Affective, Cognitive, and Behavioral Components of Identity

Identities have affective, cognitive, and behavioral components. Persons have emotions and feelings attached to identities. Such emotions change depending upon the situation. Sometimes, a particularly strong or violent avowal of an identity is a signal of the importance of that identity and the degree to which it is perceived to be threatened. Perhaps this knowledge can help us interpret why rioting occurred in South Central Los Angeles after the Rodney King verdict.

The cognitive component of identity relates to the beliefs we have about that identity. Persons hold a range of beliefs about each culture group to which they belong, but certain similarities in beliefs become evident when you ask people to talk about what it means to be U.S. American or Thai or a member of Earth First!, an environmentalist group. Members of Earth First! share beliefs in the value of ancient forests, distrust of executives who run the logging companies, politicians who support the lumber industry, and the view that spiking trees and sabotaging logging equipment is sometimes necessary as a form of protest. Such beliefs can be summarized into a core symbol, here the name of the organization, *Earth First!*

The behavioral component of cultural identity focuses on the verbal and nonverbal actions taken by group members. We come to be members of a group through our actions with one another and our reactions to one another. These verbal and nonverbal actions can be studied, and patterns described. The dimensions of cultural variability described by Hofstede (1980) such as collectivism and individualism are patterns of communicative conduct evident when particular cultural identities are enacted. Comparing what groups say and do allows us as researchers to begin to understand why some groups experience frequent misunderstandings or conflict.

## Content and Relationship

Identities comprise both content and relationship levels of interpretation. When persons communicate with each other, messages carry information as well as implications for who is in control, how close the conversational partners feel to each other or conversely how hostile they feel toward each other, how much they trust each other, or the degree of inclusion or exclusion they feel.

Sometimes persons use their in-group language to reinforce their in-group status and establish distance from the out-group (Giles, Coupland, & Coupland, 1991). At other times they may use the language of the out-group in order to adapt and align with the out-group. Mexican Americans may speak Spanish when in neighborhood communities to preserve their history and roots and to reinforce their identification and bond as a people. The same persons may speak English at school or at work because the supervisor and executives of the company demand it.

## Salience and Intensity Differences

Identities differ in their salience in particular contexts, and identities are enacted with different intensities at different times. The intensities provide markers of strong involvement, and investment in the identity. As a white U.S. American female professor visiting South Africa there were times in which I was most aware of being a white minority among the black majority, times when I was aware of being a U.S. American who was stereotyped

somewhat negatively, and times when I was most aware of being a college professor. But, when I learned that female employees in South Africa do not receive maternity leave and receive a lower housing allowance than males, my feminist identity became more salient, causing me to adopt a stronger tone and assert my views about equal pay for equal work in a more direct manner when talking with male executives in corporations.

## Cultural Identity and Communication Competence

Using cultural identity as an approach can help us better analyze others' conduct and decide how to do what is mutually competent. Spitzberg and Cupach (1984) point out that communication competence requires motivation and knowledge, as well as skills to demonstrate what behavior is appropriate and effective.

**Cultural competence** is the demonstrated ability to enact a cultural identity in a mutually appropriate and effective manner. Intercultural competence becomes a bit more complex. **Intercultural competence** is the reinforcement of culturally different identities that are salient in the particular situation. Intercultural competence occurs when the avowed identity matches the identity ascribed. For example, if you avow the identity of an assertive, outspoken U.S. American and your conversational partner avows himself or herself to be a respectful, nonassertive Vietnamese, then each must ascribe the corresponding identity to the conversational partner. You must jointly negotiate what kind of relationship will be mutually satisfying. Some degree of adjustment and accommodation is usually necessary.

A common problem in intercultural communication occurs when persons who describe themselves as the same nationality or ethnicity do not share ideas about how to enact their identity and disagree about the norms for interaction. Chicanos in the United States may differ from second- and third-generation Mexican Americans about the need to speak Spanish or call attention to their heritage. Nonetheless, understanding the identity being avowed and ascribed and noting the intensity with which the identity is avowed, enables us to understand why a particular cultural identity emerges salient in particular situations and therefore what contextual, social, or psychological factors are operating in the situation.

Some benefits of the cultural identity approach in intercultural communication situations include the following: We can acknowledge that all individuals have many potential cultural identities which may emerge in a particular situation. Remembering that identities change from situation to situation can be helpful in overcoming the tendency to treat others as stereotypical representatives of a particular group. Asking for information about what is appropriate for their cultural identity is an effective tool in becoming interculturally competent. Explaining what your own cultural identity norms are and why you behaved in a particular way can also be a useful way to increase the other person's understanding and can help develop relational trust.

Researchers, trainers, and practitioners can utilize the cultural identity approach to identify similarities and differences in behaviors, in interpretations, or in norms. It is possible to begin to explain why group members behave as they do or feel as they do in their conduct with others from the same and different groups. Trainers and teachers can compare group symbols, interpretations, and norms as well as teach others to develop analytical skills to use in their own situations.

Cultural identity as an approach to the study of culture and intercultural communication is only one of many approaches. Ongoing research, critique, and application will test the merit of the approach. Hopefully, the approach has sparked the beginning of a dialogue that will continue throughout all of our lifetimes.

## References

Banks, J. (1984). *Teaching Strategies for Ethnic Studies* (3d ed.) Boston: Allyn & Bacon.

Braithwaite, D. (1991). "Just how much did that wheelchair cost?": Management of privacy boundaries by persons with disabilities. *Western Journal of Speech Communication, 55,* 254-274.

Carbaugh, D. (1989). *Talking American: Cultural Discourses on* Donahue. Norwood, N.J.: Ablex.

Collier, M. J. (1989). Cultural and intercultural communication competence: current approaches and directions for future research. *International Journal of Intercultural Relations, 13,* 287-302.

Collier, M. J., and Thomas, M. (1988). "Cultural Identity: An Interpretive Perspective." In Y. Y. Kim and W. Gudykunst, (Eds.), *Theories in Intercultural Communication,* 99-122. Newbury Park, Calif.: Sage.

Doi, T. (1989). *The Anatomy of Dependence.* Tokyo: Kodansha Publishers.

Geertz, C. (1983). *Local Knowledge.* New York: Basic Books.

Giles, H., Coupland, N., and Coupland, J. (1991). "Accommodation Theory: Communication, Contexts and Consequences." In J. Giles, N. Coupland, and J. Coupland (Eds.), *Contexts of Accommodation: Developments in Applied Sociolinguistics.* Cambridge: Cambridge University Press.

Goldman, A. (1992). The Centrality of "Ningensei" to Japanese Negotiating and Interpersonal Relationships: Implications for U.S.-Japanese Communication. Paper presented at Speech Communication Association Conference, Chicago, Illinois.

Gudykunst, W., and Ting-Toomey, S. (1988). *Culture and Interpersonal Communication.* Newbury Park, Calif.: Sage.

Hecht, M., Collier, M. J., and Ribeau, S. (1993). *African-American Communication.* Newbury Park, Calif.: Sage.

Hecht, M., Larkey, L. K., Johnson, J. N., and Reinard, J. C. (1991). A Model of Interethnic Effectiveness. Paper presented at the International Communication Association Conference, Chicago, Illinois.

Hecht, M., Ribeau, S., and Alberts, J. K. (1989). An Afro-American perspective on interethnic communication. *Communication Monographs, 56,* 385-410.

Hofstede, G. (1980). *Culture's Consequences.* Newbury Park, Calif.: Sage.

Marin, G., and Marin, B. V. (1991). *Research with Hispanic Populations.* Newbury Park, Calif.: Sage.

Schneider, D. (1976). "Notes Toward a Theory of Culture." In K. Basso and H. Selby (Eds.), *Meaning in Anthropology.* Albuquerque: University of New Mexico Press.

Spitzberg, B. H., and Cupach, W. R. (1984). *Interpersonal Communication Competence.* Newbury Park, Calif.: Sage.

# Context and Meaning

## EDWARD T. HALL

One of the functions of culture is to provide a highly selective screen between man and the outside world. In its many forms, culture therefore designates what we pay attention to and what we ignore.[1] This screening function provides structure for the world and protects the nervous system from "information overload."[2] Information overload is a technical term applied to information processing systems. It describes a situation in which the system breaks down when it cannot properly handle the huge volume of information to which it is subjected. Any mother who is trying to cope with the demands of small children, run a house, enjoy her husband, and carry on even a modest social life knows that there are times when everything happens at once and the world seems to be closing in on her. She is experiencing the same information overload that afflicts business managers, administrators, physicians, attorneys, and air controllers. Institutions such as stock exchanges, libraries, and telephone systems also go through times when the demands on the system (inputs) exceed capacity. People can handle the crunch through delegating and establishing priorities; while institutional solutions are less obvious, the high-context rule seems to apply. That is, the only way to increase information-handling capacity without increasing the mass and complexity of the system is to program the memory of the system so that less information is required to activate the system, i.e., make it more like the couple that has been married for thirty-five years. The solution to the problem of coping with

increased complexity and greater demands on the system seems to lie in the preprogramming of the individual or organization. This is done by means of the "contexting" process....

The importance of the role of context is widely recognized in the communication fields, yet the process is rarely described adequately, or if it is, the insights gained are not acted upon. Before dealing with context as a way of handling information overload, let me describe how I envisage the contexting process, which is an emergent function; i.e., we are just discovering what it is and how it works. Closely related to the high-low-context continuum is the degree to which one is aware of the selective screen that one places between himself and the outside world.[3] As one moves from the low to the high side of the scale, awareness of the selective process increases. Therefore, what one pays attention to, context, and information overload are all functionally related.

In the fifties, the United States government spent millions of dollars developing systems for machine translation of Russian and other languages. After years of effort on the part of some of the most talented linguists in the country, it was finally concluded that the only reliable, and ultimately the fastest, translator is a human being deeply conversant not only with the language but with the subject as well. The computers could spew out yards of printout but they meant very little. The words and some of the grammar were all there, but the sense was distorted. That the project failed was not due to lack of application, time, money, or talent, but for other reasons, which are central to the theme of this [article].

The problem lies not in the linguistic code but in the context, which carries varying proportions of the meaning. Without context, the code is incomplete since it encompasses only part of the message. This should become clear if one remembers that the spoken language is an abstraction of an event that happened, might have happened, or is being planned. As any writer knows, an event is usually infinitely more complex and rich than the language used to describe it. Moreover, the writing system is an abstraction of the spoken system and is in effect a reminder system of what somebody said or could have said. In the process of abstracting, as contrasted with measuring, people take in some things and unconsciously ignore others. This is what intelligence is: paying attention to the right things. The linear quality of a language inevitably results in accentuating some things at the expense of others. Two languages provide interesting contrasts. In English, when a man says, "It rained last night," there is no way of knowing how he arrived at that conclusion, or if he is even telling the truth, whereas a Hopi cannot talk about rain at all without signifying the nature of his relatedness to the event — firsthand experience, inference, or hearsay. This is a point made by the linguist Whorf[4] thirty years ago. However, selective attention and emphasis are not restricted to language but are characteristic of the rest of culture as well.

The rules governing what one perceives and [what one] is blind to in the course of living are not simple; at least five sets of disparate categories of events must be taken into account. These are: the subject or activity, the situation, one's status in a social system, past experience, and culture. The patterns governing juggling these five dimensions are learned early in life and are mostly taken for granted. The "subject" or topic one is engaged in has a great deal to do with what one does and does not attend. People working in the "hard" sciences, chemistry and physics, which deal with the physical world, are able to attend and integrate a considerably higher proportion of significant events observed than scientists working with living systems. The physical scientist has fewer variables to deal with; his abstractions are closer to the real events; and context is of less importance. This characterization is, of course, oversimplified. But it is important to remember that the laws governing the physical world, while relatively simple compared to those governing human behavior, may seem complex to the layman, while the complexity of language appears simple to the physicist, who, like everyone else, has been talking all his life. In these terms it is all too easy for the person who is in full command of a particular behavioral system, such as language, to confuse what he can *do* with a given system, with the unstated rules governing the way the system operates. The conceptual model I am using takes into account not only what one takes in and screens out but what one does not know about a given system even though one has mastered that system. The two are *not* the same. Michael Polanyi[5] stated this principle quite elegantly when he said, "The structure of a machine cannot be defined in terms of the laws which it harnesses."

What man chooses to take in, either consciously or unconsciously, is what gives structure and meaning to his world. Furthermore, what he perceives is "what he intends to do about it." Setting aside the other four dimensions (situation, status, past experience, and culture), theoretically it would be possible to arrange all of man's activities along a continuum ranging from those in which a very high proportion of the events influencing the outcome were consciously considered to those in which a much smaller number were considered. In the United States, interpersonal relations are frequently at the low end of the scale. Everyone has had the experience of thinking that he was making a good impression only to learn later that he was not. At times like these, we are paying attention to the wrong things or screening out behavior we should be observing. A common fault of teachers and professors is that they pay more attention to their subject matter than they do to the students, who frequently pay too much attention to the professor and not enough to the subject.

The "situation" also determines what one consciously takes in and leaves out. In an American court of law, the attorneys, the judge, and the jury are compelled by custom and legal practice to pay attention only to what is legally part of the record. Context, by design, carries very little weight. Contrast this with a situation in which an employee is trying to decipher the boss's behavior — whether he is pleased or not, and if he is going to grant a raise. Every little clue is a story in itself, as is the employee's knowledge of behavior in the past.

One's status in a social system also affects what must be attended. People at the top pay attention to different things from those at the middle or the bottom of the system. In order to survive, all organizations, whatever their size, have to develop techniques not only for replacing their leader but for switching the new leader's perceptions from the internal concerns he focused on when he was at the lower and middle levels to a type of global view that enables the head man or woman to chart the course for the institution.

The far-reaching consequences of what is attended can be illustrated by a characteristic fault in Western thinking that dates back to the philosophers of ancient Greece. Our way of thinking is quite arbitrary and causes us to look at ideas rather than events—a most serious shortcoming. Also, linearity can get in the way of mutual understanding and divert people needlessly along irrelevant tangents. The processes I am describing are particularly common in the social sciences; although the younger scientists in these fields are gradually beginning to accept the fact that when someone is talking about events on one level this does not mean that he has failed to take into account the many other events on different levels. It is just that one can talk about only a single aspect of something at any moment (illustrating the linear characteristic of language).

The results of this syndrome (of having to take multiple levels into account when using a single-level system) are reflected in a remark made by one of our most brilliant and least appreciated thinkers in modern psychiatry, H. S. Sullivan,[6] when he observed that as he composed his articles, lectures, and books the person he was writing to (whom he projected in his mind's eye) was a cross between an imbecile and a bitterly paranoid critic. What a waste. And so confusing to the reader who wants to find out what the man is really trying to say.

In less complex and fast-moving times, the problem of mutual understanding was not as difficult, because most transactions were conducted with people well known to the speaker or writer, people with similar backgrounds. It is important for conversationalists in any situation—regardless of the area of discourse (love, business, science)—to get to know each other well enough so that they realize what each person is and is not taking into account. This is crucial. Yet few are willing to make the very real effort—life simply moves too fast—which may explain some of the alienation one sees in the world today.

Programming of the sort I am alluding to takes place in all normal human transactions as well as those of many higher mammals. It constitutes the unmeasurable part of communication. This brings us to the point where it is possible to discuss context in relation to meaning, because what one pays attention to or does not attend is largely a matter of context. Remember, contexting is also an important way of handling the very great complexity of human transactions so that the system does not bog down in information overload.

Like a number of my colleagues, I have observed that meaning and context are inextricably bound up with each other. While a linguistic code can be analyzed on some levels independent of context (which is what the machine translation project tried to accomplish), *in real life the code, the context, and the meaning can only be seen as different aspects of a single event.* What is unfeasible is to measure one side of the equation and not the others.[7]

Earlier, I said that high-context messages are placed at one end and low-context messages at the other end of a continuum. A high-context (HC) communication or message is one in which most of the information is either in the physical context or internalized in the person, while very little is in the coded, explicit, transmitted part of the message. A low-context (LC) communication is just the opposite; i.e., the mass of the information is vested in the explicit code. Twins who have grown up together can and do communicate more economically (HC) than two lawyers in a courtroom during a trial (LC), a mathematician programming a computer, two politicians drafting legislation, two administrators writing a regulation, or a child trying to explain to his mother why he got into a fight.

Although no culture exists exclusively at one end of the scale, some are high while others are low. American culture, while not on the bottom, is toward the lower end of the scale. We are still considerably above the German-Swiss, the Germans, and the Scandinavians in the amount of contexting needed in everyday life. While complex, multi-institutional cultures (those that are technologically advanced) might be thought of as inevitably LC, this is not always true. China, the possessor of a great and complex culture, is on the high-context end of the scale.

One notices this particularly in the written language of China, which is thirty-five hundred years old and has changed very little in the past three thousand years. This common written language is a unifying force tying together half a billion Chinese, Koreans, Japanese, and even some of the Vietnamese who speak Chinese. The need for context is experienced when looking up words in a Chinese dictionary. To use a Chinese dictionary, the reader must know the significance of 214 radicals (there are no counterparts for radicals in the Indo-European languages). For example, to find the word for star one must know that it appears under the sun radical. To be literate in Chinese, one has to be conversant with Chinese history. In addition, the spoken pronunciation system must be known, because there are four tones and a change of tone means a change of meaning; whereas in English, French, German, Spanish, Italian, etc., the reader need not know how to pronounce the language in order to read it. Another interesting sidelight on the Chinese orthography is that it is also an art form.[8] To my knowledge, no low-context communication system has ever been an art form. Good art is always high-context; bad art, low-context. This is one reason why good art persists and art that releases its message all at once does not.

The level of context determines everything about the nature of the communication and is the foundation on which all subsequent behavior rests (including symbolic behavior). Recent studies in sociolinguistics have demonstrated how context-dependent the language code really is. There is an excellent example of this in the work of the linguist Bernstein,[9] who has identified what he terms "restricted" (HC) and "elaborated" (LC) codes in which vocabulary, syntax, and sounds are all altered: In the restricted code of intimacy in the home, words and sentences collapse and are shortened. This even applies to the phonemic structure of the language. The individual sounds begin to merge, as does the vocabulary, whereas in the highly articulated, highly specific, elaborated code of the classroom, law, or diplomacy, more accurate distinctions are made on all levels. Furthermore,

the code that one uses signals and is consistent with the situation. A shifting of code signals a shift in everything else that is to follow. "Talking down" to someone is low-contexting him — telling him more than he needs to know. This can be done quite subtly simply by shifting from the restricted end of the code toward the elaborated forms of discourse.

From the practical viewpoint of communications strategy, one must decide how much time to invest in contexting another person. A certain amount of this is always necessary, so that the information that makes up the explicit portions of the message is neither inadequate nor excessive. One reason most bureaucrats are so difficult to deal with is that they write for each other and are insensitive to the contexting needs of the public. The written regulations are usually highly technical on the one hand, while providing little information on the other. That is, they are a mixture of different codes or else there is incongruity between the code and the people to whom it is addressed. Modern management methods, for which management consultants are largely responsible, are less successful than they should be, because in an attempt to make everything explicit (low-contexting again) they frequently fail in their recommendations to take into account what people already know. This is a common fault of the consultant, because few consultants take the time (and few clients will pay for the time) to become completely contexted in the many complexities of the business.

There is a relationship between the worldwide activism of the sixties and where a given culture is situated on the context scale, because some are more vulnerable than others. HC actions are by definition rooted in the past, slow to change, and highly stable. Commenting on the need for the stabilizing effect of the past, anthropologist Loren Eiseley[10] takes an anti-activist position and points out how vulnerable our own culture is:

*Their world (the world of the activist), therefore, becomes increasingly the violent, unpredictable world of the first men simply because, in lacking faith in the past, one is inevitably forsaking all that enables man to be a planning animal. For man's story,[11] in brief, is essentially that of a creature who has abandoned in-stinct and replaced it with cultural tradition and the hard-won increments of contemplative thought. The lessons of the past have been found to be a reasonably secure construction for proceeding against an unknown future.*[12]

Actually, activism is possible at any point in the HC–LC continuum, but it seems to have less direc-tion or focus and becomes less predictable and more threatening to institutions in LC systems. Most HC systems, however, can absorb activism without being shaken to their foundations.

In LC systems, demonstrations are viewed as the last, most desperate act in a series of escalating events. Riots and demonstrations in the United States, particularly those involving blacks,[13] are a message, a plea, a scream of anguish and anger for the larger society to *do something.* In China (an HC culture), the Red Guard riots apparently had an en-tirely different significance. They were promulgated from the top of the social order, not the bottom. They were also a communication from top to bot-tom: first, to produce a show of strength by Mao Tse-tung; second, to give pause to the opposition and shake things up at the middle levels – a way of mobilizing society, not destroying it. Chinese friends with whom I have spoken about these riots took them much less seriously than I did. I was, of course, looking at them from the point of view of one reared in a low-context culture, where such ri-ots can have disastrous effects on the society at large.

Wherever one looks, the influence of the subtle hand of contexting can be detected. We have just spoken of the effects of riots on high- and low-context political systems, but what about day-to-day matters of perception? On the physiological level of color perception, one sees the power of the brain's need to perceive and adjust everything in terms of context. As any interior designer knows, a powerful painting, print, or wall hanging can change the perceived color of the furnishings around it. The color psychologist Faber Birren[14] demonstrated experimentally that the perceived shade of a color depends upon the color context in which it occurs. He did this by systematically vary-ing the color of the background surrounding dif-ferent color samples.

Some of the most impressive demonstrations of the brain's ability to supply the missing informa-tion – the function of contexting – are the experi-ments of Edwin Land, inventor of the Land camera. Working in color photography using a single red filter, he developed a process that is simple, but the explanation for it is not. Until Land's experiments, it was believed that color prints could be made only by superimposing transparent images of three separate photographs made with the primary colors – red, blue, and yellow. Land made his color photographs with two images: a black-and-white image to give light and shadow, and a single, *red* filter for color. When these two images were pro-jected, superimposed on a screen, even though red was the only color, they were perceived in full color with all the shades, and gradations of a three-color photograph![15] Even more remarkable is the fact that the objects used were deliberately chosen to provide no cues as to their color. To be sure that his viewers didn't unconsciously project color, Land photographed spools of plastic and wood and geometric objects whose color would be un-known to the viewer. How the eye and the visual centers of the brain function to achieve this re-markable feat of internal contexting is still only partially understood. But the actual stimulus does only part of the job.

Contexting probably involves at least two entirely different but interrelated processes – one inside the organism and the other outside. The first takes place in the brain and is a function of either past ex-perience (programmed, internalized contexting) or the structure of the nervous system (innate context-ing), or both. External contexting comprises the sit-uation and/or setting in which an event occurs (situational and/or environmental contexting).[16]

One example of the growing interest in the rela-tionship of external context to behavior is the widespread interest and concern about our public-housing disasters. Pruitt-Igoe Homes in St. Louis is only one example. This $26-million fiasco imposed on poor blacks is now almost completely aban-doned. All but a few buildings have been dyna-mited, because nobody wants to live there.

Objections and defects in high-rise public housing for poor families are legion: Mothers can't supervise their children; there are usually no community service agencies nearby and no stores or markets; and quite often there is no access to any public transportation system. There are no recreation centers for teenagers and few places for young children to play. In any budget crunch, the first thing to be cut is maintenance and then the disintegration process starts; elevators and hallways turn into death traps. The case against high-rise housing for low-income families is complex and underscores the growing recognition that environments are not behaviorally neutral.

Although situational and environmental context has only recently been systematically studied, environmental effects have been known to be a factor in behavior for years. Such men as the industrialist Pullman[17] made statements that sounded very advanced at the time. He believed that if workers were supplied with clean, airy, well-built homes in pleasant surroundings, this would exert a positive influence on their health and general sense of well-being and would make them more productive as well. Pullman was not wrong in his analysis. He simply did not live up to his stated ideals. The main street of his company town, where supervisors lived, was everything he talked about. But his workers were still poorly housed. Being isolated in a company town in close proximity to the plush homes of managers made their inadequate living conditions more obvious by way of contrast, and the workers finally embarked on a violent strike. There were many other human, economic, and political needs, which Pullman had not taken into account, that led to worker dissatisfaction. Pullman's professed idealism backfired. Few were aware of the conditions under which his laborers actually lived and worked, so that the damage done to the budding but fragile environmentalist position was incalculable and gave ammunition to the "hard-nosed," "practical" types whose minds were focused on the bottom-line figures of profit and loss.

Quite often, the influence of either programmed contexting (experience) or innate contexting (which is built in) is brushed aside. Consider the individual's spatial needs and his feelings about certain spaces. For example, I have known women who needed a room to be alone in, whose husbands did not share this particular need, and they brushed aside their wives' feelings, dismissing them as childish. Women who have this experience should not let my talking about it raise their blood pressure. For it is very hard for someone who does not share an unstated, informal need with another person to experience that need as tangible and valid. Among people of northern European heritage, the only generally accepted proxemic needs are those associated with status. However, status is linked to the ego. Therefore, while people accept that the person at the top gets a large office, whenever the subject of spatial needs surfaces it is likely to be treated as a form of narcissism. The status and organizational aspects are recognized while internal needs are not.

Yet, people have spatial needs independent of status. Some people can't work unless they are in the midst of a lot of hubbub. Others can't work unless they are behind closed doors, cut off from auditory and visual distractions. Some are extraordinarily sensitive to their environments, as though they had tentacles from the body reaching out and touching everything. Others are impervious to environmental impact. It is these differences, when and if they are understood at all, that cause trouble for architects. Their primary concern is with aesthetics, and what I am talking about lies underneath aesthetics, at a much more basic level.

As often happens, today's problems are being solved in terms of yesterday's understanding. With few exceptions, most thinking on the man-environment relationship fails to make the man-environment (M-E) transaction specific, to say nothing of taking it into account. The sophisticated architect pays lip service to the M-E relationship and then goes right on with what he was going to do anyway, demonstrating once more that people's needs, cultural as well as individual – needing a room of one's own – are not seen as real. Only the building is real! (This is extension transference again.)

Of course, the process is much more complex than most people think. Until quite recently, this whole relationship had been unexplored.[18] Perhaps those who eschewed it did so because they unconsciously and intuitively recognized its complexity. Besides, it is much easier to deal with such simple facts as a balance sheet or the exterior design of a building. Anyone who begins to investigate context and contexting soon discovers that much of what is examined, even though it occurs before his eyes, is altered in its significance by many hidden factors. Support for research into these matters is picayune. What has to be studied is not only very subtle but is thought to be too fine-grained, or even trivial, to warrant serious consideration.

One hospital administrator once threw me out of his office because I wanted to study the effects of space on patients in his hospital. Not only was he not interested in the literature, which was then considerable, but he thought I was a nut to even suggest such a study. To complicate things further, proxemics research requires an inordinate amount of time. For every distance that people use, there are at least five major categories of variables that influence what is perceived as either correct or improper. Take the matter of "intrusion distance" (the distance one has to maintain from two people who are already talking in order to get attention but not intrude). How great this distance is and how long one must wait before moving in depends on: what is going on (activity), your status, your relationship in a social system (husband and wife or boss and subordinate), the emotional state of the parties, the urgency of the needs of the individual who must intrude, etc.

Despite this new information, research in the social and biological sciences has turned away from context. In fact, attempts are often made to consciously exclude context. Fortunately, there are a few exceptions, men and women who have been willing to swim against the main currents of psychological thought.

One of these is Roger Barker, who summarized twenty-five years of observations in a small Kansas town in his book *Ecological Psychology*.[19] Starting a generation ago, Barker and his students moved into the town and recorded the behavior of the citizens in a wide variety of situations and settings such as classrooms, drugstores, Sunday-school classes, basketball games, baseball games, club meetings, business offices, bars, and hangouts. Barker discovered that much of people's behavior is situation-dependent (under control of the setting), to a much greater degree than had been supposed. In fact, as a psychologist, he challenged many of the central and important tenets of his own field. In his words:

*The view is not uncommon among psychologists that the environment of behavior is a relatively unstructured, passive, probabilistic arena of objects and events upon which man behaves in accordance with the programming he carries about within himself. . . . When we look at the environment of behavior as a phenomenon worthy of investigation for itself, and not as an instrument for unraveling the behavior-relevant programming within persons, the situation is quite different. From this viewpoint the environment is seen to consist of highly structured, improbable arrangements of objects and events which coerce behavior in accordance with their own dynamic patterning. . . . We found . . . that we could predict some aspects of children's behavior more adequately from knowledge of the behavior characteristics of the drugstores, arithmetic classes, and basketball games they inhabited than from knowledge of the behavior tendencies of particular children. . . . (emphasis added) (p. 4)*

Later Barker states,

*The theory and data support the view that the environment in terms of behavior settings is much more than a source of random inputs to its inhabitants, or of inputs arranged in fixed array and flow patterns. They indicate, rather, that the environment provides inputs with controls that regulate the inputs in accordance with the systemic requirements of the environment, on the one hand, and in accordance with the behavior attributes of its human components, on the other. This means that the same environmental unit provides different inputs to different persons, and different inputs to the same person if his behavior changes; and it means, further, that the whole program of the environment's inputs changes if its own ecological properties change; if it becomes more or less populous, for example. (p. 205)[20]*

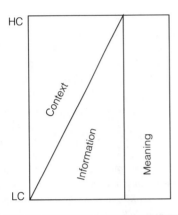

**Figure 1**

Barker demonstrates that in studying man *it is impossible to separate the individual from the environment in which he functions.* Much of the work of the transactional psychologists Ames, Ittelson, and Kilpatrick,[21] as well as my earlier work,[22] leads to the same conclusion.

In summary, regardless of where one looks, one discovers that a universal feature of information systems is that meaning (what the receiver is expected to do) is made up of: the communication, the background and preprogrammed responses of the recipient, and the situation. (We call these last two the internal and external context.)

Therefore, what the receiver actually perceives is important in understanding the nature of context. Remember that what an organism perceives is influenced in four ways — by status, activity, setting, and experience. But in man one must add another crucial dimension: *culture.*

Any transaction can be characterized as high-, low-, or middle-context [Figure 1]. HC transactions feature preprogrammed information that is in the receiver and in the setting, with only minimal information in the transmitted message. LC transactions are the reverse. Most of the information must be in the transmitted message in order to make up for what is missing in the context (both internal and external).

In general, HC communication, in contrast to LC, is economical, fast, efficient, and satisfying; however, time must be devoted to programming. If this programming does not take place, the communication is incomplete.

HC communications are frequently used as art forms. They act as a unifying, cohesive force, are long-lived, and are slow to change. LC communications do not unify; however, they can be changed easily and rapidly. This is why evolution by extension is so incredibly fast; extensions in their initial stages of development are low-context. To qualify this statement somewhat, some extension systems are higher on the context scale than others. A system of defense rocketry can be out of date before it is in place and is therefore very low-context. Church architecture, however, was for hundreds of years firmly rooted in the past and was the material focus for preserving religious beliefs and ideas. Even today, most churches are still quite traditional in design. One wonders if it is possible to develop strategies for balancing two apparently contradictory needs: the need to adapt and change (by moving in the low-context direction) and the need for stability (high-context). History is replete with examples of nations and institutions that failed to adapt by holding on to high-context modes too long. The instability of low-context systems, however, on the present-day scale is quite new to mankind. And furthermore, there is no reservoir of experience to show us how to deal with changes at this rate.

Extensions that now make up most of man's world are for the most part low-context. The question is, how long can man stand the tension between himself and his extensions? This is what *Future Shock*[23] and *Understanding Media*[24] are all about. Take a single example, the automobile, which completely altered the American scene in all its dimensions — exploded communities, shredded the fabric of relationships, switched the rural-urban balance, changed our sex mores and churchgoing habits, altered our cities, crime, education, warfare, health, funerals. (One undertaker recently experimented with drive-in viewing of the corpse!) In summary:

*The screens that one imposes between oneself and reality constitute one of the ways in which reality is structured.*

*Awareness of that structure is necessary if one is to control behavior with any semblance of rationality. Such awareness is associated with the low-context end of the scale.*

*Yet there is a price that must be paid for awareness – instability; obsolescence, and change at a rate that may become impossible to handle and result in information overload.*

*Therefore, as things become more complex, as they inevitably must with fast-evolving, low-context systems, it eventually becomes necessary to turn life and institutions around and move toward the greater stability of the high-context part of the scale as a way of dealing with information overload.*

## Notes

1. *The Hidden Dimension* discusses this quality of culture in more detail.

2. Meier (1963)

3. Man also imposes a selective screen between the conscious part of his mind and the unconscious part. Sullivan (1947) and Freud (1933)

4. Whorf (1956)

5. Polanyi (1968)

6. Sullivan (1947)

7. The linguist Noam Chomsky (1968) and his followers have tried to deal with the contexting feature of language by eliminating context and going to so-called "deep structure." The results are interesting but end up evading the main issues of communication and to an even greater extent stress ideas at the expense of what is actually going on.

8. For further information on Chinese, see Wang (1973).

9. Bernstein (1964)

10. Eiseley (1969)

11. I do not agree with Eiseley's generalizing about all of mankind, because activism, like everything else, has to be taken in context. As we will see, LC cultures appear to be more vulnerable to violent perturbations than HC cultures.

12. Saul Bellow's (1974) article on the role of literature in a setting of changing times is also relevant to this discussion. Bellow makes the point that for some time now there has been a conscious effort on the part of avant-garde Western intellectuals to obliterate the past. "Karl Marx felt in history the tradition of all dead generations weighing like a nightmare on the brain of the living. Nietzsche speaks moving of 'it was,' and Joyce's Stephen Daedalus also defines history as a 'nightmare from which we are trying to awaken.'" Bellow points out, however, that there is a paradox that must be met, for to do away with history is to destroy one's own part in the historical process. It is reasonably certain, however, that what these men were trying to do was to redefine context in order to reduce its influence on men's actions. Simply to do away with the past would lead to an incredibly unstable society, as we shall see.

13. Black culture is much higher on the context scale than white culture, and one would assume from our model that riots do not have the same meaning for blacks as they do to the white society in which the blacks are imbedded.

14. Birren (1961)

15. For further details on this fascinating set of experiments, see Land (1959).

16. These distinctions are completely arbitrary and are for the convenience of the writer and the reader. They do not necessarily occur in nature. The inside-outside dichotomy has been struck down many times, not only by the perceptual transactionalists (Kilpatrick, 1961) following in Dewey's footsteps but in my own writings as well. Within the brain, experience (culture) acts on the structure of the brain to produce mind. It makes little difference *how* the brain is modified; what is important is that modification does take place and is apparently continuous.

17. Buder (1967)

18. See Hall (1966) for a comprehensive treatment of man's relationship to the spaces he builds as well as a bibliography on the subject.

19. Barker (1968) and Barker and Schoggen (1973)

20. The interested reader will find it worthwhile to consult Barker's works directly.

21. Kilpatrick (1961)

22. Hall (1966)

23. Toffler (1970)

24. McLuhan (1964)

## Bibliography

Barker, Roger G. *Ecological Psychology.* Stanford, Calif.: Stanford University Press, 1968.
———, and Schoggen, Phil. *Qualities of Community Life.* San Francisco: Jossey-Bass, 1973.
Bellow, Saul. "Machines and Story Books," *Harper's Magazine,* Vol. 249, pp. 48-54, August 1974.

Bernstein, Basil. "Elaborated and Restricted Codes: Their Social Origins and Some Consequences." In John J. Gumperz and Dell Hymes (eds.). The Ethnography of Communication, *American Anthropologist,* Vol. 66, No. 6, Part II, pp. 55–69, 1964.

Birren, Faber. *Color, Form and Space.* New York: Reinhold, 1961.

Buder, Stanley. "The Model Town of Pullman: Town Planning and Social Control in the Gilded Age," *Journal of the American Institute of Planners,* Vol. 33, No. 1, pp. 2–10, January 1967.

Chomsky, Noam. *Language and Mind.* New York: Harcourt, Brace & World, Inc., 1968.

Eiseley, L. "Activism and the Rejection of History," *Science,* Vol. 165, p. 129, July 11, 1969.

Freud, Sigmund. *New Introductory Lectures on Psychoanalysis.* New York: W. W. Norton & Company, Inc., 1933.

Hall, Edward T. "Art, Space and the Human Experience." In Gyorgy Kepes (ed.). *Arts of the Environment.* New York: George Braziller, Inc., 1972.

_____. *The Hidden Dimension.* Garden City, N.Y.: Doubleday, 1966.

_____. "Human Needs and Inhuman Cities." In *The Fitness of Man's Environment, Smithsonian Annual II.* Washington, D.C.: Smithsonian Institution Press, 1968. Reprinted in *Ekistics,* Vol. 27, No. 160, March 1969.

Kilpatrick, F. P. *Explorations in Transactional Psychology* (contains articles by Adelbert Ames, Hadley Cantril, William Ittelson, and F. P. Kilpatrick). New York: New York University Press, 1961.

McLuhan, Marshall. *Understanding Media.* New York: McGraw-Hill, 1964.

Meier, Richard. "Information Input Overload: Features of Growth in Communications-Oriented Institutions," *Libri* (Copenhagen), Vol. 13, No. 1, pp. 1–44, 1963.

Polanyi, M. "Life's Irreducible Structure," *Science,* Vol. 160, pp. 1308–12, June 21, 1968.

Sullivan, Harry Stack. *Conceptions of Modern Psychiatry.* New York: William Alanson White Psychiatric Foundation, 1947.

Toffler, Alvin. *Future Shock.* New York: Bantam Books, 1970.

Wang, William. "The Chinese Language," *Scientific American,* Vol. 228, No. 2, February 1973.

Whorf, Benjamin Lee. *Language, Thought, and Reality.* New York: The Technology Press of M.I.T. and John Wiley, 1956.

# *Understanding Whiteness in the United States*

## JUDITH N. MARTIN

*What does it mean to be a white person in the United States? Is there such a thing as a white identity? Is it different from an ethnic identity? Is feeling white different from feeling German American or Italian American? How does being white influence the way we communicate? How is our whiteness expressed in communication?*

For many people in the United States, there currently seems to be a degree of confusion and angst about racial and ethnic identity among white people. Some people never think about being white. Some think it seems all right to feel ethnic pride, but not pride in being white. Some feel that they are being forced to think about being white because of issues like affirmative action and "reverse discrimination." This essay attempts to sort out some of these issues and explore the contradictions and tensions in the notion of whiteness as an identity. We also examine how being white in the United States may influence communication, particularly in terms of how this identity develops and is reflected in the labels and words we use to refer to ourselves.

## A Communication Perspective of Identity

Let's start with a communication perspective on identity. That is, we all have multiple identities (such as gender, religious, ethnicity, race) that make up our self-concept and how we see our-

This original essay appears here in print for the first time. All rights reserved. Permission to reprint must be obtained from the author and the publisher. Judith Martin teaches at Arizona State University, Tempe, Arizona.

selves. Identities arise from our associations with groups, some voluntary (such as professional and religious affiliations) and some involuntary (such as age and family groups), and then develop through communication with others.

As communication scholars Michael Hecht, Mary Jane Collier, and Sidney Ribeau (1993) have noted, cultural identities are *negotiated, co-created, reinforced, and challenged through communication.* Some identities may be easier to co-create and negotiate than others. For example, does it seem easier to understand and negotiate being female than being white? How is being white negotiated and challenged through communication in today's world?

In addition, as Collier explains earlier in this chapter, our identities are expressed through *norms and labels* – the communicative behaviors and terms that reflect the core symbols or priorities of our group-associated identities. In this book, a number of essays identify the core symbols and norms of various groups like Japanese, African Americans, and Indians. Are there similar norms, labels, and core symbols that are associated with being white in the United States?

One final thing that we need to keep in mind about identities is that they are *dynamic* and *context-related.* I am not just a female, a professor, a white German American. I am all of these, and any one identity may be highlighted or suppressed depending on the situation or context. For example, in some situations, such as when I am the only white person in a conversation or when I am discussing the issue of race, my white identity is highlighted. In other conversations, my professor identity may be emphasized more. We are always in the process of becoming and unbecoming, as we negotiate, develop, and re-form our identities through communication.

Three issues need to be addressed as we apply this communication perspective to understanding white identity: the difference between white racial and ethnic identity, the characteristics of a white identity, and how whites develop a sense of being white.

## White Racial and Ethnic Identity

### Race Versus Ethnicity

What is the difference between racial and ethnic identity? Many people believe that race has to do with physical characteristics, whereas ethnicity is more a sense of a shared culture, belief system, and origin. However, most scholars now reject the biological argument in favor of a more social approach to understanding race. That is, while there may be some physiological basis for racial categories, it is the way in which these categories are constructed and the meaning attached to racial categories that have a profound influence on communication and how identities are negotiated. What are the arguments against physiological definitions?

First, racial categories vary widely in different parts of the world. One contrast is seen in the United States and South America. In the United States, there are two major racial distinctions (black and white), and this distinction is fairly rigid. People seem to have a sense of who is white and who isn't (for example, "you don't look black") and are uneasy when they are unable to categorize someone of mixed racial origin ("But are you white *or* Black?"). In contrast, people in Brazil and other South American countries recognize a variety of intermediate racial categories.

A second example of how racial categories are socially constructed is that racial categories have changed throughout U.S. immigration history and some groups have been shifted from one racial category to another at particular points in history. In the eighteenth century, British immigrants struggled to preserve their base of power and even to prevent other Europeans from entering the United States. In the nineteenth century, as more and more southern Europeans immigrated, there was an attempt to classify Irish and Jewish Europeans as nonwhite. Instead, the racial line was drawn around Europe, and those outside (such as the Chinese and Japanese) were then designated as nonwhite (Omi & Winant, 1992). So while the notion of race has some basis in physiology, it probably makes more sense to talk about race *formation* and to think about race as a complex of social meanings that get interpreted through communication, rather than as something fixed, concrete, and objective.

It should also be pointed out that as socially constructed, these categories are relational, exist in relation to each other. Could there be a white without a black category? What does it mean that we tend to see race in the United States in polar categories, white and black? If people do not fit or do not want to fit into these categories, how can they negotiate their identity?

## Bounded Versus Dominant/Normative Identities

The relationship between white racial and ethnic identity can be clarified by distinguishing between bounded and dominant identities (Frankenburg, 1993; Trinh, 1986/87). Bounded cultures are those groups we belong to that are specific and not dominant or normative (such as groups defined by religion, gender, ethnicity). For most white people, connections to these groups are clear and easy to talk about. Being Irish American means we celebrate St. Patrick's Day; being Amish means we follow the "*Ordnung*" (the community rules). Growing up German American may mean working hard for the sake of working and not being very verbally expressive. It's easy to recognize and identify these cultural behaviors.

However, what it means to belong to the dominant or *normative* white culture is a much more "slippery" construct, more difficult to define, but just as real. It is not often easy to see what cultural practices or norms link white people together. For example, we usually don't think of Thanksgiving as a white American holiday. Part of the "slipperiness" of this identity is related to the dominant or normative aspect of being white.

## Identity and Power

Sometimes the more powerful aspects of identity are the most unrecognized, and power is more strongly linked to aspects of identity that are ascribed, or involuntary. For example, when questioned about identity males will often not mention gender. They just don't think about it, whereas women are more likely to be aware of how gender is a part of their identity.

The same thing may be true about being white. One reason white people don't think about being white is that they may not need to. Communication scholars Tom Nakayama and Robert Krizek (1995) suggest that this lack of consciousness on the part of whites is possible only because of the power associated with being white. The experiences and communication patterns of whites are taken as the norm from which others are marked or measured. The universal norm then becomes invisible. For example, the news media refer to "black leaders" but never to "white leaders." There is "black on black violence," but European conflicts are not referred to as "white on white violence."

What does it mean that the category "white" is seldom referred to and that whites so rarely talk about the meaning of being white? As Krizek reflects:

*I've gone through life never consciously thinking about labels. I suppose we defined ourselves as one of those people we didn't label, although nobody every said that. We were just white, not black or brown, and I don't really know what that means. No one ever questioned it (Nakayama & Krizek, 1995, p. 292).*

On the other hand, Nakayama (1993) has written about growing up in the South as a fourth-generation Japanese American, with his identity as an American consistently challenged as people frequently asked him where he was *really* from and if he spoke English.

Nakayama and Krizek attempt to show how the "invisibility" of whiteness is related to power by analyzing the "rhetoric of whiteness" or how white people talk about being white when explicitly asked. They found that people often resisted discussing how they felt about being white, which they interpret as reflecting an invisible power in which white is not a category of identity, but black African American, or Chicana is.

A second rhetorical strategy was to say that being white was based on negation, that white is "not something else (not black, brown, yellow or red)." This seems like a neutral way to talk about being white, but they point out that in this strategy white is again the universal against which other colors are marked. Another strategy confuses whiteness with nationality. Whiteness means white American. As one of their respondents noted, "A lot of times when people think of American, I bet you they probably think of white. They probably think it's redundant" (p. 301). What does it mean for all those Americans who are not white?

We can see how difficult it is for people to pin down the meaning of whiteness, but perhaps we'll understand intercultural communication better if we apply the same scrutiny to white identity that we apply to other cultural groups. This lack of awareness on the part of whites may be changing, as we'll discuss later. As issues of race are brought up more and more frequently in the United States (in the O. J. Simpson trial, for example) white people are perhaps thinking more about being white than ever before, and perhaps it will become easier to identify those norms and core symbols of whiteness.

In Chapter 3 Edith Folb argues that there is a relative continuum of power in the United States associated with various identities, ranging from the more powerful groups (whites, males, Protestants, heterosexuals, middle/upper classes, the educated) to less powerful groups (racial minorities, females, religions other than Protestant, gays, the working class, the less educated). And we each may have aspects of our identity that are more or less powerful, depending on which is highlighted in any particular context. Those that are more involuntary or physically marked are more difficult and the most problematic to negotiate.

What happens when our identities are challenged? Growing up as an Amish/Mennonite young woman, I felt marginalized in many social contexts because I was physically marked by a distinctive dress and physical appearance. It was difficult to negotiate anything other than a bounded (Amish) identity. What are the communicative consequences when identities are challenged — when, for example, Asian Americans are asked "Where are you re-ally from?" or "Do you speak English?" How does it affect the communication between people when the identities of some are often challenged and others (whites) are rarely challenged?

## Dimensions of White Identity

An interesting question, then, is whether there is a set of cultural norms and symbols shared by most white people. Many scholars feel that there are uniquely white cultural patterns, but that they are often difficult to discern. Sociologist Ruth Frankenburg suggests that one way to understand whiteness is to view it not as simply a racial or ethnic category but rather as a set of three linked dimensions in which power is a key ingredient. These are modified to emphasize the communicative aspect of identity: a location of structural advantage, a standpoint from which to view ourselves and others, and a set of cultural practices (core symbols, labels, and norms).

## Whiteness Is a Location of Structural Privilege

Some scholars argue that white identity is linked to the structural advantage of race privilege within the United States but that the two are not synonymous. All whites do not have power and do not have equal access to power. For example, one can point to times in U.S. history when some white cultural groups were not privileged, but rather were viewed as separate or different, as were the Irish in the early part of the twentieth century and the German Americans during World War II.

However, scholars have pointed out that the memory of marginality in these instances has outlasted the marginality. In the latter part of the twentieth century, European immigrant groups are now assimilated and are "just American." Boundaries between Americanness and whiteness have been much more fluid for "white ethnic" groups than for people of color.

How is this dimension of white identity played out in the everyday lives of white people and their communication with others? Peggy McIntosh (1995) has tried to identify the ways in which white privilege affects her daily interactions. See if you can list others:

I can, if I wish, arrange to be in the company of people of my race most of the time.

I can be fairly sure of having my voice heard in a group in which I am the only member of my race.

I can talk with my mouth full and not have people put this down to my color.

I can do well in a challenging situation without being called a credit to my race.

I am never asked to speak for all people of my racial group.

I can worry about racism without it being seen as self-interest or self-seeking.

My culture gives me little fear about ignoring the perspectives and powers of people of other races.

The question then is how does this aspect of white identity influence my communication with others? Perhaps it means that I approach most interactions with a confidence that if I'm nice, most people will be nice back to me. People won't prejudge me as untrustworthy, or "different," or "angry." Or if they see me sitting with other people who are white, they won't think this means I don't want to communicate with people who aren't white. They will judge me and communicate with me as an individual.

Several studies have, in fact, found that whites and African Americans approach interethnic conversations in different ways. Whites rarely talk about issues of power when discussing interethnic communication, whereas it is a more central issue in African American frameworks (Martin, Hecht, & Larkey, 1994). So maybe this is one aspect of being white, the fact that I don't consider power issues in conversations. Perhaps you can think of other ways that privilege may be reflected in whites' communication.

While being white in the United States may mean privilege sometimes, there seems to be an increasing perception that being white does not mean "invisible privilege." Charles A. Gallagher,

who interviewed college students in a large inner-city campus found that white students thought a lot about being white and saw their whiteness not as a privilege but as a liability. They often felt that minority students were getting more breaks and more privileges. They also felt that they were prejudged by students of color as being racist because they were white.

Some whites feel that being white is not very positive, that whiteness represents blandness (like Wonder Bread), and that it is not very interesting in contrast to the cultural "richness" of other cultural groups. This sometimes leads whites to retrieve their ethnic heritage and identity (Italian American, Irish American, and so on). Ethnicity for white Americans can be almost like a garment that is put on or off at will.

Perhaps this change in identity, this growing awareness of a white identity, is occurring because the changing demographics in the United States means that whites *are beginning to perceive* themselves in the minority. Gallagher (1994) also asked students to estimate the ratio of whites to blacks on campus. Many students reported that they thought the ratio was 30 percent white students, 70 percent black students. The actual ratio was 70 percent white and 30 percent black.

The point here is not the inaccuracy of the perception, or whether whites or minorities are more privileged, but how these perceptions affect intercultural communication. How do we communicate with others if we feel that we are being prejudged as racist? or as privileged? How are these identities negotiated and confirmed or challenged in our intercultural interactions?

## Whiteness Is a "Standpoint"

A second dimension of white identity, according to Frankenburg, is a standpoint, a place from which white people look at themselves, at others, and at society. What are some perceptions shared by white people? And how do these perceptions differ from those of other cultural groups?

A dramatic example arose during the trial of the African American celebrity O. J. Simpson, accused of killing his ex-wife, Nicole Brown Simpson, and her friend Ron Goldman. An ABC News poll conducted just before the verdict was handed down showed a profound split between white and black perception: 77 percent of whites thought Simpson was guilty, 72 percent of blacks believed he was innocent (*Arizona Republic,* October 1, 1995, p. A2).

Both whites and blacks saw the same televised trial, the same evidence, heard the same legal arguments, but saw these from two different "standpoints" and arrived at two different conclusions. How could this be? Experts analyzed the two standpoints and tried to understand this dramatic difference in perception in the days immediately following the trial.

Most experts saw the roots of the different perceptions in the different life experiences of African and white Americans. As one columnist explained it:

*Most whites thought Fuhrman [the policeman accused of evidence tampering and racism] was a sick act and an exception. Most blacks, especially those in L. A. thought he was no aberration; they've known others like him. (Wilson, 1995, p. 2)*

There are numerous other, perhaps less dramatic examples of how perceptions of whites contrast with those of other U.S. groups. To give just one example, according to a CBS News poll reported in the *Arizona Republic,* 38 percent of whites versus 27 percent of blacks think race relations in the United States are generally good (October 4, 1995). So something about being white influences how we view the world and ultimately how we communicate with others. As one individual reported in Nakayama and Krizek's study:

*"I don't exactly know what it means to be white, but we all know don't we? I mean I never talk about it, but I know that we understand each other at some level. Like when a black guy gets on an elevator or when you have a choice to sit or stand next to a white person or a black person. You pick the white person and you look at each other, the whites and you just know that you've got it better. You don't say anything but you know. It's in the looks." (p. 298)*

Of course, not all whites perceive all situations in the same way. Remember that identity is dynamic, negotiated, and context-dependent. Perhaps

it is easier to see shared perceptions in dramatic situations like the Simpson trial or the Rodney King beating and the subsequent trial of white police officers. And even then, it is still difficult to understand how perceptions are related to race.

Again the question comes back to how these varying perceptions, expressions of identity, influence our communication. Are there ways to negotiate these varying perceptions?

Discussions following the O. J. Simpson trial may have presented opportunities for intercultural dialogue and finding some common ground. Blacks saw whites unanimously condemning Mark Fuhrman, and whites heard the same thing from blacks concerning Simpson's pattern of spousal abuse (*Arizona Republic,* October 1, 1995, p. A22).

## Whiteness Is a Set of Core Symbols, Norms, and Labels

*Core symbols* are those values and priorities of a cultural group that are reflected in the norms of behavior and labels used to describe the group (Hecht, Collier, & Ribeau, 1993). Often the *norms* are unmarked; they are not made explicit, and it is hard to identify what norms are uniquely shared by whites. As noted, this difficulty comes partly from the normative and dominant aspect of being white. The dilemma is that white is everything and it is nothing. It is just there, and yet it is difficult to talk about, maybe even embarrassing.

Sometimes, these cultural practices are most clearly visible to those who are not white, to those groups who are excluded. Janet Helms (1990) and others (such as M. Asante, 1973) have attempted to outline values that are shared primarily by white people. For example, they suggest that a strong belief in individualism and an emphasis on linear thinking are two patterns that are most strongly linked to being white and are not universally shared by other cultural groups in the United States.

The *labels* we attach to ourselves and others that characterize ethnicity and/or race may be seen as a category of core symbols and are another way in which identity is expressed. Labels have meaning and are not neutral.

The questions of labels and identity has been of concern to marginalized groups for a long time. One issue revolves around who has the right to name others. Who has the right to use a label? Again power comes into play, for dominant groups can exercise power in naming others. And it is often difficult for the less powerful groups to control their own labels. It is well known that Native Americans have objected to the use of tribal terms as names for sports groups (Redskins), cars (Jeep Cherokee), and other commercial products. Some African Americans object to Aunt Jemima pancake mix and Uncle Ben's rice. It is not widely known that Quakers objected strenuously to the use of the label "Quaker" in Quaker Oats. Would we like a team called "the Fighting Honkeys"? One response of marginalized groups is to take the pejorative label and make it their own, as gay and lesbian groups did in appropriating and using the label "queer."

Dolores Tanno (1994) describes how her multiple identities are reflected in various labels (Spanish, Mexican American, Latina, Chicana). The Spanish label is one she was given by her family and designates an ancestral origin (Spain). The label Mexican American reflects two important cultures that make up her identity. Latina reflects cultural and historical connectedness with others of Spanish descent (such as Puerto Ricans and South Americans) and the Chicana label promotes political and cultural assertiveness in representing her identity. She stresses that she is all these, that each reveals a different facet of her identity: symbolic, historical, cultural, and political.

Similarly, the labels and meanings for African Americans have evolved over the years. Hecht, Collier, and Ribeau (1993) claim that the shift from black to African American as a self-preferred label is founded in issues of self-determination, strength, progress, and control.

What do white people want to be called? When we asked white college students what labels they preferred to use and preferred others to use, they consistently chose the most "normative," the least specific (Martin, Krizek, Nakayama, & Bradford, 1996). They wanted to be called white, or maybe white American, but not white Anglo-Saxon Protestant. What does it mean if whites resist being

specifically "located" by geography (Anglo) or history (WASP)? Does it express the right of being the normative group, the one that names and categorizes others but is not itself categorized?

However, this may be changing as our "white" identity is being (re)negotiated and defined in contemporary U.S. society. Perhaps these issues of labels will be discussed more by whites. Perhaps we can explore the meanings for various labels — African Americans, white, European American. Or we can learn to negotiate and call people what they want to be called, as Mary Jane Collier suggests, to affirm the identity that each thinks is important.

## White Identity Development

How do we develop a sense of whiteness? This sense (just like our sense of gender) develops over time and through communication with others. There seem to be several stages of identity development, not with definite beginnings and ends, but stages nonetheless that represent different positions of understanding who we are.

In the United States, minority group members develop a sense of racial and ethnic identity much earlier than majority group members do. As psychologist Rita Hardiman (1994) describes it:

*It has frequently been the case that White students enrolled in my class on racial and cultural issues in counseling expect to be taught all about the cultures of people of color and they are almost always surprised to hear that we will be discussing the White group's experience. Some students remark that they are not White; they are female, or working-class, or Catholic or Jewish, but not White. When challenged, they reluctantly admit that they are White but report that this is the first time they have had to think about what it means for them. (p. 125)*

### Stage 1: No Social Consciousness

In Hardiman's model, the first stage of identity development is the same for whites and minority groups; in this stage children may be aware of physical differences and some cultural differences but do not feel fearful or hostile and do not feel racially superior. However, eventually they absorb the message from the social environment (family and society) about racial groups.

## Stage 2: Acceptance

The second stage, acceptance, represents the internalization of the messages about racial group membership and the acquisition of a belief in the "normalcy" (superiority) of being white. This may be either a passive acceptance or an active acceptance of the dominant socialization. An important point here is that individuals at this stage are not aware that they have been programmed to accept a particular world view about race. It is simply the way things are and is not questioned.

**Passive Acceptance.** In the passive acceptance stage, there is no conscious identification with being white. Whites at this stage may hold the following subtly racist views but do not see themselves as being racist. Rather, racism is seen as the holding of extreme attitudes, such as those espoused by the Klu Klux Klan.

1. Minority groups are culturally deprived and need help to assimilate.

2. Affirmative action is reverse discrimination because people of color are being given opportunities that whites have never had.

3. White culture, music, art, and literature is "classical"; works of art by people of color are primitive art, or "crafts."

4. People of color are "culturally different" whereas whites are individuals with no group identity, cultures, or shared experience of racial privilege.

People at this stage usually take one of two passive positions with respect to racial issues and interactions with people of color. They either *avoid* or adopt a *patronizing* stance. That is, they may avoid racial issues, avoid being around people of color, or be very polite when they are. Or they may take a patronizing stance, be very solicitous and try to help the less fortunate: "I really feel terrible about the few minority students in my classes. I know it's so hard for them to fit in. I really wish I could figure out some way to make things easier for them."

**Active Acceptance.** Those whites in the active acceptance stage are very conscious of their whiteness and may express their feelings of superiority collectively (as with a White Student Union.) There may be open resentment toward minorities who are perceived to be more advantaged: "Why do all the black students sit together in the Student Union?"

Some whites never move beyond this phase. If they do, it is usually a result of a number of cumulative events. Hardiman describes the transition of one of her students from the active acceptance stage to the next stage:

*[She took] a class in high school on African American authors. . . . She felt that the authors' experiences had happened long ago and that whatever unfairness existed then had been rectified. Later, after entering college and developing some close relationships with Asian American and African American students, she began to have other experiences that contradicted her assumptions about fairness. An incident in her residence hall involving the indiscriminate rounding up of all Black male students by police, and an ensuing protest over that incident, had a particular effect upon her. She described herself as "waking up to the reality" after this incident. (p. 127)*

## Stage 3: Resistance

The resistance stage represents a major attitudinal shift, from a position that blames victims for their conditions to one that names and blames a white's own dominant group as the source of racial problems. This resistance may take the form of passive resistance, with little behavioral change, or active resistance — an ownership of racism. Individuals may be embarrassed as they recognize that much of their behavior has been racist. Some may try to distance themselves from other whites or gravitate toward communities of color.

In the active resistance stage, whites believe that changing the white community is the responsibility of whites; they shift from being a good "liberal" helper to being an active agent of change. However, as they make the transition to the next stage, they realize that while they may appreciate communities of color, they are not members of those cultures and they feel a need to redefine whiteness.

## Stage 4: Redefinition

In this stage, energy is refocused or redirected to redefining whiteness in nonracist terms. Whites come to see that they do not have to accept the definition of white that is placed on them by society. They can move beyond the connection to racism to see positive aspects of being European American and feel more comfortable being white. However, the difficult challenge here is to identify what white culture is. Sometimes this can be done only by coming into contact with and interacting with people of color, before moving on to redefine one's own white identity. A second task is to identify the ways in which racism is harmful to whites and to move beyond thinking that racism affects only people of color.

## Stage 5: Internalization

In this stage, whites are finally able to integrate their whiteness into all other facets of their identity, and this affects other aspects of social and personal identity — sex role, religious role, and so on. At this point, there is less consciousness about identity; all aspects are internalized and manifested in spontaneous behavior.

## Summary

This essay attempts to initiate a dialogue about what it means to be white in the United States as we approach the twenty-first century. At this time, it seems that there are competing notions about what is involved in white identity. It is seen as both invisible and real. It is seen as both privilege and liability. It is seen as both positive and negative. And all of these dimensions are played out in our communication with others. Our identities are simultaneously shaping and being shaped by our communication.

It seems appropriate to conclude with some questions for reflection and discussion:

1. When was the first time you were aware of your racial identity? How was it talked about with your friends and family as you were growing up?

2. How did your family talk about ethnicity?

3. If you are white, in what contexts do you think about being white? Do you feel white when you are with only white people?

4. What are the communicative consequences of thinking about race in categories like black and white? What do you feel when you can't easily categorize someone as black or white?

## References

Asante, M. K. (aka A. L. Smith), (1973). *Transracial Communication*. Englewood Cliffs, N.J.: Prentice-Hall.

Frankenburg, R. (1993). *White Women, Race Matters: The Social Construction of Whiteness*. Minneapolis: University of Minnesota Press.

Gallagher, C. A. (1994). White construction in the university. *Socialist Review, 1/2, 167–187.*

Hardiman, R. (1994). "White Racial Identity Development in the United States." In E. P. Salett and D. R. Koslow (Eds.), *Race, Ethnicity and Self: Identity in Multicultural Perspective,* 117–142. Washington, D.C.: National MultiCultural Institute.

Hecht, M., Collier, M. J., and Ribeau, S. (1993) *African-American Communication*. Newbury Park, Calif.: Sage.

Helms, J. E. (1990). "Toward a Model of White Racial Identity Development." In J. Helms (Ed.), *Black and White Racial Identity: Theory, Research, and Practice,* 49–66. New York: Greenwood Press.

Martin, J. N., Krizek, R. L., Nakayama, T., and Bradford, L. (In press). Labels for white Americans. *Communication Quarterly.*

Martin, J. N., Hecht, M. L., and Larkey, L. K. (1994). Conversational improvement strategies for interethnic communication: African American and European American perspectives. *Communication Monographs, 61,* 237–255.

McIntosh, P. (1995). "White Privilege and Male Privilege: A Personal Account of Coming to See Correspondences Through Work in Women's Studies." In M. L. Andersen and P. H. Collins (Eds.), *Race, Class and Gender,* 76–86. Belmont, Calif.: Wadsworth.

Nakayama, T. (1993). "Dis/orienting Identities: Asian Americans, History and Intercultural Communication." In A. Gonzalez, M. Houston, and V. Chen (Eds.), *Our Voices: Essays in Culture, Ethnicity and Communication,* 12–17. Los Angeles: Roxbury.

Nakayama, T., and Krizek, R. L. (1995). Whiteness: A strategic rhetoric. *Quarterly Journal of Speech, 81,* 291–309.

Omi, M., and Winant, H. (1992). "Racial Formations." In P. S. Rothenberg (Ed.), *Race, Class and Gender in the United States,* 26–35. New York: St. Martin's Press.

Salett, E. P., and Koslow, D. R. (Eds.). (1994). *Race, Ethnicity and Self: Identity in Multicultural Perspective.* Washington, D.C.: National MultiCultural Institute.

Tanno, D. (1994). "Names, Narratives, and the Evolution of Ethnic Identity." In A. Gonzalez, M. Houston, and V. Chen (Eds.), *Our Voices: Essays in Culture, Ethnicity and Communication,* 30–33. Los Angeles: Roxbury.

Trinh, T. M. (1986/7). Difference: A special third world women issue. *Discourse,* 8.

Wilson, S. (1995). Black and white perceptions of justice are worlds apart. *The Arizona Republic,* October 4, 1995, p. A2).

# *F*ive Paradigms of Ethnic Relations

## ROD JANZEN

A major focus of contemporary American education is the nature and character of interethnic relationships. This is evident whether the analysis and debate is about global issues, the domestic multicultural agenda, or social issues in general. The views expressed in the debate reflect a diverse set of ideological assumptions, though these are often concealed rather than explicit.

The present study is based on an intensive review of the literature pertaining to interethnic relationships, as well as the author's attendance at numerous interpretive presentations on diverse forms of "multiculturalism." From this review, I have identified five different perspectives, or paradigms, on the basis of which Americans in general define ethnic relations.

Our view of different ethnic and cultural groups is conditioned by the paradigms that guide our understanding of and vision for interethnic relationships. This is the case whether one is an administrator, teacher, student, or member of the community. Educators, in particular, need to come to terms with the diversity of interethnic paradigmatic understanding. While this paper does not offer specific solutions to our national multicultural dilemma, it will hopefully help clarify some of the reasons why solutions to our problems do not come easily in this complicated time.

The first paradigm is Traditional Eurocentric Racism. In this vision, America is defined as predominantly northern and western European in its

From *Social Education,* 1994, Volume 58, Number 6, pp. 349–353. Reprinted by permission of the National Council for the Social Sciences. Rod Janzen teaches at Fresno Pacific College, Fresno, California.

culture and institutions, with a dominant Anglo-Saxon and Protestant foundation. In this vision, which reflects the actual development of American history, other "white" Europeans are always at some point (usually within the second generation) pulled into the northern European center (Novak 1971, 114).

Irish immigrants, for example, initially experienced extensive discrimination due to their ethnic uniqueness and their adherence to Catholicism. Immigrants from southern Europe experienced similar bias. Because of their later date of mass immigration, they also had to deal with discrimination related to job competition with "real" Americans. The fact that many eastern Europeans were adherents of Orthodox Christianity (a tradition with which most Americans were not familiar) further complicated matters. Still, American citizens in general wanted Irish and southern and eastern European immigrants, now that they were here, to become "like" them, i.e., to become northern and western European in customs and beliefs. If one could assist in "Protestantizing" Catholic ecclesiastical and theological traditions along the way, so much the better.

Paradigm I thus describes a way of thinking and acting which brought all "white" Americans into the national fold, with one exception. Traditional Eurocentric racism never fully accepted the Jewish people because of their non-Christian religious commitment, even though Jews tended to adhere, for the most part, to northern and western European cultural traditions (Takaki 1993, 298). Jews thus found themselves occupying a quasi-purgatorial niche in American society.

According to the Paradigm I way of thinking and acting, non-Europeans were never fully accepted as "Americans." Blacks, American Indians, Asians, and Mexicans, for example, were all considered inferior peoples, culturally and intellectually. The Irish, southern Europeans, and (to a lesser extent) Jews could at some point be recognized as "real" Americans as they were assimilated (with certain stereotypical perceptions still held and acted upon), but persons in the non-European groups were never fully accepted, due to an ethnocentric bias against the cultures from which they claimed descent. Citi-

zens of the United States wanted members of inferior ethnic groups to become "like" them with regard to customs practiced, dress, religion, and attitude toward work (though the work of the inferior peoples might be supervised by European-Americans); but they were not regarded as equals.

Paradigm I thus describes the historical American approach to latter-day non-Anglo-Saxon immigrants. This was also the approach applied to America's indigenous peoples. It established a vision still held, in different forms, by many American citizens today who fear and do not want an America which might become darker physically, less Christian religiously, and less European with regard to its understanding of the best way to design social-political institutions. Even in the field of education, there are many who hold certain Paradigm I principles, even though they do not put their thoughts in print.

Paradigm II, Melting Pot Assimilations, offers a different point of view, and an alternative interpretation of American history. In the melting pot vision, various cultural groups from all over the world, whether they originate in Europe, Asia, the United States itself, the Middle East, Africa, or South America, are treated with essential equality in the United States. In their constant interaction — one culture crossing over into another — they begin at some point to join together to create one large heterogeneous mixture (Zangwill 1909, 37, 199).

Like the tiger who runs around a tree and turns into a stack of pancakes in the well-known folk tale, the various immigrant groups rotate ever more rapidly around whatever the central but constantly fluctuating definition of America has become. In the end, the United States itself is explained as a complete mixing together of various cultural traditions with regard to language, customs, religion, economic system, and political system.

With regard to language, for example, all immigrant groups eventually accept an Americanized form of English as a common tongue. Simultaneously, capitalism is accepted as the best economic system. Even though not all Americans belong to the same religious denomination, there is general acceptance of comparable moral principles and values. The Old Testament's Ten Commandments, for example, are valued in the Christian, Jewish, and Muslim traditions.

Through the relationship with other melting pot citizens, one ceases at some point to perceive oneself in any terms other than "American." Individual ties to ethnic groups culturally rooted in other parts of the world are not considered important or relevant. These connections in fact are seen as representing potentially disruptive forces which can give the melting pot too many distinctive and distracting ingredients, leaving citizens the sense that there is no melted-together foundational understanding of what it means to be an American. Individual immigrants are expected to discard connections to ancestral homes. Further, by marrying across ethnic boundaries in the North American "new world," they assist in the creation of a new world people, the "American people."

Paradigm II suggests that most immigrants in the past jumped into the pot voluntarily and with great enthusiasm (Fitzgerald 1980, 82), ridding themselves of many remnants of past existence. As the newly-arrived cultures of the world melted into the pot, they did, of course, bring cultural traditions along with them. These customs, in various manifestations, continued to inform the debate with regard to what made someone an "American." Since everybody was equal before the law, the new immigrants could feel that they had as much ethnically-based influence on what defined America as anyone who had melted into the pot at some earlier time.

Paradigm II is a description and vision for America still held by many. Indeed, a number of educators lament the fact that this model is no longer as widely accepted in the late 20th century. The melting pot paradigm does not, however, provide an accurate account of what actually transpired in American history. That story is perhaps more adequately portrayed in Paradigm I, particularly into the 1940s.

Paradigm II suggests, in a visionary sense, the melting away of all original ethnic cultures and traditions. The best part of each theoretically becomes part of what makes America a unique and great inter-ethnic experiment. Constant interaction theoretically stirs the multicultural stew together, and a gloriously harmonious unification is the end result of such mixing.

In fact, however, most new immigrants to America found themselves pressured by the power of the institutionalized public school system and generally-accepted American cultural principles to give up most ethnic traditions, unless these happened to be Anglo-Saxon Protestant in nature, and to melt into an essentially northern and western European cultural pot. Instead of melting equitably into the American soup, immigrants had first to shed essential aspects of traditional cultural belief and practice (Alba 1981, 91).

In the end, most non-Anglo-Saxon ethnic traditions were lost, with the exception of such customs as the placing of Christmas trees in American homes during the month of December and (more recently, in California) the production of tamales during that same time of year. The fact that America's large population of ethnic Germans has had so little impact on the predominant culture in the United States is perhaps the best example of the way in which the melting pot process has actually functioned. During World War I, many states even outlawed the use of German in church services (Teichroeb 1979, 96).

Paradigm II thus denotes a melting pot which in actual fact "melted away" non-Anglo-Saxon traditions. Yet this paradigm has become an integral part of mainstream American thought. It is a worldview which has been taught and promoted in American public schools both as ideal and fact, and one which has been accepted by the media in general through much of the 20th century. A large number of Americans thus still believe strongly that this is the most accurate description of historical American inter-ethnic relationships.

Both Paradigms I and II promote philosophies which are essentially assimilationist in nature. Each paradigmatic understanding assumes a common set of cultural standards which new immigrants must accept either voluntarily or by compulsion.

Many melting pot theorists today, however, call themselves "multiculturalists." They believe in the vision of a melting pot which encourages new immigrants to add to the ever-changing, melted-together, contents of the pot significant (not superficial) aspects of their traditional ethnic cultures, even as those persons are themselves transformed into ethnic "Americans" (Glazer 1991, 18).

Generally speaking, Paradigms III, IV, and V are most often used to define the multicultural way of thinking. With these paradigms we move directly into the waters of pluralism, with its emphasis on the retention and maintenance of traditional cultural beliefs and practices. There is a significant difference of opinion, however, even among advocates of pluralism, with regard to how it should be interpreted.

Paradigm III, Ethnic Nationalism, for example, suggests that each ethnic group, regardless of origin, should preserve its unique character, customs, languages, and ways of knowing without being assimilated. In this vision, the ethnic community is the principal source of one's personal and group identity.

America itself is held together, in this model, by a collective commitment to democratic institutions and practices and by the English language, which each cultural group teaches alongside other ethnic languages. Ethnic nationalism assumes the establishment of certain relationships across cultural boundaries. It expects, however, that most immigrants and Americans who have retained strong ethnic identities will focus their attention on their own cultural groups, the source of the ethnic nationalist's primary identity (Barrera 1988, 42).

Exponents of the ethnic nationalist vision often identify their ideas with the cultural mosaic concept promoted by the Canadian government. That vision was founded historically on the basis of a bicultural, French/English confrontation. Rather than being purely "multi-cultural" in nature, primary institutional support was traditionally given to two identifiable language groups (Lipset 1990, 179). Since 1971, however, the Canadian Government through its Cabinet-level Ministry of Multiculturalism and Citizenship, has encouraged every ethnic group living in Canada to retain ideological and behavioral uniqueness via substantial government-funded programs (McConaghy 1993, 190).

Pluralists who support ethnic nationalism seek to preserve special cultural and linguistic understandings and customs which have generally diminished in cosmopolitan settings. Ethnic nationalists thus emphasize the importance of retaining, in some measure, closed ethnic enclaves within American society at large. They remind us that it is not possible to express certain beliefs and feelings outside the boundaries of specific psycho-cultural-linguistic traditions. The center, in the ethnic nationalist vision is, therefore, a weak one.

Much of the Afrocentric curriculum movement fits this particular paradigm, though when it places additional emphasis on viewing the world through the lens of a myriad of cultural perspectives it might also find itself positioned within the parameters of Paradigm IV and V definitions (Hilliard 1992, 13). Persons who suggest the viability of creating semi-independent ethnic republics within the United States follow this model most closely (Barrera 1988, 160).

It is important to note that the Paradigm III model assumes that each national grouping contains within itself a multiplicity of ethnicities. Within the Laotian group, for example, the Hmong represent a unique group of people (traditionally semi-nomadic and illiterate). Ethnic nationalism thus has major implications for schooling if educators seek to meet the psychological needs, ways of knowing, and cultural expectancies of different native groups.

Paradigm IV, Globalism, provides a different pluralist twist by suggesting that the increasing economic, ecological, and political interconnectedness of modern life demands that we reach consensus on an international ideological and behavioral center which then forms the foundation for all world cultures, rather than thinking only in terms of what might hold Americans together (Paradigms I, II, and V) or with regard to those customs which provide communally separated cultural uniqueness (Paradigm III).

In this *Star Trek* vision, a Planet Earth melting pot is formed on the basis of continuous discussion concerning that which is common in the experience of all ethnic cultures, including common elements in the beliefs and practices of the various global religions (Fersh 1989, 17). In this model, one's own cultural identity is not of primary importance, except insofar as it provides input into the establishment of the new world order's central principles.

**Table 1** Inter-Ethnic Relationships

| Categories | Paradigm I | Paradigm II | Paradigm III | Paradigm IV | Paradigm V |
|---|---|---|---|---|---|
| Language | English | English | English/ multilingualism | English/ multilingualism | English/ multilingualism |
| Religion | Christian (Protestantized) | Christian | Multireligious | Beliefs common to world religions | Multireligious |
| Culture | European (NW European Anglo-Saxon dominant) | European | Multicultural | World culture | Multicultural American |
| Race | Caucasian | Caucasian | Mixed/separate ethnic groups | Mixed | Mixed |
| Political tradition | European constitutional democracy (NW European Anglo-Saxon dominant) | Constitutional democracy | Democracy responsive to ethnic needs | World democracy | Constitutional democracy |

There is a continuous search for the center in the globalist vision, via unending discussion with regard to commonly-accepted principles. The center itself draws upon the experiential and intellectual traditions of all world cultures. Global awareness, in this vision, may be promoted for social, economic, religious, or other reasons, but a central raison d'etre is the importance of working together peaceably as world citizens.

While the global ideological center is being sought, that which separates and distinguishes each nationality is not simply overlooked. Through the process of constant inter-ethnic discussion, each ethnic group is given influential power with regard to the creation of the new earth culture. In order for this culture to be equitably based, in view of the world's political, economic, and demographic contexts, a tremendous amount of negotiation and discussion is demanded. One global model sometimes referred to is the United Nations, which is organized and functions in such a way that the rights of those nations which are not as strong militarily, economically, or demographically are still theoretically protected.

Paradigm IV appeals to those pluralists who fear the possibility of the inter-ethnic conflict which has sometimes accompanied ethnic nationalist emphases – in Yugoslavia or the former Soviet Union, for example – though supporters of Paradigm III counter that the underlying reason for conflict in those regions is indeed the historical attempt by some ethnic groups to destroy the cultural vitality of neighboring ethnic groups.

Ironically, if the global vision were actuated in the way its proponents seem to desire, it might ultimately establish a culture very similar to what some melting pot enthusiasts, in a more specifically nationalistic way, appear to envision for their ideological and interpretive position based on Paradigm II. The entire world, however, would now find itself melted together.

If there were, for example, nearly complete global inter-ethnic fusion, brought about in part by increased personal relationships, leading to cross-ethnic marriage en masse worldwide, it might be difficult eventually to distinguish one ethnic tradition from another. People might then rather define themselves in terms of highly idiosyncratic interests, behaviors, and beliefs. (This is what the melting pot model envisions on a national scale.) For this to happen, however, global citizens would have to begin thinking transformatively in terms of internationally-recognized principles and be open to almost continuous change, over a long period of time, with regard to the agreed-upon nature of those axioms.

Paradigm V, Centered Pluralism, is a more conservative and pragmatic approach to pluralistic multiculturalism than that suggested by either ethnic nationalist or global paradigms. An underlying assumption of centered pluralism, for example, is that America needs to continue to hold itself together as a vital national system, and that this will not happen, politically or socially, unless certain established central traditions are adhered to by most citizens (Banks 1992, 32).

Centered pluralists, like ethnic nationalists, therefore insist that all Americans speak a common language (English) though they simultaneously encourage both the retention of first languages (where this is relevant) and the learning of additional official languages. Centered pluralists are also committed to democratic institutions though these are not defined from an exclusively Anglo-Saxon constitutional perspective.

In both of these emphases, centered pluralism is much more prescriptive in nature than globalism. Paradigm V also goes much further than ethnic nationalism in its general support for a commonly-accepted and centrally-established knowledge base. It suggests, for example, that all Americans have a common literacy foundation. This literacy base is expected to be a multicultural one, so that not all books read and studied are those written by Europeans and European-Americans, with those particular ethnic interpretations (as different as they might be). Still there are common intellectual threads, primary readings, and conventional subjects which hold Americans to similar standards of interpretation.

This paradigm also supports a national commitment to communal as well as individual socio-economic traditions, a mixture of capitalism and socialism. Centered pluralism even allows for the possibility that democracy itself might be understood differently — and perhaps in more helpful ways — in other cultural traditions. The two-party political system and representative republicanism might therefore be reviewed with regard to operational effectiveness in the modern American context. Centered pluralism assumes, however, an underlying commitment to the kind of general principles enunciated in the United States Constitution's Bill of Rights (Haynes and Kniker 1990, 306).

Centered pluralism thus establishes a commitment to many traditional "American" beliefs and practices. At the same time, this paradigm assumes the integrity of indigenous cultural identities. A central set of beliefs and practices, previously established, undergoes continuous gradual metamorphosis through constant, desired reflective interaction between various ethnic groups and their respective traditions. In this process all ethnic communities have some impact on the slowly changing character of the American "center." Centered pluralism assumes nearly complete ethnic equality and cultural acceptance. It represents a practical response to assimilationist critics of Paradigm III who attack ethnic nationalist multiculturalism for perceived divisive tendencies.

Interestingly enough, centered pluralism, in many ways, correlates to a paradigm hinted at by Milton Gordon in the mid-1960s (in his book, *Assimilation in American Society*). It is a vision, which, if Gordon was correct in his analysis, ultimately and paradoxically establishes a melting pot. Unlike that actuated historically, this melting pot provides full cultural equality (Gordon 1964, 158).

In this way the eventual outcome of a commitment to centered pluralism appears to be similar in nature to that predicted by melting pot multiculturalists, even as the latter do not place much emphasis on retention and maintenance of ethnic uniqueness. If, for example, all cultures are treated equally, one would expect that through direct association and intermarriage most ethnic groups would eventually melt away into one new American culture, still predominantly Anglo-Saxon in its foundation but with Arab-American, African-American, Asian-American, Pacific Islander–American, and Latin-American nuances.

Centered pluralism differs from melting pot assimilationism, however, in its willingness to support affirmative action to assist in leveling out the playing field for those ethnic groups which have experienced substantial discrimination and prejudice based on their association with certain ethnic traditions in the past. In theory, most of these are people other than non-northern, non-western Europeans; in practice, most of them are non-Europeans. Centered pluralists recognize a need to eradicate ethnocentric concepts already embedded in the American psyche and social order. Paradigm V thus envisions a melting pot which incorporates much greater ethnic diversity than that anticipated by melting pot multiculturalists.

Unlike the vision presented in the globalist Paradigm IV, centered pluralism is not international in character. Though centered pluralists speak in terms of internationalization of the curriculum, for example, their primary focus is on the United States of America.

The fact that Americans tend to view interethnic relationships from the perspective of these paradigms, and that there are divergences even among those who call themselves "pluralists," makes for a very confusing situation for educators. Educators are not only asked to "multiculturalize" the curriculum but to decide, in effect, which of at least four paradigmatic understandings best describes their personal perception of multiculturalism, which then may differ from that proposed by other educators and academia. All of the paradigms discussed in this article, for example, have supporters in the public school system. Teachers are required to attend inservice workshops and often volunteer to enroll in classes which certainly expose them to some form of "multiculturalism," but which may be suggesting any one of four very different versions of that concept.

It is important to note that this article's thesis that there are five general ethnic relations paradigms does not suggest that all multiculturalists abide by these theoretical paradigms in any pure sense. They may, in fact, operate out of the perspective of one or more of these models, some rationally and with purpose, others chaotically and illogically.

In addition, teachers and educators must deal with a general public whose opinions, according to polls, are much more weighted toward assimilationist models (Paradigms I and II). It is perhaps most confusing that supporters of four of the paradigms (II through V) have representative leaders who all refer to themselves as "multiculturalists," and who all employ the same term, from Nathan Glazer to James Banks to Mario Barrera. So the following question continually arises, "Who are the real multiculturalists?" and we see constant struggle, attack, and counterattack between advocates of the various paradigmatic approaches.

It is the hope of this writer that a paradigmatic understanding of why we have reached this point of multicultural confusion will be useful in helping us to comprehend why we are doing what we are doing. Further, it will push members of the educational audience, as they listen to presentations on multiculturalism, as they read articles and curriculum documents which describe the multiculturalist vision, to be more demanding with regard to what particular philosophical position is being encouraged by presenters and writers. It is always important to know the assumptions, values, and goals of one's mentors. With this knowledge, the debate will continue with the reflective educator much more knowledgeable of the deep complexity of this issue.

## References

Alba, R. D. (1981). The twilight of ethnicity among American Catholics of European ancestry. *Annals,* 45, 86–97.

Banks, J. (1992). Multicultural education: For freedom's sake. *Educational Leadership,* 49, 32–36.

Barrera, M. (1988). *Beyond Aztlan.* Notre Dame: University of Notre Dame Press.

Fersh, S. (Ed.). (1989). *Learning About Peoples and Cultures.* Evanston, Ill.: McDougal, Littel.

Fitzgerald, F. (1980). *America Revised.* New York: Vintage Press.

Glazer, N. (1991). In defense of multiculturalism. *New Republic,* 205, 18–22.

Gordon, M. (1964). *Assimilation in American Life.* New York: Oxford University Press.

Haynes, C. C., & Kniker, C. R. (1990). Religion in the classroom. *Social Education,* 54, 305, 306.

Hilliard, A. G. (1992). Why we must pluralize the curriculum. *Educational Leadership,* 49, 12–15.

Lipset, S. (1990). *Continental Divide.* New York: Routledge.

McConaghy, T. (1993). Ontario to implement anti-racist policies. *Phi Delta Kappan, 75,* 190, 191.

Novak, M. (1971). *The Rise of Unmeltable Ethnics.* New York: Macmillan.

Takaki, R. (1993). *A Different Mirror.* Boston: Little, Brown.

Teichroeb, A. (Ed.). (1979). Military surveillance of Mennonites in World War I. *Mennonite Quarterly Review, 53,* 95–127.

Zangwill, I. (1909). *The Melting Pot.* New York: Macmillan.

## Concepts and Questions for Chapter 1

1. What is intercultural communication?

2. In what ways are intercultural communication and communication alike? In what ways are they different?

3. What is meant by the term *cultural value?* How are these values manifested within a given culture?

4. What is meant by *social perception,* and how does it relate to intercultural communication?

5. What is the relationship between culture and perception?

6. How does one's world view contribute to how she or he perceives the world? What are the major cultural influences that form and shape one's world view?

7. How does the concept of a global village affect your view of international relations and your ability to relate to world events?

8. Porter and Samovar have asserted that people are not yet prepared for life in a global village. What is meant by that statement? Do you agree or disagree with the assertion? Why?

9. What does Barnlund mean by the "collective unconscious" and how does it relate to intercultural communication?

10. How does Collier classify cultures?

11. According to Collier, in what ways do we express our cultural identities?

12. How does Hall's discussion of high- and low-context communication relate to some of the underlying premises about intercultural communication?

13. According to Judith Martin, what is the role played by communication in defining one's ethnic identity?

14. How do the dimensions of white ethnic identity differ from the ethnic identity of other co-cultures in U.S. society? Be specific in your comparisons.

15. What are the development stages of white ethnic identity? Do these stages differ in any significant way from ethnic identity development in other cultures or co-cultures?

16. What are the significant differences between the five paradigms advanced by Rod Janzen?

17. Which of the five paradigms do you believe would be the most useful model for our society in the twenty-first century? Why?

18. How would someone from an extremely different cultural background respond on a first visit to your city? to your home?

19. As the United States emerges into a pluralistic, multicultural society, what contributions can you make in preparing for this society?

# Part Two

## Sociocultural Backgrounds: What We Bring to Intercultural Communication

*All persons are puzzles until at last we find in some word or act the key to the man, to the woman; straightway all their past works and actions lie in light before us.*
*— Emerson*

One of the most important aspects of human communication is the fact that the experiences participants bring to a communication experience will affect their behavior during the encounter. Psychologists A. H. Hastorf and H. Cantril underscore this issue when they note that each person acts according to the personal uniqueness he or she brings to the occasion. Think about those countless situations when you and some friends shared an experience and found that there were major differences in your reactions. What you deemed dull your companions found exciting; what you considered pointless they found meaningful. The messages received were the same for all participants; yet, because each of you has a unique personality and background, you experienced a variety of feelings, sensations, and responses. Each of you brought different backgrounds to the event and, as a result, attributed individual meanings to the shared experience. In short, the event meant what it did to you because of your own unique past history.

We contend that to understand any communication encounter you must appreciate the idea that there is much more to communication than the mere analysis of messages. Messages and the responses you make to them are products of your unique past experiences. And it is this uniqueness of experience that greatly contributes to the "immutable barriers in nature" between one individual's thoughts and another's.

Individual past experience takes on added significance when we introduce the many dimensions of culture. Individuals are influenced not only by personal experiences but also — and more importantly — by their culture. As we defined it in Part One, culture refers to those cumulative deposits of knowledge, beliefs, views, values, and behaviors acquired by a large group of people and passed on from one generation to the next. In this sense, culture affects you both consciously and unconsciously; it not only teaches you how to think and what to think about but also dictates such values as what is attractive and what is ugly, what is good and what is evil, and what is appropriate and what is not. In short, your culture tells you how to see and interpret your world. Furthermore, culture teaches you such things as how close to stand to strangers, how to greet friends, when to speak and when to remain silent, and even how to display your anger properly. When you are interacting with others and become disturbed by their actions, you can, for instance, cry, become physically violent, shout, or remain silent. Each of these behaviors is a manifestation of what you have learned; it is largely influenced by your culture.

These cultural influences affect your ways of perceiving and acting; they contain the societal experiences and values that are passed from generation to generation. Because these behaviors are so much a part of your persona, there is a danger that you might forget they are culturally engendered and will vary among cultures. This is why a person from Japan, for example, might remain silent if disturbed by someone's actions while an Israeli or an Italian would more likely verbalize the displeasure felt.

Whatever the culture, you can better understand your behavior and the reactions of others if you realize that what you are hearing and seeing is a reflection of that culture. As you might predict, this understanding is greatly facilitated when your cultural experiences are similar to those of the people with whom you are interacting. Conversely, when different and diverse backgrounds are brought to a communication encounter, it is often difficult to share internal states and feelings. In this section we focus on those difficulties by examining some of the experiences and perceptual backgrounds found in a variety of international cultures as well as those found in a number of American co-cultures.

# 2

## International Cultures: Understanding Diversity

In the field of intercultural communication, it is communication among members of *international* cultures that poses one of the most perplexing problems. How can we understand people who come from different sections of the global village? If we look around the world at any particular moment, we find disagreement, strife, and fighting – the locations may change, but the problems persist. Nations become prominent in the news, and what happens within them and between them directly affects the entire world. Although few of us at present are directly involved with these countries, their students may be studying in the United States; they may be our classmates or our students.

To better understand people from international cultures, we must learn to appreciate their diversity. This means that we must learn to tolerate what is different and even to appreciate diversity; such appreciation will help us develop a perspective that makes intercultural communication more likely to be successful. This chapter offers essays that introduce us to diversity in cultural values as well as to specific international cultures.

Understanding how people in other cultures view their world is crucial to successful intercultural communication. World view establishes how people perceive themselves, each other, and their places in the universe and serves as an underlying pattern for interaction within a culture. You interact with others according to how you view one another.

Perhaps one of the greatest cultural dichotomies in interaction patterns is found between North Americans and East Asians. In her article, "The Impact of Confucianism on Interpersonal Relationships and Communication Patterns in East Asia," June Ock Yum paints an intriguing picture of Confucianism's effect on how people view and interact with one another. She traces the various major components of Confucian philosophy and how they tend to determine East Asian patterns of interaction. As a counterpoint to her discussion, Yum makes continuous comparisons to prevalent North American interaction patterns so you can easily understand the differences between the two cultures.

Nemi C. Jain and Ellen D. Kussman move us geographically and shift our focus to the Indian subcontinent as they provide a glimpse of Hindu culture in their essay, "Dominant Cultural Patterns of Hindus in India." Jain and Kussman demonstrate how the Hindu world view, belief in reincarnation, concept of karma, aims of human life, paths to salvation, concept of dharma, caste system, and spirit of tolerance, which have persisted over thousands of years, permeate Indian culture. This provides a basis for the perceptual frames of reference common to much of India and a feeling for what it is to be Hindu.

Continuing our world voyage, we turn next to an examination of the Arabic culture. Janice Walker Anderson's article, "A Comparison of Arab and American Conceptions of 'Effective' Persuasion," details Arabic orientations toward discourse. She shows the differences between Arabic and American concepts of persuasion and the cultural diversity in persuasive strategies.

Journeying across the Gulf of Arabia we venture next to the continent of Africa. In their article, "Cultural Patterns of the Maasai," Lisa Skow and Larry A. Samovar give us a thoughtful and insightful view of the Maasai culture, which has shunned almost all Western influences and has tried to remain "pure" African. Unlike many other African cultures, it has almost completely rejected Western forms of government, dress, language, music, and religion. Skow and Samovar give us a clear view of the culture by tracing its history, values, and world view. They then discuss Maasai verbal and nonverbal processes and show how they are influenced by the prevailing Maasai culture.

In the next article, we move into the Mediterranean Sea and shift our attention to the Greek culture. In "*Palevome:* Foundations of Struggle and Conflict in Greek Interpersonal Communication," Benjamin J. Broome demonstrates how a sense of contest and struggle permeates everyday life in Greece and how it is an essential dynamic of Greek interpersonal communication. He uses the Greek verb *palevome* (we are struggling) to illustrate the Greek perspective on conflict and its role in everyday interaction.

We end our world journey by a visit to Ireland. In "Irish Conversations," Martin J. Gannon provides us with an insightful look at the Irish culture through an analysis of their conversational speaking. He begins by tracing the relationship between the original Irish language, Gaelic, and modern-day English. He then shows how religion functions in Irish culture by telling us about the Irish use of prayer as a mode of conversation. Irish hospitality is next demonstrated by looking at the free flow of conversation during Irish social activities. Gannon's use of the conversational forms of Irish language as a means of insightful understanding of the Irish culture is both a unique approach to cultural understanding and a useful way of making another culture come to life in the mind of the reader.

# The Impact of Confucianism on Interpersonal Relationships and Communication Patterns in East Asia

## JUNE OCK YUM

## Introduction

New communication technology has removed many of the physical barriers against communication between the East and the West, but there remain philosophical and cultural barriers, which are not well understood. The increased opportunity for interaction between different cultural groups, however, has sensitized some scholars to the need to study Eastern perspectives on communication.

Most cross-cultural studies of communication simply describe foreign communication patterns and then compare them to those of North America, rarely going beneath the surface to explore the source of such differences. This paper goes beyond these limitations and explores the philosophical roots of the communication patterns in East Asian countries, before comparing them to those of North America. The assumption here is that communication is a basic social process and that, as such, it is influenced by the philosophical foundations and value systems of the society in which it is found.

There is always a danger in generalizing certain cultural patterns to large geographical areas. Even though we often refer to "Eastern" or "Asian" perspectives, there are many patterns, sometimes contradictory, within the region. For instance, the

popular notion that Asians are more spiritual than Westerners might apply to India but not to China, Korea, or Japan. Nakamura (1964) has maintained that the Chinese and the Japanese are much more nonmetaphysical than Westerners. For this reason, this paper is limited to the East Asian countries of China, Korea, and Japan, those that have been most influenced by Confucian philosophical principles. Other countries that have been influenced by Confucianism are expected to have similar characteristics. For instance, Vietnam, the only country in Southeast Asia to have been influenced more by China than India, also exhibits the strong emphasis on social relationships and devotion to the hierarchical family relations that are the essence of Confucian doctrines (Luce & Summer, 1969).

## Social Relationships Versus Individualism

If one has to select the main difference between East Asian and North American perspectives on communication, it would be the East Asian emphasis on social relationships as opposed to the North American emphasis on individualism. According to Hofstede (1980), individualism-collectivism is one of the main dimensions that differentiate cultures. He defined individualism as the emotional independence of individual persons from groups, organizations, or other collectivities. Parsons, Shils, and Olds (1951) have suggested that self-orientation versus collectivity orientation is one of the five basic pattern variables that determine human action. Self-orientation occurs when a person gives "priority in a given situation to his own private interests, independently of their bearings on the interests or values of a given collectivity" (Parsons, Shils, & Olds, 1951, p. 81), as opposed to taking directly into account the values and interests of the collectivity before acting.

The individualism-collectivism dichotomy, however, is not identical to the difference between the East Asian emphasis on social relationships and North American emphasis on individualism. In East Asia, the emphasis is on proper social relationships and their maintenance rather than any abstract concern for a general collective body. In a sense, it is a collectivism only among those bound by social networks. For example, a recent study on the Chinese value system found that the Confucian value of reciprocity and proper relationships was not correlated with Hofstede's individualism-collectivism dimension (Chinese Culture Connection, 1987). Hui and Triandis (1986) have recommended that collectivism be treated in two different ways: (1) as a concern for a certain subset of people and (2) as a concern for a generalized collectivity of people.

In the 1830s, the French social philosopher Alexis de Tocqueville coined the term *individualism* to describe the most notable characteristic of American people. Bellah, Madsen, Sullivan, Swidler, and Tipton (1985, pp. vii, 142) agree that individualism lies at the very core of American culture, contending that "individualism . . . has marched inexorably through our history" and that "we believe in the dignity, indeed the sacredness, of the individual. Anything that would violate our right to think for ourselves, judge for ourselves, make our own decision, live our lives as we see fit, is not only morally wrong, it is sacrilegious." According to Varenne (1977), there is but one system of principles regulating interpersonal relationships in America and that is individualism.

Even though many Americans feel they must get involved, they are also committed to individualism, including the desire to cut free from the past and define one's own self. Thus, the primary mode of American involvement is choosing organizations that one can voluntarily join or voluntarily withdraw from. Varenne (1977, p. 53) said that Americans perceive social structure "not as a system made up of different groups considered to be in a symbiotic relationship, but rather of different individuals who come together to do something."

Considering this cultural orientation, it is not surprising that the dominant paradigm of communication is an individualistic one. Each communicator is perceived to be a separate individual engaging in diverse communicative activities to maximize his or her own self-interest.

In contrast, the most notable characteristic in East Asia is the emphasis on social relationships. Hall and Beadsley (1965) have maintained that, compared to East Asian countries, North America is in the Stone Age when it comes to social rela-

tionships. This East Asian preoccupation with social relationships stems from the doctrines of Confucianism.

## Confucianism

In the philosophical and cultural history of East Asia, Confucianism has endured as the basic social and political value system for over 1,000 years. One reason (and indication) that Confucianism has had such a profound impact is that it was adopted as the official philosophy of the Yi dynasty for 500 years in Korea, of the Tokugawa shogunate in Japan for 250 years, and of many dynasties in China.

Confucianism was institutionalized and propagated both through the formal curricula of the educational system and through the selection process of government officials. Confucian classics were required textbooks in the school systems throughout the history of China, Korea, and Japan before modern educational curricula were implemented. Government officials used to be selected through national exams that mostly examined the knowledge and the level of understanding of Confucian philosophy.

Another reason why Confucianism has exerted a much stronger impact than the other religious, philosophical systems of East Asia (such as Buddhism and Taoism) is that it is a pragmatic and present-oriented philosophy. When a student named Tzu-lu asked Confucius about serving spirits, Confucius said, "If one cannot yet serve men, how can he serve the spirits?" Asked about death, Confucius replied, "If you do not understand life, how can you understand death?" (McNaughton, 1974, p. 145). Max Weber commented, "Confucianism is extremely rationalistic since it is bereft of any form of metaphysics and in the sense that it lacks traces of nearly any religious basis. . . . At the same time, it is more realistic than any other system in the sense that it lacks and excludes all measures which are not utilitarian" (quoted by Nakamura, 1964, p. 16).

Confucianism is a philosophy of human nature that considers proper human relationships as the basis of society. In studying human nature and motivation, Confucianism sets forth four principles from which right conduct arises: *jen* (humanism), *i* (faithfulness), *li* (propriety), and *chih* (wisdom or a liberal education).

The cardinal principle, *jen* (humanism), almost defies translation since it sums up the core of Confucianism. Fundamentally it means warm human feelings between people. *Jen* is like a seed from which spring all the qualities that make up the ideal man. In addition, *jen* refers to the possession of all these qualities to a high degree. The actual practice or embodiment of *jen* in our daily lives is closely related to the concept of reciprocity. Confucius said that practicing *jen* is not to do to another man what you yourself don't want. In his own words: "If there's something that you don't like in the person to your right, don't pass it on to the person on your left. If there's something you don't like in the person to your left, don't pass it on to the person on your right" (McNaughton, 1974, p. 29).

It is suggested that Confucius himself once picked out reciprocity (*shu*) as the core of his thought. Confucius said, "There has never been a case where a man who did not understand reciprocity was able to communicate to others whatever treasures he might have had stored in himself" (McNaughton, 1974, p. 28). Therefore, practicing *jen* implies the practice of *shu,* which in turn means to know how it would feel to be the other person, to become like-hearted, and to be able to empathize with others.

The second principle of Confucianism is *i,* meaning faithfulness, loyalty, or justice. As the definition suggests, this principle also has strong implications for social relationships. Like *jen, i* is a difficult concept to translate. It may be easier to understand *i* through its opposite concept, which is personal or individual interest and profit. *I* is thus that part of human nature that allows us to look beyond personal, immediate profit and to elevate ourselves to the original goodness of human nature that bridges ourselves to other people (Yum, 1987). According to the principle of *i,* human relationships are not based on individual profit but rather on the betterment of the common good.

If *jen* and *i* are the contents of the Confucian ethical system, *li* (propriety, rite, respect for social

forms) is its outward form. As an objective criterion of social decorum, *li* was perceived as the fundamental regulatory etiquette of human behavior. Mencius suggested that *li* originated from deference to others and reservation of oneself. Confucius said that *li* follows from *jen,* that is, from being considerate to others. Only when people overcome themselves and so return to propriety can they reach humanness. On the other hand, propriety without humanness was perceived to be empty and useless.

## The Impact of Confucianism on Interpersonal Relationship Patterns

At least three of the four principles of Confucianism deal directly with social relationships. Under such a strong influence, East Asian countries have developed interpersonal relationship patterns that are quite different from the individualistic pattern of North America. Table 1 illustrates these five differences.

### Particularistic Versus Universalistic Relationships

Human relationships under Confucianism are not universalistic but particularistic. As we described earlier, the warm human feelings of *jen* are exercised according to one's relationship with another person. Ethics in Confucian thought, therefore, are based on relationships and situations rather than on some absolute and abstract good. Instead of applying the same rule to everybody with whom they interact, East Asians differentially grade and regulate relationships according to the level of intimacy, the status of the persons involved, and the particular context. The East Asian countries have developed elaborate social interaction patterns for those whose social position and relationship to oneself is known, but there are few universal patterns that can be applied to someone who is not known.

From a North American point of view, applying different rules to different people and situations may seem to violate the sacred code of fairness and equality that accompanies the individualistic values. In North America, human relationships are not particularized. Rather, one is supposed to treat

**Table 1** Comparison Between the North American and the East Asian Orientations to Interpersonal Relationship Patterns

| East Asian Orientations | North American Orientations |
|---|---|
| 1. Particularistic | Universalistic |
| Particular rules and interaction patterns are applied depending upon the relationship and context | General and objective rules are applied across diverse relationships and context |
| 2. Long-term and asymmetrical reciprocity | Short-term and symmetrical reciprocity or contractual reciprocity |
| 3. Sharp distinction between in-group and out-group members | In-group and out-group distinction is not as sharp |
| 4. Informal intermediaries | Contractual intermediaries |
| Personally known intermediaries Frequently utilized for diverse relationships | Professional intermediaries Utilized only for specific purposes |
| 5. Personal and public relationships often overlap | Personal and public relationships are often separate |

each person as an integral individual and apply general and objective rules. For instance, it is quite common in America for people to say "Hi" or "Good morning" to anybody they encounter during their morning walk, or to strike up a conversation with another person waiting in line. If you said "Hello" or "Good morning" to a stranger in Korea, you would be looked upon as a rather odd person.

The East Asian approach suggests that it is more humanitarian to consider the particular context and the persons involved in understanding the action and behavior rather than evaluate them according to generalized rules which to a certain extent are impersonal.

## Long-Term Asymmetrical Reciprocity Versus Short-Term Symmetrical or Contractual Reciprocity

Reciprocity as an embodiment of *jen* is the core concept in Confucianism, just as individualism is the core concept of the North American culture. While people may voluntarily join together for specific purposes in North America, each individual remains equal and independent; thus people join or drop out of clubs without any serious group sanctions. Commitments and obligations are often perceived as threats to one's autonomy or freedom of action. Relations are symmetrical-obligatory —

that is, as nearly "paid off" as possible at any given moment — or else contractual — the obligation is to an institution or to a professional with whom one has established some contractual base (Condon & Yousef, 1975).

In contrast, Confucian philosophy views relationships as complementary or asymmetrical and reciprocally obligatory. In a sense, a person is forever indebted to others, who in turn are constrained by other debts. Dependence is not looked down upon. Rather, dependency is accepted as a necessary part of human relationships. Under this system of reciprocity, the individual does not calculate what he or she gives and receives. To calculate would be to think about immediate personal profits, which is the opposite of the principle of mutual faithfulness, *i*. It is somewhat unusual in Korea, for example, for a group of friends, colleagues, or superior and subordinates to go "Dutch" and split the bill for dinner or drinks. Rather, each person takes turns and pays for the whole group. In North America, people generally insist on "paying their own way." The practice of basing relationships on complementary obligations creates warm, lasting human relationships but also the necessity to accept the obligations accompanying such relationships.

## In-group/Out-group Distinction

North American culture does not distinguish as strongly between in-group members and out-group members as East Asian countries do. Allegiance to a group and mobility among groups are purely voluntary, so that the longevity of membership in and loyalty to a particular group are both limited.

Mutual dependence as prescribed by the Confucian principle of i, however, requires that one be affiliated and identify with relatively small and tightly knit groups of people over long periods of time. These long-term relationships work because each group member expects the others to reciprocate and also because group members believe that sooner or later they will have to depend on the others. People enmeshed in this kind of network make clear distinctions between in-group and out-group members. For example, linguistic codes for in-group members are often different from those for out-group members. What is inside the group and what is outside it have drastically different meanings.

## Informal Intermediaries Versus Contractual Intermediaries

Because the distinctions between in-group and out-group members are so strict, it is imperative to have an intermediary to help one initiate a new relationship in East Asia. Confucian emphasis on propriety (li) also dictates that one has to follow proper rituals in establishing a new relationship, and an intermediary is part of such rituals. The intermediary has an in-group relationship with both parties and so can connect them. One strategy is for the intermediary to bring up an existing relationship that links the two parties, for example, explaining that "you are both graduates of so-and-so college" or "you are both from province A." Alternatively, the intermediary can use his or her own connections with them to create an indirect sense of in-groupness, for example, explaining that one is "my junior from high school" and the other "works in the same department as I do."

Intermediaries in the United States, however, are mostly professional or contractual in nature:

lawyers, negotiators, marriage counselors, and the like. The intermediary is an objective third person who does not have any knowledge of the parties' characteristics other than those directly related to the issue at hand. Also, the intermediary deals with each party as a separate, independent individual. Using personal connections to attain a desired goal does occur in the United States, but such a practice may be frowned on as nepotism and may also be perceived as giving up one's own individual freedom.

## Overlap of Personal and Public Relationships

The Confucian concept of i leads to a strong distaste for a purely business transaction, carried out on a calculated and contractual basis. Therefore, in East Asian countries there is a tendency to mix personal with public relationships. Even though the obvious purpose of a meeting is for business, both parties feel more comfortable if the transaction occurs on a more personal, human level. According to the principles of social reciprocity, there are several steps to follow if you want to develop an effective business relationship in Korea (Lee, 1983): (1) have frequent contacts over a relatively lengthy period of time, (2) establish a personal and human relationship, (3) if possible, create some common experiences such as sports, drinking, or travel, (4) foster mutual understanding in terms of personality, personal situations, and the like, and (5) develop a certain level of trust and a favorable attitude. The goal is to diminish the clear distinction between a personal relationship and a public relationship. It is implied that if one develops a warm personal relationship, a good public relationship will follow, because it is based on trust and mutual reciprocity. Such qualities are expected to endure rather than be limited to the business deal of the moment.

In the United States, there is a rather sharp dichotomy between private and public life. Since the primary task of the individual is to achieve a high level of autonomous self-reliance, there is an effort to separate the two lives as much as possible. Since the notion of "organizational man" is contradictory to the self-reliant individual, there is a certain level

**Table 2** Comparison Between the North American and the East
Asian Orientations to Communication Patterns

| East Asian Orientations | North American Orientations |
| --- | --- |
| 1. Process orientation | Outcome orientation |
| Communication is perceived as a process of infinite interpretation | Communication is perceived as the transference of messages |
| 2. Differentiated linguistic codes | Less differentiated linguistic codes |
| Different linguistics codes are used depending upon persons involved and situations | Linguistic codes are not as extensively differentiated as East Asia |
| 3. Indirect communication emphasis | Direct communication emphasis |
| The use of indirect communication is prevalent and accepted as normative | Direct communication is a norm despite the extensive use of indirect communication |
| 4. Receiver centered | Sender centered |
| Meaning is in the interpretation | Meaning is in the messages created by the sender |
| Emphasis is on listening, sensitivity, and removal of preconception | Emphasis is on how to formulate the best messages, how to improve source credibility, and how to improve delivery skills |

of anxiety about becoming an organizational man (Bellah et al., 1985). Some also perceive private life as a haven from the pressure of individualistic, competitive public life, and as such it must be protected.

## The Impact of Confucianism on Communication Patterns

Confucianism's primary concern with social relationships has strongly influenced communication patterns in East Asia. In general, it has strengthened patterns that help to build and maintain proper human relationships. Table 2 compares East Asia and North America in terms of communication patterns.

## Process- Versus Outcome-Oriented Communication

Since the main function of communication under Confucian philosophy is to initiate, develop, and maintain social relationships, there is a strong emphasis on the kind of communication that promotes such relationships. For instance, it is very important in East Asia to engage in small talk before initiating business and to communicate per-

sonalized information, especially information that would help place each person in the proper context. Communication is perceived to be an infinite interpretive process (Cheng, 1987), which cannot be compartmentalized into sender, message, channel, and receiver. It presumes that each partner is engaged in an ongoing process and that the relationship is in flux.

In contrast, when the main function of communication is to actualize autonomy and self-fulfillment, as in North America, the outcome of the communication is more important than the process. With short-term, discontinuous relationships, communication is perceived to be an action that is terminated after a certain duration and then replaced by a new communication. Tangible outcomes in terms of friends gained, opponents defeated, and self-fulfillment achieved become the primary function of communication.

## Differentiated Versus Less Differentiated Linguistic Codes

East Asian languages are very complex and are differentiated according to social status, the degree of intimacy, age, sex, and the level of formality. There are also extensive and elaborate honorific linguistic systems in East Asian languages (Brown & Levinson, 1978; Ogino, Misono, & Fukushima, 1985). These differentiations are manifested not only in referential terms but also in verbs, pronouns, and nouns. They result from Confucian ethical rules that place the highest value on proper human relationships (*i*) and on propriety (*li*). McBrian (1978) has argued that language forms an integral component of social stratification systems, and the hierarchical Confucian society is well represented by the highly stratified linguistic codes in Korea.

Martin (1964) has proposed that one of the main differences between English, Japanese, and Korean is the levels of speech. In both Korean and Japanese, there are two axes of distinction: the axis of address and the axis of reference. The axis of address is divided into plain, polite, and honorific while the axis of reference is divided into humble and neutral (Martin, 1964). An honorific form is used to refer to the receiver's action, while a humble form is used to refer to the sender's action — the reverse would not be appropriate. The most deferential form of speech combines the honorific address form for receiver and the humble form of self-reference.

The English language also employs different codes depending upon intimacy and status difference between the speaker and listener. In general, however, English forms of address are reasonably well described by a single binary contrast: first name (FN) versus title plus last name (TLN) (Brown & Ford, 1964). Certain European languages also contrast the familiar and formal forms, such as *tu* and *vous* in French. The use of FN or TLN can either be reciprocal (both sides use the same form of address) or nonreciprocal (one side uses FN and the other side uses TLN). Status and intimacy also play a role in greetings. For example, "Hi" is more common to intimates and to subordinates while "Good morning" is for distant acquaintances and superiors (Brown & Ford, 1964). In contrast, Ogino, Misono, and Fukushima (1985), working in Japan, found 210 different word forms, through 8 address situations, which can be put into 20 different categories. Moreover, in modern American English practice, the distance between the mutual FN and mutual TLN represents only a very small increment of intimacy, sometimes as small as five minutes of conversation. In East Asian communication situations, the distance between very honorific languages and very informal ones is quite large and more often than not cannot be altered even after a long acquaintance.

In English, the speech level is defined mainly by address forms, while in Korean or Japanese, pronouns, verbs, and nouns all have different levels. Thus, in English "to eat" is "to eat" regardless of the person addressed. In the Korean language, however, there are three different ways of saying "to eat": *muk-da* (plain), *du-shin-da* (polite), and *chap-soo-shin-da* (honorific). Different levels of a verb are often accompanied by different levels of a noun: Rice may be *bap* (plain), *shik-sa* (polite), or *jin-ji* (honorific).

In English, the pronoun "you" is used to refer alike to the old and young, to the president of the country, and to the child next door. In East Asian languages, there are different words for "you" depending upon the level of politeness and upon the relationship. There is also the compulsory or preferential use of a term of address instead of the pronoun, as when one says: *Jeh sh Wang.Shin.shen.de shu .ma?* (Literally, "Is this Mr. Wang's book?") instead of "Is this your book?" (Chao, 1956, p. 218). Actual role terms, such as professor, aunt, student, and so forth, are used in place of the pronoun "you" even in two-partner communication because they clarify and accentuate the relationships between the two communicators better than the simple second person reference. Since Confucianism dictates that one should observe the proprieties prescribed by a social relationship, the generalized "you" does not seem to be appropriate in most communication situations in East Asian countries.

This differentiation of linguistic codes in East Asian cultures bears out the familiar psycholinguistic principle that for language communities the degree of lexical differentiation of a referent field increases with the importance of that field to the community (Brown & Ford, 1964). The importance of social relationships in Confucian societies has therefore promoted the differentiation of linguistic codes to accommodate highly differentiated relationships.

## Emphasis on Indirect Communication Versus Emphasis on Direct Communication

Most cultures have both direct and indirect modes of communication. Metaphor, insinuations, innuendos, hints, and irony are only a few examples of the kinds of indirect communication that can be found in most linguistic communities. According to Searle (1969), indirect speech acts occur when the speaker communicates to the hearer more than he or she actually says by referring to some mutually shared background information and by relying on the hearer's powers of rationality and inference. Brown and Levinson (1978) have suggested that indirect speech acts are universal because they perform a basic service in strategies of politeness.

Even though the indirect mode of communication seems to be universal, however, the degree to which it is elaborated varies from culture to culture. For instance, the Malagasy speech community values an indirect style (Keenan, 1974), while certain Sabra culture prefers a straight-talking (*dugri*) style (Katriel, 1986). Rosaldo (1973) maintained that the Euro-American association of direct talk with a scientific and democratic attitude may not hold true in different cultural contexts. In Ilongot society, for example, direct talk is perceived as authoritarian and exclusionary while indirect language is perceived as accommodating and sensitive to individual wishes.

Brown and Levinson (1978) have suggested that politeness phenomena in language (indirectness is just one of them) derive from the notion of "face," the public self-image that every member wants to claim for himself or herself. According to Katriel (1986), indirect speech acts are the result of predominant concern for the other person's face. The Confucian legacy of consideration for others and concern for proper human relationships has led to the development of communication patterns that preserve one another's face. Indirect communication helps to prevent the embarrassment of rejection by the other person or disagreement among partners, leaving the relationship and each other's face intact. Lebra (1976) suggested that "defending face" is one of the main factors influencing Japanese behavior. She listed a number of concrete mechanisms for defending face, such as mediated communication (asking someone else to transmit the message), refracted communication (talking to a third person in the presence of the hearer), and acting as a delegate (conveying one's message as being from someone else), which are all indirect forms of communication.

The use of the indirect mode of communication in East Asia is pervasive and often deliberate. In comparing Japanese and American organizations, it has been noted that American employees strive to communicate with each other in a clear, precise, and explicit manner, while Japanese often deliberately communicate in a vague and indirect manner (Hirokawa, 1987; Pascale & Athos, 1981). The extensive nature of indirect communication is exemplified by the fact that there are sixteen evasive "maneuvers" that can be employed by the Japanese to avoid saying no (Imai, 1981).

It has also been suggested that there is a significant difference in the level of indirectness between North American and East Asian communication patterns. An American might say "The door is open" as an indirect way of asking the hearer to shut the door, while in Japan, instead of saying "The door is open," one often says "It is somewhat cold today." This is even more indirect, because no words refer to the door (Okabe, 1987). Operating at a still higher level of indirection, one Japanese wife communicated to her husband her discord with her mother-in-law by slight irregularities in her flower arrangements (Lebra, 1976).

One of Grice's maxims for cooperative conversation is "manner," which suggests that the speaker should avoid obscurity of expression and ambiguity (Grice, 1975). This direct communication is a norm in North America, despite the extensive use of indirect communication. Grice's principle would not be accepted as a norm, however, in East Asia. Okabe (1987) has shown that in Japan, the traditional rule of communication, which prescribes not to demand, reject, assert yourself, or criticize the listener straightforwardly, is a much more dominant principle than Grice's maxim of manner.

Reischauer (1977, p. 136) concluded that "the Japanese have a genuine mistrust of verbal skills, thinking that these tend to show superficiality in contrast to inner, less articulate feelings that are communicated by innuendo or by nonverbal means." Thus, even though both North American and East Asian communication communities employ indirect communication, its use is much more prevalent and accepted as normative in the former than the latter.

## Receiver Versus Sender Centeredness

North American communication very often centers on the sender, and until recently the linear, one-way model from sender to receiver was the prevailing model of communication. Much emphasis has been placed on how senders can formulate better messages, improve source credibility, polish their delivery skills, and so forth. In contrast, the emphasis in East Asia has always been on listening and interpretation.

Cheng (1987) has identified infinite interpretation as one of the main principles of Chinese communication. The process presumes that the emphasis is on the receiver and listening rather than the sender or speech making. According to Lebra (1976, p. 123), "anticipatory communication" is common in Japan, in which, instead of the speaker's having to tell or ask for what he or she wants specifically, others guess and accommodate his or her needs, sparing him or her embarrassment in case the verbally expressed request cannot be met. In such cases, the burden of communication falls not on the message sender but on the message receiver. A person who "hears one and understands ten" is regarded as an intelligent communicator. To catch on quickly and to adjust oneself to another's position before his or her position is clearly revealed is regarded as an important communication skill. One of the common puzzles expressed by foreign students from East Asia is why they are constantly being asked what they want when they are visiting in American homes. In their own countries, the host or hostess is supposed to know what is needed and serve accordingly. The difference occurs because in North America it is important to provide individual freedom of choice; in East Asia, it is important to practice anticipatory communication and to accommodate accordingly.

With the emphasis on indirect communication, the receiver's sensitivity and ability to capture the under-the-surface meaning and to understand implicit meaning becomes critical. In North America, an effort has been made to improve the effectiveness of senders through such formal training as debate and public speech, whereas in East Asia, the effort has been on improving the receiver's sensitivity. The highest sensitivity is reached when one empties the mind of one's preconceptions and makes it as clear as a mirror (Yuji, 1984).

Recently, there has been increased interest in listening in the United States as well. Both communication scholars and practitioners recognize that listening is not only necessary from the instrumental aspect of communication (comprehension) but, more importantly, for the affective aspect (satisfaction of being listened to).

## Discussion

This paper compared the East Asian emphasis on social relationships with the North American emphasis on individualism. These two emphases produce very different patterns of interpersonal relationships and communication. The conclusions drawn in this paper are not absolute, however. Each culture contains both orientations to some degree. It is simply more probable that East Asians would exhibit certain patterns of communication, such as indirect communication, more often than North Americans, and vice versa.

The North American preoccupation with individualism and related concepts, such as equality, fairness, and justice, and its far-reaching influences on the whole fiber of society are well documented. On the other hand, the importance of social relationships as a key to the East Asian countries has been recognized only recently. For instance, investigations of Japanese management styles have found that one of the fundamental differences between Japanese and American management is the personalized, interdependent relationships among employees and between managers and employees in Japan. These human relationships are related to loyalty and high productivity. It is not uncommon to explain such relationships away as merely a result of other organizational practices, such as lifelong employment. If one looks under the surface, however, one realizes that it is derived from a thousand-year-old Confucian legacy, and that similar human relationship patterns are found outside of large organizations. Consequently, attempts to transplant such a management style to North America with its philosophical and cultural orientation of individualism cannot be entirely satisfactory. The culture itself would have to be modified first.

There has been increasing concern in North America about the pursuit of individualism at the expense of commitment to larger entities such as the community, civic groups, and other organizations. It has been suggested that modern individualism has progressed to such an extent that most Americans are trapped by the language of individualism itself and have lost the ability to articulate their own need to get involved (Bellah et al., 1985). Although individualism has its own strength as a value, individualism that is not accompanied by commitments to large entities eventually forces people into a state of isolation, where life itself becomes meaningless.

If human beings are fundamentally social animals, it is necessary to balance the cultural belief system of individualism with the need to get involved with others. Americans have joined voluntary associations and civic organizations more than any other citizens of the industrialized world. However, such recent phenomena as the "me" generation and young stockbrokers who pursue only personal gain at the expense of their own organizations or the society as a whole can be perceived as pathological symptoms of individualism driven to its extreme. Bellah et al. (1985, p. 284) have maintained that "social ecology is damaged not only by war, genocide, and political repression. It is also damaged by the destruction of the subtle ties that bind human beings to one another, leaving them frightened and alone." They strongly argue that we need to restore social ecology by making people aware of our intricate connectedness and interdependence.

The emphasis of Confucianism on social relationships is conducive to cooperation, warm relaxed human relations, consideration of others,

and group harmony, but it has costs as well. Under such social constraints, individual initiative and innovation are slow to appear, and some individuals feel that their individuality is being suffocated. Because of the sharp distinction between in-groups and out-groups, factionalism may be inevitable. Within such well-defined sets of social relationships, people have a well-developed sense of obligation but a weak sense of duty to impersonal social entities.

Ironically, the solution for both the North American problems of excessive individualism and the excessive adherence to in-groupness in East Asia is the same: to be receptive to others. For the North Americans, this means accepting the limitations of self-reliance, becoming committed to a group, and putting the common good ahead of personal wants. For the East Asians, this means making their group boundaries more flexible and accepting outsiders with humanness and commitment to the common good.

There have been substantial changes in the East Asian societies since World War II. There has been an irrepressible influx of Western values; imported films and television programs are ubiquitous. However, it is not easy to change several hundred years of Confucian legacy. In Japan, for example, a greater proportion of young people than old expressed a preference for a boss endowed with the virtues of humanness and sympathy over a more efficient boss who would not ask for extra devotion (Dore, 1973). A similar finding was reported in Korea. When Korean workers, mostly in manufacturing plants, were asked their reasons for changing jobs, those who answered "a better human relationship and more humane treatment" still outnumbered those who answered "better payment" (Kim, 1984).

It seems inevitable, however, that the East Asian countries will see an increasing number of people who do not have traditional, binding relationships as the society moves further toward industrialization and higher mobility. The task will be to find a way for such people to cope with life without the protection of close in-group memberships and to learn to find satisfaction in expressing individual freedom and self-reliance.

# References

Bellah, R., Madsen, R., Sullivan, W., Swidler, A., and Tipton, S. (1985). *Habits of the Heart: Individualism and Commitment in American Life.* New York: Harper & Row.

Brown, R. W., and Ford, M. (1964). "Address in American English." In D. Hymes (Ed.), *Language in Culture and Society.* New York: Harper & Row.

Brown, R., and Levinson, S. (1978). "Universals in Language Usage: Politeness Phenomena." In E. Goody (Ed.), *Questions and Politeness.* Cambridge: Cambridge University Press.

Chao, Y. R. (1956). Chinese terms of address. *Language, 32,* 217–241.

Cheng, C. Y. (1987). "Chinese Philosophy and Contemporary Communication Theory." In D. L. Kincaid (Ed.), *Communication Theory: Eastern and Western Perspectives.* New York: Academic Press.

Chinese Culture Connection. (1987). Chinese values and the search for culture-free dimensions of culture. *Journal of Cross-Cultural Psychology, 18,* 143–164.

Condon, J., and Yousef, F. (1975). *An Introduction to Intercultural Communication.* New York: Bobbs-Merrill.

Dore, R. (1973). *British Factory, Japanese Factory: The Origins of National Diversity in Industrial Relations.* Berkeley and Los Angeles: University of California Press.

Grice, P. H. (1975). "Logic and Conversation." In P. Cole and J. L. Morgan (Eds.), *Studies in Syntax.* Vol. 3. New York: Academic Press.

Hall, J., and Beadsley, R. (1965). *Twelve Doors to Japan.* New York: McGraw-Hill.

Hirokawa, R. (1987). "Communication Within the Japanese Business Organization." In D. L. Kincaid (Ed.), *Communication Theory: Eastern and Western Perspectives.* New York: Academic Press.

Hofstede, G. (1980). *Culture's Consequences.* Newbury Park, Calif.: Sage.

Hui, C. H., and Triandis, H. C. (1986). Individualism-collectivism: A study of cross-cultural research. *Journal of Cross-Cultural Psychology, 17,* 225–248.

Imai, M. (1981). *Sixteen Ways to Avoid Saying No.* Tokyo: Nihon Keizai Shimbun.

Katriel, T. (1986). *Talking Straight: Dugri Speech in Israeli Sabra Culture.* Cambridge: Cambridge University Press.

Keenan, E. (1974). "Norm Makers, Norm Breakers: Uses of Speech by Men and Women in a Malagasy Community." In R. Bauman and J. Sherzer (Eds.), *Explorations in the Ethnography of Speaking.* Cambridge: Cambridge University Press.

Kim, S. U. (1984). *"Kong-jang no-dong-ja-ye ee-jik iyu"* ("Reasons for Changing Jobs Among Factory Workers"). *Hankook Daily Newspaper,* May 2 (in Korean).

Lebra, T. S. (1976). *Japanese Patterns of Behavior.* Honolulu: The University Press of Hawaii.

Lee, K. T. (1983). *Hankook-in ye u-shik koo-jo* (Cognitive Patterns of Korean People). Seoul: Shin-Won Moon-Wha Sa (in Korean).

Luce, D., and Sommer, J. (1969). *Viet Nam – The Unheard Voices.* Ithaca, N.Y.: Cornell University Press.

McBrian, C. (1978). Language and social stratification: The case of a Confucian society." *Anthropological Linguistics, 2,* 320–326.

McNaughton, W. (1974). *The Confucian Vision.* Ann Arbor: University of Michigan Press.

Martin, S. E. (1964). "Speech Levels in Japan and Korea." In D. Hymes (Ed.), *Language in Culture and Society.* New York: Harper & Row.

Nakamura, H. (1964). *Ways of Thinking of Eastern Peoples.* Honolulu: East-West Center Press.

Ogino, T., Misono, Y., and Fukushima, C. (1985). Diversity of honorific usage in Tokyo: A sociolinguistic approach based on a field survey." *International Journal of Sociology of Language, 55,* 23–39.

Okabe, K. (1987). "Indirect Speech Acts of the Japanese." In D. L. Kincaid (Ed.), *Communication Theory: Eastern and Western Perspectives.* New York: Academic Press.

Parsons, T., Shils, E., and Olds, J. (1951). "Categories of the Orientation and Organization of Action." In T. Parsons and E. A. Shils (Eds.), *Toward a General Theory of Action.* Cambridge, Mass.: Harvard University Press.

Pascale, R, and Athos, A. (1981). *The Art of Japanese Management: Application for American Executives.* New York: Warner Communications.

Reischauer, E. (1977). *The Japanese.* Cambridge: Harvard University Press.

Rosaldo, M. (1973). I have nothing to hide: The language of Ilongot oratory. *Language in Society, 11,* 193–223.

Searle, J. R. (1969). *Speech Acts.* Cambridge: Cambridge University Press.

Varenne, H. (1977). *Americans Together: Structured Diversity in a Midwestern Town.* New York and London: Teacher College Press.

Yuji, A. (Trans. N. Chung). (1984). *Ilbon-in ye usik koo-jo* (Japanese Thought Patterns). Seoul: Baik Yang Publishing Co. (in Korean).

Yum, J. O. (1987). Korean Philosophy and Communication. In D. L. Kincaid (Ed.), *Communication Theory: Eastern and Western Perspectives.* New York: Academic Press.

# Dominant Cultural Patterns of Hindus in India

NEMI C. JAIN
ELLEN D. KUSSMAN

For more than 3000 years, the peoples of the Indian subcontinent have sought the deepest truths in order to transform limited and imperfect human life into potential greatness. Their insights and discoveries have shaped what many consider one of the world's richest and most long-lived cultures.

India has been the cradle of several religions: Hinduism, Jainism, Buddhism, and Sikhism. The great majority of her people follow Hinduism, which can be taken to mean simply "the religion of India" (Ellwood, 1992). During the last 1200 years, India has also been influenced by Islam, Christianity, and Judaism, and thus has become one of the most culturally pluralistic societies in the world. Like any other culture, Indian culture is complex and consists of many interrelated beliefs, values, norms, social systems, and artifacts. In spite of its multiethnic, multilingual, and highly stratified nature, India is united by a set of cultural patterns that is widely shared among the Hindus living in India and abroad. The term *cultural patterns* refers to "the systematic and often repetitive nature of human behavior, interaction, and organization . . . human behavior is channeled and constrained by underlying systems that impose regularity and rules on what otherwise might be random activity" (Damen, 1987, p. 110).

This essay first appeared in the seventh edition. All rights reserved. Permission to reprint must be obtained from the authors and the publisher. Professor Jain teaches in the Department of Communication and is a Research Fellow in the Center for Asian Studies at Arizona State University. Ellen Kussman teaches at the American University in Beirut, Lebanon.

Hinduism is an amorphous body of beliefs, philosophies, worship practices, and code of conduct. In its present form, Hinduism embraces many often contradictory beliefs and practices. Its essential spirit, however, seems to be "live and let live." The very nature of Hinduism leads to a great tolerance of other religions as followers tend to believe that the highest divine powers complement one another for the well-being of humanity and the universe. Hinduism, because of its resilience, absorption, and respect for alternative ways of reaching the same goals, has maintained vitality since its inception. As a dominant force, it influences the cultural patterns and communication behavior of over a half billion Hindus in India and abroad.

India is a most suitable culture for study because of her preeminence in Asia, her leadership role among developing nations, and her increasing participation in international affairs. In addition, Indian culture provides an instructive contrast to American cultural patterns. The purpose of this article is to discuss briefly (1) the Hindu world view; (2) belief in reincarnation; (3) the concept of *karma;* (4) the aims of human life; (5) paths to salvation; (6) the concept of *dharma;* (7) the Indian caste system, and (8) the spirit of tolerance.

Each of these cultural patterns includes numerous assumptions, beliefs, values, and norms that are overlapping and closely interrelated. Within the same culture, variations of cultural patterns normally occur. In fact, contradictions among cultural patterns are probably universal throughout societies. At times we may simplify and make firm generalizations to avoid constant use of qualifiers. Despite internal variations and contradictions, we believe these eight cultural patterns provide a useful description of Hindu Indian culture.

## World View

World view refers to a set of interrelated assumptions and beliefs about the nature of reality, the organization of the universe, the purposes of human life, God, and other philosophical issues concerned with the concept of being (Samovar & Porter, 1991). India's great sages and philosophers have sought to understand the deepest level of reality and to satisfy the deep human longing for spiritual fulfillment. The quest generated the basic Indian wisdom that the fundamental energizing power of the cosmos and the spiritual energy of human beings are one and the same. Because of our participation in the ultimate energy and power of reality, it is possible to transform our superficial, suffering, and limited existence into a free and boundless one. This spiritual transformation has constituted the ultimate aim in life for most Indian people over the ages (Koller, 1982).

The origins and development of the Hindu world view can best be understood in terms of the following concepts: (1) undivided wholeness and ultimate reality; (2) levels of reality; and (3) the normative dimension of reality.

## Undivided Wholeness and Ultimate Reality

According to Hinduism, the world of distinct and separate objects and processes is a manifestation of a more fundamental reality that is undivided and unconditional. This undivided wholeness constituting the ultimate level of reality is known by various names: *Brahman, Ātman, Puruṣa, Jīva, Allah,* and Lord. What is especially important about this belief is that, first, the ultimate reality is not seen as separate and apart from ordinary things and events, but is the inner being and energizing force of everyday existence. Initially developed in the sacred ancient Hindu scriptures, the Vedas and Upaniṣads, this belief is an integral part of Hinduism, Jainism, Buddhism, and Yoga (Koller, 1982).

Second, existence at the deepest level is boundless in the sense that all possibilities may coexist without excluding or comprising one another. Time, space, the number of gods and goddesses, and so on are endless. Indian mythology especially celebrates the idea that opposites not only exist together but enrich one another with all of their differences arising simultaneously in an unrestricted universe of infinite freedom.

Third, the ultimate reality is so profound that reason is incapable of apprehending it. Human reason is an effective faculty for guiding our investigations of the empirical world and for understanding the rules of our practical and theoretical activities.

Since it operates by differentiating and comparing, however, it is incapable of comprehending the deepest dimensions of reality that are beyond all divisions and differences. This profound nature of reality underlies Indian mysticism and encourages the emphasis upon Yoga and meditation (Koller, 1982).

Finally, the ultimate reality has no form and no name. What can be given a name and form is not the ultimate. From ancient Vedic times to the present, however, the ultimate reality has been symbolized by unlimited numbers of gods and goddesses who participate partially in the higher reality that they symbolize, pointing to the fullness of that reality. This is why a Hindu can say in the same breath that there are millions of gods, only one god, and no gods. The last two statements mean, respectively, that all gods symbolize the one ultimate reality and that this reality cannot be captured entirely by one symbol. But that a deity is not the ultimate reality does not mean it is unreal. On the contrary, because the deity as symbol participates in the deeper levels of reality, its reality is greater than that of our ordinary existence. Through rituals and devotion to gods and goddesses, it is believed that one can achieve a spiritual transformation of life.

## Levels of Reality

Within the undivided wholeness of the totality of existence, there are various levels of reality. These range from nonexistence to empirical existence limited by space and time, to consciousness limited only by conditions of awareness, to an indescribable level beyond all conditions and limits whatsoever. The deeper the level of reality, the more fully one participates in the truth of being. One of the clearest examples of the tendency to distinguish between levels of reality occurs in the Taittirīya Upaniṣad, where five different levels of reality composing the "Self" are identified:

*At the lowest level the Self is material and identified with food. At the next level the Self is identified with life: "Different from and within that which consists of the essence of food is the Self consisting of life." Identifying a still higher level of reality, the text goes on to say,*

*"Different from and within that which consists of the essence of life is the Self which consists of mind (rudimentary forms of awareness that humans share with other animals)." Next, a fourth level of reality is recognized. Here is a still deeper source of consciousness and existence: the Self said to be of the nature of understanding (Vijñāna). Finally, the Self is identified with joy as the fifth and ultimate level of reality. Joy (ānanda) or bliss is regarded as the root or source of all existence, the foundation of higher consciousness, lower consciousness, life, and matter (Koller, 1982, p. 101).*

## Normative Dimension of Reality

The deepest level of reality is normative. According to Hinduism, norms for right living are an integral part of the fabric of human existence – they are not derived from human reason and are not imposed on life from the outside. The foundation of norms is much deeper than reason; it emanates from the very nature and expression of reality at its deepest level. Human reason only interprets and applies the norms of true or right living.

In the West, norms are usually conceived as rationally derived to fulfill human needs and aspirations. In India, it is generally recognized that a person who is true to the inner norms of existence has incredible power. Human existence is regarded as a manifestation and expression of a deeper reality. The fundamental norm of the universe is the orderly coursing of this deeper reality in its central being. Moral and social rules are partial expressions of this highest norm. The normative dimensions of the interconnected reality refer to the Hindu concept of *dharma*.

## Belief in Reincarnation

In Hinduism, the Supreme Being is the impersonal *Brahman,* the ultimate level of reality, a philosophical absolute, serenely blissful, beyond all ethical or metaphysical limitations. The basic Hindu view of God involves infinite being, infinite consciousness and infinite bliss. *Brahmā* is conceived of as the Supreme Soul of the universe. Every living soul is a part, a particular manifestation, of the *Brahmā.* Individual souls seem to change from generation to generation, but actually only the unimportant,

outer details change – a body, a face, a name, a different condition or status in life. The *Brahmā,* however, veiled behind these deceptive "realities," is continuous and indestructible. This hidden self or *ātman* is a reservoir of being that never dies, is never exhausted, and is without limit in awareness and bliss. *Ātman,* the ultimate level of reality at the individual level, is the infinite center of every life. Body, personality, and *ātman* together make up a human being (Smith, 1958).

The eternal *ātman* is usually buried under the almost impenetrable mass of distractions, false ideas, illusions, and self-regarding impulses that compose one's surface being. Life is ordinarily lived at a relatively superficial level, a level at which the ultimate reality is experienced only in fragmented and limited forms. These fragmented and partial forms of existence are actually forms of bondage, restricting access to the full power or energy of life flowing from the deepest level of reality. The aim of life is to cleanse the impurity from one's being to the point where its infinite center, the eternal *ātman,* will be fully manifest.

The Hindu belief in reincarnation affirms that individual souls enter the world and pass through a sequence of bodies or life cycles. On the subhuman level, the passage is through a series of increasingly complex bodies until at last a human one is attained. Up to this point, the soul's growth is virtually automatic. With the soul's graduation into a human body, this automatic, escalator mode of ascent comes to an end. The soul's assignment to this exalted habitation is evidence that it has reached self-consciousness, and with this state comes freedom, responsibility, and effort. Now the individual soul, as a human being, is fully responsible for its behavior through the doctrine of *karma* – the moral law of cause and effect. The present condition of each individual life is a product of what one did in the previous life; and one's present acts, thoughts, and decisions determine one's future states (Smith, 1958).

## Concept of Karma

*Karma* means basically action or activity. Actions always imply cause and effect, for nothing in this world acts or moves without an impelling cause. *Karma,* therefore, also refers to that chain of cause and effect, set in motion by one's deeds in the world. Sooner or later, through inexorable laws of justice built into *dharma,* they rebound to affect one's own future. As one sows, so one reaps (Ellwood, 1992, p. 64).

The concept of *karma* and the completely moral universe it implies carries two important psychological corollaries. First, it commits the Hindu who understands it to complete personal responsibility. Each individual is wholly responsible for his or her present condition and will have exactly the future he or she is now creating. Conversely, the idea of a moral universe closes the door to all appeals to chance or accident. In this world, there is no chance or accident. *Karma* decrees that every decision must have its determinate consequences, but the decisions themselves are, in the last analysis, freely arrived at. Or, to approach the matter from another direction, the consequences of a person's past decisions condition his or her present lot, as a card player is dealt a particular hand but is left free to play that hand in a number of ways. This means that the general conditions of life – rank, station, position – are predetermined by one's past *karma.* However, individual humans as carriers of a soul are free to determine actions independently of the soul (Smith, 1958).

According to Hinduism, the ultimate aim of life is to free oneself progressively from the exclusive identification with the lower levels of the self in order to realize the most profound level of existence. Since at this deepest level, the self is identical with ultimate reality – the *Brahman* – once this identity has been realized, there is nothing that can defeat or destroy the self. Thus, the soul puts an end to the process of reincarnation and merges with the *Brahman,* from whence it originated in the first place. This state for an individual soul is called *moksha, mukti, nirvāṇa* or liberation.

## Aims of Human Life

What do human beings want? What are the aims of human life? Hindu saints and philosophers have pondered these questions for a long time and have provided some interesting insights into human needs, wants, desires, motivations, and values. According to Hinduism, all people have four legitimate basic aims of human life: (1) *kāma,* pleasure or enjoyment; (2) *artha,* wealth or success; (3) *dharma,* righteousness, faithful duty or code of conduct; and (4) *moksha,* liberation or salvation. These four aims have constituted the basis of Indian values. Indian literature concerned with moral and social life accepts these four aims as fundamental in life. Taken together, these aims define the good life for a Hindu, giving a sense of direction to guide a person to what he or she may and may not aim at in life (Jain, 1991).

Hinduism recognizes the importance of enjoyment or *kāma* in human life. This is natural because we are all born with built-in pleasure-pain reactors and human senses. The concept of *kāma* is used in two ways in Indian literature. In the narrower sense, *kāma* is sexual desire and is symbolized by *Kāma,* the love god. *Kāma Sūtra,* along with a number of other texts, provides instructions on how to obtain the greatest sexual pleasures. As a basic human aim, however, *kāma* goes beyond this narrower sense of sexual pleasure to include all forms of enjoyment, including that of fame, fortune, and power.

A common stereotype of Indian people as so single-mindedly intent on religious salvation that there is no room for laughter, fun, or games is incorrect. Traditionally and currently, Hindus value stories, games, festivals, and parties filled with music, laughter, and fun! As a basic aim in life, *kāma* legitimizes the human pursuit of pleasure and recognizes that wealth and various goods are to be enjoyed as a way of fulfilling human nature.

India, however, has not taken pleasure as life's highest value. Hindus believe that the world holds immense possibilities for enjoyment through our senses. Moreover, there are other worlds above this one where pleasures mount by a factor of a million at each successive round; we shall experience these worlds too at later stages in our becoming (Smith, 1958). *Dharma* regulates the pursuit of pleasure at the various stages of life; for example, sexual activity is to be restricted to one's spouse and drugs and intoxicating beverages are regarded as wrong and sinful because of the injury they do. But, as long as the basic rules of morality are observed, one is free to seek all the pleasure one wishes.

The second aim of life is *artha* or worldly success (wealth, success, power, fame, and so on). Hinduism recognizes that worldly success is a worthy goal to be neither scorned nor condemned. Moreover, its satisfactions last longer than sensual pleasures. Unlike *kāma,* worldly success is a social achievement with implications for one's life, as well for one's family, relatives, caste group, and society. In this respect, it is a higher value than sensual pleasure. Although much of the Western world regards Indians as deliberately choosing poverty as a way of life, this is not true. The *Pañctantra,* a popular collection of Indian wisdom states: "Wealth gives constant vigor, confidence, and power. Poverty is a curse worse than death. Virtue without wealth is of no consequence. The lack of money is the root of all evil" (Koller, 1982, p. 65).

A certain limited amount of wealth is indispensable for one's living, for upkeeping a household, raising a family, and discharging civic duties. Beyond this minimum, worldly achievements bring to many a sense of dignity and self-respect. In the end, however, these too are found wanting. Like pleasure, rewards of wealth or worldly success are transient and short-lived, Humans seek the higher goals of *dharma* and *moksha* which are more lasting and fulfilling.

*Dharma,* the third aim of life, refers to the faithful performance of one's duties. Hinduism abounds in directives to men and women for performing their social roles and responsibilities. It sets forth in elaborate detail the duties that go with age, stages of life, gender, disposition, caste, and social status. Like the other two aims of human life, *dharma* also yields notable rewards but fails to satisfy the human heart completely. Faithful performance of duty brings the praise and appreciation of peers. More gratifying than this, however, is the self-respect that comes from having done one's part, of having contributed to society. In the end, even this realization cannot provide joy adequate to human spirit. The final aim of human life must still lie elsewhere (Smith, 1958).

According to Hinduism, the first three aims of life — pleasure, worldly success, and faithful duty — are never ultimate goals of human life. At best they are means that we assume will take us in the direction of what we really seek. First, we want being. Everyone wants "to be" rather than "not to be." Second, we want to know, to be aware. Third, human beings seek joy, a resolution of feelings in which the basic motifs are the opposite of frustration, futility, and boredom. Not only are these the things we want, we want each in infinite degree. To state the full truth, according to Hinduism, we must then say that what humans really want is infinite being, infinite knowledge, and infinite joy. To gather them together in a single word, what human beings really want is liberation or *moksha* (or *mukti*) — complete release from the countless limitations that press so closely upon present existence (Smith, 1958).

As the ultimate aim of human life, *moksha* guides one's efforts to realize identity with the *Brahman* but does not repudiate the other aims. Indeed, it calls for fulfilling these aims as a preparation for achieving complete freedom and fulfillment. Even when the distinction between worldly and spiritual existence becomes prominent, the tendency is to see the distinction in terms of higher and lower levels of the same reality than to postulate two different and opposing realities (Smith, 1958).

Thus, pleasure, worldly success, responsible discharge of duty, and liberation are the four aims of human life. These are what humans think they want, what they really want. What human beings most want, however, are infinite being, infinite awareness, and infinite joy. According to Hinduism, they are all within one's reach and can be attained through multiple paths to salvation (Smith, 1958).

## Paths to Salvation

Hinduism recognizes four different types of people: "Some are basically reflective. Others are primarily emotional. Still others are essentially active. Finally, some are most accurately characterized as experimental" (Smith, 1958, p. 35). A distinct path, or *yoga,* is suitable to a person's disposition and capacity for achieving salvation or *moksha.* The four paths are: (1) *jñāna yoga,* the path of knowledge; (2) *bhakti yoga,* the path of devotion; (3) *karma yoga,* the path of work; and (4) *rāja yoga,* the path of meditation.

*Jñāna yoga,* intended for individuals who have philosophical and intellectual orientations, attempts to overcome ignorance through the powers of knowledge and differentiation. Through logic and reflection, individuals strive to distinguish between the surface self and the larger Self that lies behind it. *Jñāna yoga* is the shortest but steepest path to salvation, and few people have the rare combination of rationality and spirituality required for it.

*Jñāna yoga* consists of three steps. The first, hearing, includes the study of scriptures and other philosophical writings in order to acquaint oneself with the concepts of self, the ultimate reality, and eternal being. The second step, thinking, encompasses intensive reflection and contemplation about the distinction between the self and Self. "If the *yogi* is able and diligent, such reflections will in due time build up a lively sense of the abiding Self that underlies his phenomenal personality" (Smith, 1953, p. 38). The third step, shifting self-identification from the passing to the eternal part of being, occurs through a variety of means, such as profound reflecting and thinking of one's finite self in the third person. The latter involves observing one's activities with calm detachment from a distance.

The second path to salvation, *bhakti yoga,* relies more on emotion than reason. The most powerful and persuasive emotion is love. "People tend to become like that which they love, with the name thereof progressively written on their brows. The aim of *bhakti yoga* is to direct toward God the geyser of love that lies at the base of every heart" (Smith, 1958, p. 39).

In contrast to *jñāna yoga, bhakti yoga* relies on religious worship and rituals through which people attempt to achieve the virtues of gods and goddesses. Hindus cherish gods' human incarnations, such as *Rāma* and *Krishna,* because they feel that gods can be loved most readily in human form. This is the most popular path currently followed in India.

*Karma yoga,* the third path to salvation, is intended for action-oriented people:

*Work can be a vehicle for self-transcendence. Every deed a person does for the sake of his or her own private welfare adds another coating to the ego and in thus thickening it insulates it further from God within or without. Correlatively, every act done without thought of self diminishes self-centeredness until finally no barrier remains to cloud one from the divine* (Smith, 1958, p. 45).

Depending on their dispositions, followers of *karma yoga* may choose to practice under the mode of *jñāna yoga* (knowledge) or *bhakti yoga* (devotion). For example, a *karma yogi* with an intellectual bent would engage in such activities as producing, disseminating, and utilizing knowledge. On the other hand, a *karma yogi* with a devotional outlook would be involved in activities such as social worship, religious festivals, and the construction of temples.

The final path of salvation, *rāja yoga,* is considered the royal way to salvation. Followers of *rāja yoga* are experimental in nature and believe that affairs of the spirit can be approached empirically. This path is based on the belief that " . . . our true selves are vastly more wonderful than we now realize and [on] a passion for direct experience of their full reach" (Smith, 1958, p. 51). Followers engage in physical, mental, and spiritual exercises through which they reach their inner spirits.

The four paths to salvation are not exclusive, because no person is solely of one disposition — either reflective, emotional, active, or experimental. "While most persons will, on the whole, find travel on one road more satisfactory than on others and will consequently tend to keep close to it, Hinduism encourages people to test all four and combine them as best suits their needs" (Smith, 1958, pp. 60-61). Each path of salvation, however, is guided by its appropriate *dharma.*

## Concept of Dharma

*Dharma* defines a code of conduct that guides the life of a person both as an individual and as a member of society. It is the law of right living, the observance of which secures the double objectives of happiness on earth and *moksha*. The life of a Hindu is regulated in a very detailed manner. Personal habits, social and family ties, fasts and feasts, religious rituals, obligations of justice and morality, and even rules of personal hygiene and food preparation are all conditioned by *dharma*.

*Dharma,* as a social value with a strong sense of morality, accounts for the cohesion in Hindu society. Harmony is achieved when everyone follows his or her own *dharma*. It is the system of norms supported by the general opinion, conscience, or spirit of the people. *Dharma* does not force people into virtue but trains them for it. It is not a fixed code of mechanical rules but a living spirit that grows and moves in response to the development of society (Koller, 1982).

The individual and social dimensions of *dharma* are interdependent. The conscience of the individual requires a guide, and one must be taught the way to realize one's aims of life and to live according to spirit and not senses. *Dharma,* at the social level, holds all living beings in a harmonious order. Virtue is conduct contributing to social welfare, and vice is opposite (Radhakrishnan, 1979).

*Dharma* is usually classified according to the requirements of one's state in life and one's position in society, for these two factors determine one's own specific *dharma*. Thus, at the individual level, *āśrama dharma* refers to duties attending one's particular stage in life. According to Hindu philosophy, human life consists of four stages or *āśramas:* student, householder, retiree, and renunciator (Jain, 1991, pp. 84–85). Specifically, the students' *dharma* includes obligations of sobriety, chastity, and social service. The householder stage requires marriage, raising a family, producing the goods necessary for society according to one's occupation, giving to the needy, and serving the social and political needs of the community. In the retiree stage, the individual is required to control his or her attachment to worldly possessions; it is the time for working out a philosophy for oneself, the time of transcending the sense to find and dwell at one with the timeless reality that underlies the dream of life in this world. Finally, the renunciator is a disinterested servant of humanity who finds

peace in the strength of spirit and attempts to fulfill the ultimate aim of human life, *moksha* or liberation. This is also the stage of complete renunciation of worldly objects and desires.

*Varṇa dharma,* on the other hand, refers to the duties attending one's caste, social class, or position. The Hindu caste system and its relationship with *dharma* are discussed in more detail later.

Hinduism recognizes a *universal dharma* that applies to any person regardless of caste, social class, or stage in life. For example, telling the truth, avoiding unnecessary injury to others, not cheating, and so on are common *dharmas* that all human beings share. Other *dharmas* are determined by particular circumstances and therefore cannot be specified in advance. The rules for determining specific requirements of action in unusual and unpredictable situations is that the higher *dharmas* and values should always prevail. Noninjury and compassion are basic moral principles in deciding cases of conflicting moral duties, and one must never engage in behavior that is detrimental to spiritual progress (Koller, 1982).

## Caste System

The caste system is a unique feature of Indian culture. No Indian social institution has attracted as much attention from foreign observers, nor has any other Indian institution been so grossly misunderstood, misrepresented, or maligned. Even the word *caste,* which is derived from the Portuguese *casta* (color), is a misnomer connoting some specious notion of color difference as the foundation of the system. It is a curious fact of intellectual history that caste has figured so prominently in Western thought.

The caste system began in India about 3,000 years ago. During the second millennium B.C., a host of Aryans possessing a different language and culture and different physical characteristics (tall, fair-skinned, blue-eyed, straight-haired) migrated to India. The class of differences that followed eventually established the caste system because the Aryans took for themselves the kinds of work thought to be desirable: They became the rulers, the religious leaders, the teachers, and the traders.

The other people were forced to become servants for the Aryans and to do less pleasing kinds of work. The outcome of this social classification and differentiation was a society clearly divided into four castes, hierarchically, from higher to lower:

1. *Brahmins* – seers or priests who perform such duties as teaching, preaching, assisting in the sacrificial processes, giving alms, and receiving gifts
2. *Kashtryās* – administrators or rulers responsible for protecting life and treasures
3. *Vaiśyas* – traders, business people, farmers, and herders
4. *Śūdras* – artisans such as carpenters, blacksmiths, and laborers

In the course of time, a fifth group developed that was ranked so low as to be considered outside and beneath the caste system itself. The members of this fifth "casteless" group are variously referred to as "untouchables," "outcastes," "scheduled castes," or (by Mahatma Gandhi) *Harijans* – "children of God." People in this group inherit the kinds of work that in India are considered least desirable, such as scavenging, slaughtering animals, leather tanning, and sweeping the streets (Chopra, 1977, pp. 27-29).

The caste system began as a straightforward, functional division of Hindu society. It was later misinterpreted by priests to be as permanent and as immutable as the word of God. Accordingly, the caste system was justified in terms of the "immutable and inborn" qualities of individuals, the unchangeable result of "actions in previous incarnations," and the unalterable basis of Hindu religion.

The caste system applies only to the Hindu segment of Indian society. The particular caste a person belongs to is determined by birth – one is born into the caste of his or her parents. Each caste has its appropriate status, rights, duties, and *dharma*. Detailed rules regulate communication and contact among people of different castes. A caste has considerable influence on the way of life of its members; the most important relationships of life, above all marriage, usually take place within the caste.

The merit of the caste system lay in it contribution to social stability and social security. Everyone has a known role to play and a group with whom to belong. The lower castes and outcastes are not necessarily happy with their role in the system as evidenced by the numbers who converted to other religions, especially Buddhism, Islam, and Christianity – all of which allowed them to escape from caste restrictions (Terpstra, 1978).

After India's independence in 1947, discrimination based on caste was outlawed. India has launched a massive social reform movement against "untouchability." There are numerous forms of affirmative action programs and quota systems aimed at promoting the welfare of "untouchables" and lower castes. These programs have produced many benefits for disadvantaged groups in the fields of education, employment, politics, and government. Unfortunately, there is still considerable prejudice and discrimination against untouchables, especially in the rural areas which comprise approximately 75 percent of India's population (Jain, 1992).

As any American knows, legislation is not always effective in bringing about immediate changes in social behavior. Sudden changes will not occur rapidly in India either, especially with a behavior pattern sanctioned by religion and 3,000 years of tradition. In urban areas, it is more common for one to cross caste lines in choosing occupation and in marrying. In rural areas, on the other hand, caste remains a major influence in one's life.

The implications of the caste system for communication and economy are quite obvious and quite negative. To the degree that the caste system is rigidly followed, it limits communication between caste groups and hinders free flow of information. It becomes difficult to allocate human resources efficiently. If birth and caste determine work assignments, rather than ability and performance, the output of the economy suffers. Coordination and integration of the work force and management can also be hindered by caste restrictions. Occupational caste assignments derived centuries ago in an agrarian society are not likely to mesh with today's technological, urban, industrial society.

## The Spirit of Tolerance

An outstanding feature of Indian culture is its tradition of tolerance. According to Hinduism, the reality or existence at the deepest level is boundless. No description, formula, or symbol can adequately convey the entire truth about anything. Each perspective provides a partial glimpse of reality, but none provides a complete view. Different partial — even opposing — viewpoints are regarded as complementing each other, each contributing something to a fuller understanding of reality.

Traditionally, Indian thinkers have been willing to adopt new perspectives and new positions without, however, abandoning old positions and perspectives. The new is simply added to the old, providing another dimension to one's knowledge. The new dimension may render the old less dominant or important, but it does not require the latter's rejection. The traditional storehouse of Indian ideas is like a four-thousand-year-old attic to which things were added every year but which was never once cleaned out (Koller, 1982).

Hindu culture believes in universal tolerance and accepts all religions as true. It is believed that the highest truth is too profound to allow anyone to get an exclusive grasp on it. When no beliefs can be said to be absolutely true, no beliefs can be declared absolutely false. Hindu culture is comprehensive and suits the needs of everyone, irrespective of caste, creed, color, or gender — it has universal appeal and makes room for all.

In Jainism, an offshot of Hinduism, the theory of *syādvāda,* or "may be," has further developed India's spirit of tolerance. According to this theory, no absolute affirmation or denial is possible. As all knowledge is probable and relative, another person's point of view is as true as one's own. In other words, one must show restraint in making judgments — a very healthy principle. One must know that one's judgments are only partially true and can by no means be regarded as true in absolute terms. This understanding and spirit of tolerance have contributed to the advancement of Indian culture, helping to bring together the divergent groups with different languages and religious persuasions under a common culture (Murthy & Kamath, 1973).

## Summary

This article has discussed eight dominant cultural patterns of Hindus in India: world view, belief in reincarnation, the concept of *karma,* the aims of human life, the reincarnation to salvation, the concept of *dharma,* the caste system, and the spirit of tolerance. These patterns have been integral parts of Hinduism and Indian culture for the last 3,000 years. They have a significant influence on the personality, values, beliefs, and attitudes of Hindus in India and abroad. An understanding of Hindu cultural patterns and their influence on communication behavior will improve the quality of intercultural communication between people of India and other cultures.

## References

Chopra, S. N. (1977). *India: An Area Study.* New Delhi: Vikas.

Damen, L. (1987). *Culture-Learning: The Fifth Dimension in the Language Classroom.* Reading, Mass.: Addison-Wesley.

Ellwood, R. S. (1992). *Many Peoples, Many Faiths.* 4th ed. Englewood Cliffs, N.J.: Prentice-Hall.

Jain, N. C. (1991). "World View and Cultural Patterns of India." In L. A. Samovar and R. E. Porter (Eds.), *Intercultural Communication: A Reader,* 6th ed., pp. 78–87. Belmont, Calif.: Wadsworth.

Jain, N. C. (1992). Teaching About Communicative Life in India. Paper presented at the annual meeting of the Western Speech Communication Association, Boise, Idaho, February.

Koller, J. M. (1982). *The Indian Way.* New York: Macmillan.

Murthy, H. V. S., and Kamath, S. U. (1973). *Studies in Indian Culture.* Bombay: Asia Publishing House.

Radhakrishnan, S. (1979). *Indian Religions.* New Delhi: Vision Books.

Samovar, L. A., and Porter, R. E. (1991). *Communication Between Cultures.* Belmont, Calif.: Wadsworth.

Smith, H. (1958). *The Religions of Man.* New York: Harper & Row.

Terpstra, V. (1978). *Cultural Environments of International Business.* Cincinnati: South-Western.

# A Comparison of Arab and American Conceptions of "Effective" Persuasion

## JANICE WALKER ANDERSON

This rhetorical analysis will illustrate that Americans and Saudis have different "rules" for political debate. "The rhetoric used in the Western world to describe the Arab-Israeli conflict is a prime example of the use of language, not as a means of illuminating reality," Abdel-Wahab El-Messiri (quoted by D. Ray Heisey, 1970) asserted, "but as a way of evading issues and complex historical totalities" (p. 12). In our modern global village, different conceptions of persuasion meet through the mass communication process.

Although mass media reports on events in the Middle East translate the words used by Arab leaders, the reports seldom explain the different cultural standards in Arab societies for evaluating reasonableness. "We can say that what is 'reasonable,'" intercultural communication scholars Condon and Yousef (1975) explain, "is not fully separable from cultural assumptions" (p. 213). This analysis indicates some of the differences between Arab and American cultural orientations toward what constitutes "effective" persuasion.

As Richard Barton (1982) argued in "Message Analysis in International Mass Communication Research," "the study of international media processes lags behind the general trend in mass communication study of systematically investigating the formal qualities of media discourse" (p. 82). This study is intended as a first step toward ad-dressing a gap in current research on international mass communications.

This paper compares the rhetorical tactics in a Saudi government advocacy advertisement, or paid editorial, with those in a Mobil Oil Corporation advocacy advertisement.... Advocacy advertisements promote ideas rather than products and usually argue one side of a controversial social or political issue.[1] Both paid editorials examined in this study explain to the American public the rationale behind the Arab's oil boycott in 1973. The two advocacy ads employ radically different rhetorical tactics to accomplish similar objectives.

First, the analysis will provide a brief overview of some essential aspect of Arab orientations toward discourse. Then, it will briefly set the historical context for the ads. Finally, it will compare the rhetorical tactics in the two advocacy advertisements and summarize the different basic assumptions about persuasion implicit in each artifact.

## Arab Orientations Toward Discourse

Before beginning the analysis, it is first necessary to acquaint American readers with some of the basics of Arab and Moslem orientations toward argumentation. "While only a small percentage (about 10%) of present-day Arabs are Bedouins," Gudykunst and Kim explain in *Communicating with Strangers,* "contemporary Arab culture holds the Bedouin ethos as an ideal to which, in theory at least, it would like to measure up" (p. 50). While values such as materialism, success, activity, progress, and rationality are featured in American culture, Arab societies revolve around the core values of "hospitality, generosity, courage, honor, and self-respect" (p. 50).

As H. Samuel Hamod indicated in "Arab and Moslem Rhetorical Theory and Practice," storytellers performed a vital function for the Bedouin tribes because few people could read or write: "[T]heir tribal storytellers functioned as historians and moralists in recounting battles and instances of outstanding bravery and cunning" (p. 97). These storytellers, or what we today might call poets, performed important political functions by establishing a means for interpreting and directing action.

From *The Howard Journal of Communications,* Vol. 2, No. 1 (Winter 1989–90), pp. 81–114. Reprinted by permission of the publisher. Janice Walker Anderson is in the Communication Department, College at New Paltz, State University of New York.

As A. J. Almaney and A. J. Alwan (1982) explained, a poet's poems "might arouse a tribe to action in the same manner as . . . [a politician] in a modern political campaign. . . . He was both a molder and agent of public opinion" (p. 79). Some attributed magical powers to these storytellers because they controlled the power of language which could act upon the human emotions and rouse the people to action.

To this day, poets are held in the highest esteem in Arab societies. As a result, many educated Arabs will attempt to write poetry at some time in their careers. In 1983, for example, Sheik Mani Said al-Otaiba, an oil minister from the United Arab Emirates, wrote a poem about OPEC's (Organization of Petroleum Exporting Companies) troubles maintaining oil production quotas. The *New York Times* reported that this poem "seemed to cause more hard feelings among his colleagues than the discord over prices" (Lewis, p. 6).

The reporter, Paul Lewis, discounted the importance of the Sheik's poem, asserting that his most important contribution was a passage in his dissertation "which marked him as one of the first Arabs to say publicly that it was the Nixon Administration that encouraged [OPEC] to quadruple world oil prices in 1973 by suggesting the West had few, if any, alternatives" (p. 6). In this instance, Lewis underestimated the importance that Arabs ascribe to poetry. It frequently functions in a political context to motivate action, and, as such, it is accorded as much weight as a scholarly dissertation.

In addition, Arab cultures connect inspired language and religion. Arabic plays an important religious role in Islamic societies. All Muslims, regardless of their nationality, must use Arabic in their daily prayers. The language of the Quran is considered a miracle in itself because it was produced by the Prophet Mohammed, who was illiterate. Consequently, Muslims believe that the Quran cannot be faithfully translated into other languages (Almaney & Alwan, p. 79).

The power of words lay not in their ability to reflect human experience, but in their ability to transcend it, to reach toward that which lay beyond human experience – the divine. To this day, the Quran stands as the ultimate book of style and grammar for Arabs. The cultural equivalent in the West would be using the King James Version of the Bible as our style manual.

The Arab's appreciation for the persuasive power of the rhythm and sound of words leads to a style that relies heavily on devices that heighten the emotional impact of a message. Certain words are used in speaking that have no denotative meaning. "These are 'firm' words because the audience knows the purpose behind their use, and the words are taken as a seal of definiteness and sincerity on the part of the speaker" (Hamod, p. 100). Other forms of assertion, such as repetition and antithesis, are also quite frequent. Emphatic assertions are expected, Almaney and Alwan explain: "If an Arab says exactly what he means without the expected assertion, other Arabs may still think he means the opposite" (p. 84).

Hamod explains the reasoning behind the Arab's emphasis on stylistic concerns. "He who speaks well is well educated; he who is well educated is more qualified to render judgments and it is his advice we should follow. Eloquence and effectiveness were equated" (p. 98). An Arab writer establishes credibility by displaying ability and artistry with the language.

## Setting the Historical Context

Both advocacy ads faced a potentially hostile American audience in presenting their views about the Middle East. The advocacy ads appeared in 1973, the year of the first oil crisis. "The press at the time," Anthony Sampson (1975), oil industry analyst, explained, "were sympathetic to the Israelis" (p. 100).

Mobil's ad, "The U.S. Stake in Middle East Peace: I," appeared in June of 1973 when another war was brewing in the Middle East. "This ad turned out to be one of the most controversial messages we've ever run," Herbert Schmertz (1986), Mobil's vice president for public affairs explained:

*The issue at hand was simply the future of America's oil supply, which boiled down to the need for recognizing the strategic importance of Saudi Arabia. Our critics accused us of running this ad at the behest of the Saudis, but there was no truth to this charge (p. 168).*

The *New York Times* editorial board was so concerned about the content of Mobil's ad that they did not allow it to appear in Mobil's normal position on the op-ed page. Instead, the ad was buried in the second section of the newspaper, where it was more likely to be obscured by product ads.

The Saudi ad, entitled, "An Open Letter to the American People," appeared six months later. The Saudi ad ran in the *Washington Post* two months after the 1973 war in the Middle East began.[2] The ad appeared on New Year's Day just as the consequences of the oil boycott were beginning to be felt within the United States.

Although the Saudi ad was attributed to Mr. Omar Sakkaf, Saudi minister of state for foreign affairs, he was not necessarily the sole author. In a telephone interview, Dr. Mohammed Al-Zafer, a former Saudi diplomat to the United States and now deputy director of King Khaled University in Saudi Arabia, explained that Mr. Sakkaf had died about five years before. In describing the generation of the ad, Dr. Al-Zafer stated that diplomats stationed in the United States speak fluent English. However, they would not prepare statements for publication without "having them checked ahead of time." By attributing the ad to the minister of state of foreign affairs, the Saudis indicated that it was an accurate reflection of their perspective on events in the Middle East. It is not unreasonable to assume the author(s) of the ad were probably educated, cosmopolitan Saudi officials familiar with both English and Arabic.

## Comparison of Rhetorical Strategies

The two ads demonstrated quite different responses to the hostile audience that they faced. Most immediately, the ads employed different strategies for framing their arguments. In addition, they used contrasting organizing principles. Finally, the ads provided different kinds of justifications for action.

## Framing the Argument

Mobil's ad, "The U.S. Stake in Middle East Peace: I," employed an inductive opening. Instead of launching immediately into a discussion of foreign affairs, the author(s) first defined a domestic problem immediate to their readers. The opening five paragraphs of the ad documented the growing gap between domestic oil production and trends in energy consumption.

Because oil and natural gas supplied over three-quarters of the United States' energy, the author(s) asserted: "Our society cannot live without adequate oil supplies ... much less continue as an industrial society." Although domestic consumption was increasing, domestic production was declining so that foreign oil already provided one third of the United States' energy needs. "In another seven years, or less," Mobil author(s) predicted, "we will be relying on foreign sources for more than half of our oil."

Our need for increased energy supplies provided the rationale for Mobil's discussion of the Middle East. Because only the Middle East had sufficient oil reserves to meet U.S. demand, the ad concluded: "Like it or not, the United States is dependent on the Middle East even just to maintain our present living standards in the years immediately ahead."

In framing its argument, the Mobil author(s) demonstrated a typically American tendency to assume that "the world is rational in the sense that ... events ... can be explained and the reasons for particular occurrences can be determined" (Stewart, 1972, p. 35). Statistics described the "objective" reality of energy demand. These rational "facts" created the necessity for action. "For Americans," Stewart explains, "the world is composed of facts — not ideas. Their process of thinking is generally inductive, beginning with facts and then proceeding to ideas" (p. 22).

The introduction of the Saudi ad, in contrast, was not concerned with the facts of energy supply and demand. It focused on competing perspectives. This "Open Letter to the American People" obliquely addressed the concerns of five distinct audiences: the American people, the American press, the "American friends of Israel," other Arab nations, and the "world in general." The first five paragraphs of the ad acknowledged the subgroups whose competing perspectives created the complexity of the political dynamics of the Middle East.

This complexity was reflected through the use of parallel structure to express contrasting ideas:

*We, the Arabs, wish you a Happy New Year. Your holiday season might have been marred by the hardships of the energy crisis. Ours is haunted by the threat of death and continued aggression.*

The antithesis highlighted the contrast in perspectives between the American people and the Arab people. It implicitly addressed the contrast between American materialistic values and Arab values of honor and self-respect. On the broad level of justice between nations of the world, economic hardships such as gas lines paled in comparison to displacement from a homeland.

The language structure of the opening appealed to a human tendency to respond to the rhythm of language, to enjoy, as Kenneth Burke pointed out, seeing the completion of a "form." Although American readers might not understand the content of the antithesis, they would unconsciously respond to the rhythm. The Saudi author(s) employed parallel structure to draw readers into their interpretation of the world. The literacy device illustrated the author(s)' sophistication with the language, thereby establishing their credibility through traditional means within Arab cultures.

By emphasizing the contrast between American and Arab perspectives, the opening simultaneously minimized the contrast between the Arab countries of Syria, Egypt, Jordan, and Saudi Arabia. "We, the Arabs" imposed a unitary perspective based on linguistic, religious, and cultural commonalities, not on national boundaries. "North Americans value individual centeredness and self-reliance," Gudykunst and Kim explain, "the Arabic attitude is one of mutual dependence" (p. 126). The Saudi author(s) would not perceive distinctions between individual Arab nations as particularly salient in the way that North Americans would.

*But it is not in bitterness that we address this message to you and it is our hope that there will be no bitterness in you as you read it.*

As though acknowledging that the American public might read the initial literary flourish as a stark exaggeration, the author(s) followed one verbal flourish with another designed to soften the impact of the first. This parallel structure emphasized commonalities. It indicated that the assertion in the opening was not intended to offend the American people. Overstatement simply indicated the sincerity of the author(s)' intentions and the seriousness of the topic. "To Arabs," Gudykunst and Kim explain, ". . . a soft tone implies weakness or even deviousness" (p. 161).

*We have been under continuous attack from the American Press – with notable exceptions – for two decades, and we must confess we are unable to understand the reasoning behind this overwhelming hostility. We lived in Palestine for two thousand years, and when we resisted displacement by a foreign state, the Americans branded us aggressors.*

The parallel structure was broken as this paragraph introduced two additional contrasting perspectives: the American media's portrayal of Arabs as aggressors versus the Arabs' view of themselves as victims. This paragraph employed a cultural commonplace meaningful within the Arab community. The two-thousand-year context the Saudi author(s) established and the use of the name "Palestine" emphasized the Israelis' role as interlopers. In this paragraph, the Saudi author(s) echoed the comments of Abdel-Wahab El-Messiri, arguing that the American media did not excel in describing "complex historical totalities."

"But let that pass," the fourth paragraph continued, once again backing away from the emotional tone that had been established, again indicating to the American audience that statements of Arab beliefs were not intended to initiate a hostile reaction. This single-sentence paragraph signaled a transition to a new topic:

*In the past year, we have made considerable concessions, given up much of what is rightfully ours, for the sole purpose of promoting peace in the Middle East and the world in general. These concessions appear to have had no effect whatsoever on the American attitude. Indeed, wild accusations against the Arabs are increasing in volume and intensity, and all of them are so baseless that we have begun to wonder if the American people really know what the Arabs want.*

The Saudi author(s) asserted the Arabs' bewilderment at the reaction of Americans toward Arabs and repeated the question that prompted the letter: "Do the American people know what we are asking for?"

The opening of the Saudi ad alluded to a range of subgroups implicit in the international mass media audience. The introduction played upon the theme of competing perspectives on events in the Middle East. Parallel structure highlighted the contrasts. A break in the rhythm indicated a redefinition offered to the American people; Arabs were victims of displacement by a foreign state, not aggressors as the American media portrayed them. While the Saudi author(s) made an effort to accommodate Americans who might not know how to interpret the assertions offered, the primary focus of the introduction was on establishing a perspective for interpretation, on naming the victims and aggressors in the region rather than on explaining principles of supply and demand.

## Organizing Principles

As a result, the Saudi author(s) were not concerned with the linear development of factual premises. The organizing principle of the Saudi ad was on the implicit level of metaphoric association, not on the level of explicit meaning. The unifying thread through the opening of the Saudi ad was the portrayal of the Arabs as victims. The unifying theme in the next section of the ad was the portrayal of the Israelis as aggressors.

Rather then mention the most recent conflict in 1973, the ad turned back to the 1967 Six-Day War. The Saudi author(s) did not provide historical explanations of the conflicts in the region. Instead, the ad simply quoted UN Resolution 242, which called for a "just and lasting peace in the Middle East based on the 'withdrawal of Israel Armed Forces from territories occupied in the recent conflict' and 'termination of all claims or states of belligerency.'" The term "recent" was used equivocally. Did it refer to the last few months or to the last five years?

"This is what we are asking for," the next paragraph of the ad explained. The simple language

structure of this statement reinforced the impression that the Arabs' demands were similarly uncomplicated. By quoting an official UN resolution that the United States had approved, the ad implied that world opinion sided with the Arabs. Yet, the equivocal language in the ad made it vague in terms of the Arabs' specific demands.

The next paragraph documented that United States officials had previously criticized Israeli expansionism in the region: "President Lyndon Johnson stated in September, 1968, that 'boundaries cannot and should not reflect the weight of conquest.'" The subsequent paragraph continued the parallel structure that had been established in this section: "This is what we are asking for, and we want nothing more."

Parallel structure and repetition were employed quite consistently in the next two paragraphs: "Israel says it wants peace. So do we. Israel says it wants security. So do we." The problem was that Israel wanted peace and the Arab lands it occupied in 1967: "Israel wants peace and *lebensraum,* security and Arab land, and Israel cannot have both," the ad explained. "Leben" is a traditional drink among Arabs that consists of coagulated sour milk. If viewed as a *double entendre,* between German and Arabic, Israel wanted the milk of Arab land as well as peace. An American might translate the phrase as Israel wanted to have its cake and eat it too.

The ad consistently alternated between long, complicated paragraphs and short, single-sentence paragraphs. The variety between complexity and simplicity combined with parallel structure and repetition made the ad quite rhythmic. One result of this method of organization, however, was that an American reader needed a broad knowledge of the conflicts in the region. Those who did not share the author(s)' historical perspective would have to read between the lines.

Americans are accustomed to greater explicitness in message design, while Arabs are more accustomed to reading implicit meanings. Intercultural communication scholars use the term "contexting" to "describe the perceptual process of recognizing, giving significance to, and incorporating contextual cues in interpreting the total meaning of any stimulus in a particular communication transaction"

(Gudykunst & Kim, p. 120). American culture (low context) places greatest emphasis on explicit meaning. Arab cultures (high context), on the other hand, make greater use of subtle, contextual clues in interpreting messages. In explaining what the Arabs wanted, the Saudi author(s) demonstrated a cultural tendency to rely on an implicit understanding of the history of conflicts in the region.

In comparison to the Saudi ad, Mobil's argument marched forward with the precision of a military parade. The ad operated almost exclusively in the realm of explicit meaning. Each paragraph advanced the argument one step further, and there was little variety in the length of these paragraphs. Establishing a rhythm was less important than supporting premises with factual references and statistics. By using such a structure, the Mobil author(s) consistently narrowed the range of feasible options for dealing with the situation.

The opening five paragraphs of Mobil's ad established the "facts" of America's energy needs. The next section of the ad documented the "facts" about oil supplies. After dismissing other possible oil sources such as Venezuela, the North Sea, and Mexico, the author(s) concentrated on Saudi Arabia because this country had more oil than any other nation in the world. Its "reserves can support an increase in production from the present level of about 8 million barrels a day to 20 million barrels daily," the author(s) explained. Saudi Arabia's huge oil reserves made it central to America's future economic growth.

Mobil's position as the major oil company with the smallest domestic reserves and the largest reliance on Saudi oil meant that Mobil's continued economic health depended on the Saudis (Sampson, p. 202). The "fact" of Mobil's significant self-interest in Middle Eastern oil was not mentioned. Instead, the Mobil author(s) attempted to generalize the company's concerns to the oil industry and to the nation as a whole. The lockstep logic of Mobil's argument obscured the company's unique constraints that made it particularly vulnerable to a boycott of Middle Eastern oil.

Overall, Mobil's argument was quite linear in its organization. Increased oil supplies were necessary for continued economic growth. Only the Middle East had sufficient reserves to meet increased energy needs in the United States. We needed Middle Eastern oil more than they needed our money. Therefore, we could no longer ignore Arab political concerns. Each premise was supported with statistics or examples. The step-by-step progression foreclosed from consideration alternatives such as conservation, alternative energies, or non-Middle Eastern sources of oil.

In organizing their argument, the Mobil authors reflected the cause-effect thinking that Steward asserts is typical of Americans. As he explains, "In the ideal form, the world is seen as a unilateral connection of causes and effects projecting into the future. Since the American focuses on the future rather than the present or the past, the isolation of the critical cause becomes paramount" (p. 35). The critical cause for the Mobil author(s) was access to supplies of Saudi Arabian oil.

The majority of the Mobil ad operated in the realm of explicit meaning. Implicit meaning and stylistic devices were only employed in the ending call-to-action. This ending was cast in general terms to avoid specifically mentioning either the Israelis or the Palestinians:

*So we say: It is time now for the world to insist on a settlement in the Middle East. . . . A settlement that will bring justice and security to all the peoples and all the states in that region. Nobody can afford another war in the Middle East. Nobody. Nobody.*

The repetition in this section emphasized the seriousness of Mobil's concern. Who could object to a call for peace and justice for all peoples in the region? Only those who read between the lines and recognized that such a general statement might include the Palestinians.

## Types of Justifications

Mobil's ad conspicuously avoided discussing the political implications of economic decisions until after its detailed delineation of oil supplies and demand. "If our country's relations with the Arab world . . . continue to deteriorate," the author(s) warned, "Saudi Arabia may conclude it is not in its interest to look favorably on U.S. requests for increased petroleum supplies." Mobil executives were concerned because "we will need the oil more than Saudi Arabia will need the money."

Without specifying what political concerns might motivate Saudi Arabia, Mobil concentrated on examining the Saudi's economic constraints. Development programs in Saudi Arabia could proceed without increased production because of the country's small population and large foreign reserves already over three billion dollars, the ad explained. Since the Saudis had no financial incentive to increase oil production, the Mobil author(s) concluded: "It is therefore time for the American people to begin adapting to a new energy age, to a vastly changed world situation, to the realities with which we will have to learn to live."

Rather than deal in the treacherous realm of political affairs, the Mobil author(s) chose the terra firma of economic concerns. Throughout the ad, Mobil offered eminently practical justifications that revolved around economic necessities. The ad twice reminded Americans that they needed to act in order to preserve their current lifestyles. Americans, Steward asserts, assume that "the things worthy of effort are material" (p. 35).

Similarly, in explaining the Saudis' motivations, the Mobil author(s) did not concentrate on the Arabs' political concerns. Instead, Mobil executives outlined the economic resources of Saudi Arabia that allowed it to enforce its political views. Mobil's practical, economic justification did not allow room for considering abstract concepts such as justice or honor.

Justice and national honor, however, were central concerns in the Saudi ad. The Arabs initiated the boycott, the ad explained, because "our national interests demanded it." The use of the personal pronoun "our" once again reinforced the identity among all Arab nations. "In the Arab world honorable behavior is that 'which is conducive to group cohesion.' . . . [S]hameful behavior is that which tends to disrupt, endanger, impair, or weaken the social aggregate" (Patai quote by Gudykunst & Kim, p. 51).

The United States had used economic boycotts in the past, the Saudi ad reminded readers. The

Arabs had been provoked into a boycott when the United States, "which had repeatedly assured us of our rights to our lands, made massive arms deliveries to the Israelis to help them remain in our lands." Although the Arabs wanted peace, they could not allow Israel to take their lands. "Nor would any just people anywhere in the world expect us to do so." The ad concluded: "We are asking the American people, especially the American friends of Israel, to understand this and to help us attain the peace we are after."

Throughout the ad, the Saudi author(s) offered justifications based on national honor and self-respect. The ad briefly acknowledged but did not discuss the economic consequences of the oil boycott, which tripled oil prices in the space of a few months and triggered one of the largest transfers of wealth in the century. In the face of displacement from a homeland, pragmatic, economic concerns such as the price of oil were secondary.

The Saudis' abstract justifications for their actions were predicated upon the past. Previous grievances against the Arabs constrained the present and limited the future. A past orientation was central to the Saudis' explanation of the boycott. The purpose of the boycott was "not to impose a change in U.S. policy in the Middle East but to demand the *implementation* of U.S. policy in the Middle East, as it has been repeatedly defined." The distinction between imposing a change in U.S. policy and asking for an existing policy to be implemented was a fine one, but it grounded the Saudis' statement that the oil boycott was not an attempt to "blackmail" the American people.

In demanding that past policies be implemented, the Saudis attributed their own orientation to the Americans, neglecting the fact that each new American political administration established new foreign policy priorities. Richard Nixon would not necessarily be constrained by the comments of Lyndon Johnson. The Saudis did not acknowledge that Americans lacked a historical memory similar to their own.

While the Saudis were concerned with the past, Mobil concentrated on the future. Mobil's ad frequently referred to "the coming years" or the "years immediately ahead." The primary motivation for action for the Mobil author(s) was future supplies of oil. In contrast, the Arabs, Steward explains, believe "it is insane to attempt to predict future events; only God knows what the future will bring" (p. 88).

Interestingly, each ad assumed the other culture's orientation was synonymous with its own. Mobil talked about the Saudis' future economic motives, while the Saudis turned to the United States' previous foreign policy statements and appealed to Americans' sense of national honor and justice. Each ad demonstrated rhetorical ethnocentrism in attributing its orientation to the other culture.

## Conclusion

As this analysis has indicated, the differences between these two ads go far beyond superficial contrasts between a florid style and a plain style (Glenn, Witmeyer, & Stevenson, 1977). While Mobil imposed a unitary perspective based on "objective facts," the Saudi ad concentrated on illustrating competing interpretations of reality. Images that clarified an emotional climate were most important for the Saudi author(s); statistics clarifying "objective" reality were most important in the Mobil ad. Mobil's author(s) concentrated on practical, economic justifications predicated on future events; the Saudi author(s) emphasized abstract justifications that focused on the past. In sum, the ads were mirror images of each other in terms of their selections of rhetorical tactics.

These different rhetorical tactics implied different conceptions about the nature of reality. The Mobil author(s), employing traditional Neo-Aristotlelian conceptions of argumentation, assumed an objective reality that could be accurately known and verified by systematic observation. The author(s) attempted to muster factual data and logical proof to support their argument that Arab concerns should be accorded a greater role in American foreign policy. "Reasonableness" was determined by the argument's consistency in replicating the structure of objective reality. The goal of Mobil's argument was to explain how the world of energy supply and demand worked. The advocacy advertisement's reliance on linear progression, practical justifications, and a focus on the future as an extension of the present sprang from the assumption of an objective reality.

The Saudi ad, on the other hand, focused not on objective reality, but on reality as apprehended and mediated through the intensifying and distorting prism of language. The Saudi author(s) assumed that reality could not be separated from the structure of language through which we understand reality. Consequently, they focused on naming the victims and aggressors in the region. Establishing the Arab's perspective for interpretation was more important than explaining principles of oil supply and demand. "Effectiveness" in this case was determined by the author(s)' ability to employ the rhythm and sounds of the language to advance an evaluative perspective, thereby controlling the prism through which reality was viewed.[3] Considered in such a light, the Saudi author(s) were remarkably effective.

Despite these different orientations toward the role of discourse in society, the ads were similar in their use of strategic ambiguity. The Saudis ignored the economic consequences of the oil boycott, while Mobil was obscure when it came to discussing its self-interest in the region and in considering the feasibility of other alternatives, such as conservation. The Saudis projected an image of Arabs as a unified group rather than competing nations and ignored their contributions to aggression in the region. Each ad concealed "facts" that it did not wish to emphasize. The ads were equally cognizant of the ability of language to conceal as well as to reveal. In this sense, both ads were equally self-serving

While the Saudi author(s) made efforts to accommodate American readers, these attempts at adaptation were likely to go unrecognized by American readers lacking an understanding of different cultural rules for political debate. A Neo-Aristotelian would argue that the Saudi ad was sloppy at best, devious at worst. Arguable premises were introduced but not developed. The ad circled around issues rather than proceeding in a linear fashion from one topic to the next. Americans, with their preference for "rational," cause-effect arguments, were likely to view such an approach as deliberately deceptive.

Arabs, on the other hand, criticized Americans because they lacked the sense of historical perspective that motivated Arabs. An Arab would view Americans' insistence on a unitary perspective based on "objective" facts as deliberately deceptive in neglecting the broader historical context behind the immediate issues. It is this American lack of a sense of "historical totalities" that contributes to Arab complaints that American portrayals are arrogant, one-sided, and simplistic.

In the end, this analysis illustrates in specific detail how "the truism of one nation becomes an argument for another" (Starosta, 1984, p. 231). Each approach to political debate makes legitimate assumptions about the nature of persuasive power. Yet, given the vastly different assumptions about the role of persuasion in society, it is not surprising that misunderstandings occur between Americans and Arabs, even when the same "language" is used. Communicating across a cultural gap requires more than just a knowledge of respective vocabularies. It also requires an understanding of the different cultural rules for what constitutes "reasonable" political debate.

## Notes

1. In the United States, advocacy advertisements mushroomed in the early seventies, as executives complained about media bias against business. By purchasing their own space, business representatives circumvented the typical editorial process, taking their case directly to the public through their own editorials. Advocacy advertising became a frequent adjunct to more traditional forms of political lobbying, offering executives total control over the final message. For a more detailed discussion of the genre, see Sethi's *Advocacy Advertising and Large Corporations* or Heath and Nelson's *Issues Management: Corporate Public Policy Making in an Information Society.*

2. The territory in the Middle East that Israel now occupies was originally called Palestine, a name taken from the Philistines who occupied the coastal part of the country in the twelfth century B.C. A Hebrew kingdom established in 1000 B.C. was subsequently controlled by Assyrians, Babylonians, Egyptians, Persians, Macedonians, Romans, and Byzantines. The Arabs took control of Palestine from the Byzantine

Empire in A.D. 634–40. The Arabs maintained control until the twentieth century, when Britain captured Jerusalem in 1917.

Jewish immigration to the area increased throughout Britain's time of control, as British Foreign Secretary Arthur Balfour promised support for a Jewish state in Palestine. Discussions on partitioning the area were tabled during World War II. In 1946, the Jewish population in the region numbered 678,000 compared to 1,269,000 Arabs. Unable to resolve the problem, Britain turned it over to the United Nations in 1947, which voted for partition in the face of strong Arab opposition.

War began with the founding of the State of Israel in 1948. A cease-fire was negotiated in 1949, which increased Israeli territory by fifty percent. The simmering conflict erupted again in 1956 with the Suez crisis and in 1967, when Israel increased its territory two hundred percent by occupying the Golan Heights, the West Bank of the Jordan river, the Old City of Jerusalem, and parts of the Sinai Peninsula. These occupied territories provided the impetus for the 1973 war, which began on October sixth, Yom Kippur, the Israelis' holiest day of the year. Initial Arab gains were reversed, and a cease-fire was negotiated two weeks later.

3. This dichotomy in metaphysical first principles has been identified and discussed in detail by a variety of theorists. Walter J. Ong (1980), for example, contrasted the linear conventions of a written culture with the holistic perspective of an oral culture. Jacqueline De Romilly (1975), in *Magic and Rhetoric in Ancient Greece,* argued that these different formulations of the wellspring of symbolic power coexisted in ancient Greece. John Poulakos (1984) in *Rhetoric, the Sophists and the Possible* provides an excellent contrast between the perspective offered by Aristotelian and sophistic rhetoric. He examines the basic assumptions of each rhetoric in light of modern philosophers such as Nietzsche, Heidegger, and Foucault. What has not typically been done, however, is to illustrate how different basic assumptions about the nature of rhetoric and reality play themselves out in actual discourse.

## References

Al-Zafer, Mohammed. (1985, Dec.). Telephone interview with author.

Almaney, A. J., & Alwan, A. J. (1982). *Communicating with the Arabs: A handbook for the business executive.* Prospect Heights, IL: Waveland Press.

Barton, R. L. (1982). Message analysis in international mass communication research. In M. Mander (Ed.), *Communication in transition* (pp. 81–101). New York: Praeger.

Condon, J., & Yousef, F. (1975). *An introduction to intercultural communication.* New York: Bobbs-Merrill.

De Romilly, J. (1975). *Magic and rhetoric in ancient Greece.* Cambridge, MA: Harvard University Press.

Glenn, E. A., Witmeyer, D., & Stevenson, K. A. (1977). Cultural styles of persuasion. *International Journal of Intercultural Relations,* 1(3), 52–66.

Gudykunst, W., & Kim, Y. (1984). *Communicating with strangers: An approach to intercultural communication.* Reading, MA: Addison-Wesley.

Hamod, H. S. (1963). Arab and Moslem rhetorical theory. *Central States Speech Journal,* 14, 97–102.

Heisey, R. D. (1970). The rhetoric of the Arab-Israel conflict. *Quarterly Journal of Speech,* 46, 12–21.

Lewis, P. (1983, March 20). An oil minister's poem stole the show. *New York Times,* Sec. 6, p. 6.

The Mobil Oil Corporation. (1973, June 30). The U.S. Stake in Middle East peace: I. *New York Times,* Sec. 2, p. 30.

Ong, W. J. (1980). Literacy and orality in our times *Journal of Communications,* 30, 197–204.

Poulakos, J. (1984). Rhetoric, the sophists and the possible. *Communication Monographs,* 51, 215–226.

Sakkaf, O. (1973, Dec. 31). Open letter to the American people. *Washington Post,* Sec. 1, p. 9.

Sampson, A. (1975). *The seven sisters.* New York: Viking Press.

Schmertz, H. with Novak, W. (1986). *Good-bye to the low profile: The art of creative confrontation.* Boston: Little, Brown.

Sethi, S. P. (1977). *Advocacy advertising and large corporations.* Lexington, MA: Lexington Books.

Starosta, W. (1984). On intercultural rhetoric. In W. Gudykunst & Y. Y. Kim (Eds.), *Methods for intercultural communication research.* (pp. 229–238). Beverly Hills: Sage.

Stewart, E. (1972). *American cultural patterns: A cross-cultural perspective.* Yarmouth, ME: Intercultural Press.

# Cultural Patterns of the Maasai

LISA SKOW
LARRY A. SAMOVAR

For many years critics of intercultural communication have charged that the field focuses on a handful of cultures while seriously neglecting others. For example, the literature abounds with material concerning Japan and Mexico, but there is very little to be found if one seeks to understand the cultures of India or black Africa. As economics and politics force a global interdependence, it behooves us to examine cultures that were previously excluded from our scrutiny.

The motivation for such analysis can take a variety of forms. Our desire for more information might be altruistic, as we learn that 40,000 babies die of starvation each day in developing countries. Or we may decide that we need to know about other cultures for more practical reasons. Strong ties with African countries can lead to economic, educational, and technological exchanges beneficial to individuals on both sides of the globe. Regardless of our motives, the 1990s and beyond will offer countless examples that demand that we look at cultures that we have ignored in the past. This article is an attempt to explore one of those cultures, specifically, that of the Maasai of East Africa.

If we accept the view of culture held by most anthropologists, it becomes nearly impossible to discover all there is to know about any one group of people. That is to say, how does one decide what is important about a culture if Hall (1976) is cor-

This original article appeared in print in the sixth edition. All rights reserved. Permission to reprint must be obtained from the authors and the publisher. Lisa Skow is a former Peace Corps volunteer and a graduate of San Diego State University. Larry Samovar teaches at San Diego State University.

rect when he writes, "there is not one aspect of human life that is not touched and altered by culture" (p. 14)? The decision as to what to include and exclude in any analysis of a culture is usually based on the background of the researcher. Someone interested in the music of a culture would obviously look at the portion of the culture relating to that specific topic and, in a sense, abstract only part of the total phenomenon called culture.

A researcher interested in intercultural communication is also faced with the problem of what to select from the total experiences of a people. What, in short, do we need to know if our goal is to understand the behavior of another culture? One answer to this question is found in the work of Samovar and Porter (1988). They have proposed a model of intercultural communication that can be used as a guide in selecting what aspects of culture need to be incorporated into any discussion of intercultural communication. This article will address the three major components of that model: perception, verbal processes, and nonverbal processes.

## Background

The East African countries of Kenya and Tanzania know firsthand about Western culture. They have lived through Western government, language, culture, and, unfortunately, oppression. Even today, more than two decades after each country received its independence, Western culture still has a profound influence on the people of Kenya and Tanzania. However, because there are so many different ethnic groups in these countries, it has not had the same impact and influence on each group. The Kikuyu of Kenya have adopted Western culture with such enthusiasm that one wonders what are "proper" Kikuyu traditions and customs and what are Western influences. On the other end of the Western continuum are the Maasai of southern Kenya and northern Tanzania, who have, for a number of reasons, rejected much of the culture presented by the West. They have largely shunned Western forms of government, dress, language, music, religion, and frequently even assistance. The

Maasai are often referred to as "true Africans" because of their "purity" – a purity of which they are very proud.

Africa may be changing at an extraordinarily fast pace, but the Maasai are one group of people who seem content to continue their own way of life. This article hopes to offer some insight into that way of life.

## Perception

One of the basic axioms of intercultural communication, and one that is part of the Samovar and Porter (1988) intercultural model, is that culture and perception work in tandem. That is to say, our cultural experiences determine, to a large extent, our view of the world. Those experiences that are most important are transmitted from generation to generation as a means of assuring that the culture will survive beyond the lifetime of its current members. Therefore, to understand any culture it is necessary to examine those experiences that are deemed meaningful enough to be carried to each generation. One way to study those experiences is through the history of a culture. The history of any culture can offer insight into the behaviors of the culture as well as explain some of the causes behind those behaviors. Let us therefore begin our analysis of the Maasai people by looking at those aspects of their history that link current perceptions to the past.

## History

While the history of any culture is made up of thousands of experiences, there are often a few significant ones that serve to explain how that culture might view the world. In the case of the Maasai, there are three historical episodes that have greatly influenced their perception of themselves, other people, and events. These historical occurrences center on their creation, fierceness, and reaction to modernization.

The history of the Maasai is the history of a people with an oral tradition. Like all cultures who practice the oral tradition, the content and customs that are transmitted are largely found within the stories, poetry, and songs of the people. To the outsider they appear vague and only loosely based on facts. Some historians, along with the aid of Maasai elders, have attempted to link the stories and folklore with the available information about the Maasai's past, a past that helps explain many of the perceptions and values held by the Maasai.

Most accounts of the origin of the Maasai as a unique culture begin with the belief that they were part of a larger group that was migrating south during a severe drought (Kipury, 1983). The group found themselves trapped in a deep valley so they constructed a bridge that was to transport them out of the valley. Folk tales and history go on to tell the story of how the bridge collapsed before all the people escaped. Those who were left behind are now thought to be the Somali, Borana, and Rendile peoples. Those who managed to escape the dryness of the valley went on to be the true Maa-speaking people.

While the above rendition of early Maasai history is uncertain in answering questions regarding the origins of the Maasai, it does reveal one very important aspect of how history and perception are linked. This story helps explain how the Maasai perceive themselves compared to other tribes. It also helps an outsider understand the strong feelings of pride that are associated with the Maasai culture. For the Maasai, the story of their origin, even if it is speculation, tells them they are better than other tribes of East Africa who did not come from the north nor escape across the bridge — regardless of how long ago that arrival might have been.

The Maasai's history of warfare and conflict is yet another source of knowledge about the perception of themselves and non-Maasai. Before the advent of colonialism in the latter part of the nineteenth century, other tribes in Kenya such as the Kikuyu, Akamba, and Kalenjin were often attacked by the Maasai. The attacks were fierce and usually resulted in their enemies being forced from their lands. Some Maasai, particularly the elders, still see themselves as the conquerors of other tribes, and even today, the Maasai still have the reputation of being warlike. Non-Maasai Kenyans may warn visitors of the "terrible" Maasai and their propensity for violence. A former colleague of one of the authors often expressed her distrust of the Maasai, believing that they would harm her simply because she was from the Kikuyu tribe. She had heard about the Maasai's fierceness and their dislike of other tribes who dressed in Western clothes. Whether entirely accurate or not, this perception of them as warlike influences both the behavior of the Maasai and the behavior of those who come in contact with them.

A third historical period that has shaped the perceptions of the Maasai is the preindependence period of Kenya. Because the Maasai occupied vast areas of land in Kenya, the British colonialists turned an eye toward acquiring this valuable property. Through numerous agreements, great parcels of land were turned over to the colonialists. The Maasai were settled on new tracts of land that were much less desirable than the ones they were leaving, and they soon began to realize that not only were they giving up their prime land but they were also seeing a number of promises made by the colonialists being broken. In response to these two conclusions, the Maasai adopted an attitude of passive resistance to all Western innovations and temptations to become "modern." While most other parts of Kenya were altering their culture through education and technology, the Maasai had become disillusioned with those who were seeking to alter their way of life, and hence they refused to change (Sankan, 1971).

The rejection of cultural conversion by the Maasai has had immense consequences on them and the people around them. On one hand it has caused the government and other tribes to perceive them as stubbornly traditional, backward, uneducated, and isolated. However, for the Maasai, resistance to change is yet another indication of their strength and long history of power. Other more Westernized tribes, such as the Kikuyu, feel the Maasai are backward and not in tune with changing Kenya. Ironically, the Kikuyu seem to have a love-hate relationship with the Maasai: scorn for their refusal to be more modern yet respect for their retaining their traditional customs.

## Values

What a culture values, or doesn't value, also helps determine how that culture perceives the world. Therefore, understanding what the Maasai regard as good or bad, valuable or worthless, right or wrong, just or unjust, and appropriate or inappropriate can help explain the communication behavior of their culture.

**Children** For a Maasai man or woman to be without children is a great misfortune. The Maasai strongly believe that children continue the race, and more important, they will preserve the family — hence, children are highly valued. The Maasai embrace the idea that a man can "live" even after death if he has a son who can carry on his name, enjoy his wealth, and spread his reputation. In addition, they value children because they offer the senior Maasai a continuous supply of workers. The Maasai have a saying that illustrates this point: "More hands make light the work." Children supply those hands. Unfortunately, this value is in direct conflict with the Kenyan government's family planning program to curb Kenya's dangerously high population growth. While the central government tries to emphasize the need to control the population, for the Maasai the man with the most children, no matter how poor he is, is the wealthiest and happiest of all men.

**Cattle** The Maasai culture revolves around the cow, on which they greatly depend for their food, clothing, housing, fuel, trade, medicine, and ceremonies. Cattle have given the Maasai their traditionally nomadic lifestyle. The more cattle a man has the more respected he is. Cattle are usually killed only on designated occasions such as for marriage and circumcision ceremonies or when special guests visit. The Maasai believe that all cattle were originally given to them by God. There is even a folk tale that tells of the Maasai descending to earth with cattle by their sides. This belief justifies their taking cattle from other tribes, even if it is in violation of the law.

**Groups** Families and life-stage groups are at the core of the Maasai community. Because children are so highly valued, the family must be strong and central in their lives. An overwhelming portion of a Maasai child's education is still carried out in the home, with the grandparents, not the schools, providing the content of the culture.

Life-stage groups are specifically defined periods in the lives of all Maasai, particularly males. Traditionally, all men must go through four stages of life: childhood, adolescence (circumcision), moranship (warriorhood — junior and senior), and elderhood (junior and senior). Women must pass through childhood, circumcision, and then marriage. Each of these stages places a strong emphasis on the group. Attempts to get Maasai students to raise their hands and participate in formal classrooms are often futile. Drawing attention to oneself in a group setting is unacceptable because the tribe and the life-stage group are far more valuable than the individual (Johnstone, 1988).

**Elders: Male and Female** Maasai children must give respect to any person older than themselves, whether a sibling, grandmother, or older member of the community. They must bow their heads in greeting as a sign of humility and inferiority. Even young circumcised men and women (aged fifteen to twenty-five years) must bow their heads to male elders, particularly if the elders are highly respected in the community.

The Maasai believe the older you become the wiser you become and that a wise individual deserves a great deal of deference and respect. Part of the strong emphasis placed on elders is that the Maasai hold their history in such high regard, and it is the oldest members of the tribe who know most of the history. Young people cannot know the "truth" until they progress through each of the life-stage groups.

For Maasai youths getting older indicates a change in social status. When male Maasai students return from a school holiday with their heads shaved, this indicates that they have just gone through circumcision and initiation into another life-stage. They have become men and are instantly perceived by other students and themselves as different, even older, and deserving of more respect.

**Pride** Pride for the Maasai means having the virtues of obedience, honesty, wisdom, and fairness. A man may be an elder in name only, for if he does not exhibit these characteristics, he is not a respected man in the community. A woman's pride is often defined by how well she keeps her home, by whether she is an obedient wife, and by the number of children she has.

Outsiders, whether black or white, perceive the Maasai loftiness and pride as a kind of arrogance. The Maasai themselves, because they are traditionally pastoralists, still look down on strictly agricultural tribes such as the Kikuyu.

Their strong sense of pride is also fueled by their view of themselves as warriors. As noted earlier, they have always been feared by other tribes and the colonialists. Their folklore is replete with tales of their fighting with incredible fearlessness, even when their primitive weapons faced their enemies' modern bullets. For them the battles were to preserve the "true African" way of life and to protect their cattle.

**Beauty** Beauty is yet another value that is important to the Maasai. Both men and women adorn themselves with elaborate beads, body paint, and other jewelry. Maasai children, especially girls, begin wearing jewelry almost from the moment of birth. One of the primary duties a woman has is to make necklaces, bracelets, bangles, belts, and earrings for their husband, children, friends, and herself. Adornment is also a way for a woman to attract a husband, and Maasai women are very meticulous in selecting jewelry for special celebrations. Maasai warriors still spend much of their day painting themselves with red ochre, and they also plait and braid their hair, which is grown long as a sign of warriorhood.

Beauty and bodily adornment are so valued in the Maasai culture that they have distinctive jewelry and dress to wear during certain periods of each life-stage. For example, one can tell if a boy has just recently been circumcised because he wears a crown of bird carcasses. Thus, we can conclude that beauty is more than superficial for the Maasai; it is a reflection of a very important value that often steers perception in one direction or another.

## World View

The world view of a culture is yet another factor that greatly modifies perception. In the Samovar and Porter (1988) model, world view deals with a culture's orientation toward such things as God, humanity, the universe, death, nature, and other philosophical issues that are concerned with the concept of being. In short, it is that perception of the world that helps the individual locate his or her place and rank in the universe. It influences nearly every action in which an individual engages. Our research would tend to agree with this observation. The Maasai's world view has three components that greatly control their life and hence their perception of the universe: coexistence with nature, religion, and death.

**Nature** For the Maasai, nature must always be held in the highest regard. They believe that their very existence depends solely on nature's benevolence. Their lifestyle is one that sees them interacting with the elements: Without rain their cattle will die, and in a sense so will they, for as we pointed out earlier, cattle supply most of the basic needs of the Maasai.

The Maasai also embrace the view that nature cannot be changed; it is too powerful. But they do acknowledge that nature itself changes without their intervening, and what they must do is change as nature fluctuates. Adapting to nature is most evident in the Maasai's seminomadic lifestyle. They carry coexistence to the point where they will not kill or eat wild animals unless they pose a threat or there is a severe drought. For the Maasai cultivating and hunting are seen as destructive to nature: Cultivation forces humans to deal directly with nature, changing and altering it to their specifications and needs; hunting for food is seen as something even worse, for then nature is not only being changed but it is being destroyed (Rigby, 1985).

**Religion** The second aspect of world view, religion, is closely tied to the Maasai perception of nature. The Maasai have one god called "Engai," but this god has two very distinct personalities and therefore serves two purposes: "Engai Narok," the black god, is benevolent and generous and shows himself through rain and thunder; "Engai Nanyokie," the red god, is manifested in lightning. To the Maasai, God encompasses everything in nature, friendly or destructive (Saitoti and Beckwith, 1980). In fact, the word "Engai" actually means "sky." Cattle accompanied the Maasai people to earth from the sky and thus cattle are seen as mediators between humans and God as well as between humans and nature. Therefore, herding is traditionally the only acceptable livelihood, since it is God's will. Not to herd would be disrespectful to Engai and demeaning to a Maasai (Salvadon and Fedders, 1973).

There is a Maasai proverb that states, "The one chosen by God is not the one chosen by people" (Rigby, 1985, p. 92). Thus, not surprisingly, the Maasai have no priests or ministers; there is no one who represents God or purports to speak for God. There are "laiboni" who are considered the wisest of the elders and often cast curses and give blessings, but they do not represent God or preach. The Maasai have no religious writings, only oral legends, therefore the elders are important in the religious life of the people.

What is most significant is that God (Engai) is found in nature. Some Maasai households rise at dawn to pray to the sun, which is seen as a manifestation of Engai. God is found in many other forms in nature for the Maasai: rain, grass, and even a particularly beautiful stone. God is nature and cannot be artificially symbolized in a cross or a building. Since nature is God, people must live in harmony with God and the Maasai must work together. This is a different view of God than the one offered by Christianity, in which God is separate from humans and is even from a different world.

**Death** The third aspect of the Maasai world view is how they perceive death. As with most cultures, death brings sorrow to those left behind by the deceased; however, cultures differ in how they respond to death. The response of the Maasai directly coincides with their belief in the coexistence of nature and human beings; therefore, except for the "laiboni" (wise man), all corpses are left out in the open to be devoured by hyenas and other scavengers. The assumption behind this action is clear, at least to the Maasai, who believe that after they have had a full life and enjoyed the benefits of nature, it is only fitting that their bones go back to the earth so they can be used to prepare the land for future life. For the Maasai there is a circular, mutually beneficial relationship between nature and humanity.

## Verbal Processes

In the most basic sense, language is an organized, generally agreed upon, learned symbol system used to represent human experiences within a geographic or cultural community. Each culture places its individual imprint on words — how they are used and what they mean.

Language is the primary vehicle by which a culture transmits its beliefs, values, and norms. Language gives people a means of interacting with other members of their culture and a means of thinking, serving both as a mechanism for communication and as a guide to social reality. Anyone interested in studying another culture must therefore look at the way a culture uses language and also the experiences in their environment they have selected to name. Research on the Maasai culture reveals two language variables that offer a clue into the workings of this particular group of people: their use of metaphors and their reliance on proverbs.

## Metaphors

Wisdom in the Maasai culture is marked not just by age and prudence but also by language use. Elders make decisions at tribal meetings based on speeches offered by various members of the group. The most successful speakers are those whose eloquence is embellished and ornate. The metaphor offers the gifted speaker a tool to demonstrate his mastery of words. Heine and Claudi (1986) explain the importance of metaphor to the Maasai when they write:

*Maa people frequently claim that their language is particularly rich in figurative speech forms. Nonliteral language, especially the use of metaphors, is in fact encouraged from earliest childhood on, and the success of a political leader depends to quite a large extent on the creative use of it (p. 17).*

**Table 1**

| Category | Maasai Word | Basic Meaning | Metaphorical Meaning |
|---|---|---|---|
| Object + Animal | Olmotonyi | Large bird | Eagle shoulder cape |
| Person + Animal | Enker | Sheep | Careless, stupid person |
| Person + Object | Sotua | Umbilical cord | Close friend |
| Quality + Object | Olpiron | Firestick | Age-set generation |

Because of the value placed on the metaphors, Johnstone (1988) writes, "Whenever there were big meetings to decide important matters, the men always spoke in proverbs, metaphors, and other figurative language." Messages are full of elaborate symbolism — blunt and simple words are rarely used.

The information in Table 1, developed by Heine and Claudi (1986), helps clarify some of the types of metaphors employed by the Maasai. These few examples demonstrate how most of the metaphors in the Maa language reflect what is important in their culture. For example, the use of the umbilical cord to refer to a very close friend is indicative of the value placed on childbirth and of the strong bonds between members of the same age-set. In addition, an age-set generation is formally established when a select group of elders kindles the fire on the day that a new generation of boys will be circumcised (Heine & Claudi, 1986). These age-sets form both a unique governing body and a social hierarchy in all Maasai communities.

## Proverbs

Like metaphors, proverbs are an integral part of the Maasai language. Massek and Sidai (1974) noted that "a Maasai hardly speaks ten sentences without using at least one proverb" (p. 6). These proverbs have common elements and themes that are directly related to the Maasai value system.

Proverbs convey important messages to the members of a culture because they often deal with subjects that are of significance. Therefore, the assumption behind examining the proverbs is a simple one — discover the meaning of the proverb and you will understand something of what is important to its user. This axiom is exceptionally true for the Maasai, for here one encounters proverbs focusing on respect, parents, children, wisdom, and proper conduct. Let us look at some of these proverbs as a way of furthering an understanding of the Maasai culture.

1. "Meeta enkerai olopeny." (The child has no owner.) Maasai children are expected to respect all elders, not just those in the immediate family. It is very common for children to refer to older men as "Father" and to older women as "Mother."

2. "Memorataa olayoni oataa menye." (One is never a man while his father is still alive.) Even as junior elders, Maasai men do not always leave their father's homestead. It is not until a man attains the full status of senior elder that he usually establishes his own home with his wife (wives) and children. In addition, the very name of male children is indicated with the word "ole," which means "son of," placed between the first and last names. A Maasai male is very often characterized by his father's name and reputation.

3. "Eder olayioni o menye, neder entito o notanye." (A boy converses with his father while a girl converses with her mother.) This proverb is representative of both the restricted relationships between the opposite sexes in a family and the strict divisions of labor found in the Maasai culture. Young girls learn to do household chores at an early age, and by age seven their brothers are responsible for tending the family herd.

4. "Menye marrmali, menye maata." (Father of troubles, father without.) In the Maasai culture there is a conviction that a man with no children has more problems than a man with many children.

They believe that even a man with a fine herd of cattle can never be rich unless he also has many children. This proverb simply serves to underscore those facts.

5. "Ideenya taa anaa osurai oota oikati." (You are as proud as lean meat with soot on it.) Being proud is a well-known characteristic of the Maasai. So strong is this value that the Maasai are often criticized by other African tribes. To sustain the reality and the perception of pride, a Maasai must always add to his accomplishments, and courageous acts and large families are two common behaviors that present an image of a proud person. It should be noted, however, that foolish pride is looked down upon as a sign of arrogance.

6. "Medany olkimojino obo elashei." (One finger does not kill a louse.) The need to cooperate is crucial to the Maasai culture, and this proverb reinforces that belief. As noted earlier, the Maasai community is a highly communal one, one that is well-structured and based on group harmony and decision making. The family unit is particularly dependent on cooperation and accord. On most occasions wives care for each other's children. Cattle are kept together and shared, with ownership only a secondary consideration.

In this section on proverbs we see the connection between what a culture talks about and what it embraces and acknowledges to be true. This link between words and behavior only serves to buttress the belief that verbal symbols represent a device by which a culture maintains and perpetuates itself.

## Nonverbal Processes

Nonverbal systems represent yet another coding system that individuals and cultures use as a means of sharing their realities. Like verbal symbols, nonverbal codes are learned as part of the socialization process — that is, each culture teaches its members the symbol and the meaning for the symbol. In the case of the Maasai, there are a number of nonverbal messages that, when understood, offer the outsider some clues as to the workings of this foreign culture.

## Movement and Posture

The Maasai show their pride and self-regard by the way they carry themselves. They are tall and slender and have a posture that reflects an appearance of strength and vigor. There is, at first glance, a regal air about them and at times they appear to be floating. "The morans [warriors], especially, walk very erect and relatively slowly. It's like they are in so much command of their environment that they are absolutely at ease" (Johnstone, personal correspondence, 1988).

The posture and movement of Maasai women also mirrors an attitude of pride and self-assurance. They are also tall and slender and have a gait that is slow and self-confident. Their heads are held high as a way of emphasizing their confidence and superiority over other tribes.

## Paralanguage

The Maasai people utilize a number of sounds that have special meanings. The most common is the "eh" sound, which is used extensively, even though the Maasai language is ornate and metaphorical. When uttered, the sound is drawn out and can have a host of different interpretations; it can mean "yes," "I understand," or "continue." Although similar to the English regulators "uh huh" and "hmmm," "eh" is used more frequently and appears to dominate short, casual conversations among the Maasai.

## Touching

While public touching between the sexes among the Maasai is usually limited to a light handshake, same-sex touching is common. Simple greetings between the sexes consist of a very light brush of the palms; in fact, so light is the touch, the hands appear barely to touch. If two women are good friends, however, they may greet each other with a light kiss on the lips. If they have not seen each other recently, they may embrace and clutch each other's upper arms. Men will frequently drape their arms around each other while conversing. When children greet an elder, they bow their heads so that the elder may place his or her hand on the young person's head, which is a sign of both respect and fondness. There is a great deal of affection to be found among the Maasai, and touching is one way of displaying that affection.

## Time

The meaning cultures attach to time also reveals something of their view toward life and other people. The Maasai are unique in their treatment of time. Unlike the Westerner, for the Maasai there is always enough time: Their life is not governed by the clock; they are never in a hurry. This casual attitude produces a people who are self-possessed, calm, and most of all, *patient*.

Children are taught very early that there is never a need to rush. The vital chore of tending the family cattle requires that children stay alert and attentive to the herd's needs and safety, but such a chore also requires eight to ten hours of patient solitude.

This endless display of patience by the Maasai people is in direct contrast to time-conscious Americans. For example, public transportation in Kenya is not run on a firm schedule; buses and "matatus" (covered pick-up trucks) leave for their destinations when they are full. As do most Kenyans, the Maasai understand this. Inquiries from Americans as to when a vehicle will be departing are often answered with "just now." "Just now," however, can mean anywhere from five minutes to an hour.

Even though the present is fully enjoyed, the Maasai culture is very past-oriented. This strong tie to the past stems from the view that wisdom is found not in the present or the future, but rather in the past. The future is governed by the knowledge of the elderly, not by the discoveries of the young. The insignificance of the future is apparent in how the Maasai perceive death: There is nothing after death unless one is a "laiboni" (wise man).

## Space

Space, as it relates to land and grazing, is truly communal. Traditionally nomadic pastoralists, the Maasai did not regard any land as theirs to own but rather perceived all land as theirs to use. Rigby (1985) explains that the pastoral Maasai "do not conceive of land as 'owned' by any group, category, community or individual" (p. 124). He explains,

however, that today most Maasai practice a subtle marking of territory. Each clan now has its own area and for the most part, clan boundaries are observed. Yet concepts of "land rights" and "trespassing" are still viewed as Western notions.

The Maasai's perception of private space is very different from Western perceptions. Maasai do not need or ask for much private space while in public settings. Lining up in a systematic order, and taking one's turn, is not part of the Maasai experience — public facilities, therefore, at least to the outsider, often appear disorderly. It is not uncommon to see a vehicle designed to hold fifteen packed with thirty occupants, and none of them complaining. For the Maasai, space is like time — there is always enough of it.

## Conclusion

It has been the intent of this article to offer some observations about the Maasai culture. It is our contention that by knowing something about the perceptions and language systems of a culture, one can better understand that culture. This increased understanding provides us with a fund of knowledge that can be helpful in formulating messages directed to a group of people different from ourselves. It can also aid in interpreting the meanings behind the messages we receive from people who appear quite different from us. As Emerson wrote, "All persons are puzzled until at last we find some word or act, the key to the man, to the woman; straightaway all their past words and actions lie in light before us."

## References

Hall, E. (1976). *Beyond Culture*. Garden City, N.Y.: Anchor.

Heine, B., and Claudi, U. (1986). *On the Rise of Grammatical Categories*. Berlin: Deitrich Reimer Verlag.

Johnstone, J. (1988, March 30). Personal correspondence.

Kipury, N. (1983). *Oral Literature of the Maasai*. Nairobi: Heinemann Educational Books.

Massek, A. O., and Sidai, J. O. (1974). *Eneno oo Lmaasai — Wisdom of the Maasai*. Nairobi: Transafrica Publishers.

Rigby, P. (1985). *Persistent Pastoralists: Nomadic Societies in Transition.* London: Zed Books.

Saitoti, T. O., and Beckwith, C. (1980). *Maasai.* London: Elm Tree Books.

Salvadon, C., and Fedders, A. (1973). *Maasai.* London: Collins.

Samovar, L. A., and Porter, R. E. (1988). "Approaching Intercultural Communication." In L. A. Samovar and R. E. Porter (Eds.), *Intercultural Communication: A Reader,* 5th ed. Belmont, Calif.: Wadsworth.

Sankan, S. S. O. (1971). *The Maasai.* Nairobi: Kenya Literature Bureau.

# *P*alevome: Foundations of Struggle and Conflict in Greek Interpersonal Communication

## BENJAMIN J. BROOME

**Conflict** is most often defined as a struggle between parties who are linked in an interdependent manner over incompatible goals, interests, or resources. In Western societies the term *conflict* usually elicits negative images; it is associated with intensity of feelings, damaged relationships, and inefficient use of time and energy. Cooperation, friendly relations, and smooth transactions are put forth as ideals. Conflict signals that something is wrong and needs to be corrected. Much of the literature on conflict management and conflict resolution, published primarily in the United States, reflects this negative image of conflict (Coser, 1956; Fink, 1968; Freud, 1949; Pruitt & Lewis, 1977; Roloff, 1976).

This view of conflict is however, culture-bound. Even though many researchers recognize the possibility of productive uses of conflict (Deutsch, 1973; Folger & Poole, 1984; Kilmann & Thomas, 1977; Putman & Wilson, 1982), the existence of conflict in a relationship is usually discussed as an irregularity; relationships in conflict are "out of balance" and need to be restored to normalcy. In contrast to this view of conflict as an abnormality, other cultural groups view struggles between parties as a way of life. This is particularly true of both traditional and contemporary Hellas, better known to

From the *Southern Communication Journal,* Vol. 55, No. 2 (Spring, 1990), pp. 260–275. Reprinted by permission of the Southern States Communication Association. Benjamin J. Broome teaches at George Mason University in Fairfax, Virginia.

English language users as the country of Greece.[1]

Permeating almost every facet of everyday life in Greece is a sense of contest. To the Western mind,[2] Greece appears to be a "maddening mobile, elusive, paradoxical world, where there seems nothing solid enough to grasp save splinters, yet where no part is less than the mystical whole and where past and present, body and soul, ideal and reality blend and struggle and blend again with each other so that the most delicate scalpel can scarcely dissect them" (Holden, 1972, p. 34). However, for Greeks, this struggle can bring with it feelings of stimulation, excitement, and genuine human contact. Even the painful feelings that are often the result of conflict are not viewed as aberrations, but rather are seen as part of the natural course of human relations. In Greece, conflict is an aspect of everyday transactions that is unavoidable.

This paper discusses the Greek approach to conflict in interpersonal communication, exploring the traditional foundations of struggle as a way of life. The views presented here are based on anthropological, sociological, linguistic, and communication literature about Greece and the author's research in Greece during 1980 to 1989.

## Struggle as the Essence of Life: Traditional Greek Culture and Orientations Toward Interpersonal Conflict

Ernestine Friedl (1962), in describing life in a traditional Greek village at that time, reports that when one walks through the fields and inquires about how the work is going, the people generally respond with "palevome" or "we are struggling." The villagers' use of the verb *palevo* expresses the difficult conditions confronting farmers trying to make a living from the predominantly rocky soil and mountainous terrain. At the same time, it reflects the predominate worldview and orientation toward interpersonal relations characteristic of Greek reality. Triandis (1972) reports that even a positive term such as *success* is linked by Greeks with struggle, whereas for North Americans it is linked with careful planning and hard work. Nickolas Gage, author of the best-selling book *Eleni*

(Gage, 1983), describes Greece as a place with "joy and tragedy straight out of Aeschylus, Sophocles, and Euripides, and it is expressed with the same classic gestures. . . . the same tendency to use strong words and violent gestures; . . . the same warm heart, the disdain for time, and the delight in life lived fully, with all the senses awake" (Gage, 1987, p. 24).

While Greece is a land of unparalleled scenic beauty, it is also a land of contrasts. Physically, the mountains and the sea meet each other throughout the country, often resulting in dramatic settings. Culturally, there are contrasts between the island inhabitants and the mountain villagers (Sanders, 1962). Historically, the Greek character has always fought over the opposing poles of a more feminine Ionian makeup and a more masculine Dorian outlook. Geographically, Greece sits between the Near East and Europe and has been invaded and occupied by forces from both, resulting in cultural influences from East and West. In politics there have been both military dictatorships and socialist governments, although the dictatorships were not the choice of the people. These contrasts and the resulting struggle between opposites are deeply embedded in the nature of Greek reality:

> . . . *Greek identity as a whole (is) best seen as a constant oscillation between just such opposites as these. The spirit and the flesh, ideal and reality, triumph and despair – you name them and the Greeks suffer or enjoy them as the constant poles of their being, swinging repeatedly from one to the other and back again, often contriving to embrace both poles simultaneously, but above all never reconciled, never contented, never still. This perennial sense of tension between diametrically opposed forces is the essence of their existence – the one absolutely consistent feature of their identity since Greek history began. In the phrase of the Cretan novelist, Kazantzakis, they are truly double-born souls.* (Holden, 1972, pp. 27 - 28, emphasis added)

Tension and struggle in interpersonal relations are contextually embedded in several aspects of Greek history and social reality. Traditionally, Greece has revolved around village culture, even though from pre-classical times Greeks have traveled all over the world to both satisfy their curiosity and to search for new resources. Hundreds of villages have always dotted the mostly mountainous countryside and the island ports, with relatively few urban centers.

Today the situation has changed, with the majority of the population living in three or four major cities and 40% of the population residing in Athens. However, in many cases the suburbs of these urban centers resemble villages. The majority of the population of Athens are migrants from the villages and small towns of the countryside and the islands, and most residents of the capital were not born in that city (Campbell, 1983). More importantly, the majority of city residents remain closely tied to their traditional villages, often maintaining a village house and returning to the village for important religious occasions. Even with voting, most Greeks prefer to keep their registration in their villages rather than move it to their city of residence, maintaining their ties and status within remote villages. Thus, while externally many Greeks conform to more contemporary Western life-styles, they are psychologically and socially bound to a traditional culture that influences their lives in a myriad of ways (Triandis, 1986).

In order to understand the Greek approach to conflict and struggle as a way of life, it is necessary to explore two aspects of traditional Greek culture that have a strong influence on contemporary Greek thought and actions. The following section will discuss (a) the distinction between "ingroup" and "outgroup" in Greek society, and (b) the influence of "philotimo" on interpersonal relations.

## The Contextual Foundations of Interpersonal Struggle

### Ingroup-Outgroup Distinctions

Traditionally Greek culture is more collectivist than individualistic in nature (Doumanis, 1983) and emphasizes distinctions between ingroup and outgroup to a much larger extent than do Western societies. The major differences between ingroup

behavior and outgroup behavior have been extensively examined by Triandis (1972), who describes the Greek as defining his universe in terms of the triumphs of the ingroup over the outgroup. Social behavior is strongly dependent on whether the other person is a member of the ingroup or the outgroup. This affects relations with people in a wide variety of situations, such as interaction with authority figures and with persons with whom one is in conflict.

The definition of the ingroup in traditional Greek society includes family, relatives, friends, and even friends of friends. Guest and other people who are perceived as showing appropriate warmth, acceptance, and assistance quickly become friends and thus part of the ingroup. Outgroup members include those in the community outside the immediate family, the extended family, and the network of ingroup affiliations. While a traditional village community is sharply divided into subgroups on the basis of these affiliations, the structure is not entirely rigid; people who are at one point outgroup members could become ingroup members through marriage or by establishing links of cooperative interdependence (Doumanis, 1983). An individual is attached to these different groupings with varying degrees of intimacy, ranging from total identification to outward hostility.

A great deal of commitment exists between ingroup members, requiring intimacy, concern, and good conduct. It is required that an individual behave toward members of his or her ingroup with self-sacrifice, as the well-being of the ingroup is more important than that of the individual. In the context of a highly competitive social world, the ingroup provides protection and help for its members. Feelings of trust, support, cooperation, sympathy, and admiration are exchanged frequently among members of the ingroup.

Relations with outgroup members are characterized by a great deal of suspicion and mistrust. Influence and pressure from the outgroup is rejected. The relationship between authority figures and subordinates is also dependent on ingroup/outgroup considerations. For example, in larger organizations, managers, who are usually viewed by employees in Greece as part of the outgroup, are treated with avoidance and hostility. On the other hand, managers who are identified as part of the employees' ingroup are usually given submissive acceptance and warmth.

Concealment and deception play important roles in relations with the outgroup. They serve as important means for upholding ingroup honor and prestige. In a world where ingroup honor must be protected and competition is a way of life, deception becomes a useful means of fulfilling one's duties. The phrase is often heard "You can't live without lies." For Greeks, however, the word for lies, *psemata,* does not carry with it the negative connotations assigned by most Westerners. It is used more freely and with less emotional intensity (Friedl, 1959). It does not have the overtones of morality found in English, and it is sometimes even justified on religious grounds by declaring it the desire of God (du Boulay, 1976). In fact, villagers are not humiliated because someone tries to deceive them, although they become angry if the deception succeeds (Friedl, 1962).

The suspicion and mistrust of outgroup members lead to a general lack of helpfulness toward those not part of the ingroup. This is illustrated in a study reported by Triandis (1986). Comparisons were made between how people in the United States, Europe, and Greece behave toward foreign strangers and toward strangers who are fellow nationals.[3] A number of situations were used in which either a fellow national or a foreigner interacted with a sample of local people. In one situation, where the stranger asks for help from a local person, approximately 50 percent of those asked in Europe and the United States provided the assistance, regardless as to whether the request came from a foreigner or a fellow national. However, in Greece, this degree of help was only provided to the foreigner (a potential ingroup member) requesting assistance. Only 10 percent of locals agreed to help a fellow Greek whom they did not know, as this person was clearly an outgroup member.

Even cheating, while it is completely unacceptable with the ingroup, is acceptable when it is directed toward members of the outgroup. When it occurs with the outgroup, cheating is treated in the context of competition, where it is required that the outgroup member be taken advantage of if he or she is weak. The outgroup member is expected to be on guard against cheating.

The ingroup-outgroup distinction leads to a continuous struggle between members of the two groups. Actions that are inappropriate within the ingroup are applied without hesitation to relations with the outgroup. The distinction provides for the support and safety necessary to carry on the struggle, and at the same time it provides the focus for the struggle itself. Loyalty to the ingroup and feelings ranging from mild disregard to intense animosity for the outgroup provide the background upon which many conflicts are staged.

## Philotimo: The Essence of Ingroup Behavior

Perhaps the most cherished term for a Greek is *eleftheria,* which means freedom. For much of its long and sometimes glorious history, Greece has been under foreign domination. For example, the Ottoman Empire ruled Greece for 400 years, and during the Second World War it suffered tremendously under German occupation. Despite this history of domination by external forces, Greeks have always maintained a strong sense of personal freedom that transcends the circumstances. Much of this can be attributed to a central aspect of Greek self-concept called *philotimo.*

Philotimo is not translatable with a single English word; it is a concept that refers to several aspects of Greek character and social relations. First, it refers to a sense of responsibility and obligation to the ingroup, particularly to the family. The most important social unit in Greece is the family, and Greeks take their family obligations seriously. They are obliged to uphold the family honor and to provide assistance to family members. This extends in various ways to other members of the ingroup. Lee (1959) says that loyalty can only be evoked in personal relations, with the result that Greeks cannot be impartial in distributing resources that are at their disposal, whether those resources are jobs or material goods. It is one's duty to take care of family and friends first, irrespective of merit or order of priority.

Second, philotimo refers to appropriate behavior within the ingroup. As Triandis (1972) indicates, a person who is considered "philotimos" behaves toward members of his ingroup in a way that is "polite, virtuous, reliable, proud, . . . truthful, generous, self-sacrificing, tactful, respectful, and grateful" (pp. 308–309). The principle of philotimo requires a person to sacrifice himself or herself to help ingroup members and to avoid doing or saying things that reflect negatively on family or friends. Appropriate ingroup behavior should be seen and felt not only by the ingroup but by the outgroup as well, thus increasing prestige for the ingroup in the eyes of the outgroup.

Third, philotimo is strongly related to a person's sense of personal honor and self-esteem. As Lee (1959) stated: "Foremost in the Greek's view of the self is his self-esteem. It is impossible to have good relations with Greeks unless one is aware of this, the Greek philotimo. It is important to pay tribute to it, and to avoid offending it, or as the Greeks say, "molesting it" (p. 141). The Greek philotimo is easily bruised, and there is constant emphasis on both protecting the philotimo and enhancing it. Protecting one's philotimo leads to a concern with losing face, with shielding the inner core of the self from ridicule, and with avoiding actions that would cause loss of respect. There is constant guard against being outsmarted by the outgroup, and it is seldom that Greeks put themselves in a position of being in less than full control of their senses in order to avoid personal abuse and damage to the ingroup.

Offense against one's philotimo brings retaliation rather than feelings of self-criticism of self-blame. As Friedl (1962) relates, the avoidance of self-blame does not have the connotation of irresponsibility, because it is a necessary part of the maintenance of self-esteem. In the same vein, philotimo is not related to feelings of remorse or guilt, and it is not strongly tied to notions of ethical morality (Holden, 1972). If actions are taken in defense of philotimo that bring harm to outgroup members, responsibility is not accepted for what occurs following the actions. If the demands of philotimo have been satisfied, the person taking action against others is entitled to reject any blame for subsequent misfortune.

Safeguarding of philotimo promotes a sense of equality between individuals, and thus it is seldom that a Greek feels inferior to another. Even differences in status levels and role responsibilities are not cast in terms of superiority or inferiority in Greece. However, the philotimo of the Greek is very different from the notion of pride. The philotimo of the Greek is promoted by actions that bring honor and respect to the family and the ingroup, not simply to the individual. Lee (1959) points out that the expression of pride carries with it the connotation of arrogance, which is detested by the Greeks. A common proverb states that "the clever (proud) bird is caught by the nose."

In many ways, interpersonal struggle is driven by concerns of philotimo. Philotimo is the key to behavior within the ingroup, and it frames much of one's behavior toward the outgroup. Requirements of philotimo lead to actions that enhance the position of the ingroup, and at the same time trigger actions in defense of the ingroup. Many conflicts occur because of the demands of philotimo. Perhaps it is because of the Greek's strong sense of philotimo that conflicts can continue over long periods of time and at a high level of intensity without feelings of guilt or remorse.

## Interpersonal Struggle in Social Transactions

Greek social life has been described by du Boulay (1976) as a type of "see-saw," continuously in motion. Friedl (1962) used the word *tension* to capture the feelings of Greek villagers toward each other and the world, saying that a large number of social encounters feature a "sense of contest, of struggle, of agony, of a kind of pushing and pulling" (Friedl, 1962, p. 76). She used the metaphor of a "battle" to describe Greek social life in the village, arguing that the Greek search for identity in a culture that seeks so strongly to preserve ingroup honor and integrity is carried out to a large extent by pitting oneself against another. It is through contrast, with others that one learns to know oneself, and this leads to the necessity of maintaining differences and emphasizing contrasts. She says that "contrasts, and the tension contrasts create, become expected and desired" (Friedl, 1962, p. 76). Struggle and contrasts are evident in several related aspects of Greek social reality: (a) conversation style, (b) competitive nature of social relationships, and (c) process nature of relational struggle.

## Conversation Style and the Role of Couvenda

The conversation style of Greeks has been described as "contrapuntal virtuosity, incisive, combative, loud" (Lee, 1959, p. 146). To the unaccustomed ear, every conversation appears to be an argument, and gentleness seems to play no part in dialogue. The substance of conversation is less important than the style because it is the process that counts (Holden, 1972). Discussion can be described as "a battle of personal opinion, and its end is neither to reach the truth nor to reach a conclusion; its end is sheer enjoyment of vigorous speech" (Lee, 1959, p. 146). Indeed, the Western visitor to Greece is immediately struck by the intensity of the conversation:

*A city neighborhood or a village can be compared to a stage, and friends, neighbors, and kin to a Greek chorus commenting on unfolding marriages, hospitality, or sexual infidelity. No one can remain solely in the audience; however, neutrality is impossible to maintain. No one can expect to receive support of his or her reputation unless he or she defends that of allies. Manipulation of opinion depends on gossip, which in turn depends on the breaking of confidences, amusement derived from ridicule, and malicious attempts to exploit the situation. (Greece: A Country Study, 1985, p. 145).*

Challenges, insults and attacks are, within appropriate limits, almost synonymous with conversing. Friedl (1962) says that conversation "has some of the quality of an arena in which each man displays himself as an individual and waits for an audience response. People talk at each other rather than with each other" (p. 83). It is not unusual for several monologues to be going on simultaneously at a table as different individuals struggle to hold center stage and assert their personalities.

*Couvenda,* or conversation, is extremely important in Greek society. As Triandis (1972) puts it,

"Greeks love to discuss, to argue, and to match their wits with other debaters" (p. 323). Gage (1987) reports a conversation with a ship owner who believes that "to exercise the tongue and provoke the mind is the most fulfilling pastime of all" (p. 30). Davenport (1978) describes Athens as a city where social activity — eating out, drinking, dancing, singing and, above all, conversing — permeates everyday life to an extraordinary degree. From childhood, everyone receives a great deal of verbal stimulation, for conversation is a skill that no one can live without.

Couvenda plays a number of important functions in Greek society. First, it is through conversation that personal relationships are developed and maintained. Hirschon (1978) says that "company with others has an intrinsic value, solitude is abhorred and the personality type most approved is that of the open and warm individual, while someone described as closed is also seen as cold" (p. 77). Isolation and withdrawal, she says, are equivalent to social death; to engage in intense verbal exchange is thus a recognition of the other's existence.

Moreover, many Greeks feel degrees of obligation toward others, even non-relatives, from their native village or surrounding area (Gage, 1987). When two strangers meet they will immediately try to discover if they share any common roots. More often than not they find they have common acquaintances or that one of their relatives is married to one of the other's relatives. Establishing this social bond through such a ritual allows each of them to place the other at least tentatively within the ingroup, thus promoting warmer feelings and a greater degree of trust.

Second, couvenda serves as a means of asserting a sense of equality in encounters with others. This equality is not necessarily related to status, education, or economic level, but rather refers to equality as a human being. As Friedl (1962) emphasizes: "The right to a certain give-and-take underlies all relationships and serves to keep each situation unique and each relationship one of equality on at least some level" (p. 83). This sense of equality is demanded by one's philotimo, and it is through couvenda that it is established and maintained.

This may even lead one to present strong views on a topic with which she or he is unfamiliar and then to stubbornly defend these views even in the face of clear evidence against them. To lose an argument on the basis of the facts or logic presented by the other would show weakness and would put the person in an inferior position. Asserting one's personality by providing strong opinions and engaging in sometimes heated argument is a common means of elevating the philotimo on an individual level.

Third, couvenda provides a source of entertainment. Traditional village life is quite routine and repetitive, and especially before the advent of television it was through conversation that freshness and uniqueness were brought to commonplace events. Variation and uncertainty are imposed on aspects of life that otherwise have no intrinsically adventurous elements. Entertainment is enhanced by the rich oral tradition of the Greeks, whose language allows a precision of expression that promotes unsurpassed storytelling.

Gage (1987) shows how everyday language is rich in proverbs, myths, legends, and humor. He says that "even the most uneducated Greek sprinkles his speech liberally with proverbs, many of them reflecting the wry cynicism of a people who have become accustomed to hardship, yet have managed to retain their spiritual strength and sense of humor" (pp. 59-60). Holden (1972) shows how boasting sometimes takes the form of "apparently harmless rhetorical embroidery to make actual situations seem grander, more significant and more self-flattering than they really are" (p. 94).

Finally, couvenda is important in asserting one's personality and maintaining self-esteem. Hirschon (1978) points out that social life is vital, because prestige and reputation, which depend on the opinion of others, are the measure of both the individual's merit and that of his or her family. Friedl (1962) considers couvenda as the way men and women boast of their own and their family's achievements and as the vehicle for men to display their political knowledge and engage in political argument. Boasting is socially acceptable, and Davenport (1978) believes that it is a means of promoting philotimo.

Despite the high level of intensity reflected in couvenda, arguments, debates, and other verbal disputes are not viewed as aberrations, and they do not necessarily affect relationships negatively or lead to negative feelings within relationships. Rather, they are viewed as integral aspects of daily existence. Couvenda, while it *reflects* the interpersonal struggle that is the essence of Greek reality, functions on center stage in full view of any audience. Behind the scenes lies relational struggle in which rivalry and *competition* play key roles.

## Competition and Relational Struggle

Holden (1972) writes about the "deep current of rivalry and suspicion" running between Greeks. He says that relationships are in a constant state of flux because of the competitive nature of the Greek's social orientation. Greeks tend to believe that "the friend of my enemy is my enemy, and the enemy of my enemy is my friend," so they are constantly making, dissolving, and remaking coalitions as different "enemies" appear on the scene. From Holden's (1972) viewpoint, "the prospect of life without an enemy generally seems intolerable" (p. 89), so new relational struggles are constantly developing.

The ongoing struggles in Greek social life are fueled by a competitive orientation that is different from that found in most Western societies. It is often noted that whereas in Europe and the United States people compete with each other by trying to "run faster" to get ahead of the other, the Greeks compete with each other by grabbing onto their competitor to "hold them back," thus keeping them from getting ahead. The tendency to compete by bringing down one's foe signals a very different approach to conflict that can significantly affect the manner in which conflicts are managed.

The approach to competition in Greece reflects the collectivist nature of traditional Greek culture. Whereas in individualistic cultures such as the United States and most of Europe competition is between individuals, Greek competition is primarily between the ingroup and the outgroup (Triandis, 1986). The requirements of philotimo that the Greek feels toward the ingroup help prevent forms of competition that would damage the basic ties holding the ingroup together. However, the need to defend the ingroup against harm from outside can lead to intense conflicts between the ingroup and the outgroup. Doumanis (1983) states that in traditional Greek communities "social relationships were either positive or negative, with no room for neutral gradation in between. Families were either co-operating with one another, closely and intimately, or were competing aggressively, cunningly and sometimes fiercely" (p. 28).

## Process Focus of Relational Struggle

Despite the competitive nature of relations with the outgroup, the interpersonal struggle characteristic of Greek relationships is not totally focused on *outcome* but rather tends to center on *process*. Heard often is the phrase "Perazmena Ksehazmena" or "What is past is forgotten." Applying not only to unpleasant events but equally to success, it points to the short-lived nature of victory and defeat. Without a competitor, life would not be very stimulating, so new relational struggles are constantly taking shape.

It can be argued that interpersonal battles provide a great deal of personal and social satisfaction to Greeks. Friedl (1962) says that it is the continuing *aghonia* (anxiety or agony) that provides for the Greek a feeling of being alive. Holden (1972) describes conflict as "generating the leaping spark of tension that is the only certain characteristic of Greekness. Tension, movement, change, process; these are the essence of Greek life" (p. 33).

Not only do struggles provide some degree of stimulation and satisfaction for Greeks, they also play an important role in strengthening ingroup solidarity. The hostility and opposition directed toward the outgroup serves as a complement to the cooperation necessary within the ingroup. Through competition with the outgroup, ingroup members attest to their allegiance with the ingroup. As Doumanis (1983) states: "The values of prestige and honor so central in the traditional Greek culture rested on the attention and opinion of friends *and* enemies, on the concerned interest of kin *and* the grudging acceptance of competitors" (p. 29, emphasis added).

In many ways, interpersonal communication and relationships in Greece mirror a description of the contrasts in the physical world. Just as the Greek countryside is dominated by mountainous and often rough terrain, conversations and relationships are characterized by transactions that seem to the outsider harsh and rocky. Physical, spiritual, and social struggles are built into the Greek landscape, psyche, and relationships in ways that are difficult for the Western European mind to comprehend. Although these struggles would.exhaust the Westerner, they seem to invigorate the Greek. Differences such as these make the current Western notion of what constitutes conflict incomplete and perhaps inappropriate in describing cultures such as those in traditional and contemporary Hellas.

## Implications for Future Research

Greece is a society in transition, moving rapidly from a traditional village and island culture to a more westernized and cosmopolitan environment. While the traditional Greek cultural milieu exerts extensive influence on the communication patterns of contemporary urban Greeks, there are only a few reported studies that examine the urban environment (Campbell, 1983; Doumanis, 1983; Hirschon, 1983; Triandis, 1986).

The need exists to conduct additional field studies and empirical investigations of communication patterns in contemporary Greece. While this study has concentrated on *palevome* and its implications for interpersonal conflict in Greece, there are other cultural factors that impact on interpersonal communication. The time is ripe for studies examining phenomena such as time orientation, male and female role distinctions, and influence of religious worldviews in the context of contemporary Greece.

Research also needs to be conducted that examines the impact of Greek interpersonal communication on relations between Greeks and Western Europeans, North Americans, and other Westerners. While it is beyond the scope of this paper to explore such applications, the consequences for intercultural interaction are numerous. A concept like palevome can be instructive to both Western

Europeans, North Americans, and Greeks as improved interpersonal relations are sought.

Finally, this examination points to a deficiency in the literature on conflict and conflict management. Much of the theoretical and research literature on conflict published in the United States must be reexamined and broadened. The culture-bound paradigm of conflict represented in the literature limits the extent to which the nature of this important phenomenon can be understood. While calls have been made for culture-specific research on communication processes (Broome, 1986), there are few reported studies in the communication literature that examine communication patterns in societies other than the United States (Shuter, 1990). Only through culture-specific research conducted in a culturally sensitive manner can we gain insight into the nature of a conflict and culture from a global perspective.

## Notes

1. The name "Greece" comes from the Latin term given by the Romans during their occupation of Greece. Greeks refer to their country as "Hellas" or "Ellada."

2. While Greece is part of the European Economic Community and is usually included geographically as part of Europe, the culture blends the traditions of both West and East in a unique way (see Woodhouse, 1983). Geographically, it sits between the west of Europe and the east of Turkey.

3. In Greece a foreign stranger is a potential ingroup member because of the emphasis the culture places on "philoxenia," or "kindness to strangers."

## References

*Area handbook for Greece.* (1970). Washington, DC: American University.

Barnlund, D. C. (1975). *Public and private self in Japan and the United States.* Tokyo: Simul Press.

Broome, B. J. (1986). A context-based approach to teaching intercultural communication. *Communication Education, 35*(3), 296–306.

Campbell, J. K. (1964). *Honor, family and patronage.* Oxford: Clarendon Press.

Campbell, J. K. (1983). Traditional values and continuities in Greek society. In R. Clogg (Ed.), *Greece in the 1980's.* St. Martin's Press, 184–207.

Coser, L. (1956). *The functions of conflict.* New York: Free Press.

Crimes of honor still the pattern in rural Greece. *New York Times,* Sect. 1, February 10, 1980, 22.

Davenport, W. W. (1978). *Athens.* New York: Time-Life Books.

Deutsch, M. (1973). *The resolution of conflict.* New Haven: Yale University Press.

Doumanis, M. (1983). *Mothering in Greece: From collectivism to individualism.* London: Academic Press.

de Boulay, J. (1976). Lies, mockery and family integrity. In J. G. Peristiany (Ed.), *Mediterranean Family Structure.* Cambridge University Press, 389–406.

Fink, C. F. (1968). Some conceptual difficulties in the theory of social conflict. *Journal of Conflict Resolution, 12,* 412–460.

Folger, J. P., and Poole, M. S. (1984). *Working through conflict: A communication perspective.* Glenview, IL: Scott, Foresman.

Freud, S. (1949). *An outline of psychoanalysis* (J. Strachey, trans.). New York: Norton.

Friedl, E. (1962). *Vasilika: A village in Modern Greece.* New York: Holt, Rinehart & Winston.

Gage, N. (1987). *Hellas: A portrait of Greece.* Athens: Efstathiadis Group.

Gage, N. (1983). *Eleni.* New York: Random House.

*Greece: A Country Study.* (1985). Washington, DC: American University.

Hirschon, R. B. (1978). Open Body/Closed Space: The Transformation of Female Sexuality. In Shirley Ardener (Ed.), *Defining Females: The Nature of Women in Society.* London: Croom Helm, 66–87.

Hirschon, R. B. (1983). Under one roof: Marriage, dowry, and family relations in Piraeus. In Michael Kenny and David I. Kertzer (Eds.), *Urban life in Mediterranean Europe: Anthropological perspectives.* Urbana: University of Illinois Press, 299–323.

Hirschon, R. B., and Gold, J. R. (1982). Territoriality and the home environment in a Greek urban community. *Anthropological Quarterly, 55*(2), 63–73.

Holden, D. (1972). *Greece without columns: The making of the modern Greeks.* Philadelphia: J. B. Lippincott, 1–36.

Kilmann, R. H., and Thomas, K. W. (1977). Developing a forced choice measure of conflict-handling behavior: The MODE instrument. *Educational and Psychological Measurement,* 309–325.

Lee, D. (1959). *Freedom and culture.* Englewood Cliffs, NJ: Prentice-Hall, Inc.

Pruitt, D., and Lewis, S. (1977). The psychology of interactive bargaining. In D. Druckman (Ed.), *Negotiations.* Beverly Hills: Sage.

Putman, L., and Wilson, D. E. (1982). Development of an organizational communication conflict instrument. In M. Burgoon (Ed.), *Communication Yearbook* (Vol. 6). Beverly Hills: Sage.

Roloff, M. E. (1976). Communication strategies, relationships, and relational changes. In G. R. Miller (Ed.), *Explorations in interpersonal communication*. Beverly Hills: Sage.

Sanders, I. T. (1962). *Rainbow in the rock*. Cambridge, MA: Harvard University Press.

Shuter, R. (Spring, 1990). The Centrality of Culture. *The Southern Communication Journal,* 55, 237–249.

Triandis, H. C. (1986). *Education of Greek-Americans for a pluralistic society*. Keynote address to the Conference on the Education of Greek Americans, New York, May.

Triandis, H. C. (1972). A comparative analysis of subjective culture. From *The Analysis of Subjective Culture*. New York: John Wiley & Sons, 299–335.

Woodhouse, C. M. (1983). Greece and Europe. In R. Clogg (Ed.), *Greece in the 1980's*. St. Martin's Press, 1–8.

too many generalizations

# *I*rish Conversations

## MARTIN J. GANNON

It is a truism that the use of language is essential for the development of culture, and most, if not all, cultural groups take great pride in their native languages. Thus it is not surprising that voice is one of the four essential elements of opera, the metaphor for Italy. In the case of Ireland, it was the brutal English rule over the nation extending over several centuries that essentially made the Irish an aural people whose love of language and conversation was essential for the preservation of their heritage. More specifically, the intersection between the original Irish language, Irish Gaelic, and English has made the Irish famous for their eloquence, scintillating conversations, and unparalleled success in fields where the use of the English language is critical, such as writing, law, and teaching.

Ireland as we know it today began to emerge in 1916 when a small group of Irish patriots commandeered the old post office building in Dublin on Easter Sunday. The English executed the rebellion's 15 leaders, which sparked a war against the English that led to the modern division of Ireland into two parts: the Protestant north with a minority Catholic population and the Catholic south. The focus of this chapter is the Catholic south, which occupies five sixths of the land.

Supposedly, everybody knows everybody else's business in a country village. Ireland largely comprises such small country villages and its culture reflects this fact. Whenever the Irish meet, one of the first things they generally do is determine one another's place of origin. The conversation usually helps to identify common relatives and friends.

From Martin J. Gannon and Associates, *Understanding Global Cultures* (Thousand Oaks, CA: Sage Publications, 1994), pp. 179–194. Reprinted by permission of Sage Publications.

Given the wide circle of friends and acquaintances that the Irish tend to make in their lives, it is usually not difficult to find a link.

Ireland's size is little more than 1% of that of the continental United States. It lies to the west of Great Britain, to which it is economically tied. Ireland has four major cities: Dublin, Cork, Limerick, and Galway. In the early 1970s, more than 60% of the workforce was employed in agriculture, but today only 16% can be found in that line of work because of the transition to a more industrialized society. Although the country has modernized significantly in the past 20 years, it is still far behind many of its European neighbors. Also, many of its young people emigrate, largely because of a lack of jobs, an expensive welfare system, and a correspondingly high tax rate. Most Irish families have sons, daughters, or close relatives who have emigrated.

Because of the high level of education in modern Ireland, Irish immigrants do well in other countries, but many would like to return to Ireland simply because it is a "being" society in which the quality of life is valued more than the pursuit of monetary gain. Ireland did become part of the EC in 1973, which should help the country economically in the long run.

The importance of conversation to the Irish makes it a fitting metaphor for the nation. However, to understand the metaphor fully, we need to explore the intersection of Irish Gaelic and English, after which we can focus on an essential Irish conversation, praying to God and the saints. The free-flowing nature of Irish conversation is also one of its essential characteristics, as are the places where conversations are held.

## Intersection of Gaelic and English

The Irish are a people who tend to enjoy simple pleasures, but the complexity of their thought patterns and culture can be baffling to outsiders. They generally have an intense love of conversation and storytelling and have been accursed often of talking just to hear the sound of their own voices. The Irish use the English language in ways that are not found in any other culture. They do not just give a verbal answer, they construct a vivid mental picture that is pleasing to the mind as well as the ear. With the transition from Gaelic to English, the Irish created vivid images in Gaelic and expressed them in English; the vivid imagery of many Irish writers originated in the imaginative storytelling that was historically a critical part of social conversation. To the Irish, Gaelic was a graphic, living language that was appropriate for expressing the wildest of ideas in a distinctive and pleasing manner.

Because of the slow arrival of electronic technology in Ireland and the country's long suppression and isolation, the talent for conversation is an art form that has not yet been lost. Among the Irish, food tends to be secondary to conversation, and a visitor will often observe that the Irish seem to forget about their food until it is almost cold. If, however, an Irishman admonishes a countryman for eating too much or too quickly, the witty reply is frequently to the effect that one never knows when the next famine will occur. This emphasis on the primacy of conversation is in contrast to the practice found in other cultures, such as the Italian and French, where not only conversation but also food is prized.

If the size of the population is taken into account, it seems that Ireland has produced many more prominent essayists, novelists, and poets than any other country since approximately 1870. This prominence reflects the intersection of the Gaelic and English languages and the aural bias of the Irish. They also have produced great musicians who combine music and words in a unique way. Conversely, the Irish have not produced a major visual artist equal to those of other European countries, and their achievements in science are modest.

There are countless examples that could be used to illustrate this intersection, but the opening words of James Joyce's (1964) *Portrait of the Artist as a Young Man,* in which he first introduced the technique of stream of consciousness, aptly serve the purpose:

*"Once upon a time and a very good time it was there was a moocow coming down along the road and this*

*moocow that was coming down along the road met a nicens little boy named baby tuckoo."*

*His father told him that story; his father looked at him through a glass; he had a hairy face.*

*"He was a baby tuckoo. The moocow came down the road where Betty Byrne lived: She sold lemon platt.*

*"O, the wild rose blossoms*
*"On the little green place.*
*"He sang that song. That was his song.*
*"O, the green wothe botheth." (p. 1)*

There are several points about this brief but pertinent passage that deserve mention. It expresses a rural bias that befits Ireland, and it reflects the vivid Gaelic language in which Joyce was proficient. Also, it immediately captures the imagination but leaves the reader wondering what is going to happen: He must read further if he wants to capture the meaning, and it seems that the meaning will become clear only in the most circuitous way. Further, although the essence of the passage is mundane, it is expressed in a captivating manner. The reader is pleasantly surprised by the passage and eagerly awaits additional pleasant surprises. In many ways this passage is an ideal example of the manner in which Gaelic Irish and English intersect. And, although some of the modern Irish and Irish-Americans may not be aware of these historical antecedents, their patterns of speech and thought tend to reflect this intersection.

Perhaps the most imaginatively wild of the modern Irish writers to incorporate the intersection of the Gaelic and English languages in his work is Myles na gCopaleen, who also used the pseudonym Flann O'Brien. He wrote some of his novels and stories in Gaelic and others in English. Even the titles of his books are indicative of this imaginative focus: for example, *The Poor Mouth: A Bad Story About The Hard Life* (O'Brien, 1974). "Putting on the poor mouth" means making a pretense of being poor or in bad circumstances to gain advantage for oneself from creditors or prospective creditors, and the book is a satire on the rural life of western Ireland. His masterpiece, *At Swim-Two-Birds* (O'Brien, 1961), sets the scene for a confrontation between "Mad Sweeny" and "Jem Casey" in the following way:

*Synopsis, being a summary of what has gone before, FOR THE BENEFIT OF NEW READERS: Dermit Trellis, an eccentric author, conceives the project of writing a salutary book on the consequences which follow wrongdoing and creates for the purpose*

*The Pooka Fergus MacPhellimey, a species of human Irish devil endowed with magical power. He then creates John Furriskey, a depraved character, whose task is to attack women and behave at all times in an indecent manner. By magic he is instructed by Trellis to go one night to Donnybrook where he will by arrangement meet and betray. . . . (p. 563)*

The remaining characters are sequentially introduced in the same imaginative way.

In the area of music, the Chieftains, who have performed together for more than 25 years, represent the distinctive approach of the Irish to music. Their songs, played on traditional instruments, are interspersed with classic Irish dances and long dialogues that sometimes involve the audience. Similarly, Thomas Moore, who lived in the 19th century, is sometimes cited as the composer who captured the essence of the intersection of the Gaelic and English languages in such poetic songs as "Believe Me If All Those Endearing Young Charms," which he wrote for a close friend and beautiful woman whose face was badly scarred in a fire (Moore, 1857):

*Believe me, if all those endearing young charms*
*Which I gaze on so fondly today*
*Were to fade by tomorrow and fleet in my arms*
*Like fairy gifts fading away.*
*Thou woust still be ador'd*
*As this moment thou art*
*Let thy loveliness fade as it will.*
*And upon the dear ruin*
*Each wish of my heart*
*Would intwine itself verdantly still. (p. 214)*

A constant reminder that the Irish are radically different from the English and Americans is their brogue. When the conversion from speaking Gaelic to speaking English was occurring, this brogue was an embarrassment for many Irish. The English looked down on these "inferior" people who were unable to speak "proper" English (Waters, 1984). Today, the brogue is prized by the Irish and appreciated throughout the world.

Given that Ireland is a rural society in which unhurried conversation is prized, it should be no surprise that it is more of a "being" than a "doing" society in which there is a balanced approach to life. In fact, many of the Irish are astonished at the "doing" entrepreneurial activities of their 44 million Irish-American counterparts who have made St. Patrick's Day, which remains a holy day in Ireland, into a fun-loving time for partying that embraces all people (Milbank, 1993). The Irish generally take life much more slowly than Americans, who tend to watch the clock constantly and rush from one activity to another. No matter how rushed the Irish may be, they normally have time to stop and talk.

The Irish also tend to place more importance on strong friendships and extended family ties than do Americans. Nothing illustrates this emphasis more than the behavior of many early Irish immigrants when they first arrived in the United States. They settled near other friends or relatives who had preceded them to the United States and developed a reputation for being very clannish. But slowly the Irish love of conversation and curiosity about all things led to their interaction with others and their Americanization.

## Prayer as Conversation

Prayer or a conversation with God is one of the most important parts of an Irish life. More than 95% of the population is Roman Catholic, and regular attendance at Sunday mass is estimated at 87% of the population, the highest percentage of any country in the world. Almost every Catholic household contains crucifixes and religious pictures. These serve as outward reminders of the people's religious beliefs and duties.

Further, this prayer is accompanied by acts of good works that stem directly from the strong ethical and moral system of the Irish. They are recognized as having made the highest per capita donation to relief efforts in countries such as

Ethiopia, and they are quick to donate their time, energy, and even lives to help those living in execrable conditions. The extent of the crisis in Somalia, for instance, was first reported to the United Nations by Mary Robinson, president of Ireland, and an Irish nurse was killed after arriving in Somalia to help out.

The separation between church and state found in most countries does not exist in Ireland. Until 1972 when Ireland joined the EC, a constitutional amendment guaranteed a special status to the Roman Catholic church. The Church did not oppose the removal of this amendment because it was secure in its majority (Bell, 1991). Such a secure outlook was well justified because little has changed except for the working of the constitution, and the Church plays an important role throughout the life of the Irish.

The state relies on the works of the Catholic church to support most of its social service programs. For example, most of the hospitals are run by the Catholic church rather than by the state. These hospitals are partially funded with state money and are staffed with nuns, when possible. The state has little control over how the money is spent, especially because it lacks the buildings and the power to replace the Church-run system that was in place when the state was formed.

The national school (state) system is also under the control of the various religious dominations in Ireland. It is the primary source of education for primary schoolchildren. The state funds the system, but the schools are run by local boards, which are almost always controlled by the clergy. There is a separate national school for each major religion. The local Catholic national school is managed by the local parish priest, whereas the Protestant vicar has his own separate school. Many instructors in these schools are nuns or brothers who work very inexpensively and keep the costs much lower than the state could. Conversely, in the United States it is no longer lawful even to pray in public schools. In exchange for these lower costs, the state has relinquished control. This is really the Church's last line of defense, because it has the ability to instill Catholic morality and beliefs in almost every young Irish child in the country.

In many ways the Catholic church does not actually influence the state's actions. Rather, it relies on Catholic lay groups to uphold the Church's teachings and to pressure the state. These watchdog groups can be quite vocal and often wield considerable power in their communities. Many times they are more conservative than the local parish priest. As the Irish become better educated and gain greater exposure to the rest of Europe, the preeminent position of the Church is slowly being eroded. However, as long as the Catholic church continues to control the primary school system, it will have a significant influence on the people's attitudes.

The Church also influences society by censoring books and artistic material, which has caused many Irish artists such as James Joyce and Sean O'Casey to leave Ireland to enjoy greater freedom in their work. The Irish have to travel to Britain or to Northern Ireland to purchase outlawed books or to see movies written by their Irish countrymen.

Sunday Mass is a special occasion in Ireland, and the entire family attends. On this occasion everyone wears his or her Sunday best. One Irish woman tells the story of returning home for a visit from the United States and, on Sunday morning, being asked by her mother if she did not have a better dress to wear to church; she had become lax in her church dress after spending several years in the United States. During Mass it is not unusual to see all the women and children sitting in the front of the church and the men standing or sitting in the back. This dichotomy does not mean that the Irish believe religion should be left to women and children; it only reflects the specific gender roles in Ireland, which are gradually changing, but at a rate that is slower than in other Western countries.

The Irish tend to begin and end their day with prayer. This is their opportunity to tell God their troubles and their joys. One of the more common prayers is that Ireland may one day be reunited. This act of talking to God helps to form a personal relationship between the Irish and their God. It is difficult to ignore the dictates of God, because He is such a personal and integral part of the daily Irish life. God is also present in daily life in the living personification of the numerous priests, brothers, and sisters found in Ireland. They are not shut away in cloisters, but interact with the laity throughout the day.

Entering the religious life is seen as a special calling for the Irish. In the past when families were very large, it was common for every family to give at least one son or daughter to the religious life. It was the greatest joy for an Irish mother to know that her son or daughter was in God's service, which was prized more highly than a bevy of grandchildren. Vocations to religious life have decreased in recent years, but Ireland still has many more priests per capita than most other Catholic countries.

In the Republic of Ireland there are few problems between Catholics and other religious groups, unlike the situation that exists in Northern Ireland. In fact, Catholics enjoy having Protestants in their communities, and they treat them with great respect. In one rural area where the Protestant congregation had dwindled, the Catholic parish helped Protestants with fund raising to make repairs to their church. This act of charity illustrates the great capacity for giving that the Irish possess, because generally they are not greatly attached to material possessions and are quite willing to share what they have with the world.

## A Free-Flowing Conversation: Irish Hospitality

Conversations with the Irish are known to take many strange turns, and one may end up discussing a subject and not knowing how it arose. Also, it is not only what is said that is important, but also the manner in which it is expressed. The Irish tend to be monochronic, completing one activity before going on to another, yet they cannot resist divergences and tangents in their conversations or their lives. They often feel that they are inspired by an idea that must be shared with the rest of the world regardless of what the other person may be saying. The Irish tend to respect this pattern of behavior and are quite willing to change the subject, which can account for the breadth of their conversations as well as their length.

Like their conversations, the Irish tend to be curious about all things foreign or unfamiliar, and they are quick to extend a hand in greeting and to start a conversation, usually a long one.

It is not unusual for the Irish to begin a conversation with a perfect stranger, but for most of the Irish there are no strangers – only people they have not had the pleasure of conversing with. The Irish do not usually hug in public, but this in no way reduces the warmth of their greeting. They often view Americans as too demonstrative and are uncomfortable with public displays of affection. The tend to be a very hospitable, trusting, and friendly people. Nothing illustrates this outlook more than their national greeting, "Cead mile failte" ("One hundred thousand welcomes"), which is usually accompanied by a handshake.

In addition, the Irish are famous for their hospitality toward both friends and strangers. As Delany (1974) points out: "In the olden days, anyone who had partaken of food in an Irishman's home was considered to be secure against harm or hurt from any member of the family, and no one was ever turned away" (p. 103). This spirit of hospitality still exists in Ireland. In the country, the Irish tend to keep their doors not only unlocked but also open. Whenever someone is passing by or asking for directions, it is difficult for them to leave without being asked into the house to have something to eat or drink. It is not unusual for the Irish to meet someone in the afternoon and invite him or her to their home for supper that evening, and this happens not only in the country but also the cities. They welcome people into their family and bring out their best china, linen, and the finest foods. Meals are accompanied by great conversation by both young and old.

Many of the Irish do not believe in secrets and, even if they did, it would be hard to imagine them being able to keep one. They seem quite willing to tell the world their business and expect their visitors to do the same.

However, the Irish are often unwilling to carry on superficial conversations. They enjoy a conversation that deals with something of substance, and they are well-known for breaking the often-quoted American social rule that one should not discuss politics or religion in public. The Irish enjoy nothing more than to discuss these subjects and to spark a deep philosophical conversation.

## Places of Conversations: Irish Friends and Families

There really is no place where the Irish would find it difficult to carry on a conversation. They are generally quite willing to talk about any subject at any time, but there are several places that have a special meaning for the Irish. Conversation in the home is very important for an Irish family. It is also one of the major social activities of an Irish public house or pub.

The typical Irish family is closely knit, and its members describe their activities to one another in great detail. Meal time is an event in the Irish household that should not be missed by a family member, not so much because of the food but the conversation. In fact, as noted previously, the food is really secondary to the conversation, and sometimes the Irish even forget to eat or delay doing so until the food is cold. Supper is the time of day when family members gather together to pray, eat, and update one another on their daily activities. The parents usually ask the children about their day in school and share the events of their own day.

Education and learning have always been held in high regard by the Irish. Teachers are treated with great respect in the community, and their relatively high salaries reflect their worth to the community. Ireland has a literacy rate of 99% because of compulsory national education. College education is available to all through government grants for those who cannot afford university fees. Given the dearth of employment opportunities, college students often complete a postgraduate degree before entering the job market. The Irish who emigrate normally bring with them a well-rounded education that is valued by employers abroad. Still, even when the Irish have advanced formal training, they generally do not flaunt it.

A frequent topic of conversation at family dinners is news of extended family, friends, or neighbors. The Irish have an intense interest in the activities of their extended family and friends, but this interest is not for the pure sake of gossip. They generally are quick to congratulate on good news and even quicker to rally around in times of trouble or need. When someone is sick, it is not unusual for all of the person's friends and family to spend almost all of their time at the hospital. They help the family with necessary tasks and entertain one another with stories and remembrances. Many of the Irish have a difficult time understanding the American pattern in which the nuclear family handles emergencies and problems by itself.

This practice holds true whenever there is a death in the community. Everyone gathers together to hold an Irish wake, which combines the viewing of the body with a party that may last for two or three days. There is plenty of food, drinking, laughing, conversation, music, games, and storytelling. Presumably the practice of a wake originated because people had difficulty traveling in Ireland over poor roads and by nonmechanized means of transportation, and the wake afforded an opportunity not only to pay respect to the deceased but also to renew old friendships and reminisce. Although the problems of travel have been solved, the Irish still cling to this ancient way of saying goodbye to the deceased and uplifting the spirits of those left behind.

An event that is as important as the wake is a wedding; it is a time of celebration for the entire family and neighborhood. There is customarily a big church wedding followed by a sit-down dinner and an evening of dancing and merriment. Registry office weddings are very rare in Ireland, as might be expected in this conservative and Catholic-dominated nation. Young people usually continue to live with their parents until they are married, and then they frequently buy a home close to them.

Irish parents are generally quite strict with their children. They set down definite rules that must be followed. Irish children are given much less freedom than American children, and they usually spend all day with their parents on Sunday and may accompany them to a dance or to the pub in the evening. Parents are usually well acquainted with the families of their children's friends and believe in group activities. The tight social community in which the Irish live makes it difficult for children to do anything without their parents' knowledge. There is always a third cousin or kindly neighbor who is willing to keep tabs on the behavior of children and report back to parents, some of whom have even managed to stretch their watchful eyes across the Atlantic to keep tabs on their children living in the United States. This close control can sometimes be difficult for young people, but it creates a strong support network that is useful in times of trouble.

A frequent gathering place for men, women, and children is the local pub, because the drinking age is not enforced throughout most of Ireland. There are two sections in most pubs: The plain working-man's part and the decorated part where the cost of a pint of beer is slightly higher. In the not-too-distant past, it was seen as unbecoming for a woman to enter a pub; there are still some pubs in which women are comfortable only in the decorated part, and they typically order half-pints of beer, whereas the men order pints. Normally, the pubs do not serve food, which may reflect the Irish de-emphasis of food noted previously.

Pubs tent to be very informal, often without waiters or waitresses and with plenty of bar and table space. Young and old mingle in the pub, often conversing with one another and trading opinions. The Irish are raised with a great respect for their elders and are quite comfortable carrying on a conversation with a person of any age or background. They tend to be a democratic people by nature and, although they may not agree with a person's opinion, they will usually respect him or her for having formed one.

Irish pubs are probably the site of the most lively conversations held in Ireland. The Irish tend to be a very sociable people who generally do not believe in drinking alone. This pattern of behavior has often resulted in their reputation for being alcoholics. Many Irish drink more than they should, but the problem often appears worse than it is because almost all of their drinking takes place in public. Further, co-workers and their superiors frequently socialize in pubs, and they tend to evaluate one another in terms of not only on-the-job performance but also their ability to converse skillfully in such a setting. The favorite drink of the Irish is Guinness, a strong black stout. It is far more popular than the well-known Irish whiskey.

Even more important than a good drink in a pub is good conversation. The Irish are famous for their storytelling, and it is not unusual to find an entire pub silent while one man tells an ancient folktale or what happened to him that afternoon. It is also not unusual for someone to recite a Shakespearean play from memory in its entirety.

Besides stories, many a heated argument can erupt in a pub. The Irish seem to have a natural love of confrontation in all things, and the conversation does not even have to be about something that affects their lives. They are fond of exchanging opinions on many abstract issues and world events. It is during these sessions at the pub that the Irish sharpen their conversational skills. However, although these conversations can become heated, they rarely become violent.

Irish friends, neighbors, and families visit one another on a regular basis. As indicated above, rarely if ever is one turned away from the door. In fact, the door is usually kept open, and visitors are expected to walk right in. Family and friends know that they are always welcome and that they will be given something to eat and drink. It is not unusual for visitors to arrive late in the evening and stay until almost morning. Such visits are usually not made for any special purpose other than conversation, which is the mainstay of the Irish life no matter where it is held.

### Ending a Conversation

A conversation with an Irishman can be such a long and exciting adventure that a person thinks it will never end. It will be hard to bring the conversation to a close because the Irish always seem to have the last word. Ireland is a country that welcomes its visitors and makes them feel so comfortable and accepted that it is hard to break free and return home after an afternoon or evening of conversation.

Geert Hofstede's (1980) research profiling the value orientation of 40 nations includes Ireland, and his analysis confirms many of our observations.

Ireland is a masculine-oriented society in which sex roles are clearly differentiated, but the status of women clearly has improved during the past 20 years. However, it is not an acquisition-oriented society, as Hofstede's classification might suggest, but a "being-oriented" society in which the quality of life is given precedence over material rewards.

Further, Ireland clusters with those countries emphasizing individualism, as we might expect of a people who are willing and eager to explore and talk about serious and conflict-laden topics. Individualism is expressed through conversation and views on issues that affect society; major tasks are unlikely to be performed by the individual, and entrepreneurship is not a strong trait among the Irish. Individualism is also expressed in other talents such as writing, art, and music. As suggested previously, music offers its own means of conversation, and Ireland reportedly has one of the highest number of musicians per capita of all countries. Still, the Irish tend to be collectivist in their emphasis on the family, religion, a very generous welfare system, and the acceptance of strong labor unions.

Ireland also falls into the category of countries emphasizing a strong desire to meet new people and challenges (low uncertainty avoidance). And, with the possible exception of the high status accorded to the clergy, the Irish cluster with those countries that attempt to diminish social class and power differences as much as possible.

In short, the Irish tend to be an optimistic people who are ready to accept the challenges that life presents, although there is a melancholy strain in many of the Irish that is frequently attributed to the long years of English rule and the rainy weather. They usually confront things head-on and are ready to take on the world if necessary. They can be quite creative in their solutions, but also quite stubborn when asked to compromise, and they tend to be truly happy in the middle of a heated but stimulating conversation. Given their history and predilections, it is not surprising that the Irish prefer personal situations and professional fields of work where their aural-focused approach to reality can be given wide reign, even after they have spent several generations living in countries such as the United States and Australia.

## References

Beckett, J. D. (1986). *A Short History of Ireland*. London: Cresset Library.

Bell, B. (1991). *Insight Guides: Ireland*. Singapore: APA Publications.

Delany, M. (1974). *Of Irish Ways*. Minneapolis: Dillon.

Hofstede, G. (1980). *Culture's Consequences*. Beverly Hills: Sage.

Joyce, J. (1964). *Portrait of the Artist as a Young Man*. New York: Viking Press.

Melbank, D. (1993). "We Make a Bit More of St. Patrick's Day Than the Irish Do." *Wall Street Journal,* March 17, pp. A1, A8.

Moore, T. (1857). *The Poetical Works of Thomas Moore*. Boston: Philips, Sampson.

O'Brien, F. (1961). "At swim-two-birds." In U. Mercier and D. Greene (Eds.), *1000 Years of Irish Prose*. New York: Grosset and Dunlap.

O'Brien, F. (1974). *The Poor Mouth: A Bad Story About the Hard Life*. New York: Seaver.

Waters, M. (1984). *The Comic Irishman*. Albany: State University of New York Press.

## Concepts and Questions for Chapter 2

1. In terms of communication behavior, compare an orientation toward social relationships with an orientation toward individualism.

2. What are the four Confucian principles of right conduct? How do they contribute to communicative behavior?

3. How do East Asian concepts of in-group and out-group differ from those of North Americans? How might these differences affect intercultural communication?

4. How does Confucianism affect linguistic codes?

5. What are the major differences in the ways in which interpersonal bonding takes place in Eastern and Western cultures?

6. How do Eastern values concerning equality differ from Western values?

7. How does the rate of self-disclosure differ in Eastern and Western cultures?

8. What unique perspectives of world view are inherent in the Hindu culture of India?

9. How might the Hindu perspective of the universe and of humankind's role in the universe affect intercultural communication between Indians and North Americans?

10. To what do Jain and Kussman refer when they discuss the Hindu spirit of tolerance? How might this spirit affect social perception and human interaction?

11. How do Arab concepts of advocacy differ from those of North Americans?

12. How do North American and Arab rhetorical strategies differ? How might these differences affect business negotiations?

13. What historical antecedents of Maasai culture contribute to their current world view?

14. How does the Maasai's orientation to children affect their world view?

15. In what ways might the Maasai world view affect intercultural communication?

16. How does the Maasai use of metaphor differ from the North American use? How could this difference affect intercultural communication?

17. What significant role does conflict play in Greek interaction?

18. What are the major differences between Greek and American cultures in the relationship to and the utilization of conflict?

19. Describe the conversational style of Greek interaction.

20. How does the intersection of Gaelic and English affect Irish culture?

21. What role does conversation occupy in Irish culture?

22. What influence does the Catholic church have in Irish conversation and communication patterns?

23. How might the Irish form of conversation affect intercultural communication?

# 3

Co-Cultures: Living
in Two Cultures

In Chapter 2, we focused on international cultures – cultures that exist beyond the immediate borders of the United States. However, numerous domestic co-cultures exist within U.S. society itself. The groups that make up these co-cultures may share a common religion, economic status, ethnic background, age, gender, sexual preference, or race. These diverse co-cultures have the potential to bring new experiences to a communication encounter, but because these co-cultures exist all around us, the dominant European American culture often takes their presence for granted. Yet, anyone who is not aware of and does not understand the unique experiences of these co-cultures can experience serious communication problems.

The articles in this chapter have been selected to introduce you to a number of U.S. co-cultures and to probe some of the cultural experiences and dynamics inherent in them. Admittedly, there are many more co-cultures than we have included here. Our selection was based on three considerations. First, limited space and the necessity for efficiency prohibited a long list of co-cultures. Second, we wanted to include some social communities that are frequently in conflict with the dominant culture. And third, we wanted to emphasize the co-cultures with which you are most likely to interact. To this end, we selected a representation of the major co-cultures resident in the United States.

As the United States continues its development into a pluralistic and multicultural society, there is an increased need and opportunity for effective communication between the dominant culture and the co-cultures as well as among the co-cultures themselves. Effective communication can come about only when we remove prejudice and stereotypes from our lives and develop an understanding of what each culture is really like. Frequently, prejudices and stereotypes lead to assumptions about members of co-cultures that are false, hurtful, and insulting.

In the first reading of the chapter, "Who's Got the Room at the Top?" Edith A. Folb discusses the concept of intracultural communication, where members of the same dominant culture hold slightly different values. Folb sees the crucial characteristics of this form of communication as the interrelationships of power, dominance, and nondominance as they are manifested in the particular cultures. She carefully examines these variables as they apply to African Americans, Native Americans, Mexican Americans, women, the aged, the physically challenged, and other groups that have been "caste-marked and more often negatively identified when it comes to issues of power, dominance, and social control."

The next essay leads us to an examination of communication involving the African American co-culture. In "An African American Communication Perspective," Sidney A. Ribeau, John R. Baldwin, and Michael L. Hecht examine the communicative style of the African American. The authors are particularly concerned with identifying satisfying and dissatisfying conversational themes, conversational strategies, and communication effectiveness from an intercultural communication perspective. They identify seven issues — negative stereotypes, acceptance, personal expressiveness, authenticity, understanding, goal attainment, and power dynamics — that impact intercultural communication. They then offer several strategies for improving intercultural communication between the African American community and the dominant culture.

In recent years it has become apparent that disabled persons are a co-culture in our society. While there are approximately 11 million disabled Americans between the ages of 16 and 64, they often find themselves either cut off from or misunderstood by the dominant culture. Dawn O. Braithwaite and Charles A. Braithwaite look at some of the reasons for this isolation in "Understanding Communication of Persons with Disabilities as Cultural Communication." They specifically examine how disabled persons view their communication relationships with able-bodied persons. Reviewing research embracing over a hundred in-depth interviews with physically disabled adults, the Braithwaites have discovered that these disabled people go through a process of redefinition that involves three steps: (1) redefining the self as part of a "new" culture, (2) redefining disability, and (3) redefining disability for the dominant culture. By becoming familiar with these steps, we can improve our communication with members of the disabled co-culture.

Recently much attention has been focused on a social community previously taken for granted by many segments of American society. Because women are so much a part of everyone's perceptual field and daily life, few perceived that the experience of being female was a viable area of investigation. Events such as the Clarence Thomas confirmation hearings, charges of sexual harassment against prominent members of Congress, and successful campaigns for local, state, and national political office by women in unprecedented numbers have resulted in recognition that a co-culture of women does indeed exist and that society must give serious consideration to this feminine culture and how it differs from the masculine culture.

One of the major differences between the feminine and masculine communities is their communicative behaviors. These differences, and some of the reasons behind them, are the major concern of Julia T. Wood's essay, "Gender, Communication, and Culture." Wood points out the conceptual differences between sex and gender, explains how communication contributes to the social-symbolic construction of gender, and shows how gender differences are formed very early in life and thereby constrict gender cultures. She then provides examples of men and women in conversation demonstrating how gender differences in communicative rules and purposes lead to frequent misunderstandings. She ends by providing excellent advice on how to achieve effective communication between gender cultures.

During the congressional debates of 1995, the elderly were the focus of much attention in terms of their well-being and security. The vocal opposition raised to proposed changes in Social Security and Medicare by this group and its advocates (such as the American Association of Retired People) has focused national attention on the co-culture of the senior citizen. In the next essay, "Understanding the Co-culture of the Elderly," Valerie C. McKay describes the cultural dimensions and dynamics of the elderly in the United States. She introduces us to both the positive and negative stereotypes associated with the elderly and the consequences those stereotypes have on understanding the co-culture of the elderly. She then discusses the communication aspects of grandparent-grandchild relationships and the communication dynamics prevalent in this unique intergenerational relationship.

# Got the Room at the Top? Issues of Dominance and Nondominance in Intracultural Communication

EDITH A. FOLB

"If a phenomenon is important, it is perceived, and, being perceived, it is labeled." So notes Nathan Kantrowitz, sociologist and student of language behavior. Nowhere is Kantrowitz's observation more apparent than in that realm of communication studies concerned with the correlates and connections between culture and communication — what the editors of this text have termed "intercultural communication." Our contemporary technology has brought us into immediate and voyeuristic contact with diverse cultures and customs, from Stone Age dwellers of South America's rain forests to modern-age inhabitants along the information superhighway. Domestic liberation movements of the past and the diverse voices of present-day immigrants continue to focus our attention on the existence and needs of a multiplicity of groups within our own nation. So the phenomenon of culture-linked communication is pervasive among us. And, as scholars concerned with culture and communication, we have tried to identify and characterize what we see. This attempt to "label the goods," as it were, has generated, over time, a profusion of semantic labels and categories — international communication, cross-cultural communication, intercultural communication, co-cultural communication, multicultural communication, intracultural communication, interracial communication, interethnic communication. What we perceive to be important, we label.

Some may chide us for our penchant for classifications — an example of Aristotelian excessiveness, they may say. However, I see it as a genuine attempt to understand what we do individually and collectively, what we focus on within the field of communication studies. I believe this effort to characterize what we do serves a useful function: It continually prods us to examine and expand our vision of what culture-linked communication is, and, at the same time, it helps us bring into sharper focus the dimensions and differences within this area of study. As Samovar and Porter (1994) remind us, "there is a need to specify the nature of intercultural communication and to recognize that various viewpoints see it somewhat differently . . . that there are a variety of ways in which the topic of intercultural communication can be explored" (p. 2). It is my intention in this essay to look at the correlates and connections between culture and communication from a particular viewpoint, one that examines the properties and issues of dominance and nondominance in communicative exchange. The essay is speculative and sometimes polemical. And the focus of my interest and discussion is the realm of intracultural communication.

## The Concept of Intracultural Communication

The label "intracultural communication" is not unknown within the field of communication studies, although it is one that has not been widely used. Early on, Sitaram and Cogdell (1976) identified intracultural communication as "the type of communication that takes place between members of the same dominant culture, but with slightly differing values" (p. 28). They go on to explain that there are groups ("subcultures") within the dominant culture who hold a minimal number of values that differ from the mainstream, as well as from other sub-

This essay was revised for the eighth edition. It first appeared in the third edition. All rights reserved. Permission to reprint must be obtained from the author and the publisher. Professor Folb teaches at San Francisco State University.

groups. These differences are not sufficient to identify them as separate cultures but are diverse enough to set them apart from each other and the culture at large. "Communication between members of such subcultures is intracultural communication" (p. 28).

In another vein, Sarbaugh (1988) saw intracultural communication as an indicator of the degree of cultural experience shared (or not shared) by two people—the more culturally homogeneous the participants, the greater the level of "intraculturalness" surrounding the communicative act. For Sitaram and Cogdell, then, intracultural communication is a phenomenon that operates within a given culture among its members; for Sarbaugh, it is a measure of homogeneity that may well transcend country or culture.

More recently, Byrd (1993) has looked at intracultural communication as that which "occurs among people who are citizens of the same geopolitical system, and also hold membership in one or more tributary groups" (p. 1). Byrd goes on to identify tributary groups in terms of specific characteristics that distinguish them from the "power dominant/general population"—characteristics such as race, ethnicity, religion, gender, sexual orientation, age and ableness (p. 1).

Like Sitaram and Cogdell, I see intracultural communication as a phenomenon that functions within a single designated culture. However, like Sarbaugh, I am concerned with the particular variables within that context that importantly influence the degree and kind of cultural homogeneity or heterogeneity that can and do exist among members of the culture. Along with Byrd, the variables of particular interest to me are those which illuminate and underscore the interrelationship of power, dominance, and nondominance in a particular culture.[1] Finally, I believe that the concept of hierarchy, as it functions within a culture, has a deep impact on matters of power, dominance, and nondominance and, therefore, on both the form and content of intracultural communication.

As a backdrop for the discussion of dominance and nondominance in an intracultural context, I would like to formulate a frame of reference within which to view the discussion.

## A Frame of Reference for Intracultural Communication

### Society and Culture

Thomas Hobbes, the seventeenth-century political philosopher, left us an intriguing legacy in his work *Leviathan*. He posited a hypothetical starting point for humankind's march to political and social organization. He called it "the state of nature." In this presocietal state, the biggest club ruled. Kill or be killed was the prevailing modus operandi. Somewhere along the evolutionary road, our ancestors began to recognize a need to change their ways—if any of them were to survive for very long. The principle of enlightened self-interest became the name of the game. Our forebears, however grudgingly, began to curb their inclination to kill, maim, steal, or otherwise aggress upon others and joined together for mutual survival and benefit. The move was one of expediency, not altruism. "Do unto others as you would have them do unto you," whatever its religious import, is a reiteration of the principle of enlightened self-interest.

So, this aggregate of beings came together in order to survive and, in coming together, gave up certain base instincts, drives, and predilections. "Society" was formed. But it was not sufficient merely to form society; it must be maintained. Controls needed to be established to ensure its stability. Thus, the social contract was enacted. It was, indeed, the social contract that ensured mutual support, protection, welfare, and survival for the society's members—"law and order."

Those who may scoff at this postulated state of nature need only turn on their television on any given night to see it in very real terms—in Haiti, in Bosnia, on the angry streets of a riot-racked Los Angeles, in daily occurrences of drive-by-warfare. The media show us, in all too brutal detail, the rapidity with which a society's fabric can disintegrate and we can return to the force of the club.

But let us continue with the telling of humankind's tale. Social maintenance and control did not ensure the perpetuation of the society as an intact entity, carrying along its cumulative and collective experiences, knowledge, beliefs, and attitudes, as well as the emergent relationship of self to other, to the group, to the universe, to matters of time and space. That is, it did not ensure the perpetuation of society's accoutrements – its culture. Institutions and structures were needed to house, as it were, the trappings of culture. So, culture was embodied not only in the precepts passed on from one generation to another, but also in the artifacts created by society to safeguard its culture. Looked at in a different light, culture is both a blueprint for continued societal survival and the pervasive cement that holds the social mosaic together. Culture daily tells us and shows us how to be in the universe, and it informs future generations how to be.[2]

From the moment we begin life in this world, we are instructed in the cultural ways that govern and hold together our society, ways that ensure its perpetuation. Indeed, the social contract that binds us to our society and our culture from the moment of birth is neither of our own choice nor of our own design. For example, we are labeled by others almost immediately – John, Jamal, Mika, Maria. Our gender is determined at once and we are, accordingly, swaddled in appropriate colors and treated in appropriate ways.[3]

As we grow from childhood, the socialization process is stepped up and we rapidly internalize the rules of appropriate and inappropriate societal behavior. Family, religion, education, recreation, health care, and many other cultural institutions reinforce our learning and shape and regulate our behaviors and thoughts so they are orderly and comprehensible to other members of our society. Through the socialization process the human animal is transformed into the social animal. Thus, society is maintained through instruction and indoctrination in the ways of the culture.

But the question that pricks and puzzles the mind is, Whose culture is passed on? Whose social order is maintained? Whose beliefs and values are deemed appropriate? Whose norms, mores, and folkways are invoked?

## Hierarchy, Power, and Dominance

In most societies, as we know them, there is a hierarchy of status and power. By its very nature, hierarchy implies an ordering process, a sense of ranking and rating of those being ordered. Our own vernacular vocabulary abounds with references to hierarchy and concomitant status and power: "top gun," "top dog," "main man," "king of the mountain," "numero uno."

High status and attendant power may be accorded to those among us who are seen or believed to be great warriors or hunters; those invested with magical, divine, or special powers; those who are deemed wise; or those who are in possession of important, valued and/or vital societal resources and goods. Of course, power and high status are not necessarily – or even usually – accorded to these specially designated members of the society in some automatic fashion. Power, control, and subsequent high status are often forcibly wrested from others and forcibly maintained. Not everyone abides by the social contract, and strong-arm rule often prevails, as conquered, colonized, and enslaved people know too well.

Whatever the basis for determining the hierarchy, the fact of its existence in a society assures the evolution and continued presence of a power elite – those at the top of the social hierarchy who accrue and possess what the society deems valuable or vital. And, in turn, the presence of a power elite ensures an asymmetrical relationship among the members of the society. In fact, power is often defined as the ability to get others to do what you want and the resources to force them to do your bidding, if they resist – the asymmetrical relationship in its extreme form.

But the perpetuation of the power elite through force is not the most effective or efficient way of ensuring one's position at the top of the hierarchy. It is considerably more effective to institute, encourage, and/or perpetuate those aspects of culture – knowledge, experiences, beliefs, values, pattens of social organization, artifacts – that subtly and manifestly reinforce and ensure the continuation of the power elite and its asymmetrical relationship within the society. Though we may dismiss Nazism as a malignant ideology, we should attend to the fact that Hitler well understood the maintenance of the power elite through the manipulation and control of culture – culture as propaganda.

Though I would not imply that all power elites maintain themselves in such an overtly manipulative way, I would at least suggest that the powerful in many societies — our own included — go to great lengths to maintain their positions of power and what those positions bring them. And to that end, they support, reinforce, and, indeed, create those particular cultural precepts and artifacts that are likely to guarantee their continued power. To the extent that the culture reflects implicitly or expressly the need and desires of the power elite to sustain itself, it becomes a vehicle for propaganda. Thus, cultural precepts and artifacts that govern such matters as social organization and behavior, values, beliefs, and the like can often be seen as rules and institutions that sustain the few at the expense of the many.

So, we come back to the question of whose rules, whose culture? I would suggest that when we in communication studies refer to the "dominant culture," we are, in fact, not talking about numbers. That is why the label "minorities" is misleading when we refer to cultural or demographic groups within the larger society. For example, women in the United States are not the numerical minority — quite the contrary. Yet they are far from being "in the majority" among the true power elite.[4] In fact, when we talk about the concept of dominant culture, we are really talking about power — those who *dominate* culture, those who historically or traditionally have had the most persistent and far-reaching impact on culture, on what we think and say, on what we believe and do in our society. We are talking about the culture of the minority and, by extension, the structures and institutions (social, political, economic, legal, religious, and so on) that maintain the power of this minority. Finally, we are talking about rules of appropriate and inappropriate behavior, thought, speech, and action for the many that preserve power for the few. Dominant culture, therefore, significantly reflects the precepts and artifacts of those who dominate culture and is not necessarily, or even usually, a reference to numbers, but rather to power. Though those who "look like" the power elite can be said to be "cultural beneficiaries" of the system,

it is still those who dominate culture who call the shots — and reap the biggest rewards.

So, coming full circle, I would suggest that our socialization process, our social introduction to this aggregate of people who form society, is an introduction to a rule-governed milieu of asymmetrical societal organization and relationship, and the communicative behaviors and practices found there are likewise asymmetrical in nature. As the witticism goes, "All men (perhaps even women) are created equal — some are just more equal than others."

Given this frame of reference, I would now like to explore some definitions and concepts that, I believe, emerge from this perspective. It is my hope that the discussion will provide the reader with another way to look at intracultural communication.

## A Nomenclature for Intracultural Communication

### The Concept of Nondominance

As already indicated, I view intracultural communication as a phenomenon that operates within a given cultural context. However, my particular focus, as suggested, is not a focus on numbers but an attention to dominance, nondominance, and power in the cultural setting. That is, how do nondominant groups intersect and interact with the dominant culture membership (with those who enact the precepts and support the institutions and systems of the power elite)? For purposes of discussion and analysis, I will take most of my examples from the geopolitical configuration called the United States.

By "nondominant groups" I mean those constellations of people who have not historically or traditionally had continued access to or influence upon or within the dominant culture's social, political, legal, economic, and/or religious structures and institutions. Again, by dominant culture, I mean those who dominate culture. Nondominant groups include people of color, women, gays and lesbians, the physically challenged, and the aged poor, to name some of the most prominent. I use the expression "nondominant" to characterize these people because, as suggested, I am referring to power and dominance, not numbers and dominance. Within the United States, those most likely to hold and control positions of real – not token – power and those who have the greatest potential ease of access to power and high status are still generally white, male, able-bodied, heterosexual, and youthful in appearance, if not in age.[5]

Nondominant people are also those who, in varying degrees and various ways, have been "invisible" within the society of which they are a part and at the same time bear a visible caste mark. Furthermore, it is this mark of caste identity that is often consciously or habitually assigned low or negative status by members of the dominant culture.

The dimensions of invisibility and marked visibility are keen indicators of the status hierarchy in a given society. In his classic novel, *The Invisible Man*, Ralph Ellison instructs us in the lesson that nondominant people – in this instance, African Americans – are figuratively "invisible." They are seen by the dominant culture as no one, nobody, and therefore go unacknowledged and importantly unperceived.[6] Furthermore, nondominant peoples are often relegated to object status rather than human status. They are viewed as persons of "no consequence," literally and metaphorically. Expressions such as "If you've seen one, you've seen them all," "They all look alike to me," and "If you put a bag over their heads, it doesn't matter who you screw" attest to this level of invisibility and dehumanization of nondominant peoples (people of color or women, for instance). Indeed, one need only look at the dominant culture's slang repertory for a single nondominant group, women, to see the extent of this object status: "tail," "piece of ass," "side of beef," "hole," "gash," "slit."

At the same time that nondominant peoples are socially invisible, they are often visibly caste-marked. Though we tend to think of caste in terms, say, of East Indian culture, we can clearly apply the concept to our own culture. One of the important dimensions of a caste system is that it is hereditary – you are born into a given caste and are usually marked for life as a member. In fact, we are all born into a caste, we are all caste-marked. Indeed, some of us bear multiple caste marks. In the United States, the most visible marks of caste relate

to gender, race, age, and the degree to which one is able-bodied.

As East Indians do, we also assign low to high status and privilege to people within our society. The fact that this assignment of status and privilege may be active or passive, conscious or unconscious, malicious or unthinking does not detract from the reality of the act. And one of the major determinants of status, position, and caste marking relates back to who has historically or traditionally had access to or influence upon or within the power elite and its concomitant structures and institutions. So, historically, African Americans, Native Americans, Hispanics, women, the aged poor, the physically challenged have at best been neutrally caste-marked and more often negatively identified when it comes to issues of power, dominance, and social control.

Low status has been assigned to those people whom society views as somehow "stigmatized." Indeed, we have labels to identify such stigmatization: "deviant," "handicapped," "abnormal," "substandard," "different" – that is, different from those who dominate. As already suggested, it is the white, male, heterosexual, able-bodied, youthful person who both sets the standards for caste marking and is the human yardstick by which people within the United States still are measured and accordingly treated. As Porter and Samovar (1994) remind us, in the instance of race: "Although there has been a lessening of overt racial violence since the 1960s, the enduring racist-ethnocentric belief system has not been appreciably affected. . . . The result is a structured domination of people of color by the white Anglo power structure" (p. 6). Again, our language is a telling repository for illuminating status as it relates to subordination in the social hierarchy: "Stay in your place," "Don't get out of line," "Know your place," "A woman's place is on her back," and "Know your station in life" are just a few sample phrases.

It is inevitable that nondominant peoples will experience – indeed be subjected to and suffer from – varying degrees of fear, denial, and self-hatred of their caste marking. Frantz Fanon's (1963) vivid characterization of the "colonized native" – the oppressed native who has so internalized the power elite's perception of the norm that he or she not only serves and speaks for the colonial elite but is also often more critical and oppressive of her or his caste than is the colonial – reveals this depth of self-hatred and denial.

In a parallel vein, the concept of "passing," which relates to a person of color attempting to "pass for" white, is a statement of self-denial. Implicit in the act of passing is the acceptance, if not the belief, that "white is right" in this society, and the closer one can come to the likeness of the privileged caste, the more desirable and comfortable one's station in life will be. So, people of color have passed for white – just as Jews have passed for gentiles or gay males and lesbians have passed for straight, often with the fear of being discovered "for what they are." Physical impairment, too, has often been hidden from public view by those so challenged. Even so powerful a figure as a president of the United States – Franklin Delano Roosevelt – refused to be photographed in any way that would picture him as a "cripple."

If the act of passing is a denial of one's caste, the process of "coming out of the closet" is a conscious acceptance of one's caste. It is an important political and personal statement of power, a vivid metaphor that literally marks a rite of passage. Perhaps the most striking acknowledgment of one's caste marking in our society relates to sexual or affectional preference. For gay males or lesbians to admit their respective preferences is for them to consciously take on an identity that mainstream society has deemed abnormal and deviant – when measured against the society's standard of what is appropriate. They become, quite literally, "marked people."

In an important way, most liberation or freedom movements are devoted to having their membership come out of the closet. That is, these movements demand not only to have their people heard and empowered by the power elite, but also to have their membership reclaim and assert their identity and honor their caste. Historically, slogans embraced by domestic liberation movements in the United States have told the story of positive identification with one's caste: "Black is beautiful," "Brown power," "Sisterhood is powerful," "Gay pride," "I am an Indian and proud of it." More

graphic and contemporary assertions of caste identification can be seen in the "inverting" of society's pejorative labels into positive, "in-your-face" marks of identity.[7] So, for example, there is the gay activist group, Queer Nation, or the African American rap group, NWA – Niggers With Attitude.

The nature and disposition of the social hierarchy in a given society, such as the United States, is reflected not only in the caste structure, but also in the class structure and the role prescriptions and expectations surrounding caste and class. Although the power structure in the United States is a complex and multileveled phenomenon, its predominant, generating force is economic. That is, the power elite is an elite that controls the material resources and goods in this country as well as the means and manner of production and distribution. Though one of our national fictions is that the United States is a classless society, we have, in fact, a well-established class structure based largely on economic power and control. When we talk of lower, middle, and upper classes in this country, we are not usually talking about birth or origins, but about power and control over material resources and the attendant wealth, privilege, and high status.

There is even a kind of status distinction made within the upper-class society in this country that again relates to wealth and power, but in a temporal rather than a quantitative way – how long one has had wealth, power, and high-class status. So distinctions are made between the old rich (the Harrimans, the Gores, the Pews) and the new rich (the Hunt family, Norton Simon, and their ilk).

Class, then, is intimately bound up with matters of caste. Not all, or even most, members of our society have the opportunity – let alone the caste credentials – to get a "piece of the action." It is no accident of nature that many of the nondominant peoples in this country are also poor peoples. Nor is it surprising that nondominant groups have been historically the unpaid, low-paid, and/or enslaved workforce for the economic power elite.

Finally, role prescriptions are linked to both matters of status and expectations in terms of one's perceived status, class, and caste. A role can be defined simply as a set of behaviors. The set of behaviors we ascribe to a given role is culture-bound and indicative of what has been designated as appropriate within the culture vis-à-vis that role. They are prescriptive, not descriptive, behaviors. We hold certain behavioral expectations for certain roles. It is a mark of just how culture-bound and prescriptive these roles are when someone is perceived to behave inappropriately — for example, the mother who gives up custody of her children in order to pursue her career has "stepped out of line."

Furthermore, we see certain roles as appropriate or inappropriate to a given caste. Though another of our national myths — the Horatio Alger myth — tells us that there is room at the top for the industrious, bright go-getter, the truth of the matter is that there is room at the top if you are appropriately caste-marked (that is, are white, male, able-bodied, and so on).

The resistance, even outright hostility, nondominant peoples have encountered when they aspire to or claim certain occupational roles, for example, is a mark of the power elite's reluctance to relinquish those positions that have been traditionally associated with privileged status and high caste and class ranking. The concept of the "glass ceiling," so popular in today's vocabulary, is an apt metaphor to describe not only the sense of thwarted advancement in the workplace, but also the implied resistance of the power elite to incursions from the up-and-coming "outsider." In the public arena, the idea of the presidency being held by a member of a visible, nondominant group is still just that — an idea. Whether or not a popular public figure, like Colin Powell, will or can transform idea to reality is still to be seen.[8] For that matter, even the vice-presidency has not been held by a woman or a person of color.

The cultural prescription to keep nondominant peoples "in their place" is reinforced by and reinforces what I refer to as the "subterranean self" — the culture-bound collection of prejudices, stereotypes, values, and beliefs that each of us embraces and employs to justify our world view and the place of people in that world. It is, after all, our subterranean selves that provide fuel to fire the normative in our lives — what roles people ought and ought not to perform, what and why certain individuals

are ill- or well-equipped to carry out certain roles, and why people should be kept in their places, as we see them (through righteously stated rationalizations). Again, it should be remembered that those who dominate the culture reinforce and tacitly or openly encourage the perpetuation of those cultural prejudices, stereotypes, values, and beliefs that maintain the status quo; that is, the asymmetrical nature of the social hierarchy.

Those who doubt the fervent desire of the power elite to maintain things as they are need only ponder the intense and prolonged resistance to the defunct Equal Rights Amendment. If women are already "equal," why not make their equality a matter of record? Recall the hue and cry for an "English as Official Language" Amendment. After more than 200 years without such a "statement" on the books, why now? Perhaps it's a response to the perceived threat — linguistic and cultural — from the influx of "all those foreign immigrants" (read immigrants of color). And whose civil rights would be "secured" by the proposed California Civil Rights initiative?

The foregoing discussion has been an attempt to illuminate the meaning of nondominance and the position of the nondominant person within our society. By relating status in the social hierarchy to matters of caste, class, and role, it has been my intention to highlight what it means to be a nondominant person within a culture that is dominated by the cultural precepts and artifacts of a power elite. It has also been my intention to suggest that the concept of "dominant culture" is something of a fiction, as we in communication studies traditionally use it. Given my perspective, it is more accurate to talk about those who dominate a culture rather than a dominant culture per se. Finally, I have attempted to point out that cultural dominance is not necessarily, or even usually, a matter of the numbers of people in a given society, but of those who have real power in a society.

## Geopolitics

The viewpoint being developed in this essay highlights still another facet of dominance and nondominance as it relates to society and the culture it generates and sustains — namely, the geopolitical aspect. The United States is not merely a territory with certain designated boundaries — a geographical entity — but is also a geopolitical configuration. It is a country whose history reflects the clear-cut interrelationship of geography, politics, economics, and the domination and control of people. For example, the westward movement and the subsequent takeover of indigenous peoples' lands and chunks of Mexico were justified by this country's doctrine of Manifest Destiny, not unlike the way Hitler's expansionism was justified by the Nazi doctrine of "geopolitik." It is not accident that the doctrine of Manifest Destiny coincides with the rapid growth and development of U.S. industrialization. The U.S. power elite wanted more land in which to expand and grow economically, so it created a rationalization to secure it.

Perhaps nowhere is a dominant culture's ethnocentrism (the ethnocentrism of those who dominate culture) more apparent than in the missionary-like work carried on by its members — whether it be to "civilize" the natives (that is, to impose the conquerors' cultural baggage on them), to "educate them in the ways of the white man," or to "Americanize" them. Indeed, the very term *America* is a geopolitical label as we use it. It presumes that those who inhabit the United States are the center of the Western hemisphere, indeed its only residents.[9] Identifying ourselves as "Americans" and our geopolitical entity as "America" — in light of the peoples who live to the north and south of our borders — speaks to both our economic dominance in this hemisphere and our ethnocentrism.

Identifying the United States in geopolitical terms is to identify it as a conqueror and controller of other peoples and suggests both the probability of nondominant groups of people within that territory and a polarized, even hostile, relationship between these groups and those who dominate culture. What Rich and Ogawa (1982) have pointed out in their model of interracial communication is applicable to most nondominant peoples: "As long as a power relationship exists between cultures where one has subdued and dominated the other . . . hostility, tension and strain are introduced into the communicative situation" (p. 46).

Not only were Native American lands, as well as parts of Mexico, conquered and brought under the colonial rule of the United States, but in its industrial expansionism, the United States also physically enslaved black Africans to work on the farms and plantations of the South. Throughout its short history, the United States also has economically enslaved large numbers of East European immigrants, Chinese, Irish, and Mexicans in its factories, on its railroads, and in its mines and fields through low wages and long work hours. It co-opted the cottage industries of the home and brought women and children into the factories under abysmal conditions and the lowest of wages.

And economic servitude continues today. Refugees, fleeing from war, poverty, and oppressive regimes in East and Southeast Asia, Latin America, and the Caribbean have become the invisible, low-paid nannies, maids, day laborers, and caretakers of the old and sick. So, the pool of cheap labor stays full and "in place."

Indeed, many of the nondominant peoples in this country today are the very same ones whom the powerful have historically colonized, enslaved, disenfranchised, dispossessed, discounted, and relegated to poverty and low caste and class status. The asymmetrical relationship between the conqueror and the conquered continues uninterrupted. Although the form of oppression may change through time, the fact of oppression — and coexistent nondominance — remains.

It has been my desire throughout this essay to speculate about the complex ways in which society, culture, position, and place in the societal hierarchy affect and are affected by the matters of dominance, power, and social control. To this end, I have chosen to identify and characterize configurations of people within a society not only along a cultural axis but along a socioeconomic and a geopolitical axis as well. I have tried to reexamine some of the concepts and definitions employed in discussions of culture-linked communication in a particular light. And I have chosen the issues and conditions surrounding dominance and nondominance as points of departure and return. As I said at the beginning of this essay, the content is intended to encourage ongoing dialogue and exchange about the conditions and constraints surrounding intracultural communication.

## Notes

1. See Folb (1980) for another perspective on the intersection of power, dominance, and nondominance as they operate within a discrete microcultural group, the world of the African American teenager, living in the inner city.

2. For a fascinating account of how and what kind of culture is transmitted from person to person, see Margaret Mead's classic text, *Culture and Commitment* (1970).

3. J. T. Wood's book, *Gendered Lives: Communication, Gender and Culture* (1994), provides an informative and lively discussion of the ways in which females and males are catalogued, characterized, and compartmentalized through their communicative behavior. She focuses on the intersection of gender, culture, and communication as it affects what we say and do, as well as how others perceive us.

4. Contrary to the belief that white males are fast losing power in the United States, they are still very much in the "cat bird seat." In a *Newsweek* article (1993) entitled "White Male Paranoia," the writers bring this fact into sharp relief: "It's still a statistical piece of cake being a white man, at least in comparison with being anything else. White males make up just 39.2 percent of the population [in the U.S.], yet they account for 82.5 percent of the Forbes 400 (folks worth at least $265 million), 77 percent of Congress, 92 percent of state governors, 70 percent of tenured college faculty, almost 90 percent of daily-newspaper editors, 77 percent of TV news directors. They dominate just about everything but NOW and the NAACP" (p. 49).

5. In a country as youth conscious as the United States, advanced age is seen as a liability, not as a mark of honor and wisdom as it is in other cultures. For example, whatever other reservations people had about Ronald Reagan's political aspirations in 1980, the one most discussed was his age. His political handlers went to great lengths—as did Reagan himself—to "prove" he was young in spirit and energy, if not in years. It was important that he align himself as closely as possible with the positive mark of youth we champion and admire in this country. The same scenario is repeating itself in the 1996 election. Septuagenarian Bob Dole's handlers are trying to package him much the same as Reagan was some 16 years ago.

6. It is no mere coincidence that a common thread which binds together the domestic liberation movements of the past with the immigrant protest groups of the present in the United States is the demand to be seen, heard, and empowered.

7. Grace Sims Holt was one of the first to talk about the concept of inversion as an empowering force in language use. See her pioneering article "'Inversion' in Black Community," in Kochman (1972).

8. The issue of Colin Powell's race "will matter"—at least, according to a pre-election *Newsweek* article: "Even today the presidency is a mythic office and letting a black man be 'daddy' is a huge Freudian leap for many white Americans. (Recall that voters told pollsters in 1982 that they preferred Tom Bradley, who is black, for governor of California, but enough of them apparently changed their minds in the privacy of the polling booth to cost him the election.)" (September 25, 1995).

9. The bumper sticker, "Get the United States Out of North America," was a pointed reference to U.S. hemispheric self-centeredness.

## References

Byrd, M. L. (1993). *The Intracultural Communication Book*. New York: McGraw-Hill.

Fanon, F. (1963). *Wretched of the Earth*. New York: Grove Press.

Folb, E. A. (1980). *Runnin' Down Some Lines: The Language and Culture of Black Teenagers*. Cambridge: Harvard University Press.

Holt, G. S. (1972). "'Inversion' in Black Community." In T. Kochman (Ed.), *Rappin' and Stylin' Out: Communication in Urban Black America*. Urbana: University of Illinois Press.

Porter, R. E., and Samovar, L. A. (1994). "An Introduction to Intercultural Communication." In L. A. Samovar and R. E. Porter, *Intercultural Communication: A Reader*, 7th ed., 4–26. Belmont, Calif.: Wadsworth.

Rich, A. L., and Ogawa, D. M. (1982). "Intercultural and Interracial Communication: An Analytical Approach." In L. A. Samovar and R. E. Porter (Eds.), *Intercultural Communication: A Reader*, 3d ed. Belmont, Calif.: Wadsworth.

Samovar, L. A., and Porter, R. E. (Eds.). (1994). *Intercultural Communication: A Reader*, 7th ed. Belmont, Calif.: Wadsworth.

Sarbaugh, L. E. (1988). *Intercultural Communication*, 2d ed. New Brunswick: Transaction Books.

Sitaram, K. S., and Cogdell, R. T. (1976). *Foundations of Intercultural Communication*. Columbus, Ohio: Merrill.

Wood, J. T. (1994). *Gendered Lives: Communication, Gender and Culture*. Belmont, Calif.: Wadsworth.

# An African American Communication Perspective

SIDNEY A. RIBEAU
JOHN R. BALDWIN
MICHAEL L. HECHT

African American communication is as complex as
the culture from which it emerges. Taken from the
shores of Africa, the enslaved captives were forced
to create a means of expression consistent with an
African cultural tradition, yet responsive to life in
the new world. The fusion of past traditions with
slavery, and post-slavery experiences in the rural
South and North, created a unique ethnic culture
for the group known as African Americans.

The communicative style of African American
ethnic culture is captured in a number of studies
that investigate linguistic characteristics, social relationships, and verbal and nonverbal messages. This
early research, which is primarily descriptive, provides an introduction to a rich and promising line
of inquiry. Our work expands the discussion of
African American discourse to include empirical investigations of the interpersonal dimensions that
characterize this unique ethnic communication
system. We are particularly interested in (1) the
identifications of satisfying and dissatisfying conversational themes, (2) conversational improvement
strategies, and (3) communication effectiveness. A
few important assumptions support our work and
provide a context for this research.

## Underlying Assumptions

We consider communication to be problematic —
an interactive event during which persons assign
meanings to messages and jointly create identities
and social reality. This process is multi-dimensional
and extremely complex. Attribution of meaning to
symbols requires the interpretation of messages
and negotiation of social worlds. The process is replete with the potential for failure which is magnified when ethno-cultural factors are introduced.
Ethnic cultures consist of cognitive (for example,
values, beliefs, norms) and material (for example,
food, dress, symbols) characteristics that distinguish them from mainstream American culture. For
successful communication to occur, these potential
problems must be anticipated and managed.

Here we use an interpretive approach that uti-
lizes the perceptions of cultural actors to explain
their communicative behavior. The descriptions
and narrative accounts provided by interactions
enable one to glimpse a world normally reserved
for members of the shared community. It is this
world that we seek to unfold.

Culture and ethnicity are the concepts that govern our exploration of African American communication. **Culture** consists of the shared cognitive and
material items that forge a group's identity and ensure its survival. Culture is created, shared, and
transmitted through communication. **Ethnicity**
pertains to the traditions, heritage, and ancestry
that define a people. It is particularly apparent in a
group's expressive forms. (We take as axiomatic the
existence of ethnic cultures in America, and recognize African American culture as a fundamental element of life in America.)

Our early work is governed by the conceptual assumptions listed, and practical concern: *research on
African American communication should assist the
practitioner in improving relationships between African
Americans and European Americans.* It is our belief
that the communication discipline has much to offer
the area of human relations. This line of research is
intended to make a contribution to that effort. To
that end we began with studies of (1) intragroup
communication issues, (2) interethnic communication issues, and (3) conversational improvement

strategies. The remainder of this paper will report our findings and discuss their implications. First, however, we frame these studies within an understanding of communication effectiveness.

## Communication Effectiveness

Many scholars have provided valuable information about what behaviors and communication people believe to be effective (Martin, 1993; Martin & Hammer, 1989; Pavitt & Haight, 1985; Ruben, 1977, 1989). "Competent" or "effective" communication has been defined in many ways (Spitzberg & Cupach, 1984; Spitzberg & Hecht, 1984; Wiemann & Bradac, 1989). One way to define **effective** behavior is that which is productive and satisfying for both partners. Communication is appropriate if it follows the rules and expectations the partners have; these expectations vary depending on the context the speakers are in or the relationship between them. The positive feelings the communicators have when their expectations are met make up the "satisfying" part of our definition (Hecht, 1978, 1984). The expectations may be met because a relationship is satisfying (McLaughlin & Cody, 1982), or because the communicators were able to function effectively in a new situation (Vause & Wiemann, 1981).

In view of effective communication, we see *communication issues* as "the agenda for effective communication held in common by members of the group" (Hecht, Collier, & Ribeau, 1993, p. 127). That is, they are aspects of communication, which, if missing, pose problems for the communication; they are expectations about communication. Since different ethnic groups have different shared histories and ways of seeing the world, we believe that the unspoken, often subconscious, rules that one co-culture has for effective or satisfying communication may differ from those imposed by another. Further, given the impact of historical race and power relationships in the United States, it seems likely that African Americans (and other American cultures) would apply differing rules for measuring effective communications with in-group and out-group members.

## Intragroup Communication Issues

We started by trying to understand how African Americans communicate among themselves. We asked African Americans, Mexican Americans, and European Americans to describe satisfying or dissatisfying conversations they had experienced with a member of their own ethnic group (Hecht & Ribeau, 1984). We found that the expectations of the groups were in some ways different, in others similar. Mexican Americans differed the most, with African Americans and European Americans responding more similarly.

Mexican Americans, for example, tended to seek closely bonded relationships, seeing the relationship itself as rewarding. Within this ethnic group, satisfying communication involved nonverbal communication and acceptance of self. In comparison, African Americans, and to a greater extent, European Americans, were self-oriented – that is, they saw the reward in something the other partner might provide for them, instead of in the existence of the relationship.

In keeping with this idea of potential reward, European Americans tended to look more to the future of the relationship. This echoes a previous study in which European Americans found communication with friends more satisfying when there were signs of intimacy that confirmed the future of the relationship (Hecht, 1984). At the same time, European Americans demonstrated less concern and interest for the partner in the conversation (other orientation) than did African Americans.

African Americans, on the other hand, found greater satisfaction in conversations where both partners were more involved in the topic. Intimacy was therapeutic and foundational to the relationship, and trust was highly important. While conversation was goal-oriented, at the same time it was important that ideas and feelings be exchanged. Where the Mexican Americans found bonding a priority for relationships, the African Americans surveyed found bonding conditional – to be established only if that exchange of ideas took place. In light of this, genuineness ("being real") and expressiveness were important, and were communicated through expressive style, passion, and deep involvement with the topic. Helping one another was an integral part of satisfying interaction, supporting goal-oriented relationships. Because both parties may be trying to meet the same goals, it is necessary that those goals be clearly understood; thus, understanding is also important. African Americans found satisfaction when they knew where the conversation was going.

## Intergroup Communication Issues

We next sought to understand the agenda for effective interethnic communication – specifically, communication between blacks and whites (Hecht, Collier, & Ribeau, 1993, Hecht, Larkey, & Johnson, 1992; Hecht & Ribeau, 1987; Hecht, Ribeau, & Alberts, 1989; Hecht, Ribeau, & Sedano, 1990). In this research, we identified seven primary issues important to those African Americans studied: (1) negative stereotyping, (2) acceptance, (3) personal expressiveness, (4) authenticity, (5) understanding, (6) goal attainment, and (7) power dynamics. In describing these issues, we provide quotes from African American responses to interviews and surveys to illuminate the findings.

## Negative Stereotyping

*Negative stereotyping* is "the use of rigid racial categories that distort an African American's individuality. This violates the concept of uniqueness, something research has shown to be very important to African Americans" (Hecht, Collier, & Ribeau, 1993). Negative stereotyping occurred in two ways. The first, and more obvious, was when European Americans in the study racially categorized African Americans – that is, when they treated them as a member of a group, or ascribed to them characteristics of the group, instead of treating them like individuals.

Indirect stereotyping occurred when European Americans talked to African Americans about what were seen to be "African American topics," such as sports or music. Some African Americans reported that this type of behavior made them want to withdraw, or caused them to see their conversational partner with disdain. One male African American, while seeing the introduction of such topics as an

attempt to find common interests, saw those who brought them up as "patronizing or unaware," and felt that other African Americans felt the same way. Another type of indirect stereotyping is when European Americans ask or expect African Americans to speak on behalf of all African Americans. One participant *did feel satisfied* about her conversation because she "didn't feel put on the spot to speak for the whole of the black race." Another female was satisfied when the other person spoke to her "as another person and didn't let my color interfere with the conversation."

## Acceptance

The second issue is *acceptance,* "the feeling that another accepts, confirms, and respects one's opinions" (Hecht, Collier, & Ribeau, 1993, p. 131). Frequently, African Americans did not feel accepted by European Americans. For example, some persons interviewed said African Americans sometimes try to make up for "cultural deprivation" and "talk rather than listen in order to cover up." They act "cool," flippant, or talkative, sometimes using stylized speech. Some of the participants saw these behaviors as responses to stereotypes, either in the sense that the African Americans were trying to control the conversation to preempt the stereotypes, or that they were trying to avoid recognizing them. One person strongly volunteered that African Americans are no longer concerned about what European Americans feel or accept. At the same time, many of those interviewed felt that acceptance was a characteristic of satisfying conversations. This acceptance might be shown by positive nonverbal behaviors, similar dress, feeling comfortable with the conversation, "mutual respect for each other's beliefs," and even, at times, acting "cool" or removed.

## Personal Expressiveness

*Personal expressiveness* refers to the verbal and nonverbal expression of thoughts, ideas, or feelings. While many African Americans mentioned some aspect of expressiveness, how that expressiveness is played out varies from person to person. Some saw honesty, integrity, and the open sharing of ideas as valuable; others felt it important to keep their feelings hidden in intercultural communications. For example, one African American woman expressed dissatisfaction with a conversation because "I maintained control and did not curse her out." Opinions are important, but the emphasis is on expressing feelings — "talking from the heart, not the head." In contrast, non-expressive European Americans might be seen as racist or standoffish. Interestingly, many participants — more females than males — expressed the need to portray a tough exterior. African Americans need to "be cool," and not let European Americans know what they are thinking or feeling. History had an impact here with some of the women participants, pointing out that African American women have had to be strong both in response to prejudice and often as the head of the household. A possible explanation for the contrasting answers is that some African Americans value toughness and "coolness" until barriers of fear and mistrust are broken down; then, it becomes important to express who one really is.

## Authenticity

*Authenticity* is tied directly to the concept of being oneself, of being genuine. Both African and European Americans perceived authenticity on the part of their conversational partner when the other was seen as revealing personal information — being honest, "being real," "being themselves," or expressing personal feelings freely. One African American male complained about "so many phony conversations — white people trying to impress African Americans with their liberalness." Straightforwardness, or "telling it like it is," is one aspect of authenticity; the opposite of this is avoidance of the truth through double talking or fancy language.

At the same time, many African American males engage in self-presentation; they try to create an acceptable image of themselves through "high talk" and "stylin'." "You dress as if you had money even if you don't." Creating an acceptable self-image becomes critical when a demeaning image has been externally imposed by European American society. In this light, stylized behavior to African Americans emerges as a sign of strength, not a lack of authenticity.

## Understanding

*Understanding* is the feeling that messages are successfully conveyed. This theme was expressed when people felt that information was adequately exchanged or learning took place. One person noted that "there was a genuine exchange of thinking, feeling, and caring." Unfortunately, understanding can be hampered by cultural differences or differences in upbringing. One female commented that "if people don't share the same life experiences, they can't be expected to truly understand each other. If whites haven't been exposed to blacks, there will be a 'fear of the unknown.'"

## Goal Attainment

*Goal attainment,* or achieving desired ends from a conversation, was mentioned more in satisfying than in dissatisfying conversations. It is closely linked to understanding in that without some mutual understanding no goals will be met. Goals might include finding the solution to some problem, exchanging information, or finishing some project. But cultural misunderstandings can get in the way of goals. As one male responded: "Blacks and whites may come away with different meanings from a conversation because concepts aren't defined in the same way. The members of the ethnic groups tend to think in a different manner." Because of this, African Americans often find conversations with European Americans unrewarding, but those rewarding conversations are "like gates opening."

## Power Dynamics

*Power dynamics,* the last category, contains two main themes: powerlessness and assertiveness. *Powerlessness,* a feeling of being controlled, manipulated, or trapped, resulted from behaviors that rob African American conversational partners of the right to express their ideas freely. One participant objected to the term "powerlessness" as "putting things in white terms"; the label is not as important to us as the behaviors it describes. European Americans were seen as manipulating when they tried to control the topic, tried to persuade through subtlety, or would not let the African Americans finish their thoughts. One European American communicator "tried to carry on the conversation all by himself . . . he would keep talking and interrupted me whenever I tried to say something."

Extreme assertiveness and confrontation used by African Americans, called "Mau Mauing," by one participant is the other half of power dynamics. African Americans, it was commented, often talk with one another in a way that "whites would consider antagonistic or brutal." For this reason, many African Americans *code switch,* or change their communication style and language, when they interact with European Americans. Assertive speaking among some African Americans is exemplified by "the dozens," a put-down game in which one person puts down or makes fun of another person. It should be emphasized, however, that this type of assertiveness is by no means universal to all African Americans.

## Communication Improvement Strategies

While interethnic communication issues are characteristics or behaviors that can help or hurt these communications, the African American participants believed *improvement strategies* can enhance conversation. These are things communicators can do to help make the interaction more satisfying. While our initial research found six strategies (Hecht & Ribeau, 1987; Hecht, Ribeau, & Alberts, 1989; Martin, Larkey, & Hecht, 1991), later research has expanded the list to twelve: (1) asserting one's point of view, (2) positive self-presentation, (3) be open and friendly, (4) avoidance, (5) interaction management, (6) other-orientation, (7) inform/educate, (8) express genuineness, (9) confront, (10) internal management, (11) treat others as individuals, and (12) language management. We describe these again with quotes from African Americans to expound.

### Asserting One's Point of View

*Assertiveness,* in both style and substance, includes using such expressions as "stress," "assert," or "emphasize my point." This strategy grew out of dissatisfying conversations and was recommended for aiding African Americans' persuasion or argumentation efforts. The purpose is not simply to inform, but to gain agreement. Examples of this point of view are expressed in these comments: "Just simply be more vocal in the conversation. This in itself will give you a sense of control or power." "I continue to put across what I believe."

### Positive Self-Presentation

Two methods of positive self-presentation attempt to reverse the other person's impressions. One method of self-presentation is to deliberately contradict stereotypes: "I just make sure my actions and conversation don't fit the negative stereotype." The other method is to point out positive attributes or accomplishments: "I try to make others see what I know, that is, when I'm being talked down to I try to show my intelligence."

### Be Open and Friendly

This strategy, used most often to improve dissatisfying conversations, is similar to positive self-presentation, but without the deliberate desire to impress. Again, the participants varied in their views on openness, or open-mindedness. Some respondents felt European Americans should "be more patient, not assume anything, find out first." However, some African Americans rejected openness as a European American, middle-class female attribute, preferring to present themselves as strong, more closed. Friendliness includes being considerate of the other, polite, and courteous.

### Avoidance

In a dissatisfying conversation, one might avoid either the conversation itself (by leaving), or the topics that are sensitive or demeaning. The first strategy is indicated by those who "terminate the conversation," or "remove myself from the conversation." The second is used when an African American perceives that some topics just cannot be discussed with certain individuals. Possible methods of avoidance include "not bringing up the subject," or changing the subject. ("I don't think it's beneficial to try to change the other person.")

## Interaction Management

Either the African or the European American can attempt to manage the flow of the interaction. This might be done to reduce problems or just to improve a conversation. Possible strategies within this category include managing immediate interaction ("take turns," "work toward a compromise"), postponing the problem ("request a time to talk it over"), or finding different means of communication ("write a note"). Sometimes the conversation can be better managed by "just talking a little more" or spending "more time" together.

## Other-Orientation

A concern for or interest in the other person was a sign of satisfying relationships, and might be created in different ways. Involving the other person in the conversation or finding common ground was one method suggested: "Think or talk about something that both can identify with." Others emphasized listening to the other person's thoughts and opinions: "learn by listening," "placing them in our shoes," and "try to look at it from both sides." Either party can improve the conversation with this strategy.

## Inform/Educate

Information was often shared to educate or inform the conversational partner, in contrast to "asserting one's point of view." One should "tactfully educate by giving more information," and "if the conversation is that important, try and explain whatever you feel is being misunderstood." More facts should be given, sometimes specifically citing African American history to help others understand. At the same time, African Americans sometimes mentioned the need to ask European Americans more questions. This strategy attempts to resolve the issues raised by stereotyping and lack of understanding.

## Express Genuineness

This strategy, genuineness, addresses the issue of authenticity, of "being yourself." Comments in this category valued honesty and expressing feelings.

Some participants opened up in hopes that their conversation partner would follow. Others saw it in terms of a need to "share your feelings of a lack of accomplishment," in attempting to have a satisfying conversation or to "ask the person to be for real." While these suggestions seem confrontational, they are geared toward moving the other into more honest expression.

## Confront

Confrontation implies "either a direct confrontation of the issue or using questions to place the burden back on the other person" (Hecht, Collier, & Ribeau, 1993). Strategies in this category include "Correct misconceptions in a shrewd, effective manner," or opposing "I believe you must always confront stereotyping by saying, 'It sounds as if you are making generalizations that may not be applicable to me.'" Examples of direct questions are "Just say, 'but how do *you* feel about it?' If they don't answer, it's obvious that it at least makes them feel uncomfortable," or "Ask why and how they got that stereotype."

## Internal Management

Rather than focusing on specific behaviors to improve interaction, these comments described ways for African Americans to think about or deal with the situation. Some of these suggestions included acceptance, objectivity, and nondefensiveness: "I do my best to control my thoughts," "Think first of who you are, how you feel about yourself," and "Put the situation in proper perspective, that is, lose a battle to win the war."

## Treat Others As Individuals and Equals

Leave race, color, or stereotypical beliefs entirely out of the conversation some suggested: "Talk to each other without having the sense of color in the conversation." Treat people based on who they are, and nothing else: "Decisions should be made based on each individual" or "Get to know me then judge me." This strategy, voiced most often to fight the stereotyping issue, primarily advocates desired behavior by the European American conversation partner.

## Language Management

A few strategies that did not fit in the other categories are grouped here including: avoid slang or jargon and use clear articulation. "Refrain from using unfamiliar jargon" and "talk the same language" are examples of comments in this area. This strategy was used to resolve problems of a lack of understanding.

Note that the African American participants recommended some of these strategies primarily as things they should do (for example, assertiveness, positive self-presentation, avoidance, internal management, inform/educate, confront, language management); some as things European Americans should do (treat others as individuals); and some as things both should do (be more open and friendly, interaction management, express genuineness, other-orientation). Second, it should be noted that within each category (for example, be more open and friendly) there is a diversity of thought among African Americans as to how or if that strategy should be used.

The African Americans we interviewed felt that these strategies might be successful for improving a conversation, but not always. When stereotyping or lack of acceptance takes place, for example, no strategies are seen as effective — it is like "bouncing off a brick wall." If African Americans "see signs of racism, patronizing behavior, or other put downs, they turn off quickly." The first few minutes of a conversation can make or break the conversation — and the relationship.

## Conclusion

It is often tempting to state communication effectiveness theories (or others) as if they applied to the way all people behave. However, the studies described here demonstrate that rules for effective or satisfying communication behavior vary, depending on the ethnicity of the group, as well as the situation. Further, the research shows a diversity and complexity among African Americans (Hecht & Ribeau, 1991). Finally, African Americans' own descriptions reveal clear suggestions, both for African Americans and European Americans, for how to make interethnic communication more rewarding for all concerned.

## References

Hecht, M. L. (1978). Toward a conceptualization of interpersonal communication satisfaction. *Quarterly Journal of Speech, 64,* 47–62.

Hecht, M. L. (1984). Satisfying communication and relationship labels: Intimacy and length of relationship as perceptual frames of naturalistic conversation." *Western Journal of Speech Communication, 48,* 201–216.

Hecht, M. L., Collier, M. J., and Ribeau, S. (1993). *African American Communication: Identity and Cultural Interpretations.* Newbury Park, Calif.: Sage.

Hecht, M. L., Larkey, L. K., and Johnson, J. N. (1992). African American and European American perceptions of problematic issues in interethnic communication effectiveness. *Human Communication Research, 19,* 209–236.

Hecht, M. L., and Ribeau, S. Ethnic communication: A comparative analysis of satisfying communication. *International Journal of Intercultural Relations, 8,* 135–151.

Hecht, M. L., and Ribeau, S. (1987). Afro-American identity labels and communicative effectiveness. *Journal of Language and Social Psychology, 6,* 319–326.

Hecht, M. L., and Ribeau, S. (1991). Sociocultural roots of ethnic identity: A look at Black America. *Journal of Black Studies, 21,* 501–513.

Hecht, M. L., Ribeau, S., and Alberts, J. K. (1989). An Afro-American perspective on interethnic communication. *Communication Monographs, 56,* 385–410.

Hecht, M. L., Ribeau, S., and Sedano, M. V. (1990). A Mexican American perspective on interethnic communication. *International Journal of Intercultural Relations, 14,* 31–55.

Martin, J. N. (1993). "Intercultural Communication Competence." In R. Wiseman and J. Koester (Eds.), *International and Intercultural Communication Annual, 17.*

Martin, J. N., Larkey, L. K., and Hecht, M. L. (February, 1991). An African American Perspective on Conversational Improvement Strategies for Interethnic Communication. Paper presented to the Intercultural and International Communication Conference, Miami, Florida.

Martin, J. N., and Hammer, M. R. (1989). Behavioral categories of intercultural communication competence: Everyday communicators' perceptions. *International Journal of Intercultural Relations, 13,* 303–332.

McLaughlin, M., and Cody, M. J. (1982). Awkward silences: Behavioral antecedents and consequences of the conversational lapse. *Human Communication Research, 8,* 229–316.

d Haight, L. (1985). The "competent
    ...ator" as a cognitive prototype. *Human
    ...tion Research, 12,* 225 – 242.
        ....1977). Guidelines for cross-cultural
    ...munication effectiveness. *Group and Organiza-
    tional Studies, 12,* 225 – 242.
Ruben, B. D. (1989). The study of cross-cultural
    competence: Traditions and contemporary issues.
    *International Journal of Intercultural Relations, 13,*
    229 – 239.
Spitzberg, B. H. (1989). Issues in the development of
    a theory of interpersonal competence in the inter-
    cultural context. *International Journal of Intercul-
    tural Relations, 13,* 241 – 268.
Spitzberg, B. H., and Cupach, W. R. (1984). *Interper-
    sonal Communication Competence.* Beverly Hills,
    Calif.: Sage.
Spitzberg, B. H., and Hecht, M. L. (1984). A compo-
    nent model of relational competence. *Human Com-
    munication Research, 10,* 575 – 600.
Vause, C. J., and Wiemann, J. M. (1981). Communica-
    tion strategies for role invention. *Western Journal of
    Speech Communication, 45,* 241 – 251.
Wiemann, J. M., and Bradac, J. J. (1989). "Metatheoret-
    ical Issues in the Study of Communication Compe-
    tence: Structural and Functional Approaches." In
    B. Dervin and M. J. Voight (Eds.), *Progress in Com-
    munication Sciences,* Vol. 9, 261 – 284. Norwood,
    N.J.: Ablex.

# *Understanding Communication of Persons with Disabilities as Cultural Communication*

## DAWN O. BRAITHWAITE
## CHARLES A. BRAITHWAITE

Jonathan is an articulate, intelligent, thirty-five-year-old professional man who has used a wheelchair since he became paraplegic at age twenty. He recalls taking an able-bodied woman out to dinner at a nice restaurant. When the waitress came to take their order, she looked only at his date and asked, in a condescending tone, "And what would *he* like to eat for dinner?" At the end of the meal the waitress presented Jonathan's date with the check and thanked her for her patronage.[1]

Jeff, an able-bodied student, was working with a group that included Helen, who uses a wheelchair. He related an incident that really embarrassed him. "I wasn't thinking and I said to the group, "Let's run over to the student union and get some coffee." I was mortified when I looked over at Helen and remembered that she can't walk. I felt like a real jerk." Helen later described the incident with Jeff, recalling:

*At yesterday's meeting, Jeff said, "Let's run over to the union" and then he looked over at me and I thought he would die. It didn't bother me at all; in fact, I use that phrase myself. I felt bad that Jeff was so embarrassed, but I didn't know what to say. Later in the*

This original essay appears here for the first time. All rights reserved. Permission to reprint must be obtained from the authors and the publisher. Dawn O. Braithwaite and Charles A. Braithwaite teach in the Department of Communication Studies, Arizona State University West, Phoenix, Arizona.

*group meeting I made it a point to say, "I've got to be running along now." I hope that Jeff noticed and felt OK about what he said.*

Although it may seem hard to believe, these scenarios represent common experiences for people with physical disabilities and are indicative of what often happens when disabled and able-bodied people communicate.

The passage of the Americans with Disabilities Act (ADA), a "bill of rights" for persons with disabilities, highlighted the fact that they are now a large, vocal, and dynamic group within the United States (Braithwaite & Labrecque, 1994). Disabled people represent one group within American culture that is growing in numbers. Persons with disabilities constitute as much as 7 percent of the population and are the largest minority group in certain states (Wheratt, 1988). There are two reasons for increases in the numbers of persons with disabilities. First, as the American population ages and has a longer life expectancy, more people will live long enough to develop age-related disabilities. Second, advances in medical technologies now allow persons with disabilities to survive life-threatening illnesses and injuries where survival was not possible in earlier times. For example, when actor Christopher Reeve became quadriplegic after a horse-riding accident in May 1995, newer advances in medical technology allowed him to survive his injuries and to live with a severe disability.

In the past, most people with disabilities were sheltered, and many were institutionalized; but today they are very much a part of the American mainstream. Each of us will have contact with people who have disabilities within our families, among our friends, or within the workplace. Some of us will develop disabilities ourselves. Says Marie, a college student who became paralyzed after diving into a swimming pool:

*I knew there were disabled people around, but I never thought this would happen to me. I never even knew a disabled person before I became one. If before this happened, I saw a person in a wheelchair, I would have been uncomfortable and not known what to say.*

Marie's comment highlights the fact that many able-bodied people feel extremely uncomfortable interacting with disabled people. But as people with disabilities continue to move into mainstream culture, both able-bodied and disabled persons will need to know how to communicate with one another.

## Disability and Cultural Communication

The goal of this essay is to focus on communication between able-bodied persons and persons with disabilities as *intercultural communication* (Carbaugh, 1990). The claim for the term *intercultural* is made because, as will be demonstrated later, persons with disabilities use a distinctive speech code which implicates specific models of personhood, society, and strategic action that are qualitatively different from those models used by able-bodied persons. Because persons with disabilities are treated so differently in American society, distinctive meanings, rules, and speech habits develop that act as a powerful resource for creating and reinforcing perceptions of cultural differences between those with disabilities and those who are able-bodied. The distinctive verbal and nonverbal communication used by persons with disabilities creates a sense of cultural identity that constitutes a unique social reality.

Several researchers have described the communication of disabled and able-bodied persons as cultural communication (Braithwaite, 1990, 1996; Emry & Wiseman, 1987; Padden & Humphries, 1988). That is, we recognize that persons with disabilities develop certain unique communicative characteristics that are not shared by the majority of able-bodied individuals in U.S. society. In fact, except for individuals who are born with disabilities, becoming disabled means assimilating from being a member of the able-bodied majority to being a member of a minority co-culture (Braithwaite, 1990). In other words, the onset of a physical disability requires learning new ways of talking about the self and developing new ways of engaging in interaction with others.

Adopting a cultural view in this essay, we start by introducing communication problems that can arise between persons in the able-bodied culture and those in the disabled culture. Second, we discuss some of the weaknesses of the earlier research on communication between able-bodied and disabled persons. Third, we discuss research findings from interviews with people who have physical disabilities. Results from these interviews show that people with disabilities are engaged in a process of redefinition; that is, they critique the prevailing stereotypes about disability, and they communicate strategically in order to redefine what it means to be disabled. Finally, we will talk about important contributions both scholars and students of intercultural communication can make to improving relations between disabled and able-bodied people.

## Challenges for Disabled Communicators

When we adopt a cultural view and attempt to understand the communicative challenges faced by people with disabilities, it is useful to distinguish between *disability* and handicap. Even though the two terms are often used interchangeably in everyday speech, their meanings are quite different. The two terms implicate different relationships between persons with disabilities and society. People with disabilities are challenged to overcome the barriers associated with their disability as it affects all areas of their lives. Crewe and Athelstan (1985) identified five "key life functions" that may be affected by disability: (1) mobility, (2) employment, (3) self-care, (4) social relationships, and (5) communication. People are often able to compensate for physical challenges associated with the first three key life functions through assisting devices, such as wheelchairs or canes, through training on how to take care of one's personal needs, and through occupational therapy to find suitable employment.

A disability becomes a handicap when the physical or social environment interacts with it to impede a person in some aspect of his or her life (Crewe & Athelstan, 1985). For example, a disabled individual with paraplegia can function well in the physical environment using a wheelchair, ramps, and curb cuts, but he or she is handicapped when buildings and/or public transportation are not accessible to wheelchairs. When a society is willing and/or able to create adaptations, disabled persons have the ability to achieve increasingly independent lives (Cogswell, 1977; DeLoach & Greer, 1981). Higgins (1992) highlights the drive toward independence and the political activism of disabled people, which has resulted in laws like the ADA. He goes on to say that disabled citizens themselves are "'standing up' . . . and working to revise the disabling practices and policies that have remade disability" (p. 249).

In fact, it is important to realize that adaptations are regularly made to the physical environment and that these are used by *all* people, not just people who are disabled. Most of us are unaware of just how handicapped we would be without these physical adaptations. For example, our offices are located on the second floor of a three-story building. We know that stairs take up a significant amount of space in a building. Space used for the stairwell on each level takes the place of at least one office. The most space-efficient way to get people to the second floor would be a climbing rope, which would necessitate a relatively small opening on each floor. However, very few of us could climb a rope to reach our offices on the second story, so we would be handicapped without stairs or elevators. Similarly, physical adaptations made to accommodate people with disabilities are also useful for nondisabled people as well. When a parent is out with a baby in a stroller or when a student is walking with a heavy load of library books, automatic door openers, ramps, curb cuts, elevators, and larger doorways become important environmental adaptations. Physical limitations become disabilities for all of us when the physical environment cannot be adapted to preempt our shortcomings.

## Challenges to Relationships Between Disabled and Able-Bodied Persons

While it is possible to identify and cope with the physical challenges associated with mobility, self-care, and employment, disabled persons often find the two key life functions of social relationships and communication to be much more formidable. It is less difficult to detect and correct physical barriers than it is to deal with the insidious social barriers facing people with disabilities. Coleman and DePaulo (1991) would label social barriers as "psychological disabling," which is even more common in Western culture where "much value is placed on physical bodies and physical attractiveness" (p. 64).

When nondisabled and disabled people begin to get to know one another, the challenges associated with forming any new relationship are greater. For able-bodied people, this may be due to high uncertainty about how to talk with a person who is disabled. They feel uncertain about what to say or how to act because they are afraid of saying or doing the wrong thing or of hurting the disabled person's feelings. As a result, they may feel overly self-conscious, and their actions may be constrained, self-controlled, and rigid because they feel uncomfortable and uncertain (Belgrave & Mills, 1981; Braithwaite, 1990; Higgins, 1992; Weinberg, 1978). Higgins (1992) points out that the able-bodied person may try and communicate appropriately; however, "Wishing to act in a way acceptable to those with disabilities, they may unknowingly act offensively, patronizing disabled people with unwanted sympathy" (p. 105). Interestingly, researchers have found that the type of disability a person possesses does not change the way able-bodied persons react. Able-bodied persons' trepidation about communicating with a disabled person does not differ significantly across different types of disabilities (Fichten, Robillard, Tagalakis, & Amsel, 1991).

Even when an able-bodied person tries to "say the right thing" and communicate verbal acceptance to the person with the disability, his or her nonverbal behavior may communicate rejection and avoidance (Thompson, 1982). For example, it is not uncommon for disabled people to report that an able-bodied person who talks to them may also stand at a greater distance than usual, avoid eye contact, avoid mentioning the disability, or cut the conversation short (Braithwaite, 1990, 1991). In this case, a disability becomes a handicap in the social environment, and it can block the development of a relationship with a nondisabled person. In all, able-bodied people hold many stereotypes of people from the disabled culture. Coleman and DePaulo (1991) discuss some of these stereotypes:

*For example they often perceive [disabled people] as dependent, socially introverted, emotionally unstable, depressed, hypersensitive, and easily offended, especially with regard to their disability. In addition, disabled people are often presumed to differ from able-bodied people in moral character, social skills, and political orientation. . . . (p. 69)*

Our experience has shown us that many able-bodied people recognize what we have just described as representative of communication experiences with, or attitudes toward, people who are disabled. Able-bodied persons may find themselves given conflicting advice, and they often do not know what is expected of them or how to act. On the one hand, they have been taught to "help the handicapped," and, on the other hand, they have been told to "treat all people equally." Americans usually conceptualize people as "individuals" who "have rights" and "make their own choices" (Carbaugh, 1988). However, when able-bodied persons encounter a person with a disability, this model of personhood creates a serious dilemma. For example, should one help people with disabilities open a door or try to help them up if they fall? Able-bodied persons greatly fear saying the wrong thing, such as "See you later!" to a blind person or "Why don't you run by the store on your way home?" to a person using a wheelchair. In the end, it seems to be easier to avoid situations where one might have to interact with a disabled person rather than face feelings of discomfort and uncertainty.

People with disabilities find these situations equally problematic and are well aware of the discomfort of able-bodied people. They are able to describe in great detail both the verbal and nonverbal signals of discomfort and avoidance that able-bodied persons portray (Braithwaite, 1985, 1990). People with disabilities report that when they meet able-bodied persons, they want to get the discomfort "out of the way," and they want the able-bodied person to treat them as a "person like anyone else," rather than focus solely on their disability (Braithwaite, 1985, 1991).

## Problems with the Present Research

When we first began looking at the research on communication between able-bodied and disabled persons, three problems came clearly to the fore-front. First, very little is known about the communication behavior of disabled people. While a few researchers have studied disabled persons' communication, most of them have studied able-bodied persons' reactions to disabled others. These studies on "attitudes toward disabled persons" are analogous to the many studies that look at majority members' attitudes toward other minority groups. A look at the intercultural literature as a whole reveals few studies from the perspective of the minority.

A second, and related, problem was that most researchers talked *about* persons with disabilities, not *with* them. Disabled persons rarely have been represented in survey data; most often these consist of able-bodied people reporting their impressions of disabled people. In experimental studies the disabled person is most often "played" by an able-bodied person using a wheelchair.

Third, and most significantly, the research has been conducted most often from the perspective of the able-bodied person; that is, what should people with disabilities *do* to make able-bodied others feel more comfortable? Coming from this perspective, researchers do not give much consideration to the effects of communication on the person with the disability. For example, several studies revealed that able-bodied persons are more comfortable when disabled persons disclose about their disability, so they suggest that disabled people should self-disclose to make able-bodied others more comfortable. Braithwaite (1991) points out that these researchers have forgotten to look at how self-disclosing might affect disabled persons. Therefore, research oriented toward the able-bodied displays an *ethnocentric bias* that ignores the perspective of the disabled minority. While more recent research has taken the perspective of disabled interactants, we still have an incomplete picture of the communication of disabled persons.

The remainder of this essay presents selected findings from ongoing studies being conducted from the perspectives of disabled people and concerning their communication with able-bodied others. To date, over 100 in-depth interviews have been completed with adults who are physically disabled. All of these people have disabilities that are visible to an observer, but they have no significant communication-related disabilities (such as deafness or speech impairments). The research aims to describe communication with nondisabled people from the frame of reference of people who are disabled. Doing research by talking *with* disabled people helps to bring out information important to them; the researcher strives to describe patterns of responses from the interviews. These studies represent a departure from what most other researchers have done insofar as (1) the interview format allows participants to describe their experiences in detail and (2) the focus is on the perspective of people in the disabled minority.

## Process of Redefinition

A central theme emerging from the interviews was what we call *redefinition;* that is, people who are disabled are critiquing the prevailing stereotypes about being disabled, and they are creating new ways of perceiving themselves and their disability. We were able to see three types of redefinition: (1) redefining the self as part of a "new" culture, (2) redefining the concept of disability, and (3) redefining disability for the dominant culture.

### Redefining the Self as Part of the Disabled Culture

People with disabilities often report seeing themselves as a minority group or a culture. For some of the interviewees, this definition crosses disability lines; that is, their definition of *disabled* includes all those who have disabilities. For others, the definition is not as broad; when they think of disability, they are thinking exclusively about others with the same type of disability they have. For example, some people with mobility-related disabilities also talked about blind and deaf people with whom they discussed disability, and others talked only about other wheelchair users. However narrowly or broadly they defined it, however, many interviewees do see themselves as part of a minority culture. For example, one said that being disabled "is like West Side Story. Tony and Maria; white and Puerto Rican. They were afraid of each other; ignorant of each other's cultures. People are people." Another man explained his view:

*First of all, I belong to a subculture (of disability) because of the way I have to deal with things, being in the medical system, welfare. There is the subculture. . . . I keep one foot in the able-bodied culture and one foot in my own culture. One of the reasons I do that is so that I don't go nuts.*

This man's description of the "balancing act" between cultures demonstrates that membership in the disabled culture has several similarities to the experiences of other American cultural groups. Many of the interviewees have likened their experiences to those of other cultural groups, particularly to the experiences of American ethnic minorities. Interviewees recognized the loss of status and power that comes from being disabled, and they expressed their feeling that many people are uncomfortable with them simply because they are different.

When taking a cultural view, it is important to recognize that not everyone comes to the culture the same way. Some people are born with disabilities, and others acquire them later. For those people who are not born with a disability, membership in the culture is a process that emerges over time. For some, the process is an incremental one, as in the case of a person with a degenerative disease like multiple sclerosis that develops over many years. For a sudden-onset disability, such as breaking one's neck in an accident and "waking up as quadriplegic," moving from the majority (a "normal" person) to the minority (a person who is disabled) may happen in a matter of seconds. This sudden transition into the disabled culture presents many challenges of redefinition and readjustment in all facets of an individual's life (Braithwaite, 1990, 1996; Goffman, 1963).

If disability is a culture, when does one become part of that culture? Even though a person is physically disabled, redefinition of the self, from "normal" or able-bodied to disabled, is a process that develops over time. Braithwaite (1990, 1996) argues that becoming physically disabled does not mean one immediately has an awareness of being part of the disabled culture. In fact, for most people, adjusting to disability happens in a series of stages or phases (DeLoach & Greer, 1981; Padden & Humphries, 1988). First, after becoming disabled, the individual focuses on rehabilitation and all of the physical changes and challenges being experienced. A second phase occurs when the disabled person realizes that his or her life and relationships have changed dramatically and he or she tries to find ways to minimize the effects of their disability. The individual may try to return to normal routines and old relationships. This can be a frustrating phase, because often things have changed more than the person realizes. Especially when trying to reestablish old relationships the recently disabled person may find that old friends are no longer comfortable with him or her or that, without shared activities, the friendships may lapse. It is at this point that the person starts to become aware of operating as a member of a different culture than he or she had belonged to earlier — and assimilation into the new culture begins (Braithwaite, 1990, 1996).

It is in this third phase, what DeLoach and Greer (1981) call Stigma Incorporation, that the individual begins to integrate being disabled into a personal definition of self. Seeing both the positive and negative aspects of being disabled, the person develops ways to cope with the negative aspects of it (DeLoach & Greer, 1981). In this stage of adjustment people with disabilities develop ways of behaving and communicating that allows them to function successfully in the able-bodied culture (Braithwaite, 1990, 1996). This is what Morse and Johnson (1991) call "Regaining Wellness," when individuals regain control of themselves, their relationships, and adapt to new ways of doing things in their lives. It is at this point that they are able to develop communication strategies that help them live successfully in the majority culture (Braithwaite, 1985, 1990, 1991, 1996; Braithwaite & Labrecque, 1994; Emry & Wiseman, 1987; Fox & Giles, in press).

In this phase, then, people incorporate the role of disability in their life. One man said, "You're the same person you were. You just don't do the same things you did before." Another put it this way: "If anyone refers to me as an amputee, that is guaranteed to get me madder than hell! I don't deny the leg amputation, but I am me. I am a whole person. One." It is during this phase that people can come to terms with both the negative and positive changes in their lives. One woman said:

*I find myself telling people that this has been the worst thing that has happened to me. It has also been one of the best things. It forced me to examine what I felt about myself . . . confidence is grounded in me, not in other people. As a woman, not as dependent on clothes, measurements, but what's inside me.*

Finally, in an interview with Barbara Walters, four months after his accident, actor Christopher Reeve demonstrates the concept of Stigma Incorporation:

*You also gradually discover, as I'm discovering, that your body is not you. The mind and the spirit must take over. And that's the challenge as you move from obsessing about "Why me?" and "It's not fair" and move into "Well, what is the potential?" And, now, four months down the line I see opportunities and potential I wasn't capable of seeing back in Virginia in June . . . genuine joy and being alive means more. Every moment is more intense than it ever was.*

## Redefining Disability

A second type of redefinition discussed by interviewees was redefining the concept of disability. For example, to help others redefine disability, one interviewee will say to them: "People will say, 'Thank God I'm not handicapped.' And I'll say, 'Let's see, how tall are you? Tell me how you get something off that shelf up there!'" His goal in this interchange is to make others see disability as one of many *characteristics* of a person. From this perspective, everyone is handicapped in one way or another, by race, sex, height, or physical attributes; and people must work to overcome their handicapping conditions. Short people may need a stool to reach something on a high shelf, and people who

are very tall may be stared at and certainly will not be able to drive small, economy-size cars. Similarly, people with disabilities will be working to adapt to the physical challenges presented to them. One interviewee, who conducts workshops in disability awareness, talked about how he helps able-bodied people redefine disability:

*I will say to people "How many of you made the clothes that you're wearing?" "How many of you grew the food that you ate yesterday?" "How many of you built the house that you live in?" Nobody raises their hand . . . and then after maybe five of those, I'll say "And I bet you think you're independent." . . . And I'll say, "I'll bet you, if we could measure how independent you feel in your life versus how independent I feel in mine, then I would rate just as high you do. And yet here I am 'depending' to have people get me dressed, undressed, on and off the john, etc. It's all in our heads, folks. Nobody is really independent." I can see them kind of go, "Yeah, I never thought of it that way." And they begin to understand how it is that somebody living with this situation can feel independent. That independence really is a feeling and an attitude. It's not a physical reality.*

Redefinition of disability can also be achieved through changing the language we use. One interviewee objected to being called a "handicapped person," preferring the label "persons with a handicapping condition." He explained why: "You emphasize that person's identity and then you do something about the condition." The goal is to speak in ways that emphasize the *person,* rather than their disability. One interviewee who had polio as a child rejected the term "polio victim" and preferred to label herself as "a person whose arms and legs do not function very well." One way we have found to accentuate the person is to talk about "*people* with disabilities" rather than "disabled people." The goal is to stress the person first, before introducing their disability. These are all forms of strategic action that help to create and maintain a sense of unique cultural identity among persons with disabilities.

Redefining disability is also reflected in sensitizing oneself to commonly used labels for being disabled, such as being "a polio victim," "an arthritis sufferer," "confined to a wheelchair," or "wheelchair bound." When trying to redefine disability as a characteristic, one could change these phrases to "a person with polio," "a person who has arthritis," or a "wheelchair user." While, at first glance, some may think this is no more than an attempt at political correctness, those who study language know that the words we use do affect perception. The way people with disabilities are labeled will affect how they are seen and how they see themselves. One of the interviewees discussed her dislike of all the labels that stereotype disabled people negatively. She used a humorous example, talking about what is commonly referred to as "handicapped parking." She explained, "I'd like to call it 'acceptable parking' because there's nothing wrong with the parking — it's not handicapped! The point is, I'd like to stresss more positive terms."

There have also been changes in the terms that refer to able-bodied people. In the interviews it was common to refer to the majority in terms of the minority, talking about "nondisabled" or "nonhandicapped" rather than "able-bodied" or "normal." Several interviewees used the phrase "TABs" as a humorous reference term for able-bodied people. "TAB" is short for "*Temporarily Able-Bodied*." One interviewee joked, "Everyone is a TAB. . . . I just got mine earlier than you!" Being called a TAB serves to remind able-bodied persons that no one is immune from disability. Finally, researcher Susan Fox has suggested that we avoid talking about the communication of disabled and able-bodied people and instead use the phrase "interability communication" (see Fox & Giles, in press). However we do it, whether we are disabled or able-bodied, it is clear that the language we use both creates and reflects our view of people with disabilities.

In addition to redefining disability, the interviewees also redefined "assisting devices" like wheelchairs or canes. For example, one man told the following story about redefining his prosthetic leg:

*Now there were two girls about eight playing and I was in my shorts. And I'll play games with them and say "which is my good leg?" And that gets them to thinking. Well this one (he pats artificial leg) is not nearly as old as the other one!*

Another interviewee redefined assisting devices this way: "Do you know what a cane is? It's a portable railing! The essence of a wheelchair is a seat and wheels. Now, I don't know that a tricycle is not doing the exact same thing."

In these examples, then, the problem is not the disability or the assisting device, but how one views them. Redefining assisting devices also helps us see how they might mean different things to disabled and able-bodied persons. Several interviewees expressed frustration with people who played with their wheelchairs. One interviewee exclaimed, "This chair is not a toy, it is *part of me*. When you touch my chair, you are touching *me*." Another woman, a business executive, expanded on this by saying, "I don't know why people who push my chair feel compelled to make car sounds as they do it."

## Redefining Disability Within the Dominant Culture

Finally, as the interviewees redefine themselves as members of a culture, and as they redefine what it means to have a disabling condition, they are also concerned with trying to change the view of disability within the larger culture (Braithwaite, 1990). From the interviews it was clear that most people with disabilities view themselves as public educators on disability issues. People told stories about taking the time to educate children and adults on what it means to be disabled. They are actively working to change the view of themselves as helpless, as victims, or as ill and to change as well the ensuing treatment such a view brings. One wheelchair user said:

*People do not consider you; they consider the chair first. I was in a store with my purchases on my lap and money on my lap. The clerk looked at my companion and not at me and said, "Cash or charge?"*

This incident with the clerk is a story told by *every* person interviewed in some for or another. Recall Jonathan and his date from the beginning of this essay. One woman, who has multiple sclerosis and uses a wheelchair, told of shopping for lingerie with her husband accompanying her. When they were in front of the lingerie counter, the clerk repeatedly talked only to her husband saying, "And what size does she want?" The woman told her the size, and the clerk looked at the husband and said, "And what color does she want?"

Those with disabilities recognize that able-bodied persons often see them as disabled first and as a person second (if at all). The most common theme expressed by people with disabilities in all of the interviews is that they want to be *treated like a person first*. One man explained what he thought was important to remember: "A lot of people think that handicapped people are 'less than' and I find that it's not true at all." The interviewees rejected those things that would not help them be seen as persons. A man with muscular dystrophy talked about the popular Labor Day telethon:

*I do not believe in those goddamned telethons . . . they're horrible, absolutely horrible. They get into the self-pity, you know, and disabled folk do not need that. Hit people in terms of their attitudes; then try to deal with and process their feelings. And the telethons just go for the heart and leave it there.*

One man suggested what he thought was a more useful approach:

*What I am concerned with is anything that can do away with the "us" versus "them" distinction. Well, you and I are anatomically different, but we're two human beings! And, at the point we can sit down and communicate eyeball to eyeball; the quicker you do that, the better!*

Individually and collectively, people with disabilities do identify themselves as part of a culture. They are involved in a process of redefining themselves, redefining disability, and they want to help nondisabled people internalize a redefinition of people with disabilities as "people first."

## Conclusion

The research we have discussed highlights the usefulness of viewing disability from a cultural perspective. People with disabilities do see themselves as members of a culture, and viewing communication between able-bodied and disabled people from this perspective sheds new light on the communication problems that exist. Emry and Wiseman (1987) argue for the usefulness of intercultural training about disability issues. They call for unfreezing old attitudes about disability and refreezing new ones. Clearly, the interviews indicate that people who have disabilities would seem to agree.

The interviewees were asked whether they had received any sort of training concerning communication – during or after their rehabilitation. We anticipated that they would have been given information to prepare them for changes in their communication and relationships due to being disabled. We speculated that this education would be especially critical for those who experience sudden – onset disabilities because their self-concepts and all of their relationships would undergo sudden, radical changes. Surprisingly, we found that less than 30 percent of the interviewees received disability-related communication training. Clearly, there are some important gaps in the rehabilitation process, and we would argue that intercultural communication scholars have relevant background and experience for the kind of research and training that could help make the transition from majority to minority an easier one (Braithwaite, 1990; Emry & Wiseman, 1987). We also believe that students of intercultural communication should have an advantage in being able to better understand the perspective of people with disabilities, as presented in this essay, and will be able to adapt to communicating with persons in this culture.

As for able-bodied persons who communicate with disabled persons, this intercultural perspective leads to the following proscriptions and prescriptions:

*Don't:*

*assume* persons with disabilities cannot speak for themselves or do things for themselves

*force* your help on persons with disabilities

*avoid* communication with persons who have disabilities simply because you are uncomfortable or unsure *use terms* like "handicapped," "physically challenged," "crippled," "victim," and so on, unless requested to do so by persons with disabilities

*assume* that a disability defines a person

*Do:*

*assume* persons with disabilities can do something unless they communicate otherwise

*let persons with disabilities tell you* if they want something, what they want, and when they want it. If a person with a disability refuses your help, don't go ahead and help anyway. The goal is to give the person with the disability control in the situation

*remember* that persons with disabilities have experienced others' discomfort before and understand how you might be feeling

*use terms* like "*people* with disabilities" rather than "disabled people." The goal is to stress the person first, before introducing their disability

*treat* persons with disabilities as *persons first,* recognizing that you are not dealing with a disabled person but with *a person* who *has* a disability. This means actively seeking the humanity of the person you are speaking with, and focusing on the person's characteristics instead of the superficial physical appearance. Without diminishing the significance of a physical disability, you can selectively attend to many other aspects of a person during communication.

## Note

1. The quotes and anecdotes in this essay come from in-depth interviews with people who have visible physical disabilities. The names of the participants in these interviews have been changed to protect their privacy.

## References

Belgrave, F. Z., and Mills, J. (1981). Effect upon desire for social interaction with a physically disabled person of mentioning the disability in different contexts. *Journal of Applied Social Psychology, 11*(1), 44–57.

Braithwaite, D. O. (1985). Impression Management and Redefinition of Self by Persons with Disabilities. Paper presented at the annual meeting of the Speech Communication Association, Denver, Colorado, February.

Braithwaite, D. O. (1990). From majority to minority: An analysis of cultural change from ablebodied to disabled. *International Journal of Intercultural Relations, 14,* 465–483.

Braithwaite, D. O. (1991). Just how much did that wheelchair cost?: Management of privacy boundaries by persons with disabilities. *Western Journal of Speech Communication, 55,* 254–274.

Braithwaite, D. O. (1996). "Persons First: Exploring Different Perspectives on the Communication of Persons with Disabilities." In E. B. Ray (Ed.), *Communication and Disenfranchisement: Social Health Issues and Implications.* Hillsdale, N.J.: Lawrence Erlbaum.

Braithwaite, D. O., and Labrecque, D. (1994). Responding to the Americans with Disabilities Act: Contributions of interpersonal communication research and training. *Journal of Applied Communication, 22*(3), 287–294.

Carbaugh, D. (1988). *Talking American.* Norwood, N.J.: Ablex.

Carbaugh, D. (Ed.). (1990). *Cultural Communication and Intercultural Contact.* Hillsdale, N.J.: Lawrence Erlbaum.

Cogswell, B. E. (1977). "Self Socialization: Readjustments of Paraplegics in the Community." In R. P. Marinelli and A. E. Dell Orto (Eds.), *The Psychological and Social Impact of Physical Disability,* 151–159. New York: Springer.

Coleman, L. M., and DePaulo, B. M. (1991). "Uncovering the Human Spirit: Moving Beyond Disability and 'Missed' Communications." In N. Coupland, H. Giles, and J. M. Wiemann (Eds.), *Miscommunication and Problematic Talk,* 61–84. Newbury Park, Calif.: Sage.

Crewe, N., and Athelstan, G. (1985). *Social and Psychological Aspects of Physical Disability.* Minneapolis: University of Minnesota, Department of Independent Study and University Resources.

DeLoach, C., and Greer, B. G. (1981). *Adjustment to Severe Disability.* New York: McGraw-Hill.

Emry, R., and Wiseman, R. L. (1987). An intercultural understanding of ablebodied and disabled persons' communication. *International Journal of Intercultural Relations, 11,* 7–27.

Fichten, C. S., Robillard, K., Tagalakis, V., and Amsel, R. (1991). Casual interaction between college students with various disabilities and their nondisabled peers: The internal dialogue. *Rehabilitation Psychology, 36*(1), 3–20.

Fox, S. A., and Giles, H. (in press). "Let the Wheelchair Through!" In W. P. Robinson (Ed.), *Social Psychology and Social Identity: Festschrift in Honor of Henri Tajfel.* Amsterdam: Elsevier.

63). *Stigma: Notes on the Management* ntity. New York: Simon & Schuster.
992). *Making Disability: Exploring the mation of Human Variation.* Spring-les C. Thomas.

, and Johnson, J. L. (1991). *The Illness Experience: Dimensions of Suffering.* Newbury Park, Calif.: Sage.

Padden, C., and Humphries, T. (1988). *Deaf in America: Voices from a Culture.* Cambridge: Harvard University Press.

Thompson, T. L. (1982). Disclosure as a disability-management strategy: A review and conclusions. *Communication Quarterly, 30,* 196-202.

Weinberg, N. (1978). Modifying social stereotypes of the physically disabled. *Rehabilitation Counseling Bulletin, 22*(2), 114-124.

Wheratt, R. (1988). "Minnesota Disabled to Be Heard." *Star Tribune,* August 1, pp. 1, 6.

# Gender, Communication, and Culture

## JULIA T. WOOD

*"MEN AND WOMEN: CAN WE GET ALONG? SHOULD WE EVEN TRY?"*

Blazing across the cover of a January 1993 popular magazine, this headline announces the drama of gender, communication, and culture. Asking whether we should *even try* to get along, the magazine suggests the effort to build relationships between women and men may require more effort than it's worth. Useful as this media hype might be in selling the magazine, it's misleading in several respects. One problem is that the headline focuses on sex as the source of differences when actually, as we will see in this article, sex has very little to do with how people get along. Gender, however, has a great deal of impact on human interaction. The magazine's cover also exaggerates the difficulty of creating and sustaining satisfying relationships between the genders. If you understand why feminine and masculine cultures differ and how each communicates, it's likely you won't have a great deal of trouble getting along with people of both genders. It's also likely you'll decide it is worth the effort of trying to get along!

This article will help you understand how differences between gender cultures infuse communication. We follow the drama of culture, communication, and gender in two ways. In Act I of this drama, we consider how communication produces and reproduces cultural definitions of mas-

This essay first appeared in the seventh edition. All rights reserved. Permission to reprint must be obtained from the author and the publisher. Julia T. Wood teaches at the University of North Carolina at Chapel Hill.

culinity and femininity. Act II explores masculine and feminne cultures to discover why the genders differ in when, how, and why they use communication. To conclude, Act III offers suggestions for ways we might bridge communication gaps that sometimes interfere with effective interaction in cross-cultural gender communication.

What makes something a culture instead of just a quality common to a number of individuals? For instance, although all people with blue eyes share a common characteristic, we don't consider them a culture. Why then would we regard masculinity and femininity as different cultures? What are feminine and masculine gender cultures, and how are they created? How do differences in gender cultures affect communication? How do we learn to translate each other's communication and to develop a second language ourselves? These are the questions we pursue in this reading.

## The Social-Symbolic Construction of Gender

Perhaps you have noticed that I use the terms *feminine* and *masculine* rather than women and men. The former refer to gender and the latter to sex, which are distinct phenomena. *Women, men, male,* and *female* are words that specify sexual identities, which biology determines. In contrast, feminine and masculine designate genders, which are socially constructed meanings for sex. Before we can understand why gender is a culture, we need to clarify what gender is and how it differs from sex.

### Sex

*Sex* is determined by genetic codes that program biological features. Of the forty-nine pairs of human chromosomes, one pair controls sex. Usually this unit has two chromosomes, one of which is always an X chromosome. If the second chromosome is a Y, the fetus is male; if it is an X, the fetus is female. (Other combinations have occurred: XYY, XXY, XO, and XXX.) During gestation, genetic codes direct the production of hormones so that fetuses receive hormones that develop genitalia and secondary sex characteristics consistent with their genetic makeup. (Again there are exceptions, usu-

ally caused by medical interventions. See Wood, 1993a for a more thorough discussion.)

Aided and abetted by hormones, genetics determine biological features that we use to classify male and female sex: external genitalia (the clitoris and vagina for a female, the penis and testes for a male) and internal sex organs (the uterus and ovaries in females, the prostate in males). Hormones also control secondary sex characteristics such as percentage of body fat (females have more fat to protect the womb when a fetus is present), how much muscle exists, and amount of body hair. There are also differences in male and female brains. Females generally have greater specialization in the right hemisphere which controls integrative and creative thinking, while males typically have more developed left lobes, which govern analytic and abstract thought. Generally, females also have better developed corpus callosa, which are the bundles of nerves connecting the two brain lobes. This suggests women may be more able to cross to the left hemisphere than men are to cross to the right. All of these are sex differences directed by genetics and biology.

### Gender

*Gender* is considerably more complex than sex. For starters you might think of gender as the cultural meaning of sex. A culture constructs gender by arbitrarily assigning certain qualities, activities, and identities to each sex and by then inscribing these assignments into the fabric of social life. Cultural constructions of gender are communicated to individuals through a range of structures and practices that make up our everyday world. From birth on, individuals are besieged with communication that presents cultural prescriptions for gender as natural and right. Beginning with the pink and blue blankets still used in many hospitals, gender socialization continues in interactions with parents, teachers, peers, and media. Throughout our interaction with others, we receive constant messages that reinforce females' conformity to femininity and males' to masculinity. This reveals gender is a social creation, not an individual characteristic.

The process of gender socialization is constant and thorough, so it generally succeeds in persuading individuals to adopt the gender society endorses for them. This means that individuals are not born with a gender, but we *become* gendered as we internalize and then embody our society's views of femininity and masculinity. Although some people resist gender socialization, the intensity and pervasiveness of social prescriptions for gender ensure most females will become feminine and most males will become masculine. This article should give you insight into your own gender so that you may decide whether you are masculine, feminine, or a combination of genders.

Gender refers to social beliefs and values that specify what sex *means* and what it allows and precludes in a particular society at a specific time. Because cultures vary and each one changes over time, the meaning of gender is neither universal nor stable. Instead, femininity and masculinity reflect the beliefs and values of particular cultures at certain points. The pervasive presence of socially constructed meanings of gender in our lives makes them seem natural, normal, right. Since cultures systematically normalize arbitrary definitions of gender, we seldom reflect on how *unnatural* it is that half of humans are assumed to be more passive, emotional, and interested in caring for others than the other half. If we do reflect on social definitions of masculinity and femininity, they don't make a great deal of sense (Janeway, 1971; Miller, 1986)!

In summary, gender and sex are not synonymous. Sex is biological, while gender is socially constructed. Sex is established by genetics and biology, while gender is produced and reproduced by society. Barring surgery, sex is permanent, while gender varies over time and across cultures. Sex is an individual property, while gender is a social and relational quality which gains meaning from prevailing social interests and contrast with the other gender. What we've covered so far explains the first relationship among gender, communication, and culture: We see that societies create meanings of gender that are communicated through an array of cultural structures and practices; in turn, individuals become gendered as they embody social prescriptions in their personal identities. We turn now to the second relationship, which concerns how social-symbolic constructions of gender establish

codes of conduct, thought, and communication that create distinct gender cultures.

## Feminine and Masculine Communication Cultures

Beginning in the 1970s scholars noticed that some groups of people share communication practices not common to outsiders. This led to the realization that there are distinctive speech communities, or communication cultures. William Labov (1972, p. 121) defined a communication culture as existing when a set of norms regarding how to communicate is shared by a group of people. Within a communication culture, members embrace similar understandings of how to use talk and what purposes it serves.

Once scholars realized distinctive communication cultures exist, they identified many, some of which are discussed in this book: African Americans, older people, Indian Native Americans, gay men, lesbians, and people with disabilities. Members in each of these groups share perspectives that outsiders don't have, and their distinctive values, viewpoints, and experiences influence how each culture uses language. This holds true for gender cultures since women and men in general have different perspectives on why, when, and how to communicate.

Feminine and masculine communication cultures have been mapped out by a number of scholars (Aries, 1987; Beck, 1988; Coates & Cameron, 1989; Johnson, 1989; Kramarae, 1981; Spender, 1984; Tannen, 1990a, b; Treichler & Kramarae, 1983; Wood, 1993a, b, c, d; Wood & Inman, 1993). Their research reveals that most girls and women operate from assumptions about communication and use rules for communicating that differ significantly from those endorsed by most boys and men. I use the qualifying word, "most," to remind us we are discussing general differences, not absolute ones based on sex. Some women are not socialized into feminine culture or they reject it; likewise, some men do not identify with masculine culture. For the most part, however, females are socialized into feminine culture and males into masculine culture. How that transpires is our next consideration.

mother — must pull away from the first relationship to establish selfhood. We see, then, a basic difference in the foundation of the sexes' identities: Girls tend to define self in relation to others, while boys typically define self independent of others.

Whether we think of ourselves as fundamentally connected to others (within relationship) or separate from them (independent of relationship) influences how we perceive ourselves and how we interact with others (Gilligan, 1982; Riessman, 1990; Surrey, 1983). In general, males (children and adults) maintain a greater degree of distance between themselves and others than do females. This makes sense since closeness with mothers facilitates daughters but interferes with sons in their efforts to define a self. Given these different bases of identity, it's hardly surprising that girls and women are generally comfortable building close relationships and disclosing to others, while most boys and men are reserved about involvements and disclosures (Aries, 1987; Wood, 1993a). Important as the mother-child relationship is, however, it isn't the only factor that cultivates gender identities.

## The Games Children Play

Augmenting psychodynamic influences on gender identity is communication that occurs in childhood games. Insight into this area was pioneered by Daniel Maltz and Ruth Borker (1982), who studied children at play. The researchers noticed recreation was usually sex-segregated, and boys and girls tended to favor discrete kinds of games. While girls were more likely to play house, school, or jump rope, boys tended to play competitive team sports like football and baseball. Because different goals, strategies and relationships characterize girls' and boys' games, the children learned divergent rules for interaction. Engaging in play, Maltz and Borker concluded, contributes to socializing children into masculine and feminine communication cultures.

**Girls Games.** Most girls' games require just two or three people so they promote personal relationships. Further, these games don't have preset or fixed rules, roles, and objectives. While touchdowns and home runs are goals in boys' games and roles such as pitcher, lineman, and blocker are clearly

Gender is not merely a role; it is a core aspect of identity which is central to how we perceive ourselves and how we act in the world (Rakow, 1986; Zimmerman & West, 1975). In her classic book, *The Reproduction of Mothering,* psychiatrist Nancy Chodorow (1978) claims that gender identity is profoundly shaped by psychological dynamics in families and most particularly by mother-child relationships in the early years. According to Chodorow, it is significant that the primary caregiver for most children is a female, usually the mother. Mothers form different relationships with sons and daughters, and these differences cultivate masculine and feminine gender identities.

Between a mother and daughter, argue Chodorow and other clinicians (Eichenbaum & Orbach, 1983; Miller, 1986; Surrey, 1983), there is a basic identification as members of the same sex. Because daughters identify with mothers, they can develop their identities inside of that primary relationship. A son, however, cannot identify fully with the mother because she is female. Thus, to develop a gender identity, sons must differentiate from specified, how to play house is open to negotiation. To make their games work, girls talk with each other and agree on rules, roles, and goals: "You be the mommy and I'll be the daddy, and we'll clean house." From unstructured, cooperative play, girls learn three basic rules for how to communicate:

1. Be cooperative, collaborative, inclusive. It's important that everyone feel involved and have a chance to play.

2. Don't criticize or outdo others. Cultivate egalitarian relationships so the group is cohesive and gratifying to all.

3. Pay attention to others' feelings and needs and be sensitive in interpreting and responding to them.

In sum, girls' games occur within a gender culture that emphasizes relationships more than outcomes, sensitivity to others, and cooperative, inclusive interpersonal orientations.

**Boys' Games.** Unlike girls' games, those that boys tend to play involved fairly large groups (baseball requires nine players plus extras to fill in) and proceed by rules and goals that are externally established and constant. Also, boys' games allow for individual stars—MVP, for instance—and, in fact, a boy's status depends on his rank relative to others. The more structured, large, and individualized character of boys' games teaches them three rules of interaction:

1. Assert yourself. Use talk and action to highlight your ideas and to establish your status and leadership.

2. Focus on outcomes. Use your talk and actions to make things happen, to solve problems, and achieve goals.

3. Be competitive. Vie for the talk stage. Keep attention focused on you, outdo others, and make yourself stand out.

Boys' games, then, emphasize achievement—both for the team and the individual members. The goals are to win for the team and to be the top player on it. Interaction is more an arena for negotiating power and status than for building relationships with others, and competitiveness eclipses cooperativeness as the accepted style in masculine communication cultures.

The characteristics of boys' and girls' games lead to distinctive understandings of what talk does and how we should use it. Differences Maltz and Borker identified in children's play are ones that we carry forward into adulthood so they punctuate communication between adult women and men. So divergent are some of women's and men's understandings of communication that linguist Deborah Tannen (1990b, p. 42) claims "communication between men and women can be like cross culture communication, prey to a clash of conversational styles."

In combination, psychodynamic theories and social science research offer a coherent picture of how gender cultures are produced and what they entail. Feminine socialization emphasizes relationships and sensitivity to people and the process of interaction, while masculine socialization stresses independence, power, and attention to outcomes. Table 1 summarizes how these differences in gender cultures affect communication.

## Men and Women in Conversation: Cross-Cultural Communication

As males and females learn the rules of distinctive gender cultures, they embody them in their personal identities, and this reproduces prevailing social meanings of the genders. One implication of being socialized into gendered identities is that there are generalizable differences in feminine and masculine styles of communication. These differences frequently lead to misunderstandings in cross-gender interaction.

### Gender Gaps in Communication

To illustrate the practical consequences of differences we've identified, let's consider some concrete cases of cross-cultural gender communication. Following are five examples of common problems in communication between women and men. As you read them, you'll probably find that several are familiar to you.

**Table 1** Differences Between Feminine and Masculine Communication Culture

| Feminine Talk | Masculine Talk |
|---|---|
| 1. Use talk to build and sustain rapport with others. | 1. Use talk to assert yourself and your ideas. |
| 2. Share yourself and learn about others through disclosing. | 2. Personal disclosures can make you vulnerable. |
| 3. Use talk to create symmetry or equality between people. | 3. Use talk to establish your status and power. |
| 4. Matching experiences with others shows understanding and empathy ("I know how you feel.") | 4. Matching experiences is a competitive strategy to command attention. ("I can top that.") |
| 5. To support others, express understanding of their feelings. | 5. To support others, do something helpful — give advice or solve a problem for them. |
| 6. Include others in conversation by asking their opinions and encouraging them to elaborate. Wait your turn to speak so others can participate. | 6. Don't share the talk stage with others; wrest it from them with communication. Interrupt others to make your own points. |
| 7. Keep the conversation going by asking questions and showing interest in others' ideas. | 7. Each person is on her or his own; it's not your job to help others join in. |
| 8. Be responsive. Let others know you hear and care about what they say. | 8. Use responses to make your own points and to outshine others. |
| 9. Be tentative so that others feel free to add their ideas. | 9. Be assertive so others perceive you as confident and in command. |
| 10. Talking is a human relationship in which details and interesting side comments enhance depth of connection. | 10. Talking is a linear sequence that should convey information and accomplish goals. Extraneous details get in the way and achieve nothing. |

*What counts as support?* Rita is really bummed out when she meets Mike for dinner. She explains that she's worried about a friend who has begun drinking heavily. When Mike advises her to get her friend into counseling, Rita repeats how worried she feels. Next, Mike tells Rita to make sure her friend doesn't drive after drinking. Rita explodes that she doesn't need advice. Irritated at her lack of appreciation for his help, Mike asks, "Then why did you ask for it?" In exasperation Rita responds, "Oh, never mind, I'll talk to Betsy. At least she cares how I feel."

*Tricky feedback* Roseann and Drew are colleagues in a marketing firm. One morning he drops into her office to run an advertising play by her. As Drew discusses his ideas, Roseann nods and says "Um," "Un huh" and "Yes." When he finishes and asks what she thinks, Roseann says "I really don't think that plan will sell the product." Feeling misled, Drew demands, "Then why were you agreeing the whole time I presented my idea?" Completely confused, Roseann responds, "What makes you think I was agreeing with you?"

*Expressing care* Dedrick and Melita have been dating for two years and are very serious. To celebrate their anniversary Melita wants to spend a quiet evening in her apartment where they can talk about the relationship and be with just each other. When Dedrick arrives, he's planned a dinner and concert. Melita feels hurt that he doesn't want to talk and be close.

*I'd rather do it myself.* Jay is having difficulty writing a paper for his communication class, because he's not sure what the professor wants. When he mentions this to his friend Ellen, she suggests he ask the professor or a classmate to clarify directions. Jay resists, saying "I can figure it out on my own."

*Can we talk about us?* Anna asks her fiancé, Ben. "Can we talk about us?" Immediately Ben feels tense – another problem on the horizon. He guards himself for an unpleasant conversation and reluctantly nods assent. Anna then thanks Ben for being so supportive during the last few months when she was under enormous pressure at her job. She tells him she feels closer than ever. Then she invites him to tell her what makes him feel loved and close to her. Although Ben feels relieved to learn there isn't any crisis, he's also baffled: "If there isn't a problem, why do they need to talk about the relationship? If it's working, let it be."

You've probably been involved in conversations like these. And you've probably been confused, frustrated, hurt, or even angry when a member of the other sex didn't give you what you wanted or didn't value your efforts to be supportive. If you're a woman, you may think Mike should be more sensitive to Rita's feelings and Dedrick should cherish time alone with Melita. If you're a man, it's likely that you empathize with Mike's frustration and feel Rita is giving him a hard time when he's trying to help. Likewise, you may think Melita is lucky to have a guy willing to shell out some bucks so they can do something fun together.

Who's right in these cases? Is Rita unreasonable? Is Melita ungrateful? Are Dedrick and Mike insensitive? Is Jay stubborn? Did Roseann mislead Drew? When we focus on questions like these we fall prey to a central problem in gender communication: the tendency to judge. Because Western culture is hierarchical, we're taught to perceive differences as better and worse not simply as different. Yet, the inclination to judge one person as right and the other wrong whenever there's misunderstanding usually spells trouble for close relationships.

But judging is not the only way we *could* think about these interactions, and it's not the most con-

structive way if our interest is building healthy relationships. Disparaging what differs from our own style only gets in the way of effective communication and satisfying relationships. All of the energy invested in fixing fault or defending our behaviors diminishes what we can devote to learning how to communicate better. What might be more productive than judging is understanding and respecting unique styles of communication. Once we recognize there are different and distinctly valid styles of interacting, we can tune into others' perspectives and interact more constructively with them.

## Understanding Cross-Gender Communication

Drawing upon earlier sections of this article, we can analyze the misunderstandings in these five dialogues and see how they grow out of the different interaction styles cultivated in feminine and masculine communication cultures. Because men and women typically rely on distinct communication rules, they have different ways of showing support, interest, and caring. This implies they may perceive the same communication in dissimilar ways.

In the first scenario, Rita's purpose in talking with Mike isn't just to tell him about her concern for her friend; she also sees communication as a way to connect with Mike (Aries, 1987; Riessman, 1990; Tannen, 1990b; Wood, 1993b). She wants him to respond to her and her feelings, because that will enhance her sense of closeness to him. Schooled in masculinity, however, Mike views communication as an instrument to do things, so he tries to help by giving advice. To Rita it seems he entirely disregards her feelings, so she doesn't feel close to Mike, which was her primary purpose in talking with him. Rita might welcome some advice, but only after Mike responds to her feelings.

In the second example, the problem arises when Drew translates Roseann's feedback according to rules of communication in masculine culture. Women learn to give lots of response cues – verbal and nonverbal behaviors to indicate interest and involvement in conversation – because that's part of using communication to build relationships with others. Masculine culture, however, focuses on outcomes more than processes, so men tend to use feedback to signal specific agreement and disagreement (Beck, 1988; Fishman, 1978; Tannen, 1990b; Wood, 1993a). When Drew hears Roseann's "ums," "uh huhs," and "yeses," he assumes she is agreeing. According to her culture's rules, however, she is only showing interest and being responsive, not signaling agreement.

Dedrick and Melita also experience culture clash in their communication. With feminine culture, talking is a way – probably the primary way – to express and expand closeness. For women there is closeness in dialogue (Aries, 1987; Riessman, 1990; Wood, 1993b). Masculine socialization, in contrast, stresses doing things and shared activities as primary ways to create and express closeness (Cancian, 1987; Swain, 1989; Wood & Inman, 1993). A man is more likely to express his caring for a woman by doing something concrete for her (washing her car, fixing an appliance) or doing something with her (skiing, a concert, tennis) than by talking explicitly about his feelings. Men generally experience "closeness in doing" (Swain, 1989). By realizing doing things is a valid way to be close, feminine individuals can avoid feeling hurt by partners who propose activities. In addition, women who want to express care in ways men value might think about what they could do for or with the men, rather than what they could say (Riessman, 1990).

Masculinity's emphasis on independence underlies Jay's unwillingness to ask others for help in understanding his assignment. As Tannen (1990b) points out rather humorously, men invariably resist asking directions when they are lost on the road while women don't hesitate to ask strangers for help. What we've discussed about gender identity helps us understand this difference. Because women initially develop identity within relationships, connections with others are generally sought and welcomed – even the casual connection made in asking for directions or help with an assignment. In contrast, men differentiated from their first relationship to develop identity, so relationships have an undertone of danger – they could jeopardize independence. So Jay's refusal to ask others for help reflects the masculine emphasis on maintaining autonomy and not appearing weak or incompetent to others.

Unless Ellen realizes this difference between them, Jay will continue to baffle her.

In the final case we see a very common example of culture-clash in gender communication. Feminine culture prioritizes relationships so they are a constant source of interest, attention, and communication. In contrast, within masculine culture relationships are not as central and talk is perceived as a way to do things such as solve problems rather than a means to enhance closeness (Wood, 1993a, b, c). Given these disparate orientations, "talking about us" means radically different things to most men and women. As Tannen (1986) points out, men generally feel a relationship is going along fine if there's no need to talk about it, while women tend to feel a relationship is good as long as they are talking about it! Anna's wish to discuss the relationship because it's so good makes no sense to Ben, and his lack of interest in a conversation about the relationship hurts Anna. Again, each person errs in relying on inappropriate rules to interpret the other's communication.

Most problems in cross-cultural gender communication result from faulty translations. This happens when men interpret women according to rules of masculine culture and when women interpret men according to rules of feminine culture. Just as we wouldn't assume Western rules apply to Asian people, so we'd be wise not to imagine one gender's rules pertain to the other. When we understand there are distinct gender cultures and when we respect the logic of each one, we empower ourselves to communicate in ways that enhance our relationships.

## Communicating Effectively Between Gender Cultures

Whether it's a Northern American thinking someone who eats with hands is "uncouth" or a woman assuming a man is "closed" because he doesn't disclose as much as she does, we're inclined to think what differs from our customs is wrong. Ethnocentric judgments seldom improve communication or enhance relationships. Instead of debating whether feminine or masculine styles of communication are better, we should learn to see differences as merely that – differences. The information we've covered, combined with this book's emphasis on understanding and appreciating culturally diverse communication, can be distilled into six principles for effective cross-gender communication.

1. *Suspend judgment.* This is first and foremost, because as long as we are judging differences, we aren't respecting them. When you find yourself confused in cross-gender conversations, resist the tendency to judge. Instead, explore constructively what is happening and how you and your partner might better understand each other.

2. *Recognize the validity of different communication styles.* In cross-gender communication, we need to remind ourselves there is a logic and validity to both feminine and masculine communication styles. Feminine emphases on relationships, feelings, and responsiveness don't reflect inability to adhere to masculine rules for competing any more than masculine stress on instrumental outcomes is a failure to follow feminine rules for sensitivity to others. It is inappropriate to apply a single criterion – either masculine or feminine – to both genders' communication. Instead, we need to realize different goals, priorities, and standards pertain to each.

3. *Provide translation cues.* Now that you realize men and women tend to learn different rules for interaction, it makes sense to think about helping the other gender translate your communication. For instance, in the first example Rita might have said to Mike, "I appreciate your advice, but what I need first is for you to deal with my feelings." A comment such as this helps Mike interpret Rita's motives and needs. After all, there's no reason why he should automatically understand rules that aren't a part of his gender culture.

4. *Seek translation cues.* We can also improve our interactions by seeking translation cues from others. If Rita didn't tell Mike how to translate her, he could have asked "What would be helpful to you? I don't know whether you want to talk about how you're feeling or ways to help your friend. Which would be better?" This message communicates clearly that Mike cares about Rita and he wants to support her if she'll just tell him how. Similarly, in-stead of blowing up when Roseann disagreed with him and assuming she had deliberately misled him, Drew might have taken a more constructive approach and said, "I thought your feedback during my spiel indicated agreement with what I was saying. What did it mean?" This kind of response would allow Drew to learn something new.

5. *Enlarge your own communication style.* Studying other cultures' communication teaches us not only about other cultures, but also about ourselves. If we're open to learning and growing, we can enlarge our own communication repertoire by incorporating skills more emphasized in other cultures. Individuals socialized into masculinity could learn a great deal from feminine culture about how to support friends. Likewise, people from feminine cultures could expand the ways they experience intimacy by appreciating "closeness in the doing" that is a masculine speciality. There's little to risk and much to gain by incorporating additional skills into our personal repertoires.

6. *Suspend judgment.* If you're thinking we already covered this principle, you're right. It's important enough, however, to merit repetition. Judgment is so thoroughly woven into Western culture that it's difficult not to evaluate others and not to defend our own positions. Yet as long as we're judging others and defending ourselves, we're probably making no headway in communicating more effectively. So, suspending judgment is the first and last principle of effective cross-gender communication.

## Summary

As women and men, we've been socialized into gendered identities, ones that reflect cultural constructions of femininity and masculinity. We become gendered as we interact with our families, childhood peers, and others who teach us what gender means and how we are to embody it in our attitudes, feelings, and interaction styles. This means communication produces, reflects, and reproduces gender cultures and imbues them with a taken-for-granted status that we seldom notice or question. Through an ongoing, cyclical process communication, culture, and gender constantly recreate one another.

Because we are socialized into distinct communication cultures, women and men tend to communicate for different reasons and in different ways. When we fail to recognize that genders rely on dissimilar rules for talk, we tend to misread each other's meanings and motives. To avoid the frustration, hurt, and misunderstandings that occur when we apply one gender's rules to the other gender's communication, we need to recognize and respect the distinctive validity and value of each style.

## "Men and Women: Can We Get Along? Should We Even Try?"

Chances are pretty good we will keep trying to get along. Relationships between women and men are far too exciting, frustrating, and interesting not to! What we've covered in this article provides a good foundation for the ongoing process of learning not just how to get along with members of the other gender, but to appreciate and grow from valuing the different perspectives on interaction, identity and relationships that masculine and feminine cultures offer.

## References

Aries, E. (1987). "Gender and Communication." In P. Shaver (Ed.), *Sex and Gender,* 149-176. Newbury Park, Calif.: Sage.

Beck, A. (1988). *Love Is Never Enough.* New York: Harper & Row.

Cancian, F. (1987). *Love in America.* Cambridge: Cambridge University Press.

Chodorow, N. J. (1978). *The Reproduction of Mothering: Psychoanalysis and the Sociology of Gender.* Berkeley: University of California Press.

Coates, J., and Cameron, D. (1989). *Women in Their Speech Communities: New Perspectives on Language and Sex.* London: Longman.

Eichenbaum, L., and Orbach, S. (1983). *Understanding Women: A Feminist Psychoanalytic Approach.* New York: Basic Books.

Fishman, P. M. (1978). Interaction: The work women do. *Social Problems, 25,* 397-406.

Gilligan, C. (1982). *In a Different Voice: Psychological Theory and Women's Development.* Cambridge: Harvard University Press.

Janeway, E. (1971). *Man's World, Woman's Place: A Study in Social Mythology.* New York: Dell.

Johnson, F. L. (1989). "Women's Culture and Communication: An Analytic Perspective." In C. M. Lont

and S. A. Friedley (Eds.), *Beyond Boundaries: Sex and Gender Diversity in Communication.* Fairfax, Va.: George Mason University Press.

Kramarae, C. (1981). *Women and Men Speaking: Frameworks for Analysis.* Rowley, Mass.: Newbury House.

Labov, W. (1972). *Sociolinguistic Patterns.* Philadelphia: University of Pennsylvania Press.

Lakoff, R. (1975). *Language and Woman's Place.* New York: Harper & Row.

Maltz, D. N., and Borker, R. (1982). "A Cultural Approach to Male-Female Miscommunication." In J. J. Gumpertz (Ed.), *Language and Social Identity,* 196-216. Cambridge: Cambridge University Press.

Miller, J. B. (1986). *Toward a New Psychology of Women.* Boston: Beacon Press.

Rakow, L. F. (1986). Rethinking gender research in communication. *Journal of Communication, 36,* 11-26.

Riessman, J. M. (1990). *Divorce Talk: Women and Men Make Sense of Personal Relationships.* New Brunswick: Rutgers University Press.

Spender, D. (1984). *Man Made Language.* London: Routledge and Kegan Paul.

Surrey, J. L. (1983). "The Relational Self in Women: Clinical Implications." In J. V. Jordan, J. L. Surrey, and A. G. Kaplan (Speakers), *Women and Empathy: Implications for Psychological Development and Psychotherapy,* 6-11. Wellesley, Mass.: Stone Center for Developmental Services and Studies.

Swain, S. (1989). "Covert Intimacy: Closeness in Men's Friendships." In B. J. Risman and P. Schwartz (Eds.), *Gender and Intimate Realtionships,* 71-86. Belmont, Calif.: Wadsworth.

Tannen, D. (1986). *That's Not What I Meant! How Conversational Style Makes or Breaks Relationships.* New York: Ballantine.

Tannen, D. (1990a). "Gender Differences in Conversational Coherence: Physical Alignment and Topical Cohesion." In B. Dorval (Ed.), *Conversational Organization and Its Development: XXXVIII,* 167-206. Norwood, N.J.: Ablex.

Tannen, D. (1990b). *You Just Don't Understand: Women and Men in Conversation.* New York: William Morrow.

Treichler, P. A., and Kramarae, C. (1983). Women's talk in the ivory tower. *Communication Quarterly, 31,* 118-132.

Wood, J. T. (1993a). *Gendered Lives.* Belmont, Calif.: Wadsworth.

Wood, J. T. (1993b). "Engendered Relationships: Interaction, Caring, Power, and Responsibility in Close Relationships." In S. Duck (Ed.), *Processes in Close Relationships: Contexts of Close Relationships.* Vol. 3. Beverly Hills: Sage.

Wood, J. T. (1993c). "Engendered Identities: Shaping Voice and Mind Through Gender." In D. Vocate

(Ed.), *Intrapersonal Communication: Different Voices, Different Minds*. Hillsdale, N.J.: Lawrence Erlbaum.

Wood, J. T. (1993d). *Who Cares?: Women, Care, and Culture*. Carbondale: Southern Illinois University Press.

Wood, J. T., and Inman, C. C. (1993). In a different mode: Masculine styles of communicating closeness. *Journal of Applied Communication Research*.

Zimmerman, D. H., and West, C. (1975). "Sex Roles, Interruptions, and Silences in Conversation." In B. Thorne and N. Henley (Eds.), *Language and Sex: Difference and Dominance*, 105–129. Rowley, Mass.: Newbury House.

# Understanding the Co-Culture of the Elderly

## VALERY C. McKAY

On January 24, 1995, in his State of the Union Address, President Clinton declared that "our senior citizens have made us what we are today." Who are our senior citizens? Why were they mentioned in a keynote address such as the State of the Union message? Do they deserve a commendation such as Mr. Clinton provided, or is this simply an indication that politicians presume senior citizens to have political power that is not to be ignored? What contributions have senior citizens made to the progress of our society and culture? Are they a culture of their own?

The purpose of this essay is to illustrate, through research literature and example, the characteristics of the co-culture of the elderly. This will be accomplished first by discussing the concept of culture and why the population of senior citizens in our society can be conceptualized *culturally* and not just as a subgroup of our society; second, by noting both the negative and positive stereotypes associated with older adulthood, their origin and their falsity; and third, by illustrating the communicative relationship between grandparents and grandchildren that goes beyond the stereotypes and fears inherent in other relations between young and old generations.

## The Concept of Culture

If we define culture as a "form or pattern for living," then it logically follows that the lifestyle of

This original essay appears here for the first time. All rights reserved. Permission to reprint must be obtained from the author and the publisher. Valery C. McKay teaches at California State University, Long Beach.

our senior citizens might have a character all its own. As a co-culture, senior citizens can certainly be distinguished from the larger culture of which they are a part. If our definition becomes even more specific to include the nature of "language, friendships, eating habits, communication practices, social acts, economic and political activities" (Porter & Samovar, 1985, p. 19), then we may discover valid evidence to substantiate our claim that older adults are a co-culture of their own.

The limitation inherent in conceptualizing a culture or co-culture is the assumption of the homogeneity of the group; in other words, we assume that most people within the co-culture behave *similarly* based upon our *generalized* notion of the group. The result of this assumption is, of course, our tendency to stereotype or form "rigid preconceptions which are applied to all members of a group . . . over a period of time, regardless of individual variations" (Atkinson, Morten, & Sue, 1985, p. 172). Although some may view stereotyping as a means by which we can *generally* understand, or become familiar with, peoples of other cultures or co-cultures, this process often prevents us from really getting to know those individuals whom we encounter in our day-to-day lives. As a result, we don't ask the key questions that get us past the uncertainty and unfamiliarity and into the preliminary stages of relationship (friendship) development. In many cases, the diversity (or heterogeneity) within a culture or co-culture is of more significance than the comparison with an entirely different culture altogether (Catchen, 1989).

## Why We Consider Our Senior Citizens as a Co-Culture

Although this question will be addressed in further detail later in this essay, let's take a moment to find some preliminary evidence for this claim. The first characteristic associated with culture is *language*. Do the elderly speak a different language? That depends, of course, upon which group of older adults you are talking about; there are as many languages being spoken by the elderly as there are cultures represented in our nation today. But if we focus on English, which is the most common language spoken in the United States, we may or may not find

that we are all speaking the same language. Do you know what the term GAP means? (GAP is senior citizen argot, an acronym which stands for "grandparent as parent.")

Our next characteristic is *friendship*. Friendships among the elderly are a source of social support, care giving, transportation and household help, social networking, and emotional satisfaction. Many elderly friendships are long term – the result of many years of development and nurturance. While elderly friendships do not differ significantly in their quality in comparison with other groups, they are especially significant for elderly women who, after the loss of their spouse, are alone, are experiencing a reduction in the quality of life, and are sometimes physically and emotionally isolated from family. In contrast, elderly men, who find themselves alone after the loss of their spouse or with the onset of retirement, are less likely to develop and maintain friendships. For some of these men, the risk of suicide increases with age, accounting for a rate three times that of the general population (Perkins & Tice, 1994). Friendships among older adults appear to be especially significant in meeting both physical and emotional needs.

One more example will suffice to provide preliminary evidence of the existence of our co-culture of older adult citizens: *political activity*. According to Binstock (1992, p. 331), "persons 65 and older do constitute a large block of participating voters. They represent 16.7 – 21% of those who actually voted in national elections during the 1980s. And this percentage is likely to increase in the next four decades because of projected increases in the proportion of older persons." Although an initial interpretation of this statistic might compel visions of an elderly voting conglomerate with only self-interest in mind, the statistic itself fails to reveal the heterogeneity of the older-adult constituency with regard to opinions and interest in political issues (Hess, 1992). "Diversity among older persons may be at least as great with respect to political attitudes and behavior as it is in relation to economic, social, and other characteristics" (Binstock, 1992, p. 331). Nonetheless, in relation to the total voting population, they constitute a significant proportion of participating voters.

We must be cautious in our generalities, however, as these characteristics do differ by factors such as gender, ethnicity, housing and income status, and geographical location. What we are going to find is that our senior citizens are as unique and diverse as most members of the younger population in our society perceive themselves to be (Ade-Ridder & Hennon, 1989). Unfortunately, our negative stereotypes of older adulthood and our persistent pursuit of a youth-oriented society combine to prevent many of us from recognizing the value of the wisdom and experience our seniors have to offer us. What are some of the images that we as a society hold of our aging population?

## The Co-Culture of the Elderly

Who are our senior citizens? Are they really greedy, lonely, afraid, incompetent, senile, sexless, inarticulate, forgetful, depressed, stubborn, and all of the other characteristics composing the negative stereotypes previously mentioned? Let's take a moment to find out who they really are.

## Stereotypes of the Elderly

As previously mentioned, stereotypes are rigid generalities that members of society impose on others with whom they are unfamiliar or whom they do not understand. Stereotypes function as a system of categorization; we often fail to recognize those individuals who do not fit the stereotype. Members of the dominant culture (in this case our youth-oriented culture) commonly stereotype the subordinate and minority culture (the aging population) and draw negative stereotypical inferences both preceding and during intergenerational interaction (Giles, Coupland, Coupland, Williams, & Nussbaum, 1992). Two severe consequences of stereotyping have been noted: First, "those who have preconceived notions about minority group members may unwittingly act upon these beliefs" (Atkinson, Morten, & Sue, 1985, p. 172). Stereotyping might function to unknowingly and unintentionally impose limitations or standards upon a group of people (such as when younger adults use elderspeak or view the elderly as feeble and infirm). Secondly, the group may engage in self-fulfilling

behavior as a consequence of the limitations being imposed upon them (for example, the elderly become reclusive and isolated, unwilling to interact for fear of negative evaluation or embarrassment). Overcoming the tendency to stereotype, though difficult, offers us the opportunity to become familiar with and better understand members of another culture or co-culture and also helps enhance their self-esteem.

Interestingly, social stereotypes of older adults before 1980 are in stark contrast to those after 1980; according to Rosenbaum and Button (1993), this evolution is due, in part, to the Reagan era and political sensitivity to the needs of our aging population. Prior to 1980, the aged were seen as frail, in need of assistance, lacking political strength; in general, they were viewed as a group of deserving poor that had been largely ignored given the prejudices of a youth-oriented society. After 1980 and the years of Reaganomics, the aged were seen as relatively well off, as a potent political force, significantly increasing in numbers, and ready and willing to claim their portion of the federal budget with regard to health and Social Security benefits (Binstock, 1992). As we will see, very few of these stereotypes can be validated with evidence — except, perhaps, for the increasing numbers of baby boomers reaching middle and older adulthood.

At a more interpersonal level, stereotypes of the elderly held by young, middle-aged, and elderly adults were investigated by Hummert, Garstka, Shaner, and Strahm (1994). While both negative and positive stereotypes emerged across all three age groups (young, middle-aged, and elderly), similarities as well as differences in stereotypical characterizations by age groups were noted. A detailed description of this study is beyond the scope of this article; however, some of the characteristics of the stereotypes will be illustrated.

**Positive Stereotypes** Among the positive stereotypes, the "golden ager" is described as active, adventurous, healthy, lively, wealthy, interesting, liberal, and future-oriented (to name only a few characteristics). "Perfect grandparents" are wise, kind, trustworthy, loving, understanding, and family-oriented. The "John Wayne conservative" is retired, conservative, old-fashioned, nostalgic, and religious. The "activist" (a stereotype identified *only* by elderly adults) is political, sexual, health-conscious, and liberal. Finally, the "small-town neighbor" (also identified by elderly adults *only*) is old-fashioned, quiet, conservative, tough, and nostalgic. How many television advertisements can you recall that depict at least one of these elderly stereotypes needing or using their products? Do you find it easy to picture an elderly individual who fits any of these stereotypes? How about one who does not?

Hummert, Gartska, Shaner, and Strahm (1994) found that all three of the age groups (young, middle-aged, and elderly) identified the "golden ager," "perfect grandparent," and "John Wayne conservative" as positive stereotypes of the elderly. The middle-aged group added "liberal matriarch/patriarch," which is described as liberal, mellow, and wealthy. (Is this the way individuals in middle adulthood picture their own parents?) The elderly adult group, as previously mentioned, added "activist" and "small-town neighbor" categories comprising sexuality, political activity, health consciousness, and a strong sense of the past.

**Negative Stereotypes** The negative stereotypes include the "shrew/curmudgeon," who is described as bored, complaining, ill-tempered, bitter, and a hypochondriac. The "despondent" is depressed, hopeless, sick, neglected, and afraid. Those who are "severely impaired" are described as senile, incompetent, incoherent, feeble, sick, slow-thinking, and sexless; "mildly impaired" are tired, frustrated, worried, and lonely. The "recluse" is quiet, timid, dependent, forgetful, and naive. A "self-centered" elder is greedy, miserly, snobbish, emotionless, and humorless. Finally, the "elitist" (identified by elderly adults *only*) is demanding, prejudiced, and wary.

Again, similarities in negative stereotypes across age groups were noted: All three groups identified "shrew/curmudgeon," "despondent," "severely impaired," and "recluse." The middle-aged group added "self-centered," and the elderly adult group, as previously mentioned, added "elitist" and "mildly impaired." While these stereotypes seem harmless and, in some cases, humorous, we must not fail to realize the consequences of perpetuating these positive and negative images of older adults. "Any minority community that is not well understood generates myths both in its own and the host community. These myths serve functions for both communities — they demystify, they make life more tolerable, they allow subtle discrimination to continue" (Ebrahim, 1992, p. 52). They may prevent members of one culture from getting to know members of another.

## What Are the Consequences of Stereotyping the Aging?

The consequences of healthy and frequent interaction between generations have been documented in research from the early 1960s. For children with living grandparents — and sometimes great-grandparents — perceptions toward older persons, the aging process, and their own aging are enhanced by intergenerational relationships. In contrast, children who have limited contact with elders are more likely to develop stereotypical images of the elderly and develop increasing concern for their own aging process. Unfortunately, interaction with older adults has not been found to reduce the negative effects of stereotypical images of older adults in young children; once the stereotypes have been firmly fixed in their minds, they are difficult to eradicate. Not surprisingly, negative stereotypes of the elderly can create fear of aging and the aged that, although unfounded, does impede and inhibit effective and quality communication between generations.

Does stereotyping function to unknowingly and unintentionally impose limitations or standards upon a group of people? Does the group being stereotyped engage in self-fulfilling behavior as a consequence of the limitations being imposed upon them? Utilizing *accommodation theory* as the framework for analysis of accommodating behavior found in communication between generations, Ryan, MacLean, and Orange (1994, p. 273) found that "negative nonverbal behaviors were rated as significantly more likely to occur with patronizing style" and that these behaviors were frequently based on stereotyped expectations of the elderly interactants. The accommodating nonverbal behaviors included simplification and exaggeration of key components of messages, short topics, elder-speak (baby talk directed toward elders), shorter and less complex utterances, and imperatives/interrogatives/repetitions.

Focusing upon a comparison of social skills between young and older interactants, Segrin (1994) found that elders may see themselves as impaired or less skilled especially in interaction with younger people, more as a result of self-comparison than of real inability. This misperception, in turn, leads to lower self-esteem and perhaps less self-confidence in such interactions. These results and those found by Ryan, MacLean, and Orange (1994) suggest (1) that young people tend to interact with their elderly counterparts based upon stereotypical notions of older adults (often in relation to perceptions of impaired physical and mental abilities) and (2) that acting upon these stereotypes results in deleterious effects upon the self-esteem and self-confidence of the elderly.

In fact, in a recent study conducted by Giles et al. (1992), intergenerational talk between young and old was explored in order to identify characteristics and effects of stereotypical images of the elderly. The study focused upon the sociolinguistic behavior of both the older adults and young adults functioning in the roles of initiator and respondent in interaction. These researchers concluded that "the message transmitted (i.e., what is attended to, encoded, produced, and responded to) is affected by beliefs, assumptions, and stereotypes"; and specifically, in the case of the aging population, the stereotypes of decrement, incompetence, and inability transcend both the way in which the message is processed, and the way the response is produced (Giles et al., 1992, p. 290). Furthermore, older adults were seen to accommodate these stereotypes by engaging in language that depicted them as helpless, dependent, immobile, and victims of old age. This behavior is referred to as "instant aging," for many of the older individuals participating in the study described themselves as active and independent prior to engaging in interaction with their youthful counterparts.

How can we transcend the barriers between cultures that stereotypes so systematically place in our way? First, we familiarize ourselves with the other culture; then, we try communicating with its members.

## Communication Aspects of the Grandparent-Grandchild Relationship

One intergenerational relationship that seems to transcend the negative stereotypes of the aging, and perhaps even the fear of aging itself, is that between grandparents and grandchildren. Although the nature of this relationship is as diverse as the individuals who embrace this intergenerational bond, it engenders a unique communicative character all its own. The diversity characterizing the grandparent-grandchild relationship is influenced by factors such as the age(s) of grandparent and grandchild, sex of relationship participants (as well as maternal or paternal grandparenthood), ethnicity and cultural background, grandparents' work/retirement status, geographic proximity, marital status of both parents and grandparents, and, of course, grandparents' physical health.

Two decades of research exploring the quality, individuality, and character of this distinctive relationship depict a continuum of grandparental involvement. Early research into the nature of this relationship focused primarily on the enjoyable aspects of the relationship for grandparents, especially in relation to recreational activities and presence on holidays. Recent investigations have found some grandparents taking a more participative role in their grandchildren's lives; this is especially evident in situations of divorce, surrogate child care, and grandparents acting as primary child-care providers (grandparents as parents) (McKay, 1989; McKay & Caverly, 1995).

The intensity and degree of responsibility accepted by the grandparents is largely dependent upon their own life situation, their age, and relations with their own children. Grandparents' concern for the welfare of their granchild(ren) must often supersede the welfare of, or relations with, their own child (the grandchild's parent) in addition to concerns for their own health or financial status, as they accept full responsibility for grandchild care (Jendrek, 1994). Grandparents' full acceptance of responsibility for grandchild care is often the result of neglect or abuse effected by mothers' emotional problems, drug addiction, and/or alcoholism; partial acceptance usually stems from the desire to assist with child day care (due to mothers' employment) and the need for self-fulfillment or being useful (Jendrek, 1994). These circumstances seem to occur across ethnic groups and geographical areas. Within the Apache culture, for instance, grandmothers welcome the active family role of the parenting grandparent, in contrast to some who accept the role only under circumstances beyond their control (Bahr, 1994).

Focusing upon the communicative nature of the grandparent-grandchild relationship, interviews with numerous grandmothers, grandfathers, grandsons, and granddaughters of various ages and ethnicities, and in several geographical areas, have provided a plethora of knowledge and understanding about this unique bond. Interestingly, the common thread, no matter what the nature of the relationship, is the desire on the part of grandparents to impart, and the desire by grandchildren to listen to, grandparents' stories of their life experiences, family history, and advice. "Inasmuch as life stories function to help people make, shape, and preserve history, the shared stories between grandparent and grandchild provide some common ground in which to negotiate and maintain a relationship" (Nussbaum & Bettini, 1994, p. 78).

Perhaps there is no communicative event more salient to the grandparent-grandchild relationship as the sharing of stories, events, advice, or family history. The benefits intrinsic to this type of information exchange, for both grandparents and grandchildren, have been the focus of much research. For example, grandparents provide grandchildren with a source of identity development by sharing stories about their past experiences and other accounts of family history (Baranowski, 1982). Moreover, grandparents achieve a sense of continuity and satisfaction in knowing that the ideas, beliefs, values, and memories shared are carried on into the future (Mead, 1974). Of particular significance, however, is the storyteller, the grandmother or grandfather who plays an integral part in both the characterization and content of the story told (McKay, 1993). These individuals have a life-time of wisdom and experience to impart; to be unable to do so is a loss not only to the listener, but to the teller as well.

## Conclusions and Implications

Who are our senior citizens? Can we transcend the stereotypes of our aging population and reap the benefits of their wisdom and experience?

First: Who are our senior citizens? To summarize, they are a co-culture of individuals who engender patterns of friendship and social interaction that are distinct from other forms. Their attitudes toward work and retirement vary with their needs, their life and social status, their work history. They are unique in that many can boast long-term marriage in contrast to a younger generation overwhelmed by high divorce rates. They are both politically active *and* politically diverse; their interest in political, economic and social issues is heterogeneous, even though they participate in the political process in significant proportions. Today's senior citizen has participated in at least one (and possibly two) World Wars, the Depression, and other significant historical events. They have seen dramatic innovations in electronics and technology, television and computers. They are as varied and diverse as the younger generations perceive themselves to be.

Second: Can we transcend the stereotypes of our aging population and reap the benefits of their wisdom and experience? The answer to this question is beyond the scope of this article. Beginning with the grandparent-grandchild relationship, however, we can ask the questions and listen to the answers that may penetrate the obstacles that stereotypes of our elderly have so securely placed in our way.

One easy but inappropriate way to understand the culture of the elderly is to accept and perpetuate the predominantly negative stereotypes so easily accepted by our youth-oriented society. A better alternative, however, is the recognition that, like many other cultures, there exists as much diversity within the elderly population as between it and any other group (Triandis, 1979). The objective of this chapter has been to introduce members of our elderly population; to make the reader aware of the complex and interesting lives they lead; and, at the very least, to dispel some of the negative myths and stereotypes our society embraces rather than think about aging and face the fear that such thoughts provoke.

## References

Ade-Ridder, L., and Hennon, C. B. (1989). "Diversity of Lifestyles Among the Elderly." In L. Ade-Ridder and C. B. Hennon (Eds.), *Lifestyles of the Elderly: Diversity in Relationships, Health, and Caregiving,* 1–8. New York: Human Sciences Press.

Atkinson, D. R., Morten, G., and Sue, D. W. (1985). "Minority Group Counseling: An Overview." In L. A. Samovar and R. E. Porter (Eds.), *Intercultural Communication: A Reader,* 7th ed. Belmont, Calif.: Wadsworth.

Bahr, K. S. (1994). The strengths of Apache grandmothers: Observations on commitment, culture, and caretaking. *Journal of Comparative Family Studies, 25,* 233–248.

Baranowski, M. D. (1982). Grandparent-adolescent relations: Beyond the nuclear family. *Adolescence, 17,* 375–384.

Binstock, R. H. (1992). "Aging, Politics, and Public Policy." In B. B. Hess and E. W. Markson (Eds.), *Growing Old in America,* 325–340. New Brunswick, N.J.: Transaction Books.

Catchen, H. (1989). "Generational Equity: Issues of Gender and Race." In L. Grau (Ed.), *Women in the Later Years: Health, Social, and Cultural Perspectives,* 21–38. New York: Haworth Press.

Ebrahim, S. (1992). "Health and Ageing Within Ethnic Minorities." In K. Morgan (Ed.), *Gerontology: Responding to an Ageing Society,* 50–62. London: The British Society of Gerontology.

Giles, H., Coupland, N., Coupland, J., Williams, A., and Nussbaum, J. (1992). Intergenerational talk and communication with older people. *International Journal of Aging and Human Development, 34,* 271–297.

Hess, B. B. (1992). "Growing Old in America in the 1990's." In B. B. Hess and E. W. Markson (Eds.), *Growing Old in America,* 5–22. New Brunswick, N.J.: Transaction Books.

Hummert, M. L., Garstka, T. A., Shaner, J. L., and Strahm, S. (1994). Stereotypes of the elderly held by young, middle-aged, and elderly adults. *Journal of Gerontology, 49,* 240–249.

Jendrek, M. P. (1994). Grandparents who parent their grandchildren: Circumstances and decisions. *The Gerontologist, 34,* 206–216.

McKay, V. C. (1989). "The Grandparent-Grandchild Relationship." In J. F. Nussbaum (Ed.), *Life-Span Communication: Normative Processes,* 257–282. Hillsdale, N.J.: Lawrence Erlbaum.

McKay, V. C. (1993). "Making Connections: Narrative as the Expression of Continuity Between Generations of Grandparents and Grandchildren." In N. Coupland and J. Nussbaum (Eds.), *Discourse and Lifespan Identity,* 173–185. London: Sage.

McKay, V. C., and Caverly, R. S. (1995). "Relationships in Later Life: The Nature of Inter- and Intragenerational Ties Among Grandparents, Grandchildren, and Adult Siblings." In J. Nussbaum (Ed.), *Handbook of Communication and Aging,* 207–225. Hillsdale, N.J.: Lawrence Erlbaum.

Mead, M. (1974). Grandparents as educators. *Teachers College Record, 76,* 240–249.

Nussbaum, J., and Bettini, L. M. (1994). Shared stories of the grandparent grandchild relationship. *International Journal of Aging and Human Development, 39,* 67–80.

Perkins, K., and Tice, C. (1994). Suicide and older adults: The strengths perspective in practice. *Journal of Applied Gerontology, 13,* 438–454.

Porter, R. E., and Samovar, L. A. (1985). "Approaching Intercultural Communication." In L. A. Samovar and R. E. Porter (Eds.), *Intercultural Communication: A Reader,* 7th ed., 15–30. Belmont, Calif.: Wadsworth.

Rosenbaum, W. A., and Button, J. W. (1993). The unquiet future of intergenerational politics. *The Gerontologist, 33,* 481–490.

Ryan, E. B., MacLean, M., and Orange, J. B. (1994). Inappropriate accommodation in communication to elders: Inferences about nonverbal correlates. *International Journal of Aging and Human Development, 39,* 273–291.

Segrin, C. (1994). Social skills and psychosocial problems among the elderly. *Research on Aging, 16,* 301–321.

Triandis, H. C. (1979). Values, attitudes, and interpersonal behavior. *Nebraska Symposium on Motivation,* 195–259.

## Concepts and Questions for Chapter 3

1. By what means can you approach interaction with members of co-cultures without making erroneous assumptions that may be harmful to their sense of self-worth?

2. What does Edith Folb mean by the term *intracultural* communication? How does this form of communication differ from intercultural communication?

3. What role or influence does hierarchy, power, and dominance have in the process of intracultural communication?

4. What does Folb mean by *nondominant groups*? How does the role or position of nondominance affect one's position in the larger culture?

5. Can you think of other co-cultures that fall into Folb's category of nondominant groups?

6. How do you suppose someone from a foreign culture would respond to one of our co-cultures? Be specific.

7. How would you set about trying to make people realize that their stereotypes of other cultures and co-cultures are probably erroneous and that they need to be changed or eliminated?

8. What are the basic assumptions Ribeau, Baldwin, and Hecht make regarding African American communication?

9. What recommendations do Ribeau, Baldwin, and Hecht make to improve intercultural communication between whites and African Americans? How can you incorporate these recommendations into your own communicative behavior?

10. How does becoming disabled change a person's communication patterns?

11. What are some of the cultural problems inherent in communication between able-bodied and disabled persons?

12. What does Wood mean when she asserts that communication constructs gender cultures?

13. What methods does Wood suggest to help improve understanding in cross-gender communication?

14. How does the co-culture of the elderly differ from the dominant culture in the United States?

15. How do the elderly's own positive and negative stereotypes differ from the stereotypes held by the younger members of the dominant culture?

16. How do stereotypes of the elderly affect intergenerational communication?

17. What social dynamics affect grandparent-grandchild communications?

# Part Three

## Intercultural Interaction: Taking Part in Intercultural Communication

*If we seek to understand a people we have to put ourselves, as far as we can, in that particular historical and cultural background. . . . One has to recognize that countries and people differ in their approach and their ways, in their approach to life and their ways of living and thinking. In order to understand them we have to understand their way of life and approach. If we wish to convince them, we have to use their language as far as we can, not language in the narrow sense of the word, but the language of the mind.*

*—Jawaharlal Nehru*

In Part Three we are concerned with participation in intercultural communication. We focus on both verbal and nonverbal forms of symbolic interaction as well as on the social and physical context in which it occurs. As we pointed out in introducing Part Two, meanings reside within people, and symbols serve as stimuli to which these meanings are attributed. Meaning-evoking stimuli consist of both verbal and nonverbal behaviors. Although we consider these forms of symbolic interaction separately for convenience, we hasten to point out their interrelatedness. As nonverbal behavior accompanies verbal behavior, it becomes a unique part of the total symbolic interaction. Verbal messages often rely on their nonverbal accompaniment for cues that aid the receiver in decoding the verbal symbols. Nonverbal behaviors not only serve to amplify and clarify verbal messages but can also serve as forms of symbolic interaction without verbal counterparts. In addition, the context in which verbal and nonverbal behaviors occur adds to the evocation of meanings.

When we communicate verbally, we use words with seeming ease, because there is a high consensus of agreement about the meanings our words evoke. Our experiential backgrounds are similar enough that we share basically the same meanings for most of the word symbols we use in everyday communication. But even within our culture we disagree over the meanings of many word symbols. As words move farther from the reality of sense data, they become more abstract; and then there is far less agreement about appropriate meanings. What do highly abstract words such as *love, freedom, equality, democracy,* or *good time* mean to you? Do they mean the same things to everyone? If you are in doubt, ask some friends; take a poll. You will surely find that people have different notions of these concepts and consequently different meanings for these words. Their experiences have been different, and they hold different beliefs, attitudes, values, concepts, and expectations. Yet all, or perhaps most, are from the same culture. Their backgrounds, experiences, and concepts of the universe are really quite uniform. When cultural diversity is added to the process of decoding words, however, much larger differences in meanings and usage are found.

Culture exerts no small influence over our use of language. In fact, it strongly determines just what our language is and how we use it. In the narrowest sense, language is a set of symbols (vocabulary) that evoke more or less uniform meanings among a particular population and set of rules (grammar and syntax) for using the symbols. In the broadest sense, language is the symbolic representation of a people, and it includes their historical and cultural backgrounds as well as their approach to life and their ways of living and thinking.

What comes to be symbolized and what the symbols represent are very much functions of culture. Similarly, how we use our verbal symbols is also a function of culture. What we think about or speak with others about must be capable of symbolization, and how we speak or think about things must follow the rules we have for using our language. Because the symbols and rules are culturally determined, how and what we think or talk about are, in effect, a function of our culture. This relation between language and culture is not unidirectional, however. There is an interaction between them — what we think about and how we think about it also affect our culture.

As we can see, language and culture are inseparable. To be effective intercultural communicators requires that we be aware of the relationship between culture and language. It further requires that we learn and know about the culture of the person with whom we communicate so that we can better understand how his or her language represents that person.

Another important aspect of verbal symbols or words is that they can evoke two kinds of meanings: *denotative* and *connotative*. A denotative meaning indicates the referent or the "thing" to which the symbol refers. For example, the denotative meaning of the word *book* is the physical object to which it refers; or, in the case of the set of symbols *Intercultural Communication: A Reader,* the referent is the book you are now reading. Not all denotations have a physical correspondence. As we move to higher levels of abstraction, we often deal with words that represent ideas or concepts, which exist only in the mind and do not necessarily have a physical basis. For example, much communication research is directed toward changes in attitude. Yet *attitude* is only a hypothetical construct used to explain behavior; there is no evidence of any physical correspondence between some group of brain cells and a person's attitudes.

The second type of meaning – connotative – indicates a valuative dimension. Not only do we identify referents (denotative meaning), but we also place them along an evaluative dimension that can be simply described as positive-neutral-negative. Where we place a word on the dimension depends on our prior experiences and how we "feel" about the referent. If we like books, we might place *Intercultural Communication: A Reader* near the positive end of the dimension. When we are dealing with more abstract symbols, we do the same thing. In fact, as the level of abstraction increases, so does our tendency to place more emphasis on connotative meanings. Most will agree that a book is the object you are holding in your hand, but whether books are good or bad or whether this particular book is good or bad or in between is an individual judgment based on prior experience.

Culture affects both denotative and connotative meanings. Consequently, a knowledge of how these meanings can differ culturally is essential to effective intercultural communication. To make the assumption that everyone uses the same meanings is to invite communication disaster.

There are other ways in which culture affects language and language use. We tend to believe that our way of using language is both correct and universal and that any deviation is wrong or substandard. This belief can and does elicit many negative responses and judgments when we encounter someone from another culture whose use of language deviates from our own specifications.

What we are trying to point out with these examples should be quite obvious – language and culture are inseparable. In fact, it would be difficult to determine which is the voice and which is the echo. How we learn, employ, and respond to symbols is culturally based. In addition, the sending and the receiving of these culturally grounded symbols are what enable us to interact with people from other cultures. Hence, it is the purpose of this part of the book to highlight these verbal and nonverbal symbols: to help you understand some of the complexities, subtleties, and nuances of language and, at the same time, to acquaint you with how the social and physical contexts influence verbal and nonverbal behavior.

It is obvious that communication involves much more than the sending and receiving of verbal and nonverbal messages. Human interaction takes place within some social and physical setting that influences how we construct and perceive messages. The sway of context is rooted in three interrelated assumptions. First, communication is *rule*-governed; that is to say, each encounter has implicit and explicit rules that regulate our conduct. These rules tell us everything from what is appropriate attire to what topics can be discussed. Second, the *setting* helps us define what "regulations" are in operation. Reflect for a moment on your own communication behavior as you move to and from the following arenas: classroom, courtroom, church, hospital, and dance hall. Visualize yourself behaving differently as you proceed from place to place. Third, most of the communication rules we follow have been *learned* as part of cultural experiences. While cultures might share the same general settings, their specific notion of proper behavior for each context manifests the values and attitudes of that culture. Concepts of turn taking, time, space, language, manners, nonverbal behavior, silence, and control of the communication flow are largely an extension of each culture.

In this part of the book we offer some readings that demonstrate the crucial link that exists between context, culture, and communication. What emerges from these essays is the realization that to understand another culture you must appreciate the rules that govern that culture's behavior in a specific setting. Although intercultural communication occurs in a variety of contexts, we have selected environments related to business, education, and health care to discuss in this part of the book.

# 4

## Verbal Processes:
## Thinking and Speaking

Some people have suggested that as a species our most unique feature is our ability to receive, store, manipulate, and generate symbols. All 5.6 billion of us deal with the past, take part in the present, and prepare for the future. By simply making certain sounds or marks on paper, we are able to share experiences with other people. Language is that simple yet complex instrument that gives us the gift of sharing ourselves with other people. This chapter looks at that gift.

It is the premise of this chapter that a culture's use of language involves much more than sounds and meanings. It also involves forms of reasoning, techniques of problem solving, specialized linguistic devices such as analogies and idioms, and ways of perceiving the world. Hence, to understand the language of any culture means you must look beyond the vocabulary, grammar, and syntax of that culture. This broad view of culture has guided us in our selection of readings. We urge you to view language from this larger perspective both as you read these articles and as you confront people from different cultures. This eclectic outlook toward language will help you understand the interaction patterns of cultures that are different from your own. The first two articles will examine this relationship between language and culture.

We begin with an essay by Devorah A. Lieberman, "Culture, Problem Solving, and Pedagogical Style," that advances the claim that thinking, problem solving, and language are not only interrelated but are also grounded in culture. She maintains that an understanding of differences among cultures in cognitive processing and right- and left-brain hemisphere dominance can help explain variations in problem-solving strategies. To facilitate that understanding Lieberman develops three major themes in her essay. First, she explores the possible reasons for and approaches to differences among cultures in problem solving and cognitive processing. Second, as a means of demonstrating these differences she examines some culture-specific problem-solving approaches. Finally, by means of the case study method, five culturally different teachers and classrooms (Japanese, Hebrew, French, Spanish, and English) are examined to determine what problem-solving approaches are encouraged in each of these learning environments.

In the next reading, "The Crossroads of Language and Culture," Mary Fong introduces us to some fundamental ideas about the relationship between language and culture. She begins with a brief review of the Sapir-Whorf hypothesis, which proposed linguistic relativity and was one of the first modern observations of the relationship between language and culture. She then traces later developments in this area that have led to ethnographic research approaches to the study of language and culture. Applying these techniques in two studies of Chinese language use, Fong shows not only the ways in which ethnographic approaches are employed, but also the rich linguistic practices of the Chinese.

As we noted in the introduction to this section of the book, language involves attaching meanings to world symbols, whether they are sounds or marks on a piece of paper. If those symbols have to be translated to or from a foreign language, numerous problems can arise. Without accurate translations, those trying to communicate often end up simply exchanging meaningless sounds and vague images. What usually happens is that the interpretations lack a common vocabulary and familiar referents. Our next two selections examine some of the difficulties in dealing with foreign languages. In these cases, however, communication problems occur because one of the parties is not only from a foreign culture and speaks a foreign language, but also has English as a second language. One of the most blatant examples of the problems associated with English as a second language is found in our persistent use of idioms. Idioms, by their very nature, can be perplexing and confusing. They are culture-bound and not readily understandable from their grammatical construction. Imagine how frustrating it would be if English were your second language and you heard someone say "Peter has dropped the ball again by dilly-dallying over this hot potato." It is this topic of idioms that is the focus of Wen-Shu Lee in "That's Greek to Me: Between a Rock and a Hard Place in Intercultural Encounters." Lee begins by reminding us that idioms are both treacherous and important in intercultural communication because they are figurative in nature, depend on a common background for their definition, are often not explained in detail, and frequently "hold one of the keys to interpersonal closeness." To assist us in our use of idioms, Lee advances a four-step process for using idioms: (1) cultivating a supportive conversational decorum, (2) learning to differentiate goal-oriented talk from metatalk, (3) applying the principle of double-multiple description, and (4) finding relational relevance in a speaker's lifeworld.

Our next essay also emphasizes some obstacles that need to be examined when English is the second language of one of the participants. This time, however, the issues center on differences in linguistic rules. In his essay "Finnish and American Linguistic Patterns: A Cultural Comparison," Donal Carbaugh maintains that "some rules that Americans use and invoke when speaking in public are quite different from those supplied by Finns for similar public contexts." By comparing these conversational rules, Carbaugh believes that we can gain a better understanding of the "dynamics that transpire when one cultural system of expression contacts another." It is important to keep in mind as you read this essay that even though Carbaugh is examining only the Finnish culture, his advice regarding linguistic patterns can be applied to all cultures. For, as we have said elsewhere, all cultures use language in a specialized manner.

We have attempted to stress the idea that language is more than words and meanings; it is also a mirror of one's cultural experience. In no instance is this point more vivid than in the African American community, where "talk" is important. And, according to the author of the next article, Mark P. Orbe, it also is a community that "most non-African Americans — especially European American males — have great difficulty comprehending." In his article, "Utilizing an Inductive Approach to Studying African American Male Communication," Orbe presents six essential themes that reflect the communication process of African American men. According to Orbe, these six themes depict the "lived experiences" of this co-cultural group. By learning about these experiences and how they reflect communicative behavior, the author believes intercultural communication can be improved.

In the last essay, we consider the language of a very large and prominent co-culture: the co-culture of the Mexican American. This co-culture is quite diverse, containing numerous members whose Mexican heritage precedes the fact of U.S. sovereignty over the Southwest as well as Mexicans who immigrated from Mexico within their lifetime or whose parents immigrated from Mexico. Such cultural diversity make it difficult to perceive and understand the central values of this co-culture.

In order to help us better understand the Mexican American co-culture and to further focus our vision on the interrelationship between culture and language, Shelly M. Zormeier and Larry A. Samovar introduce us to this culture through an examination of its proverbs. In "Language as a Mirror of Reality: Mexican American Proverbs," they introduce us to the notions of proverbs and the relationship between proverbs and culture. It is in this relationship between culture and proverbs that we see how proverbs contain the values and world views of a culture. Through their examination of specific Mexican American proverbs, we gain insight into the significant values of this co-culture. This examination shows how proverbs relate to such cultural dynamics as collectivism, fatalism, present-time orientation, being orientation, and family values.

The purpose of this chapter is to introduce you to the various forms of verbal communication found among and between cultures. We encourage you to see that there are almost as many communication styles as there are cultures and that, with an understanding of some of these styles, you can improve the quality of your own communication when you are interacting with people from different cultures.

# Culture, Problem Solving, and Pedagogical Style

## DEVORAH A. LIEBERMAN

Intercultural communication theory is grounded in the concept that participants in any interaction bring with them "a system of symbols and meanings" (Schneider, 1976, p. 297) that shapes their perceptions of a shared phenomenon. Additionally, a culture is not a characteristic of individuals, but rather a "collective mental programming of the people in an environment" (Hofstede, 1980, p. 42). Based upon this approach to intercultural communication, researchers in the field and the teachers of intercultural communication in our own college classrooms claim that differences (such as values, beliefs, attitudes, frames of reference) are the basic variables that influence perceptions and assumptions (Kohls, 1984). However, few scholars have addressed culture-based approaches to problem solving. Condon and Yousef (1975) and Samovar and Porter (1988, 1991, 1994) are notable exceptions. Much research has addressed the different ways cultures vary in values, beliefs and ways of classifying, but "there is a lack of research addressing differences in problem solving by culture. This research needs to be done" (Cole & Scribner, 1974, p. 174). The debate among ethnocognitivists over "cultural differences in problem-solving" (Bogen, Dezare, TenHousten, & Marsh, 1972; Cole & Scribner, 1974) ranges from whether there are inherent cultural differences in cognitive abilities to whether cultures merely teach culture-specific cognitive process. Based upon the premise that individuals

in cultures tend to encourage and reward certain problem-solving approaches, this article has a threefold purpose. First, it explores the possible reasons for and differences in problem-solving approaches across cultures. Second, it examines teaching styles that reinforce these culture-specific problem-solving approaches. Third, it identifies pedagogical styles and differences across culturally disparate classrooms.

## Culture and Problem-Solving Approaches

"Cognitive processes" are universal cerebral means employed to handle a specific task or problem at hand. According to Luria (1966) everyone has the same cognitive components but learns to use them differently throughout life. Cole and Scribner (1974) support Luria, contending that it is the cultural influence that conditions the alternative cognitive process chosen to complete tasks and resolve problems. Each culture teaches, trains, and models those within its system to exhibit what is considered the most appropriate range of problem-solving methods. For example, "Research on cultural difference . . . indicates that members of industrialized societies and members of nonindustrial societies respond to visual illusions quite differently" (Reid, 1987, p. 87).

Kleinfeld (1994) reminds us that for more than twenty-five years research on cultural differences in learning has been unable to conclude that one method of teaching works better for children of one cultural group while another method of teaching works better for children of a different cultural group. The pitfall scholars often experience in this line of research is the assumption that a cognitive strategy for problem solving is inherent within a culture, rather than examining the possibility that teachers within a culture teach what they believe is "the best method for solving problems."

Anthropological research has traditionally examined culture and problem solving from a group, content-observation, field-description approach. Psychological research has examined cognition, elementary functions, process, the individual laboratory, and explanation (Cole, 1985). This chapter integrates both culture and cognition by examining problem-solving approaches encouraged by teachers in different cultures. These approaches range from concrete participative problem solving to abstract individualistic problem solving.

## Cognitive Styles

Cultures tend to encourage and reinforce the cognitive style individuals employ when faced with refining information during the problem-solving process. Mestenhauser (1981) explains that learning as well as problem solving involves "the way a person abstracts information from the environment, remembers it, [and] classifies it into concepts and categories . . ." (p. 161). Furthermore, "Logic [problem solving approach] . . . is evolved out of a culture; it is not universal" (Kaplan, 1988, p. 208). Thus, a particular problem-solving approach may be considered either the "most logical" or the "most common sensical" within a particular culture and situation (Lieberman, Kosokoff, & Kosokoff, 1988). Witkin and Goodenough (1981) claim that there are stark differences in the global and abstract functioning of individuals in different cultures and that particular modes of thinking may vary by culture. Cognitive styles considered in this article are field-dependent–field-independent, reflective–impulsive, tolerance–intolerance of ambiguity, and left hemisphere–right hemisphere.

Individuals who employ the field-dependent cognitive style tend to focus on elements or non-centralized variables from the environment. These individuals tend to perceive the event holistically, including the emotionality and the feelings associated with the entire event. Scarcella (1990) claims that individuals who operate from a field-dependent perspective enjoy working with others to solve problems. They tend to be sensitive to the feelings and opinions of the others in the group. He also asserts that Hispanic and African American students seem to employ more field-dependent rather than field-independent strategies in learning and problem solving. Delpit (1995) claims that the Southern Black Baptist [field-dependent] style is intricately connected to context, with a dependence on paralinguistic features. "Rhythm, intonation, gesture, emotion, humor, use of metaphor, indirect

personalized message to individuals, and audience participation are crucial to communication in the black church, features which are but slightly modified reflections of secular black communication style" (p. 137). Scarcella explains these cognitive behaviors as resulting from cultures that are more group-oriented and more sensitive to the social environment.

The individual who employs the field-independent cognitive style tends to isolate given details of the field, placing the elements into a cause-effect, linear, or sequential frame. This style emphasizes the logic of the problem, while deemphasizing feelings or emotion within the field. Brown (1980) claims that the field-dependent cognitive style is encouraged and reinforced in more traditional societies that also reinforce high-context and authoritarian behavior. The field-independent cognitive style is more prominent in highly industrialized, low-context, competitive societies.

Reflectivity and impulsivity refer to the length of time individuals are encouraged to spend "thinking about a problem." Certain cultures expect an individual to reflect on multiple variables surrounding a problem to ascertain the most correct answer. Impulsivity in these cultures traditionally is not rewarded. "To make a mistake is painful; to guess is to admit not having spent enough time in finding the correct answer. Being only partially 'right,' which may be acceptable to the impulsive learners and in other cultures, is often seen as totally 'wrong' by those whose reflective learning styles are culturally sanctioned" (Damen, 1987, p. 302).

Tolerance of ambiguity describes cultures that downplay bipolar language. The English language emphasizes bipolarity. In a problem-solving situation, bipolar language might be: "This is either right or wrong," "black or white," "good or bad," "yes or no," "correct or incorrect." Bipolar language encourages cause-effect thinking and linearity (Korzybsky, 1933). Consequently, there is less tolerance for ambiguity where there is greater bipolarity in the structure and meaning embedded in the language itself.

Linguistic contradictions are not as glaring in cultures that have a greater tolerance of ambiguity. "Tolerance of ambiguity, as a cognitive style, is ill-

| Left Hemisphere | Right Hemisphere |
| --- | --- |
| Verbal, analytic, symbolic, abstract, temporal, rational, digital, logical, linear, cause-effect, sequential, theoretical, auditory | Nonverbal, synthetic, concrete analogic, nontemporal, holistic, intuitive, nonrational, spatial, tactile, creative, emotive, global |
| Field-independent | Field-dependent |
| Intolerance of ambiguity | Tolerance of ambiguity |
| Impulsivity | Reflectivity |
| Low context<br><br>Individualistic | High context<br><br>Collectivistic |

**Figure 1** Types of Cognitive Problem-Solving Styles

received in the scientifically oriented, competitive ambiance of the average classroom in the United States. On the contrary, particularly at higher levels of education, field-independence, impulsivity, and intolerance of ambiguity are generally rewarded" (Damen, 1987, p. 302).

Positive relationships exist among these three problem-solving cognitive styles. Cultures that tend to encourage and reward individuals who display field-independence also may reward impulsivity and intolerance of ambiguity, whereas, cultures that tend to encourage field-dependence also may reward reflectivity and tolerance of ambiguity (see Figure 1).

Even as I write this particular essay and make sense out of the information which I choose to integrate into the content, it is important for me to attempt to avoid a culturally encouraged Aristotelian "intolerance of ambiguity," in which I categorize cultures and individuals as "either field-independent of field-dependent," "impulsive or reflective," or "high-context or low-context." "The English language and its related thought patterns have evolved out of the Anglo-European cultural

pattern. The expected sequence of thought in English is essentially a Platonic-Aristotelian sequence, descended from the philosophers of ancient Greece and shaped subsequently by Roman, medieval European, and later Western thinkers" (Kaplan, 1988, p. 208). As a result, it is nearly impossible for me to report findings other than in a linear, cause-effect reasoning style.

You might find it helpful to try reading this essay from a perspective other than your culturally learned one. Try to examine ranges of cognitive styles and approaches to problem solving that are encouraged and reinforced within other cultures. For example, categorizing individual thought and behavior as either "left hemisphere" or "right hemisphere" "reflective" or "impulsive," and so on, encourages "either-or" thinking. Try to avoid categorical labels by substituting continua which then lead to the thinking that behaviors may occur anywhere along a dimension in relation to different contexts and situations.

## Cultural Differences

Two culture-based continua that directly relate to the investigation of culture and pedagogical style are low context – high context and individualism – collectivism. Triandis (1994) asserts that "the contrast between collectivism and individualism is one of the most important cultural differences in social behavior" (p. 169).

Hall (1976) classified cultures as exhibiting high-context or low-context behavior. In high-context communication, most of the meaning of the message is "either in the physical context or internalized in the person, while very little is in the coded, explicit, transmitted part of the message" (p. 91). Low-context communication finds most of the information "vested in the explicit code" (p. 91).

Similarly, cultures that encourage and reward low-context communication tend to advocate individualism while those that encourage and reward high-context communication tend to advocate collectivism (Gudykunst & Ting-Toomey, 1988). Individualistic cultures invite individuality of thought and personal achievement of the individual as supraordinate to the group. Stewart and Bennett

(1991) maintain that the U.S. culture reflects values that are dominantly low-context and individualist. Collectivistic cultures promote group goals and the belief that the group is supraordinate to the individual. The goals of the group take precedence, with interdependence and reciprocal obligations highly valued (Hofstede, 1986). Hofstede (1991, p. 62) writes of the collectivistic classroom: "the virtues of harmony and the maintenance of face reign supreme. Confrontations and conflicts should be avoided, or at least formulated so as not to hurt anyone; even students should not lose face if this can be avoided."

## Problem Solving of the Kpelle, Fiji, Pomo, and Trobriand

The Kpelles of Liberia, Fijians, Native Americans, and Trobriands use problem-solving techniques acquired through group participation, field dependence, and reflectivity. Each is a relatively high-context culture (Hall, 1976), gathering information from the immediate environment and employing concrete approaches to attend to unsolved tasks. In each, there seems little leeway for inferential problem solving.

The Kpelle rice farmers from central Liberia work together clearing land and raising rice, and they cooperate in the forest, gathering materials for building, tools, and medicine. The researcher seated two of the Kpelles at a table facing each other with a small partition between them. In front of each were ten sticks (pieces of wood of different kinds); each stick matched one stick in the other pile. The researcher chose a stick from one of the men and told him to describe the stick so that the other Kpelle farmer could choose the matching stick from his pile. The procedure continued until all ten sticks had been described and selected.

When the partition was lifted, the men compared the two rows of sticks and described and discussed errors. The barrier was replaced and they repeated the entire process of choosing one stick and describing it to the other. Examples of the descriptions on the first trial were "one of the sticks," "not a large one," "piece of bamboo," "one stick," "one of the thorny." Examples of the de-

scriptions on the second trial were "one of the sticks," "curved bamboo," "large bamboo," and "has a thorn."

The problem-solving technique of "hit and miss" description used to transfer information did not take into account the precise information the other person needed to know to choose the stick. These farmers, through observation of one another, always participate together in tasks; one does not need to share the information the other lacks. All information is observable and available to all individuals (Cole, Gay, & Glick, 1969). In this high-context culture, where information is gathered from the environment, the Kpelles seem to problem-solve in a concrete manner.

Griffin (1983) found that the Fijian language does not allow for abstract problem solving as there is inadequate verbal coding to identify a new problem. When a problem arises that has not been previously confronted, the Fijian is "unable to think out new rules, verbalize problems, and generate options" (p. 60). Anxiety and frustration often follow as outlets for the problem-solving barrier. The Fijians employ field dependence as their cognitive style, drawing from the immediate environment to address solutions.

Another concrete approach to reasoning is evident in the Native American (Freedle, 1981). When Pomo Native Americans were asked to recall a story and could not remember a piece of information, their response was that they could not recount the story at all. A subject's recall was either null or perfect. Similarly, a problem could be perceived as either solvable or not, depending on information availability. All pieces of the puzzle were required for problem solving to occur. Other Native American languages (for example, Hopi and Navajo) also lend themselves to concrete rather than abstract thinking, leading to less analytic and more absolute problem solving.

The Trobriand, also concrete in language, do not problem-solve from the cause-and-effect approach that usually is associated with linear-thinking cultures. They do not have the traditional stimulus-response system; consequently, when they are confronted with a problem, their approach to the solution is oriented to the present. Because the language has no "to be" verbs, the concept of delayed gratification — a solution emerging in the future — does not exist. Therefore, sequential logic is not a part of their cognitive process. Trobriand students represent an example of negative consequences for cultures that contradict the mainstream problem-solving styles. Trobriand students have been refused entrance to colleges solely because of the autobiographic sketches accompanying their applications. They have been assessed as lacking purposefulness and ability to plan and have been rated as questionable in character as well as intellectually inadequate (Lee, 1950).

## Problem Solving in Mainstream Cultures

Kaplan (1970) examined problem-solving approaches and patterns of thought in more mainstream cultures. He concluded that different languages have different rhetorical norms, representing different ways of organizing. Specifically, English-Speaking persons from the United States tend to be more linear and direct than do Semitic, Asian, Romance, or Russian speakers. The Semitic individuals solved problems using a combination of tangential and semidirect approaches. Asians employed a circular approach. Romance cultures used a more consistently circuitous approach, and Russians employed a combination of direct and circuitous approaches. Though current researchers assert that his seminal article on "contrastic rhetoric" took an oversimplistic approach to cultural differences, there is basis for continued dialogue about differences in problem solving and organizing information.

Kaplan asserts that in learning another language, one must learn the logic and problem-solving approach encouraged in that culture. A basis for identifying the problem-solving approach is to study the paragraph format of a particular culture. "Each language and each culture has a paragraph order unique to itself, and that part of the learning of a particular language is mastering its logical system" (Kaplan, 1988, p. 222). Kaplan cites an activity performed in U.S. schools that exemplifies how the educational system encourages linear, sequential cognition (Figure 2). Students are told

I. Programs of Serious Interest
  A. News Broadcasts:
    1. _____
    2. _____

  B. Special Features:
    1. _____
    2. _____

II. Programs Intended Primarily as Entertainment
  A. Variety Shows:
    1. _____
    2. _____

  B. Situational Comedies:
    1. _____
    2. _____

  C. Adventure Tales:
    1. _____
    2. _____

III. Advertising
  A. _____
    1. _____
    2. _____
  B. _____
    1. _____
    2. _____

**Figure 2** Outlining in the U.S. Educational System

to categorize commercial television (for example) by type and purpose (p. 219). The instructor provides the programming types for the student and supplies supporting spaces that the student is expected to fill in. However, the essential category and format is designed by the instructor. It is apparent that there is no room for nonlinear, nonsequential thought on the part of the students.

Patterns of thought, first identified by Pribram (1949), vary situationally within and among cultures. Each culture teaches its members which patterns of thought and problem-solving approaches are most appropriate when confronted with particular situations (Condon & Yousef, 1975). A few of these patterns have been identified by various authors as universalistic, nominalistic, hypothetical, intuitional, organismic, dialectical, temporal, axiomatic, affective, inductive/deductive, analytic, global, sequential, concrete sequential, and abstract random (Condon & Yousef, 1975; Felder & Silverman, 1988; Gregorc, 1979; Pribram, 1949).

Particular patterns are dominant within specific cultures. For example, U.S. society encourages faculty-inductive reasoning (ascertain facts, find similarities, and formulate conclusions); the cultures within the former Soviet Union stress axiomatic-deductive reasoning (move from general principles to particulars, which can be easily deduced); and Arab cultures encourage intuitive-affective reasoning (facts are secondary to emotions).

An extension of the cognitive process for problem solving is an individual's style of presentation. Confronted with a problem, an individual from the United States potentially might respond with two or three specific alternative solutions. U.S. culture perpetuates either thinking in threes (for example, "Tom, Dick and Harry," "I came, I saw, I conquered," and, when telling a joke, "and then the third man came up and said") or in dichotomies (for example, either/or; right or wrong; good or bad). Conditioning to perceive a situation or problem from a particular style as well as from a particular perspective dictates the appropriate response (Condon & Yousef, 1975).

Though individuals have the ability to use any process, the culture stresses only two or three (Gregorc, 1979). Even though these styles and patterns are idiosyncratic to the individual, "they must be heavily influenced by cultural transmission" (Collings & Dedre, 1987, p. 263).

Intercultural communication research that addresses cultural patterns of thought and problem-solving approaches has only scratched the surface of cognitive functioning and differences among cul-

tures. Springer and Deutsch (1985, p. 241) contend that different languages (whether oriented toward concrete or abstract thought) are very likely responsible for differential hemispheric involvement. They maintain that particular cognitive functions are hemisphere-specific. If a culture produces individuals who exhibit predominant problem-solving patterns and these patterns have been associated with particular hemisphericity, then it follows that ethnocognitivism (thought patterns dominant within a culture) and hemisphericity (hemisphere dominance in the brain) should be a greater consideration in the examination of intercultural interactions.

## The "Cultural Cognition" Paradox

The left hemisphere has traditionally been associated with the following processes: sequential, verbal, auditory, analytic, symbolic, abstract, temporal, rational, digital, logical, theoretical, cause-effect, and linear (see Figure 1). Left-hemisphere processing is systematic. "Analysis and planning are key strategies. Problems are solved by looking at the parts, and sequence is critical" (McCarthy, 1990, p. 32). The right hemisphere has traditionally been associated with the following processes: nonverbal, visual, synthetic, concrete, analogic, emotional, creative, nontemporal, nonrational, spatial, intuitive, tactile, holistic, and global (Edwards, 1979; Springer & Deutsch, 1985). "Right-mode processing seeks patterns and solves problem by looking at the whole picture. Intuition, beliefs, and opinions are key processing strategies" (McCarthy, 1990, p. 32).

The "cultural cognition" paradox asks whether a culture trains its individuals to have dominant left or right hemispheres or whether cultures are inherently left- or right-hemisphere dominant (Paredes & Hepburn, 1976). Springer and Deutch (1985) resolve the paradox by suggesting that "every human brain is capable of more than one kind of logical process, but cultures differ with respect to the process used with various situations." Certain researchers within the cultural paradox literature (Tsunoda, 1979) claim that the Japanese brain, as opposed to the Western brain, actually functions differently. Tsunoda asserts that the Japanese left hemisphere processes nonverbal human sounds, animal sounds, and Japanese instrumental music, while the right hemisphere processes Western instrument music. Previous research claimed all nonverbal sounds (human, animal, and musical) were processed in the right hemisphere. Also, he contends that Westerners process emotion in their right hemisphere, the Japanese in the left. The language first learned develops the person's pattern of thought and influences how the brain's two halves process language (Tsunoda). Furthermore, Western children raised in the Japanese culture speaking Japanese acquire typically Japanese brains, and the opposite is true of Japanese children raised in Western culture. Very little of this research has been translated from Japanese into English, and understandably "much more work is needed to determine if cultural differences in hemispheric utilization are real and, if so, to what they are attributable" (Springer & Deutsch, 1985, p. 242). Though this research has not been corroborated it raises exciting questions regarding culture as it relates to hemisphericity and problem solving.

Considering the problem-solving cognitive styles discussed within this chapter, a pattern emerges for style and hemisphericity. Researchers caution that cultures encourage individuals to apply particular cognitive tools (for example, reflectivity or impulsivity), though not necessarily to the exclusion of others. For example, McCarthy (1990) addresses four styles of learning and problem solving, each with a preference, though not exclusively, for either right- or left-hemisphere skills. The four styles are (1) imaginative, (2) analytic, (3) common sense, and (4) dynamic. The imaginative approach (primarily right hemisphere) "perceives information concretely and processes it reflectively." The analytic approach (which emphasizes left- and right-hemisphere processing) "perceives information abstractly and processes it reflectively." The commonsense approach (which emphasizes left- and right-hemisphere processing) integrates theory and practice, by perceiving information abstractly and immediately applying it to concrete situations. The dynamic approach (primarily right hemisphere) perceives information concretely and applies it immediately to concrete situations (McCarthy, 1990, p. 32).

## Culture, Hemisphericity, and Pedagogy

Given the potential for cultural influence on hemisphere dominance and problem-solving patterns, it is essential to understand the responsibility educational systems have toward understanding their effect on developing students' patterns of thought, approaches to problem solving, and communication styles. For example, Blakeslee (1980) contends that the U.S. educational system has not realized that it is teaching its students to process information and formulate responses almost singularly using traditionally accepted left-hemisphere skills (for example, linear, analytic, rational, and nonemotional processes). Qualities of the right hemisphere, often termed the "unconscious hemisphere," are not only deemphasized but also often are associated with less important or irrelevant qualities. "Because we operate in such a sequential world [the United States] and because the logical thought of the left hemisphere is so honored in our culture, we gradually damp out, devalue, and disregard the input of our right hemispheres. It is not that we stop using it altogether; it just becomes less and less available to us because of established patterns" (Prince, 1978, p. 57). Blakeslee (1980) goes so far as to contend that "there is a decadence in the field of higher education that is the natural result of ignorance of the unconscious side of the brain. . . . The system thus feeds itself and becomes more and more scholarly and less and less intuitive" (p. 76).

Consequently, because patterns of thought develop accompanying world views, the educational system is encouraging a particular world view and world interpretation constructed by the individual and the culture (Ong, 1973, p. 36). This world view will be influenced by the mode of thought most condoned and rewarded by a particular culture. Hale-Benson (1969) asserts that U.S. schools encourage analytic approaches to learning and problem solving. He claims that U.S. children "who have not developed these skills and those who function with a different cognitive style will not only be poor achievers early in school, but . . . also become worse as they move to higher grade levels" (p. 31).

The researchers cited in this article claim that cultures encourage problem-solving approaches viewed as "most appropriate for particular situations." Furthermore, where particular cognitive styles may be encouraged, others may be discouraged. The discouraged styles are considered "less effective," "less suitable," or "less reasonable." In some cases, particular approaches might fly in the face of what individuals from a particular culture would label "common sense reasoning" (Lieberman, Kosokoff, & Kosokoff, 1988). Claxton and Murrell (1987) go so far as to ask the question, "Are the learning styles [problem-solving styles] of minority students different from those of students of the dominant culture?" (p. 69). Numerous researchers suggest that reasoning and problem-solving approaches are encouraged in the classroom (Gregorc, 1979; Kolb, 1984; Kaplan & Kaplan, 1981). Though their explanations of the various reasoning and problem-solving approaches may differ, each asserts that classroom education reinforces the dominant thinking patterns of that particular culture (Hooks, 1994; Wallace & Grave, 1995).

Felder and Silverman (1988) claim that most college students, either of traditional college age or older, respond well to teaching methods that stress right-hemisphere visual information. Unfortunately, the information usually is presented via predominantly auditory methods (lecturing) or visual representations of auditory information (words and mathematical symbols) written in texts and handouts, on transparencies, or on chalkboard). Silverman (1987) found that U.S. students retain 10 percent of what they read; 26 percent of what they hear; 30 percent of what they see; 50 percent of what they see and hear; 70 percent of what they say; and 90 percent of what they say as they do something.

Hegelsen (1988) claims that the teacher usually teaches in the style he or she has been trained in (traditionally left hemisphere in the United States) and that the student tries to match his or her learning style to that of the teacher. This frequently leads to learning some material, missing some material, and often tuning out. Numerous educators suggest that teachers learn to "understand the duality of their students' minds" (Blakeslee, 1980, p. 59), in this way stimulating both the verbal and nonverbal minds.

## Analysis of Teaching Styles: Five Case Studies

Few researchers have compared and contrasted the problem-solving approaches encouraged by teachers of various cultures. Ideally, this would be accomplished by observing teachers and classrooms in cultures around the globe. Unable to undertake this global endeavor, I observed culturally disparate teachers in the Pacific Northwest and identified the problem-solving approaches they encourage.

In Spring of 1991, my assistant researcher and I contacted five private elementary schools in the Pacific Northwest of the United States. Each employs teachers who instruct in the language and adhere to the academic philosophy of their original country. The five private schools represented are: Japanese-speaking, Hebrew-speaking, French-speaking, Spanish-speaking, and English-speaking. The Japanese-speaking instructors are from Japan. The Hebrew-speaking instructors are from Israel. The French-speaking instructors are from France and Belgium. The Spanish-speaking instructors are from Colombia and Peru. The English-speaking instructors are from the United States.

Each of the five schools granted us permission to videotape teachers of math and art classes; the Japanese school was the exception, as they do not offer art classes. Each teacher was told that he or she was being observed and videotaped as part of a research endeavor identifying different ways of teaching throughout the Pacific Northwest private school system. The videotapes were subsequently translated in English (for analysis purposes) by speakers fluent in English and the language of the videotaped teacher. Though it is impossible to generalize any of these findings to the cultures of the respective instructors, the study takes a step toward noting differences in teaching styles of five teachers trained in different cultures and languages.

Math classes were chosen because of the basic left-hemisphere skills utilized for arithmetic understanding; art classes were chosen because of the basic right-hemisphere skills utilized for visualization and tactility. Specific math classes were chosen that addressed numbers and formulae on the day of observation taping.

**Table 1** Analysis of Nonverbal Differences Among Classrooms

| | Room Adornments | Room Arrangement |
|---|---|---|
| Japanese Math | Very little on walls | Desks in rows<br>Individual desks<br>Teacher in front |
| Art (not offered) | Pictures of scenery | Chalkboard<br>Students called up |
| Israeli Math | Math projects by students on walls | All on floor<br>Common project<br>At desks at times |
| Art | Art projects by students on walls | All on floor<br>Group project |
| French Math | No numbers on walls<br>Projects on walls | Teacher in front<br>Student desks in rows<br>3 or 4 per row/desk |
| Art | Student projects on walls | Common project on floor and at desks |
| U.S. Math | Math as appears in other projects | One teacher in front<br>Group project at separate desks |
| Art | Art projects combined with other subjects | One teacher<br>Individual projects at desks, instructed by teacher |
| Spanish Math | Picturesque scenes | Desks pushed together |
| Art | Student work individualized | Partly on floor, partly at desks<br>No obvious order |

The basic analysis addresses verbal and nonverbal differences among the various teachers and schools. The nonverbal differences focus on room adornment, teacher-student interactive behaviors, teacher-student ratio, teacher-student haptics (touch behaviors), and teacher-student vocalics. The verbal differences focus on differences in encouraging problem solving, tolerance or intolerance of ambiguity, impulsivity or reflectivity, and individualistic or collectivistic reasoning. A summary analysis of the five classroom observations follows.

## Nonverbal Elements in the Classrooms

Even though the teachers were responsible for adorning the classroom walls in whatever style they desired, there were some practical limitations to doing so (see Table 1). Specifically, the Japanese classrooms were shared with the public schools during the week and the U.S. classrooms were used for several different classes throughout the day, so these teachers may have been limited in how and whether they could adorn the classroom wall.

**Table 2** Analysis of Nonverbal Differences Among Classrooms

|  | Teacher/Student Ratio | Teacher/Student Haptics | Teacher/Student Vocalics |
|---|---|---|---|
| Japanese | 1 to approximately 20 | No touching | Little noise. No speaking unless directly asked a question. No group verbal interaction. |
| Israeli | 1 to approximately 12 | Hugging to reinforce answer. Touching to discipline. | Dyad and triad interaction when responding to teacher questions. Group interaction while teacher addressed other students. |
| French | 1 to approximately 20 | Few touches. Touching of shoulders. | Very little student/student interaction in math. Much student socio-emotional interaction during art. |
| U.S. | 1 to approximately 20 | Some touching: shoulders, back of hands, middle of back to direct student movements. | Some student interaction during math. Primarily focused on teacher/student questions. Small group interaction during art. |
| Spanish | 1 to approximately 10 | Many hugs to display affection and reinforce positive behavior. | Students discussing answers before speaking out loud. Little structured interaction. Greatest noise level. |

Interestingly, the U.S., French, and Israeli teachers' math classes were each adorned with projects that included math as one of their functions. The projects were holistic, nonlinear, and collectivistic. For example, some projects were geographically oriented; these examined particular countries, and the math focused on percentages of the population that were male or female, of specific age groups, and of particular occupations. The Japanese math class had very little on the walls, other than photographed landscape scenes. There were no humans in the scenes and nothing to identify what subject was studied in this classroom. The Spanish teacher's walls were adorned with students' individualized work and pictures of scenes from various countries in Central and South America.

Each of the art classes displayed individual art projects completed by the students in the class. However, the U.S. class combined the art projects with other subjects. Art theory, presented by the art teacher, was displayed on the walls.

Each of the classes had only one teacher with no teacher aides (see Table 2). The Japanese, U.S., and French teachers taught approximately 20 children for one hour per academic subject. The Israeli and Spanish teachers each taught between 10 and 12 students for one hour per academic subject.

The classroom observations data included teacher-initiated haptics (touch behavior). On a continuum, the Japanese instructor initiated the least amount of touch and the Spanish teachers the most. The Japanese instructor did not touch any of the students throughout the math lesson. The U.S. teachers used touch functionally as part of their teaching, with both the math and art teachers touching the shoulders and backs of the students to guide them in a particular direction or touching their hands to demonstrate how to hold a particular art tool. They used no emotive haptics to reinforce or discipline. The French teachers touched infrequently – to encourage physical movement, for positive reinforcement, and to lead a few students back to their desks. The French art class teacher touched a few students on their shoulders to positively reinforce their participation and work. The Israeli and Spanish teachers used touching, hugs, and hand pats as positive reinforcement and for disciplining. Disciplining was done when children were on the floor, as in touching the foot or shoulder and asking the child to pay attention or to stop talking to fellow students. The Israeli teachers each sat with their arms loosely around students who had been repeatedly told to pay more attention.

I also analyzed the teacher-student vocalics and noise level during the class. Specific attention was paid to the teacher's nonverbal encouragement of group interaction or the amount of student-student interaction tolerated while the teacher was addressing a question to another student. The Japanese teacher's class exhibited the least unstructured interaction among the students and the least amount of noise as opposed to the Spanish classes, which exhibited the greatest unstructured interaction among the students and the loudest noise level. The Japanese students interacted only with the teacher and answered questions only when called upon. The Spanish students discussed the problems posed by the teacher among themselves and responded without definite order. For example, the art teacher asked a student what colors she thought would go nicely in the art project. Four of her fellow students all started to discuss what they thought would be appropriate for the project. Each then responded to the teacher with opinions, speaking for the group. Music played in the background during the art and music classes, adding to the overall noise levels.

## Analysis of Verbal Differences Among Classrooms

The student problem-solving styles encouraged by the teachers varied among the classes observed (see Tables 3 and 4). The math class teaching styles varied from very theoretical with almost no application to pure application with almost no theory introduced. The Japanese and French math classes were the most theoretical. The Japanese teacher wrote equations on the board and then called on students with their hand raised to come up to the board and write the answer. Similarly, the French teacher wrote a formula on the board and then gave a signal for all the students to hold up their individual slates with the formula and answer they had written.

The U.S. math class employed a combination of theoretical, linear, and verbal with nonverbal, visual, tactile problem solving. First, the students each wrote a formula for percentage and ratio on their individual papers. The teacher then directed each student to stand and emulate a bird, flapping his or her wings a specific number of times per minute. After the activity, the student applied his or her "wing flapping" behavior to the formula written on the paper. The teacher then explained the theory behind the formula.

Both the Israeli and Spanish teachers discussed math problems with their students; neither teachers nor students wrote formulas. Teachers used different colors of paper to represent different sizes, ratios, or percentages. Students solved the number, ratio, and percentage problems as a group, based upon the figures, shapes, and sizes presented to them.

Both the Japanese and French math instructors encouraged reflectivity among the students, by

**Table 3** Analysis of Verbal Differences Among Classrooms

| | Impulsivity/Reflectivity | Individualistic/Collectivistic |
|---|---|---|
| Japanese<br>Math | Reflectivity encouraged<br>Impulsivity discouraged | Individualistic |
| Israeli<br>Math | Impulsivity encouraged | Collectivistic and individualistic |
| Art | Impulsivity encouraged | Collectivistic |
| French<br>Math | Reflectivity encouraged<br>Impulsivity discouraged | Individualistic |
| Art | Reflectivity encouraged | Collectivistic |
| U.S.<br>Math | Impulsivity encouraged | Collectivistic and individualistic |
| Art | Reflectivity encouraged | Individualistic |
| Spanish<br>Math | Impulsivity encouraged | Collectivistic |
| Art | Impulsivity encouraged | Collectivistic |

writing the formula on the board and directing "Think about your answer as you solve it." The Japanese instructor added, "Remember all that I have taught you." Both teachers emphasized phrases such as "Don't answer too quickly. You want to be correct." The French teacher waited for everyone to complete their response and then announced "Hold up your answers now." In the other three classrooms, impulsivity was encouraged. Teachers verbalized the problems with students responding quickly either verbally or by raising their hands. A few even raised their hands before the teachers had finished the questions. This type of impulsivity did not occur in either the Japanese or French math classes.

Both the Japanese and the French teachers encouraged reflectively among their students; however, neither greatly rewarded or chastised the students for correct or incorrect answers. The students worked individually on the problems but "face" was always saved when a student offered an incorrect answer. The teacher would ask the other students, "Does anyone else have the answer?"

Collectivistic and individualistic collaboration on solving problems and separating behaviors were examined in the classroom. No teachers in this research chastised a student for incorrect answers, thereby singling out (or individualizing) him or her from the rest of the group. However, the Spanish math and art teachers and the French art teacher all encouraged collectivistic student involvement when working on a math problem or an art project. The U.S. art class was the only art class observed that had no collectivistic-collaborative approach. Each student worked on his or her own art project. The teacher circulated among the students to answer questions and offer suggestions on their particular "sponge" art projects, but students did not ask each other for information. The teacher also offered bits of art theory throughout the assignment.

Tolerance of ambiguity (concerning how a problem was solved) varied in the classrooms. This research examined whether the various teachers expected students to solve a problem employing a particular method, rather than allowing students to

**Table 4** Analysis of Verbal Differences Among Classrooms

|  | Types of Reasoning Encouraged | Tolerance of Ambiguity |
|---|---|---|
| Japanese Math | Linear Sequential Digital | High intolerance of ambiguity |
| Israeli Math | Holistic Tactile | Some tolerance of ambiguity |
| Art | Tactile Abstract | |
| French Math | Analytic Linear Rational | High intolerance of ambiguity |
| Art | Analogic Intuitive Tactile | |
| U.S. Math | Verbal, logical Nonverbal Abstract | Some intolerance of ambiguity |
| Art | Tactile, cause-effect, temporal | |
| Spanish Math | Spatial, holistic, digital, symbolic | High tolerance of ambiguity |
| Art | Nonrational, tactile, spatial | |

apply various methods. In other words, was there a tolerance or intolerance for choice of solution format selected by the students? The Japanese math class, Israeli math and art classes, and French math class seemed to tolerate little ambiguity in method chosen to solve the problem presented. The teachers explained how the problem was to be solved and expected the students to employ that particular approach. The French art class and the Spanish art and math classes allowed students to choose various methods for solving the problem, and each student suggested his or her method to the rest of the group.

Finally, the type of reasoning encouraged by the teachers varied. The Japanese and French math teachers encouraged linear, sequential, rational, and digital processing of math problems. They presented theory in digital formula, with little association to application, verbally giving students the format for its solution. The English math class mirrored the theory of the Japanese and French classes, but encouraged cognitive processing of theory to visual, application-oriented events (for example, number of times a bird flaps its wings). The Israeli and Spanish math classes promoted relationship of symbols to other functions, presented tactilely and holistically.

Honest research must address the obvious limitations in this cursory study: these classroom tapings were of a limited number of teachers (not generalizable to a larger population), on a particular day, teaching a particular subject matter. However, patterns do emerge among this sample in regard to type of problem solving encouraged. The French and Japanese math instructors encouraged the least collaboration among the students, the most reflectivity, and the greatest adherence to a single linear, theoretical method of problem solving. The Spanish and Israeli math teachers encouraged the greatest collaboration among students, the most impulsivity, and the greatest adherence to a holistic and application-oriented approach to methods of problem solving. The U.S. math class used the strongest combination of theory and application.

## Comparing Chinese and U.S. University Instructors

A replication of the "five case studies research" (Samovar & Porter, 1994) was conducted (Sun, 1995) comparing teaching styles of three Chinese male instructors, each videotaped during three classes of instruction in a Chinese University, and three U.S. male instructors videotaped during three classes of instruction in a university of the Pacific Northwest. The researcher and research assistant observed each of the eighteen tapes identifying instructor behaviors that encouraged or rewarded particular student problem-solving or communication behaviors. The data analysis was guided by categories previously established by Gudykunst (1988), Hofstede (1986), and Lieberman (1994) as behavioral indicators of cultural styles. The specific categories were collectivistic behaviors, individualistic behaviors, large power distance, and small power distance.

Examples associated with each category that guided the videotape observation analysis follow. Behaviors that encourage individualism are (1) individual students speaking up in class in response to a general invitation by the instructor; (2) students being expected to learn how to learn – What do you think about that ___?"; (3) students being

encouraged to debate an issue in class. Behaviors that encourage collectivism are (1) individual students speaking up in class only when called upon personally by the teacher; (2) students being expected to learn how to complete tasks; for example, "Do you remember what we learned?" (3) formal harmony in learning situations being maintained at all times; for example, "You don't need to question the writer, just understand his meaning"; (4) students not questioning teachers in class; for example, "If you have any questions, please see me after class." Behaviors that encourage small power distance between student and instructor are (1) student-centered teaching in which the premium is on student initiative, such as much student participation; (2) teacher encouraging critical thinking; for example, "What is your opinion of this article, and why do you think this?"; (3) teacher breaking to respond positively to spontaneous comments or questions from students. Behaviors that encourage large power distance between student and instructor are (1) teacher-centered education, such as information presented by teacher with little expectation for discussion or response; (2) students speaking up in class only when invited by the teacher; (3) students expecting teachers to initiate communication, discussion, and direction of the class; (4) teacher being neither contradicted nor criticized.

A chi-square test for homogeneity established reliability for tape observation within each of the two cultural groups. A chi-square for frequency of behaviors exhibited by the two cultural groups suggested significance for each of the categories (see Table 5). A chi-square for proportion also suggested no significance difference in proportions within each of the cultural groups.

The findings in this research strongly support previous findings that U.S. university teachers exhibit significantly more individualist/direct behaviors and more small power distance/personal behaviors with their students than do Chinese teachers. Comparatively, Chinese teachers exhibited significantly more collectivistic/indirect behaviors and more large power distance/contextual behaviors with their students than did U.S. teachers (see Table 5).

**Table 5** Pearson Chi-Square ($\chi^2$) for Frequency of U.S. and Chinese Behaviors Exhibited

| Culture of Teacher | Types of Behavior Encouraged | | | | |
|---|---|---|---|---|---|
| | Collectivist | Individualist | Large Power Distance | Small Power Distance | Total |
| Chinese | 112 | 30 | 132 | 20 | 294 |
| U.S. | 8 | 461 | 6 | 376 | 851 |
| Total | 120 | 491 | 138 | 396 | 1,145 |

| Value | Df | p< |
|---|---|---|
| 828.697 | 3 | .001* |

Note: Statistically significant for frequency of U.S. and Chinese behaviors by each dimension.

Sun (1995, Appendix B) observed that Chinese university instructors rarely directed questions to any individual students in particular but posed questions to the entire class. Examples of specific questions asked were "Do you remember what we learned last time?" "Who can remember well and talk about that?" "What do you think about the article after I explained it?" "How do you evaluate the article?" The questions were more rhetorical, and students were not expected to respond individually. Questions were not posed by students to the instructor. They were guided through silent problem solving without student-to-student interaction or dialogue.

U.S. university instructors asked more open-ended questions and generally waited for student responses. Types of questions asked were "How many of you feel stress about this class?" "How and why did you know about that?" "How many people feel much better than before the discussion?" "Good question . . . I had not thought of that point." "Let's talk this through to see if we shed light on something we never addressed before."

Though this research cannot begin to support academic and neurological research addressing hemisphericity, cultures, pedagogy, and problem solving, it is an initial step in the direction of understanding differences in methods of problem solving encouraged within the classroom. This basic project suggests that more extensive research be completed addressing patterns of problem solving encouraged cross-culturally, dependent upon the cultures of the students and instructors and the subjects taught.

Whether the intercultural interactants are in the classroom, socializing, or in a business environment, differences in cognitive processing and problem solving are inherent within the interaction. Hofstede (1986) claims that in the multicultural classroom "the focus of the teacher's training should be on learning about his or her own culture: getting intellectually and emotionally accustomed to the fact that in other societies, people learn [problem-solve] in different ways. This means taking one step back from one's values and cherished beliefs, which is far from easy" (p. 315). Consideration and understanding of differences among cultures in cognitive processing and presentation styles in problem solving constitute a major step toward successful intercultural communication.

## References

Blakeslee, T. R. (1980). *The Right Brain: A New Understanding of the Unconscious Mind and Its Creative Powers*. New York: Anchor.

Bogen, J., Dezare, W., TenHousten, W., and Marsh, J. (1972). The other side of the brain. IV: The A/P ration. *Bulletin of the Los Angeles Neurological Societies, 37*, 49–61.

Brown, H. (1980). *Principles of Language Learning and Teaching.* Englewood Cliffs, N.J.: Prentice-Hall.

Claxton, C., and Murrell, P. (1987). *Learning Styles: Implications for Improving Educational Practices.* Washington, D.C.: George Washington University, ASHE (Association for the Study of Higher Education).

Cole, M. (1985). "The Zone of Proximal Development: Where Culture and Cognition Create Each Other." In J. Wertsch (Ed.), *Culture, Communication and Cognition: Vygotskian Perspectives,* 146–162. Cambridge: Cambridge University Press.

Cole, M., Gay, J., and Glick, J. (1969). Communication Skills Among the Kpelle of Liberia. Paper presented at the Society for Research in Child Development Meeting, Santa Monica, Calif.

Cole, M., and Scribner, S. (1974). *Culture and Thought: A Psychological Introduction.* New York: Wiley.

Collins, A., and Dedre, G. (1987). "How People Construct Mental Models." In D. Holland and N. Quinn (Eds.), *Cultural Models in Language and Thought,* 243–269. New York: Cambridge University Press.

Condon, J., and Yousef, F. (1975). *An Introduction to Intercultural Communication.* Indianapolis: Bobbs-Merrill.

Damen, L. (1987). *Culture Learning: The Fifth Dimension in the Language Classroom.* Reading, Mass.: Addison-Wesley.

Delpit, L. (1995). *Other People's Children: Cultural Conflict in the Classroom.* New York: New Press.

Edwards, B. (1979). *Drawing on the Right Side of the Brain.* Los Angeles: J. P. Tarcher.

Felder, R., and Silverman, L. (1988). Learning and teaching styles in engineering education. *Engineering Education,* 674–681.

Freedle, R. (1981). "The Need for a Cross-Cultural Perspective." In J. Harvey (Ed.), *Cognition, Social Behavior and the Environment.* Hillsdale, N.J.: Lawrence Erlbaum.

Gregorc, A. F. (1979). Learning/Teaching Styles: Potent Forces Behind Them. *Educational Leadership, 36,* 234–236.

Griffin, C. (1983). "Social Structure, Speech and Silence: Fijian Reactions to the Problems of Social Change." In W. Maxwell (Ed.), *Thinking: The Expanding Frontier,* 57–69. Philadelphia: The Franklin Institute.

Gudykunst, W. B. (1988). "Uncertainty and Anxiety." In Y. Kim and W. Gudykunst (Eds.), *Theories in Intercultural Communication.* Newbury Park, Calif.: Sage.

Gudykunst, W. B., and Ting-Toomey, S. (1988). *Culture and Interpersonal Communication.* Newbury Park, Calif.: Sage.

Hale-Benson, J. (1969). *Black Children: Their Roots, Culture and Learning Styles.* Baltimore, Md.: Johns Hopkins University Press.

Hall, E. (1976). *Beyond Culture.* New York: Doubleday.

Helgesen, M. (1988). *Natural Style and Learning Style Preferences: Their Effect on Teaching and Learning.* University of Illinois at Urbana-Champaign: Instruction and Management Services.

Hofstede, G. (1980). Motivation, leadership, and organization: Do American theories apply abroad? *Organizational Dynamics,* Summer, 42–63.

Hofstede, G. (1986). Cultural differences in teaching and learning. *International Journal of International Relations, 10,* 301–320.

Hofstede, G. (1991). *Cultures and Organizations: Software of the Mind.* London: McGraw-Hill.

Hooks, B. (1994). *Teaching to Transgress.* New York: Routledge.

Kaplan, R. (1988). "Cultural Thought Patterns in Inter-Cultural Education." In J. Wurzel (Ed.), *Toward Multiculturalism: A Reader in Multicultural Education,* 207–222. Yarmouth, Me.: Intercultural Press.

Kaplan, R. B. (1970). Cultural thought patterns in intercultural education. *Language Learning, 16* (Vols. 1 & 2), 1–20.

Kaplan, S., and Kaplan, R. (1981). *Cognition and Environment.* New York: Pergamon Press.

Kleinfeld, J. (1994). "Learning Styles and Culture." In W. Lonner and R. Malpass (Eds.), *Psychology and Culture,* 151–156. Boston: Allyn & Bacon.

Kohls, L. (1984). *Survival Kit for Overseas Living,* rev. ed.. Yarmouth, Me.: Intercultural Press.

Kolb, D. (1984). *Experiential Learning.* Englewood Cliffs, N.J.: Prentice-Hall.

Korzybsky, A. (1933). *Science and Sanity: An Introduction to Non-Aristotelian Systems and General Semantics.* Lakeville, Conn.: Institute of General Semantics.

Lee, D. (1950). Codifications of Reality: Lineal and Nonlineal. *Psychosomatic Medicine, 12*(2), 89–97.

Lieberman, D. (1994). "Ethnocognitivism, Problem Solving and Hemisphericity." In L. Samovar and R. Porter (Eds.), *Intercultural Communication: A Reader,* 7th ed., 178–193. Belmont, Calif.: Wadsworth.

Lieberman, D., Kosokoff, S., and Kosokoff, J. (1988). What is common about common sense? *ORTESOL, 9,* 13–28.

Luria, A. R. (1966). *Higher Cortical Function in Man.* New York: Basic Books.

McCarthy, B. (1990). Using the 4MAT System to Bring Learning Styles to Schools. *Educational Leadership,* 31–37.

Mestenhauser, J. (1981). "Selected Learning Concepts and Themes." In G. Althen (Ed.), *Learning Across Cultures: Intercultural Communication and Interna-*

*tional Educational Exchange.* Washington, D.C.: National Association for Foreign Student Affairs.

Ong, W. (1973). "World as View and World as Event." In M. Prosser (Ed.), *Intercommunication Among Nations and Peoples,* 27 – 45. New York: Harper & Row.

Paredes, J., and Hepburn, K. (1976). The split brain and the culture-and-cognition paradox. *Current Anthropology, 17,* 121 – 127.

Prince, G. (1978). Putting the other half of the brain to work. *Training: The Magazine of Human Resources Development, 15,* 57 – 61.

Pribram, K. (1949). *Conflicting Patterns of Thought.* Washington, D.C.: Public Affairs Press.

Reid, J. (1987). The learning style preferences of ESL students. *TESOL Quarterly,* 87 – 111.

Samovar, L., and Porter, R. (Eds.). (1988). *Intercultural Communication: A Reader,* 5th ed. Belmont, Calif.: Wadsworth.

Samovar, L., and Porter, R. (Eds.). (1991). *Intercultural Communication: A Reader,* 6th ed. Belmont, Calif.: Wadsworth.

Samovar, L., and Porter, R. (Eds.) (1994). *Intercultural Communication: A Reader,* 7th ed. Belmont, Calif.: Wadsworth.

Scarcella, R. (1990). *Teaching Language Minority Students in the Multicultural Classroom.* Englewood Cliffs, N.J.: Prentice-Hall.

Schneider, D. (1976). "Notes Toward a Theory of Culture." In K. Basso and H. Silby (Eds.). *Meanings in Anthropology.* Albuquerque: University of New Mexico Press.

Silverman, L. (1987). Global Learners: Our Forgotten Gifted Children. Paper presented at the Seventh World Conference on Gifted and Talented Children, Salt Lake City, Utah.

Springer, S., and Deutsch, G. (1985). *Left Brain, Right Brain.* New York: W. H. Freeman.

Stewart, E., and Bennett, M. (1991). *American Cultural Patterns – A Cross-Cultural Perspective.* Yarmouth, Me.: Intercultural Press.

Sun, X. (1995). *Behavioral Differences in the Classroom: U.S. University Teachers and Chinese University Teachers.* Master's Thesis. Portland, Ore.: Portland State University.

Triandis, H. (1994). "Culture and Social Behavior." In W. Lonner and R. Malpass (Eds.), *Psychology and Culture,* 169 – 173. Boston: Allyn & Bacon.

Tsunoda, T. (1979). Difference in the mechanism of emotion in Japanese and Westerner. *Psychotherapy and Psychosomatics, 31,* 367 – 372.

Wallace, B., and Grave, W. (1995). *Poisoned Apple: The Bell-Curve Crisis and How Our Schools Create Mediocrity and Failure.* New York: St. Martin's Press.

Witkin, H., and Goodenough, D. (1981). *Cognitive Styles: Essence of Origins.* New York: International University Press.

# The Crossroads of Language and Culture

MARY FONG

Since the dawning of humanity, scholars have been interested in the concept of language and its relationships to human endeavor. Confucius's observation that "if language not be in accordance with the truth of things, affairs cannot be carried on to success" and Saint-Exupery's comment that "to grasp the meaning of the world of today we use a language created to express the world of yesterday" reflect this concern. In the current era, anthropologists, linguists, psychologists, and philosophers continue to try to fathom the role of language in human activity and its connection to culture. In this essay, I examine briefly some basic perspectives about the relationship between language and culture. I begin with a brief description of the Sapir-Whorf hypothesis and then review the more current ethnographic directions of culture and language research. And, then, in order to demonstrate some of the relationships between language and culture using ethnographic methodologies, I draw from research on the Chinese culture to demonstrate the intersection of language and culture in examples from both cultural interaction and intercultural interaction.

## Perspectives on Language and Culture

### Sapir-Whorf Hypothesis

A major proponent of linguistic relativity and one of the first modern observations of the relationship between language and culture is the Sapir-Whorf hypothesis. This notion proposes a deterministic view that language structure is necessary in order to produce thought. In other words, language and its categories – grammar, syntax, and vocabulary – are the only categories by which we can experience the world. Simply stated: language influences and shapes how people perceive their world, their culture. This vision dominated scholarly thinking as a point of discussion, research, and controversy for over five decades.

The Sapir-Whorf hypothesis also holds that language and thought covary with one another. That is, diversity in language categories and structure lead to cultural differences in thought and perceptions of the world. This position is known as linguistic relativity. Sapir (1951) believed that the "real world" is largely built upon the unconscious language habits of the group.

Benjamin Whorf, who was a student of Edward Sapir's in the early 1930s, initially published (Whorf, 1956) the views he and Sapir held about language and culture in a series of articles in 1940–41. He stated:

*We cut nature up, organize it into concepts, and ascribe significances as we do, largely because we are parties to an agreement to organize it in this way – an agreement that holds throughout our speech community and is codified in the patterns of our language. (p. 213)*

Sapir and Whorf's ideas have been understood to mean that people who speak different languages segment their world differently. Thus, any language, such as Russian, Chinese, or German, structures a "Russian," "Chinese," or "German" reality by framing and screening what these cultural members attend to. If there is a word for "it" in their language, then cultural members know that "it" exists; and if not, "it" is nonexistent to them.

Brown (1958) in part disagreed with Sapir-Whorf and argued that a cultural member's world view is not determined by language. He held, rather, that people categorize their world by attaching labels to what is out there. People use language to do what they need it to do. Brown's position does support the idea of linguistic relativity because the perceptual categories that are frequently used receive labels, while unused or insignificant categories may not be labeled.

Several research studies on color terms and color perception tested the Sapir-Whorf hypothesis (Berlin & Kay, 1967; Bruner, Olver, & Greenfield, 1966; Greenfield & Bruner, 1966; Kay and Kempton, 1984). Eastman (1990) reviewed these studies that supported the idea of linguistic relativity and stated that "it appears to be the case that world view is a matter more of linguistic relativity than linguistic determinism" (p. 103).

Other researchers have found it difficult to test how strongly the structure of a language influences the world view of people because reliable methods for assessing the world view of a cultural people independently of the language they speak are needed (Brown, 1976; Carroll, 1967; Kay & Kempton, 1984). "In general, the Sapir-Whorf hypothesis has come to be regarded as either unconfirmable or incorrect . . . most linguists and psychologists believe that evidence offered in its support is flawed. . . . If the hypothesis can be sustained at all, it implies only a weak influence of language structure on thought" (Carroll, 1992).

## Ethnographic Research Approaches

In 1974, Hymes described the development of linguistic research:

*the first half of the century was distinguished by a drive for the autonomy of language as an object of study and a focus upon description of [grammatical] structure, [while] the second half was distinguished by a concern for the integration of language in sociocultural context and a focus upon the analysis of function. (p. 208)*

Hymes's description was quite accurate because the second half of the century has marked a number of qualitative research methods, such as discourse analysis, pragmatics, and ethnography of communication, as ways to investigate the interrelationship of language and culture. For some researchers, the controversy over whether language determines or reflects thought or thought determines or reflects language has not been the primary concern. To Sherzer (1987), what is at issue is the analysis of discourse as the "embodiment of the essence of culture and as constitutive of what language and culture relationship is all about." Sherzer (1987) also views discourse as the intersection where language and culture interrelate. He states, "It is discourse that creates, recreates, focuses, modifies, and transmits both culture and language and their intersection" (p. 295).

For Sherzer (1987), culture is the organization of individuals who share rules for production and interpretation of behavior. Language represents an individual's symbolic organization of the world. Language is a medium that reflects and expresses an individual's group membership and relationships with others. Discourse analysis derives from pragmatics and speech act theory (Saville-Troike, 1989). Pragmatics or speech act theory refers to the study of the connotative (inner) and denotative (outer) meanings of "expressions when used in a conversation or a written work" (Paul, 1987, p. 101). To Silverstein (1976), pragmatics is "the study of the meaning of linguistic signs relative to their communicative functions (p. 20)." Pragmatics also entails cultural members applying their knowledge of the world to the interpretation of what is said and done in interaction (Fromkin & Rodman, 1983; Gumperz, 1982).

The ethnography of communication provides the researcher with a framework of observation and interviewing techniques to facilitate capturing interlocutors' meanings in various communicative acts both culturally and interculturally. The ethnographer endeavors to describe the communicative choices that interlocutors make. This involves describing and accounting for the interpretive systems and practices through which members construct actions and deal with behaviors.

Hymes (1962), an originator of the ethnography of communication, states that the "study of speech as a factor in cognitive and expressive behavior leads to concern with the ethnographic patterning of the uses of speech in a community" (p. 102). Investigating language and culture is finding not only linguistic structural regularities, but also regularities of usage that have motives, emotions, desires, knowledge, attitudes, and values attached to them. An essential aim of studies on language and culture using the ethnography-of-communication approach is to make implicit cultural beliefs, attitudes, values, norms of interpretation, rules of speaking, norms of interaction, and so forth explicit in order to understand and to practice communicative competence within a particular culture.

## Language Studies

Some of the sample findings in the cultural and intercultural studies that follow are illustrations of language and culture analysis. The qualitative methods – discourse analysis, pragmatics, and ethnography of communication – jointly provide tools and perspectives to make possible an in-depth examination of communicative phenomena.

## A Cultural Study

An ethnographic study of the Chinese New Year celebration in Hong Kong (Fong, 1993) provides an example of the manner in which the Chinese employ language to reverse bad luck. By examining the speaking pattern used when someone breaks a glass object during the Chinese New Year, it is possible to understand how Chinese people "play" with words and their meanings through the use of implied statements that represent a positive idea. The unfortunate incident of breaking an object is transformed to a fortunate incident when a person orally uses a positive expression to describe the unfortunate act. The expression of the positive statement counteracts the negative occurrence. One informant from Fong's (1993) study explained:

*Be careful not to break any cups or glass things. It's bad luck to break something on the New Year. I remember seeing some old Chinese films; some child was so careless, he broke a bowl, a glass. The adult would say, "We cannot change what has happened. How can we reverse it?" By saying:* /lɔk⁹ dei⁶ hɔi¹ fa¹/, *which means falling down to the ground, may the flowers blossom. This expression implies* /fu³ gwei³ wiŋ⁴ wa⁴/, *that is, being prosperous and becoming wealthy. So you see the Chinese are very clever. They would say something to change it to good.* /lɔk⁹ dei⁶ hɔi¹ fa¹/ *is to fall to the ground,* /hɔ i¹ fa¹/ *is, it will blossom.*

/Fu$^3$ gwei$^3$/, *will be wealthy.* /Wiŋ/$^4$ /wa/$^4$, *is prosperous. When you drop something, once it touches the floor, it blossoms up. Once the flowers blossom, you'll have wealth. This is related to the new year.* [Ed. note: *The author has phonetically translated Cantonese Chinese using the symbol system of the International Phonetic Alphabet. The superscript numbers indicate various tone levels found in the nine-tone Cantonese language.*]

Because the expression is meant to reverse the bad luck, the positive linguistic concepts such as prosperous and wealthy contained in these expressions can be considered as good luck attributes. Possible antonyms of these linguistic concepts are misfortune and poverty, which are considered attributes of bad luck.

To understand what linguistic devices the Chinese employ, it is necessary to understand a few rules of behavior and speaking. Shimanoff (1980) proposes an "If . . . , then . . ." method of concisely stating a rule of behavior. To develop Shimanoff's method of stating behavioral rules, I will add a "because . . . , meaning . . ." sequence in order to add a meaning component to a formulation of a communication rule.

In this situation, the sequential rule statement begins with the initial linguistic "If . . ." slot, which provides information on the particular context, condition, or situation, like a speech event, speech act, or genre. It is followed by the "then . . ." slot, which refers to the speaking and/or behavioral interaction pattern discovered from the researcher's ethnographic data analysis.

The third linguistic device, the "because . . ." slot provides a concise rationale for why people of a particular culture behave the way they do. Here, an underlying belief or value system or cultural principle may be revealed to provide an explanation for a people's way of communicating. The final linguistic device, is the "meaning . . ." slot, which serves as the speaking and/or behavioral interaction pattern, a particular speech act, speech event, scene, and so forth.

These sequential rules statement provide the formula:

**If** . . . (context, condition, or situation like a speech event, speech act, or genre),

**then** . . . (speaking and/or interaction pattern)

**because** . . . (belief or value system or cultural principle),

**meaning** . . . (norm of interpretation of: a symbol, speaking pattern, interaction pattern, particular speech act, speech event, scene, etc.)

Applying these sequential rules to the Chinese custom of reversing the negative effect of an object that has been shattered can be expressed in a concise rule statement using the formula:

**If** a person breaks a glass item on Chinese New Year Day,

**then** a Hong Kong Chinese person should say: /lɔk$^9$ dei$^6$ hɔi$^1$ fa$^1$/ (falling down to the ground, may the flowers blossom)

**because** this is believed to counteract the bad luck and to create good luck,

**meaning** that prosperity and wealth may come about

## An Intercultural Study

An intercultural study on compliment interactions between Chinese immigrants and European Americans from the perspective of Chinese immigrants (Fong, 1994) found that both cultural groups have differing ways of speaking in compliment interactions (Chen, 1993; Chiang & Pochtrager, 1993; Fong, 1994). European Americans on the West Coast and in the Midwest generally accept a compliment (Chen, 1993; Chiang & Pochtrager, 1993; Fong, 1994). On the other hand, the literature reports that Chinese have the tendency to deny compliments in order to give an impression of modesty (Chen, 1993; Chiang & Pochtrager, 1993; Gao, 1984; Zhang, 1988). Four adaptations by Chinese immigrant participants (CIPs) to European American compliments were found. An orientation is a state or condition that is changeable from one interaction to another depending on the Chinese immigrant's adaptation to intercultural communication differences. Four orientations in which the CIP can be located are (1) intercultural shock state, (2) intercultural resistance state, (3) intercultural accommodation state, and (4) bicultural competence state. In this essay, I will examine the intercultural shock state in order to convey a sense of Chinese immigrants' thinking and speaking.

Affectively, CIPs reported feeling uncomfortable, unnatural, stressed, embarrassed, surprised, shocked, or afraid, uneasy, nervous when a European American complimented them. The situational outcome of the intercultural compliment interaction for CIPs, however, was an appreciation of receiving praise because they felt accepted, liked, and welcomed by European Americans. CIPs reported that compliments helped them to reduce some of their stress as a newcomer to the United States.

Cognitively, CIPs in the intercultural shock state have minimum knowledge of the intercultural communication differences in compliment interactions with European Americans. Prior to coming to the United States, CIPs reported that they were not familiar with the European Americans' generosity in (1) giving compliments, (2) giving compliments containing strong positive adjectives, (3) giving compliments intended to encourage a person after an unsatisfactory performance, (4) giving compliments on a wide variety of topics, (5) accepting compliments, and (6) giving compliments face-to-face in all types of relationships.

Behaviorally, five speaking patterns were found, and two examples are provided here. The first example is one type of compliment response that Chinese immigrants used: the Direct Denial + Verbal Corrective/Prescriptive response. Here is a reported intercultural compliment interaction:

*(American) roommate:* You look very lovely today, Bei Sha.

*(Taiwan) roommate:* Oh, no, no, no. It's not necessary to say that. I just look ordinary.

Because Chinese immigrants value indirectness and modesty in conversation, the compliment was interpreted as being direct, face-to-face, expressed openly with very positive adjectives on Bei Sha's appearance. This is contrary to the normal Chinese forms of compliment interactions. The response

was made to avoid self-praise and to suggest to the American roommate that such a direct compliment should not be given.

In the second example, CIPs who were in the intercultural shock state were found to use a Silence response. Below is an intercultural compliment interaction reported to have occurred at an American host family's home during a dinner:

*(American) hostess:* You must be very prepared, mature to come here by yourself.

*(Hong Kong) student:* [silence]

Chinese immigrants highly value modesty, but they are also aware that Americans directly accept and appreciate compliments. The compliment was interpreted as being direct, face-to-face, and as expressing openly positive thoughts with very positive adjectives, which is contrary to Chinese forms of compliment interactions. The Chinese immigrant recipient reported feeling ambivalent about which cultural response to use and so remained silent.

## Conclusion

The excerpt from the cultural study (Fong, 1993) illustrates the Chinese way of thinking and speaking. When an object is shattered during the Chinese New Year holiday, the Chinese interpret the incident as bad luck. Through speech, however, the perceived bad luck is reversed to good luck.

The intercultural compliment interaction study (Fong, 1994) sheds light on the way Chinese immigrants in the intercultural shock state reveal patterns of thinking and speaking. The denial response is a pattern of speaking that is commonly used in the intercultural shock state. CIPs in this orientation essentially perceive European Americans as being generous in giving compliments with relatively strong positive adjectives and in accepting compliments.

Current ethnographic methods hold that the best way to capture a view of language and culture is to observe the communicative phenomenon in a naturalistic setting and to have cultural members identify and classify the interaction or event as being culturally significant. The crossroads of language and culture are found in the culturally shared meaning of ideas and behaviors that are voiced as symbolic utterances, expressions, dialogue, and conversations in such various contexts as interpersonal and group interactions, research interviews, and public speaking forums.

In the two language and cultural studies described in this essay, the ways of speaking and thinking were the two primary interrelated foci that reveal and reflect the outer and inner shared substances of communications that primarily make up a speech community. To examine a speech community's patterns of speaking without also discovering the norms of interpretation or the shared sociocultural knowledge of cultural members is to silence their cultural humanness as a speech community. To study only the shared sociocultural knowledge of cultural members and not attend to how it is relevant to their way of speaking is to lose an opportunity to understand more about different cultural communication styles — potential sources of intercultural conflict.

Both examples of findings from the language and cultural studies illuminate, in part, what Hymes (1974) has suggested:

*It has often been said that language is an index to or reflection of culture. But language is not simply passive or automatic in its relation to culture. . . . Speaking is itself a form of cultural behavior, and language, like any other part of culture, partially shapes the whole; and its expression of the rest of culture is partial, selective. That selective relation, indeed, is what should be interesting to us. Why do some features of a community's life come to be named – overtly expressible in discourse – while others are not?* (p. 127)

## References

Berlin, B., and Kay, P. (1967). Universality and Evolution of Basic Color Terms. Working Paper #1, Laboratory for Language Behavior Research, University of California, Berkeley.

Bruner, J., Olver, R. R., and Greenfield, P. M. (1966). *Studies in Cognitive Growth*. New York: Wiley.

Brown, R. (1958). *Words and Things*. New York: Free Press.

Brown, R. (1976). Reference. In Memorial Tribute to Eric Lennenberg. *Cognition, 4,* 125–153.

Carroll, J. B. (1967). "Bibliography of the Southwest Project in Comparative Psycholinguistics." In D. Hymes (Ed.), *Studies in Southwestern Ethnolinguistics,* 452–454. The Hague: Mouton.

Carroll, J. B. (1992). "Anthropological Linguistics: An Overview." In W. Bright (Ed.), *International Encyclopedia of Linguistics*. New York: Oxford University Press.

Chen, R. (1993). Responding to compliments: A contrastive study of politeness strategies between American English and Chinese speakers. *Journal of Pragmatics, 20,* 43–75.

Chiang, F., and Pochtrager, B. (1993). A Pilot Study of Compliment Responses of American-Born English Speakers and Chinese-Born English Speakers. (available in microfiche only: ED 35GG49)

Eastman, C. M. (1990). *Aspects of language and culture,* 2d ed. Novato, Calif.: Chandler & Sharp.

Fong, M. (1993). Speaking Patterns Related to Luck During the Chinese New Year. Paper presented at the annual meeting of the Speech Communication Association, Miami, Florida.

Fong, M. (1994). Patterns of occurrences of compliment response types. In unpublished doctoral dissertation, *Chinese Immigrants' Interpretations of Their Intercultural Compliment Interactions with European-Americans*. (Chapter 6). Seattle: University of Washington.

Fromkin, V., and Rodman, R. (1983). *An Introduction to Language, 3d ed.* New York: CBS Publishing.

Gao, W. (1984). Compliment and Its Reaction in Chinese and English Cultures. *Working Papers in Discourse in English and Chinese*. Canberra: Canberra College of Advanced Education, 32–37.

Greenfield, P. M., and Bruner, J. S. (1966). Culture and cognitive growth. *International Journal of Psychology, 1,* 89–107.

Gumperz, J. J. (1982). *Discourse Strategies*. New York: Cambridge University Press.

Hymes, D. (1962). "The Ethnography of Speaking." In T. Gladwin and W. Sturtevant (Eds.), *Anthropology and Human Behavior,* 99–137. Washington, D.C.: Anthropological Society of Washington.

Hymes, D. (1964). Toward ethnographies of communication: The analysis of communicative events. *American Anthropologist, 66,* 21–41.

Hymes, D. (1974). *Foundations in Sociolinguistics: An Ethnographic Approach*. Philadelphia: University of Pennsylvania Press.

Kay, P., and Kempton, W. (1984). What is the Sapir-Whorf hypothesis? *American Anthropologist, 86,* 65–73.

Paul, A. (1987). Review of Joseph H. Greenberg, *Language in the Americas. The Chronicle of Higher Education,* July 15, p. 6.

Sapir, E. (1951). "The Status of Linguistics as a Science." In D. Mandelbaum (Ed.), *Collected Writings.* Berkeley: University of California Press.

Saville-Troike, M. (1989). *The Ethnography of Communication,* 2d ed. New York: Basil Blackwell.

Sherzer, J. (1987). A discourse-centered approach to language and culture. *American Anthropologist, 89,* 295–309.

Shimanoff, S. B. (1980). *Communication Rules: Theory and Research.* Beverly Hills: Sage.

Silverstein, M. (1976). "Shifters, Linguistic Categories, and Cultural Description." In K. H. Basso and H. A. Selby (Eds.), *Meaning in Anthropology,* 11–56. Albuquerque: University of New Mexico Press.

Whorf, B. L. (1956). *Language, thought, and reality.* Cambridge: M.I.T. Press.

Zhang, Z. (1988). A discussion of communicative culture. *Journal of Chinese Language Teacher Association, 23,* 107–112.

# *That's Greek to Me: Between a Rock and Place in Intercultural Encounters*

## WEN-SHU LEE

It was fall 1983, my first year in the United States as a foreign student pursuing a master's degree at the Department of Communication Arts and Sciences, University of Southern California. Even after ten years of studying English to pass entrance examinations in Taiwan, I had a hard time jotting down notes in graduate seminars. To solve this problem, I would summarize what I heard in the seminar in Chinese. During a seminar break, I was frantically adding Chinese characters to my notes. One of my fellow American students watched over my shoulder and said, "That's *Greek* to me!" I promptly corrected him: "No, it's Chinese." He was shocked for about one second and then burst into laughter. We spent 20 minutes or so clarifying that "Greek" did not mean "Greek," that "Greek" meant "foreign, difficult, and mysterious stuff," and I finally *agreed* that my Chinese was "Greek" to him.

This article will address problems caused by incomprehension of idiom or slang during communication between people from different cultures. I will first explore the reasons why this is an important subject in intercultural communication. Second, I will redefine idiom incomprehension problems by integrating theories proposed by Gregory Bateson, Mikhail Bakhtin, and Jurgen Habermas. Finally, I will propose a four-step process to help people get

...from between a rock and a hard place in intercultural encounters.

## Why Should We Study Idiom in Intercultural Communication?

There are four reasons why idioms should be an important subject in intercultural communication. First, idioms are figurative in nature. Second, figurative meanings often cause comprehension problems for people from different cultures. Third, we do not explain idioms completely. Finally, idioms open up an avenue to interpersonal closeness. Let me explain these related reasons in detail for you.

### Idiomatic Meaning Is Figurative

First, an idiom and its meaning often do not match because they have a *figurative* rather than a *literal* relationship. The meaning of an idiom is rarely predictable from its constituent components; consider, "bought the farm," "get your feet wet," "get your hands dirty," "a wild goose chase," "like a duck on a June bug." Like the "It's Greek to me" example, "bought the farm" has no literal relationship with "someone died," and "like a duck on a June bug" has no literal relationship with "I will confront you immediately with what you have done."

### Idioms Cause Comprehension Problems for Those from Different Cultures

Second, communication breakdowns often occur when people use idioms in communicating with those who do not comprehend the idiomatic meanings. For people who use idioms "naturally," the figurative link between an idiom and its meaning often goes unnoticed. But this link becomes problematic for those who do not share the lifeworld with the idiom users.[1] This problem is more easily solved by those who speak English as a first language (hereafter, L1 speakers) than those who speak English as a second language (hereafter, L2 speakers). For example, a young college student, Susan, living in San Jose uses "Check it out, there's a stud muffin" with her friend, Jenny, while shopping with her Mom. Her mother, an L1 speaker in her fifties who does not share the lifeworld of "col-

lege life" with Susan and Jenny, may ask "What do you mean by a 'stud muffin'?" knowing that it is an expression among young people that she is not familiar with. But if Susan and Jenny are shopping with an L2 speaker, Huei-Mei, the problem becomes more complex. She may not hear "stud muffin" clearly. Or, she may hear the idiom but remain quiet about it, suspecting that her English is not good enough. Even if she has the courage to ask for the meaning of "stud muffin," Huei-Mei may still have a hard time linking "a handsome guy" with "a male breeding horse" and "English breakfast food." Finally, even if she knows the linguistic meaning of "stud muffin," she may use it in an inappropriate relational context. For example, she may want to compliment her handsome seminar professor: "Professor Spano, you are a stud muffin." Therefore, the study of idioms is important to intercultural communication competence.

### We Rarely Explain an Idiom Completely, Especially Its Relational Meaning

Third, as is apparent in the stud muffin, a complete explanation of an idiom requires a linguistic discussion about the meaning of idiom words and a relational discussion about the association between the two people who use an idiom together. Most of us engage in a linguistic explanation but leave out the relational one. For example, Susan forgets to tell Huei-Mei that "stud muffin" is used between friends (usually females) to comment on a third person, a handsome male. We do not use it with someone who has a formal, professional relationship with us. Huei-Mei, as a result, needs to know that one should not use "stud muffin" with a professor. For this reason, we need to study idiom explanations more carefully in intercultural encounters.

### Idioms Enable People to Relate Closely

Finally, idioms hold one of the keys to interpersonal closeness. Idioms are commonly used in informal situations between casual acquaintances, friends, and pals (Knapp, 1984, pp. 225–228). The ability to use idioms accepted by a group may not guarantee closeness, but it can increase the possibilities of shortening interpersonal distance if so desired. That is, if people from different cultural backgrounds can use each other's idioms, formal and awkward discomfort may be replaced by a sense of informality and even closeness. This may facilitate intercultural relationships in a variety of contexts — interpersonal relationships between classmates and friends, working relationships in a company, and teaching-learning relationships in the classroom.

Idioms are an important subject in intercultural communication because they create problems as well as closeness. Idioms create problems because idiom users often are unaware of the potential for confusing those who do not share their lifeworld. Idioms have the potential to create closeness because of the informality and fun associated with them. In the following sections, I will take on the most dramatic and difficult case — between L1 and L2 speakers[2] — and propose a four-step process to help them make sense of their confusion through dialogue. It is important to note that the following method may help anyone who encounters idiom problems when coming into a new environment because of marriage or relocation; when dealing with someone of a different sexual orientation; and when moving between ethnic, professional, religious groups, and so on. It is to this process I now turn.

## A Process for Intercultural Understanding of Idioms and Lifeworld

This method is composed of four steps. They are based upon concrete life experiences and theories proposed by Gregory Bateson (Ruesch & Bateson, 1951; Bateson, 1972, 1979; Bateson & Bateson, 1987) and Mikhail Bakhtin (1981, 1986). The goal of these steps is to provide a guide to *a new way of talking,* remove idiom problems between L1 and L2 speakers (and those who do not share lifeworlds), and link mutually unintelligible lifeworlds through the use of dialogue.

### Step 1: Establishing a New Conversational Decorum

Some L1 adult speakers live by an etiquette system which consists of tacit rules dictating how they should speak — be polite and cordial, do not comment on another's speech errors or pronunciation problems, and so on. Discussions about idioms in this case are difficult. In fact, problems with idioms are regularly ignored. Other L1 speakers may abide by a different set of rules — bolder and more honest — correcting another's speaking problems on the spot. This correction is sometimes awkward or snide, turning off the other's desire to learn.

L2 speakers also face problems regarding rules of speaking. Some L2 speakers may feel that asking questions about incomprehensible messages is a sign of weakness and stupidity, and they may turn to more private ways of learning (such as reading magazines, watching television programs, looking words up in a dictionary). This also makes discussions about idioms difficult. Other L2 speakers may be more forthright and ask for clarifications on a regular basis if they encounter problems in a conversation. At least, they start the process of learning. However, they tend to focus more on linguistic meanings than on relational meanings.

The point here is that in order to resolve idiom problems in daily conversations, both L1 and L2 speakers need to work together to establish a conversational decorum in which it is all right or socially acceptable to bring up problems. When we have a safe space to talk about idiom problems,[3] we may move next to learn how to ask questions and how to explain in a friendly and nonintimidating way. It is to this second step I will turn.

### Step 2: Learning to Differentiate Goal-Oriented Talk from Metatalk

In this section, I will discuss two ways of labeling ordinary talk — metatalk and goal-oriented talk. Then I will use these labels to explain how the process of idiom explanation involves the use of metatalk to fix comprehension problems so that people can resume their goal-oriented talk to do daily business together.

People engage in *goal-oriented talk,* when their shared lifeworld (that is, language and culture) is unproblematic. That is, they do not have to worry about whether they understand each other's words and meanings. They can just use language to communicate what goals they intend to accomplish. Consider an example of goal-oriented talk:

*Jerry:* Hey dude, whatz up?

*Tony:* Not much. Wanna go grab a bite?

*Jerry:* No. I'm under the wire....

*Tony:* Take a chill pill. Don't worry about it so much....

When lifeworld cannot be assumed, when idiomatic expressions such as "chill pill" cause comprehension problems, goal-oriented talk cannot continue. At this juncture, people need to learn to talk about talk. Talk about talk is called metatalk.[4] We use metatalk to talk about idioms. That is, we use metatalk to fix problems caused by idioms in goal-oriented talk. Ultimately, this may help people resume their goal-oriented talk. For example, the goal-oriented conversation between Jerry and Tony aim at the goals of greeting, grabbing a bite, and then calming the partner down. It may not have gone so smoothly if Tony were an L2 speaker:

*Jerry:* Hey dude, whatz up?

*Tony:* *What* did you just say?

Here Jerry and Tony find themselves between a rock and a hard place in their intercultural encounter. They need to use metatalk to get out of this dilemma. To obtain a complete knowledge of metatalk, we need to learn two sub-labels subsumed under metatalk – linguistic metatalk and relational metatalk (Bateson, 1972). They both are metatalk; however, they differ in the aspect of talk they try to deal with. Linguistic metatalk discusses talk as "linguistic codes." Relational metatalk discusses talk as "linguistic codes used by two people." Simply put, linguistic metatalk talks about *words* while relational metatalk talks about *relationship between the two people who use an idiom with each other*. Let me use an example to clarify these two concepts:

*Jerry:* Hey dude, whatz up? (*goal-oriented* talk)

*Tony:* What do you mean by "dude"? (*linguistic metatalk*)

*Jerry:* Oh, "dude" means guy, friend, a person (*linguistic metatalk*), and "Hey dude" means saying hello (*linguistic metatalk*).

*Tony:* What is the relationship between two people, let's say John and Steve, who use "Hey dude" with each other? (*relational metatalk*)

*Jerry:* Oh ... John and Steve are younger, good pals (*relational metatalk*). This term became popular among surfers in Santa Cruz, and later, we hear it used in movies like *Wayne's World, Bill & Ted's Most Excellent Adventure*. Those who watch these movies and like them, especially young people, tend to use "Hey dude" or "most excellent" with their pals (*relational metatalk* in a historical context).

Linguistic metatalk centers on "dude" and "Hey dude," while relational metatalk focuses on "John and Steve," "surfer with pals," and "Bill & Ted." The former is talk about *words* only, while the latter is talk about *people* who use these words with each other.

This is a problem — most people, when called upon to explain an idiom, probably know about linguistic metatalk only. Most people do not know that relational metatalk is crucial for those who try to learn idioms from them. Let me give you a real case reported by my student in an intercultural communication class.

*An L2 student of mine, Ming-Huei, learned an idiom "kick the bucket." It had nothing to do with "kick" or "bucket." She learned that it meant somebody is dead. She also learned that idioms have the potential to shorten interpersonal distance. The next day, she was told that her president's father just passed away. When the president walked into the general office, Ming-Huei made a point to approach him saying, "I am so sorry that your father just kicked the bucket!"*

Oh boy! Ming-Huei was linguistically correct, but relationally inappropriate. This case illustrates the importance of using both linguistic and relational metatalk to accomplish intercultural competence. There are still problems. Even if L1 speakers become aware and capable of both types of metatalk, their L2 partners may still "miss the boat" by failing to understand relational meanings, even when they are explained. The next step explains how to get across relational meanings of idioms in terms of Gregory Bateson's principle of double/multiple description.

## Step 3: The Principle of Double/Multiple Description

Bateson indicates that human communication grows out of *perceived difference* (Bateson & Bateson, 1987). That is, when we say something, it is because we have perceived a "noticeable difference." For example, if someone put a bouquet of roses on a podium in a classroom, an instructor walking into the room might say, "Oh! Roses." Following Bateson's thesis, this communication, "Oh! Roses" reflects a perceived difference between what the classroom had had (no roses) and what it had at this particular moment (roses).

Yet, human communication is predominantly single-descriptive in nature. That is, it does not spell out the comparison point. Let's juxtapose a single-descriptive talk and a double-descriptive talk to clarify the point:

*Professor:* Oh! Roses. (*single-descriptive talk*)

*Professor:* Oh! In comparison with what the room looked like before, we have roses today. (*double-descriptive talk*)

Pay attention to these examples again. We may note that single-descriptive talk seems to refer to "things" — in this case, roses. Double-descriptive talk seems to refer to "difference between two states" — in the case, the classroom before versus the classroom now. Since people, due to differences in upbringing, communication patterns, cultures, and so on may come up with different comparison points, double-descriptive talk offers a better opportunity to understand the rationale behind one's talk. That is, people may comment on the same phenomenon in a different way, not because of differences in "the single thing" observed but in differences between "two-somethings."[5]

Returning to our discussion on idioms, I want to combine double-descriptive talk with metatalk. Because relational meanings are most difficult to explain, we need to practice double-descriptive relational metatalk. Let's use "kicked the bucket" as an example. Jenny, an L1 speaker, may engage in relational metatalk and say:

*The relationship between two people, let's say Bob and Betsy, who use "kicked the bucket" to indicate that George just died, is kind of rural and informal, and their relationship with George was casual, not very respectful.*

But what does Jenny mean by "rural"? "Rural" in comparison with what? "Informal" in comparison with what? "Casual" in comparison with what? And, "not very respectful" in comparison with what? To answer these questions is to reconstruct multiple ways of saying "someone just died" and to compare and contrast the similarities and differences among these relationships. For example, we may came up with the following idioms to express the same "linguistic" meaning as "kicked the bucket":

bought the farm

bit the dust

croaked

no longer with us

died

passed away

The preceding idioms together are called "alternates" (Labov, 1966; Gumperz, 1970), the term refers to different expressions/words available to a speaker to express an intent. In the preceding case, they are alternates used to express "Someone just died." The purpose of constructing a list of alternates is to enable someone explaining an idiom to do multiple-descriptive relational metatalk. Let's continue with our example. Jenny may replace her single-descriptive relational metatalk listed earlier with the following multiple/double-descriptive relational metatalk:

In comparison with the *relationship* between people who use "passed away" to indicate George's death, the *relationship* between Bob and Betsy who use "kicked the bucket" is more informal and rural.

In comparison with the *relationship* between George and those who use "no longer with us" to talk about George's death, the *relationship* between George and Bob and Betsy, who use "kicked the bucket," was not as full of respect.

"Kicked the bucket," shares a similar *relationship* assumption with "bought the farm," "bit the dust," and "croaked," while "passed away" shares a similar *relationship* assumption with "no longer with us."

By engaging in multiple/double-descriptive relational metatalk, the meanings of various relationships — "rural," "informal," and "not respectful" — become clear relative to one another. Such discussions may bring out the "heteroglossia" in a culture.[6] From dyads to families, to a work unit, to a region, a gender, sexual orientation, social class, ethnicity, state, and a certain part of a country, relational meanings vary. Linguistic metatalk gives "words" *uniform meanings* (for example, "They all mean 'someone died'"), the kind of meaning authorized in dictionaries and high-culture genres. Meanings here are rendered faceless, authorless, and nonidiosyncratic! Multiple/double-descriptive relational metatalk, on the other hand, gives words *idiosyncratic meanings* (for example, "Some are more rural and informal; others are used by people in more formal relationships"). An ability to engage in multiple/double-descriptive relational metatalk gives people from different cultures a more refined and contextualized understanding of each other.

But we are not out of the woods yet! To accomplish mutual intercultural understanding, we need to learn about the last step in our process.

## Step 4: Finding Relevance in L2 Speakers' Lifeworld

The final step centers on the concept of "relevance." That is, it aims at making multiple-descriptive relational metatalk relevant to an L2 speaker's lifeworld. To accomplish relevance, L1 speakers need to ask their L2 partners to talk about their lifeworld back in the native land. Then, the L1 idiom explainers have to connect "an American idiom" to a specific relationship in the L2 partners' home world. If a real relationship cannot be

located to link up an idiom, hypothetical relationships in the L2 partners' lifeworld may be used.

Let us continue with our "kicked the bucket" example. Jenny (L1) needs to ask Ming-Huei (L2) about a relationship in Taiwan that occurs in a rural area and in an informal situation versus a relationship in Taiwan that occurs in a metropolitan area and in a formal situation. Ming-Huei may reply:

*I have an uncle who lives in Ping-Dong, which is a small rural town in southern Taiwan. My parents live in Taipei. Ping-Dong to Taipei is like Fresno to San Francisco. A rural and informal relationship would be between my uncle and my father, and a metropolitan and formal relationship would be between my father and his boss in an export-import firm.*

Then Jenny should ask Ming-Huei to think of people who had died in Taiwan. One should be a person whom her father respected, and one less respected. Ming-Huei may reply,

*We had a person, Mr. Wang, living in the community. He was a miser and was always very mean to people. Most of us did not like him. We did not respect him. My grandfather died when I was a fourth grader. It was about twenty-two years ago. All of us respected grandpa very much.*

At this moment, Jenny has two pairs of relationships: father and uncle, and father and his boss. She also has two people who died: Mr. Wang (not respected) and grandpa (respected). Jenny may go ahead creating hypothetical situations:

*When your grandpa died, your father wanted to tell his boss about it, he would say, "My father just passed away"; to your uncle, he could say, "My father died" (or "passed away" or "is no longer with us"). When Mr. Wang died, your father wanted to tell his boss about it, he could say, "Mr. Wang died"; to your uncle, he could say, "Mr. Wang bought the farm" (or "bit the dust," or "kicked the bucket," or "croaked").*

At this moment, Ming-Huei may start telling Jenny about Chinese idioms used to mean "someone died," according to different relational situations. For example, the group of informal, rural, and disrespectful idioms may find their counterparts in these Chinese expressions:

pig tail pricked up[7]
went to see Yen Lwou Wang (the king of hell)[8]

The formal idioms may find their Chinese counterpart as follows:

godly[9] died
passed the world[10]
thanked the world

Alternates and multiple-descriptive relational metatalk mark the beginning of an exciting intercultural exchange. As the reader may have noticed, intercultural conversation may go off from idiom discussions to topics related to "pig tail and dynasty," "Yen Lwou Wang and heaven versus hell," and religions in China.

We can relate the preceding to our earlier discussion about lifeworld, goal-oriented talk, and metatalk. Jenny and Ming-Huei set aside their "goal-oriented talk" and used "linguistic metatalk and multiple-descriptive relational metatalk" to connect their lifeworlds (American and Taiwanese) that become problematic by various idioms concerning death. After laborious explanations in analogous situations, Ming-Huei and Jenny start to share a small portion of a common world cultivated through various idioms. They, at this moment, are prepared to resume their "goal-oriented talk," using idioms accurately and appropriately in going about their daily business. That is, they are able to move in and out of idiom explanations through the use of goal-oriented talk and metatalk.

## Summary

This chapter discusses four reasons why it is important to study idioms in intercultural communication. It provides a process for L1 and L2 speakers to work together to get out from between a rock and a hard place in intercultural communication — idiom incomprehension. It suggests four steps to accomplish this goal. First, L1 and L2 speakers need to establish a conversational decorum that facilitates the talk about idiom problems. Second, L1 and L2 speakers need to learn to differentiate goal-oriented talk from metatalk. They especially need to learn to engage in linguistic metatalk and relational metatalk. Third, to make explanations relative rather than absolute, both L1 and L2 speakers need to understand the principle of double/multiple comparison. By engaging in multiple-descriptive relational metatalk, we bring out different voices and heteroglossia in a culture. Finally, all explanations about idioms should be made relevant to the L2 speakers' lifeworld. This step finalizes the goal of having L2 speakers (or anyone coming into a new [sub]culture) learn to use idioms in a linguistically accurate and relationally appropriate way.

## Reflections

Interacting with people from the same culture, we take a lot of things for granted without jeopardizing goal coordination. As habituation grows, we become increasingly incurious. Edmund Husserl (1973) calls this orientation "the natural attitude." To overcome this attitude, Husserl encouraged people to bracket various phenomena, suspend judgment, and explore phenomenologically the ultimate meaning of person-in-relation-to-the-world. Applying Husserl's thesis to intercultural encounters, we come to realize that even words (idioms, for example) cannot be taken for granted. In intercultural encounters, the shared ground of coordinated actions shrinks to the minimal. We are, therefore, forced to abandon our natural attitude. That is, intercultural encounters become involuntarily bracketed. Our four-step process may be thought of, in this context, as a heuristic guideline for a dialogical sense-making process of two "phenomenologically bracketed minds." In other words, our method helps people who have little in common to talk with each other.

This chapter suggests a radical reinterpretation of a dominant concept in intercultural communication, high- and low-context cultures (Gudykunst & Kim, 1984; Hall, 1976, 1983). When two people from different cultural backgrounds meet, whether they are labeled high-context (like Chinese culture) or low-context (like American culture), they have little to share. If the meaning of "low context" means people's sharing of tacit knowledge is low or little, intercultural encounters are inherently "low context" in nature. Explicit and elaborated communication, which often characterizes low-context cultures, becomes necessary to bridge the gap resulting from the merger of two different lifeworlds. Multiple types of talk and relevance discussed in this chapter represent the kind of intercultural talk that is conducive to the creation of sharing and, it is to be hoped, close relationships. The four-step process helps transform a "low-context" strange intercultural encounter into a qualitatively new "high-context" interaction between L1 and L2 speakers.

Idioms are central to our participation in a multicultural and multiethnic environment (including women and men, children and adults, adults and old people, professors and students, gay and straight people, Asian Americans, African Americans, Euro-Americans) at home and abroad. An ability to talk about and play with idioms means that we will be less likely to share polite smiles and later say, "It was all Greek to me" and will be more likely to have fun, ask honest questions, and share deep thoughts with each other.

## Notes

1. This notion comes from Jurgen Habermas's work (1987). Lifeworld, which is also called common horizon (Todorov, 1984), means the taken-for-granted context in which people act and speak. Language and culture are part and parcel of our lifeworld. Those who share a lifeworld can leap from an idiom to a collectively intended meaning without too much trouble. Those who are not privy to this arbitrary link between idiom and its meaning are often paralyzed at the edge of idiomatic words, uncertain about where to dive in.

2. During three years of teaching idiom explanation in my intercultural communication classes, I have often encountered students amazed at the fact that their co-workers, friends, or significant others, who are L2 speakers and have been in America for a long period of time (ranging from 5 to 14 years), can speak very good English but still fail to comprehend common idioms in this culture. The project aiming at identifying and removing idiom problems often draws them closer together.

3. The new decorum called for in this chapter assumes an *ideal conversational situation*. Daily encounters are often far from perfect due to different cultural, regional, and institutional norms; assumptions about male and female relationships; sexual preferences, etc., that regualte who can speak, when, and how. That is, some people have more internal motivation and external encouragement than others to learn and practice this new/ideal decorum. Others – due to power imbalance, discrimination, or oppression – may have to work harder to achieve this ideal situation.

4. Meta means "about." For example, metaunderstanding means understanding about understanding. Metatalk, therefore, is a term used to mean "talk about talk."

5. For detailed definition and different forms of double description, see Bateson, 1979, pp. 69–93.

6. Heteroglossia is a concept central to Mikhail Bakhtin's work. It emphasizes the primacy of context over text. This chapter examines the relational context surrounding a special type of text (i.e., idioms).

7. Pig tail was a male hairstyle in the Ching dynasty, the last dynasty in China (see the movie, *The Last Emperor*). When a person did awful deeds, he was often beheaded, which made his pig tail prick up. Hence, "Mr. Wang's pig tail pricked up" is used to show disrespect, because he had done some awful deeds when he was alive.

8. In Chinese mythology, the person who controls hell is called "Yen Lwou Wang." He is equivalent to Satan in bibilical literature. "Mr. Wang went to see Yen Lwou Wang" means he died and went to hell.

9. Chinese culture has had tremendous tolerance for different religions (with the exception of the Cultural Revolution between 1966 and 1976). As a result, the concept of "god" may be religious as well as secular. The expression "godly died" takes on a more secular meaning. That is, "godly" (Shien) describes a person who died as *spiritual* and *desireless*. "My father godly died," therefore, is a very respectful idiom in the Chinese culture.

10. The world here means the world of the living. A person who passed or thanked the world of the living was usually one who was respected. These two idioms belong to high-culture, classic Chinese.

## References

Bakhtin, M. (1981). *The Dialogic Imagination*. Austin: University of Texas Press.
Bakhtin, M. (1986). *Speech Genres and Other Late Essays*. C. Emerson & M. Holquist (Eds.). V. W. McGee (Trans.). Austin: University of Texas Press.

Bateson, G. (1972). *Steps to an Ecology of Mind*. New York: Ballantine.

Bateson, G. (1979). *Mind and Nature*. New York: Bantam.

Bateson, G., and Bateson, M. C. (1987). *Angels Fear*. New York: Macmillan.

Gudykunst, W., and Kim, Y. Y. (1984). *Communicating with Strangers*. New York: Random House.

Gumperz, J. (1970). *Sociolinguistics and Communication in Small Groups*. Working Paper No. 33, Language-Behavior Research Laboratory. Berkeley: University of California.

Habermas, J. (1987). *The Theory of Communicative Action* (Vol. II): *Lifeworld and System – A Critique of Functionalist Reason*. Thomas McCarthy (Trans.). Boston: Beacon Press.

Hall, E. T. (1976). *Beyond Culture*. New York: Doubleday.

Hall, E. T. (1983). *The Dance of Life*. New York: Doubleday.

Husserl, E. (1973). *Cartesian Meditations. An Introduction to Phenomenology*. D. Cairns (Trans.). The Hague: M. Nijoff.

Knapp, M. (1984). *Interpersonal Communication and Human Relationships*. Boston: Allyn & Bacon.

Labov, W. (1966). *The Social Stratification of English in New York City*. Washington, D.C.: Center for Applied Linguistics.

Ruesch, J., and Bateson, G. (1951). *Communication: The Social Matrix of Psychiatry*. New York: W. W. Norton.

Todorov, T. (1984). *Mikhail Bakhtin: The Dialogical Principle*. W. Godzich (Trans.). Minneapolis: University of Minnesota Press.

# *F*innish and American Linguistic Patterns: A Cultural Comparison

## DONAL CARBAUGH

### KIRSTI

Kirsti, an 18 year old Finnish female, had just arrived in the United States as an exchange student. Having been in the United States for two weeks, she had met a few people, including Mary. On a sunny afternoon, as Kirsti walked down Main Street in her adopted American town, she saw Mary.

*Mary:* Hi Kirsti!!! How are you?

*Kirsti:* Thank you, good.

*Mary:* Are you enjoying your stay?

*Kirsti:* Yes, very much.

*Mary:* It's a beautiful (!) day outside isn't it?

*Kirsti:* Yes.

They talk for a while longer, then say "Good bye."

The next day, Kirsti saw Mary across the street. She moved toward Mary smiling and waving at her. Mary smiled and waved in return, but kept walking quickly toward her car.

These two exchanges between Kirsti and Mary led Kirsti to conclude "Americans are friendly, but superficial."

From *Tempus* (April, 1995), 6-9. Published by the Federation of Foreign Language Teachers in Finland. Reprinted by permission of the publishers and author. Donal Carbaugh teaches at the University of Massachusetts.

## ULLA

A 22 year old Finnish female, Ulla, had just returned to Finland from the United States, and had this to say about Americans:

"Well, Americans are friendly. There's this small talk thing that they do. It's really nice. The person comes up to you and says 'how are you' and you talk for awhile and it's nice."

Immediately she added: "But then they're superficial. I saw this person (whom she had had small talk with the day before) the next day and they just waved and acted like they didn't even know me. I don't understand that."

## BILL

An American male who was a student at a Finnish University, after hearing this kind of story repeatedly, exclaimed in exasperation, with a hint of anger: "If I hear that Americans are superficial one more time . . ."

Clearly he, and perhaps his Finnish contemporaries, had heard enough of this kind of thing.

How is it that some Finns, upon interacting with Americans, find them to be "superficial"? Perhaps this has something to do with the ways Americans and Finns use language, but more importantly, it might have something to do with the ways each uses language, even the same language (e.g., English), in culturally distinctive ways. Let's explore this possibility in some detail.

## Different Social Obligations

In the exchange between Kirsti and Mary above, we could notice in the first seven lines that the exchange had gone relatively smoothly. We could also notice that Kirsti's comment "Thank you, good," shows that she might be rather new to uses of English. Where many users of English might say "Fine, thanks" or simply "good," Kirsti is supplying an utterance close to a Finnish one that is often produced in this conversational place, "Kittos, hyvin." But her utterance of "thank you, good" presents no

problem in the exchange. Even if Kirsti is relatively new to English, she appears to be using English quite ably, and nicely converses with Mary in it.

However, the interaction on the following day between Mary and Kirsti might be a source of some puzzlement for Kirsti. Upon seeing Mary, she presumes Mary will be available for at least some limited conversation. When, however, a simple and hurried wave was supplied by Mary, instead of some verbal exchange, Kirsti was surprised and disappointed. So, if there is some difficulty created in these interactions between Mary and Kirsti, one source of that difficulty might be the differences in the kind of groundwork each presumed was getting done in the course of their earlier encounter. (The observations made here of Finnish conversational features are very preliminary and tentative, and are based upon field work currently in progress.)

If we take this exchange between Mary and Kirsti, and consider also the comments of Ulla, we might be able to identify one kind of slippage, or asynchrony, between Finnish and American communication patterns. It appears a Finnish pattern of action presumes that if one talks with another for a period of time, perhaps in small talk, there is a slight social obligation upon seeing the other again, to talk with them. That obligation, if rather weak, presumes upon meeting again, if it is at all possible, one would stop and exchange a few words. This subsequent interaction, when forthcoming, continues a Finnish pattern as it solidifies the link with the other that was presumably forged during the earlier exchange. Further, the subsequent interaction reaffirms that the earlier exchange was something important and worthy of one's time and attention.

Note the consequences, from this Finnish point of view, if subsequent interaction is not forthcoming, as it was not from Mary, nor apparently not also from other Americans that Ulla encountered. There is some perhaps slight sense of violation (of Finnish expectations) on several counts. As noted above, subsequent sociable interaction was not forthcoming (a wave was not sufficient as a "subsequent sociable interaction"): lacking that, the link with the American was called into question (e.g., perhaps we are not friends like I thought we were); further, the status of the previous "small talk" is called into question (e.g., it was not what it seemed). Upon a kind of Finnish reflection, Americans like Mary and others seem not to take such obligations at all seriously. Consequently, links with Americans can seem to be weak, and exchanges with them to be shallow. Thus, Americans can seem (to Finns) to be "superficial."

## Finnish Rules for Speaking

There are other possible sources of the Finnish claim about "superficial Americans" that are evident in the kind of exchange described above. Some of these relate to what might be called rules for speaking. For Finns, especially when in public with people one does not know [really] well, but sometimes with close friends, it is important to speak properly. One kind of proper speech is guided by some loose configuration of these rules:

1. Don't state the obvious.
2. If speaking, say something worthy of everyone's attention.
3. Don't invoke topics or themes that are contentious or conflictual (or more positively, keep present relations on harmonious ground).
4. Be personally committed to or invested in what you say.
5. What you say properly – the unobvious, socially worthwhile, noncontentious, personally involving themes – forms a basis for subsequent interactions.

These rules can function in a very demanding way. With just the first rule, one feels one ought to say something that is not obvious. This requires some thought, sometimes considerable thought and silence depending upon one's co-participants, prior to speaking. Add to that, that one ought to say something socially worthwhile, and that it ought to be non-contentious, and something that reflects one's personal commitments, and one's speech is subject to considerable demands. These conditions, when met, of course constrain the production of talk, making it something that is considered and thoughtful, and thus can lay social ground in a potent cultural way.

When these Finnish conversational rules contact other systems of communication practice, like an American one, difficulties can arise. For example, in the exchange above, on a beautiful sunny day, Mary, the American, says, "It's a beautiful day." Finns might think, on the basis of the first Finnish rule, that saying such an obvious thing is "rather silly," and perhaps such things should "go without saying" or "are better left unsaid." After all, as one Finn said to me when we discussed an American propensity to use first names when addressing each other, "Why say such things when they are so damn obvious?" In social exchanges like these, especially during American small talk, one might hear (and produce) all kinds of obvious things, like "nice day," "got your hair cut," "rainy isn't it," "hi, Chuck," that to Finns could "go without saying." Because Americans sometimes talk about such things that are on the surface, and because Finns as a rule prefer the talk go beyond that surface, Americans can seem, to Finns, to be "superficial." (The formulation of these rules and their use will be the subject of future work. The rules do however seem linked to what some Finns call "the no name culture" or the minimal use of personal names, to a general devaluing of "small talk" {as Americans produce it}, and to a unique Finnish form of it, to many uses of silence {because of the need to produce proper speech}, to Finnish themes of modesty and distance, as well as to the cultural status of talk itself.)

## American Use of Superlatives

Another source of possible intercultural difficulty can be related to the use of superlatives such as the "beautiful" that Mary spoke on line 5. The free use of superlatives by Americans can be troubling to some Finnish ears. One Finnish woman who lived in America for a couple of years described an encounter with her American aunt: "She would describe things saying, 'It's magnificent' or 'It's absolutely gorgeous!' I would reply genuinely by saying, 'it's nice,' but then my aunt would say, 'don't you like it?' It would drive me crazy." She went on saying, "I just can't say things like, 'it's so fabulous.' That runs against my grain."

If this is a typical pattern, it suggests, relative to Americans, that Finnish uses of such superlatives are rather guarded, or reserved, if existent at all. This becomes especially the case since superlatives statements can sound to Finns a bit presumptuous, and can possibly be heard as immodest, or as being too impressionable, reflecting a person whose inner being falls prey to overstatement, or quick, evaluative whims. As Mary exclaimed the obvious, the "beautiful day outside," she may have run a bit against Kirsti's Finnish "grain." American use of superlatives are perhaps, relative to Finns, more frequent and intense, thus giving the impression of saying more, and speaking more intensely, than is necessary, or accurate. Because Americans can use superlatives very freely, and because Finns use them less freely and perhaps more cautiously, Americans can sound to Finns again as "superficial," when saying more than the social situation perhaps properly and rightfully warrants.

## Finnish Standards

With the above patterns in mind, we have now established perhaps a better understanding of the sources of the Finnish sense that Americans are, at times, "superficial." Part of the sense of this stereotype reflects some Finnish standards of practice that are used to evaluate communication of Finns, and Americans. The standards evident so far are:

1. that people who engage in talk should follow-up on it

2. that people should not freely and continually state the obvious, and

3. that people should not overstate the case

Americans, on some occasions, violate all of these Finnish expectations, or rules. This gives cultural grounds to the accusation of superficiality from the vantage point of Finnish patterns of communication.

## Friendliness Versus Friendship

Presumably Americans, who act as above, are not trying to be superficial, nor would they say they value superficiality. What, then, are these Americans doing? Or, what do they intend to be doing? What features of American communication are evident here?

In contemporary America, encounters like the one between Mary and Kirsti are quite common. People greet, and follow-up their greetings with friendly exchanges. . . . The functions of such encounters are varied, but perhaps generally, in America, they have something to do simply with verbally acknowledging the existence of each participant (thus the frequent use of first names), and establishing a momentary link between them (thus the importance given to "relationships"). The tone is typically quite friendly. And often in the process, given the backdrop of variety in types of people in the American scene today (e.g., Blacks, Anglos, Native Americans, Chicanos, Chinese, Vietnamese, Irish, German, Italian, East Indian, etc.), the result is the verbal demonstration or disclosure of some common experience. Because people in America are presumably different and unique, both culturally and personally, such encounters are not trivial, but constant daily efforts to acknowledge the presence of each other, and to forge some kind of civil links among them. Friendly interaction, therefore, as this, is forceful culturally partly because it so often occurs upon a cultural fabric of considerable variety and difference.

American "friendliness" thus should not be confused with "friendship," for the former is required routinely in public encounters with an eye to linking people who are presumably different, while the latter stems from other forms of action, deemed more "personal" than "public."

After engaging in such civil, sociable encounters, the obligation one incurs to follow them up is, relative to Finns, quite minimal, if existent. One might engage in similar encounters with the same people again, but one would typically feel a minimal obligation to do so. If possible, or timely, one might engage with others one has met with earlier, but such would be done more out of kindness or courtesy, and less because one would feel a duty to meet with them. . . . Some recent research into American communication patterns has demonstrated that Americans differentiate "small talk" from "really communicating" (Carbaugh 1988: Philipsen 1992). Small talk or chit-chat, as perhaps was that between Mary and Kirsti, is generally less valued than "real communication," and is, relative to it, rather closed, distant, neutral, and rigid. To many Americans, chit-chat is important as a form of sociability, but it is also less valued, less potent relationally, and less penetrating as a means of self-expression. As a result, engaging in it incurs little by way of obligation.

## American Rules for Speaking

Some rules that Americans use and invoke when speaking in public are quite different from those supplied by Finns for similar public contexts. Americans believe that one should express one's self, with very few constraints being placed upon that expressiveness. In fact, participants often state the rule that people are free to say whatever they please, and it is not up to those present – thinking perhaps it is only up to God – to evaluate or judge those expressions. Such rules lay bases for great amounts of talk, since the belief is that everyone should have the opportunity to speak, or be heard from. Such speaking often elaborates one's personal experiences, thoughts and feelings. Americans are often, in public speech, then, less preoccupied with the social worthiness of their expression, than they are with its personal importance. . . . Together, the dynamic produces much public talk that is close to the surface, but does so as an important means of producing public information, common resources, and a social mosaic of differences, if doing so in a less than deeply penetrating way (Carbaugh 1990).

The above American rules for speaking can create much talk that is, from the vantage point of the Finnish system, quite suspect. Saying things that are obvious, paying more attention to personal matters, and less attention to the social worthiness of a topic of discussion they introduce, all of this can appear "superficial" to Finns. This might be because Americans often talk as if they presume very

little in common among those present. Furthermore, some Americans might playfully speak contentiously, introducing a controversial topic in order to "get someone/something going," to turn up the heat and intensity of an ongoing social encounter. Offense at this is not necessarily taken; in fact some even delight at the airing of diverse and competing views. And more puzzling perhaps, to many Finns, is the extent to which some Americans might say things (e.g., make proposals or propositions) that they do not agree with, or are not all that personally committed to, or invested in. Such talk is sometimes used to test ideas, or as a mode of thought (e.g., "thinking out loud"), than it is a demonstration of one's deeper convictions or beliefs. Such American rules can produce many and varied personal disclosures and opinions, assertions that are not personally held, obvious statements and the like, for the sake of generating information and discussion. Yet all of this, from the outside can also be easily heard as lacking "conviction" and thus as being "superficial."

So, are Americans "superficial" when they fail to follow-up social encounters, speak about the obvious, make statements they don't personally believe in, and overstate for the sake of discussion, or argument? From a Finnish point of view perhaps so. But if taken as intended, from their own frame of reference, they are up to something else: To getting the conversation going; to producing information; to airing a diversity of views; in the process, to acknowledging each other's presence and linking with each other; to exhibiting some common life, some civility, if sometimes preoccupied with personal themes, or if sometimes contentious. Such is often done in the spirit of friendliness, of getting along with each other, even if this doesn't appear, from outside, to go very deep.

The depth of such American encounters is not necessarily in the content of these encounters – they can produce many varied sayings – but in the cultural form used for their expression. Through this form of social life, a common forum for American people is created, a forum where anyone can have a say, where a civil routine is created, where information is produced, and differences among people are both a warrant and theme in its production (Carbaugh 1988). This might appear peculiar from abroad, as it sometimes does from within, but the pieces of it that might seem that way from afar are a part of another puzzle closer to it's home. There, the larger picture is one that presumes verbal information should be freely available, and great differences among people must be heard.

Thus talk about things that are never deemed all that obvious, becomes part of a form that routinely creates a common life. This picture, a mosaic in motion, of course differs from others, painted in other places. In Finland, the picture is perhaps one that presumes people hold much in common, and thus should not be preoccupied with the obvious surfaces of life, the all too apparent commonness of things, but should move beyond that.

## Culturally Distinctive Patterns

The above are preliminary observations and in need of much further consideration, which in the future I look forward to doing. But hopefully they demonstrate ways that communication is patterned in culturally distinctive ways. For example, it shows how similar forms of sociable speaking, especially initial encounters, are erected on culturally distinctive premises; it shows that rules for producing sociable speech vary from cultural communicative system to cultural communicative system; it shows that the use of particular linguistic devices like superlatives varies in culturally distinctive ways; and finally, it shows that each of these differences can be the source of miscommunication and negative cultural stereotypes.

With regard to the relationship between language use and culture, note that the above demonstrates how a single language, in this case English, can be used to express two different cultural meaning systems. In the other direction, the Finnish language is also used to express American, Russian, and of course Finnish cultures. The crucial variable when treating culture and communication is not fundamentally the language that is used, but the patterned ways in which the language is used, and the cultural meanings associated with them. This requires careful description of linguistic interaction, and nonverbal means of expression, as shown above in the dialogue between Mary and Kirsti. It requires that one interpret the cultural meaning systems that are being presumed and created in those interactions, with those means of expression.

While the cultural interpretation in the above "notes" is very thin, a deeper look would explore what such patterns implicate by way of beliefs about being a person, about societal life, about acting with others. In the way, following these leads, we can come to hear cultures in linguistic, and nonlinguistic, action, to hear what such interaction presumes, what it says and means. Such leads can help develop our understanding of our own cultural conduct, and that of others, while also enabling a better understanding of the dynamics that transpire when one cultural system of expression contacts another.

## References

Carbaugh, D. 1988. *Talking American*. Norwood, NJ: Ablex.

Carbaugh, D. 1990. Communication rules in Donahue discourse. In: D. Garbaugh (Ed.), *Cultural Communication and Intercultural Contact,* Hillsdale, NJ: Lawrence Erlbaum, pp. 119-149.

Philipsen, G. 1992. *Speaking Culturally*. Albany: SUNY Press.

# Utilizing an Inductive Approach to Studying African American Male Communication

## MARK P. ORBE

At the forefront of many discussions of "race" is the positioning of African American men. In the early 1980s, social science researchers described African American men as visible figures, yet the least understood and studied of all sex and ethnic groups in the United States (Staples, 1982). Most recently, they have been framed as an "endangered species" (Gibbs, 1988), whose "plight" (Dyson, 1989) reflects a "crisis situation" (Wiley, 1990) of "epidemic" (Mc-Jamerson, 1991) proportions. This "crisis terminology" reflects the lived reality for African American men, one which has found them over-represented in every major social ill and problem category in the country, including unemployment, mental disorders, poverty, cases of AIDS, illiteracy, violent crimes, and divorce (Kunjufu, 1991).

Most non-African Americans—especially European American males—have great difficulty comprehending the lived reality of African American men (Dreyfus, 1992). In part, their views are tainted by the concentration of negative attention that is given to this group (as indicated by the "crisis terminology" described above). With the majority of information focusing primarily on the social prob-lems of African American men—without much attention to how many lead productive lives despite social barriers—non-African Americans often receive a "commuter's view" (Elise & Umoja, 1992) of the African American male experience. This superficial perception is based on statistics, flashes of stereotypical images in the media, and limited personal contact. Without question, such a lack of concrete understanding greatly reduces communication effectiveness during interethnic interactions that include African American men. Communication scholars are in a unique position to provide insight into the relationship of ethnicity and communication and, in the process, enhance and promote effective interethnic communication. This article summarizes the findings from a series of research projects that attempt to heighten the awareness of the issues surrounding African American male communication.

The findings reported here were arrived at inductively. The research did not begin with a set of preconceived hypotheses regarding African American male communication. Instead, the project sought to gain insight into one (general) question: How do African American men communicate with non-African Americans? Instead of trying to force African American men under a microscope—as some researchers might attempt—specific attempts were made to create a process by which African American men could describe what they view as salient within their lived experiences *in their own words*. In this regard, the men involved in the research described here were considered "co-researchers," not merely subjects or participants. The co-researchers were involved in every aspect of the research process: creating research questions, formulating interview/focus-group protocols, developing the themes, as well as interpreting themes. Specifically, this essay describes the process of a series of phenomenological inquiries into the lived experiences of African American men. The essay concludes with an interpretation of these guiding themes, discussion of emerging considerations of this area of research, and description of the implications for future research.

## Research of African American Communication: Advancing an Inductive Approach

The research projects described here represent a move away from the traditional (empirical, positivist) approach to studying African American communication as urged by Hecht, Collier, and Ribeau (1993, pp. 173–174). A phenomenological approach is utilized in order to reveal the essence of African American communication; the insight sought after here is not easily obtained through traditional quantitative methods (Orbe, 1995a).

Phenomenology focuses on the conscious experience of a person as he or she relates to the lived world (Lanigan, 1979). Within this holistic approach, people are viewed as multidimensional and complex beings whose particular social, cultural, and historical life circumstance is acknowledged (Van Manen, 1990).

Phenomenological studies involve a three-step process: (1) gathering descriptions of lived experience (description), (2) reviewing data in order to reveal essential themes (reduction), and (3) determining the interrelatedness of the themes and how they reflect the essence of the phenomena (interpretation) (Lanigan, 1988; Nelson, 1989; Peterson, 1987).

### Six Themes Related to the African American Male Experience

The research reported here can be best understood within six themes that depict the lived experiences of African American men in this society: (1) needing to communicate with other African Americans, (2) learning how to interact with non-African Americans, (3) playing the part, (4) keeping a safe distance, (5) testing the sincerity of non-African Americans, and (6) feeling an intense social responsibility. Because these descriptions may or may not accurately recount the lived experiences of other African American men, they are not offered here as "facts" that can be generalized to all African American men. Instead, these six themes recapitulate what thirty-five African American male co-researchers involved in a series of projects had to say in regard to their communication.

**Needing to Communicate.** One clear essential theme that emerged from the transcripts of interviews and focus groups involved the crucial need that African American men have to interact with other African Americans. As one co-researcher simply put it:

*I like to talk to people . . . who can relate to me and I can relate to them. . . . We have been through some common experiences.*

The African American men involved in this study felt that other African Americans were able to better understand common problems, situations, and pressures that non-African Americans – particularly European Americans – had difficult identifying and understanding.

Co-researchers delineated intra-ethnic communication with a variety of people as especially important. Nuclear and extended family members – mothers, fathers, grandmothers, siblings, cousins, and so on – were described as important sources of support by co-researchers. Other narrators cited their "boys" and significant others as African American persons whose interaction was instrumental in successfully coping with everyday life experiences. While discussing a close friend, one man sentimentally offered the following explanation:

*I like to talk to him because we kind of grew up together, so he knows. . . . We think basically the same, so whatever is on my mind, he knows what it is and knows what I am feeling . . . and doesn't try to minimize [it].*

Interestingly, the reference of "growing up together" here does not refer to a lengthy history together, but simply to their college experiences with one another. "We kind of grew up together" can be seen as a reference to the common bond that all African American men share – a multigenerational history of lived experiences that revolve around acts of racism, discrimination, and oppression based on their ethnic and gender identity. Many of the African American men involved in this project also described intra-ethnic communication as a means to measure one's success. The "American

Dream" was seen as unobtainable, even for those persons with impressive credentials and "relative success." Instead, co-researchers described interactions revolving around activities of competition and comparison with other African Americans — interactions that served as a means of measurement, motivation, and reinforcement. For instance, one co-researcher, in referring to another African American man, stated:

*He has gotten me to a point where I am competitive, because he is extremely competitive. . . . I hate to lose to him. I don't mind losing, but when it comes to him, I hate to lose.*

Another co-researcher described a typical interaction that reiterates this perspective.

*A lot of our conversations are centered on him doing better than I or me doing better than him. It is just like the competitiveness going back and forth.*

Although often fierce, but seldom destructive, this aggressive interaction assists African American men in negotiating the response to the question, "What are the realities of the *African* American Dream?" One African American man articulated his relationship with other African American males in quite simple terms:

*It is a matter of looking at what they have been through and changing it around to fit my situation . . . and using that as an inspiration to excel.*

**Learning How to Interact with Non–African Americans.** A few African American men had difficulty articulating exactly how they learned to communicate with non–African Americans. They acknowledged that their communication with other African Americans was vastly different from their communication with European Americans but attributed their different communication styles to an unconscious, indescribable process. Most of the African American male co-researchers, however, attributed their education in this area to three sources: *direct talks with others, observation,* and *trial and error.*

Co-researchers described direct talks with other African Americans — family, friends, mentors, and even acquaintances — that addressed how they should interact with non–African Americans. These discussions started early in life and continue to occur. "Be careful and watch what people tell you," "Be careful of what you say and how you say it," and "Whites are not on your side, so always watch your back" represent typical warnings from other African Americans.

Other co-researchers related that they were never sat down and told how to communicate with non–African Americans; instead they learned the process through observing others. Specifically, co-researchers described instances when they watched how others — mothers, grandmothers, fathers, aunts, uncles, co-workers, and older siblings — interacted with European Americans. One African American man indicated that he learned this intricate process by "constantly watching people . . . how people interact, listening to what they say to other people."

However, other co-researchers recognized that their learning process was more of a trial-and-error process: trying different strategies, learning from past mistakes, and constantly putting themselves in risky and awkward positions. This process was one that could be highly frustrating, as one co-researcher described:

*I remember in high school, I was frustrated because they were teaching me how to dress, to be professional, but no one was teaching me . . . how to interact with people outside our own community . . . I didn't know how to act.*

While some co-researchers quickly figured out specific strategies, others had difficulty maintaining a balance between preserving their ethnicity and assimilating into a different speech community. One man confessed that

*it took a long time for me to learn this [interethnic communication skill], because I was one of the hardheaded people. . . . It took a while before I understood exactly.*

Although these African American men described a variety of processes in learning *how* to interact with non-African Americans, *what* they learned was generally consistent from co-researcher to co-researcher.

**Playing the Part (SNAP!).** Several co-researchers recalled observing instances when a magical transformation would occur when their African American relatives would communicate with European Americans. Respondents with great pleasure retold humorous stories where the change would come so quickly that it would appear that two different people were communicating. For instance, one eighteen-year-old African American man shared the following narrative:

*My aunts in my family, they all have law degrees . . . and whenever they had [white] people over, I could tell a certain change – snap! – that they would go through . . . the biggest difference was – snap! – she would come up to par, you know, play the part.*

While recalling this instance, my co-researcher would loudly snap his fingers to signify the quickness of the change. Another reading of this gesture can be seen within Johnson's (1995) work on "SNAP! culture." In this respect, the co-researcher's inclusion of a series of prominent "snaps!" could signify his pleasure on how African Americans often fool unsuspecting non-African Americans while "playing the part."

"Playing the part" involves abandoning the communication styles of the African American community and adopting those associated with the dominant European American culture. This strategy was one that was well-learned from others, as African American men described times when they "definitely talk white" in business settings, "tend to straighten up" in meetings, are "careful not to use any slang," or, as one African American man put it, "talk the part."

"For the most part, it's not acceptable to be yourself," one African American man told me without hesitation. Clearly, African American men have developed a double consciousness (DuBois, 1969) where they can effectively interact in two distinct cultures. In short, my co-researchers found themselves "playing the part" in order to communicate effectively with non-African Americans and avoid being stigmatized by racial stereotypes. However, this assimilative style of code switching involved some risks. For instance, African American men who "played the part" *too* well risked being ostracized as a "sell-out" or "Uncle Tom." Clearly, the dialectic of "playing the part" and being yourself involved an ever present tension, as articulated by one co-researcher:

*It is a constant struggle. . . . You have to play a double role if you're a black male on campus. You have to know when not to do things and when to do things.*

**Keeping a Safe Distance.** Within this project, African American men frequently described conscious efforts to maintain a specific distance from non-African Americans. The emergence of this theme was revealed in descriptions of interethnic communication characterized by "a tremendous amount of skepticism," "lack of trust," "suspicion," "confusion," "an unbelievable tension," "lack of respect," and "fear." When asked for a word or phrase that would typify their interaction with non-African Americans, African American men offered adjectives such as "superficial," "professional," "cautious," "selective [in speech]," "reserved," and "choosey" [with whom to communicate]. Communication with European Americans was generally described as work-related, involving "a very polite face" but "nothing real." African American men felt compelled to maintain a distance during interethnic interactions in light of the history of injustice, discrimination, and oppression of African Americans at the hands of European Americans. One man recalls a situation where he was the only African American male:

*The whole time I was there [a new job in a predominantly European American environment] I separated myself and . . . trusted no one. . . . I always felt suspicious and didn't trust anyone.*

This distance was especially maintained when interacting with European American males and/or persons in authority. These persons were perceived by co-researchers to be "less personable," "the most intimidated" and threatened by the presence of capable African American men. One co-researcher disclosed that he

*taps into this cautious state of mind that [he is] typically in when around white individuals . . . especially [those] in authority positions.*

Some European American men were even perceived as "avoiding contact" with African American men unless absolutely necessary. Co-researchers felt that this tendency may be due to an "uncomfortableness due to lack of interaction [with African American males]," but also related it to their uneasiness and "paranoia" in regard to the "successes of black men."

Although described as a survival technique, maintaining a professional distance with non–African Americans had some disadvantages. Information needed to succeed is often channeled through interpersonal, rather than organizational, networks. Many co-researchers described instances where their professional careers suffered because they lacked information that was generated through informal—mostly European American—channels. For some, "keeping a safe distance" from European Americans has some negative consequences in regard to personal and professional advancement. African American men therefore find themselves needing to identify those European Americans who can be trusted as confidants.

**Testing the Sincerity of Non-African Americans.**
In today's climate of "political correctness," identifying non–African Americans who are genuinely interested in understanding under-represented groups is no easy task. Frequently, it means shifting through an abundance of rhetoric and "PC jargon" to determine sincerity and genuine sensitivity. One African American man hesitantly confessed his "struggle":

*I guess that I have found it very difficult to distinguish when they [whites] are sincere versus when they are trying to be politically correct. . . . I struggle with that.*

Another African American man confided that he is "once bitten, twice shy" when it comes to some European Americans. His experiences with having been deceived by some "slick talkers" in the past have made him more suspicious of European Americans who appear sincere.

The majority of African American male co-researchers described processes by which they identified those persons who were sensitive to the issues important to the African American community. Some descriptions offered by co-researchers expressed a "God-given talent . . . where I'm able to tell if [a] person is true or not." For others, it seems as if years of experience in dealing with European Americans have resulted in a process of evaluating the sincerity of co-workers, classmates, and others. Several co-researchers described "watching how people interact," while others talked about "asking certain questions" that would indicate levels of sensitivity. Certain phrases were perceived as problematic, as one co-researcher explained:

*My flag always goes up whenever I hear someone say "some of my best friends are black" or "my cousin's married to one."*

Another co-researcher jokingly, but honestly, shared that "one way for me to test people is to invite [them] to my house." Generally, responses to this invitation provided a clearer perspective on which European Americans were sincere in their intentions. In other words, those persons practicing "lip service" to the call for diversity always managed to have conflicting plans that made it difficult to accept this invitation.

Testing non–African Americans to determine their attitudes toward African Americans can take days or years. Some co-researchers described instances where they immediately recognized a European American who could be trusted, where other African American men recalled experiences where a relationship had to develop over the period of years before they began to "let some of those walls down." European Americans who were perceived as allies were those persons who came across as sensitive, sincere, honest, and "open with their feelings."

These individuals were also people who were "not afraid to ask questions," who "admit that they had some biases," and who were "willing to take responsibility for their wrongdoings." Generally, these European Americans could be counted as allies even when difficult situations arose.

**Feeling an Intense Social Responsibility** The African American men that I spoke with felt an urgency to uplift other African Americans in their struggles. Co-researchers felt a genuine responsibility to educate younger African Americans, especially African American males, about the intricacies of surviving (and succeeding) in a society dominated by European American males. One forty-three-year-old African American man recalled the assorted times older African Americans took time to explain certain things about interacting with "whites" that he did not understand. Feeling a sense of responsibility to younger African Americans, he concluded that "I am now trying to pass that on." Another African American man discussed "the brother/sister thing – [where] everyone is family." Co-researchers expressed an urgent sense that younger people needed to be given a realistic portrayal of how society operates. One African American college administrator believed that giving the youth a "candy-coated" picture is not effective; instead he was up front about the racial tendencies on campus:

*That's why I've started a discussion, support group . . . for black students. . . . I sit them down and tell them: it's sad, it's wrong, but this is the way it is.*

A second aspect of this social responsibility is making non-African Americans aware of different lived experiences, especially those of African American men that counter negative stereotypes. It is important to have non-African Americans realize that they "in reality, are part of the problem *and* solution," explained one high-school-aged African American male. Many co-researchers were optimistic that their efforts in educating others – through workshops, training sessions, or simply more personal means – would help to create a better environment

for younger African Americans. For some, educating others represented an avenue to "redirect a lot of anger and frustration." Others, however, recognized their efforts as a means to become empowered. One college-aged co-researcher wrote that:

*It is my belief that if I can educate one person to change or see their views differently, then some good came out of it.*

Others validated this personal philosophy as a concrete avenue to advance the positioning of African American men in this country. Representative of several African American men involved in this project, one co-researcher explained that "I know that I am only one, but I think that I can [make a change]." Although at least one co-researcher expressed his skepticism that "whites just don't understand," most of the African American men involved in this project had some optimism for future relations between African Americans and European Americans. As one co-researcher, at the ripe age of twenty, concluded, "I finally realized, that okay, it is going to be a long process."

## A Dose of Reality: "Remember, It's Always Whites' Ball"

One experience recalled by an African American man during a focus-group discussion emerged as especially relevant as a central issue to African American male communication:

*I'll never forget this story. I was officiating a basketball game and one team had shirts and the other team had no shirts. They were playing and the ball went out of bounds and I said, "It's skin's ball." And [my coach] was walking by, and he said "Remember, it's always whites' ball." I guess that at that point I began to realize, maybe to a certain extent, it is a white man's world. I guess that I knew that even if I worked hard, it would still be the white man's world.*

"Remember, it's always whites' ball" emerged as a revelatory phrase that worked to capture the interconnectedness of the six essential themes and reveal the essence of communication for African American men. This one phrase, in the form of a sports competition metaphor, reveals the underlying basis for the issues described above. In a society largely controlled by European American men, African American men find that they are attempting to perform on "unequal playing fields" where they are "fighting an uphill battle." It seems as if European Americans never "relinquish control of the ball" for any significant length of time and always "get the close calls." When asked about a summer basketball tournament, one African American man recently shared with me that:

*We played really well and shoulda won . . . but it was impossible because we were playing five on seven. . . . [Responding to my puzzled looks, he added] . . . the two refs were on their side!*

The analogy of "playing five on seven" seems especially fitting when attempting to describe the experiences of African American people in this society. Many African American men never have the opportunity to "play" on the same levels with European Americans. However, when they are able to overcome great obstacles to participate in various competitions, their chances for success are limited because the "officials," who are supposed to be impartial and unbiased in their rulings, are seen as simply "members of the opposing team."

Within this framework, each theme – needing to communicate with other African Americans, learning how to communicate with non–African Americans, keeping a safe distance, playing the part (SNAP!), testing the sincerity of non–African Americans, and feeling an intense social responsibility – represents an effective strategy for coping with the reality of a European American male-dominated society. In a sense, the themes described here reflect a culture common to African American men. Culture, according to Korzenny (1991), refers to a "social product [which] allows humans to function and strive in the pursuit of order and survival" (p. 56).

## Conclusion

The issues that emerged from this project appear central in describing the cultural mores created and maintained by African American males. Many co-researchers described living in this society as "craziness," referring to the illogical systems (personal, institutional, societal) of discrimination based on "race" (Spickard, 1992). I believe the essential themes revealed here describe a cultural communication system that African men have embraced in order to survive amidst a society which proclaims that "all men are created equal," while the realities of everyday life paint a different picture. In no uncertain terms, they can never forget that "it's always whites' ball." So, how might African American men manage in an oppressive society? They communicate with other African Americans for support, motivation, and reassurance. The affirmation gained through the African American community is typically not available from other outlets. They also learn how to interact with non–African Americans, but this interaction involves a number of dialectal struggles: Should I maintain co-cultural barriers while playing the part? Or can I identify non–African Americans who are sincere and trustworthy? Finally, in order to cope with reality, African American men assume an intense social responsibility to help others contend with life in an oppressive society. Such efforts encourage a sense that African American men can promote change within and outside the African community. From this perspective, the six issues described in this essay depict a cultural reality adopted by African American men in this society.

Further inquires need to investigate how issues of socioeconomic status, age, or sexual/affectional orientation might influence the lived experiences of African American men. Further inquiries need to avoid research that dichotomizes interethnic communication as "black/white," but instead need to begin to address the broad array of issues – age, gender, class, sexual orientation, and so on – that complicate the issue of interethnic communication beyond such a simplistic discernment. A "co-cultural communication perspective" articulated by Orbe (1995b) provides a framework for research at the macro- and micro-levels of analysis.

# References

Dreyfus, J. (1992). "White Men on Black Power." *Essence,* November, 67–70, 124–128.

DuBois, W. E. B. (1969). *The Souls of Black Folks.* New York: New American Library.

Dyson, M. (1989). "The Plight of Black Men." *ETA Magazine,* February, 51–56.

Elise, S., and Umoja, A. (1992). Spike Lee constructs the new black man: Mo' better. *Western Journal of Black Studies, 16,* 82–89.

Gibbs, J. T. (Ed.) (1988). *Young, Black and Male in America: An Endangered Species.* Dover, Mass.: Auburn House.

Hecht, M. L., Collier, M. J., and Ribeau, S. A. (1993). *African American Communication: Ethnic Identity and Cultural Interpretation.* Newbury Park, Calif.: Sage.

Johnson, E. P. (1995). SNAP! culture: A different kind of "reading." *Text and Performance Quarterly, 15,* 122–142.

Korzenny, F. (1991). "Relevance and Application of Intercultural Communication Theory and Research." In L. Samovar and R. Porter (Eds.), *Intercultural Communication: A Reader,* 6th ed., 56–62. Belmont, Calif.: Wadsworth.

Kunjufu, J. (1991). The real issue about the male academy. *Black Issues in Higher Education,* October 10, p. 88.

Lanigan, R. L. (1979). The phenomenology of human communication. *Philosophy Today, 23,* 3–15.

Lanigan, R. L. (1988). *Phenomenology of Communication: Merleau-Ponty's Thematics in Communicology and Semiology.* Pittsburgh: Duquesne University Press.

McJamerson, E. M. (1991). The declining participation of African-American men in higher education: Causes and consequences. *Sociological Spectrum, 11,* 45–65.

Nelson, J. (1989). "Phenomenology as Feminist Methodology: Explicating Interviews." In K. Carter and C. Spitzack (Eds.), *Doing Research on Women's Communication: Perspectives of Theory and Method,* 221–241. Norwood, N.J.: Ablex.

Orbe, M. (1955a). African American communication research: Toward a deeper understanding of interethnic communication. *Western Journal of Communication, 59,* 61–78.

Orbe, M. (1995b). Discovering Co-cultural Communication Strategies: The Negotiation of Muted Group Status. Paper presented at the annual conference of the International Communication Association, Albuquerque, New Mexico, May.

Peterson, E. E. (1987). Media consumption and girls who want to have fun. *Critical Studies in Mass Communication, 44,* 37–50.

Spickard, P. (1992). "The Illogic of American Racial Categories." In M. P. Root (Ed.), *Racially Mixed People in America,* 12–23. Newbury Park, Calif.: Sage.

Staples, R. (1982). *Black Masculinity: The Black Male's Role in American Society.* San Francisco: Black Scholar Press.

Van Manen, M. (1990). *Researching Lived Experience: Human Science for Action Sensitive Pedagogy.* Albany: State University of New York Press.

Wiley, E. (1990). Institutional concern about the implications of black male crisis questioned by scholars. *Black Issues in Higher Education,* July 5, 33–39.

# Language as a Mirror of Reality: Mexican American Proverbs

SHELLY M. ZORMEIER
LARRY A. SAMOVAR

## Proverbs and Culture

Over a century ago, the English writer Tennyson observed that "Proverbs sparkle forever." Tennyson, like countless other historians and philosophers, was fascinated by the enduring quality of proverbs. Jewish tradition even suggests that nine hundred years before Christ, Solomon (973–933 B.C.) authored more than 3,000 proverbs (Kent, 1913, p. 191). The persistent power of proverbs gives testimony to their impact on human behavior. In one or two lines and through the use of vivid images, they capture what a culture deems important. As Haskins and Butts (1973) note, "Proverbs contain the wisdom of nations" (p. 16). Regardless of the culture, proverbs teach children what to expect from life and what life extracts in return. From a very young age children are taught those proverbs that are generally accepted as true. Encased in the "truths" are important cultural values that are handed down by tradition from one generation to the next. As Campa (1947) states, "The collection of proverbs is of paramount importance in all the great literatures of the world, because they are the folklore fossils of all languages" (p. 19). They are, as the English proverb reminds us "the child of experience."

Through the wisdom of proverbs, important aspects of culture become transmissible (Samovar &

Porter, 1995). The spoken word as a symbol is an excellent means of teaching because it can succinctly summarize events and predict outcomes. In this way the past, present, and future are fused. Proverbs impart important messages to the members of a culture because these perceptions receive ongoing reinforcement for the most important aspects of a culture. The assumption behind examining proverbs is a simple one – discover the meaning of the proverb and you will understand something of what is important to its user. Because proverbs repeat those assumptions on which a culture operates, they offer valuable insight into the culture. Perhaps more importantly, those insights deal with meaningful cultural values.

It should be noted at the outset that while thousands of proverbs speak to specific cultural values, there are just as many values that are universal. That is to say, because proverbs describe common human experiences, many of the same proverbs can be found in nearly all cultures. In addition, through the thousands of social contacts with ancient and modern civilizations, many proverbs have been transferred from one country to another, always constituting a particular element of folklore that is common to all people. Proverbs connect the listener with his or her ancestors; they give witness to the ancient human fables that continue to plague us to this day. Even ancient philosophers have noted their importance (Sellers, 1994). Aristotle, for example, referred to proverbs as remnants and relics of the truest ancient philosophy.

Because proverbs are both universal and specific, they are normally divided into two classes (Paredes, 1970). First are those that possess a truth independent of time and place. In other words, they are universal. For instance, all cultures believe that the family is a reflection of the individual. Hence, the Chinese have a proverb that notes "Know the family and you will know the child." In the United States we hear "The apple does not fall far from the tree." In nearly every culture hard work is stressed. In Germany the proverb states "One that does not honor the penny is not worthy of the dollar." Americans are told "A penny saved is a penny earned." Most cultures place strong emphasis on honesty. Its importance can be seen in many cultural proverbs. In the Anglo culture, when someone is not honest, the proverb is stated as "Your nose is growing longer than Pinocchio's." In the Mexican culture the saying is "You grew a longer tail than a monkey." Likewise, there is the universal notion that once an event has transpired there is nothing that can be done. In the Anglo culture, this notion can be found in the proverb that states "Don't cry over spilled milk." In Mexican culture the saying is "After the rabbit is gone, why throw stones at the bush?" Yet other cross-cultural proverbs deal with the notion of taking precautions. For instance, in the Anglo culture people say "An ounce of prevention is worth a pound of cure." In the Mexican culture this proverb is stated as "Withstand the beginning, remedies came too late.

The second category into which proverbs can be divided are those that are written or spoken particularly for one culture and are transmitted to the members of that culture. We now focus on this type of proverb. More specifically, we will audit some important values of the Mexican American culture. By examining both the proverb and the message contained within the proverb, we can become aware of some of the perceptions and behaviors found within this culture.

## Mexican American Proverbs

The Mexican culture has a long tradition of employing proverbs as a tool for carrying significant values. Mexican "proverbios" originated in the primitive stages of the Spanish language for conversational purposes rather than for literary purposes (Campa, 1947). They have been used to sharpen the wits, stimulate interest, test the wisdom of the learned, or entertain at festive occasions (Aranda, 1977). "They are of most ancient and honorable parentage, being the direct descendent of the oldest didactic and moral philosophy" (p. 5). Proverbs may explicitly contain advice or may describe a scene and leave the implications to be inferred. In any case, these proverbs are a large part of the Mexican American culture. They condense the wisdom, experience, and explanations of well-known truths.

In ancient times, as well as today, these proverbs can be found in Mexican American wedding songs, Christmas carols, lyrics, and poems. Since the majority of Mexican Americans are Catholic, these popular sayings can also be found within the Bible in the "Book of Proverbs," as well as in their prayers. Wherever they are found, they are primitive forms of popular art and knowledge. In them we find the fundamental elements of history, religion, and values that are important to the Mexican American culture (Campa, 1947). According to Sellers (1994), Mexican proverbs

*are the verbal property of common people. They are . . . sayings, some pithy remark from a man leaning on his plow or a woman with her elbow up on a table as she listens to the chisme-gossip of a neighbor. These sayings may inform and advise, or offer an arguable point to life. It is amusement and it is wisdom itself. It is the snappy scolding of a naughty child. It is the soothing remedy to loss and the loss of hope. . . . It is the unwritten literature and philosophy of the poor, particularly rural folk. While the wealthy and educated have Carols Fuentes and Octavio Paz, the man or woman on the street has songs, limericks, folklore, chisme, cuentos, and proverbs. (p. 6)*

As a way of linking Mexican American proverbs to perception and behavior, we have selected those proverbs that represent the most important values of the Mexican American culture: collectivism, fatalism, present-time orientation, being orientation, and family. The proverbs in the following sections are located in the works of Sellers (1994).

## Collectivism

The first prominent value that can be seen in Mexican American proverbs is collectivism.

*Better to be a fool with the crowd than wise by oneself.* In a collectivistic culture, it is much more important to show loyalty to one's in-group than to strive for individual success. It is meaningful to achieve the goals and needs of the group. Cooperation and affiliation are emphasized rather than competition or aggressiveness (Eshleman, 1985). In an individualistic culture, individuals work hard for personal accomplishments. These cultures place a strong emphasis on individual goals (Hofstede, 1980). In fact, if a person does not achieve individual success, he or she is often seen as having less academic, monetary, or social power. This is because personal identity and self-worth are derived from individual accomplishments. The opposite, of course, is the case with collectivistic cultures.

*A solitary soul neither sings nor cries.* People in collectivistic cultures are born into extended families and join organizations that protect them (Hofstede, 1984). "Collectivistic cultures are interdependent and as a result they work, play, live, and sleep in close proximity" (Andersen, 1989, p. 169). Therefore, it is better to be part of a collectivistic in-group because one will have others to share happiness or sorrow. An individual who is not part of a collectivistic group will have no one to rejoice with him or her in times of happiness. Likewise, there will be no one to comfort the individual during difficult times. If one belongs to a collectivistic in-group, there will always be many friends and family members who will try to understand one's feelings and provide support. Those who are not part of a collectivistic in-group will not experience the rich drama of life, which includes participating in others' joys and sorrows.

*He who divides and shares is left with the best share.* As part of a collectivistic society, Mexican Americans maintain a "we" consciousness. The needs of the group take precedence over individual needs. If someone is lacking a material necessity, it will be provided by others within the in-group. In this way, everyone will always be taken care of. Sharing with others will ensure that one's own needs will also be taken care of in the future.

*Bewail your poverty, and not alone.* Members of collectivistic societies are emotionally dependent on the institutions and organizations to which they belong. During economically difficult times, people within the Mexican American in-group will protect each other's interests. If this is not possible, at least the in-group will be able to offer support.

## Fatalism

This section will discuss those proverbs that exemplify the fatalistic world view of Mexican Americans.

*God gives it and God takes it away.* Catholicism is manifested in the fatalistic view of Mexican Americans. They conceive of God as all-powerful and of humans as simply part of nature that is subject to His will (Schreiber & Homiak, 1981). Since God sends people to this earth, people must leave when He calls. Through creation and destruction, God maintains the balance of the world. One must suffer to deserve.

*If God is going to give you something, it will come easy.* Good or bad fortune is predestined. If God wishes an individual to have something, he or she will receive it. If God does not want an individual to have something, it will not be given to him or her.

*He who is born to suffer will start from the cradle.* God has already decided the fate of every individual (Gomez, 1972). One's fate is decided even before birth. If one's fate is to suffer, there is nothing one can do to change it. Therefore, one should submit to the allotted level of suffering.

*He who is born to be a potted plant will not go beyond the porch.* One has little control over the situation, environment, or world; each person has a certain place in life that cannot and should not be changed. Therefore if one's destiny is to be a "potted plant," he or she will never go beyond the porch because it was not meant to be.

*Everywhere the ox goes he is put to plow; everywhere the poor man goes he must work.* Also, *He who is a parrot will be green wherever he is.* These proverbs suggest that when a person is meant to do or be something in life, there is no way to change the situation. It does not matter how industrious one is, for he or she will receive only what God dictates. Just as the ox was meant to plow, the poor person will always work because it is what God has predestined. Likewise, those born to be parrots will remain parrots.

*We are like well buckets, one goes up and the other comes down.* Although difficulties are a part of life, the Mexican American sees a balance of opposites (Gomez, 1972). Pain is balanced by pleasure, life by death, creation by destruction, and illness by health. God maintains this balance by seeing that no extreme exists without a counterbalance. For example, "pain must follow pleasure just as a hang-over must follow a drunk" (p. 170). One must suffer to deserve. Therefore if one suffers (the well bucket comes down), God will be sure to balance this suffering with pleasure (the well bucket goes up). However, this pleasure may not be seen in this world. It may be that one's pleasure will be received after death (that is, in securing a place for oneself in heaven).

*Submit to pain because it is inevitable.* Difficulties are a part of life (Gomez, 1972). Everyone will experience some type of pain in life because people must suffer to deserve. People must bear illness with dignity and courage. Fate should be accepted without complaint.

## Present-Time Orientation

Proverbs discussed in this section exemplify the prominence of the Mexican American present-time orientation.

*Don't move the water; the river is already flooding.* This proverb is interpreted to mean that one should leave matters as they are. A culture that maintains a present-time orientation is not as concerned with meeting deadlines and conforming to schedules. Acceptance and appreciation of things as they are constitute primary values. If the river is already flooding, just be content to leave it as it is.

*Give time to time.* One should not rush in life. There is time for everything because there is always tomorrow. While a person from a culture with a future orientation may have a clear plan of where he or she wishes to be in five or ten years, Mexican Americans are not overly concerned with obtaining a "blue print for life" (Flores, 1982). There is not as much concern for how much is accomplished today because there will eventually be time for everything.

*There is more time than life.* Also, *Tomorrow will be another day.* Although Mexican Americans maintain respect for the past, it is gone. Likewise, the future remains uncertain due to their fatalistic orientation. One must live for the here and now, for the moment, for that is all that can be done. If something is not completed today, do not worry because there will always be time tomorrow.

*Don't do today what you can put off until tomorrow.* Since the future is so uncertain and one never

knows if tomorrow will really come, there is no need to rush to complete everything in one day.

## Being Orientation

The being orientation is another important value in the Mexican American culture. It is therefore not surprising that many proverbs reinforce this cultural value.

*He who lives a hurried life will soon die.* Also, *Don't worry so much so you can last longer.* These proverbs refer to the value of focusing on the present moment. In contrast, the doing orientation is dominated by time schedules and goals, which require one to hurry to meet deadlines and complete tasks. If one is always hurrying, there will be no time for the important things in life, such as God and family.

*He who gets drenched at dawn has the rest of the day to dry out.* Do not be overly concerned with completing a task because there is an entire day to finish. If one gets wet in the morning, it is no problem because there is the rest of the day to dry.

*He who wants everything will lose everything.* Those who try to obtain everything in life will lose sight of what is really important, such as God and family. In the end, these people will be left with nothing, by neglecting God and family, people lose them. Therefore, just be content and satisfied to leave things as they are rather than focus on everything that could be gained.

## Family Values

The family is of utmost importance to Mexican Americans. The traditional Mexican American family is described as patriarchal, religious, and cohesive (Eshleman, 1985). Mexican American values are taught and maintained by the family. The family teaches each person his or her responsibilities as well as characteristics and behavior appropriate for his or her gender. These responsibilities, characteristics, and behaviors can be seen in the following proverbs.

*A tree that grows crooked cannot be straightened.* Mexican Americans are extremely familistic (Diaz-Guerrero, 1975). To maintain harmony in this collectivistic unit, children are taught that their responsibility is to maintain obedience and loyalty from a very young age. Children who are not taught these values from a young age and are not disciplined will never learn them.

*Better to die on your feet than to live on your knees.* These proverbs relate to the concept of machismo. The value of machismo governs male behavior in almost every facet of social life but wields its greatest influence in connection with the concept of honor (Grebler, Moore, & Guzman, 1970). The conduct of a male in any social situation must support his public image as a person of honor and integrity. A situation that might compromise his image as a man is avoided at all costs.

*A man is king in his home.* The father is the autocratic head of the household (Murillo, 1976). Few decisions can be made without his approval or knowledge. All the other family members are expected to be respectful of him and to accede to his will. The mother must be completely devoted to her husband. Fulfillment is seen in helping her husband to achieve his goals as he sees fit.

## Summary

The symbols of a culture enable values to be passed from one generation to the next. The spoken word as a symbol is a way to enforce what is most important to a culture. Proverbs are unique because they contain a condensed piece of wisdom that can be easily used by anyone in that culture. These proverbs may be repeated by a mother scolding her children, a father offering advice, or even by a person singing or praying. Studying Mexican American proverbs allows one to see that the most important aspects of the Mexican American culture are collectivism, fatalism, present-time orientation, being orientation, and familism.

## References

Andersen, P. A. (1989). Directions in Nonverbal Intercultural Communication Research. Paper presented to the Graduate Honors Seminar, Arizona State University, Tempe. April.

Aranda, C. (1977). *Dichos: Proverbs and Sayings from the Spanish.* New York: Greenwood Press.

Campa, A. L. (1947). Sayings and Riddles in New Mexico. *The University of New Mexico Bulletin, 15,* pp. 5-67.

Diaz-Guerrero, R. (1975). *Psychology of the Mexican.* Austin: University of Texas Press.

Eshleman, J. R. (1985). *The Family,* 4th ed. Boston: Allyn & Bacon.

Flores, Y. G. (1982). *The Impact of Acculturation of the Chicano Family.* Ann Arbor, Mich.: Xerox University Microfilms International.

Gomez, R. (1972). *Mexican-American: A Reader.* El Paso: University of Texas.

Grebler, L., Moore, J. W., and Guzman, R. C. (1970). *The Mexican American People.* Newbury Park, Calif.: Sage.

Haskins, J., and Butts, H. F. (1973). *The Psychology of Black Language.* New York: Barnes & Noble.

Hofstede, Geert (1980). *Culture's Consequences: International Differences in Work-Related Values.* Beverly Hills: Sage.

Hofstede, Geert (1984). National Cultures and Corporate Cultures. Paper presented on LIFIM Perspective Day, Helsinki, Finland, December 4, 1984.

Kent, C. F. (1913). *The Anchor Bible: Proverbs and Ecclesiastes.* Garden City, N.Y.: Doubleday.

Murillo, N. (1976). *Chicanos: Social and Psychological Perspectives.* Saint Louis: Mosby.

Paredes, Americo (1970). *Folktales of Mexico.* Chicago: University of Chicago Press.

Samovar L. A., and Porter, R. E. (1995). *Communication Between Cultures,* 2d ed. Belmont, Calif.: Wadsworth.

Schreiber, J. M., and Homiak, J. P. (1981). "Mexican-Americans." In A. Harwood (Ed.), *Ethnicity and Medical Care,* 265-335. Cambridge: Harvard University Press.

Sellers, J. M. (1994). *Folk Wisdom of Mexico.* San Francisco: Chronicle Books.

## Concepts and Questions for Chapter 4

1. Drawing from your own experiences, can you think of any examples that demonstrate the proposition that cultures often use different problem-solving techniques?

2. What might be some additional cultural differences in left- and right-brain hemisphere activity not mentioned by Lieberman?

3. What is the difference between field-dependent and field-independent cognitive styles?

4. What does Fong mean when she writes, "language and thought covary with one another"? Do you agree?

5. Can you think of examples, such as the one involving the Chinese culture employed by Fong, that explains the link between culture and language?

6. Can you think of five or six common English idioms that might cause communication problems when speaking with someone who has English as a second language?

7. What is there about idioms that often make them troublesome and confusing?

8. What can we do to overcome some of the problems associated with using idioms in intercultural settings?

9. Can you think of some American superlatives that might be sources of difficulty for the Finnish?

10. What American rules of conversation, not included in Carbaugh's essay, might cause problems when Americans are speaking to members of other cultures?

11. What does Orbe mean by the phrase "lived reality of African American men"?

12. Is "communicating with other men" an essential characteristic of white males?

13. What does Orbe mean by the phrase "playing the part"?

14. As used by Orbe, what does the phrase "remember, it's always whites' ball" mean?

15. How do proverbs help us understand the deep values of a culture?

16. Are the proverbs seen relating to Mexican values applicable to other cultures?

17. Can you think of proverbs from your own culture and specify what values they represent?

# 5

## Nonverbal Interaction: Action, Sound, and Silence

It is indeed a truism that we communicate with our actions as well as our words. Therefore, successful participation in intercultural communication requires that we recognize and understand culture's influence not only on verbal interaction but on nonverbal interaction as well. Our nonverbal actions constitute yet another symbol system that enables other people to gain insight into our thoughts and feelings. Because nonverbal symbols are derived from such diverse behaviors as body movements, postures, facial expressions, gestures, eye movements, physical appearance, the use and organization of space, the structuring of time, and vocal nuances, these symbolic behaviors often vary from culture to culture. An awareness of the role of nonverbal behaviors is crucial, therefore, if we are to appreciate all aspects of intercultural interaction.

Nonverbal behavior is largely unconscious. We use nonverbal symbols spontaneously, without thinking about what posture, what gesture, or what interpersonal distance is appropriate to the situation. These factors are critically important in intercultural communication because, as with other aspects of the communication process, nonverbal behaviors are subject to cultural variation. These nonverbal behaviors can be categorized in two ways.

In the first, culture tends to determine the specific nonverbal behaviors that represent or symbolize specific thoughts, feelings, or states of the communicator. Thus, what might be a sign of greeting in one culture could very well be an obscene gesture in another. Or what might be a symbol of affirmation in one culture could be meaningless or even signify negation in another. In the second, culture determines when it is appropriate to display or communicate various thoughts, feelings, or internal states; this is particularly evident in the display of emotions. Although there seems to be little cross-cultural difference in the behaviors that represent emotional states, there are great cultural differences in which emotions may be displayed, by whom, and when or where they may be displayed.

As important as verbal language is to a communication event, nonverbal communication is just as, if not more, important. Nonverbal messages can stand alone or they can tell us how other messages are to be interpreted. For example, they often indicate whether verbal messages are true, uttered in jest, serious, threatening, and so on. Nonverbal communication is especially important because as much as 90 percent of the social content of a message is transmitted paralinguistically, or nonverbally.

Chapter 5 deals with nonverbal interaction. More specifically, it deals with how one's culture influences both the perception and use of nonverbal actions. These readings will demonstrate the variety of culturally derived nonverbal behaviors and the underlying value structures that produce these behaviors.

We begin this chapter with an overview of the topic of nonverbal communication rather than with a critique of a single culture. Peter Andersen's essay, "Cues of Culture: The Basis of Intercultural Differences in Nonverbal Communication," begins with an analysis of how culture determines our nonverbal communicative behavior. He then discusses the following fundamental dimensions of cultural variability: (1) immediacy and expressiveness, (2) individualism, (3) gender, (4) power distance, (5) uncertainty, and (6) high and low context. The motivation driving Andersen's analysis is one that is at the heart of this entire book. Simply stated, if you understand the nonverbal codes used by various cultures you can better interact with people from those cultures.

Our next essay moves us from a discussion of cultures in general to an analysis of a specific culture. Edwin R. McDaniel, in his piece titled "Nonverbal Communication: A Reflection of Cultural Themes," examines some nonverbal communication patterns found in the Japanese culture. As a means of demonstrating the link between culture and communication, McDaniel not only examines the communication behaviors of the Japanese culture, but also traces the reasons for these behaviors. By presenting what he refers to as "cultural themes," McDaniel is able to explain how Japan's social organizations, historical experiences, and religious orientations are directly connected to how the Japanese perceive and use kinesics (movement), oculesics (eye contact), facial expressions, proxemics (space), touch, personal appearance, time, paralanguage, silence, and olfactics (smell).

Our next essay examines a culture's use of space as yet another aspect of human interaction. The assumption behind this analysis is that our use of space is a message that transmits meaning to those around us.

As noted in several selections in this chapter, our perception of space and the use we make of it are directly related to our culture. This relationship is documented and illustrated by Carol Zinner Dolphin in her essay "Variables in the Use of Personal Space in Intercultural Transactions." Dolphin, like the editors of this book, conceives of a culture as more than simply the country one calls home; she therefore includes the influence of age, sex, relationships, environment, and ethnicity on the communication encounter. Dolphin concludes by presenting a number of suggestions for further research. She believes that the issues raised by these questions will increase our understanding of the link between culture, communication, and space.

In our final essay, "Monochronic and Polychronic Time," Edward T. Hall looks at the conscious and unconscious ways culture uses time. Hall maintains that cultures organize and respond to time in two different ways, which he refers to as Polychronic (P-time) and Monochronic (M-time). While these systems are not meant to be perceived as either/or categories, they do offer two distinct approaches to time. Cultures such as those found in the Mediterranean, Africa, and South America are P-time cultures in that they do many things at the same time, are more concerned with people and the present moment than with schedules, and believe that they are in command of time rather than being controlled by it. M-time cultures of Northern Europe and North America, on the other hand, emphasize schedules, the segmentation of time, and promptness. It is easy to imagine the potential for misunderstanding when people from these diverse orientations come together. Hall's essay helps us avoid communication problems by introducing us to the many forms these two interaction patterns take.

# Culture:
## of Intercultural Differences in Nonverbal Communication

## PETER ANDERSEN

Culture may be the central topic of the next millennium. At one time most people spent their lives within their own culture, interacting with people from their own group. Only rarely across the generations did sojourners, traders, or warriors encounter people from other cultures – usually with disastrous effects. People with different customs were thought to be crazy, rude, sinful, promiscuous, uncivilized, or subhuman. Today some of these attitudes toward people from other cultures still persist. In California ballot measures are being passed restricting the rights of illegal immigrants. Among many nations, trade wars, ethnic cleansing, and genocide still occur.

As we enter the third millennium, contact between people from various cultures is increasing. International migration is at an all-time high. International trade increased 100 percent between 1985 and 1995 and nearly 400 percent between 1965 and 1995 (Brown, Kane, & Roodman, 1994). International tourism is an increasingly common phenomenon. The number of official refugees topped 18 million for the first time ever (Brown et al., 1994). In short, the amount of intercultural contact in today's world is unprecedented, making the study of intercultural communication more important than ever.

This essay is an extensive revision of an essay first published in the fifth edition. All rights reserved. Permission to reprint must be obtained from the publisher and the author. Peter Andersen teaches at San Diego State University.

While language differences are most apparent, they are only the tip of a very large cultural iceberg. Culture is primarily an implicit nonverbal phenomenon, for most aspects of one's culture are learned through observation and imitation rather than explicit verbal instruction or expression. The primary level of culture is communicated implicitly, without awareness, chiefly by nonverbal means (Andersen, 1988; Hall, 1984; Sapir, 1928). In most situations intercultural interactants do not share the same language. But languages can be learned, and larger communication problems occur in the nonverbal realm. Nonverbal communication is a subtle, nonlinguistic, multidimensional, spontaneous process (Andersen, 1986). Indeed, individuals are aware of little of their own nonverbal behavior, which is enacted mindlessly, spontaneously, and unconsciously (Andersen, 1986; Burgoon, 1985; Samovar & Porter, 1985). Since we are not usually aware of our own nonverbal behavior, it becomes extremely difficult to identify and master the nonverbal behavior of another culture. At times we feel uncomfortable in other cultures because we intuitively know something isn't right. "Because nonverbal behaviors are rarely conscious phenomena, it may be difficult for us to know exactly why we are feeling uncomfortable" (Gudykunst & Kim, 1984, p. 149). Indeed, Edward Sapir stated long ago that

*We respond to gestures with an extreme alertness and, one might almost say, in accordance with an elaborate and secret code that is written nowhere, known to none and understood by all. (1928, p. 556)*

Indeed, culture is so basic, learned at such a tender age, and so taken-for-granted, that it is often confused with human nature itself.

This article will briefly explore the subtle codes of nonverbal communication, locate culture as a part of interpersonal behavior, and then discuss six primary dimensions of cultural variation, including immediacy, individualism, gender, power distance, uncertainty-avoidance, and cultural contextualization. It is argued that each of these dimensions explains the fundamental differences in a culture's communication, particularly in a culture's nonverbal communication.

## Nonverbal Codes

Most discussions of nonverbal intercultural communication have been antecdotal, descriptive, and atheoretical, where numerous examples of intercultural differences for each nonverbal code are discussed in detail. Recapitulation of the various nonverbal codes of intercultural communication is not a primary purpose here. Thus the basic code of nonverbal communication will be discussed only briefly along with references that provide detailed and excellent analyses of how each nonverbal code differs interculturally.

Two of the most fundamental nonverbal differences in intercultural communication involve space and time. *Chronemics,* or the study of meanings, usage, and communication of time, is probably the most discussed and well-researched nonverbal code in the intercultural literature (Bruneau, 1979; Burgoon, Buller, & Woodall, 1989; Gudykunst & Kim, 1984; Hall, 1959, 1976, 1984; Malandro & Barker, 1983). These analyses suggest that the time frames of cultures differ so dramatically that if only chronemic differences existed, intercultural misunderstandings would still be considerable. In the United States time is viewed as a commodity that can be wasted, spent, saved and used wisely. Of course, many cultures have no such concept of time. In many third-world cultures life moves to the rhythms of nature, the day, the seasons, the year. Human inventions like seconds, minutes, hours, or weeks have no real meaning. Things are experienced polychronically and simultaneously, whereas in Western culture time is modularized and events are scheduled sequentially, not simultaneously.

A second nonverbal code that has attracted considerable attention is *proxemics,* the communication of interpersonal space and distance. Research has documented that cultures differ substantially in their use of personal space, the distances they maintain, and their regard for territory as well as the meanings they assign to proxemic behavior (Burgoon, Buller, & Woodall, 1989; Gudykunst & Kim, 1984; Hall, 1959, 1976; Malandro & Barker, 1983; Scheflen, 1974).

Considerable intercultural differences have been reported in people's *kinesic* behavior, including their facial expressions, body movements, gestures, and conversational regulators (Burgoon, Buller, & Woodall, 1989; Gudykunst & Kim, 1984; Hall, 1976; Jensen, 1985; Malandro & Barker, 1983; Rich, 1974; Samovar, Porter, & Jain, 1981; Scheflen, 1974). Gestures differ dramatically in meaning, extensiveness, and intensity. Stories abound in the intercultural literature of gestures that signal endearment or warmth in one culture, but that may be obscene or insulting in another culture.

Interpersonal patterns of tactile communication called *haptics* also reveal substantial intercultural differences (Andersen & Leibowitz, 1978; Malandro & Barker, 1983; Prosser, 1978; Samovar, Porter, & Jain, 1981). Recent research has shown vast differences in international and intercultural touch in amount, location, type, and public or private manifestation (Jones, 1994; McDaniel & Andersen, 1995).

Other important codes of nonverbal communication have attracted considerably less space in publications on nonverbal and intercultural communication. *Physical appearance,* the most important nonverbal code during initial encounters, is of obvious importance, since many intercultural encounters are based on stereotypes and are of short duration. Some discussion of intercultural differences in appearance are provided by Scheflen (1974) and Samovar, Porter, and Jain (1981). Though blue jeans and business suits have become increasingly accepted attire internationally, local attire still abounds. Recently, while collecting intercultural communication data at an international airport, I witnessed Tongans in multicultural ceremonial gowns, Sikhs in white turbans, Hasidic Jews in blue yarmulkes, and Africans in white dashikis, alongside Californians in running shorts and halter tops.

*Oculesics,* the study of messages sent by the eyes — including eye contact, blinks, eye movements, and pupil dilation — has received only marginal attention by intercultural communication scholars (Gudykunst & Kim, 1984; Jensen, 1985; Samovar, Porter, & Jain, 1981). Since eye contact has been called an "invitation to communicate," its variation cross-culturally is an important communication topic.

*Vocalics,* or *paralanguage,* the nonverbal elements of the voice, also has received comparatively little attention from intercultural researchers (Gudykunst & Kim, 1984; LaBarre, 1985; Rich, 1974; Samovar, Porter, & Jain, 1981; Scheflen, 1974). Music and singing, universal forms of aesthetic communication, have been almost completely overlooked in intercultural research, except for an excellent study (Lomax, 1968) that identified several groups of worldwide cultures through differences and similarities in their folk songs. Finally, *olfactics,* the study of interpersonal communication via smell, has been virtually ignored in intercultural research despite its importance (Samovar, Porter, & Jain, 1981).

| | Location of Influence | |
|---|---|---|
| Time Frame | **Social Environment** | **Internal Forces** |
| Enduring Phenomena | Culture | Traits |
| Transient Phenomena | Situation | State |

**Figure 1** Sources of influence on interpersonal behavior.

## Locating Culture in Interpersonal Behavior

Culture is a critical concept to communication scholars because every communicator is a product of her/his culture. Culture, along with traits, situations, and states, is one of the four primary sources of interpersonal behavior (Andersen, 1987, 1988; see Figure 1). Culture is the enduring influence of the social environment on our behavior, including our interpersonal communication behavior. Culture is a learned set of shared perceptions about beliefs, values, and needs that affect the behaviors of relatively large groups of people (Lustig & Koester, 1993). Culture exerts a considerable force on individual behavior through what Geertz (1973) called "control mechanisms – plans, recipes, rules, instructions (what computer engineers call 'programs') – for the governing of behavior" (p. 44). Culture has similar, powerful, though not identical, effects on all residents of a cultural system. "Culture can be behaviorally observed by contrasting intragroup homogeneity with intergroup heterogeneity" (Andersen, Lustig, & Andersen, 1986, p. 11).

Culture has been confused with personal traits because both are enduring phenomena (Andersen, 1987, 1988). Traits have multiple causes (Andersen, 1987), only some of which are the result of culture. Culture has also been confused with situation, for both are part of one's social environment. However, culture is an enduring phenomenon, while situation is a transient one with an observable beginning and end. Culture, along with genetics, is the most enduring, powerful, and invisible shaper of our communication behavior.

## Dimensions of Cultural Variation

Thousands of anecdotes regarding nonverbal misunderstandings between persons from different cultures have been reported. While it may be useful to know that Arabs stand closer than Americans, the Swiss are more time-conscious than Italians, and Orientals value silence more than Westerners, more than this approach is necessary. Because the number of potential pairs of cultures are huge and the number of possible nonverbal misunderstandings between each pair of cultures is similarly large, millions of potential intercultural anecdotes are possible (Andersen, 1988). What is needed is some way to organize, explain, and understand this plethora of potential problems in intercultural communication. Some initial research has shown that cultures can be located along dimensions that help explain these intercultural differences. Most cultural differences in nonverbal behavior are a result of variations along the dimensions discussed below.

## Immediacy and Expressiveness

Immediacy behaviors are actions that simultaneously communicate warmth, closeness, and availability for communication and also signal approach rather than avoidance and closeness rather than distance

(Andersen, 1985; Hecht, Andersen, & Ribeau, 1989). Examples of immediacy behaviors are smiling, touching, eye contact, closer distances, and more vocal animation. Some scholars have labeled these behaviors as "expressive" (Patterson, 1983).

Cultures that display considerable interpersonal closeness or immediacy have been labeled "contact cultures," since people in these countries stand closer and touch more (Hall, 1966). People in low-contact cultures tend to stand apart and touch less. According to Patterson (1983):

*These habitual patterns of relating to the world perme-ate all aspects of everyday life, but their effects on so-cial behavior define the manner in which people relate to one another. In the case of contact cultures, this general tendency is manifested in closer approaches so that tactile and olfactory information may be gained easily. (p. 145)*

Interestingly, contact cultures are generally located in warmer countries and low-contact cultures in cooler climates. Considerable research has shown that high-contact cultures comprise most Arab countries, including North Africa; the Mediter-ranean region, including France, Greece, Italy, Por-tugal, and Spain; Jewish people from both Europe and the Middle East; Eastern Europeans and Rus-sians; and virtually all of Latin America (Condon & Yousef, 1983; Jones, 1994; Jones & Remland, 1982; Mehrabian, 1971; Patterson, 1983; Samovar, Porter, & Jain, 1981; Scheflen, 1972). Australians are moderate in their cultural contact level, as are North Americans, though North Americans tend toward low contact (Patterson, 1983). Low-contact cultures comprise most of Northern Europe, in-cluding Scandinavia, Germany, and England; British-Americans; white Anglo-Saxons (the primary culture of the United States); and virtually every Asian country, including Burma, Korea, China, Japan, In-donesia, the Philippines, Thailand, and Vietnam (Andersen, Andersen, & Lustig, 1987; Heslin & Alper, 1983; Jones, 1994; Jones & Remland, 1982; McDaniel & Andersen, 1995; Mehrabian, 1971; Patterson, 1983; Samovar, Porter, & Jain, 1981; Scheflen, 1972). Indeed, McDaniel and Andersen's data on public touch suggest the big difference is between Asians, who rarely touch in public, and virtually every other culture, which all manifest higher degrees of public touching. These findings are consistent with other research suggesting that China and Japan are distinctly non-touch cultures (Barnland, 1978; Jones, 1994). However, two recent studies (McDaniel & Andersen, 1995; Remland, Jones, & Brinkman, 1991) report that the English engage in considerable touch and maintain rela-tively close distances. Indeed, both studies ques-tion Hall's (1966) original designation of some cultures as "low contact" as an oversimplification.

Explanations for these latitudinal variations have included energy level, climate, and metabo-lism (Andersen, Lustig, & Andersen, 1990). Evi-dently, cultures in cooler climates tend to be more task-oriented and interpersonally "cool," whereas cultures in warmer climates tend to be more inter-personally oriented and interpersonally "warm." Even within the United States, the warmer lati-tudes tend to be higher-contact cultures. Andersen, Lustig, and Andersen (1990) report a .31 correla-tion between latitude of students' university and touch avoidance. These data suggest students at Sun Belt universities are more touch-oriented. Re-cently, Pennebaken, Rimé, and Sproul (1994) found a correlation between latitude and expressiveness within dozens of countries. Northerners are more expressive, according to their data, in Belgium, Croatia, France, Germany, Italy, Japan, Serbia, Spain, Switzerland, and the United States, with an overall difference within the entire northern hemi-sphere. Pennebaken et al. (1994) conclude:

*Logically, climate must profoundly affect social pro-cesses. People living in cold climates devote more time to dressing, to providing warmth, to planning ahead for food provisions during the winter months. . . . In warm climates, people are more likely to see, hear, and inter-act with neighbors year around. Emotional expressive-ness, then would be more of a requirement. (pp. 15–16)*

Similarly, Andersen, Lustig, and Andersen (1990) conclude:

*In Northern latitudes societies must be more struc-tured, more ordered, more constrained, and more orga-nized if the individuals are to survive harsh weather forces. . . . In contrast, Southern latitudes may attract or produce a culture characterized by social extravagance and flamboyance that has no strong inclination to constrain or order their world. (p. 307)*

Without a doubt, cultures differ in their immediacy. In general, northern countries, northern parts of individual countries, traditional cultures, and Asians are the least immediate and expressive. Southern people, modern countries, and non-Asian cultures are the most expressive and immediate. Obviously, these findings are painted with a fairly broad brush and will await a more detailed cultural portrait.

## Individualism

One of the most fundamental dimensions along which cultures differ is their degree of individualism versus collectivism. This dimension determines how people live together (alone, in families, or tribes; see Hofstede, 1982), their values, and how they communicate. As we will see, Americans are individualists for better or worse. We take individualism for granted and are blind to its impact until travel brings us in contact with less individualistic, more collectivistic cultures.

Individualism has been applauded as a blessing and has been elevated to the status of a national religion in the United States. Indeed, the best and worst in our culture can be attributed to individualism. Proponents of individualism have argued that it is the basis of liberty, democracy, freedom, and economic incentive and also serves as protection against tyranny. Individualism has been blamed for our alienation from one another, loneliness, selfishness, and narcissism. Indeed, Hall (1976) has claimed that as an extreme individualist, "Western man has created chaos by denying that part of his self that integrates while enshrining the part that fragments experience" (p. 9).

There can be little doubt that individualism is one of the fundamental dimensions that distinguish cultures. Likewise, "there is little doubt that Western culture is individualistic so people rely on personal judgments. Eastern cultures emphasize harmony among people, between people and nature, and value collective judgments" (Hecht, Andersen, & Ribeau, 1989, p. 170). Tomkins (1984)

demonstrated that an individual's psychological makeup is the result of this cultural dimension. He stated, "Human beings, in Western Civilization, have tended toward self-celebration, positive or negative. In Oriental thought another alternative is represented, that of harmony between man and nature" (p. 182). Prosser (1978) suggested that the Western emphasis on individuality finds its culmination in contemporary North American cultures where the chief cultural value is the role of the individual. This idea is verified in the landmark intercultural study of Hofstede (1982). In his study of individualism in forty non-communist countries the nine most individualistic (in order) were the United States, Australia, Great Britain, Canada, Netherlands, New Zealand, Italy, Belgium, and Denmark, all of which are Western or European cultures. The ten least individualistic (starting with the least) were Venezuela, Colombia, Pakistan, Peru, Taiwan, Thailand, Singapore, Chile, and Hong Kong, all Asian or South American cultures. Similarly, Sitaram and Codgell (1976) reported individuality to be of primary importance in Western cultures, of secondary importance in black cultures, and of lesser importance in Eastern and Muslim cultures.

While the United States is the most individualistic country on earth (Hofstede, 1982), regions of the United States and particular ethnic groups vary in their degree of individualism. Elazar (1972) has shown that the central Midwest and the mid-Atlantic states have the most individualistic political culture, whereas the Southeast is the most traditionalistic and least individualistic. But this is all relative and, by world standards, even Mississippi is an individualistic culture. Bellah et al. (1985) stated:

*Individualism lies at the very core of American culture. . . . Anything that would violate our right to think for ourselves, judge for ourselves, make our own decisions, live our lives as we see fit, is not only morally wrong, it is sacrilegious. (p. 142)*

Different ethnic groups may vary within a culture. African Americans, for example, place a great deal of emphasis on individualism, whereas Mexican

Americans place a greater emphasis on group and relational solidarity (Hecht, Andersen, & Ribeau, 1989). Indeed, our extreme individualism makes it difficult for Americans to interact with and understand people from other cultures. We are unique; all other cultures are less individualistic. As Condon and Yousef (1983) stated, "The fusion of individualism and equality is so valued and so basic that many Americans find it most difficult to relate to contrasting values in other cultures where interdependence greatly determines a person's sense of self" (p. 65).

The degree to which a culture is individualistic or collectivistic affects the nonverbal behavior of that culture in every way. First, people from individualistic cultures are more remote and distant proximally. Collectivistic cultures are interdependent; and, as a result the members work, play, live, and sleep in close proximity to one another. Hofstede (1982) cites research suggesting that as hunters and gatherers, people lived apart in individualistic, nuclear families. As agricultural societies developed, the interdependent extended family began living in close proximity in large family or tribal units. Urban-industrial societies returned to a norm of individualism, nuclear families, and lack of proximity to one's neighbors, friends, and coworkers.

Kinesic behavior tends to be more synchronized in collectivistic cultures. Where families work collectively, movements, schedules, and actions need to be highly coordinated (Argyle, 1975). In urban cultures family members often do their "own thing," coming and going, working and playing, eating and sleeping on different schedules. People in individualistic cultures also smile more than people in normatively oriented cultures, according to Tomkins (1984). This is probably due to the fact that individualists are responsible for their relationships and their own happiness, whereas normatively or collectively oriented people regard compliance with norms as a primary value and personal or interpersonal happiness as a secondary value (Andersen, 1988). Matsumoto (1991) contends that "collective cultures will foster emotional displays of their members that maintain and facilitate group cohesion, harmony, or cooperation, to a greater degree

than individualistic cultures" (p. 132). Similarly, Lustig & Koester (1993) maintain that "people from individualistic cultures are more likely than those from collectivistic cultures to use confrontational strategies when dealing with interpersonal problems; those with a collectivist orientation are likely to use avoidance, third-party intermediaries, or other face-saving techniques" (p. 147). People in collectivistic cultures may suppress both positive and negative emotional displays that are contrary to the mood of the group, since maintaining the group is a primary value (Andersen, 1988). Recently, Bond (1993) found the Chinese culture to be lower in frequency, intensity, and duration of emotional expression. Bond asserts that "the expression of emotion is carefully regulated out of a concern for its capacity to disrupt group harmony and status hierarchies" (p. 245).

People in individualistic cultures are encouraged to express emotions since individual freedom is a paramount value. Research suggests that people in individualistic cultures are more nonverbally affiliative. Intuitively, the reason for this is not obvious, since individualism doesn't require affiliation. However, Hofstede (1982) explained that

*In less individualistic countries where traditional social ties, like those with extended family members, continue to exist, people have less of a need to make specific friendships. One's friends are predetermined by the social relationships into which one is born. In the more individualistic countries, however, affective relationships are not socially predetermined but must be acquired by each individual personally. (p. 163)*

In individualistic countries, like the United States, affiliativeness, dating, flirting, small talk, smiling, and initial acquaintance are more important than in collectivistic countries where the social network is more fixed and less reliant on individual initiative. Bellah et al (1985) maintain that for centuries in the individualistic and mobile United States society, people could meet more easily and their communication was more open. However, their relationships were usually more casual and transient.

Finally, in an impressive study of dozens of cultures, Lomax (1968) found that song and dance styles of a country were related to its level of social cohesion and collectivism. Collectivistic cultures are higher in "groupiness" and cohesion found in their singing styles. Collectivistic cultures show both more cohesiveness in singing and more synchrony in their dance style (Lomax, 1968). It isn't surprising that rock dancing, which emphasizes separateness and "doing your own thing," evolved in individualistic cultures like England and the United States. These dances may serve as a metaphor for the whole U.S. culture, where individuality is more prevalent than in any other place (Andersen, 1988).

## Gender

The gender orientation of culture has a major impact on many aspects of nonverbal behavior, including the types of expressions permitted by each sex, occupational status, nonverbal aspects of power, the ability to interact with strangers or acquaintances of the opposite sex, and all aspects of interpersonal relationship between men and women. "While numerous studies have focused on gender as an individual characteristic, gender has been neglected as a cultural dimension" (Hecht, Andersen, & Ribeau, 1989, p. 171). As conceptualized here, gender refers to the rigidity of gender rules. In rigid cultures, masculine traits are typically attributes such as strength, assertiveness, competitiveness, and ambitiousness, whereas feminine traits are attributes such as affection, compassion, nurturance, and emotionality (Bem, 1974; Hofstede, 1982). In less rigid cultures both men and women can express more diverse, less stereotyped sex-role behaviors. Cross-cultural research shows that young girls are expected to be more nurturant than boys, though there is considerable variation from country to country (Hall, 1984). Hofstede (1982) has measured the degree to which people of both sexes in a culture endorse masculine or feminine goals. Masculine cultures regard competition and assertiveness as important, whereas feminine cultures place more importance on nurturance and compassion. Not surprisingly, the masculinity of a culture is negatively correlated with the percentage of women in technical and professional jobs and positively correlated with segregation of the sexes in higher education (Hofstede, 1982).

Countries with the nine highest masculinity index scores, according to Hofstede (1982) are, respectively, Japan, Austria, Venezuela, Italy, Switzerland, Mexico, Ireland, Great Britain, and Germany. The nine countries with the lowest masculinity scores (respectively) are Sweden, Norway, Netherlands, Denmark, Finland, Chile, Portugal, and Thailand. Not surprisingly, high-masculinity countries have fewer women in the labor force, only recently have afforded voting privileges to women, and are less likely to consider wife-rape a crime than are low masculinity countries (Seager & Olson, 1986).

Why would South American cultures not manifest the Latin pattern of machismo? Hofstede (1982) suggests that machismo is more present in the Caribbean region than in the remainder of South America. In fact, South America, as compared to Central America, has a much higher percentage of working women, much higher school attendance by girls, and more women in higher education (Seager & Olson, 1986).

Considerable research suggests the androgynous patterns of behavior (that are both feminine and masculine) result in more self-esteem, social competence, success, and intellectual development for both males and females (Andersen, 1988). Nonverbal styles where both men and women are free to express both masculine traits (such as dominance, anger) and feminine traits (such as warmth, emotionality) are likely to be both healthier and more effective. Buck (1984) has demonstrated that males may harm their health by internalizing emotions rather than externalizing them as women usually do. Internalized emotions that aren't expressed result in more stress and higher blood pressure. Interestingly, more masculine countries show higher levels of stress (Hofstede, 1982).

Considerable research has demonstrated significant vocal differences between egalitarian and nonegalitarian countries. Countries where women are economically important and where sexual standards for women are permissive show more relaxed vocal patterns than do other countries (Lomax, 1968). Moreover those egalitarian countries show less tension between the sexes, more vocal solidarity and coordination in their songs, and more synchrony in their movement (Lomax, 1968).

It is important to note that the United States tends to be a masculine country, according to Hofstede (1982), though it is not among the most masculine. Intercultural communicators should keep in mind that other countries may be either more or less sexually egalitarian than the United States. Because most countries are more feminine (that is, nurturant, compassionate), Americans of both sexes frequently seem loud, aggressive, and competitive by world standards. Likewise, Americans' attitude toward women may seem sexist in extremely feminine locations like Scandinavia.

## Power Distance

A fourth fundamental dimension of intercultural communication is power distance. Power distance, the degree to which power, prestige, and wealth are unequally distributed in a culture has been measured in a number of cultures using Hofstede's (1982) Power Distance Index (PDI). Cultures with high PDI scores have power and influence concentrated in the hands of a few rather than more equally distributed throughout the population. Condon and Yousef (1983) distinguish among three cultural patterns: democratic, authority-centered, and authoritarian. The PDI is highly correlated (.80) with authoritarianism (as measured by the F-Scale) (Hofstede, 1982).

High-PDI countries (highest first) are the Philippines, Mexico, Venezuela, India, Singapore, Brazil, Hong Kong, France, and Colombia (Hofstede, 1982), all of which are south Asian, South American or Caribbean countries with the exception of France. Gudykunst and Kim (1984) report that both African and Asian cultures generally maintain hierarchical role relationships. Asian students are expected to be modest and deferent nonverbally in the presence of their instructors. Likewise, Vietnamese consider employers to be their mentor and will not question orders. Low-PDI countries (lowest first) are Austria, Israel, Denmark, New Zealand, Ireland, Sweden, Norway, Finland, and Switzerland (Hofstede, 1982), all of which are European-origin, middle-class, democracies located at high latitudes. The United States is slightly lower than the median in power distance, indicating smaller status differentials than in many other

countries. Cultures differ in terms of how status is acquired. In many countries, such as India, one's status is determined by class or caste. In the United States power and status is typically determined by money and conspicuous material displays (Andersen & Bowman, 1990).

A primary determiner of power distance is the latitude of a country. Hofstede (1982) claims that latitude and climate are one of the major forces shaping a culture. He maintains that the key intervening variable is that in colder climates technology is needed for survival. This produces a chain of events in which children are less dependent on authority and learn from people other than authority figures. Hofstede (1982) reports a .65 correlation between PDI and latitude! In a study conducted at 40 universities throughout the United States, Andersen, Lustig, and Andersen (1990) report a −.47 correlation between latitude and intolerance for ambiguity, and a −.45 correlation between latitude and authoritarianism. This suggests that residents of the northern United States are less authoritarian and more tolerant of ambiguity. Northern cultures may have to be more tolerant and less autocratic to ensure cooperation and survival in harsher climates.

It is obvious that power distance would affect the nonverbal behavior of a culture. High-PDI cultures, such as India, with a rigid caste system may severely limit interaction, as in the case of India's "untouchables." Over 20 percent of India's population are untouchables who lie at the bottom of India's five-caste system (Chinoy, 1967). Any contact with untouchables by members of other castes is strictly forbidden and considered "polluting." Certainly, tactile communication between castes is greatly curtailed in Indian culture. High-PDI countries with less rigid stratification than India may still prohibit free interclass dating, marriage, and contact — all of which are taken for granted in low-PDI countries.

Social systems with large power discrepancies also produce different kinesic behavior. Cultures with high power distance will foster and encourage emotions that present status differences. For instance, in high-power-distance cultures people would be expected to show only positive emotions to high-status others and only negative emotions to low-status others (Matsumoto, 1991). According to Andersen and Bowman (1990), subordinates' bodily tension is more obvious in power-discrepant relationships. Similarly, Andersen and Bowman (1990) report that in power-discrepant circumstances subordinates smile more in an effort to appease superiors and appear polite. The continuous smiles of many Asians are a culturally inculcated effort to appease superiors and smooth social relations that are appropriate to a high-PDI culture.

Vocalic and paralinguistic cues are also affected by the power distance in a culture. Citizens of low-PDI cultures are generally less aware that vocal loudness may be offensive to others. American vocal tones are often perceived as noisy, exaggerated, and childlike (Condon & Yousef, 1983). Lomax (1968) has shown that in countries where political authority is highly centralized, singing voices are tighter and the voice box is more closed, whereas more permissive societies produce more relaxed, open, and clear sounds.

## Uncertainty

Uncertainty is a cultural predisposition to value risk and ambiguity (Hecht, Andersen, & Ribeau, 1989). At the individual level this quality is often called tolerance for ambiguity (Martin & Westie, 1959). People with intolerance of ambiguity or high levels of uncertainty avoidance want clear, black and white answers. People with tolerance of ambiguity and low levels of uncertainty avoidance are more tolerant, accept ambiguous answers, and see many shades of gray. Similarly, Hofstede (1982) reports that a country's neuroticism or anxiety scores are strongly correlated with uncertainty avoidance. High uncertainty avoidance is negatively correlated with risk taking and positively correlated to fear of failure.

Countries vary greatly in their tolerance for uncertainty. In some cultures, freedom leads to uncertainty, which leads to stress and anxiety. Hofstede (1982) maintained that intolerance of ambiguity and dogmatism are primarily a function of the uncertainty-avoidance dimension rather than the power-distance dimension. Countries with the highest levels of uncertainty avoidance are Greece, Portugal, Belgium, Japan, Peru, France, Chile, Spain,

and Argentina (Hofstede, 1982). The list is dominated by southern European and South American countries. Countries lowest in uncertainty avoidance and most tolerant are Singapore, Denmark, Sweden, Hong Kong, Ireland, Great Britain, India, the Philippines, and the United States. This list is dominated by northern European and south Asian cultures. Hofstede (1982) also reports that Catholic countries are high in uncertainty avoidance whereas Protestant, Hindu, or Buddhist countries tend to be more accepting of uncertainty. Eastern religions and Protestantism tend to be less "absolute" while Catholicism is a more "absolute religion." Andersen, Lustig, and Andersen (1990) report that intolerance for ambiguity is much higher in the southern United States than in the northern states, tending to reflect the international pattern of latitude and tolerance.

We know relatively little about nonverbal behavior associated with uncertainty. Hofstede (1982) maintains that countries high in uncertainty avoidance tend to display emotions more than countries low in uncertainty avoidance. Furthermore, he reports that the emotional displays of young people are tolerated less in countries with high uncertainty avoidance. Certainly, disagreement and nonconformity are not appreciated if uncertainty avoidance is high. Nonverbal behavior is more likely to be codified and rule-governed in countries with high uncertainty avoidance. This seems to fit a country like Japan, but the hypothesis remains to be tested and is somewhat speculative. Hofstede (1982) found that nations high in uncertainty avoidance report more stylized and ritual behavior, so we should expect that nonverbal behavior is more prescribed in these cultures. When people from the United States communicate with people from a country like Japan or France (both high in uncertainty avoidance), the Americans may seem excessively nonconforming and unconventional, whereas their Japanese or French counterparts might seem too controlled and rigid to the Americans (Lustig & Koester, 1993).

## High and Low Context

A final important dimension of intercultural communication is that of context. Since nonverbal cues often provide context, this is a very important dimension. Hall (1976, 1984) has described high- and low-context cultures in considerable detail. "A high context (HC) communication or message is one in which most of the information is either in the physical context or internalized in the person, while very little is in the coded, explicit, transmitted parts of the message" (Hall, 1976, p. 91). Lifelong friends often use HC or implicit messages that are nearly impossible for an outsider to understand. The situation, a smile, or a glance provides implicit meaning that doesn't need to be articulated. In HC situations or cultures, information is integrated from the environment, the context, the situation, and nonverbal cues that give the message meaning unavailable in the explicit verbal utterance.

Low-context (LC) messages are just the opposite of NC messages; most of the information is in the explicit code (Hall, 1976). LC messages must be elaborated, clearly communicated, and highly specific. Unlike personal relationships, which are relatively high-context message systems, institutions such as courts of law and formal systems such as mathematics or computer language require explicit, LC systems, for nothing can be taken for granted (Hall, 1984).

Cultures vary considerably in the degree of context used in communication. The lowest-context cultures are probably Swiss, German, North American, and Scandinavian (Gudykunst & Kim, 1984; Hall, 1976, 1984). These cultures are preoccupied with specifics, details, literalness, and precise time schedules at the expense of context. They utilize behavior systems built around Aristotelian logic and linear thinking (Hall, 1984) and may be pathologically verbal. Cultures that have some characteristics of both HC and LC systems would include the French, English, and Italian (Gudykunst & Kim, 1984), which are somewhat less explicit than Northern European cultures.

The highest-context cultures are found in Asia. China, Japan, and Korea are extremely HC cultures (Elliott et al., 1982; Hall, 1976, 1984). Languages are some of the most explicit communication systems, but the Chinese language is an implicit high-context system. To use a Chinese dictionary one must understand thousands of characters that change meaning in combination with other characters. Zen Buddhism, a major influence in Asia, places a high value on silence, lack of emotional expression, and on the unspoken, nonverbal parts of communication (Burgoon, Buller, & Woodall, 1989; McDaniel & Andersen, 1995). Americans frequently complain that the Japanese never "get to the point" but fail to recognize that HC culture must provide a context and setting and let the point evolve (Hall, 1984). In a recent study of airport departures, McDaniel and Andersen (1995) found Asians to be least tactile of any cultural group on earth. The influence of Buddhism and the value placed on context rather that emotional expression probably explain this finding. American Indian cultures with ancestral migratory roots in East Asia are remarkably like contemporary Asian culture in several ways, especially in its need for high context (Hall, 1984). Not surprisingly, most Latin American cultures, a fusion of Iberian (Portugese-Spanish) and Indian traditions, are also high-context cultures. Southern and eastern Mediterranean people such as Greeks, Turks, and Arabs tend to be HC cultures as well.

Obviously, communication is quite different in high- and low-context cultures. First, explicit forms of communication such as verbal codes are more prevalent in low-context cultures such as the United States and northern Europe. People from LC cultures are often perceived as excessively talkative, belaboring of the obvious, and redundant. People from HC cultures may be perceived as nondisclosive, sneaky, and mysterious. Second, HC cultures do not value verbal communication the same way that LC cultures do. Elliot et al. (1982) found that more verbal people were perceived as more attractive by people in the United States, but less verbal people were perceived as more attractive in Korea, an HC culture.

A third implication for communication is that HC cultures are more reliant on and tuned in to nonverbal communication. LC cultures, particularly men in LC cultures, fail to perceive as much nonverbal communication as do members of HC cultures. Nonverbal communication provides the context for all communication (Watzlawick, Beavin, & Jackson, 1967), but people from HC cultures are particularly affected by these contextual cues.

Thus, facial expressions, tensions, movements, speed of interaction, location of the interaction, and other subtle "vibes" are likely to be perceived by and have more meaning for people from high-context cultures. Finally, people in HC cultures expect more than interactants in LC cultures (Hall, 1976). People in HC cultures expect communicators to understand unarticulated feelings, subtle gestures, and environmental clues that people from low-context cultures simply do not process. Worse, both cultural extremes fail to recognize these basic differences in behavior, communication, and context and are quick to misattribute the causes for their behavior.

## Conclusions

Reading about these six cultural dimensions cannot ensure intercultural communication competence. The beauty of international travel and even travel within the United States is that it provides a unique perspective on one's own behavior and the behavior of others. Combining cognitive knowledge from intercultural readings and courses with actual encounters with people from other cultures is the best way to gain intercultural competence.

A full, practical understanding of the dimensions along which cultures differ – along with knowledge of how specific communication acts differ cross-culturally – has several practical benefits. First, such knowledge will highlight and challenge assumptions about our own behavior. The structure of our own behavior is invisible and taken for granted until it is exposed and challenged through study of cultures and actual intercultural encounters. Indeed, Hall (1976) stated that ethnic diversity in interethnic communication can be a source of strength and an asset from which one's self can be discovered.

Second, this discussion should make it clear that attributions about the nonverbal communication of people from other cultures are bound to be wrong. No dictionary or code of intercultural behavior is available. You cannot read people like books, not even people from your own culture. Understanding that someone is from a masculine, collectivistic, or high-context culture, however, will make his or her behavior less confusing and more interpretable.

Finally, understanding about intercultural communication and actually engaging in intercultural encounters is bound to reduce ethnocentrism and make strangers from other cultures seem less threatening. Fear is often based on ignorance and misunderstanding. The fact of intercultural diversity should produce joy and optimism about the number of possible ways to be human.

## References

Andersen, J. F., Andersen, P. A., and Lustig, M. W. (1987). Opposite-sex touch avoidance: A national replication and extension. *Journal of Nonverbal Behavior, II,* 89 – 109.

Andersen, P. A. (1985). "Nonverbal Immediacy in Interpersonal Communication." In A. W. Siegman and S. Feldstein (Eds.), *Multichannel Integrations of Nonverbal Behavior,* 1 – 36. Hillsdale, N.J.: Lawrence Erlbaum.

Andersen, P. A. (1986). Consciousness, cognition, and communication. *Western Journal of Speech Communication, 50,* 87 – 101.

Andersen, P. A. (1987). "The Trait Debate: A Critical Examination of the Individual Differences Paradigm in Intercultural Communication." In B. Dervin and M. J. Voigt (Eds.), *Progress in Communication Sciences,* Vol. VIII, 47 – 82. Norwood, N.J.: Ablex.

Andersen, P. A. (1988). "Explaining Intercultural Differences in Nonverbal Communication." In L. A. Samovar and R. E. Porter (Eds.), *Intercultural Communication: A Reader,* 5th ed. 272 – 281. Belmont, Calif.: Wadsworth.

Andersen, P. A., and Bowman, L. (1990). "Positions of Power: Nonverbal Influence in Organizational Communication." In J. A. DeVito and M. L. Hecht (Eds.), *The Nonverbal Reader,* 391 – 411. Prospect Heights, Ill.: Waveland Press.

Andersen, P. A., and Leibowitz, K. (1978). The development and nature of the construct touch avoidance. *Environmental Psychology and Nonverbal Behavior, 3,* 89 – 106.

Andersen, P. A., Lustig, M. W., and Andersen, J. F. (1986). *Communication Patterns Among Cultural Regions of the United States: A Theoretical Perspective.* Paper presented at the annual convention of the International Communication Association, Chicago.

Andersen, P. A., Lustig, R., and Andersen, J. F. (1990). Changes in latitude, changes in attitude: The relationship between climate and interpersonal communication predispositions. *Communication Quarterly, 38,* 291 – 311.

Argyle, M. (1975). *Bodily Communication*. New York: International Universities Press.

Barnland, D. C. (1978). "Communication Styles in Two Cultures: Japan and the United States." In A. Kendon, R. M. Harris, and M. R. Key (Eds.), *Organization of Behavior in Face to Face Interaction*, 427–456. The Hague: Mouton.

Bellah, R. N., Madsen, R., Sullivan, W. M., Swidler, A., and Tipton, S. (1985). *Habits of the Heart: Individualism and Commitment in American Life*. New York: Harper & Row.

Bem, S. L. (1974). The measurement of psychological androgny. *Journal of Consulting and Clinical Psychology, 42,* 155–162.

Bond, M. H. (1993). Emotions and their expression in Chinese culture. *Journal of Nonverbal Behavior, 17,* 245–262.

Brown. L. R., Kane, H., and Roodman, D. M. (1994). *Vital Signs 1994: The Trends That Are Shaping Our Future*. New York: W. W. Norton.

Bruneau, T. (1979). "The Time Dimension in Intercultural Communication." In D. Nimmo (Ed.), *Communication Yearbook 3,* 423–433. New Brunswick, N.J.: Transaction Books.

Buck, R. (1984). *The Communication of Emotion*. New York: Guilford Press.

Burgoon, J. K. (1985). "Nonverbal Signals." In M. L. Knapp and G. R. Miller (Eds.), *Handbook of Interpersonal Communication*, 344–390. Beverly Hills, Calif.: Sage.

Burgoon, J. K., Buller, D. B., and Woodall, W. G. (1989). *Nonverbal Communication: The Unspoken Dialogue*. New York: Harper & Row.

Chinoy, E. (1967). *Society*. New York: Random House.

Condon, J. C., and Yousef, F. (1983). *An Introduction to Intercultural Communication*. Indianapolis: Bobbs-Merrill.

Elazar, D. J. (1972). *American Federalism: A View from the States*. New York: Thomas P. Crowell.

Elliot, S., Scott, M. D., Jensen, A. D., and McDonough, M. (1982). "Perceptions of Reticence: A Cross-Cultural Investigation." In M. Burgoon (Ed.), *Communication Yearbook 5,* 591–602. New Brunswick, N.J.: Transaction Books.

Geertz, C. (1973). *The Interpretation of Cultures*. New York: Basic Books.

Gudykunst, W. B., and Kim, Y. Y. (1984). *Communicating with Strangers: An Approach to Intercultural Communication*. New York: Random House.

Hall, E. T. (1959). *The Silent Language*. New York: Doubleday.

Hall, E. T. (1966). A system of the notation of proxemic behavior. *American Anthropologist, 65,* 1003–1026.

Hall, E. T. (1976). *Beyond Culture*. Garden City, N.Y.: Anchor.

Hall, E. T. (1984). *The Dance of Life: The Other Dimension of Time*. Garden City, N.Y.: Anchor.

Hecht, M. L., Andersen, P. A., and Ribeau, S. A. (1989). "The Cultural Dimensions of Nonverbal Communication." In M. K. Asante and W. B. Gudykunst (Eds.), *Handbook of International and Intercultural Communication,* 163–185. Newbury Park, Calif.: Sage.

Heslin, R., and Alper, T. (1983). "Touch: A Bonding Gesture." In J. M. Wiemann and R. Harrison (Eds.), *Nonverbal Interaction,* 47–75. Beverly Hills, Calif.: Sage.

Hofstede, G. (1982). *Culture's Consequences,* abridged ed. Beverly Hills, Calif.: Sage.

Jensen, J. V. (1985). "Perspectives on Nonverbal Intercultural Communication." In L. A. Samovar and R. E. Porter (Eds.), *Intercultural Communication: A Reader,* 4th ed. 256–272. Belmont, Calif.: Wadsworth.

Jones, S. E. (1994). *The Right Touch: Understanding and Using the Language of Physical Contact*. Cresshill, N.J.: Hampton Press.

Jones, T. S., and Remland, M. S. (1982). *Cross-Cultural Differences in Self-Reported Touch Avoidance*. Paper presented at the annual convention of the Eastern Communication Association, Hartford, Conn., May.

Knapp, M. L., and Hall, J. A. (1992). *Nonverbal Communication in Human Interaction,* 3d ed. Fort Worth: Harcourt Brace.

LaBarre, W. (1985). "Paralinguistics, Kinesics, and Cultural Anthropology." In L. A. Samovar and R. E. Porter (Eds.), *Intercultural Communication: A Reader,* 272–279. Belmont, Calif.: Wadsworth.

Lomax, A. (1968). *Folk Song Style and Culture*. New Brunswick, N.J.: Transaction Books.

Lustig, M. L., and Koester, J. (1993). *Intercultural Competence: Interpersonal Communication Across Culture*. New York: HarperCollins.

Malandro, L. A., and Barker, L. (1983). *Nonverbal Communication*. Reading, Mass.: Addison-Wesley.

Matsumoto, D. (1991). Cultural influences on facial expressions of emotion. *Southern Communication Journal, 56,* 128–137.

Martin, J. G., and Westie, F. R. (1959). The intolerant personality. *American Sociological Review, 24,* 521–528.

McDaniel, E. R., and Andersen, P. A. (1995). Intercultural Variations in Tactic Communication: An Empirical Field Study. Paper presented at the International Communication Association Convention, Albuquerque, N.M., May.

Mehrabian, A. (1971). *Silent Messages*. Belmont, Calif.: Wadsworth.

Patterson, M. L. (1983). *Nonverbal Behavior: A Functional Perspective*. New York: Springer-Verlag.

Pennebaken, J. W., Rimé, B., and Sproul, G. (1994). Stereotype of Emotional Expressiveness of Northerners and Southerners: A Cross-Cultural Test of Montesquieu's Hypotheses. Unpublished paper, Southern Methodist University.

Prosser, M. H. (1978). *The Cultural Dialogue: An Introduction to Intercultural Communication*. Boston: Houghton Mifflin.

Remland, M. S., Jones, T. S., and Brinkman, H. (1991). Proxemic and haptic behavior in three European countries. *Journal of Nonverbal Behavior, 15,* 215–232.

Rich, A. L. (1974). *Interracial Communication*. New York: Harper & Row.

Samovar, L. A., and Porter, R. E. (1985). "Nonverbal Interaction." In L. A. Samovar and R. E. Porter (Eds.), *Intercultural Communication: A Reader*. Belmont, Calif.: Wadsworth.

Samovar, P. A., Porter, R. E., and Jain, N. C. (1981). *Understanding Intercultural Communication*. Belmont, Calif.: Wadsworth.

Sapir, E. (1928). "The Unconscious Patterning of Behavior in Society." In E. S. Drummer (Ed.), *The Unconscious,* 114–142. New York: Knopf.

Saral, T. (1977). "Intercultural Communication Theory and Research: An Overview." In B. D. Ruben (Ed.), *Communication Yearbook I,* 389–396. New Brunswick, N.J.: Transaction Books.

Scheflen, A. E. (1972). *Body Language and the Social Order*. Englewood Cliffs, N.J.: Prentice-Hall.

Scheflen, A. E. (1974). *How Behavior Means*. Garden City, N.Y.: Anchor.

Seager, J., and Olson, A. (1986). *Women in the World Atlas*. New York: Simon & Schuster.

Sitaram, K. S., and Codgell, R. T. (1976). *Foundations of Intercultural Communication*. Columbus: Charles E. Merrill.

Tomkins, S. S. (1984). "Affect Theory." In K. R. Scherer and P. Ekman (Eds.), *Approaches to Emotion,* 163–195. Hillsdale, N.J.: Lawrence Erlbaum.

Watzlawick, P., Beavin, J. H., and Jackson, D. D. (1967). *Pragmatics of Human Communication*. New York: W. W. Norton.

# Nonverbal Communication: A Reflection of Cultural Themes

## EDWIN R. McDANIEL

Modern technology has made the world a much smaller place. An increasingly mobile population is a direct outgrowth of contemporary technological advances. Growing international economic interdependencies and expanding multinational security alliances have significantly increased the importance of effective intercultural encounters. Individuals from diverse cultures are interacting with each other more and more frequently — in professional, diplomatic, and social venues.

The most critical aspect of this burgeoning international intercourse is, of course, communication. The ability to understand and be understood is central to successful transnational activities. Competent comprehension, however, must go beyond a topical awareness of another culture's communicative practices and behaviors. An appreciation of the cultural antecedents and motivations shaping an individual's communication conventions is necessary for understanding *how* and *why* a particular practice is used.

An established method of explicating the cultural motivations of human behavior is to identify and isolate consistent themes among a social grouping. Anthropological writings have posited that each culture manifests a "limited number of dynamic affirmations" (Opler, 1945, p. 198), referred to as themes. According to Opler (1945), these cul-

This essay appears here for the first time. All rights reserved. Permission to reprint must be obtained from the publisher and the author. Edwin R. McDaniel teaches at Arizona State University.

tural themes promote and regulate human behavioral activities that are societally encouraged and condoned. To illustrate the approach, Opler (1946) examined the social relations of the Lipan Apaches to demonstrate how thematic study could provide insight into cultural beliefs and behaviors.

In communication studies, the concept of thematic commonality has been utilized by Burgoon and Hale (1984, 1987) to help explicate relational communications. They conceptualized a series of "interrelated message themes" (Burgoon & Hale, 1987, p. 19), which have purported application to both verbal and nonverbal exchanges. These proposed themes, or *topi,* have become a supposition cited in subsequent studies of interpersonal relations communication (for example, Buller & Burgoon, 1986; Coker & Burgoon, 1987; Spitzberg, 1989).

Burgoon and Hale's (1984) concept of identifying consistent themes to assist in the explanation of a communication process possesses significant utility for additional, more comprehensive employment. The innovation has clear application to the study of culture-specific communication predisposition.

Using the Japanese as a cultural model, this essay makes practical application of the thematic consistency concept advanced by Opler (1945, 1946) and Burgoon and Hale (1984, 1987). The objective is to illustrate how nonverbal communication practices function as a reflection, or representation, of societal cultural themes. Employing a standard taxonomy of nonverbal communication codes and addressing each individually, cultural themes influencing and manifested by the code are discussed in a propositional format. Additionally, the essay strives to demonstrate how cultural influences can subtly shape a society's communication conventions.

## Japanese Cultural Themes

Japan's predominantly homogeneous indigenous population embodies a particularly rich array of cultural themes. The more prevalent themes include collectivism and group affiliation, hierarchy, social balance or harmony (*wa*), empathy, mutual-dependency, *gaman* (perseverance and sacrifice),

humility, and formality (ritual, tradition, and protocol) (Caudill, 1973; Lebra, 1976; Reischauer, 1988).

Confucian-based collectivism exerts a significant influence on Japanese communication patterns. The nation's racial and cultural homogeneity creates a strong identity bond and facilitates intra-group and interpersonal familiarity. This societal closeness promotes an instinctive, nonverbal understanding between Japanese people. Their cultural similitude abets an intuitive, nonverbal comprehension by diminishing the requirement to orally specify numerous details (Barnlund, 1989; Ishii, 1984; Kinosita, 1988; Kitao & Kitao, 1985; Morsbach, 1988a; Nakane, 1970; Westwood & Vargo, 1985; Yum, 1988).

The Japanese concept of collectivism is epitomized by use of the term *nihonjinron* to express self-perceived uniqueness as both a nation and a people. This idea of distinctive originality provides the Japanese a focus for social cohesiveness. Their propensity for group affiliation has created a social context referred to as *uchi-soto,* or inside-outside. The context can also be viewed as ingroup (possessing membership) and out-group (no involvement). Within the security of their respective in-group (*uchi*), the Japanese can be quite expressive and display considerable nonverbal affiliation with other members. Much less interaction will occur in an out-group (*soto*) situation (Gudykunst & Nishida, 1984; Gudykunst, Nishida, & Schmidt, 1989; Gudykunst, Yoon, & Nishida, 1987; Lebra, 1976, 1993).

The hierarchical nature of Japanese society and an inexorable compulsion for social balance or harmony (*wa*) increase the reliance on nonverbal behaviors and concomitantly discourage verbal exchanges. A hierarchy exists in every instance of group or personal interaction. In this superior-subordinate environment, the junior is socially compelled to assume a passive role, awaiting and hopefully anticipating the senior's desires or actions. The senior, desiring to exemplify humility and avoid any social or personal discord, will endeavor to nonverbally ascertain the junior's expectations.

The cultural pressure for social balance dictates the course of all Japanese activities and creates a pervasive acceptance of ambiguity and vagueness during any communication endeavor. Reluctant to advance personal opinions or attitudes, a Japanese will draw on the situational context and attempt to instinctively discern what the other person is thinking (Hall & Hall, 1990; Ishii, 1984; Ishii & Bruneau, 1991; Kitao & Kitao, 1985; Lebra, 1976; Morsbach, 1988a; Munakata, 1986; Reischauer, 1988).

The cultural trait of empathy (*omoiyari*) also lessens the Japanese reliance on verbal exchanges. In Japan, considerable value is placed on an individual's ability to empathetically determine the needs of another person. During interpersonal encounters, the Japanese will frequently use indirect or vague statements and depend on the other person's sensitivity to ascertain the desired meaning of the interaction (Doi, 1988; Ishii, 1984; Lebra, 1976).

## Propositional Survey

Considered in isolation, a nonverbal code normally provides only partial interpretation of the intended message. This study, however, is not concerned with the code's proposed message, but instead attempts to demonstrate how the code is culturally based and motivated. To this end, in each of the following propositions, specific nonverbal communication codes are shown to reflect one or more cultural themes common to Japanese society.

H1: Japanese kinesics reflect the cultural themes of (1) group orientation, (2) hierarchy, (3) social balance, (4) formality, and (5) humility.

The Japanese enjoy a wide array of kinesic activities, especially gestures (Caudill & Weinstein, 1969; March, 1990; Seward, 1983; Sherman, 1989). Usage, however, is situational and often limited to males (Richie, 1987). A Japanese manager, for instance, might rely on gestures to communicate with subordinates (Sethi, 1974), thereby demonstrating the cohesive familiarity common among in-group (uchi) members.

The Japanese are more relaxed and expressive within their in-group. Away from the in-group, however, the use of body language is usually remarkably restrained (Cohen, 1991; Ishii, 1975). In public, it is quite common to see both Japanese men and women sitting quietly and unobtrusively, with hands folded (March, 1990). This self-restraint of body movement in out-group (soto) environments is designed to avoid attention and maintain situational harmony or balance.

As another example of concern for social balance, Japanese hand gestures are never used in reference to a person who is present at the time. Instead, they are employed to refer to some absent party (Richie, 1987). This, quite naturally, reduces the opportunity for offending anyone present and helps sustain contextual harmony.

The most common activity associated with Japanese kinesics is the bow, an integral and repetitive part of daily social interaction. A Japanese will bow when meeting someone, when asking for something, while apologizing, when offering congratulations, when acknowledging someone else, and when departing, to mention just a few occurrences. Historically a sign of submission, the bow is a contemporary ritual that continues to convey respect and denote hierarchical status. The junior person bows first, lowest, and longest. An improperly executed bow can be a significant insult (Hendry, 1989; Ishii, 1975; Kitao & Kitao, 1987, 1989; Morsbach, 1988b; Ramsey, 1979; Richie, 1987; Ruch, 1984; Sherman, 1989).

Traditional Japanese women exhibit a very distinct kinesic activity by obscuring facial areas with their hands or some object (Ishii, 1975; Ramsey, 1981). Ramsey's (1981) investigation of this phenomenon concluded that women utilized these adaptors for impression management. A very explicit intent of these actions is to evoke a perception of humility when in the presence of a social superior.

H2: Japanese oculesics reflect the cultural themes of (1) hierarchy, (2) social balance, and (3) humility.

In Japan, prolonged eye contact is considered rude, threatening, and disrespectful. The Japanese are taught, from childhood, to avert their gaze or look at a person's throat. When one is part of an audience, looking away or simply sitting silently with eyes closed indicates attention to, and possibly agreement with, the speaker. Direct, sustained eye contact is normally avoided, unless a superior wants to admonish a subordinate (Hall & Hall, 1990; Ishii, 1975; Kasahara, 1986; Kitao & Kitao, 1987, 1989; March, 1990; Morsbach, 1973; Richie, 1987; Ruch, 1984; Watson, 1970).

By avoiding eye contact, the participants in communication simultaneously evince an air of humility and sustain situational wa. The employment of direct eye contact by a superior is a clear exercise of hierarchical prerogative (March, 1990).

H3: Japanese facial expressions reflect the cultural themes of (1) social balance and (2) gaman.

As is common to all aspects of their social behavior, the Japanese do not evince any significant emotion through public facial displays. The most commonly observed expressions are either a placid, unrevealing countenance or a nondescript smile, whose actual meaning, or intent, may be totally indecipherable. A smile can indicate happiness or serve as a friendly acknowledgement. Alternatively, it may be worn to mask negative emotions, especially displeasure, anger, or grief (Gudykunst & Nishida, 1993; Kitao & Kitao, 1987, 1989; Morsbach, 1973; Sherman, 1989).

For the Japanese, the smile is simply a part of social etiquette, designed to help sustain harmony. In a social environment, a Japanese would consider it unpardonable to burden someone else with an outward show of irritation or anguish. Eschewing any external display of negative emotion is an example of perseverance or self-sacrifice (gaman) to avoid disrupting the social balance (wa). The smile is also used to avoid conflict; a Japanese might simply smile in order to avoid answering an awkward question (Ishii, 1975; Kitao & Kitao, 1987, 1989; Nakane, 1970; Ruch, 1984; Seward, 1972).

H4: Japanese proxemic behaviors reflect the cultural themes of (1) in-group affinity, (2) hierarchy, and (3) balance.

The Japanese attitude toward personal space is, on the surface, quite complex and seemingly contradictory. In uncrowded situations, they assidu-

ously strive to maintain personal space intervals that are even greater than those maintained by Americans. Conversely, when on a train or bus, they offer no resistance to frequent or even prolonged body contact from total strangers. Personal space is also very close among friends or family members (Hall, 1990; Richie, 1987).

This apparent dichotomy is the result of their societal group orientation, vertical structure, and constant concern for social balance. In an uncrowded out-group environment, the Japanese maintain their personal space, which also provides a psychological barrier against the unknown, such as the hierarchical status and group affiliation of others (Ishii, 1975; Morsbach, 1973; Watson, 1970). If forced into close proximity with an out-group, the Japanese will assume a façade of unperturbable passivity in an effort to maintain situational harmony. I have often observed the Japanese projecting an air of composed detachment while being subjected to near suffocation in the crowd aboard a Tokyo subway car.

Among in-group members, where strong social ties exist, personal space is dramatically reduced. Family members commonly sleep in the same room, within easy touching distance (Caudill & Plath, 1966). Male white-collar coworkers (salarimen) sitting close and patting each other on the back during after-work drinking excursions are a common sight in Japanese bars.

Japanese proxemic behavior has been the subject of several investigations. In a study involving status manipulation, Japanese subjects exhibited signs of anxiety in reaction to an interviewer's forward lean (Bond & Shiraishi, 1974). Iwata's (1979) study of Japanese female students disclosed that individuals with high self-esteem evinced a negative reaction to crowding. This is consistent with the Japanese concept of hierarchy. Self-esteem would be proportional with social status, which would predicate greater interpersonal distance in out-group situations.

H5: Japanese tactile conventions reflect the cultural themes of (1) in-group affinity and (2) social balance.

Studies of Japanese maternal care have disclosed that children experience considerable touch from their mothers (Caudill & Plath, 1966; Caudill & Weinstein, 1969). The amount of public tactile interaction drops dramatically, however, after childhood, and the individual is expected to conform to societal non-touch standards (Barnlund, 1975; Montague, 1978). Indeed, adult Japanese actively avoid public displays of interpersonal physical expressiveness (Barnlund, 1989; Malandro & Barker, 1983) unless in a close-knit in-group setting.

For adults, in-group (uchi) touching is quite acceptable (Lebra, 1976). This is especially evident when male coworkers are drinking (Miyamoto, 1994). In an out-group (soto) situation, touch is highly uncommon unless it results inadvertently from crowding, and then it is simply ignored (Ishii, 1975; Morsbach, 1973; Ramsey, 1985). These conventions are again indicative of the value placed on group affiliation and harmony.

H6: Japanese personal appearance reflects the cultural themes of (1) collectivism, (2) group affiliation, (3) social balance, and (4) hierarchy.

The central theme of Japanese external appearance is, quite simply, group identity and status. The ubiquitous dark suit dominates the business world, and everyone, both men and women, opt for conservative styles. Small lapel pins or badges identifying the individual's company are frequently worn. Blue-collar workers normally wear a uniform (such as coveralls or smocks) distinctive to their corporation (Condon & Yousef, 1983; Hall, 1981; Harris & Moran, 1979; March, 1990; Morsbach, 1973; Ruch, 1984).

The proclivity for conservative dress styles and colors emphasizes the nation's collectivism and, concomitantly, lessens the potential for social disharmony arising from nonconformist attire. Lapel pins and uniforms signal a particular group affiliation, which in turn facilitates easy determination of social position.

While not specifically nonverbal, the Japanese business card, or meshi, must be discussed. It exerts considerable influence on Japanese nonverbal behavior and communication in general. The initial impression of an individual is derived from his or her meshi. The card must be of the appropriate size and color and list the person's company and position. This facilitates rapid determination of the individual's group affiliation and personal station, which dictates the correct deportment and appropriate speech levels for participants engaging in interpersonal dialogue (Craft, 1986; Morsbach, 1973; Ruch, 1984; Sherman, 1989).

H7: Japanese use of space reflects the cultural themes of (1) hierarchy and (2) group orientation.

The Japanese hierarchical contextualization of space is best exemplified by the standard spatial array of their business and corporate offices. Numerous desks, occupied by lower-level employees, are lined hierarchically in the center of a large, common room, without walls or partitions. The supervisors and managers are positioned nearest the windows. This organization encourages the exchange of information, facilitates multi-task accomplishment, promotes group cooperation and solidarity, and facilitates rapid discernment of the work-center rank structure. Seating arrangements at any formal or semiformal function are also based on hierarchy (Hamabata, 1990; Ramsey, 1979; Ramsey & Birk, 1983; Ruch, 1984; Takamizawa, 1988).

In explaining the Japanese perception of space as a hierarchical concept, Hall (1990) offers an insightful illustration. Neighborhood houses in Japan are numbered in the order they are constructed, regardless of actual location along the street.

H8: Japanese use of time reflects the cultural themes of (1) hierarchy, (2) group orientation, and (3) social balance.

Hall and Hall (1990) have indicated that the Japanese use time polychronically among themselves and monochronically when conducting business with foreigners. The rigid adherence to schedules when dealing with foreigners is in contrast with the temporal flexibility exhibited during interactions with other Japanese. This demonstrates an ability to adjustment to dynamic situations. For example, schedules may have to be altered in order to accommodate the desires of a senior, which reflects hierarchical sensitivities.

The Japanese decision-making process characterizes the influence of group orientation and social balance on the usage of time. In almost every interpersonal context, it is necessary to build a consensus before announcing a decision. This process, concerned with maintaining social balance among group members, can take days, weeks, or even months (Hall, 1988; Nakane, 1970; Stewart, 1993).

H9: Japanese vocalics reflect the cultural themes of (1) hierarchy, (2) balance, and (3) empathy.

The Japanese make ample use of paralanguage in their conversations. During interpersonal discussions, the Japanese will constantly nod and make small utterances (such as *hai, soo, un,* or *ee*) to demonstrate their attentiveness (Harris & Moran, 1979; Sherman, 1989). These vocalics possess a cultural motivation. Hierarchy is demonstrated by the adjustment of voice tone and pitch to fit the speaker's position of junior or senior (Morsbach, 1973).

For the Japanese, laughter can possess a variety of meanings. Laughter can signal joy, of course, but it is also used to disguise embarrassment, sadness, or even anger (Seward, 1972). Use of laughter in the latter modes is designed to maintain situational harmony and avoid any potential for interpersonal discord.

In a 1989 study, White analyzed tape-recorded English-language conversations of Americans and native Japanese. The Japanese participants employed significantly more feedback responses that the Americans. Unable to ascertain a linguistic reason for this greater use of vocalics, White concluded it was a cultural influence. The listener was believed to be exhibiting a sensitivity to the speaker's viewpoint and feelings (in other words, was expressing empathy).

H10: Japanese use of silence reflects the cultural themes of (1) hierarchy, (2) social balance, and (3) empathy.

The salient role of silence in the Japanese communication process is attributed to a general mistrust of spoken words and an emphasis on emotionally dis-

cerning the other person's intentions (empathy). Silence is considered a virtue as well as a sign of respectability and trustworthiness (Buruma, 1985; Cohen, 1991; Hall & Hall, 1990; Ishii, 1975, 1984; Lebra, 1976, 1993; Morsbach, 1988a).

A pronounced feature of Japanese conversations is the many short pauses or breaks, referred to as *ma*. According to Matsumoto (1988), the Japanese closely attend to these brief conversational breaks. The pauses can convey meaning, demonstrate respect, or be an attempt to assess the other person or the situation (Di Mare, 1990; Doi, 1973, 1988; Hall, 1988).

Instances of ma in a Japanese discourse can impart a variety of messages, with the context supplying the actual meaning. Silence is employed to tactfully signal disagreement, nonacceptance, or an uncomfortable dilemma. A period of silence can be used to consider an appropriate response or formulate an opinion. Also, a junior may remain silent in deference to a senior (Graham & Herberger, 1983; Morsbach, 1973; Ramsey & Birk, 1983; Ueda, 1974).

H11: The Japanese use of olfactics reflects the cultural theme of social balance.

Little information is available concerning the Japanese attitude toward odors. Kasahara (1986) asserted that the Japanese propensity for cleanliness creates a preference for an environment totally absent of odors. Although there is no supporting evidence, the near ritualistic tradition of frequent baths and the desire to refrain from personal offense lends credence to this contention.

## Conclusions

The preceding propositions suggest that the use of, and reliance on, nonverbal communication is actually a part of Japanese behavioral psychology motivated by cultural imperatives. If this supposition is accepted, the benefits of employing cultural motivations to investigate a society's nonverbal communication habits, or other communication patterns, become self-evident. Application of cultural themes to communicative dispositions would provide a salient methodology for examining, and better understanding, both cultural-specific and intercultural communication phenomena.

Potential benefits derived from practical application of this approach are especially promising. Greater appreciation of the cultural imperatives behind communicative behaviors would directly enhance intercultural communication competence. An individual engaged in an intercultural communication exchange could better understand both *what* the other person was doing and *why* she or he was doing it.

The suggested design is not, however, free of limitations. Several perceived impediments exist that require additional investigation and clarification before implementation of wider theoretical application.

A particularly important aspect that demands greater inquiry relates to the identification of cultural themes. As earlier discussed, Japan presents an unusually homogeneous culture. This societal similitude facilitates discernment of both cultural themes and their motivations. Moreover, the cultural themes can then be reliably applied across almost all dimensions of Japanese society.

Other societies, such as the United States, do not enjoy the degree of cultural congruency extant in Japan. For these cases, identification and application of consistent cultural themes to the composite ethnicities is fraught with considerable difficulty and potential peril. Any motivation to stereotype themes across an entire heterogeneous populace must be tempered by a resolve to treat ethnic divisions as both separate entities and as integral parts of the greater societal whole.

Another dilemma requiring meditation concerns units of measurement. The nonverbal communication patterns of a culture are, for the most part, observable and measurable. Culture, as an entity itself and as a motivator of communication behaviors, is not, however, readily quantifiable. The majority of studies dealing with cultural influences have relied on recitations of personal experience and observations (anecdotal documentation).

Many studies incorporate "culture" as a somewhat ethereal, abstract manifestation of humankind's imagination. Others have approached "culture" empirically and attempted to employ scientific measurements. Hofstede, for instance, used survey questionnaires and statistical analysis in an effort to determine the role of culture in the formation of value systems that affect "human thinking, organizations, and institutions in predictable ways" (1980, p. 11). Similarly, Osgood, May, and Miron have made noteworthy progress in statistically quantifying intangible attributes, what they term "subjective culture" (1975, p. 4).

The progress of Hofstede (1980) and Osgood, May, and Miron (1975) suggest that culture is not entirely beyond the scope of objective quantification. Their achievements provide benchmarks for empirical examination of the influence of cultural themes on communication behaviors.

Thematic universality is also an area of potential peril for theoretical application of cultural themes to communicative practices. Specifically, the investigator must not axiomatically assume that similar themes beget similar behaviors when moving between cultures. A theme prompting a specific behavioral action in one culture may generate an entirely different pattern in another cultural environment. To obviate this possible pitfall, each culture must be examined as a unique entity. The identification of common cultural themes and communication practices across a substantial number of societies is needed before theoretical application can be made on unexamined cultures.

Further investigation is also needed to determine if any of the cultural themes are codependent. For example, if hierarchy is manifested by a culture, will formality or another theme also be present?

The preceding constraints should not be interpreted as a repudiation of the proposed approach to explaining communicative practices. Rather, they are simply areas of concern that must be investigated and clarified before cultural themes can be reliably employed to help discern and understand societal communication predispositions. Resolution of these concerns will only serve to instill the concept with increased application, additional rigor, and greater parsimony.

## Appendix: Propositions

H1: Japanese kinesics reflect the cultural themes of (1) group orientation, (2) hierarchy, (3) social balance, (4) formality, and (5) humility.

H2: Japanese oculesics reflect the cultural themes of (1) hierarchy, (2) social balance, and (3) humility.

H3: Japanese facial expressions reflect the cultural themes of (1) social balance and (2) *gaman*.

H4: Japanese proxemic behaviors reflect the cultural themes of (1) in-group affinity, (2) hierarchy, and balance.

H5: Japanese tactile conventions reflect the cultural themes of (1) in-group affinity and (2) social balance.

H6: Japanese personal appearance reflects the cultural themes of (1) collectivism, (2) group affiliation, (3) social balance, and (4) hierarchy.

H7: Japanese use of space reflects the cultural themes of (1) hierarchy, and (2) group orientation.

H8: Japanese use of time reflects the cultural themes of (1) hierarchy, (2) group orientation, and (3) social balance.

H9: Japanese vocalics reflect the cultural themes of (1) hierarchy, (2) balance, and (3) empathy.

H10: Japanese use of silence reflects the cultural themes of (1) hierarchy, (2) social balance, and (3) empathy.

H11: The Japanese use of olfactics reflects the cultural theme of social balance.

## References

Barnlund, D. (1975). *Public and Private Self in Japan and United States*. Tokyo: Simul.

Barnlund, D. (1989). *Communicative Styles of Japanese and Americans*. Belmont, Calif.: Wadsworth.

Bond, M. H., and Komai, H. (1976). Targets of gazing and eye contact during interviews: Effects on Japanese nonverbal behavior. *Journal of Personality and Social Psychology, 34*(6), 1276–1284.

Bond, M. H., and Shiraishi, D. (1974). The effect of body lean and status of an interviewer on the nonverbal behavior of Japanese interviewees. *International Journal of Psychology, 9*, 117–128.

Buller, D. B., and Burgoon, J. K. (1986). The effects of vocalics and nonverbal sensitivity on compliance. *Human Communication Research, 13*(1), 126–144.

Burgoon, J. K., and Hale, J. L. (1984). The fundamental topic of relational communication. *Communication Monographs, 51*, 193–214.

Burgoon, J. K., and Hale, J. L. (1987). Validation and measurement of the fundamental themes of relational communication. *Communication Monographs, 54*, 19–62.

Buruma, I. (1985). *A Japanese Mirror*. New York: Penguin.

Caudill, W. (1973). General culture: The influence of social structure and culture on human behavior in modern Japan. *The Journal of Nervous and Mental Disease, 157*, 240–257.

Caudill, W., and Plath, D. (1966). Who sleeps with whom? Parent-child involvement in urban Japanese families. *Psychiatry, 29*, 344–366.

Caudill, W., and Weinstein, H. (1969). Maternal care and infant behavior in Japan and America. *Psychiatry, 32*, 12–43.

Cohen, R. (1991). *Negotiating Across Cultures*. Washington, D.C.: United States Institute of Peace.

Coker, D. A., and Burgoon, J. K. (1987). The nature of conversational involvement and nonverbal encoding patterns. *Human Communication Research, 13*(4), 463–494.

Condon, J. C., and Yousef, F. (1983). *An Introduction to Intercultural Communication*. Indianapolis: Bobbs-Merrill.

Craft, L. (1986). All in the cards: The mighty *meishi*. *Tokyo Business Today*, May, 61–64.

Di Mare, L. (1990). Ma and Japan. *Southern Communication Journal, 55*(3), 319–328.

Doi, T. (1973). The Japanese patterns of communication and the concept of *amae*. *The Quarterly Journal of Speech, 59*, 180–185.

Doi, T. (1988). "Dependency in Human Relationships." In D. I. Okimoto and T. P. Rohlen (Eds.), *Inside the Japanese System: Readings on Contemporary Society and Political Economy*, 20–25. Stanford: Stanford University Press.

Graham, J. L., and Herberger, R. A. (1983). Negotiations abroad: Don't shoot from the hip. *Harvard Business Review, 83*(4), 160–168.

Gudykunst, W. B., and Nishida, T. (1984). Individual and cultural influences on uncertainty reduction. *Communication Monographs, 51*, 23–36.

Gudykunst, W. B., and Nishida, T. (1993). "Interpersonal and Intergroup Communication in Japan and the United States." In W. B. Gudykunst (Ed.), *Communication in Japan and the United States*, 149–214. Albany: State University of New York Press.

Gudykunst, W. B., Nishida, T., and Schmidt, K. (1989). The influence of culture, relational, and personality factors on uncertainty reduction processes. *Western Journal of Speech Communication, 53,* 13 - 29.

Gudykunst, W. B., Yoon, Y. C., and Nishida, T. (1987). The influence of individualism-collectivism on perceptions of communication in ingroup and out-group relationships. *Communication Monographs, 54,* 295 - 306.

Hall, E. T. (1981). *Beyond Culture.* New York: Anchor. (Original work published 1976)

Hall, E. T. (1988). "The Hidden Dimensions of Time and Space in Today's World." In F. Poyatos (Ed.), *Cross-cultural Perspectives in Nonverbal Communication,* 145 - 152. Lewiston, N.Y.: C. J. Hogrefe.

Hall, E. T. (1990). *The Hidden Dimension.* New York: Anchor. (Original work published 1966)

Hall, E. T., and Hall, M. R. (1990). *Hidden Differences: Doing Business with the Japanese.* New York: Anchor. (Original work published 1987)

Hamabata, M. M. (1990). *Crested Kimono: Power and Love in the Japanese Business Family.* Ithaca, N.Y.: Cornell University Press.

Harris, P. R., and Moran, R. T. (1979). *Managing Cultural Differences.* Houston: Gulf.

Hendry, J. (1989). *Becoming Japanese: The World of the Pre-school Child.* Honolulu: University Press of Hawaii. (Originally published in 1986)

Hofstede, G. (1980). *Culture's Consequence: International Differences in Work-Related Values.* Newbury Park, Calif.: Sage.

Ishii, S. (1975). Characteristics of Japanese nonverbal communicative behavior. *Occasional Papers in Speech.* Honolulu: Department of Speech, University of Hawaii.

Ishii, S. (1984). *Enyro-Sasshi* communication: A key to understanding Japanese interpersonal relations. *Cross Currents, 11,* 49 - 58.

Ishii, S., and Bruneau, T. (1991). "Silence and Silences in Cross-cultural Perspective: Japan and the United States." In L. A. Samovar and R. E. Porter (Eds.), *Intercultural Communication: A Reader,* 6th ed., 314 - 319. Belmont, Calif.: Wadsworth.

Iwata, O. (1979). Selected personality traits as determinants of the perception of crowding. *Japanese Psychological Research, 21,* 1 - 9.

Kasahara, Y. (1986). "Fear of Eye-to-Eye Confrontation Among Neurotic Patients in Japan." In T. S. Lebra and W. P. Lebra (Eds.), *Japanese Culture and Behavior: Selected Readings,* Rev. ed., 379 - 387. Honolulu: University of Hawaii Press.

Kinosita, K. (1988). Language habits of the Japanese. *Bulletin of the Association for Business Communication, 51*(3), 35 - 40.

Kitao, K., and Kitao, S. K. (1985). *Effects of Social Environment on Japanese and American Communication.* (ERIC Document Reproduction Service No. ED 260 579)

Kitao, K., and Kitao, S. K. (1987). *Differences in the Kinesic Codes of Americans and Japanese.* Department of Communication, Michigan State University. (ERIC Document Reproduction Service No. ED 282 400)

Kitao, K., and Kitao, S. K. (1989). *Intercultural Communication Between Japan and the United States.* Tokyo: Eichosha Shinsha Co. (ERIC Document Reproduction Service No. ED 321 303)

Lebra, T. S. (1976). *Japanese Patterns of Behavior.* Honolulu: University Press of Hawaii.

Lebra, T. S. (1993). "Culture, Self, and Communication in Japan and the United States." In W. B. Gudykunst (Ed.), *Communication in Japan and the United States,* 51 - 87. Albany: State University of New York Press.

Malandro, L. A., and Barker, L. L. (1983). *Nonverbal Communication.* Menlo Park, Calif.: Addison-Wesley.

March, R. M. (1990). *The Japanese Negotiator: Subtlety and Strategy Beyond Western Logic.* New York: Kondansha. (Original work published 1989)

Matsumoto, M. (1988). *The Unspoken Way: "Haragei": Silence in Japanese Business and Society.* New York: Kondansha. (Original work published 1984 in Japanese under the title *Haragei*)

Miyamoto, M. (1994). *Straitjacket Society: An Insider's Irreverent View of Bureaucratic Japan.* New York: Kodansha.

Montagu, A. (1978). *Touching: The Human Significance of the Skin,* 2nd ed. New York: Harper & Row.

Morsbach, H. (1973). Aspects of nonverbal communication in Japan. *Journal of Nervous and Mental Disease, 157,* 262 - 277.

Morsbach, H. (1988a). "The Importance of Silence and Stillness in Japanese Nonverbal Communication: A Cross-cultural Approach." In F. Poyatos (Ed.), *Cross-cultural Perspectives in Nonverbal Communication,* 201 - 215. Lewiston, N.Y.: C. J. Hogrefe.

Morsbach, H. (1988b). "Nonverbal Communication and Hierarchical Relationships: The Case of Bowing in Japan." In F. Poyatos (Ed.), *Cross-cultural Perspectives in Nonverbal Communication,* 189 - 199. Lewiston, N.Y.: C. J. Hogrefe.

Munakata, T. (1986). "Japanese Attitudes Toward Mental Illness and Mental Health Care." In T. S. Lebra and W. P. Lebra (Eds.), *Japanese Culture and Behavior: Selected Readings,* Rev. ed., 369 - 378. Honolulu: University Press of Hawaii.

Nakane, C. (1970). *Japanese Society.* Berkeley: University of California Press.

Opler, M. E. (1945). Themes as dynamic forces in culture. *American Journal of Sociology, 51,* 198 – 206.

Opler, M. E. (1946). An application of the theory of themes in culture. *Joural of the Washington Academy of Sciences, 36*(5), 137 – 166.

Osgood, C. E., May, W. H., and Miron, M. S. (1975). *Cross-cultural Universals of Affective Meaning.* Urbana: University of Illinois Press.

Ramsey, S. J. (1979). "Nonverbal Behavior: An Intercultural Perspective." In M. K. Asante, E. Newmark, and C. A. Blake (Eds.), *Handbook of Intercultural Communication,* 105 – 143. Beverly Hills: Sage.

Ramsey, S. (1981). The kinesics of femininity in Japanese women. *Language Sciences, 3*(1), 104 – 123.

Ramsey, S. (1985). "To Hear One and Understand Ten: Nonverbal Behavior in Japan." In L. A. Samovar and R. E. Porter (Eds.), *Intercultural Communication: A Reader* (4th ed.), 307 – 321. Belmont, Calif.: Wadsworth.

Ramsey, S. J., and Birk, J. (1983). "Training North Americans for Interaction with Japanese: Considerations of Language and Communication Style." In D. Landis and R. W. Brislin (Eds.), *The Handbook of Intercultural Training: Vol. III. Area Studies in Intercultural Training,* 227 – 259. New York: Pergamon Press.

Reischauer, E. O. (1988). *The Japanese Today: Change and Continuity.* Cambridge, Mass.: Belknap Press.

Richie, D. (1987). *A Lateral View: Essays on Contemporary Japan.* Tokyo: The Japan Times.

Ruch, W. (1984). *Corporate Communication: A Comparison of Japanese and American practices.* Westport, Conn.: Quorum Books.

Sethi, S. P. (1974). Japanese management practices: Part I. *Columbia Journal of World Business, 9*(4), 94 – 104.

Seward, J. (1972). *The Japanese.* New York: William Morrow.

Seward, J. (1983). *Japanese in Action* (rev. ed.). New York: Weatherhill.

Sherman, J. (1989). *Japan: Body Language and Etiquette as a Means of Intercultural Communication.* Paper presented at the 8th Annual Eastern Michigan University Conference on Languages and Communications for World Business and the Professions, Ann Arbor, Michigan. (ERIC Document Reproduction Service No. ED 324 837)

Spitzberg, B. H. (1989). Issues in the development of a theory of interpersonal competence in the intercultural context. *International Journal of Intercultural Relations, 13,* 241 – 268.

Stewart, L. P. (1993). "Organizational Communication in Japan and the United States." In W. B. Gudykunst (Ed.), *Communication in Japan and the United States,* 215 – 248. Albany: State University of New York Press.

Sussman, N., and Rosenfeld, H. (1982). Influences of culture, language and sex on conversational distance. *Journal of Personality and Social Psychology, 42,* 67 – 74.

Takamizawa, H. (1988). *Business Japanese: A Guide to Improved Communication.* New York: Kondansha.

Ueda, T. (1974). "Sixteen Ways to Avoid Saying "No" in Japan." In J. C. Condon and M. Saito (Eds.), *Intercultural Encounters with Japan,* 185 – 192. Tokyo: Simul.

Watson, M. O. (1970). *Proxemic Behavior: A Cross-cultural Study.* The Hague: Mouton.

Westwood, M. J., and Vargo, J. W. (1985. "Counselling Double-Minority Status Clients." In R. J. Samuda (Ed.), *Intercultural Counselling and Assessment: Global Perspectives,* 303 – 313. Lewiston, NY: C. J. Hogrefe.

White, S. (1989). Backchannels across cultures: A study of Americans and Japanese. *Language in Society, 18*(1), 59 – 76.

Yum, Y. (1988). The impact of Confucianism on interpersonal relationship and communication patterns in East Asia. *Communication Monographs, 55,* 374 – 388.

# Variables in the Use of Personal Space in Intercultural Transactions

## CAROL ZINNER DOLPHIN

### I. Background

The concept of personal space has been the subject of numerous analogies. David Katz compared it to the shell of a snail. Stern developed the concept of a personal world. Von Uexkull used the graphic analogy of people "surrounded by soap bubble worlds" (Sommer, 1959). Hayduk (1983), on the other hand, suggests that the bubble is not a good analogy since it does not characterize the gradual acceptance of space intrusion under varying circumstances and prefers Sundstrom's (1976) alternate analogy, which compares personal space to an electrical field which is three dimensional, possesses force which decreases with distance, and has positive/negative signs to account for attraction and repulsion of certain bodies.

Forston (1968) defined *proxemics* as "the study of how man communicates through structuring microspace — the distance that man consciously maintains between himself and another person while relating physically to others with whom he is interacting" (p. 109). *Personal space* may be viewed as "the way in which individuals expect the immediate space around them to be used," translating the "more general interpersonal goals into spatial and behavioral terms..." (Liebman, 1970, p. 211). Personal space differs from *territory,* "an area controlled by an individual, family or other face-to-face collectivity," principally by virtue of its mobility (Sommer, 1966, p. 59). Whereas territory tends to remain stable with somewhat definable boundaries, personal space is carried with the individual. "Personal space has the body as its center; territory does not" (Sommer, 1959, p. 247). Hall (1966) adds another dimension to the concept of proxemics by terming it "the interrelated observations and theories of man's use of space as a specialized elaboration of culture" (p. 1).

Edward Hall (1966) maintains that "it is in the nature of animals including man to exhibit behavior which we call territoriality. In doing so, they use the senses to distinguish between one space or distance and another" (p. 128). The anthropologist's formal observations of interpersonal transactions led him to propose a system of classifying the use of personal space. Subjects in Hall's United States sample (middle class adults, mainly natives of the northeastern seaboard) exhibited four distance zones, marked particularly by shifts in vocal volume. The intimate zone (contact to eighteen inches) usually is reserved for spouses, lovers and close friends, people engaged in lovemaking, comforting, nursing and conversations of a private nature. The personal zone (eighteen inches to four feet) includes activities such as chatting, gossiping, playing cards and casual interactions and is the territory of friends and acquaintances. Those whom one does not know well are often kept in the social zone (four to twelve feet), the domain of interviews, business transactions and professional exchanges. The public zone (beyond twelve feet) makes interpersonal communication nearly impossible and often denotes a status difference between the speaker and listener. "Spatial changes," writes Hall (1959, p. 204), "give a tone to a communication, accent it, and at times can even override the spoken word. The flow and shift of distance between people as they interact with each other is part and parcel of the communication process."

Emphasizing the impact of culture on communication behaviors, Hall specifies that the above distances are relevant only for those who fit into his sample category and notes that, in the United States and Northern Europe, individuals are guided in their use of space according to their concept of a partner as a stranger or as a familiar. Other cultures demonstrate other patterns such as the family/

From *The Howard Journal of Communications*, Volume 1 (Spring 1988), 23–38. Reprinted by permission of the publisher. Professor Dolphin teaches at the University of Wisconsin Center, Waukesha County.

nonfamily distinction in Portugal and Spain or the caste/outcaste system of India (Hall, 1966, p. 128).

It is in this vein that Hall (1963), based upon Heidiger's division of animals into contact and noncontact species, expands his theories in the use of personal space to identify differences between contact and noncontact cultures. It is hypothesized that people from contact cultures, i.e. Arabs, Southern Europeans and Latin Americans, will use closer distances, maintain more direct axes and eye contact, touch each other more frequently, and speak more loudly than those from noncontact cultures, i.e. Northern Europeans, Asians, Americans and Indians.

According to Hall, then, culture inevitably plays *the* definitive role in determining how different individuals use personal space. People from different cultures are seen as not only speaking different languages, but inhabiting different sensory worlds. "Selective screening of sensory data admits some things while filtering out others, so that experience as it is perceived through one set of culturally patterned sensory screens is quite different from experience perceived through another" (Hall, 1966, p. 2). Moreover, cultural conditioning is seen as difficult if not impossible to overcome. "Cultural irrationality," writes Hall in *Beyond Culture* (1976, p. 192), "is deeply entrenched in the lives of us, and because of culturally imposed blinders, our view of the world does not normally transcend the limits imposed by culture. We are, in effect, stuck with the program culture imposes." Giving support to Hall's earlier theories were experiments by Baltus (1974) which led him to characterize proxemic behavior as "culturally conditioned and entirely arbitrary . . . binding on all concerned" (p. 7).

Early support for Hall's hypotheses was provided in experiments conducted by Watson and Graves in 1966 and by Watson in 1970. The 1966 study, which observed proxemic distances in dyads of male Arab students (from a contact culture) and male American students (from a noncontact culture), concluded that Arab subjects sat close to one another, faced each other more directly, maintained higher degrees of eye contact, touched each other more frequently, and were generally more involved with one another during interaction than the American students. Watson expanded his work in his 1970 study which included a greater number of students from a wider range of locations. Added to the original sample of only sixteen individuals were an additional one hundred and ten male students, all of whom were involved in pairs speaking their own native languages and were observed through a one-way glass. Contact cultures were represented primarily by subjects from Saudi Arabia, Latin America and Southern Europe, while those from Northern Europe, East Asia and India/Pakistan represented natives of noncontact cultures. Again, Hall's hypotheses were generally supported with there being no overlap in mean scores between contact and noncontact groups in the areas of directness of axis, frequency of touch, and maintenance of direct eye contact. A slight variance was noted in the use of proxemic distances where Indians/Pakistanis maintained a closer mean distance than all other groups except Arabs.

Other researchers, however, have not been as supportive of Hall's theories. Forston (1968) observed eight dyads of male Latin American students and eight dyads of male North American (United States) students, all of whom had been asked to work together to solve a problem. Contrary to Forston's expectations, the North Americans (noncontact culture) sat closer to one another than the Latin Americans (contact culture); no touch interaction occurred whatsoever except that of a single handshake between two North Americans. Similarly, studies conducted by Shuter (1977), Mazur (1977), and Sanders (1985), all cited later in this paper, produced results which raise serious questions about Hall's contact/noncontact theory and his view of culture as the primary factor in behavior, "the backdrop against which all other events are judged" (Hall, 1966, p. x).

In 1972, Madeline Schmitt proposed a theoretical network which identified culture as but one of five variables to predict social distance: (1) Social Identity (the identity of a particular individual and/or his/her social role), (2) Status, (3) Cultural Distance (difference in values influenced by cultural variations), (4) Physical Distance (actual proximity and/or ecological position), and (5) Personal Distance (emotional differences and/or interpersonal closeness). Bochner (1982) believes that the determination of the "correct" distance in a relationship depends upon two things: the type of activity and the relationship of the individuals involved (p. 14). He proposes nine variables in the use of personal space, specifically considering cross-culture contacts: (1) On whose territory the interaction occurs, (2) Time span of the contact, (3) Purpose of the meeting, (4) Type of involvement, (5) Frequency of contact, (6) Degree of intimacy, (7) Relative status and power, (8) Numerical balance, and (9) Visible distinguishing characteristics (such as race and sex). Significantly, Bochner suggests that a major difference may exist if the exchange is between two individuals from the same culture or if the individuals come from different cultures.

Finally, Canter (1975) cautions that the amount of space necessary in order for an individual to perform a certain task must be distinguished from the use of space by individuals in their daily transactions. It is the failure to separate these two concepts, he maintains, which have led some (notably Hall) to conclude that generalizations can be made about humans' spacial requirements across a sweeping cross-section of cultures (p. 132).

*Hall, an anthropologist, has gone to some pains to point out the differences in the use of space between cultures. He rather confuses the argument by detailed categorizations of the spatial zones whilst still insisting that there are large cultural and, presumably, subcultural variations. Large individual differences combined with large subcultural variations could easily find two people using similar spatial distances in quite different ways. This makes the notion of tying distances to zones of space (or "proxemic behavior," as Hall calls it) quite inappropriate (p. 142).*

The purpose of the remainder of this paper is not to disprove or to devalue the theories of Edward Hall, but rather to substantiate the claim that variables other than the broad scale categorization of a country into contact- or noncontact-oriented may play equally important roles in determining inhabitants' use of space. Furthermore, evidence will be offered which suggests that some of these variables do not rely to any extent whatsoever upon cultural conditioning but might be proposed as culture-general principles.

## II. Age and Sex

Certainly the most obvious of these additional variables are those of the age and sex of the individuals involved in an interact. Of the two areas, age appears to be the more culture-general characteristic. Studies by both Baxter (1970) and Aiello and Jones (1971) indicate that the need for personal space increases with age. Both experiments were conducted by unobtrusively observing subjects in natural settings, and both found that children interacted the most proximally, adolescents at an intermediary distance, and adults at the greatest distance. Furthermore, Dean (1976) found that adults tend to respond more favorably to their space being invaded by smaller children, with a reduction of tolerance as the age of the uninvited visitor increases.

Pegán and Aiello (1982) observed 284 Puerto Rican children (138 males and 146 females) in grades one, six, and eleven in both New York City and Puerto Rico. In each location, a confederate who appeared to be a young teacher invited dyads of children to discuss their favorite television shows; each twenty seconds, she recorded the pair's distance and axis (shoulder orientation to one another). In both samples, older pairs used more space, with first graders using a mean distance of seven inches, sixth graders twelve inches, and eleventh graders twenty-four inches, thus moving out of Hall's "intimate" range into the close range of "personal" distance. It is important that both groups, whether in the United States or Puerto Rico, showed similar results; however, it is impossible to ascertain whether this was due primarily to the children's ages or familiar cultural environment.

Of more cultural significance, then, are the results of two studies done by Richard Lerner (1975 and 1976), who asked similar groups of kindergarten through third grade children in the United States and in Japan to illustrate comfortable interaction distances by the placement of figures on a flannel board. Despite cultural differences, the two groups yielded identical findings with mean distances between subjects increasing as the ages of the children increased. Additionally, Lerner determined that, beginning in the first grade, both male and female children used greater distances between opposite sex dyads than same sex dyads, illustrating the early influences of sex upon proxemic conditioning. Finally, children with endomorphic body types were given more surrounding space than either ectomorphs or mesomorphs, with males giving more space to endomorphs than females.

The observations of Heshka and Nelson (1972) focused on the behavior of adult dyads in an outdoor environment in London, England. Following each observation, which was also unobtrusively photographed, each individual was asked to fill out a brief questionnaire revealing his/her age and relationship to the other person. While Heshka and Nelson confirmed the hypothesis that distances are closer with young people and tend to increase, they have proposed that distance may vary in a curvilinear pattern, with spatial needs beginning to decrease at about age forty and continuing to decrease into old age.

Although the use of space by persons of certain ages appears to have some culture-general applications, the same can surely not be said about the sex variable. Use of personal space as influenced by the sex(es) of interacting individuals tends to differ dramatically from one culture to another. Whereas one culture may expect physical contact between males, in another it may be a taboo. While one country may expect females to maintain distances, the same behavior may be interpreted as coldness or disinterest in another. The examples which follow confirm two hypotheses: (1) Behavioral expectations for male/male, female/female, and male/female dyads differ according to the sex of the participants, and (2) These expectations are culture-specific but do not necessarily correspond to the contact or noncontact categorization of a culture.

For example, Jeffrey Sanders (1985) and his colleagues examined personal space zones by measuring distances maintained between 32 male and 32 female Arab students (a contact culture) and 32 male and 32 female American students (a noncontact culture). In the dyads, he varied the degree of relationship between the two participants as well as using both same sex and opposite sex pairs. Although Hall's theories would lead one to expect closer interactions between the Arabs than the Americans, the experimenters found very little difference between Arab males and Americans in general (male and female). Arab females, on the other hand, showed dramatic differences from the other three groups. Male friends were kept at a much farther distance than were female friends. For these females, the primary variable appeared to be sex, as male friends were kept nearly as far away as male strangers.

Studies conducted by Julian and Nancy Edney (1974) in the United States and by H. Smith (1981) in France and Germany examined crowding patterns on the beaches in these countries. Although the personal space needs were less for the French (a contact culture) than for the Germans and Americans (noncontact cultures) and thus confirmed Hall's hypothesis, similar variations were noted in all three cultures according to sex. Larger groups, mixed sex groups, and females tended to claim less space per person than small groups and males. In general, lone females used less space than lone males; similarly they used less space within their groups, placing themselves closer to other female groups than to male groups. These results are consistent with Smith's suggestion that "cross national commonalities in territorial patterns are more important than within cultural variations" (Smith, p. 132).

Curt and Nine (1983) noted that in Puerto Rico (a contact culture), people of the same sex and age touch a great deal and stand quite close together; whereas, people of the opposite sex and age do not touch at all and tend to stand farther apart than Americans do. Upon closer observation, Curt and Nine realized that, in closer male/female relationships, women may touch the males; however the men do not reciprocate. On the other hand, females tend to avoid direct eye contact with males, with many Puerto Rican wives never looking directly at their husbands.

Latin Americans from three contact nations — Costa Rica, Panama and Colombia — were observed by Robert Shuter (1976) to note their proxemic angles toward one another, their proxemic distances, and their frequency of physical contact (touch). Shuter found that the mean axis score and the mean distance for Costa Ricans were significantly smaller than for those of Panamanians and Colombians; similarly, a greater number of Costa Ricans touched each other than did the two other cultures. Shuter's results indicate that the directness of interactions diminishes as one travels from Central to South America, despite the classification of all three as contact cultures. Across all three cultures, however, females tend to relate most directly, followed by male/female dyads, and, finally, by males. Accordingly, the mean distance score for females was considerably smaller than for male/female or male/male dyads — regardless of culture. Finally, in each of the three countries, female/female dyads were the most likely to make physical contact, followed by male/male and male/female in Costa Rica and Colombia (where 0% of the male/female pairs exhibited touch) and male/female, male/male in Panama.

Shuter (1977) conducted a similar study by observing interactions in Venice Mastre, Italy, Heidelberg, Germany, and Milwaukee, Wisconsin, to determine if sex and/or culture have an impact on distance, axis orientation and/or contact. Contrary to Hall's theories, Shuter's data suggest that a single culture may be both contact and noncontact oriented. For example, Italians, normally viewed as contact oriented, exhibited the greatest amount of tactility in male/male dyads; however, in male/female and female/female groupings, they did not differ significantly from the Germans (a noncontact culture). Furthermore, although male/male pairs exhibited a more active contact pattern, Italian males did not converse more closely nor more directly than the non-touching German male. Additionally, American females were as tactile as Italian women, while both were surpassed by the German female.

Based on this research, Shuter (1977) seriously questioned the validity of Hall's hypothesis:

*Contrary to Hall's position, it appears that each of the cultures examined is so diverse that it cannot be classified as strictly contact or noncontact oriented. In fact, sex pairs within Germany, Italy and the United States displayed such a wide range of distance, axis, and tactile behaviors that gender-free culture statements could not be advanced on any tested variable. Unsurprisingly, when sex pair behavior is compared across the three cultures, the limitation of Hall's categories is dramatically revealed (p. 304).*

Upon an examination of even a limited number of contact and noncontact cultures, it is apparent that male/male, female/female, and male/female dyads most often respond differently within a single culture and that these patterns often vary from culture to culture. A recent experiment by Lombardo (1986) introduced yet another confounding factor, namely the influence of sex role (orientation toward androgyny) upon American males and females in their use of space. His results led Lombardo to propose that sex roles, as well as sex itself, may have an impact over how an individual uses space and his or her perception of space needs and space invasion. Clearly, it is impossible to make culture-general statements about "typical" behaviors when referring to the variable of sex.

## III. Relationships and Environment

Other than culture, age and sex, the interaction distance between two individuals can be affected by a host of other variables: relationship between the two, the environment of the transaction, attitudinal differences, occupation and/or status, the language used, etc. Of these, the first two, relationship and environment, will be considered in more detail.

In the presentation of his theory of the four distance zones, Hall (1966) notes that "how people are feeling toward each other at the time (of a meeting) is a decisive factor in the distance used" (p. 114). Yet, Hall effectively eliminates this consideration of relationships in his intercultural work. A theoretical model of personal space and interpersonal relationships, developed by Sundstrom and Altman (1976), follows three assumptions: that people seek an optimal distance for each interaction, that discomfort results from interaction outside of the optimal

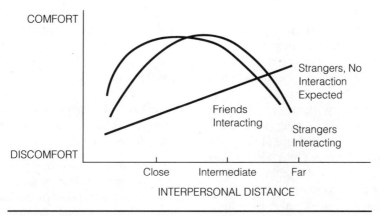

COMFORT

DISCOMFORT

Strangers, No
Interaction
Expected

Friends
Interacting

Strangers
Interacting

Close    Intermediate    Far

INTERPERSONAL DISTANCE

**Figure 1** Sundstrom and Altman (1976, p. 61)

range (too close or too far) and that the optimal zone, as well as reactions to violations, will depend upon the interpersonal situation. Their model (Figure 1) diagrams levels of comfort/discomfort in distances, based upon interactions with friends, strangers, and strangers where no interaction is anticipated, indicating that the highest degree of comfort at close distances occurs with friends interacting. The studies cited below support this model and suggest the basic for a culture-general hypothesis concerning the variable of relationship.

In 1968, Little studied social interaction distances by asking individuals from five countries (United States, Sweden, Scotland — noncontact cultures — and Greece and Southern Italy — contact cultures) to place figures of their own sex on a flannel board to represent various communication situations. Although Hall's contact/noncontact culture theory was supported, there was a general tendency across cultures for subjects to indicate closer proxemic distances as the indicated relationship became closer and the subjects more pleasant, leading Little to conclude that "the major single factor determining distances in dyadic schemata appears to be the relationship between the members, with the specific content or affective tone of the transaction as next important" (Little, p. 1). Identical results were noted by Watson (1970, also cited in Part I) who observed male college students from the noncontact cultures of North America, East Asia, India, Pakistan, and Northern Europe

and the contact cultures of the Middle East, Latin America and Southern Europe. In Waston's expansive study, the rankings of cultural groups on interpersonal distance (far to near) was nearly identical to their rankings on average intensity of friendships within the pairs. That is, the more friendly the pairs representing a given culture, the closer their average interpersonal distance, regardless of culture. In a study cited earlier, Heshka and Nelson (1972) found that, in London, strangers, particularly females, stood farther apart than friends.

Lomranz (1976) tested three groups of sixteen to seventeen year old male sojourners (Argentineans, Iraqis, and Russians) who had lived in Israel for approximately one year. He found that proxemic distance in all three cultures varied along a continuum toward progressive greater distances as the level of friendship declined. Significantly, in dealing with a close friend, only a small variance was noted across these three very distinct cultures, a fact which did not hold true for meetings with strangers. A later study by Carolyn and E. Gregory Keating (1980) in yet another culture documented the behavioral pattern of dyads on park benches in Nairobi, Kenya. In this African culture also, the Keatings observed that those who appeared to be acquainted (spoke to each other, approached or left together) sat closer together than strangers.

Acceptable spatial distances may also vary according to the environment of a given interaction, as well as to people's (probably) cultural perception of crowding and privacy. Moreover, their use of space and tolerance for crowding may not be at all related to the concept of contact and noncontact cultures. Studies done by Robert Sommer as early as 1962 illustrate that the proxemic distances chosen by individuals may vary according to the placement of furniture, the specific setting (such as a living room or an office), and the size of the space. In the latter situation, Sommer (1962) determined that people feel more comfortable sitting at closer distances in a large room than in an intimate setting. Nasar and his colleagues (1984) further hypothesized that feelings of crowding may be affected by the amount of light available in a room. An experiment conducted by Mazur (1977), in which he observed the spacing of male strangers on park benches in the United States, Spain, and Morocco, led him to offer an alternate hypothesis to Hall's: "Under a given set of physical constraints (e.g. bench length, room dimensions, number of people per square yard, etc.), the spacing pattern of noninteracting strangers is similar across cultures" (p. 58).

On the other hand, culturally influenced privacy needs may complicate the establishment of such culture-general rules. "In the strictest sense," writes Canter (1975, p. 139), "privacy may be seen as the establishing of a physical and/or psychological barrier against the world." In Western societies, the need for privacy may take the form of territoriality and/or the setting up of physical barricades against others, thus creating the sense of aloneness. In Eastern societies, however, the feeling of privacy may be reached even in a crowded room, as the individual simply retreats into him or herself. Neither the Arabs (a contact culture) nor the Japanese (a noncontact culture) have a word for "privacy" as we understand it in their languages. In public situations, both groups demonstrate a tolerance for crowding, pushing, and close proximity which is uncomfortable to the American. The homes of both peoples tend to be open and flexible, emphasizing a need to be with one another. (Arab homes are usually constructed without specific room dividers; whereas Japanese walls are flexible, and activity in the center of the space is emphasized.) In the use of personal interaction distance, on the other

hand, the two cultures differ significantly with the Arab approaching close enough to smell the partner's breath, while maintaining direct eye contact, and the Japanese adopting a much more distant position with averted eyes.

Condon and Yousef (1975) offer a warning about careless attempts to categorize and predict nonverbal behaviors based on overly simplistic categorizations:

*. . . one wonders, however, if it might be possible to anticipate relations between proxemic behavior and other cultural patterns of communication before completing detailed proxemic descriptions of many different societies. For example, are there likely to be some common value orientations among cultures which are characterized by frequent physical contact . . . ? Do relatively noncontact cultures reveal different value orientations? Or is there no more connection between values and the sound system of the language spoken in any given culture? . . . Perhaps the best we can do at this point is to warn of pushing analogies too far and point out that many codes of nonverbal interaction cannot be treated adequately by analogies to other forms of behavior (p. 141).*

## IV. Ethnicity

The characteristics of age, sex, relationships, and environment can be seen as universal variables, possibly influenced by, but not dependent upon, a particular culture. The final aspect of this paper, on the other hand, focuses on an aspect of culture, namely ethnicity, which may supercede the categorization of a country or geographical area as a contact or noncontact culture. For example, will a group of Japanese Italian citizens living in a predominantly Japanese extended family group in Italy be more influenced by their ethnic background (the noncontact Japanese) than by the geographical area (the contact Italian) in which they live? This concept has particularly sweeping implications for countries such as the United States which, despite its "melting pot" composition, has been described as a noncontact culture by Hall.

In his description of the four spatial distances (public, social, personal, and intimate), Hall (1966) carefully explains the limitations of his sample:

*It should be emphasized that these generalizations are not representative of human behavior in general – or even of American behavior in general – but only of the group included in the sample. Negroes and Spanish Americans as well as persons who come from southern European cultures have very different proxemic patterns (Hall, 1966, p. 116).*

Interestingly, the anthropologist has had considerable experience in working with the Native Americans of United States Southwest, whom he often identifies as unique in their conceptualizations and use of time (1976, 1983). It is particularly ironic, then, that, in his writings about contact and noncontact cultures, Hall appears to adopt but two molds into which countries of the world must fit, apparently overlooking the multitude of co-cultures and subcultures which exist in most geographical areas.

Even more importantly, most researchers have been painstakingly cautious in separating contact culture and noncontact culture subjects. Studies and anecdotes abound which portray the classic behavioral patterns when two Arabs meet or when two Japanese converse. It is apparently assumed that, by studying such isolated examples, the individual from another culture can internalize and adapt to the use of personal space in countries other than his/her own. What is sorely lacking in intercultural research are experiments and observations which survey the results of interactions between individuals from two different cultures or from two co-cultures within the same country. If age, sex, and a host of other variables can affect an interaction, it stands to reason that the presence of two cultures or co-cultures interacting side-by-side may carry an even greater impact. Studies of different ethnic groups within a single country, most notably blacks and whites in the United States, imply support of this hypothesis.

As early as 1970, Baxter noted differences for personal space needs in Hispanic-American, White-American, and Black-American children, with mixed race dyads exhibiting greater distances than any single-race pairs. In studies of black and white children, Severy (1979) determined that, by age seven, black children require less personal space than

white children, with mixed sex dyads needing more space than same sex dyads. Somewhat paradoxically, through observations of fifth grade boys at play, Zimmerman (1975) noted that black boys talked to each other significantly less, faced each other less directly and interacted at greater distances than white boys. Racially mixed dyads appeared to attempt to adjust to each other's needs and interacted at an intermediate distance.

Based on Hall's contact/noncontact culture theory, Aiello and Jones (1971) observed 210 same sex (male/male, female/female) first and second grade dyads from three diverse New York City subcultures: blacks, whites, and Puerto Ricans; they hypothesized that blacks and Puerto Ricans would interact at closer distances than the white children. In this study, in contrast to that of Zimmerman, the hypothesis was confirmed with whites maintaining distances nearly twice that of blacks and Puerto Ricans. An additional correlation was found, however, between distance and sex of the dyad. Both Puerto Rican and white female/female dyads stood closer than male/male dyads, with the opposite being true of blacks. Additionally, the axis orientation of white children was more direct than that of blacks or Puerto Ricans, with the latter being the least direct. Across cultures, males tended to face their partners more directly than females. In a similar vein, Jones (1971) found that Chinese in New York City interacted at greater distances than either Puerto Ricans or Italians.

Perhaps related to their comfortability with closer proximities, there is also some indication that blacks will more readily invade the personal space of another black than will whites intrude upon the personal space of another individual of either race. When Bauer (1973) instructed blacks and whites to approach a same sex/same race confederate "as close as comfortable," white males chose the fartherest distance, followed by white females, black males, and black females. An experiment by William Dick (1976) netted similar results. Four male confederates (two blacks, aged 20 and 30 years, and two whites, aged 20 and 30 years) were positioned individually on a university campus in front of a bubble gum machine so that subjects would need to invade their space in order to turn the knob to receive free gum. Significantly more black subjects invaded the space of the black confederates. Females tended to be more cautious than males, indicating that both race and sex influenced the subject's decision to "invade space."

Although conducted in the unlaboratory-like setting of the New York subway, the work of David Maines (1977) makes a unique contribution in his observation of mixed sex/mixed race dyads. In observing the elbow placement of individuals, either to the side or out to the front, Maines discovered that there was a general tendency for individuals to locate their elbows to their sides in noncrowded conditions and to the front in more crowded contexts. Movement to the front was particularly significant in mixed race and mixed sex dyads where individuals are apparently more reluctant to actually touch another person. A similar pattern was noticed in observing the physical contact patterns of the hands of passengers sharing a "balance strap." In these situations, there was an especially noticeable pattern of avoidance in the case of mixed race/same sex groupings. While Maines' observations did not include verbal interactions, his results are important in suggesting further implications for mixed ethnic pairings. Unfortunately, studies of mixed race or mixed subculture groups in other cultures are difficult to locate.

A final significant contribution is that of Sussman and Rosenfeld (1982) who looked at the influence of culture and language on conversational distance. The researchers hypothesized that theories for contact/noncontact societies hold true primarily in same-culture interactions in which individuals speak in their native tongues and that, correspondingly, adopting the use of another language serves to create a distance which is evidenced through proxemics. Observations of Japanese, Venezuelan, and American student dyads substantiated their hypothesis, with all three groups maintaining further distances when speaking a foreign tongue than when using their native language. Although this study used dyads of individuals from the same culture, hypotheses might be suggested about the potential implications for interactions in mixed-culture pairs with differing native tongues.

## V. Conclusions

The research in this paper holds suggestions for further study in the use of space in several different areas:

Can culture-general hypotheses for the following be substantiated?

A curvilinear pattern of proxemic distances according to age

A continuum of progressively smaller distances as relationships move from that of stranger to that of close friend

Can culture-specific theories for the following be generated?

Interaction differences between male/male, female/female, and male/female dyads in different cultures

The impact of environment and the perceptions of crowding and privacy in different cultures

Can (and should) Hall's theory of contact/noncontact cultures be redefinded and refined?

More significantly, however, this research indicates a serious gap in the study of "intercultural" proxemics; indeed, there appears to be very little work with a truly intercultural focus being done. While anecdotal accounts are sometimes cited to explain the "East Meets West" phenomenon, I was unable to locate a single example of a study which used a scientific approach to examine interaction behaviors between individuals from different cultures. Only one (the Maines subway study) even touched upon United States patterns in racially mixed pairs. The experiments and hypotheses to date, then, have been based nearly totally on intracultural or, at best, cross-cultural studies. Some of the areas which might be probed are the following:

Can any hypotheses be substantiated for intercultural interactions based upon contact/noncontact, noncontact/noncontact, contact/contact dyads?

Can any hypotheses be substantiated in terms of the distance control factor for the host or the sojourner?

Can any hypotheses be substantiated about the distance behaviors of two sojourners from different cultures interacting in a third culture?

Can any hypotheses be substantiated about the impact of language choice in a transaction? Is there a correlation between use of the native tongue and the distance control factor?

In any of the above cases, how might the sex, sex roles, age, relationship, status and ethnicity of the individuals influence the interaction patterns?

"Proxemics research" admits Edward Hall (1976, p. 86), "requires an inordinate amount of time." Because of the many variables present, he says, few studies have been done which examine its impact. In his first book, *The Silent Language* (1959), Hall offers this simplistic advice to the sojourner: "Watch where people stand and don't back up." In this world of multinational companies and jet travel, however, we cannot afford to be so easily placated.

## References

Aiello, J. R. and S. E. Jones (1971). Field study of proxemic behavior of young school children in three subcultural groups. *Journal of Personality and Social Psychology,* 19: 351–356.

Baltus, D. (1974). Proxemics. Conference paper.

Bauer, E. A. (1973). Personal space: A study of blacks and whites. *Sociometry,* 36(3): 402–408.

Baxter, J. (1970). Interpersonal spacing in natural settings. *Sociometry,* 33(4): 444–456.

Birdwhistell, R. (1970). *Kinesics and Context: Essays on Body Motion Communication.* Philadelphia: University of Pennsylvania Press.

Bochner, S. (1982). The social psychology of cross-cultural relations. In S. Bochner (Ed.) *Cultures in Contact.* New York: Pergamon Press: 5–44.

Canter, D. *et al.* (1975). *Environmental Interactions: Psychological Approaches to Our Physical Surroundings.* London: Surrey Press.

Condon, J. C. and F. Yousef (1975). *An Introduction to Intercultural Communication.* Indianapolis: Bobbs-Merrill.

Curt, C. and J. Nine (1983). Hispanic-Anglo conflicts in nonverbal communication. In Isidora Albino (Ed.) *Perspectives Pedagogicas.* San Juan, Puerto Rico: Universidad de Puerto Rico.

Dean, L. M., F. N. Willis, and J. N. la Rocco (1976). Invasion of personal space as a function of age, sex and race. *Psychological Reports,* 38(3)(pt.1): 959–965.

Dick, W. E. (1976). Invasion of personal space as function of age and race. *Psychological Reports,* 39(1): 281–282.

Edney, J. and N. Jordon-Edney (1974). Territorial spacing on a bench. *Sociometry,* 37(1): 92–104.

Edwards, D. J. (1980). Perception of crowding and tolerance of interpersonal proxemics and separation in South Africa. *Journal of Social Psychology,* 110(1): 19–28.

Engebretson, D. and D. Fullmer (1970). Cross-cultural differences in territoriality. *Journal of Cross-Cultural Psychology,* 1: 261–269.

Evans, G. W. (1978). Human spatial behavior: The arousal model. In Andrew Baum and Yakov M. Epstein (Eds.) *Human Response to Crowding.* N.J.: Erlbaum Associates.

Felipe, N.J. and R. Sommer (1966). Invasions of personal space. *Social Problems,* 14: 206–214.

Forston, R. and C. Larson (1968). The dynamics of space. An experimental study in proxemic behavior among Latin Americans and North Americans. *Journal of Communication,* 18: 109–116.

Goffman, E. (1971). *Relations in Public.* New York: Basic Books.

Hall, E. T. (1959). *The Silent Language.* New York: Doubleday.

Hall, E. T. (1960). The silent language in overseas business. *Harvard Business Review,* 38(3): 87–96.

Hall, E. T. (1963). A system for the notation of proxemic behavior. *American Anthropologist,* 65: 1003–1026.

Hall, E. T. (1964). Silent assumptions in social communication. *Disorders of Communication,* 42: 41–55.

Hall, E. T. (1966). *The Hidden Dimension.* New York: Doubleday.

Hall, E. T. (1976). *Beyond Culture.* New York: Anchor Press.

Hall, E. T. (1983). *Dance of Life.* New York: Doubleday.

Hayduk, L. A. (1983). Personal space: Where we now stand. *Psychological Bulletin,* 94: 293–335.

Heaton, J. (1978). Teaching culture as a second language. Private culture and kinesics. University of California, Los Angeles: Research Report.

Heshka, S. and Y. Nelson (1972). Interpersonal speaking distances as a function of age, sex, and relationship. *Sociometry,* 35(4): 491–498.

Jensen, J. V. (1972). Perspectives on nonverbal intercultural communication. In Larry A. Samovar and Richard E. Porter (Eds.) *Intercultural Communication: A Reader.* Belmont, Calif.: Wadsworth.

Jones, S. E. (1971). A comparative proxemics analysis of dyadic interaction in selected subcultures of New York City: *Journal of Social Psychology,* 84: 35–44.

Keating, C. E. and E. G. Keating (1980). Distance between pairs of acquaintances and strangers on public beaches in Nairobi, Kenya. *Journal on Social Psychology,* 110(2): 285–286.

Kinloch, G. C. (1973). Race, socio-economic status and social distance in Hawaii. *Sociology and Social Research,* 57(2): 156-167.

Lerner, R. M., *et al.* (1975). Effects of age and sex on the development of personal space schemata toward body build. *Journal of Genetic Psychology,* 127: 91-101.

Lerner, R. M., *et al.* (1976). Development of personal space schemata among Japanese children. *Developmental Psychology,* 15(5): 466-467.

Liebman, M. (1970). The effects of sex and race norms on personal space. *Environmental Behavior,* 2: 208-246.

Little, K. B. (1968). Cultural variations in social schemata. *Journal of Personality and Social Psychology,* 10(1): 1-7.

Lombardo, J. P. (1986). Interaction of sex and sex role in response to violations of preferred seating arrangements. *Sex Roles,* 15: 173-183.

Lomranz, J. (1976). Cultural variations in personal space. *Journal of Social Psychology,* 99(1): 21-27.

Maines, D. R. (1977). Tactile relationships in the subway as affected by racial, sexual and crowded seated situations. *Environmental Psychology and Nonverbal Behavior,* 2(2): 100-108.

Mazur, A. (1977). Interpersonal spacing on public benches in contact vs. noncontact cultures. *Journal of Social Psychology,* 101: 53-58.

Nasar, J. L., *et al.* (1984). Modifiers of perceived spaciousness and crowding among different cultural groups. Research report, November.

Noesjirwan, J. (1978). A laboratory study of proxemic patterns in Indonesians and Australians. *Journal of Social and Chemical Psychology,* 17(4):333-334.

Pegán, G. and J. R. Aiello (1982). Development of personal space among Puerto Ricans. *Journal of Nonverbal Behavior,* 7(2): 59-68.

Sanders, J., *et al.* (1985). Personal space amongst Arabs and Americans. *International Journal of Psychology,* 20(1): 13-17.

Schmitt, M. H. (1972): Near and Far: A re-formulation of the social distance concept. *Sociology and Social Research,* 57(1): 85-97.

Severy, L. J., *et al.* (1979). A multimethod assessment of personal space development in female and male, black and white children. *Journal of Nonverbal Behavior,* 4(2): 68-86.

Shuter, R. (1976). Nonverbal communication: Proxemics and tactility in Latin America. *Journal of Communication,* 26(3): 46-52.

Shuter, R. (1977). A field study of nonverbal communication in Germany, Italy and the United States. *Communication Monographs,* 44(4): 298-305.

Singer, M. R. (1987). *Intercultural Communication: A Perceptual Approach.* N.J.: Prentice-Hall.

Six, B., *et al.* (1983). A cultural comparison of perceived crowding and discomfort: The United States and West Germany. *Journal of Psychology,* 114(1): 63-67.

Smith, A. G. (Ed.) (1966). *Communication and Culture: Readings in the Codes of Human Interaction.* New York: Holt, Rinehart and Winston.

Smith, H. (1981). Territorial spacing on a beach revisited: A crossnational exploration. *Social Psychology Quarterly,* 44: 132-137.

Sommer, R. (1959). Studies in personal space. *Sociometry,* 22: 247-260.

Sommer, R. (1962). The distance for comfortable conversation: A further study. *Sociometry,* 25: 111-125.

Sommer, R. (1966). Man's proximate environment. *Journal of Social Issues,* 22(4): 59-70.

Sommer, R. (1969). *Personal Space.* N.J.: Prentice-Hall.

Sommer, R., and F. D. Becker. Territorial defense and the good neighbor. *Journal of Personality and Social Psychology,* 11: 85-92.

Speelman, D. and C. D. Hoffman (1980). Personal space assessment of the development of racial attitudes in integrated and segregated schools. *Journal of Genetic Psychology,* 136(2): 307-308.

Sundstrom, E. and I. Altman (1976). Interpersonal relationships and personal space: Research review and theoretical model. *Human Ecology,* 4: 46-67.

Sussman, N. and H. M. Rosenfeld (1982). Influence of culture, language and sex on conversational distance. *Journal of Personality and Social Psychology,* 42(1): 66-74.

Thayer, S. and L. Alban. A field experiment on the effect of political and cultural factors in the use of personal space. *Journal of Social Psychology,* 88(2): 267-272.

Watson, O. M. (1970). *Proxemic Behavior: A Cross-Cultural Study.* The Hague: Mouton.

Watson, O. M. and T. D. Graves (1966). Quantitative research in proxemic behavior. *American Anthropologist,* 68: 971-985.

Wysocki, B., Jr. (1986). Closed society: Despite global role, many Japanese try to avoid foreigners. *Wall Street Journal,* 68(23): 1, 18.

Yousef, F. S. (1974). Cross-cultural communication aspects of contrastive social values between North Americans and Middle Easterners. *Human Organization,* 33(4): 383-387.

Zimmerman, B. and G. H. Brody (1975). Race and modeling influence in the interpersonal play pattern for boys. *Journal of Educational Psychology,* 67(5): 591-598.

# Monochronic and Polychronic Time

## EDWARD T. HALL

Lorenzo Hubbell, trader to the Navajo and the Hopi, was three quarters Spanish and one quarter New Englander, but culturally he was Spanish to the core. Seeing him for the first time on government business transactions relating to my work in the 1930s, I felt embarrassed and a little shy because he didn't have a regular office where people could talk in private. Instead, there was a large corner room – part of his house adjoining the trading post – in which business took place. Business covered everything from visits with officials and friends, conferences with Indians who had come to see him, who also most often needed to borrow money or make sheep deals, as well as a hundred or more routine transactions with store clerks and Indians who had not come to see Lorenzo specifically but only to trade. There were long-distance telephone calls to his warehouse in Winslow, Arizona, with cattle buyers, and his brother, Roman, at Ganado, Arizona – all this and more (some of it quite personal), carried on in public, in front of our small world for all to see and hear. If you wanted to learn about the life of an Indian trader or the ins and outs of running a small trading empire (Lorenzo had a dozen posts scattered throughout northern Arizona), all you had to do was to sit in Lorenzo's office for a month or so and take note of what was going on. Eventually all the different parts of the pattern would unfold before your eyes,

From Edward T. Hall, *The Dance of Life: The Other Dimension of Time* (New York: Doubleday and Company, 1983), pp. 41-54. Copyright © 1983 by Edward T. Hall. Used by permission of Doubleday, a division of Bantam, Doubleday, Dell Publishing Group, Inc.

as eventually they did before mine, as [ ] worked on that reservation over a five-y[ ]

I was prepared for the fact that the I[ ] things differently from AE cultures bec[ ] spent part of my childhood on the Uppe[ ] Rio Grande River with the Pueblo Indians as friends. Such differences were taken for granted. But this public, everything-at-once, mélange way of conducting business made an impression on me. There was no escaping it, here was another world, but in this instance, although both Spanish and Anglos had their roots firmly planted in European soil, each handled time in radically different ways.

It didn't take long for me to accustom myself to Lorenzo's business ambiance. There was so much going on that I could hardly tear myself away. My own work schedule won out, of course, but I did find that the Hubbell store had a pull like a strong magnet, and I never missed an opportunity to visit with Lorenzo. After driving through Oraibi, I would pull up next to his store, park my pickup, and go through the side door to the office. These visits were absolutely necessary because without news of what was going on life could become precarious. Lorenzo's desert "salon" was better than a newspaper, which, incidentally, we lacked.

Having been initiated to Lorenzo's way of doing business, I later began to notice similar mutual involvement in events among the New Mexico Spanish. I also observed the same patterns in Latin America, as well as in the Arab world. Watching my countrymen's reactions to this "many things at a time" system I noted how deeply it affected the channeling and flow of information, the shape and form of the networks connecting people, and a host of other important social and cultural features of the society. I realized that there was more to this culture pattern than one might at first suppose.

Years of exposure to other cultures demonstrated that complex societies organize time in at least two different ways: events scheduled as separate items – one thing at a time – as in North Europe, or following the Mediterranean model of involvement in several things at once. The two systems are logically and empirically quite distinct. Like oil and water, they don't mix. Each has its strengths as well as its weaknesses. I have termed doing many things at once: Polychronic, P-time. The North European system — doing one thing at a time — is Monochronic, M-time. P-time stresses involvement of people and completion of transactions rather than adherence to preset schedules. Appointments are not taken as seriously and, as a consequence, are frequently broken. P-time is treated as less tangible than M-time. For polychronic people, time is seldom experienced as "wasted," and is apt to be considered a point rather than a ribbon or a road, but that point is often sacred. An Arab will say, "I will see you before one hour," or "I will see you after two days." What he means in the first instance is that it will not be longer than an hour before he sees you, and at least two days in the second instance. These commitments are taken quite seriously as long as one remains in the P-time pattern.

Once, in the early '60s, when I was in Patras, Greece, which is in the middle of the P-time belt, my own time system was thrown in my face under rather ridiculous but still amusing circumstances. An impatient Greek hotel clerk, anxious to get me and my ménage settled in some quarters which were far from first-class, was pushing me to make a commitment so he could continue with his siesta. I couldn't decide whether to accept this rather forlorn "bird in the hand" or take a chance on another hotel that looked, if possible, even less inviting. Out of the blue, the clerk blurted, "Make up your mind. After all, time is money!" How would you reply to that at a time of day when literally nothing was happening? I couldn't help but laugh at the incongruity of it all. If there ever was a case of time not being money, it was in Patras during siesta in the summer.

Though M-time cultures tend to make a fetish out of management, there are points at which M-time doesn't make as much sense as it might. Life in general is at times unpredictable; and who can tell exactly how long a particular client, patient, or set of transactions will take. These are imponderables in the chemistry of human transactions. What can be accomplished one day in ten minutes, may take twenty minutes on the next. Some days people will be rushed and can't finish;

on others, there is time to spare, so they "waste" the remaining time.

In Latin America and the Middle East, North Americans can frequently be psychologically stressed. Immersed in a polychronic environment in the markets, stores, and souks of Mediterranean and Arab countries, one is surrounded by other customers all vying for the attention of a single clerk who is trying to wait on everyone at once. There is no recognized order as to who is to be served next, no queue or numbers to indicate who has been waiting the longest. To the North European or American, it appears that confusion and clamor abound. In a different context, the same patterns can be seen operating in the governmental bureaucracies of Mediterranean countries: a typical office layout for important officials frequently includes a large reception area (an ornate version of Lorenzo Hubbell's office), outside the private suite, where small groups of people can wait and be visited by the minister or his aides. These functionaries do most of their business outside in this semipublic setting, moving from group to group conferring with each in turn. The semiprivate transactions take less time, give others the feeling that they are in the presence of the minister as well as other important people with whom they may also want to confer. Once one is used to this pattern, it is clear that there are advantages which frequently outweigh the disadvantages of a series of private meetings in the inner office.

Particularly distressing to Americans is the way in which appointments are handled by polychronic people. Being on time simply doesn't mean the same thing as it does in the United States. Matters in a polychronic culture seem in a constant state of flux. Nothing is solid or firm, particularly plans for the future; even important plans may be changed right up to the minute of execution.

In contrast, people in the Western world find little in life exempt from the iron hand of M-time. Time is so thoroughly woven into the fabric of existence that we are hardly aware of the degree to which it determines and coordinates everything we do, including the molding of relations with others in many subtle ways. In fact, social and business life, even one's sex life, is commonly schedule-dominated. By scheduling, we compartmentalize; this makes it possible to concentrate on one thing at a time, but it also reduces the context. Since scheduling by its very nature selects what will and will not be perceived and attended, and permits only a limited number of events within a given period, what gets scheduled constitutes a system for setting priorities for both people and functions. Important things are taken up first and allotted the most time; unimportant things are left to last or omitted if time runs out.

M-time is also tangible; we speak of it as being saved, spent, wasted, lost, made up, crawling, killed, and running out. These metaphors must be taken seriously. M-time scheduling is used as a classification system that orders life. The rules apply to everything except birth and death. It should be mentioned, that without schedules or something similar to the M-time system, it is doubtful that our industrial civilization could have developed as it has. There are other consequences. Monochronic time seals off one or two people from the group and intensifies relationships with one other person or, at most, two or three people. M-time in this sense is like a room with a closed door ensuring privacy. The only problem is that you must vacate the "room" at the end of the allotted fifteen minutes or an hour, a day, or a week, depending on the schedule, and make way for the next person in line. Failure to make way by intruding on the time of the next person is not only a sign of extreme egocentrism and narcissism, but just plain bad manners.

Monochronic time is arbitrary and imposed, that is, learned. Because it is so thoroughly learned and so thoroughly integrated into our culture, it is treated as though it were the only natural and logical way of organizing life. Yet, it is *not* inherent in man's biological rhythms or his creative drives, nor is it existential in nature.

Schedules can and frequently do cut things short just when they are beginning to go well. For example, research funds run out just as the results are beginning to be achieved. How often has the reader had the experience of realizing that he is pleasurably immersed in some creative activity, totally unaware of time, solely conscious of the job at hand, only to be brought back to "reality" with the rude shock of realizing that other, frequently inconsequential previous commitments are bearing down on him?

Some Americans associate schedules with reality, but M-time can alienate us from ourselves and from others by reducing context. It subtly influences how we think and perceive the world in segmented compartments. This is convenient in linear operations but disastrous in its effect on nonlinear creative tasks. Latino peoples are an example of the opposite. In Latin America, the intelligentsia and the academicians frequently participate in several fields at once — fields which the average North American academician, business, or professional person thinks of as antithetical. Business, philosophy, medicine, and poetry, for example, are common, well-respected combinations.

Polychronic people, such as the Arabs and Turks, who are almost never alone, even in the home, make very different uses of "screening" than Europeans do. They interact with several people at once and are continually involved with each other. Tight scheduling is therefore difficult, if not impossible.

Theoretically, when considering social organization, P-time systems should demand a much greater centralization of control and be characterized by a rather shallow or simple structure. This is because the leader deals continually with many people, most of whom stay informed as to what is happening. The Arab fellah can always see his sheik. There are no intermediaries between man and sheik or between man and God. The flow of information as well as people's need to stay informed complement each other. Polychronic people are so deeply immersed in each other's business that they feel a compulsion to keep in touch. Any stray scrap of a story is gathered in and stored away. Their knowledge of each other is truly extraordinary. Their involvement in people is the very core of their existence. This has bureaucratic implications. For example, delegation of authority and a buildup in bureaucratic levels are not required to handle high volumes of business. The principal shortcoming of P-type bureaucracies is that as functions increase, there is a proliferation of small bureaucracies that really are not set up to handle the problems of outsiders. In fact, outsiders travel-ing or residing in Latin American or Mediterranean countries find the bureaucracies unusually cumber-some and unresponsive. In polychronic countries, one has to be an insider or have a "friend" who can make things happen. All bureaucracies are oriented inward, but P-type bureaucracies are especially so.

There are also interesting points to be made concerning the act of administration as it is con-ceived in these two settings. Administration and control of polychronic peoples in the Middle East and Latin America is a matter of job analysis. Ad-ministration consists of taking each subordinate's job and identifying the activities that go to make up the job. These are then labeled and frequently indicated on the elaborate charts with checks to make it possible for the administrator to be sure that each function has been performed. In this way, it is felt that absolute control is maintained over the individual. Yet, scheduling how and when each activity is actually performed is left up to the em-ployee. For an employer to schedule a subordinate's work for him would be considered a tyrannical vio-lation of his individuality – an invasion of the self.

In contrast, M-time people schedule the activity and leave the analysis of the activities of the job to the individual. A P-type analysis, even though tech-nical by its very nature, keeps reminding the sub-ordinate that his job is not only a system but also part of a larger system. M-type people, on the other hand, by virtue of compartmentalization, are less likely to see their activities in context as part of the larger whole. This does not mean that they are un-aware of the "organization" – far from it – only that the job itself or even the goals of the organization are seldom seen as a whole.

Giving the organization a higher priority than the functions it performs is common in our cul-ture. This is epitomized in television, where we al-low the TV commercials, the "special message," to break the continuity of even the most important communication. There is a message all right, and the message is that art gives way to commerce – polychronic advertising agencies impose their val-ues on a monochronic population. In monochronic

North European countries, where patterns are more homogeneous, commercial interruptions of this sort are not tolerated. There is a strict limit as to the number as well as the times when commer-cials can be shown. The average American TV pro-gram has been allotted one or two hours, for which people have set aside time, and is conceived, writ-ten, directed, acted, and played as a unity. Inter-jecting commercials throughout the body of the program breaks that continuity and flies in the face of one of the core systems of the culture. The poly-chronic Spanish treat the main feature as a close friend or relative who should not be disturbed and let the commercials mill around in the antecham-ber outside. My point is not that one system is su-perior to another, it's just that the two don't mix. The effect is disruptive, and reminiscent of what the English are going through today, now that the old monochronic queuing patterns have broken down as a consequence of a large infusion of poly-chronic peoples from the colonies.

Both M-time and P-time systems have strengths as well as weaknesses. There is a limit to the speed with which jobs can be analyzed, although once analyzed, proper reporting can enable a P-time ad-ministrator to handle a surprising number of sub-ordinates. Nevertheless, organizations run on the polychronic model are limited in size, they depend on having gifted people at the top, and are slow and cumbersome when dealing with anything that is new or different. Without gifted people, a P-type bureaucracy can be a disaster. M-type organizations go in the opposite direction. They can and do grow much larger than the P-type. However, they com-bine bureaucracies instead of proliferating them, e.g., with consolidated schools, the business con-glomerate, and the new superdepartments we are developing in government.

The blindness of the monochronic organization is to the humanity of its members. The weakness of the polychronic type lies in its extreme dependence on the leader to handle contingencies and stay on top of things. M-type bureaucracies, as they grow larger, turn inward; oblivious to their own structure, they grow rigid and are apt to lose sight of their original purpose. Prime examples are the Army Corps of Engineers and the Bureau of Reclamation, which wreak havoc on our environment in their dedicated efforts to stay in business by building dams or aiding the flow of rivers to the sea.

At the beginning of this chapter, I stated that "American time is monochronic." On the surface, this is true, but in a deeper sense, American (AE) time is both polychronic and monochronic. M-time dominates the official worlds of business, government, the professions, entertainment, and sports. However, in the home – particularly the more traditional home in which women are the core around which everything revolves – one finds that P-time takes over. How else can one raise several children at once, run a household, hold a job, be a wife, mother, nurse, tutor, chauffeur, and general fixer-upper? Nevertheless, most of us automatically equate P-time with informal activities and with the multiple tasks and responsibilities and ties of women to networks of people. At the preconscious level, M-time is male time and P-time is female time, and the ramifications of this difference are considerable.

In the conclusion of an important book, *Unfinished Business,* Maggie Scarf vividly illustrates this point. Scarf addresses herself to the question of why it is that depression (the hidden illness of our age) is three to six times more prevalent in women than it is in men. How does time equate with depression in women? It so happens that the time system of the dominant culture adds another source of trauma and alienation to the already overburdened psyches of many American women. According to Scarf, depression comes about in part as a consequence of breaking significant ties that make up most women's worlds. In our culture, men as a group tend to be more task-oriented, while women's lives center on networks of people and their relations with people. Traditionally, a woman's world is a world of human emotions, of love, attachment, envy, anxiety, and hate. This is a little difficult for late-twentieth-century people to accept because it implies basic differences between men and women that are not fashionable at the moment. Nevertheless, for most cultures around the world, the feminine mystique is intimately identified with the development of the human relations side of the personality rather than the technical, cortical left-brain

occupational side. In the United States, AE women live in a world of peoples and relationships and their egos become spread out among those who are closest to them by a process we call identification. When the relationships are threatened or broken or something happens to those to whom one is close, there are worries and anxieties, and depression is a natural result.

Polychronic cultures are by their very nature oriented to people. Any human being who is naturally drawn to other human beings and who lives in a world dominated by human relationships will be either pushed or pulled toward the polychronic end of the time spectrum. If you value people, you must hear them out and cannot cut them off simply because of a schedule.

M-time, on the other hand, is oriented to tasks, schedules, and procedures. As anyone who has had experience with our bureaucracies knows, schedules and procedures take on a life all their own without reference to either logic or human needs. And it is this set of written and unwritten rules – and the consequences of these rules – that is at least partially responsible for the reputation of American business being cut off from human beings and unwilling to recognize the importance of employee morale. Morale may well be the deciding factor in whether a given company makes a profit or not. Admittedly, American management is slowly, very slowly, getting the message. The problem is that modern management has accentuated the monochronic side at the expense of the less manageable, and less predictable, polychronic side. Virtually everything in our culture works for and rewards a monochronic view of the world. But the antihuman aspect of M-time is alienating, especially to women. Unfortunately, too many women have "bought" the M-time world, not realizing that unconscious sexism is part of it. The pattern of an entire system of time is too large, too diffuse, and too ubiquitous for most to identify its patterns. Women sense there is something alien about the way in which modern organizations handle time, beginning with how the workday, the week, and the year are set up. Such changes as flextime do not alter the fact that as soon as one enters the door of the office, one becomes immediately locked into a monochronic, monolithic structure that is virtually impossible to change.

There are other sources of tension between people who have internalized these two systems. Keep in mind that polychronic individuals are oriented toward people, human relationships, and the family, which is the core of their existence. Family takes precedence over everything else. Close friends come next. In the absence of schedules, when there is a crisis the family always comes first. If a monochronic woman has a polychronic hairdresser, there will inevitably be problems, even if she has a regular appointment and is scheduled at the same time each week. In circumstances like these, the hairdresser (following his or her own pattern) will inevitably feel compelled to "squeeze people in." As a consequence, the regular customer, who has scheduled her time very carefully (which is why she has a standing appointment in the first place), is kept waiting and feels put down, angry, and frustrated. The hairdresser is also in a bind because if he does not accommodate his relative or friend regardless of the schedule, the result is endless repercussions within his family circle. Not only must he give preferential treatment to relatives, but the degree of accommodation and who is pushed aside or what is pushed aside is itself a communication!

The more important the customer or business that is disrupted, the more reassured the hairdresser's polychronic Aunt Nell will feel. The way to ensure the message that one is accepted or loved is to call up at the last minute and expect everyone to rearrange everything. If they don't, it can be taken as a clear signal that they don't care enough. The M-time individual caught in this P-time pattern has the feeling either that he is being pressured or that he simply doesn't count. There are many instances where culture patterns are on a collision course and there can be no resolution until the point of conflict is identified. One side or the other literally gives up. In the instance cited above, it is the hairdresser who usually loses a good customer. Patterns of this variety are what maintain ethnicity. Neither pattern is right, only different, and it is important to remember that they do not mix.

Not all M-times and P-times are the same. There are tight and loose versions of each. The Japanese, for example, in the official business side of their lives where people do not meet on a highly personalized basis, provide us an excellent example of tight M-time. When an American professor, business person, technical expert, or consultant visits Japan, he may find that his time is like a carefully packed trunk — so tightly packed, in fact, that it is impossible to squeeze one more thing into the container. On a recent trip to Japan, I was contacted by a well-known colleague who had translated one of my earlier books. He wanted to see me and asked if he could pick me up at my hotel at twelve-fifteen so we could have lunch together. I had situated myself in the lobby a few minutes early, as the Japanese are almost always prompt. At twelve-seventeen, I could see his tense figure darting through the crowd of arriving business people and politicians who had collected near the door. Following greetings, he ushered me outside to the ubiquitous black limousine with chauffeur, with white doilies covering the arms and headrests. The door of the car had hardly closed when he started outlining our schedule for the lunch period by saying that he had an appointment at three o'clock to do a TV broadcast. That set the time limit and established the basic parameters in which everyone knew where he would be at any given part of the agenda. He stated these limits — a little over two hours — taking travel time into account.

My colleague next explained that not only were we to have lunch, but he wanted to tape an interview for a magazine. That meant lunch and an interview which would last thirty to forty minutes. What else? Ah, yes. He hoped I wouldn't mind spending time with Mr. X, who had published one of my earlier books in Japanese, because Mr. X was very anxious to pin down a commitment on my part to allow him to publish my next book. He was particularly eager to see me because he missed out on publishing the last two books, even though he had written me in the United States. Yes, I did remember that he had written, but his letter arrived after the decision on the Japanese publisher had been made by my agent. That, incidentally, was the very reason why he wanted to see me personally. Three down and how many more to go? Oh, yes, there would be some photographers there and he hoped I wouldn't mind if pictures were taken? The pictures were to be both formal group shots, which were posed, and informal, candid shots during the interview, as well as pictures taken with Mr. X. As it turned out, there were at least two sets of photographers as well as a sound man, and while it wasn't "60 Minutes," there was quite a lot of confusion (the two sets of photographers each required precious seconds to straighten things out). I had to hand it to everyone — they were not only extraordinarily skilled and well organized, but also polite and considerate. Then, he hoped I wouldn't mind but there was a young man who was studying communication who had scored over 600 on an examination, which I was told put him 200 points above the average. This young man would be joining us for lunch. I didn't see how we were going to eat anything, much less discuss issues of mutual interest. In situations such as these, one soon learns to sit back, relax, and let the individual in charge orchestrate everything. The lunch was excellent, as I knew it would be — hardly leisurely, but still very good.

All the interviews and the conversation with the student went off as scheduled. The difficulties came when I had to explain to the Japanese publisher that I had no control over my own book — that once I had written a book and handed it in to my publisher, the book was marketed by either my publisher or my agent. Simply being first in line did not guarantee anything. I had to try to make it clear that I was tied into an already existing set of relationships with attached obligations and that there were other people who made these decisions. This required some explaining, and I then spent considerable time trying to work out a method for the publisher to get a hearing with my agent. This is sometimes virtually impossible because each publisher and each agent in the United States has its own representative in Japan. Thus an author is in their hands, too.

We did finish on time — pretty much to everyone's satisfaction, I believe. My friend departed on schedule as the cameramen were putting away their equipment and the sound man was rolling up his wires and disconnecting his microphones. The student drove me back to my hotel on schedule, a little after 3 P.M.

The pattern is not too different from schedules for authors in the United States. The difference is that in Japan the tightly scheduled monochronic pattern is applied to foreigners who are not well enough integrated into the Japanese system to be able to do things in a more leisurely manner, and where emphasis is on developing a good working relationship.

All cultures with high technologies seem to incorporate both polychronic as well as monochronic functions. The point is that each does it in its own way. The Japanese are polychronic when looking and working inward, toward themselves. When dealing with the outside world, they have adopted the dominant time system which characterizes that world. That is, they shift to the monochronic mode and, characteristically, since these are technical matters, they outshine us. . . .

## Concepts and Questions for Chapter 5

1. What does Andersen mean when he writes that "the primary level of culture is communicated implicitly, without awareness, by primarily nonverbal means"?

2. Do you agree with Andersen that two of the most fundamental nonverbal differences in intercultural communication involve space and time? From your experiences what two nonverbal areas have you found most troublesome when interacting with people from different cultures?

3. From your personal experiences can you think of different ways that people in various cultures greet, show emotion, and beckon?

4. Do you believe that intercultural communication problems are more serious when they involve nonverbal communication or verbal communication?

5. In what ways does the concept of individualism influence nonverbal communication between cultures?

6. According to McDaniel, why is it useful to study a culture by means of cultural "themes"?

7. How does Confucian-based collectivism help control Japanese nonverbal communication patterns?

8. Can you think of any American cultural themes that might influence how Americans use nonverbal communication?

9. How might cultural differences in time conceptualization lead to intercultural problems?

10. Can you think of instances where your personal space was "invaded" by someone from another culture?

11. Dolphin notes that "Other than culture, age, and sex, the interaction distance between two individuals can be affected by a host of other variables: relationship between the two, the environment of the transactions, attitudinal differences, occupation and/or status, the language used, etc." Can you think of any other variables not mentioned by Dolphin?

12. Which one of the various types of nonverbal behaviors discussed in this chapter do you think is most important to the student of intercultural communication?

13. How have you seen Hall's concept of monochronic time reflected in your culture?

14. Hall notes that "both M-time and P-time systems have strengths as well as weaknesses." What are some of these strengths and weaknesses?

# 6

## Cultural Contexts: The Influence of the Setting

All human interaction takes place within a social setting or environment that impacts the communication event. Whether you are in a classroom, dance hall, doctor's office, business meeting, or church, the setting will influence how you send and receive messages. The way you dress, what you talk about, who you talk to, and even the volume of that talk are in some way controlled by the context in which you find yourself. We call this the social context because the setting is never neutral; it influences how the participants behave. We have all learned appropriate patterns of communicative behavior for the various social contexts in which we normally find ourselves. But, as with other aspects of intercultural communication, the patterns of behavior appropriate to various social contexts are culturally diverse. When we find ourselves in an unfamiliar context without an internalized set of rules to govern our behavior or when we are interacting with someone who has internalized a different set of rules, communication problems often arise. This chapter is about those problems and the resolution of those problems.

We begin with the business setting. The growth of international business during the last thirty years has been startling. Overseas transactions that generated millions of dollars annually just a few decades ago are now multibillion-dollar operations. Furthermore, the international business community has become multinational, with culturally diverse organizational units. In fact, the study of the multinational organization has now become a viable topic within the fields of intercultural and organizational communication. Successful people functioning in international business and world markets learn about approaches to business practices that are different from their own.

Because of this economic growth and the internationalization of business, people no longer have the luxury of dealing exclusively with those who possess the same cultural background and experiences. One's associates, clients, subordinates, and even supervisors are frequently from different countries and cultures. Such aspects of business life as gift giving, methods of negotiation, decision making, policy formulation, marketing techniques, management structure, human resource management, and patterns of communication are now subject to culturally diverse influences.

While the globalization of business was taking place, changes also were occurring within the United States; the country was becoming a more pluralistic, multicultural society. As a result, the cultural diversity of the U.S. population increased, and we now often find ourselves engaged in intercultural communication in a variety of communication contexts. The workplace, schools, social service agencies, and health services, among others, are contexts that have become especially intercultural. Consequently, intercultural interaction within the United States continues to increase.

As we have indicated, the readings in this chapter deal with cultural diversity in communication contexts. We focus on a combination of international and domestic settings in which knowledge and appreciation of cultural diversity are important if successful intercultural communication is to occur.

We begin with essays that involve a setting that is truly international – the business setting. It is obvious that all business activities encompass many forms of communication, and those forms reflect the attitudes, values, and communication patterns unique to each culture. Hence, our first four essays examine how culture touches and alters organizational communication, managerial styles, negotiations strategies, and interpersonal relations.

Our first selection, "Cultural Influences on Communication in Multinational Organizations: The Maquiladora," by Edwin R. McDaniel and Larry A. Samovar, examines some of the problems organizations face when managers and workers are confronted with an array of culturally diverse customs, traditions, values, societal norms, and communication styles. In this instance the members of the organization are from Mexico, Japan, and the United States, and the specific setting is Mexican maquiladoras. Maquiladoras are plants or factories that are used to assemble products that are shipped from another nation. The finished product is then returned to the country of origin for distribution, marketing, and sales. While examining a number of maquiladoras in Mexico, McDaniel and Samovar were able to isolate seven cultural characteristics that had the potential to impact communication in these, or any, multinational workplace: (1) the social unit, (2) organizational loyalty, (3) authority structures and basis, (4) negotiations, decisions, and conflict, (5) status, formality, and appearance, (6) spatial, temporal, and contextual considerations, and (7) nonverbal communication. Through use of a table, the authors summarize and compare the three cultures in question on all seven communication dimensions.

From the title of Robert A. Friday's article, "Contrasts in Discussion Behaviors of German and American Managers," it is clear what the author is trying to explain to us. Friday traces cultural expectations of both German and American managers across a number of dimensions, pointing out the differences and how they can lead to misunderstandings and ineffective communication. Specifically, he is concerned with cultural differences as they relate to (1) the perception of business, (2) interpersonal credibility, (3) assertiveness and fair play, (4) problem solving, and (5) education and training. Friday ends his essay by offering some suggestions that he believes will increase cultural understanding when German and American managers share a common environment.

We have already made the point that the phrase "global economy" simply means that the business arena is teeming with people from all over the world. An outgrowth of this truism is that we now sit at the conference table and negotiate business and sales contracts with people from cultures different from our own. How to negotiate effectively in this international environment is the subject of our next essay. Lisa A. Stefani, Larry A. Samovar, and Susan A. Hellweg lead us through an investigation of cultural diversity in negotiating behavior. In "Culture and Its Impact on Negotiation," they highlight negotiation styles used by the American, French, German, Mexican, African, Japanese, Chinese, Brazilian, and Arabic Middle East cultures. To assist us in understanding variations in these styles they (1) explain some of the characteristics of North American negotiating practices, (2) explain how various cultures select their negotiators – including their consideration of women, (3) discuss the role of cultural values in business negotiations, (4) compare decision-solving strategies, and (5) offer some specific ideas for improving cross-cultural negotiations.

Our final business-oriented essay focuses on a series of cultures that are often referred to as the "Five Asian Dragons" (Hong Kong, Japan, Singapore, South Korea, and Taiwan). In "The Five Asian Dragons: Management Behaviors and Organizational Communication," Guo-Ming Chen and Jensen Chung maintain that to effectively communicate with people from these cultures it is crucial to have an appreciation of the role of Confucianism in interpersonal communication. According to Chen and Chung, this world view, which emphasizes hierarchical relationships, family systems, benevolence, and education, helps explain the manner in which these five cultures engage in managerial behaviors and organizational communication.

The next article, "The Group: A Japanese Context" concentrates on the specific setting of group communication. That is to say, how do cultures perceive and behave in small groups? Dolores and Robert Cathcart examine the Japanese concept of "group" to answer this question. The assumption behind their research is a simple one — a person's experience with groups changes from culture to culture, and so it follows that each culture might well bring a different way of acting to a group situation. The Cathcarts describe relevant Japanese history and analyze its influence in shaping modern Japanese culture as a basis for investigating the role of groups as the significant context for communication in Japan.

A multicultural society impacts strongly on the health care setting because cultural beliefs about health and disease are very diverse. Such a simple question as "How do you catch a cold?" can elicit a variety of answers ranging from standing in a draft to being the victim of a supernatural spell, depending upon one's cultural background. In her article, "Negotiating Cultural Understanding in Health Care Communication," Patricia Geist examines the complex and dynamic features of communication in a health care context. She begins by developing the link between culture, health, and communication and the expansion of cultural sensitivity in the health care context. She then describes cultural differences in perceptions, treatment practices, and relationships. As she notes, "All cultures have beliefs about health and illness that have been passed down from generation to generation." The difference between the belief system of the Western biomedical model and that of other cultures can result in inappropriate assessment or complications in treatment and communication in the provider-patient relationship. Geist concludes her article with suggestions for culturally sensitive health care.

Classrooms represent yet another setting where the sway of culture must be taken into consideration. Lisa A. Stefani takes this same position in an essay titled "The Influence of Culture on Classroom Communication." She bases her investigation on the simple premise that increased immigration, coupled with regional shifts in demographics, has created what is now called the "multicultural classroom." To help us understand that classroom Stefani examines (1) the need to assess acculturation levels, (2) differences in learning, relational, and cognitive styles, (3) the manner in which cultures differ with regard to motivation and the setting of educational goals, (4) the problems associated with language diversity, and (5) cultural differences regarding gender norms in the classroom.

# Cultural Influences on Communication in Multinational Organizations: The Maquiladora

EDWIN R. McDANIEL
LARRY A. SAMOVAR

Modern technological advances have significantly reduced the spatial and temporal barriers previously constraining transnational intercourse. Global communication links, coupled with the capability to effect rapid, efficient movement of goods on a worldwide scale, have created a growing international economic interdependency among nations. Geographical boundaries are no longer a concern to international commerce (Reich, 1991).

Continued movement toward an economic global village has produced a dramatic increase in the number of multinational corporations. This dynamic growth is exemplified by the *maquiladora,* or twin plant, industry along the border between the United States and Mexico. Maquiladoras are most commonly used to assemble products from materials shipped from another nation. The completed product is then returned to the country of origin for sales distribution, thereby eliminating many associated duties and tariffs (Lindsley & Braithwaite, 1994).

Although there were only twelve factories in 1965, there are now over 2,000 maquiladoras operating along the U.S.-Mexican border. Most of these firms are American-owned, but many investors come from other nations, such as Japan, South Korea, Taiwan, France, Germany, and Canada. The plants assemble a multiplicity of products, including automotive parts, electronics, garments, furniture, and pharmaceuticals. Employing a half million Mexican workers, the maquiladora industry accounted for 38.9 percent of Mexico's exports during the first quarter of 1993, surpassing domestic exports (Forero, 1993; Kraul, 1991; Lindquist, 1994; Peak, 1993; San Diego Business Journal, 1990; "Business Briefing," 1993).

Maquiladora managers and workers are confronted with an array of diverse customs, traditions, values, societal norms, and communication styles. The successful manager must be knowledgeable of the differences in cultural conventions and business protocols at national, regional, and local levels. Effective managers should also be cognizant of, and adept at, the communication rules governing each culture represented in their workforce (Samovar & Porter, 1991).

Using this premise, this essay examines cultural traits that can, and do, influence communication in a multinational organization. Employing the matrix from Table 1, we contrast selected cultural patterns, or values, from the United States, Japan, and Mexico and discuss their potential impact on communication within a multinational organization. Primary data were obtained from unobtrusive observations and interviews we conducted during a series of visits to two Japanese-owned maquiladoras in the San Diego–Tijuana area.

## Theoretical Aspects

In both theory and actuality, cultures vary in their expression of language, nonverbal behavior, perception of space and time, values, and societal norms. Commencing at birth, individuals are conditioned to exhibit behavioral standards appropriate to specific situational contexts. This enculturation process enables peoples of the same culture to successfully interact and achieve varying degrees of communication competency, both verbally and nonverbally (Kim, 1988).

**Table 1** Cultural Traits Influencing Communication in a Multinational Environment

| Trait | United States | Japan | Mexico |
|---|---|---|---|
| Social unit | Individual | Group | Family |
| Locus of organizational loyalty | Self | Group/organization | Superior/organization |
| Authority structure | Egalitarian | Hierarchical | Hierarchical |
| Basis for authority | Competence | Seniority | Trust |
| Style of negotiation | Direct | Indirect | Indirect |
| Decision making | Individualistic | Consensus | Authoritarian |
| Role of conflict/competition | Seeks | Avoids | Avoids |
| Empathy for others (emotion) | Low | High | High |
| Role of personal relations | Beneficial | Essential | Essential |
| Basis for status | Money/competence | Title/position | Title/position |
| Role of formality | Medium/low | High | High |
| Importance of appearance | Medium | High | High |
| Sense of history | Low | High | High |
| Spatial arrangements | Individual | Collective | Collective |
| Time structure | Monochronic | Polychronic | Polychronic |
| Importance of time | High | High/low* | Low |
| Type culture | Low context | High context | High context |
| Proxemics | Near | Far | Close |
| Tactility | Low | Very low | High |

*High in business; low in personal matters.

When individuals leave the familiar surroundings of their own social groups and enter another culture, the rules governing behavior and communication frequently undergo comprehensive alteration (Almaney, 1974). To function effectively in a different culture, a person must learn the social and communication patterns applicable to the host environment. To be truly productive, this learning process, or acculturation, may also require that some native habits, acquired either consciously or subconsciously, be recognized and suppressed (Kim, 1988).

In a multinational commercial environment, cultural and linguistic differences play a critical role in the failure or success of each endeavor (Hall &

Hall, 1990). This is especially true in maquiladoras, where studies have demonstrated that language and cultural diversity represent the greatest obstacles to productive operations (Boysen, Sasaki, Shields, & Nalven, 1987; Pena, 1983). This potential impediment is even more salient within a Japanese-owned maquiladora, which forms a confluence of three distinct cultures – U.S., Japanese, and Mexican. The Japanese own the business, which uses U.S. materials; the product is assembled in Mexico and shipped back to the United States. In this setting, both the native language and cultural patterns of each nation vary markedly from those of the other two nations. The confluence presents considerable opportunity for misunderstandings and conflict, unless the cultural variances are recognized and compensated for.

## Practical Application

Table 1 provides a comparison of specific U.S., Japanese, and Mexican cultural characteristics that have the potential to adversely impact intercultural communication. Using the table as a guide, the remainder of this essay uses a maquiladora as a model to demonstrate how culturally based behaviors and attitudes can impact communication in a multinational organization.

## Social Unit

The basic social unit of a culture helps shape an individual's self-perception and his or her view of others in familiar, societal, and work-related interactions. In the United States, individualism is highly prized, and individual rights are zealously protected. In contrast, the Japanese emphasize group affiliation over all other forms of social organization (Caudill, 1973). Japanese workers consider their place of employment as part of an extended family (Hall & Hall, 1990), creating a mutual dependency between employee and employer. In Mexican society, the actual family, which includes members of the extended family, constitutes the most important social component (Diaz-Guerrero, 1967) and takes precedence over work considerations.

These three dissimilar attitudes can precipitate considerable misunderstanding when consolidated in the same locale, such as a maquiladora. During one interview, for example, a Japanese supervisor complained that Mexican workers would absent themselves from work to take care of family matters.

This is an excellent illustration of how varying cultural values and social realities can affect communication between supervisor and worker. For Japanese maquiladora managers, work-group relations supersede even personal affairs. Mexican workers, however, place family considerations above work-related issues. The Mexican's perspective is dictated, in part, by the lack of an adequate social-support infrastructure. Utilities, transportation, health care, communications, and many social systems taken for granted in the United States and Japan are not available to the Mexican worker. One effect of this situation is exemplified by the statement "Absenteeism is often caused by circumstances rather than intention" (deForest, 1991, p. 39). This lack of social services creates stronger familial interdependency in the Mexican culture than exists in either Japan or the United States.

Americans' traditional insistence on personal independence can create friction between U.S. and Japanese workers. Japanese managers often equate American individualism with a lack of commitment, or team effort. For example, they have difficulty comprehending the American desire for individual bonuses, as opposed to group rewards ("Labor Letter," 1991).

## Organizational Loyalty

Factors that coalesce to form a culture's basic social unit also influence and reflect an individual's locus of organizational loyalty. Self-interest and well-being supersede work-group or company considerations in the United States. Personal concerns are constantly uppermost in the mind of the American workers. Their strong sense of individualism conflicts with the Japanese ideal of corporate loyalty.

For a Mexican, the corporation is simply a place where work is performed in order to acquire the means for supporting one's family (Peak, 1993). Within an organization, Mexican workers and their supervisors form bonds of loyalty predicated on an affirmation of trust between the overseer and subordinate. This trust is an outgrowth of the Mexican's strong sense of familial affiliation, which creates a desire for a paternalistic structure (Morris & Pavett, 1992; Ruch, 1989).

In contrast, the Japanese place immense importance on the work group. This is illustrated by the many efforts employed to encourage organizational solidarity and similitude. For example, work clothing is used to manifest group affiliation in Japanese manufacturing corporations. Assembly line workers normally wear identical coveralls or smocks to promote corporate identity. Japanese executives don identical coveralls or smocks when leaving their offices to enter a production area. One Japanese maquiladora we visited had established a similar policy at its Mexican facility. Every assembly line worker wore a colored, short-sleeved smock. The corporation president was even observed replacing his suit coat with a smock before visiting the assembly line.

There is considerable potential for miscommunication caused by these differing loci of organizational loyalty. Japanese managers complain that Americans' frequent job changes demonstrate a lack of corporate loyalty, but the Americans believe they must consider themselves first, then the organization. The Japanese also cite the high turnover rate among Mexican maquiladora workers as a lack of commitment, but a Mexican's primary sense of responsibility is to familial obligations. Consequently, if an opportunity arises to enhance support to the family, a Mexican worker will readily change jobs.

## Authority Structures and Basis

Americans' penchant for individualism is further reflected in the egalitarianism of the United States. All Americans are raised to believe that their opinions or ideas possess an equality of merit with anyone else's. Upward advancement within the U.S. labor force is, for the most part, based on individual competence and drive. Talented employees are often promoted ahead of their less capable seniors. This has created a nation of highly competitive, ambitious workers, who have little difficulty in openly disagreeing with their superiors. This world view, focusing on the individual and his or her personal achievements, can produce conflict when Americans interact with people enculturated with differing concepts of authority.

In both Japan and Mexico, authority is strongly hierarchical. Japanese workers advance to their level of competency by a system of seniority. Juniors are rarely promoted ahead of their seniors, and senior employees normally serve as mentors to junior workers.

In Mexico, authority is effectuated through trust. A Mexican manager secures the allegiance of his subordinates through both professional and social interaction, while concomitantly manifesting an authoritarian persona. In effect, the Mexican authority figure must earn the respect and trust of subordinates (Ruch, 1989).

When U.S., Japanese, and Mexican workers are all located within a single organization, these differ-

ing concepts of empowerment can create considerable communication difficulties. An American worker, for example, is seldom reluctant to express an honest, forthright opinion. The Japanese, on the other hand, place considerable emphasis on indirectness in their communication. A direct, emphatic "no" is unthinkable (Hall & Hall, 1990). Similarly, Mexican workers will endeavor to provide only positive information, even to the extent of suppressing negative data (Condon, 1985; Cohen, 1991; Ruch, 1989).

## Negotiations, Decisions, and Conflict

The authority structure of a nation can also be reflected in its negotiation style. The United States is widely known for a direct, logical, expedient, and competitive approach to business negotiations. The Japanese prefer an indirect process, where conflict is avoided and formal negotiations serve as a forum to officially acknowledge previously arranged agreements. Mexicans take a similar indirect approach and tend to base their business transactions on personal relations. Contractual details are frequently worked out informally (Weiss & Stripp, 1984).

Cultural variation in the decision-making process is another arena of potential discord. Japanese managers must seek consensual agreement prior to implementing new procedures or changing extant policies (Lange, 1982). Mexicans take an autocratic approach when making and implementing decisions. Senior managers are expected to issue policy guidance, and subordinates seldom question this authority, even when directives are known to be incorrect (Kras, 1989; Ruch, 1989). U.S. managers, however, are delegated authority appropriate to their level of responsibility and then left to their own judgments.

These three contrasting decision-making processes can create considerable difficulties for a multinational corporation if unrecognized and left unattended. To avoid potential pitfalls, one Japanese maquiladora had adopted the American and Mexican modes of decision making at the respective facilities in the United States and Mexico. In an aside, the Japanese manager of the Tijuana operation professed to prefer the Mexican system over the Japanese method, indicating it required less time than the complex consensus building necessary in Japan.

In business transactions, both Japanese and Mexicans attempt to avoid direct confrontation and place considerable emphasis and reliance on intuitive judgements. This often results in close personal relationships and empathic affiliation among business associates (Weiss & Stripp, 1984). As a result, interpersonal relations can be a significant factor in commercial matters.

American managers, however, are imbued with the cultural traits of individualism, directness, and a historically competitive spirit. Consequently, they rely strongly on logic and objective reality in conducting commercial transactions. Personal and emotional affairs are relegated to a distinctly subordinate position, exerting little or no influence on work-related matters. While personal relations may be beneficial, ability is the ultimate criterion.

These contrasting cultural values provide a ripe medium for intercultural communication conflict. To avoid incidents of conflict, a manager must be aware of how the cultural values shape and influence communicative practice.

## Status, Formality, and Appearance

Status is frequently a fundamental value in cultures, differing only in method of acquisition and mode of expression. The egalitarian culture traits in the United States emphasize individual ability. The most competent person will, in theory, reap the greatest rewards. This frequently results in status being equated to ostentatious displays of material possessions, with little regard for educational achievements or social contributions. The inflated compensation and extensive perks demanded, and received, by CEOs and professional athletes in the United States ably demonstrate this propensity.

Status also plays a significant role in the hierarchical societies of Japan and Mexico (Weiss & Stripp, 1984; Jarvis, 1990; Kras, 1989). Japanese employees attach great importance to the reputation, and concomitant social status, of their company, which is an extension of the group-affiliation syndrome. Within the company or group, however, a façade of equality is promoted. As previously discussed, uniforms are used to promote loyalty and communicate solidarity.

In the Mexican culture, status permeates every facet of organizational life. Conflict created by varying methods of communicating status is illustrated by events that transpired at one of the maquiladoras. Mexican assembly line workers wanted to wear the company-provided smocks because they protected personal clothing. Mexican managers, in contrast, thought wearing the smocks eroded recognition of their status. In this instance, the Mexican penchant for symbols to differentiate and communicate status conflicted with the Japanese effort to promote corporate solidarity and loyalty by fostering a perception of group affiliation.

During subsequent visits to this maquiladora, conducted over a two-year period, we noticed that different-colored smocks began to appear. One individual on each assembly line would be wearing a distinctive tan smock, while everyone else remained in blue. An informant indicated the tan smocks had been instituted to designate the senior technician on each assembly line. The original purpose had been to make the technician more easily recognizable when questions arose. The new colored smocks, however, had quickly become a source of hierarchical distinction and status differentiation among the Mexican assembly line workers. Subsequently, brown smocks were instituted to distinguish supervisors, who were responsible for two or three assembly lines. The Japanese and Mexican managers, however, continued to wear the blue smocks. This organizational evolution represents senior management's recognition of differing cultural values and partial realignment.

Variation in assignment of parking spaces at a maquiladora offered another example of divergent attitudes toward status. On the U.S. side, only four spaces were designated, each simply marked "Reserved." These were for the president and the three vice-presidents. The Mexican facility had a much smaller parking lot, and most employees either rode public transportation or walked to work. The parking lot, however, had designated spaces for everyone from the plant manager downward through middle management. An informant indicated that the Mexican managers had demanded this perk, which can be seen as a means of communicating their position. This attests to the importance of status in the Mexican culture and the potential for influencing employee relations in a multicultural locale.

Formality is closely aligned with status for the three cultures. Conditioned by societal values of equality and individualism, Americans evince an outward air of informality by using first names, casual dress, and eschewing ceremony. The hierarchical societies of Japan and Mexico, influenced by their strong sense of history, prize formality. This extends to business protocol, etiquette, interactions with subordinates, and personal appearance.

To accommodate American workers, one maquiladora had designated Friday as a casual dress day for the U.S. facility. The Americans quickly adopted this weekly routine. During repeated visits over a two-year-period, however, the Japanese were always observed attired in coat and tie, even on Fridays.

## Spatial, Temporal, and Contextual Considerations

**Space.** "Space is organized differently in each culture," according to Hall (1990, p. 165). This is reflected in how spatial arrangements in the workplace differ between cultures. Japanese like large, open areas that facilitate communication by allowing free and rapid exchange of data between all employees, including juniors and seniors. Mexicans also prefer similar office arrangements (Ruch, 1989). In contrast, American business organizations are often characterized by many separate offices, which can actually encumber the communication process (Hirokawa, 1987).

One of the maquiladoras studied had adopted the Japanese architectural arrangement for its offices. On the American side, only the president and vice-presidents had private offices; at the Mexican plant, the president, vice-president, and one or two Mexican managers enjoyed private spaces. At both facilities, all other employees occupied desks in a large open area. At this particular maquiladora, the arrangement had successfully endured since the company's establishment three years earlier.

An older Japanese maquiladora, however, had not experienced the same success. The Americans' office area, once spacious and unobstructed, had been partitioned with room dividers into a series of small, rabbit-warren-like cubicles, each providing a façade of individual privacy. Apparently, the openness of the original arrangement had failed to satisfy the American employee's need for perceptual isolation.

**Time.** How a culture structures and manages time has a salient influence on intercultural communication. According to Hall and Hall (1990, p. 23), "Time is a basic system of both communication and organization." A multinational manager must be aware of the varying concepts of time that exist among workers.

The Japanese treat time situationally. In interpersonal relations, they are polychronic, but they take a monchronic approach when dealing with foreigners or technology (Hall & Hall, 1990). The necessity to build a consensus before arriving at a decision can take days, weeks, or months (Hall, 1988). But once the decision is made, they are quick to act.

Mexicans also perceive time polychronically (Ruch, 1989; Weiss & Stripp, 1984). Interpersonal considerations take precedence over schedules and calendars, frequently delaying appointments and extending delivery dates. Punctuality for social events is extremely elastic. In effect, time is a secondary consideration for Mexicans.

Americans, on the other hand, are highly monochronic and place considerable importance on promptness and rigid adherence to specific itineraries. Decisions are usually made quickly, often with only a minimum of information. Having to wait for an appointment is frequently perceived as a snub. Interruptions during negotiations or delays in production delivery dates usually create considerable distress. For Americans, time is an extremely important aspect of life.

**Contextual Settings.** The influence of context is how a culture adapts communication processes to various environmental circumstances. Context can facilitate or constrain communication (Samovar & Porter, 1991). In high-context cultures, such as Japan and Mexico, considerable reliance is placed on implicit understanding. The Japanese eschew directness and depend on subtle suggestion or intuitive communication skills to convey their message. Similarly, Mexicans place considerable reliance on "body language and emotional cues" (Weiss & Stripp, 1984, p. 33). In a low-context culture, like the United States, communication competency is based on verbal skills; messages are normally direct and explicit.

Managers must be cognizant of the possible variances when supervising personnel from both high- and low-context cultures. Group and personal communication practices might require different approaches with members from each culture. Training programs and task instructions may have to be modified to accommodate the multicultural representation.

## Nonverbal Communication

Nonverbal cues vary between cultures and can assume different significance or meanings. A complimentary or benign cue in one culture may possess a decidedly offensive connotation in another. Two particularly important nonverbal aspects of cross-cultural communication are personal distance and acceptance of touch.

The distance established between people for conversational purposes will vary with situational context and degree of intimacy between the individuals, depending upon their culture. In Mexico — and Latin America in general — the personal interaction distance is significantly less than in the United States (Hall, 1990), and the Japanese expect even greater spatial separation between individuals (Barnlund, 1989).

This norm was exemplified in one maquiladora's conference rooms. At the Mexican plant, the room was laid out and furnished in the traditional Japanese fashion. Individual chairs were arranged around a low table, with participants sitting opposite each other. The distance across the table was such that an American and a Mexican were noted perched on the front edge of their chairs and leaning forward to conduct conversations. In contrast, the Japanese appeared quite at ease in this environment and were noted sitting back comfortably in their seats.

Tactile interaction also plays a role in cross-cultural communication. The Japanese, for example, actively avoid public displays of physical expressiveness (Barnlund, 1989; Malandro & Barker, 1983). The United States is considered a noncontact culture but much less so than the Japanese. American managers will shake hands with new acquaintances and, depending on locale, may engage in a light back or shoulder slap with previously known colleagues. Conversely, Mexicans are usually much more tactile. They expect to shake hands with everyone at every meeting and will exchange embraces (*abrazo*) with well-known individuals (Ruch, 1989). Sensitivity to these variations can be critical in opening and establishing effective communication channels.

## Comments

The preceding paragraphs have addressed numerous cultural traits that can affect communication in a multicultural enterprise, such as a maquiladora. The characteristics discussed represent only a portion of the number that must be considered before achieving intercultural communication competency. There are many additional cultural patterns and norms that can impact organizational and individual communication styles.

Ethics, style of argument, emotional sensitivity and expression, assumption of responsibility, type of rewards and punishments, and issues of empowerment are just some of the additional cultural features that can influence workplace communication. The most important point to understand is that managers for international businesses and transnational corporations must possess an awareness of, and appreciation for, cultural variation within their labor force. Managers can no longer rely solely on technical, statistical, and administrative expertise. They must recognize the difficulties inherent in cross-cultural communication and implement measures to prevent or ameliorate problems arising from these obstacles.

# References

Almaney, A. (1974). Intercultural communication and the MNC executive. *The Columbia Journal of World Business, 9*(4), 23–28.

Barnlund, D. C. (1989). *Communicative Styles of Japanese and Americans: Images and Realities.* Belmont, Calif.: Wadsworth.

Boysen, H., Sasaki, Y., Shields, M., and Nalven, J. (1987). "The Maquiladora Program from the United States and Japanese Perspective." In P. Ganster (Ed.), *The Maquiladora Program in Trinational Perspective: Mexico, Japan, and the United States,* 89–110. San Diego, Calif.: Institute for Regional Studies of the Californias, San Diego State University, Border Issues series, 2 (Panel Discussion).

"Business Briefing: Nation and World." (1993). *The San Diego Union-Tribune,* June 3, C-1.

Caudill, W. A. (1973). General culture: The influence of social structure and culture on human behavior in modern Japan. *The Journal of Nervous and Mental Disease, 157*(4), 240–257.

Condon, J. C. (1985). *Good Neighbors: Communicating with the Mexicans.* Yarmouth, Maine: Intercultural Press.

Cohen, R. (1991). *Negotiating Across Cultures: Communication Obstacles in International Diplomacy.* Washington, D.C.: United States Institute of Peace Press.

deForest, M. E. (1991). When in Mexico . . . Cultural awareness is key to productivity in maquiladora plants. *Business Mexico, 1*(5), 38–40.

Diaz-Guerrero, R. (1967). *Psychology of the Mexican: Culture and Personality.* Austin: University of Texas Press.

Forero, J. (1993). "Many Face Harsh Life in Shacks." *The San Diego Union-Tribune,* November 7, A-1.

Hall, E. T. (1988). "The Hidden Dimensions of Time and Space in Today's World." In F. Poyatos (Ed.), *Cross-cultural Perspectives in Nonverbal Communication,* 145–152. Lewiston, N.Y.: C. J. Hogrefe.

Hall, E. T. (1990). *The Silent Language.* New York: Anchor. (Original work published 1959)

Hall, E. T., and Hall, M. R. (1990). *Hidden Differences: Doing Business with the Japanese.* Garden City, N.Y.: Anchor. (Original work published 1987)

Hirokawa, R. Y. (1987). "Communication Within the Japanese Business Organization." In D. L. Kincaid (Ed.), *Communication Theory: Eastern and Western Perspectives,* 137–149. San Diego: Academic Press.

Jarvis, S. S. (1990). "Preparing Employees to Work South of the Border." *Personnel,* June, 59–63.

Kim, Y. Y. (1988). *Communication and Cross-cultural Adaptation: An Integrative Theory* (Intercommunication Series). Philadelphia: Multilingual Matters.

Kras, E. S. (1989). *Management in Two Cultures: Bridging the Gap Between U.S. and Mexican Managers.* Yarmouth, Maine: Intercultural Press.

Kraul, C. (1991). "Pact Nothing to Fear, Maquiladoras are Told." *Los Angeles Times,* February 19, D2A, D2B.

"Labor Letter." (1991). *Wall Street Journal,* May 21, A1.

Lange, R. (1982). "Participative Management as a Reflection of Cultural Contingencies: A Need to Reevaluate our Ethics." In S. M. Lee and G. Schwendiman (Eds.), *Japanese Management: Cultural and Environmental Considerations,* 117–134. New York: Praeger.

Lindquist, D. (1994). "Maquilas Lose Some Tax Breaks." *The San Diego Union-Tribune,* April 30, C1.

Lindsley, S. L., and Braithwaite, C. A. (1994). *"You Should 'Wear a Mask'": Cultural and Intercultural Communication in Maquiladoras.* Paper presented at the annual meeting of the Western States Communication Association Convention, Portland, Oregon.

Malandro, L. A., and Barker, L. L. (1983). *Nonverbal Communication.* Menlo Park, Calif.: Addison-Wesley.

Morris, T., and Pavett, C. M. (1992). Management style and productivity in two cultures. *Journal of International Business Studies, 23*(1), 169–179.

Peak, M. H. (1993). "Maquiladoras: Where Quality is a Way of Life." *Management Review,* March, 19–23.

Pena, D. G. (1983). *The Class Politics of Abstract Labor: Organizational Forms and Industrial Relations in the Mexican Maquiladoras.* Ph.D. dissertation, University of Texas at Austin.

Reich, R. B. (1991). *The Work of Nations: Preparing Ourselves for 21st Century Capitalism.* New York: Alfred A. Knopf.

Ruch, W. V. (1989). *International Handbook of Corporate Communication.* Jefferson, N.C.: McFarland.

Samovar, L. A., and Porter, R. E. (1991). *Communication Between Cultures.* Belmont, Calif.: Wadsworth.

San Diego Business Journal. (1990). *Maquiladoras 1990: A Guide to Binational Manufacturing in the San Diego–Tijuana, Mexico Area.* San Diego: San Diego Business Journal.

Weiss, S. E., and Stripp, W. (1984). *Negotiating with Foreign Business Persons: An Introduction for Americans with Propositions on Six Cultures.* Business Negotiations Across Cultures, Working Paper No. 1. Unpublished manuscript, New York University, Graduate School of Business Administration.

# Contrasts in Discussion Behaviors of German and American Managers

ROBERT A. FRIDAY

## American Managers' Expectation

### Business Is Impersonal

In any business environment, discussion between colleagues must accomplish the vital function of exchanging information that is needed for the solution of problems. In American business, such discussions are usually impersonal.[1] Traditionally the facts have spoken for themselves in America. "When facts are disputed, the argument must be suspended until the facts are settled. Not until then may it be resumed, for all true argument is about the meaning of established or admitted facts" (Weaver, 1953) in the rationalistic view. Much of post-WWII American business decision making has been based on the quantitative MBA approach which focuses on factual data and its relationship to the ultimate fact of profit or loss, writing strategy plans, and top-down direction. After all of the facts are in, the CEO is often responsible for making the intuitive leap and providing leadership. The power and authority of the CEO has prevailed in the past 40 years, with no predicted change in view (Bleicher & Paul, 1986, p. 10 - 11). Through competition and contact with West Germany and Japan, the more personal approach is beginning to enter some lower level decision-making practices (Peters & Waterman, 1982, pp. 35 - 118).

Another reason for the impersonal nature of American business is that many American managers do not identify themselves with their corpo-

From *International Journal of Intercultural Relations*, Vol. 13, 1989, pp. 429 - 445. Reprinted by permission of Pergamon Press, Inc., and the author.

rations. When the goals and interests of the corporation match up with those of the American manager, he or she will stay and prosper. However, when the personal agenda of the American manager is not compatible with that of the corporation, he or she is likely to move on to attain his or her objective in a more conducive environment. Most American managers can disassociate themselves from their business identity, at least to the extent that their personal investment in a decision has more to do with their share of the profit rather than their sense of personal worth.

In contrast, "the German salesman's personal credibility is on the line when he sells his product. He spends years cultivating his clients, building long-term relationships based on reliability" (Hall, 1983, p. 67). This tendency on the part of Germans is much like American business in the early part of this century.

The cohesiveness of the employees of most German businesses is evidenced in the narrow salary spread. Whereas in the United States the ratio of lowest paid to highest paid is approximately 1 to 80, in Germany this ratio is 1 to 25 (Hall, 1983, p. 74).

## German Managers' Expectation

### Business Is Not as Impersonal

The corporation for most Germans is closely related to his or her own identity. German managers at Mobay are likely to refer to "Papa Bayer" because they perceive themselves as members of a corporate family which meets most of their needs. In turn, most German managers there, as elsewhere, have made a lifelong commitment to the larger group in both a social and economic sense (Friday & Biro, 1986 - 87). In contrast to the American post-WWII trend is "the German postwar tradition of seeking consensus among a closely knit group of colleagues who have worked together for decades [which] provides a collegial harmony among top managers that is rare in U.S. corporations" (Bleicher & Paul, 1986, p. 12). Our interviews suggested that many German managers may enter a three-year-plus training program with the idea of moving on later to another corporation. This move rarely occurs.

While a three-year training program appears to be excessively long by American standards, one must understand that the longer training program works on several levels that are logical within the German culture. The three or more years of entry level training is a predictable correlation to the German and USA relative values on the Uncertainty Avoidance Index[2] (Hofstede, 1984, p. 122). The longer training period is required to induct the German manager into the more formal decision-making rules, plans, operating procedures, and industry tradition (Cyert & March, 1963, p. 119), all of which focus on the short-run known entities (engineering/reliability of product) rather than the long-run unknown problems (future market demand).

On another level the "strong sense of self as a striving, controlling entity is offset by an equally strong sense of obligation to a *code* of decency" (McClelland, Sturr, Knapp, & Wendt, 1958, p. 252). Induction into a German company with an idealistic system of obligation requires a longer training period than induction into an American company in which the corporate strategy for productivity is acquired in small group and interpersonal interaction.[3] The German manager who moves from one corporation to another for the purpose of advancement is regarded with suspicion partly because of his lack of participation in the corporate tradition, which could prove to be an unstabilizing factor.

Our preliminary interview results suggested uncertainty avoidance (Hofstede, 1984, p. 130) in everyday business relationships, especially the German concern for security. For example, most of the transfer preparation from the German home office to the USA consists of highly detailed explanations of an extensive benefits package. Since the German manager sees a direct relationship between his or her personal security and the prosperity of his or her company, business becomes more personal for him or her. Similarly, Americans who work in employee-owned companies are also seeing a clear relationship between personal security and the prosperity of their company.

## American Managers' Expectation

### Need to Be Liked

The American's need to be liked is a primary aspect of his or her motivation to cooperate or not to cooperate with colleagues. The arousal of this motivation occurs naturally in discussion situations when direct feedback gives the American the desired response which indicates a sense of belongingness or acceptance. The American "envisions the desired responses and is likely to gear his actions accordingly. The characteristic of seeing others as responses is reflected in the emphasis on communication in interaction and in the great value placed on being liked. . . . American's esteem of others is based on their liking him. This requirement makes it difficult for Americans to implement projects which require an 'unpopular' phase" (Stewart, 1972, p. 58).

For Americans, the almost immediate and informal use of a colleague's first name is a recognition that each likes the other. While such informality is common among American business personnel, this custom should probably be avoided with Germans. "It takes a long time to get on a first-name basis with a German; if you rush the process, you may be perceived as overly familiar and rude. . . . Germans are very conscious of their status and insist on proper forms of address. Germans are bewildered by the American custom of addressing a new acquaintance by his first name and are even more startled by our custom of addressing a superior by first name" (Hall, 1983, p. 57–58). When such matters of decorum are overlooked during critical discussions, an "unpopular phase" may develop.

The need to be liked is culturally induced at an early age and continued throughout life through regular participation in group activities.

*They [Americans] are not brought up on sentiments of obligation to others as the Germans are, but from kindergarten on they regularly participate in many more extracurricular functions of a group nature. In fact, by far the most impressive result . . . is the low number of group activities listed by the Germans (about 1, on the average) as compared with the Americans (about 5, on the average). In these activities the*

*American student must learn a good deal more about getting along with other people and doing things cooperatively, if these clubs are to function at all (McClelland et al., 1958, p. 250).*

This cultural orientation in relation to group participation will be revisited later in the closing discussion on "learning styles, training, instruction, and problem solving."

## German Managers' Expectation

### Need to Be Credible

The German counterpart to the American need to be liked is the need to establish one's credibility and position in the hierarchy. The contrast between American informality and mobility and German formality and class structure is a reflection of the difference between these two needs. In the absence of a long historical tradition, Americans have developed a society in which friendships and residence change often, family histories (reputations) are unknown, and, therefore, acceptance of what one is doing in the present and plans to do in the future is a great part of one's identity. In order to maintain this mobility of place and relationships, Americans rely on reducing barriers to acceptance through informality.

Germans, with their strong sense of history, tradition, family, and life-long friendships, tend to move much less often, make friendships slowly, and keep them longer than Americans. Because one's family may be known for generations in Germany, the family reputation becomes part of one's own identity, which in turn places the individual in a stable social position.[4]

The stability of the social class structure and, thus, the credibility of the upper class in Germany is largely maintained through the elitist system of higher education.

*Educational achievement has been a major factor in determining occupational attainment and socioeconomic status in the post-World War II era. University education has been virtually essential in gaining access to the most prestigious and remunerative positions. Some of the most enduring social divisions have focused on level of education (Nyrop, 1982, p. 113).*

A German's education most often places him or her at a certain level which, in turn, determines what they can and can't do. In Germany, one must present credentials as evidence of one's qualification to perform *any* task (K. Hagemann, personal communication, May–September, 1987). Thus, the German societal arrangement guarantees stability and order by adherence to known barriers (credentials) that confirm one's credibility. In Germany, loss of credibility would be known in the manager's corporate and social group and would probably result in truncated advancement (not dismissal since security is a high value).

The rigid social barriers established by education and credentials stand in direct contrast to the concepts of social mobility in American society. "Our social orientation is toward the importance of the individual and the equality of all individuals. Friendly, informal, outgoing, and extroverted, the American scorns rank and authority, even when he/she is the one with the rank. American bosses are the only bosses in the world who insist on being called by their first names by their subordinates" (Kohls, 1987, p. 8). When Germans and Americans come together in discussion, the German's drive is to establish hierarchy, the American's is to dissolve it.

## American Managers' Expectations

### Assertiveness, Direct Confrontation, and Fair Play

In comparing Americans with Japanese, Edward Stewart relates the American idea of confrontation as "putting the cards on the table and getting the information 'straight from the horse's mouth.' It is also desirable to face people directly, to confront them intentionally" (Stewart, 1972, p. 52). This is done so that the decision makers can have all of the facts. Stewart contrasts this intentional confrontation of Americans to the indirection of the Japanese, which often requires the inclusion of an intermediary or emissary in order to avoid face to face confrontation and thus, the loss of face. However, this view may leave the American manager unprepared for what he or she is likely to find in his or her initial discussion with a German manager.

The American manager is likely to approach his or her first discussion with German managers in an assertive fashion from the assumption that competition in business occurs within the context of co-operation (Stewart, 1972, p. 56). This balance is attained by invoking the unspoken rule of fair play.

*Our games traditions, although altered and transformed, are Anglo-Saxon in form; and fair play does mean for us, as for the English, a standard of behavior between weak and the strong – a standard which is curiously incomprehensible to the Germans. During the last war, articles used to appear in German papers exploring this curious Anglo-Saxon notion called "fair play," reproduced without translation – for there was no translation.*

*Now the element which is so difficult to translate in the idea of "fair play" is not the fact that there are rules. Rules are an integral part of German life, rules for behavior of inferior to superior, for persons of every status, for every formal situation. . . . The point that was incomprehensible was the inclusion of the other person's weakness inside the rules so that "fair play" included in it a statement of relative strength of the opponents and it ceased to be fair to beat a weak opponent.*

*. . . Our notion of fair play, like theirs [British], includes the opponent, but it includes him far more personally. . . . (Mead, 1975, p. 143 – 145).*

I am not implying that the American is in need of a handicap when negotiating with Germans. It is important to note however, that the styles of assertiveness under the assumption of American equality (fair play) and assertiveness under the assumption of German hierarchy may be very different. The general approach of the German toward the weaker opponent may tend to inspire a negative reaction in the American, thus reducing cooperation and motivation.

## German Managers' Expectations

### Assertiveness, Sophistication, and Direct Confrontation

The current wisdom either leaves the impression or forthrightly states that Americans and Germans share certain verbal behaviors which would cause

one to predict that discussion is approached in a mutually understood fashion.

*If North Americans discover that someone spoke dubiously or evasively with respect to important matters, they are inclined to regard the person thereafter as unreliable, if not dishonest. Most of the European low-context cultures such as the French, the Germans, and the English show a similar cultural tradition. These cultures give a high degree of social approval to individuals whose verbal behaviors in expressing ideas and feelings are precise, explicit, straightforward, and direct (Gudykunst & Kim, 1984, p. 144).*

Such generalizations do not take into account the difference between *Gespräch* (just talking about – casually) and *Besprechung* (discussion in the more formal sense of having a discussion about an issue). *Besprechung* in German culture is a common form of social intercourse in which one has high level discussions about books, political issues, and other weighty topics. This reflects the traditional German values which revere education. Americans would best translate *Besprechung* as a high level, well evidenced, philosophically and logically rigorous debate in which one's credibility is clearly at stake – an activity less familiar to most Americans.

The typical language of most Americans is not the language many Germans use in a high level debate on philosophical and political issues.

*In areas where English immigrants brought with them the speech of 16th and 17th century England, we find a language more archaic in syntax and usage than [sic] present-day English. Cut off from the main stream, these pockets of English have survived. But the American language, as written in the newspapers, as spoken over the radio (and television), . . . is instead the language of those who learned it late in life and learned it publicly, in large schools, in the factory, in the ditches, at the polling booth. . . . It is a language of public, external relationships. While the American-born generation was learning this public language, the private talk which expressed the overtones of personal relationships was still cast in a foreign tongue. When they in turn taught their children to speak only American, they taught them a one-dimensional public language, a language oriented to the description of external aspects of*

**Figure 1** Development of Discussion Behavior at a Glance

| American | Focus | German |
|---|---|---|
| Impersonal — act as own agent — will move on when business does not serve his/her needs or when better opportunity arises | Relationship to Business | Not as impersonal — corporation is more cohesive unit — identity more closely associated with position, and security needs met by corporation |
| Need to be liked — expressed through informal address and gestures | Personal Need | Need for order and establishment of place in hierarchy — expressed through formal address and gestures |
| Short-term — largely informal — many procedures picked up in progress | Orientation to Corporation | Long-term training — formal — specific rules of procedure learned |
| Based on accomplishment and image — underlying drive toward equality | Status | Based on education and credentials — underlying drive toward hierarchy |
| Assertive, tempered with fair play — give benefit of doubt or handicap | Confrontation | Assertive — put other in his/her place |
| Discussion about sports, weather, occupation: what you do, what you feel about someone. Logical, historical analysis rarely ventured. Native language sophistication usually low. | Common Social Intercourse | Besprechung — rigorous logical examination of the history and elements of an issue. Politics favorite topic. Forceful debate expected. Native language sophistication high. |

*behavior, weak in overtones. To recognize this difference one has only to compare the vocabulary with which Hemingway's heroes and heroines attempt to discuss their deepest emotions with the analogous vocabulary of an English novel. All the shades of passion, laughter close to tears, joy tremulous on the edge of revelation, have to be summed up in such phrases as: 'They had a fine time.' Richness in American writing comes from the invocation of objects which themselves have overtones rather than from the use of words which carry with them a linguistic aura. This tendency to a flat dimension of speech has not been reduced by the maintenance of a classical tradition* (Mead, 1975, pp. 81–82).

Since many Americans tend not to discuss subjects such as world politics, philosophical and ethical issues with a large degree of academic sophistication, a cultural barrier may be present even if the Germans speak American style English. In a study of a German student exchange program, Hagemann observed that "it was crucial for the Germans, that they could discuss world-politics with their American counterparts, found them in-terested in environmental protection and disarmament issues and that they could talk with them about private matters of personal importance. . . . If they met Americans who did not meet these demands the relationships remained on the surface" (Hagemann, 1986, p. 8).

This tendency not to enter into sophisticated discussions and develop deeper relationships may be a disadvantage for many Americans who are working with Germans (see Figure 1). In addition, in a society in which one's intellectual credibility[5] establishes one's position in the group and thus determines what one can and can't do, *Besprechung* can become quite heated — as is the case in Germany.

## Focus: When Besprechung and Discussion Meet

The management style of German and American managers within the same multinational corporation is more likely to be influenced by their nationality than by the corporate culture. In a study of carefully matched national groups of managers working in the affiliated companies of a large U.S.

multinational firm, "cultural differences in management assumptions were not reduced as a result of working for the same multinational firm. If anything, there was slightly more divergence between the national groups within this multinational company than originally found in the INSEAD multinational study" (Laurent, 1986, p. 95).

On the surface we can see two culturally distinct agendas coming together when German and American managers "discuss" matters of importance. The American character with its need to remain impersonal and to be liked avoids argumentum ad hominem. Any attack on the person will indicate disrespect and promote a feeling of dislike for the other, thus promoting the "unpopular phase," which, as Stewart indicates, may destroy cooperation for Americans.

In contrast, the German manager, with his personal investment in his position and a need to be credible to maintain his or her position, may strike with vigor and enthusiasm at the other's error. The American manager with his lack of practice in German-style debate and often less formal language, education, and training, may quickly be outmaneuvered, cornered, embarrassed, and frustrated. In short, he or she may feel attacked. This possible reaction may be ultimately important because it can be a guiding force for an American.

Beyond the question of character is the more fundamental question of the guidance system of the individual within his or her culture and what effect changing cultural milieu has on the individual guidance system. I define guidance system as that which guides the individual's actions. In discussing some of the expectations of German and American managers, I alluded several times to what could be construed as peer pressure within small groups. How this pressure works to guide the individual's actions, I will argue in the next section, has great implications for developing programs for American success in Germany.

Viewed as systems of argumentation, discussion and *Besprechung* both begin a social phase even though Americans may at first view the forcefulness of the Germans as anti-social (Copeland & Griggs, 1985, p. 105). However, a dissimilarity lends an insight into the difference in the guidance systems and how Germans and Americans perceive each other.

American discussion, with the focus on arriving at consensus, is based on the acceptance of value relativism (which supports the American value of equality and striving for consensus). The guidance system for Americans is partly in the peer group pressure which the individual reacts to but may not be able to predict or define in advance of a situation. Therefore, some Americans have difficulty articulating, consciously conceiving, or debating concepts in their guidance system but rather prefer to consider feedback and adjust their position to accommodate the building of consensus without compromising their personal integrity.

German *Besprechung,* with the focus on arriving at truth or purer concepts, rejects value relativism in support of German values of fixed hierarchy and social order. The German *Besprechung* is argumentation based on the assumption that there is some logically and philosophically attainable truth. The guidance system for Germans is composed of concepts which are consciously taken on by the individual over years of formal learning (a la Hall) and debate. While a German makes the concepts his/her own through *Besprechung,* his/her position is not likely to shift far from a larger group pressure to conform to one hierarchical code.

The peer pressure of the immediate group can often become a driving force for Americans. The irony is that many Germans initially perceive Americans as conformists and themselves as individualists, stating that Americans can't act alone while Germans with their clearly articulated concepts do act alone. Americans, on the other hand, often initially perceive Germans as conformists and themselves as individualists stating that Germans conform to one larger set of rules while Americans do their own thing.

## Learning Styles, Training, Instruction, and Problem Solving

### Education and Training

The ultimate function of group process in American corporations is problem solving and individual motivation (being liked). For Germans motivation

**Figure 2** Manager Background At a Glance

| American | Focus | German |
|---|---|---|
| Peer pressure of immediate group — reluctant to go beyond the bounds of fair play in social interaction — backdrop is social relativism | Guidance System | Peer pressure from generalized or larger social group — forceful drive to conform to the standard — backdrop is consistent and clearly known |
| Generally weaker higher education — weak historical perspective and integrated thought — focus is on the future results — get educational requirements out of the way to get to major to get to career success | Education | Higher education standards generally superior, speak several languages, strong in history, philosophy, politics, literature, music, geography, and art |
| More group oriented — social phase develops into team spirit — individual strengths are pulled together to act as one | Problem Solving | More individualized and compartmentalized — rely on credentialed and trained professional |
| Informal awareness — get the hang of variations — often unconscious until pointed out | Learning | Formal awareness — specific instruction given to direct behavior — one known way to act — highly conscious |

is more of a long term consideration such as an annual bonus or career advancement. Problem solving for Germans is more compartmentalized and individualized.

The contrasting elements discussed earlier and outlined in both "At a Glance" summaries (Figures 1 and 2) indicate that considerable cultural distance may have to be traveled by Germans and Americans before they can be assured that cooperation and motivation are the by-products of their combined efforts. The contrasting elements are, of course, a result of the organization and education — the acculturation — of the minds of Germans and Americans. In this section I will examine the different cultural tendencies from the perspective of Hall's definitions of formal and informal culture and discuss some implications for intercultural training and education.

The first level of concern is general preparation for the managerial position. As an educator I must take a hard look at the graduates of our colleges and universities as they compare to their German counterparts. I am not attempting to imply that Germans are better than Americans. All cultural groups excel in some area more than other cultural groups.

*Germans are better trained and better educated than Americans. A German university degree means more than its U.S. equivalent because German educational standards are higher and a smaller percentage of the population wins college entrance. Their undergraduate degree is said to be on par with our master's degree. It is taken for granted that men and women who work in business offices are well educated, able to speak a foreign language, and capable of producing coherent, intelligible, thoughtful communications. German business managers are well versed in history, literature, geography, music and art (Hall, 1983, p. 58).*

Americans tend to focus on the present as the beginning of the future, whereas Germans tend to "begin every talk, every book, or article with background information giving historical perspective" (Hall, 1983, p. 20). While Hall makes a strong generalization, a contrary incident is rare. American college graduates are not known for having a firm or detailed idea of what happened before they were born. While some pockets of integrated, sophisticated thinking exist, it is by no means the standard. Indeed, many American college students are unable to place significant (newsworthy) events within an over-all political/philosophical framework two months after the occurrence.

In contrast, college educated Germans tend to express a need to know *why* they should do something – a reasoning grounded in a logical understanding of the past. Compared to the rigorous German theoretical and concrete analysis of past events, Americans often appear to be arguing from unverifiable aspirations of a future imagined. While such vision is often a valuable driving force and the basis for American innovation and inventiveness, it may not answer the German need to explicitly know why and, thus, may fall short (from a German perspective) in group problem solving when these two cultures are represented. From the educational perspective, one must conclude that more than a few days of awareness training is needed before successful discussions can result between German and American managers, primarily because of what is not required by the American education system. The contrary may also be true in the preparation of Germans to work with Americans. Tolerance for intuitive thinking may well be a proper focus in part of the German manager's training prior to working with American managers.

## Formal and Informal Culture

The unannounced and largely unconscious agenda of small group process among Americans is usually more subtle than the German formal awareness but equally as important. American individuals come together in the initial and critical social phase, "size up" each other, and formally or informally recognize a leader. In a gathering of hierarchical equals the first to speak often emerges as the leader. At this point the embers of team spirit warm once again. As the group moves through purpose and task definition, members define and redefine their roles according to the requirements of the evolving team strategy. Fired with team spirit, inculcated through years of group activity and school sports, the group produces more than the sum of their individual promises.

"In the United States a high spontaneous interest in achievement is counterbalanced by much experience in group activities in which the individual learns to channel achievement needs according to the opinions of others. . . . Interestingly enough, the American 'value formula' appears to be largely un-

conscious or informally understood, as compared to the German one, at any rate" (McClelland et al., 1958, p. 252). Though this observation is 30 years old, it still appears to be quite accurate. The use of modeling (imitation) as a way of acquiring social and political problem-solving strategies is also a way of adjusting to regionalisms. In taking on different roles, Americans become adept at unconsciously adjusting their character to meet the requirements of different situations. In short, says Hall, "Compared to many other societies, ours does not invest tradition with an enormous weight. Even our most powerful traditions do not generate the binding force which is common in some other cultures. . . . We Americans have emphasized the informal at the expense of the formal" (Hall, 1973, p. 72).

The German learning style is often characterized by formal learning as defined by Hall (Hall, 1973, p. 68). The characteristics of German frankness and directness are echoed in Hall's example of formal learning: "He will correct the child saying, 'Boys don't do that,' or 'You can't do that,' using a tone of voice indicating that what you are doing is unthinkable. There is no question in the mind of the speaker about where he stands and where every other adult stands" (Hall, 1973, p. 68). German formal awareness is the conscious apprehension of the detailed reality of history which forms an idealistic code of conduct that guides the individual to act in the national interest as if there was no other way.[6]

American informal awareness and learning is an outgrowth of the blending of many cultural traditions, in an environment in which people were compelled to come together to perform group tasks such as clearing land, building shelter, farming, and so on. The reduction of language to the basic nouns and functions was a requirement of communication for the multilingual population under primitive conditions. Cultural variations will always be a part of the vast American society. Americans have had to "get the hang of it" precisely because whatever *it* is, *it* is done with several variations in America.

In a sense, the informal rules such as "fair play" are just as prescriptive of American behavior as the system of German etiquette is prescriptive of much of German social interaction, including forms of address (familiar *Du* and the formal *Sie*). Even the rules for paying local taxes, entering children in schools, or locating a reputable repair person vary by local custom in America and can only be known by asking.[7] The clear difference is that the rules are not overtly shared in America.

The American expectations or informal rules for group discussion are general enough to include the etiquette of American managers from different ethnic backgrounds. As long as notions of equality, being liked, respect, fair play, and so on guide behaviors things run smoothly. "Anxiety, however, follows quickly when this tacit etiquette is breached. . . . What happens next depends upon the alternatives provided by the culture for handling anxiety. Ours include withdrawal and anger" (Hall, 1973, p. 76). In the intercultural situation, the American who participates informally in group behavior may feel that something is wrong but may not be able to consciously determine the problem. Without the ability of bringing the informal into conscious awareness, which is a function of awareness and education, many Americans may flounder in a state of confusion, withdrawal, and anger.

## Conclusion

What should become apparent to intercultural trainers working with companies that are bringing German and American personnel together is that they are working with two populations with distinct learning and problem-solving styles. The American is more likely to learn from an interactive simulation. Within the situation the American can "get the hang of" working with someone who has a German style. Trainers and educators of American managers know that the debriefing of the role play, which brings the operative informal rules into conscious awareness, is the focus of the learning activity. The short-term immersion training so often used today can only supply some basic knowledge and limited role-play experience.

What must never be forgotten in the zeal to train American managers is that their basic guidance system in America is a motivation to accommodate the relative values of the immediate group.

While the general cultural awareness exercises that begin most intercultural training may make Americans conscious of their internal workings, much more attention must be given to inculcate an understanding of German social order and the interaction permitted within it.

Knowledge of the language and an in-depth orientation to the culture for the overseas manager and spouse should be mandatory for American success in Germany and German success in the United States. "The high rate of marital difficulties, alcoholism and divorce among American families abroad is well known and reflects a lack of understanding and intelligent planning on the part of American business" (Hall, 1983, p. 88). In our pilot program we became quite aware of the fact that German spouses require much more preparation for a sojourn to America. American short-term planning is in conflict with the long-term preparation needed for most Americans who are going to work with Germans. In Germany the role of the spouse (usually the female) in business includes much less involvement than in the United States. We suspect this has much to do with the lack of attention to spouse preparation that we have observed thus far.

## Recommendation

Long-term programs should be established that provide cultural orientation for overseas families at least three or four years before they start their sojourn with beginning and increasing knowledge of the language as a prerequisite for entry. Such programs should

attend to the general instructional deficiencies of Americans in the areas of history, philosophy, and politics as studied by Germans,

prepare Germans to expect and participate in an informal culture guided by value relativism in a spirit of equality,

incorporate cultural sharing of German and American managers and their families in social settings so the sojourners can come together before, during, and after their individual experiences to establish a formal support network.

Segments of such programs could be carried on outside the corporate setting to allow for a more open exchange of ideas. In America, colleges and universities could easily establish such programs. Many American colleges and universities which have served as research and development sites for business and industry are also developing alternative evening programs to meet the educational needs in the community. Also, corporate colleges are an ideal setting for extended in-house preparation. In such learning environments, professors can come together with adjunct faculty (private consultants and trainers) to produce a series of seminars which combine lecture instruction, small group intercultural interaction, networking, media presentations, contact with multiple experts over time, and even a well planned group vacation tour to the sojourner's future assignment site.

Part of the programs should be offered in the evening to avoid extensive interference with the employee's regular assignments and to take advantage of the availability of other family members who should be included in intercultural transfer preparation. Cost to the corporation would be greatly reduced in that start-up funds could be partly supplied through federal grants, travel costs would be lessened, and program costs would be covered under regular tuition and materials fees. As a final note, I strongly recommend that such programs for American managers be viewed as graduate level education since they will be entering a society in which education is a mark of status.

## Notes

1. Future references to America and Americans should be understood as referring to the North Eastern United States and the citizens thereof, while references to Germany and Germans should be understood as West Germany and the citizens thereof.

2. Actual German values were 65, with a value of 53 when controlled for age of sample, while the actual USA values were 46, with a value of 36 when controlled for age of sample.

3. For a quick overview of how small group and interpersonal communication is related to corporate success in America see Peters and Austin, 1985, pp. 233-248.

4. These comparative descriptions correspond to the German social orientation and the American personal orientation discussed by Beatrice Reynolds (1984, p. 276) in her study of German and American values.

5. "In Germany, power can be financial, political, entrepreneurial, managerial or intellectual; of the five, intellectual power seems to rank highest. Many of the heads of German firms have doctoral degrees and are always addressed as 'Herr Doktor.'" (Copeland & Griggs, 1985, p. 120). While there may be exceptions to this rule, exceptions are few and hard to find.

6. "Yet this rigidity has its advantages. People who live and die in formal cultures tend to take a more relaxed view of life than the rest of us because the boundaries of behavior are so clearly marked, even to the permissible deviations. There is never any doubt in anybody's mind that, as long as he does what is expected, he knows what to expect from others" (Hall, 1973, p. 75). "In Germany everything is forbidden unless it is permitted" (Dubos, 1972, p. 100).

7. The perplexing problem for German executives who are new in the United States is that in Germany everything is known thus, *you should not have to ask* to find your way around. But in the USA where change is the watch word, *one has to ask to survive.*

## References

Bleicher, K., & Paul, H. (1986). Corporate governance systems in a multinational environment: Who knows what's best? *Management International Review, 26,* (3) 4-15.

Copeland, L., & Griggs, L. (1985). *Going international: How to make friends and deal effectively in the global marketplace.* New York: Random House.

Cyert, R. M., & March, J. G. (1963). *A behavioral theory of the firm.* Englewood Cliffs, N.J.: Prentice-Hall.

Dubos, R. (1972). *A god within.* New York: Charles Scribner's Sons.

Friday, R. A., & Biro, R. (1986-87). [Pilot interviews with German and American personnel at Mobay Corporation (subsidiary of Bayer), Pittsburgh, PA]. Unpublished raw data.

Gudykunst, W. B., & Kim, Y. (1984). *Communicating with strangers: An approach to intercultural communication.* Reading, Mass.: Addison-Wesley.

Hagemann, K. (1986). *Social relationships of foreign students and their psychological significance in different stages of the sojourn.* Summary of unpublished diploma thesis, University of Regensburg, Regensburg, Federal Republic of Germany.

Hall, E. T. (1973). *The silent language.* New York: Doubleday.

Hall, E. T. (1983). *Hidden differences: Studies in international communication – How to communicate with the Germans.* Hamburg, West Germany: Stern Magazine Gruner + Jahr AG & Co.

Hofstede, G. (1984). *Culture's consequences: International differences in work-related values.* Beverly Hills: Sage Publications.

Kohls, L. R. (1987). *Models for comparing and contrasting cultures,* a juried paper, invited for submission to National Association of Foreign Student Advisors, June, 1987.

Laurent, A. (1986). The cross-cultural puzzle of international human resource management. *Human Resource Management, 25,* 91 – 103.

McClelland, D. C., Sturr, J. F., Knapp, R. N., & Wendt, H. W. (1958). Obligations of self and society in the United States and Germany. *Journal of Abnormal and Social Psychology, 56,* 245 – 255.

Mead, M. (1975). *And keep your powder dry.* New York: William Morrow.

Nyrop, R. F. (Ed.) (1982). *Federal republic of Germany, a country study.* Washington, D.C.: U.S. Government Printing Office.

Peters, T., & Austin, N. (1985). *A passion for excellence.* New York: Warner Communication.

Peters, T., & Waterman, R. (1982). *In search of excellence.* New York: Warner Communication.

Reynolds, B. (1984). A cross-cultural study of values of Germans and Americans. *International Journal of Intercultural Relations, 8,* 269 – 278.

Stewart, E. C. (1972). *American cultural patterns: A cross-cultural perspective.* Chicago: Intercultural Press.

Weaver, R. M. (1953). *The ethics of rhetoric.* South Bend, In.: Regnery/Gateway.

# Culture and Its Impact on Negotiation

LISA A. STEFANI
LARRY A. SAMOVAR
SUSAN A. HELLWEG

Never before in history has the business arena exhibited such global qualities. The days of manufacturing and selling products and services within the same country are gone forever. Many of our products, from the foreign cars we drive to the clothes we wear, are manufactured by foreign companies. Even Tropicana apple juice contains concentrate from Austria, Italy, Hungary, and Argentina (Acuff, 1993). This increase in globalization is a result of growth in U.S. and foreign multinational industries since the 1960s.

Examples of the global nature of the business arena abound. *Fortune*'s 1991 list of the world's largest industrial corporations included 164 for the United States, 111 for Japan, 43 for Britain, and 30 each for France and Germany (Acuff, 1993). Of the world's 15 largest banks, none is a U.S. bank and 13 are Japanese (*Information Please Almanac, 1995,* p. 60). According to the U.S. Department of Commerce, the United States exports over 350 billion dollars' worth of goods to its major trading partners, the Pacific Rim (33 percent), the European Community (27 percent), Canada (24 percent), Latin America (13 percent), and others (3 percent) (as cited in Acuff, 1993, p. 9). The United States also imports over 450 billion dollars' worth of goods from the Pacific Rim (44 percent), Canada

(21 percent), the European Community (18 percent), Latin America (11 percent), and others (6 percent) (p. 10). The Bureau of Economic Analysis (Department of Commerce) reported over 400 billion dollars in foreign direct investment in the United States in 1990 (as cited in Acuff, 1993). Trade agreements like NAFTA and GATT, as well as international business arrangements such as joint ventures, licensing agreements, and subcontracts, are now commonplace. Not only are large multinational companies doing business nationwide, but smaller domestic enterprises such as the Otis Elevator Company of Farmington, Connecticut, are also investing in places such as Russia (Van Rooy, 1994). Even our own Mickey Mouse was rescued from financial destitution in Europe by a Saudi Arabian prince (Horn, 1994)!

Having considered the widespread impact of globalization through the preceding examples, it seems reasonable to assume that many organizations, as well as the individuals employed by these organizations, will be communicating and negotiating with people from different cultures. Thus, it is not alarming to find that many large U.S. corporations rated cross-cultural negotiation training as the type of seminar they needed most (Harris & Moran, 1991, p. 55). It appears that in order for organizations to be effective in today's global marketplace, good communication and cross-cultural negotiating skills are essential. These two activities, communication and negotiation, go hand in hand. As Foster (1992) reminds us, "Negotiation is essentially about communication, and nowhere is that more clear than in business dealings across cultures in an international setting" (p. 16).

In examining the influence of culture on negotiation and how we can adapt to that influence, this chapter will (1) examine some of the characteristics of North American negotiating practices, (2) explain how various cultures select their negotiators — including their consideration of women, (3) discuss the role of cultural values in business negotiations, (4) compare decision-solving strategies, and (5) offer some ideas for improving cross-cultural negotiations.

## Understanding North American Negotiation Styles

If we are going to understand the communication behavior of other people, it is useful to have some appreciation of the way we might approach the same communication event. More specifically, it would be profitable to have some idea of how Americans behave when they confront a negotiation session. While we are all individuals, we are also products of our culture, and that culture spills over into every situation. While a complete and detailed examination of North American communication patterns is beyond the scope of this essay, we have been able to isolate five characteristics that seem to be the trademarks of North American negotiators: argumentation, informality, competition, verbal communication, and time.

### Argumentation

"The American negotiation style is basically argumentative" (Okabe, 1983, p. 37). Americans perceive the negotiation process as an arena where they will forge agreements out of debate and confrontation (Moran, 1985, p. 76). Graham and Herberger (1983) make much the same point when they tell us that Americans are "inherently competitive and argumentative during negotiations" (p. 161). Anyone who understands American culture realizes that antecedents of this argumentative style are deeply rooted in the value system of this country. The importance placed on independence, competition, and freedom of expression give rise to negotiation techniques that are often argumentative. As we shall see later, these techniques often clash with those of other cultures.

### Informality

For centuries, Americans have valued informality. Hence, it is not surprising that they bring this trait to the negotiation table. The eminence of informality often means that Americans "shun the use of formal codes of conduct, titles, honorifics, and ritualistic manner in their interactions with others. They instead prefer a first-name basis and direct address" (Okabe, 1983, p. 27). During negotiations this attitude means that "Americans typically start off the negotiation informally by emphasizing first names, playing down status distinctions such as titles, and by eliminating unnecessary formalities such as lengthy introductions" (Alston, 1990, p. 75). In short, American negotiators are quick to reject rigid protocols and unyielding formality. Again, we remind you that this feature of American negotiation style is not one that is found throughout the world.

## Competition

For some American negotiators the entire bargaining process is viewed as a combat zone or a sporting event — with a winner and a loser. The other participants are pictured as opponents, or even "the enemy." Moran (1985) contends that Americans act this way "because competition is a characteristic in the American culture" (p. 28). As we have said repeatedly, the characteristics of any culture find their way to the business setting. In this case, the characteristic is the high priority placed on competition.

## Verbal Communication

North American communication patterns rely on verbal language that is direct and open. As Ruch (1989) points out, "Americans are willing to put anything into words anytime because in their culture, the most successful people express everything verbally as quickly, concisely, and convincingly as possible. They consider it acceptably polite to be direct in conversation and social relations" (p. 37). This verbal directness is often reflected during international negotiations with phrases such as "This is our bottom line" and "This is our final offer." Using language in this form when negotiating often means "Silence is avoided in conversation, and interruptions are common" (Acuff, 1993, p. 228). Later in this chapter we will compare Americans' fondness for direct verbal communication with cultures that perceive and use language in ways that often are in conflict with this blunt approach.

## Time

There is little debate over the conclusion that "throughout the world Americans are known for their speed in business" (Foster, 1992, p. 135). This American view and use of time will, of course, be transferred into the negotiation session. As Moran (1985) noted, "American negotiators strive for and pride themselves on time efficiency during negotiations, often saying, 'time is money'" (p. 35). This same idea is echoed by Acuff (1993): "Whether a negotiation takes place over the telephone, in an office, or over a business meal, emphasis is put on getting through the content of the negotiation as efficiently as possible" (p. 226).

When we move further into this essay you will see how the Americans' use of time, with its emphasis on speed and expediency, will be yet another area of potential difficulty when negotiating with other cultures.

## The Selection of Negotiators

Having briefly examined common negotiation styles found among most Americans, we are now ready to discuss how Americans and members of other cultures select the people to attend negotiation meetings. An awareness of these differences will enable you to appreciate the place and importance of person perception in intercultural communication. "Americans typically choose their negotiators on the basis of their substantive knowledge of the issues at the table and on their negotiating experience; the gender or age of the negotiator can be incidental" (Foster, 1992, p. 275). Social status also has little to do with the selection of "team members or leaders" (Hellweg, Samovar, & Skow, 1994, p. 289). However, as we shall see, gender, age, and other key factors often play important roles in the selection of negotiators in other countries. Let us pause now and look at some of the specific variables used by these countries in selecting their negotiation teams.

We begin with age. It is a well-known fact that in Asian cultures age carries a great deal of weight (Fisher, 1980; Foster, 1992). In fact, Chinese negotiators often feel slighted if they do not negotiate with a senior person. Middle Eastern negotiators also prefer members of the team to be older. The oldest member is usually the leader, and younger members may even be ignored on Iranian teams (Soderberg, 1985).

Personal connections and social contacts are often the criteria for selection in Mexico and other parts of Latin America. This means negotiators from North America "can find themselves negotiating with someone in Latin America who may have little grasp of the issues but is at the bargaining table because of his relationship with key industrial or political figures" (Foster, 1992, p. 277). The method of selection can also influence the group dynamics of the meeting because the person of authority in these situations is not always apparent. For example, a person who might appear as a subordinate (a personal secretary) may actually command a great deal of authority and respect.

In many parts of Europe, status (that is, education, family ties, and so on) plays a key role in the selection of team members (Weiss & Stripp, 1985). As Foster (1992) notes, "Schooling and social class in France, and in other parts of Europe as well, quite often determines who conducts business" (p. 277). This strong affinity for status is especially true in class-conscious England. The Swazis of Africa represent yet another cultural group that places great capital on status. Hence, their negotiation team is usually composed of people who, because of age and loyalty, have achieved a high standing within the organization (Nwosu, 1988).

At the international level, gender is a major issue when analyzing the selection of members for the negotiation session. As we have already indicated, using such a criterion in the United States is both legally and socially unacceptable. However, this is not the case throughout the world. "There are many countries where customs, attitudes, and religion are hostile to women in business and there is no question that international business negotiations are dominated by men" (Acuff, 1993, p. 92). Acuff (1993) offers a concise and current summary of attitudes toward female negotiators in Europe, Latin America, North America, the Middle East, and the Pacific Rim.

Due to the male-dominated business environment in eastern Europe it is extremely rare to find female negotiators. On the other hand, western Europe is less chauvinistic. Sweden, for example, has one of the highest percentages of women in the workforce in the world (48 percent). Therefore, it is a profitable business atmosphere for women. While the business setting is largely male-dominated, Belgium, Greece, and the United Kingdom are also relatively satisfying places for women to conduct business. In France and Italy women can effectively negotiate, but they should expect gallant and often flirtatious behavior from males. The Dutch, at least by American standards, are somewhat chauvinistic, but American women can negotiate successfully in this male-dominated society. In Spain macho and chauvinistic attitudes prevail, and only certain roles are appropriate for women in business. Germany is one of the most difficult business environments for women. "Germans are more resistant to women working than people in some other European countries. Women who do work are unlikely to obtain key professional or management positions. Almost no sex discrimination laws exist" (Acuff, 1993, p. 157).

In Latin American countries, chauvinism, machismo, and traditional values prevail. Many men, particularly Brazilian men, can be expected to stare and make comments. Although it may be easy to establish friendships on a personal level, the business level remains difficult and elusive for females. Successful female negotiators must work hard to be polite but firm (Acuff, 1993).

Females will find Israel to be the most favorable country in the Middle East in which to conduct business. Although there is a male-dominated tradition, women have considerable influence inside and outside of the home. Egypt tends to be less sex-segregated than the remaining Middle East countries, improving the possibility of successful negotiation by women. Saudi Arabia is one of the most difficult countries for women to conduct business in. Even Western women are expected to cover their arms and legs and are encouraged to wear an *abbaya*—a black cape. If Western women are able to get a visa into the country, they can effectively conduct business with support from their male counterparts, spouses, or local networks. The United Arab Emirates are somewhat less conservative toward women than is Saudi Arabia. In the United Arab Emirates, Western women are allowed to drive cars (Acuff, 1993).

In the Pacific Rim, Hong Kong is the most favorable place for women to negotiate effectively because women are on local negotiating teams. Taiwan, Thailand, Singapore, and Japan also offer favorable business environments for women, except that Japanese men are still uncomfortable with women in positions of power. Women can negotiate in the Philippines despite some machismo, and South Koreans are more accepting of international business women than are the Japanese. However, successful negotiations may be problematic in Malaysia due to the conservative Muslim influence. Business transactions in China continue to be difficult for any Western person, but particularly for women (Acuff, 1993).

It should be clear that it is important to consider the gender attitudes of the culture with which you will be engaging in business. However, it is also important to recognize that business women from the United States may likely be considered "foreign executives" rather than solely women, thus improving their chance for effective negotiations (Acuff, 1993).

## Values and Cultural Knowledge

Because there are fundamental differences between the way various cultures view the essential facts of life, it is important to gain an understanding of the values and deep structure of the culture with which you will be negotiating. As Foster (1992) notes, "Most [negotiation] problems occur over deep cultural misunderstanding rather than specific behavior differences" (p. 30). For this reason, it is important to consider the traditional values of the culture with which you will do business.

A value may be defined as an "enduring belief that a specific mode of conduct or end-state of existence is personally or socially preferable to another" (Rokeach, 1973, p. 5). Values, then, are cultural guideposts that provide us with rules for making choices and help us determine what is

right, wrong, good, bad, appropriate, and inappropriate. When we understand the values of another culture, we can appreciate the behavior of its members and know how to treat them. For example, "knowing that the Japanese value detail and politeness might cause us to examine carefully a proffered Japanese business card, as the Japanese do, rather than immediately relegating it to a coat pocket or purse" (Samovar & Porter, 1995, p. 83). As you would suspect, a countless number of cultural values influence the negotiation process. However, we have selected four values that are often at the root of cross-cultural problems at the negotiation table. These are cultural differences with regard to (1) risk taking (often referred to as uncertainty avoidance), (2) individualism, (3) interpersonal relations, and (4) the use of language. Each of these values can be visualized as a stone being tossed into a pond. That stone, at first glance, appears to create a large wave. Yet on further inspection the stone also generates a series of ripples. This somewhat simple point serves as an analogy for the four values we have selected. They are the large stones that produce a number of critical effects (ripples).

## Risk Taking Versus Prudence

The Scandinavian researcher Hofstede (1980) coined the phrase "uncertainty avoidance" to indicate the extent to which a culture feels threatened by uncertain and ambiguous situations. Cultures with high uncertainty avoidance dislike uncertainty, the unknown, and ambiguity. They prefer security, formal and written rules, structure, and ritual in all aspects of life; they place great value on expert advice and dislike taking risks. Cultures such as Portugal, Greece, Germany, Peru, Belgium, and Japan have a strong uncertainty-avoidance tendency. In contrast, cultures such as Sweden, Denmark, Norway, and the United States have a high tolerance for uncertainty and ambiguity. They are more likely to engage in risk-taking behavior, prefer as few rules as possible, easily accept the unusual, and rely on their own common sense before expert advice (Hofstede, 1980; Samovar & Porter, 1995).

A culture's degree of uncertainty avoidance can influence the negotiating situation in a variety of ways. For example, we can observe one "ripple" in the pre-negotiation stages. Cultures who want information as a way of reducing uncertainty and ambiguity place a different emphasis on the information-gathering process than do cultures who are willing to take risks. This same point is made by Foster (1992):

*Many of the cultures we are doing business with in the rest of the world are significantly more conservative, more cautious, in their business attitudes than we, as a culture, generally are. This means, among other things, that their need for information, their need to be certain before making decisions, before taking action, can be greater than similar needs in ourselves. (p. 31)*

This attitude means that many of the cultures Americans do business with, particularly cultures with a strong uncertainty-avoidance tendency, will want to spend a great deal of time and energy finding out about the United States, its values, standard business practices, organizations, and even the specific people in those organizations. In contrast, Americans often tend to acquire just enough information to conduct the negotiation.

Not only do cultures with high uncertainty avoidance spend considerable time investigating the culture with which they will negotiate but they also require a great deal of information before they are willing to make a decision. For example, Ruch (1989) tells us that when conducting negotiations with people from Belgium we should be prepared with "facts and figures" (p. 126). He makes much the same point regarding the Dutch: "The Dutch are pragmatic and down-to-earth, so presentations must be factual and full of facts" (p. 156). The Japanese, also a high-uncertainty culture, will request very specific information from Americans at the negotiation table (Foster, 1992). They will also ask a large number of very specific questions.

The Chinese, for reasons that are somewhat different from those of the Japanese, are yet another culture that is somewhat reluctant to take risks. When writing about trade negotiations with the Chinese, Lavin (1994) observed: "In China's closed political system, no official depends on popular re-election as the reward for pursuing sound policies, so little incentive exists to risk even prudent policy changes. An overwhelming institutional bias exists in favor of the status quo" (p. 17).

## Individualism Versus Collectivism

It does not take a great deal of documentation to support the assertion that individualism is highly prized in the United States. From our literature, arts, media, sports, and history, the message to each generation is the same: individual achievement, sovereignty, and freedom are the virtues that are most glorified and canonized. Our heroes, being independent agents, tend to accomplish their goals with little or no assistance. Even God "helps those who help themselves." It is not surprising that this same value dominates American business practices – including how we negotiate. Team negotiations are very unlikely for most Americans, unless of course the "negotiation is very complex" (Acuff, 1993, p. 226). And even in these cases there is normally one person who makes the key decisions. The "lone cowpuncher syndrome," as Acuff (1993) calls it, is not found in every culture. This may explain why "the Japanese pack the negotiating table with fourteen people" (Acuff, 1993, p. 71). There are many cultures that value the group (collectivism) over the individual: "Singapore, Hong Kong, Japan and other Asian dragons" (Foster, 1992, p. 96). For these cultures, the group is perceived as a harmonious whole. Therefore, all members of the team need to be taken into account, treated with respect, and convinced of the soundness of the proposition. For many Americans this may mean a change of tactics – learning to view the group as whole instead of as individual entities.

## Content Versus People

This next value – interpersonal relations – deals with the manner in which a culture stresses the content and process of the negotiation over the participants at the meeting. The American attitude toward this value is clearly stated by Acuff (1993): "American negotiators emphasize content over the relationships involved in the negotiations. American negotiators focus on the mechanics of the deal more than on the process and emotions" (p. 48). Foster (1992) echoes the same idea in slightly different words when he writes:

*The American view of relationships in business has traditionally been quite different from the view held in the rest of the world. When it comes to business, we Americans like to do business first and only then establish relationships. For much of the rest of the world, it has traditionally been the other way around: one must first establish relationships, and only then can we do business. (p. 146)*

What this means is that while Americans are polite and casual during negotiations, they pay very little attention to issues associated with friendship and rapport building. This approach to doing business, while prevalent for Americans and many Europeans, is not the rule throughout the world. For example, the Japanese and Chinese believe that mutual interests and friendships are important in the negotiation process, so socialization during negotiation of the contract is necessary. While Americans usually spend five or ten minutes introducing each other and socializing, the Japanese – because social harmony is important when negotiating – prefer to spend much more time getting to know every person involved in the negotiation. Klopf (1991) maintains that so very strong is this need for friendship and harmony that Japanese negotiators will often avoid unnecessary confrontation.

In the Middle East personal relationships are also an important element in the negotiation process. Hospitality is a first priority in business transactions (Weiss & Stripp, 1985), and negotiations are initiated with social graces. The high value placed on friendship can be found in negotiations with Nigerians. They do not feel comfortable with a strong task orientation (Weiss & Stripp, 1985).

The general business approach utilized by Brazilians and Mexicans is similar to the approach taken by Middle Eastern negotiators (Foster, 1992). Because many countries do not have elaborate legal systems "to iron things out," they focus on establishing and maintaining personal relationships in business transactions (Graham & Herberger, 1983).

## Direct Versus Indirect Communication

Earlier in the chapter we introduced the idea that "Americans are identified throughout the world by their plain speaking and direct style of communication" (Acuff, 1993, p. 72). This means that negotiators from North America prize direct and open communication. They are likely to bluntly assert such things as "This is unacceptable," "This is our final bidding price," "Just lay it on the line," and "We have been here long enough, let's net it out." Other signs of the direct style of North American negotiators is that they often avoid silence, tend to speak loudly, interrupt frequently, and often complete sentences for others (Foster, 1992).

In Eastern European countries such as Czechoslovakia, Hungary, Poland, and Russia, communication also tends to be direct. In fact, Eastern European communication is sometimes more abrupt and aggressive than is the communication of North Americans (Acuff, 1993). Their opinions and stances are made clear because of their straightforwardness, and there is little value given to emotional displays.

European countries such as France, Germany, Italy, Switzerland, the United Kingdom, Sweden, Spain, Greece, the Netherlands, and Belgium generally conduct business in a formal and articulate manner. They expect and value the same in return. Soft tones and small to moderate displays of emotion are typical.

Pacific Rim cultures, such as Japan, Hong Kong, Indonesia, China, Thailand, Taiwan, South Korea, Singapore, the Philippines, and Malaysia, also tend to use quiet tones, but emotions are generally not visible. A great separation between the public and private self is valued. Confucian teachings encourage self-discipline and self-restraint so that any display of raw emotion is inappropriate social behavior. Instead, the Chinese tend to conceal their sentiments in the process of negotiation (Eberhard, 1971).

Communication in Pacific Rim cultures is very indirect. Confucian ethics, the teachings of the Buddha, and Taoism govern most interpersonal relationships. As a result, communication reflects great consideration for others. Face-saving is crucial because these cultures generally do not want to be responsible for causing someone to experience humiliation or fame. Because the Buddha writes, "Beware of false illusions created by words," many Pacific Rim cultures mistrust words. Members of these cultures believe there is a supreme truth that words cannot reach. Therefore, silence, humility, and modesty are valued communication characteristics.

"In high-context cultures such as Japan or China, people expect the person to whom they are talking to know what is on their mind. They give the other person all the necessary information except the crucial piece" (Acuff, 1993, p. 265). This indirect communication pattern is clearly illustrated in the way "no" is communicated. For cultures with a direct communication pattern, "no" is used often and is not to be taken personally. But a blunt "no" seems to the Japanese more as if you are saying "no" to the person himself rather than to his idea, opinion, or request. Thus, a direct denial could be potentially detrimental to the negotiation. When negotiating with cultures that practice indirect communication, good listening skills are imperative because "no" will be indicated by something other than the word "no." That is to say, the "no" might take some of the following forms: "We will examine the situation," "We will need to gather more information," "That is a good question," or "We will get back to you." The indirect "no" might also take a nonverbal form. As March (1988) suggests, in Japan your communication counterpart "may simply shake his head and smile wanly, suggesting that the question is completely beyond him, or he hasn't really understood it, or it should have been asked by someone else" (p. 141).

Most Arab cultures, with the exception of Israel, are also high-context cultures that will rarely give a direct "no." However, because Arabs value language, the "no" may not take the form of a single word. Instead, Arabs use rhetorical patterns such as exaggeration, over-assertion, repetition, and metaphor to avoid directness.

*Arabs generally have a strong feeling that information is critical, and they are therefore masters at incremental disclosures — slow at letting you know what is really on their minds. The "truth" is considered something that can be cruel, dangerous, and rude, as well as a matter of negotiation. (Acuff, 1993, p. 241)*

Negotiators from such Latin American cultures as Brazil, Argentina, Venezuela, Mexico, and Colombia are expressive and spontaneous. They are eager to share their ideas and interrupt as often as North Americans. A blunt "no" is uncommon for these cultures as well, but for a different reason. Because Latin American cultures tend to first establish a friendship with the individuals with whom they do business, they feel a blunt "no" may destroy the friendship. In fact, members of Latin American cultures often interpret a blunt "no" as the breaking of the friendship tie (Acuff, 1993).

## Cultural Variations in Decision Making

The mental processes, forms of reasoning, and approaches to problem solving prevalent in a community represent yet another major component that often separates one culture from another. People often assume that everyone thinks in much the same manner unless they have had experiences with people from other cultures who follow different patterns of thought. There are vast cultural differences in how people think and make decisions. In the inductive Western view, truth and the "correct" conclusions can be reached if we apply the correct steps of the scientific method. Americans believe that if they follow the Aristotelian modes of reasoning nearly all problems can be solved — and solved quickly. These attitudes, as you would suspect, apply even to the negotiation table. The Eastern version, best illustrated by Taoist thought, holds that truth, not the individual, is the active agent, and ways of knowing take a variety of forms. We need to remember that even the simple notion of an organization scheme that includes introduction, body, and conclusion is not found in much of the world. In short, cultural variations in decision-making and organizational patterns represent yet another series of problems facing American negotiators.

In the United States negotiators view negotiation sessions as problem-solving events, even if no real problem exists. They tend to compartmentalize issues, focusing on one issue at a time. As we have already indicated, Americans prefer to make decisions through what they believe to be rational thinking (Weiss & Stripp, 1985). However, this strong emphasis on intellect and reason is not popular throughout the world and can often create problems at the negotiation table. As Hall & Hall (1987) note: "Logic is a mode of thinking invented by the early Greeks that is integral to the Europeans and Americans, but is anathema to the Japanese. They feel that logical, linear, one-step-at-a-time arguments denote immaturity" (p. 121). This overly logical and rigid presentation makes the Japanese believe that the speaker wants to do their thinking for them.

Middle Easterners can be described as having an intuitive-affective approach to decision making. Broad issues that do not appear to be directly related to the discussion at hand are often brought up; issues are linked together on the basis of whether or not the speaker likes the topic being considered. Negotiation teams from Saudi Arabia do not make decisions on the basis of empirical reasoning. While subordinates are consulted informally, the leader always makes the final decision (Weiss & Stripp, 1985). In Swaziland (Nwosu, 1988) and in Nigeria (Weiss & Stripp, 1985), the decision-making process is controlled by authority figures with little input from subordinates.

The Mexicans use a centralized decision-making process. They view authority as being inherent within the individual, not his or her position; delegating of authority by an individual would be seen as a surrendering of assets. Making "trade-offs" is common for Mexican negotiators, including additional issues that are not part of the business at hand (Fisher, 1980).

The *pace* at which the negotiations move is also directly related to the decision-making process. We briefly alluded to this point when we discussed interpersonal relations, and noted how some cultures want to spend time getting to know all of the people at the negotiation table. However, the issue is important enough to justify some additional observations regarding the speed at which problems are solved.

As we have already suggested, the American concept of time and pace is reflected in two ways during a negotiation session. First, Americans want to "get down to business" as soon as possible and, second, they do not want the negotiation process to become elongated. Americans are not the only group that values a quick-paced negotiation process. "Australian, Swiss, British, and Singapore negotiators, for example, practice rapid-paced negotiations much like those in the United States" (Acuff, 1993, p. 78).

In contrast to cultures that seek an expeditious meeting, the Chinese have a longer view of time when engaging in cross-cultural negotiations (Weiss & Stripp, 1985). The Chinese do not mind going over the same point again and again. "Time is simply not the pressing consideration for the Chinese [that] it is for so many Americans" (Foster, 1992, p. 283). Likewise, the Japanese are not inclined to reach an agreement in order to fulfill a time constraint. An agreement will take as long as it takes for them (March, 1985). As Moran and Stripp (1991) noted, "Time is viewed more subjectively by the Japanese than their Western counterparts. A meeting that might take three days to conclude in the West will probably take two weeks in Japan" (p. 122).

The slow-paced approach to negotiations is also found in much of Latin America and Africa. For Nigerians, the simplest of dealings may take hours. Time is flexible for them. In fact, foreigners who hurry through negotiations with them may be suspected of cheating (Weiss & Stripp, 1985).

Negotiations with Saudi Arabia and other Middle Eastern cultures are also not bound by schedules. There is a sense in these cultures of timelessness. Hence, the pace is slower and delays and interruptions are common.

## Improving Cross-Cultural Negotiations

To this point in the essay we have focused on problems that may occur when cultures come together to negotiate a business contract. Let us now turn our attention to a discussion of some communication behaviors that might avoid these problems and therefore contribute to a successful business meeting. Although specific improvement strategies are numerous and often must be fashioned to each specific culture, we have nevertheless been able to isolate five positive behaviors that can apply to any culture.

First, and perhaps most important, learn to accept the idea that there are cultural differences in the manner in which nations do business. From gift giving to the use of time, each culture has its own rituals and customs that dictate how the negotiation process is perceived. By knowing that the prenegotiation period is important to Mexicans, you can better adapt your plans to a longer time frame. If you understand that some amount of "haggling" is expected in Saudi Arabia, yet frowned upon in Belgium, you can adjust to both situations.

Second, adopt a win-win approach. There is nothing built into the negotiation setting that maintains that one side has to win and the other must lose. As Foster reminds us, "Skilled negotiators tend to spend less time on defense/attack behavior and in disagreement" (Foster, 1992, p. 99). Instead, they try to create an atmosphere where both sides feel they are gaining something from the negotiations.

Third, be prepared for basic problems in communication. These problems can be either verbal or nonverbal. If English is the second language for your communication partner, you should speak slowly, repeat key points, and avoid colloquial expressions and idioms (such as "let us get down to the nitty gritty," "give me a ballpark figure," "we will toe the line if you avoid red flagging bottom line issues"). Nonverbally, you may need to learn about behaviors related to facial expressions, touching, eye contact, posture, and the like.

Fourth, practice patience. As noted earlier, not all cultures conduct business at the same pace. Learning to adapt to a different pace in the negotiation setting is a hallmark of any good international negotiator. This adjustment is as simple as learning to relax and as complicated as learning to be prepared to listen to a long list of questions from your negotiating counterpart.

Finally, develop a tolerance for ambiguity. Being around people from other cultures will involve con-

fronting ambiguous situations. How you handle that ambiguity will go a long way toward determining your success as a negotiator. For example, if your culture values talking, and you are interacting with a culture that employs a great deal of silence, you might find the silence ambiguous and confusing, for you may not understand its significance. Yet coping with this ambiguity is a key element in successful intercultural negotiations.

Remember that having a fund of knowledge about another culture can help you better decide what is appropriate and inappropriate behavior. Confucius said much the same thing in a far more eloquent manner: "The essence of knowledge is, having it, to apply it." We urge you to do both: have accurate knowledge and apply it.

## References

Acuff, F. L. (1993). *How to Negotiate Anything with Anyone Anywhere Around the World*. New York: American Management Association.

Alston, J. P. (1990). *The Intelligent Businessman's Guide to Japan*. Rutland, Vt.: Charles E. Tuttle.

Eberhand, W. (1971). *Moral and Social Values of the Chinese – Collected Essays*. Washington, D.C.: Chinese Materials and Research Aids Service Center.

Fisher, G. (1980). *International Negotiations: A Cross-cultural Perspective*. Chicago: Intercultural Press.

Foster, D. A. (1992). *Bargaining Across Borders: How to Negotiate Business Successfully Anywhere in the World*. New York: McGraw-Hill.

Graham, J. L., and Herberger, R. A. (1983). Negotiations abroad, don't shoot from the hip. *Harvard Business Review, 61,* 160 – 168.

Hall, E. T., and Hall, M. R. (1987). *Hidden Differences: Doing Business with the Japanese*. Garden City, N.Y.: Anchor.

Harris, P. R., and Moran, R. T. (1991). *Managing Cultural Differences: High Performance Strategies for a New World of Business,* 3rd ed. Houston: Gulf.

Hellweg, S. A., Samovar, L. A., and Skow, L. M. (1994). "Cultural Variations in Negotiations Styles." In L. A. Samovar and R. E. Porter (Eds.), *Intercultural Communication: A Reader,* 7th ed., 286 – 293. Belmont, Calif.: Wadsworth.

Hofstede, G. (1980). *Culture's Consequences: International Differences in Work-Related Values,* Beverly Hills: Sage.

Horn, J. (1994). "Euro Disney Finds Its Prince." *The San Diego Union Tribune,* June 2, p. C1.

*Information Please Almanac,* (1995). New York: Houghton Mifflin.

Klopf, D. W. (1991). Japanese communication practices: Recent comparative research. *Communication Quarterly, 39,* 130–143.

Lavin, F. L. (1994). "Negotiating with the Chinese." *Foreign Affairs,* July, 16–22.

March, R. M. (1985). "East Meets West at the Negotiating Table." *Winds,* April, 47–55.

March, R. M. (1988). *The Japanese Negotiator: Subtlety and Strategy Beyond Western Logic.* Tokyo: Kodansha.

Moran, R. T. (1985). *Getting Your Yen's Worth: How to Negotiate with Japan.* Houston: Gulf.

Moran, R. T., and Stripp, W. G. (1991). *Dynamics of Successful International Business Negotiations.* Houston: Gulf.

Nwosu, P. O. (1988). Negotiating with the Swazis. *The Howard Journal of Communications, 3,* 145–154.

Okabe, R. (1983). "Cultural Assumptions of East and West: Japan and the United States." In W. Gudykunst (Ed.), *Intercultural Communication Theory,* 186–195. Beverly Hills: Sage.

Rokeach, M. (1973). *The Nature of Human Values.* New York: Free Press.

Ruch, William V. (1989). *International Handbook of Corporate Communication.* Jefferson, N.C.: McFarland.

Samovar, L. A., and Porter, R. E. (1995). *Communication Between Cultures,* 2nd ed. Belmont, Calif.: Wadsworth.

Soderberg, D. C. (1985). *A Study of the Influence of Culture on Iranian and American Negotiations.* Unpublished master's thesis, San Diego State University.

Van Rooy, J. (1994). The Russian investment dilemma. *Harvard Business Review, 72,* 35–44.

Weiss, S. E., and Stripp, W. (1985). *Negotiating with Foreign Businesspersons: An Introduction for Americans with Propositions on Six Cultures.* Working paper No. 1, New York University, Graduate School of Business Administration.

# The "Five Asian Dragons": Management Behaviors and Organizational Communication

GUO-MING CHEN
JENSEN CHUNG

The progress of technology has made global markets more accessible and the business world more interrelated and international in the last decade. As Adler (1983) indicates, the increasing internationalization of business means an increasing multiculturalism within organizations and an increasing interaction between managers and employees of different cultures. This increasing multiculturalism in organizations calls for understandings among cultures and new strategies for organizational operations. From Adler's perspective the influence of Confucianism on modern Asian organizations is a case that deserves further investigation by communication scholars.

In the Pacific basin nations, the internationalization of business has occurred and in recent years in this region several newly industrializing nations have emerged in East Asia. Among these Asian nations five have been experiencing what is called an "economic miracle." These political entities, dubbed "Five Dragons," include Hong Kong, Japan, Singapore, South Korea, and Taiwan. According to a World Bank report (1988), between 1980 and 1986, the average annual growth rate of per capita gross national product (GNP) was 6.1% for Hong Kong,

From *Communication Quarterly,* (Spring 1994), 93–105. Copyright by the Speech Communication Association. Reprinted by permission of the publisher. Professor Chen teaches at the University of Rhode Island. Professor Chung teaches at San Francisco State University.

3.7% for Japan, 5.3% for Singapore, 8.2% for South Korea, and 6.8% for Taiwan, while only 1.8% for European countries and 3.1% for the United States.

Why are these particular countries so successful economically? Many scholars have attempted to answer this question from different perspectives, including the value of economic growth and the fast response to the international market (e.g., Chan, 1990; Wu, 1988). Although different scholars provide various factors to explain the unexpected economic growth of the Five Dragons, most of them agree that, for the root cause, one must turn to the domain of culture. It is the purpose of this inquiry to examine the impact of cultural environment on the economic success of the Asian Five Dragons. Because these economically successful nations in Northeast Asia share the same cultural heritage of Confucianism, this inquiry aims at investigating how Confucianism as a cultural factor contributes to the success of these nations. More specifically, this study explores the impact of Confucianism on the organizational life and organizational communication in these nations.

## Cultural Modifiers

To what degree do the cultural factors of a society influence its organizational life? Child (1981) indicates that different cultural orientations will lead to specific organizational effects. Gorden (1984) summarizes five hypotheses regarding the relationship between cultural orientations and organizational effects specified by Child: (1) If the society considers human nature as good, then the organizations will advocate employee autonomy and reliance on intrinsic motivation; (2) if the society believes that the human being is the master of nature, then the organizations will lead to adventurous and proactive management; (3) if the society orients to the future, then the organizations will emphasize long-term planning, workforce planning, and assessment centers; (4) if the society is "being" oriented, then the organizations will emphasize interpersonal sensitivity, and concern about morale and commu-

nication climate; and (5) if the society orients to individualism, then the organizations will minimize authority and hierarchy.

Hofstede's (1980) large-scale study shows the consistent relationship between cultural orientations and organizational life. The results of Hofstede's national value surveys from a multinational company in some 40 different countries reveal four dimensions of cultural values that are related to the organizational life: power distance, individualism, masculinity, and uncertainty avoidance.

Furthermore, the Chinese Culture Connection (1987) also has collected data from 22 countries and found four dimensions of cultural values that show influence on organizational life, especially in Asian countries. Three of the four dimensions are similar to Hofstede's power distance, individualism, and masculinity. The fourth one is labeled "Confucian Work Dynamism." The Chinese Culture Connection not only argues that it is this dimension that distinguishes the cultural orientation between Western and Eastern organizations, but also finds that this dimension is strongly related to the economic growth of the Asian Five Dragons over the period between 1965 and 1985. These studies indicate that a strong connection between cultural factors and the logic of organizing exists.

## The Dominant Culture of the Five Dragons

It is a common belief that specific nations possess specific cultural traits that are resistant to change. "Neo-Confucianism," rooted in the teachings of Confucius, is used by Kahn (1979) to describe the cultural traits of East Asian nations. According to Kahn, East Asian nations have common cultural roots that can be traced to Confucianism. This shared cultural heritage has contributed to the economic success of these nations in the international market over the past 30 years.

Confucius was born in China around 500 B.C. His teachings are mainly concerned with practical ethics of daily life without any addition of religion elements. Confucianism includes a set of pragmatic rules for the daily behaviors of common people. Hofstede and Bond (1988) indicate that the teachings of Confucius are comprised of four key princi-

**Table 1** Confucian Principles of Interpersonal Communication

| Four Principles | Contents |
| --- | --- |
| Hierarchical relationship | Particularistic relationship |
| | Complementary social reciprocity |
| | Ingroup/outgroup distinction |
| | Essential intermediary and formality |
| | Overlap of personal and public relationships |
| Family system | Private relationship |
| | Paternalistic leadership |
| | Harmony is the first virtue |
| | Distrust of outgroup members |
| | Loyalty and commitment |
| Jen | Jen—benevolence, self-discipline, filial piety, brotherly love, and trust |
| | Yi—righteousness, faithfulness, and justice in social interaction |
| | Li—propriety, rite, and respect for social norms |
| Education emphasis | Providing education for all people without discrimination |
| | Ethical teachings |

ples; the hierarchical relationship among people, the family as a basic unit, *Jen,* and the emphasis on education. We now use these principles as a framework to explain how Confucianism influences interpersonal relationships and organizational lives in the Asian Five Dragons (see Table 1).

## Hierarchical Relationship

According to Confucius, human relationships should be regulated by the Five Code of Ethics, *Wu Lun,* which is based on the five basic relationships: ruler/subject, father/son, husband/wife, older brother/younger brother, and between friends. These relationships are assumed to be unequal and complementary. Condon (1977) indicates that complementary relationships tend to "maximize differences in age, sex, role, or status and serve to encourage the mutuality of the relationship, the interdependency" (p. 54). Juniors are required to owe their seniors respect and obedience, and seniors owe their juniors consideration and protection. In other words, the Confucian Five Code of Ethics stipulates that the ruler has to show justice, and the subject shows loyalty; father shows love, and son shows filial piety; husband shows initiation, and wife shows obedience; the older brother shows brotherly love, and younger brother shows rever-

ence in return; and friends show mutual faith to each other.

The application of *Wu Lun* to the organizational life shows five types of ordering relationships: particularistic relationships, complementary social reciprocity, ingroup/outgroup distinction, essential intermediary and formality, and overlap of personal and public relationships (Yum, 1988). Particularistic relationships are relatively predictable. They are governed by a set of specific communication rules and patterns that provide individuals with directions concerning interaction. This kind of relationship may be extended to friends, family, co-workers, or superior/subordinate, along with many other relationships. The function of maintaining a particularistic relationship is a way for East Asians to avoid embarrassing encounters or serious conflicts (Hwang, 1988; Jacobs, 1979). Moreover, particularistic relationships are often used as a social resource which is a "potential power in persuasion, influence, and control" in the organizational life (Chung, 1991, p. 9).

Complementary social reciprocity, the second type of orderly relationship resulting from the Five Code of Ethics, refers to the process of give-and-take in a social interaction. Based on the hierarchical relationship, Confucian philosophy views interpersonal relationships as asymmetrical and reciprocally obligatory in which people always feel indebted to others. When East Asians receive a gift from others, for example, they show a deep appreciation and heartily try to find an opportunity to return the favor (Shiang, 1982). This obligation of returning the favor to others is also strongly reflected in the superior/subordinate relationship in an organization. Usually, a superior has certain responsibilities or obligations, such as protection and a holistic concern for subordinates; employees, in turn, have obligations, such as loyalty or commitment to a superior.

With the Confucian teaching of interpersonal relationships, the existence of an individual must be defined by another in East Asian societies. This characteristic of mutual interdependence between people leads to a sharp distinction between ingroup and outgroup members. Such interdependence "requires that one be affiliated with relatively small and tightly knit groups of people and have a relatively long identification with those groups" (Yum, 1987, p. 94). Individuals who join the group or an organization are assigned different positional roles, and are required to fulfill certain obligations. Moreover, they are subordinate to the group in which commitments and loyalty are required. Due to these requirements for group members, people are only able to belong to a limited number of organizations throughout their lives. This long-term, reciprocal relationship between the individual and the group is further developed into the lifetime employment system in Japanese organizations.

The Confucian principles of *Yi* (righteousness) and *Li* (propriety) dictate that individuals must follow a proper way and a proper ritual in a social interaction. An intermediary is a product of this requirement. It is a popular practice in East Asia to use an intermediary to help people initiate a new relationship or solve a conflict. This kind of indirect interaction and the formality of social life is considered a way of avoiding an embarrassing confrontation, a way of "saving face." A smooth and predictable verbal and nonverbal interaction is usu-

ally reached through the value of indirect communication and formality, factors which explain why it is very common for the East Asians to use formal codes of conduct, titles, honorifics in their interactions with others.

Finally, the Confucian idea of social reciprocity leads to a vague boundary between personal and public relationships. According to Yum (1988), this orientation leads to a strong taste for a pure business transaction in which people try to develop a personal rather than a business-like atmosphere. To build a good and warm personal relationship is the key to success in a business transaction. In Japan, for example, consensus is often reached before a meeting is summoned. Similarly, in other East Asian nations, one must develop a mutual understanding, establish a personal relationship, keep frequent contacts, develop personal trust, and build mutual interests in social activities with one's counterpart to develop an effective business relationship.

## The Family System

Confucian teachings consider "family" the prototype of all social organizations. Confucianism is like social cement that fixes family members in the network of their appropriate hierarchical relationships. Furthermore, concepts such as loyalty, obedience, and filial piety practiced in the family are transferred to social organizations in which habits of disciplined subordination and acceptance of authority are fostered (MacFarquhar, 1980).

Three discernible value orientations influenced by Confucian teachings can be identified within the family system: a lineal structure of relational orientation, a specific positional role behavior, and an authoritarian orientation (Chen, 1988). According to Hwang (1989), this collectivistic sense of the family structure that is applied to social organizations is one of the main reasons for the economic success of the Asian Five Dragons. Within this collectivistic family system, one becomes only a member of a family in which one must learn to restrain oneself, to subdue individuality in order to maintain the harmony in the family (Hofstede & Bond, 1988). The extension of the family system to business produces a popular practice of "family enterprise" in the Asian Five Dragons. Chen (1991) stipulates five characteristics of "family enterprise" that are heavily influenced by Confucian teachings:

1. Private relationship. The private relationship is based on the concept of "similarity" or "affinity," and it includes: (1) blood relationships – consisting of one's own family, relatives outside the household, wife's relatives, and relatives of different surnames (Chen, 1988); (2) demographic relationships – for those who are from the same area of the country; (3) colleague relationships – for those who work in the same organization; (4) teacher-student relationships; and (5) classmate relationships (Chiao, 1988).

2. Paternalistic leadership. In this kind of organization a manager always acts like a father who expresses concern for employees with families and the quality of the products the employees produce. This makes it difficult for workers to separate their personal and professional lives.

3. Harmony, the first virtue. Only harmony among group members can produce fortune. It is believed that personal harmony is the best way to maintain dignity, self-respect, and prestige.

4. Distrust of outgroup members. This characteristic shows that most high and middle management are selected from the network of the private relationships.

5. Relative loyalty and commitment between managers and employees. The concern with employee's personal benefit from top management usually requires the unconditional loyalty or spirit of sacrifice from employees.

## Jen (Benevolence)

Jen is one of the cardinal concepts of Confucian teachings. It is a collective concept which is comprised of various virtues, but "love" is the core meaning of Jen. To oneself, Jen is self-restraint and self-discipline; to others, benevolence; to parents, filial piety; to elders, brotherly love; to personal duty, loyalty; and to interpersonal behaviors, trust (Chen, 1987). Jen is like a seed from which all the virtuous qualities of the ideal humans are originated.

Basically, the concept of Jen interweaves with two other cardinal concepts of Confucian teachings: Yi (righteousness) and Li (propriety). Only through Yi and Li is the meaning of Jen rectified. Yi is the binding force of social interaction; it refers to the righteousness, faithfulness, loyalty, and justice in the process of social interaction. Yi serves two major functions: guidance of behavior and connection of all appropriate behaviors. As a directive behavior Yi stipulates what one ought and ought not do. In this sense, Yi is the internal criterion of appropriateness of Jen which affects all human behaviors.

Li is the external form of Jen. It refers to propriety, rite, and respect for social norms, and it is "the rule of the universe and the fundamental regulatory etiquette of human behavior" (Yum, 1988, p. 378). The practice of Li allows the intimate connections of individual character and social duties by means of rules, including propriety of conduct, propriety of speech, and propriety of example.

Based on Confucian teachings, "reciprocity," referring to mutual expectations of social responsibility among people, is the yardstick of propriety of conduct. Confucian teachings place the performance of duties due others above all other duties and treat this performance as a necessary means of self-development. Confucius explicates this idea by indicating that in order to confirm or enlarge oneself, one has to confirm and enlarge others.

Confucian teachings admonish followers to be cautious about their speech, because the "smartness" of speech elicits hatred from others. One's speech should be simple, direct, and to the point. In other words, one should express the precise meaning rather than what seems to be said or variant from it. Straightforwardness or too much candor during discourse, however, is dangerous, since it is often not regulated by the rule of appropriateness. Confucius warns that straightforwardness, without the rules of propriety, will often lead to rudeness.

Confucian teachings also emphasize the important role of a listener in the process of discourse. A listener must be able to understand accurately what a person says, because it is impossible to know men without knowing the force of words.

Moreover, the ability to know when to speak and the ability to read a speaker's facial expression are also important to the listener, especially when communicating with a superior. Confucius uses "impetuousness" to describe those who speak before spoken to; "reticence" for those who do not reply when spoken to; and "blindness" for those who speak without observing the superior's facial expression. Finally, Confucian teachings urge a superior to be cautious when giving commands to subordinates. Confucius indicates that once commands are issued, they must be carried into effect and cannot be retracted.

Lastly, the propriety of example refers to the kind of people with whom a person should associate. Confucian teachings indicate that three kinds of friends will benefit a person: the upright, the devoted, and the learned. In contrast, three kinds of friends will harm a person: the fawning, the flattering, and the too eloquent. Confucius repeatedly utters the admonition for being with those who employ artful speeches and insinuating looks. He considers that words and an insinuating appearance are barriers for being virtuous. Prudence, in regard to conversation and association with others, is strongly recommended in Confucian teachings.

An admonition to a friend or superior is encouraged in Confucian teachings, but the admonition must be regulated by appropriateness. Confucius further warns against unnecessary admonitions, because frequent remonstrances and reproofs often lead to disgrace. All these Confucian ideas provide a set of rules that guide the behaviors and relationships between superiors and subordinates in modern organizations of the Asian Five Dragons. More influences are discussed in the next section.

## The Emphasis on Education

The perfectibility and educability of human beings is central to Confucian thinking. This emphasis on education has become one of the most important characteristics of Chinese culture, and the tradition is carried over to every Asian nation, especially the Asian Five Dragons. The World Bank reports that in 1985 the number in secondary school as percentage of age group in the Asian Five Dragons is: Hong Kong, 69%; Japan, 96%; Singapore, 71%;

South Korea, 94%; and Taiwan, 99%. According to Tai (1989), the Confucian emphasis on education is considered a substantial facilitator to the process of economic modernization, which underlines a rudimentary economic principle: "Human resource development is a slow, long-term, and costly process, but the benefit is great, cumulative, and nearly always outweighs the cost" (p. 25). Only the skillful and intelligent human beings are able to use the economic resources productively.

The philosophy of Confucian education is based on the idea of "providing education for all people without discrimination," and completely emphasizes the teaching of ethics; thus, the purpose of education is to help students develop an ideal personality. Through this educational system, virtues with regard to one's tasks in life are integrated. Those virtues attributing to the economic growth of the Asian Five Dragons include skill acquisition, hard work, moderation, patience, and perseverance.

The four key principles of Confucian teachings show a direct impact on organizational communication, especially on the principle of management and interpersonal relationship and communication in the Asian Five Dragons.

## The Impact of Confucianism on Organizational Communication

A conclusion that can be drawn from the previous discussion of the four key principles of Confucian teachings is that "human" is the focal point of Confucian teachings. When applied to the process of management, the Confucian style of management is therefore termed "humanistic management" or "ethical management" (Tseng, 1991). The humanistic emphasis of Confucian teachings is parallel to the Human Relations Model of organizing developed in the West. As Conrad (1989) points out, the Human Relations Model focuses on the "individual identities and needs of employees and looks to improvements in personal relations and interpersonal communication as a way of simultaneously meeting organizational needs for control and coordination and employee needs for predictability, creativity, autonomy, and sociability" (p. 157). This

**Table 2** Confucian Influence on Management/Leadership

| Ideal State of Management | Leadership |
|---|---|
| To develop a secure working environment for all employees in the organization | Rectification of name—a process for a leader to correctly perceive his/her role behavior and the legitimate authority from it |
| Humanistic management:<br>1. Human nature is mutable<br>2. A committed employee is able to adapt to the changing environment<br>3. Mutual understanding between superior and subordinate is a key to organizational success | Sincerity—honesty to one's self and truthfulness toward employees: (1) five virtues to be pursued, and (2) five evils to be avoided |

section examines the influence of Confucian teachings on management principles and interpersonal relationships and communication in the organizations of Asian Five Dragons.

## Influence on Management Principles

Two aspects of management are discussed: the ideal state of management and leadership (see Table 2). Based on Confucian principles, the ideal state of management is to develop a secure working environment for all employees in the organization through the process of self-cultivation and self-improvement. Tseng (1986) labels this thought as "M theory." M represents three concepts: men, medium, and management. M theory indicates that management is a process of making a harmonious balance among people. M theory entails three assumptions. First, human nature is mutable. The responsibility of a manager is to lead employees to a perfect working environment through the practice of *Jen*. Second, a committed employee is able to adapt to changing environments. A manager has to inform employees clearly about the goal of and behavioral criteria in the company. The adaptability to contingencies is regulated by *Yi*. Third, the mutual understanding between a superior and subordinate is a key to organizational success. This assumption is based on the understanding of one's role and position in the organization. A manager needs to specify role behaviors and to expect the fulfillment of those role behaviors. The achievement of this goal is regulated by cooperation, reciprocity, and mutual

trust, as originated from the concept of *Li*. The ideal state of management, therefore, is the integration of practicing the three core concepts of Confucian teaching: *Jen, Yi,* and *Li*.

Although the hierarchical structure of interpersonal relationships between a superior and subordinate makes Asian social groups function smoothly with more authoritarian interaction patterns, Confucian teachings specify that an effective leadership must follow two requirements: "cheng ming" (rectification of name) and "cheng" (sincerity). Only when terms are correctly used for the positional roles of leadership and understood by employees can the reality of organizing be described. The rectification of name is a process for leaders to correctly perceive the role behaviors and gain the legitimate authority from it (Hsieh & Fang, 1991).

Sincerity is referred to as honesty to self and truthfulness toward employees. According to Chan (1952), the function of sincerity is to exercise fully one's native intelligence and good knowledge, conscience, and native ability to do good. Confucian teachings indicate that a sincere mind is the precursor of "Kan Ying" (influence and response). Sincerity is the basis for receiving from employees a positive response to a manager's influence. The practice of sincerity in leadership reveals the abilities of "esteeming the five virtues" and "avoiding the four evils" indicated by Confucius. The five virtues are: (1) To treat as advantageous what employees find advantageous, (2) to put only those able employees to work, (3) to have desires for

**Table 3** Confucian Influence on Communication in the Organization

| Interpersonal Relationship | Organizational Life |
|---|---|
| Explicit communication rules | Reduced uncertainty in organizational communication |
| Complimentary relationship | Socio-emotional communication prevails |
| Ingroup/outgroup distinction | Team building; life-time employment |
| Intermediary | Non-confrontational communication |
| Vague boundary between personal and public relationships | Conflict avoidance; consensus building; trust |
| Similar communication context | Facilitate communication and training |

achieving humanness-at-its-best without greed, (4) to be dignified but not proud of regarding quantity and size of property, and (5) to inspire awe from employees without being brutal. The four evils to be avoided are: (1) cruelty — to punish employees for the lack of instructions, (2) outrageousness — to expect accomplishment from employees without proper advisement, (3) deterioration — to insist upon completion after instruction to proceed slowly, and (4) pettiness — to promise a reward but to begrudge its payment.

## Influence on Relationship and Communication

Based on the foregoing discussions, six characteristics of interpersonal relationships and communication as a result of the Confucian influence can be identified in the organizations of the Asian Five Dragons: Explicit communication rules, complementary relationships, ingroup and outgroup distinction, use of an intermediary, vague boundary between personal and public relationships, and similar communication contexts. These characteristics and their influences on the organizational life and communication cost are discussed as follows (see Table 3):

First, explicit communication rules are predominant in interpersonal communication. Because human relationships in Confucian societies are regulated by the Five Code of Ethics (*Wu Lun*), interpersonal relationships are governed by a set of explicit communication rules and are, thus, rela-

tively predictable. Many rules in interpersonal communication are transferred to the organizational setting. The hierarchical ruler/subject and father/son relationships, for example, are applied to the superior/subordinate relationships. Since these rules are explicit, learning rules becomes important and necessary for the group members. Following these rules would lead to safer communication which minimizes uncertainty and guess work in the organization. Communication cost is then reduced.

The hierarchical superior/subordinate relationship is especially reflected in Korean and Japanese organizations. For example, according to Klopf (1991), in a Japanese business setting the relationships are usually based on rank which is determined by sex, age, educational background, and length of service in the company. Moreover, the hierarchical structure of relationship requires strict communication patterns. This explains why subordinates use honorifics and become more restrained when talking to superiors.

Second, since interpersonal relationships are complementary, the management or the superiors in the organization give holistic and fraternalistic concerns to employees or subordinates in exchange for their loyalty. Soci-emotional functions of communication are almost inherent in the management-employee or superior-subordinate relationships. For example, Chung (1992) indicates that superiors in Taiwanese and Japanese companies often get involved in the resolution of subordinates' family problems. In Japan, "when an employee dies on the job, the company would hire his wife, although not necessarily to do the same job in the same company" (p. 7). The cost of socio-emotional communication may be great, but many frustrations, dissatisfactions, or conflicts are then prevented.

Third, due to the tendency of clearly distinguishing ingroup and outgroup members, organizational members are easier to motivate toward the goal of team-building, and commitment to the group can be easily transferred to the organization as a whole. Organizational climate then is more supportive. The Japanese term "kaisha" well displays the concept of "ingroup" in Japanese organizations. According to Nakane (1970), kaisha is

*"my" or "our" company, the community to which one belongs primarily; and which is all-important in one's life. Thus in most cases the company provides the whole social existence of a person, has authority over all aspects of his life; he is deeply involved in the association. (p. 4)*

The clear distinction between ingroup and outgroup and the "we" feeling among group members also affect management-employee relationship and control system. As Rehder (1981) points out, when comparing the traditional American and Japanese organizations, Japanese organizations rely on high group motivation and standards with social work control, while, in American organizations, employment commitment depends on economic conditions and performance. As a result of this group motivation, many Japanese workers proudly identify themselves as their "company's man" (Goldhaber, 1993). The advantage of "easy motivating within group" is not without cost. Ingroup motivation is usually accomplished at the expense of outgroup exclusion. This is why, in Confucianism-influenced societies and organizations, outsiders or foreigners have greater difficulty being accepted. The input from the environment is, thus, reduced to a minimum, resulting in a relatively closed communication system.

Fourth, because an intermediary is customarily used for initiating a new relationship or resolving a conflict, communication styles become non-confrontational. This code would reduce conflicts and, thus, minimize communication costs. The non-confrontational communication style is based on the Confucian concept "Ho" (harmony). According to Chung (1992), in Chinese organizations conflict is considered harmful and leads to a negative result in the organization. For example, a superior's disciplinary action to a subordinate in the Chinese organization is usually practiced by following the saying "Extol the merit in public hall; rectify the wrongdoing in the private room."

Fifth, the vague boundary between personal and public relationships in Confucian societies makes contact with organizational members more frequent. This, in turn, functions to identify mutual interests, expand overlapping communication contexts, build trust, and reach consensus. For example, Japanese superiors often invite subordinates to have a drink or to engage in other social situations after work. These socio-emotional communication activities on a relatively personal level characteristically create a common culture, which reduces uncertainty and conflict and increases morale and effectiveness.

Lastly, the heavy emphasis on education and equal opportunity of education has produced educated communicators who can communicate within more similar contexts than if education gaps are wide. The cost of education may be enormous, but education could facilitate communication, especially in terms of the organizational socialization and organizational training. The previous discussions of emphasis on education in the Asian Five Dragons have explained the impact of education on the organizational life.

The six characteristics present a general picture of the Confucianism-influenced organizational communication, resembling the Human Relations School of organizational thought developed in the West. The emphasis on interpersonal relationships in Confucian teachings, for example, is also advocated by Follett and Barnard, the pioneers of the Human Relations School (Bostdorff, 1985). The emphasis on human relationship in Confucianism-influenced organizational communication is also echoed by Mayo, the main pioneer of the human

**Table 4** The Preventive Communication Cost and Compensation in Confucianism-Influenced Organizations

| Preventive Comm. Cost | Compensation |
| --- | --- |
| Rule-learning cost | Reduced guess work and uncertainty |
| Long-term interaction cost | Reduced apprehension and increased liking and mutual respect |
| Outgroup exclusion cost | Easier motivation |
| Intermediary cost | Reduced conflict |
| Personal contact cost | Loyalty and commitment |
| Education cost | Reduced misunderstanding and clarification efforts |

relations theory of organization. Some of his assumptions, as summarized by Eisenberg and Goodall (1993), include that employees are motivated by social needs and obtain the sense of self-identity through interactions with others.

The Human Relations School, however, does not adequately explain why communication can boost effectiveness or productivity. This investigation of Confucianism with respect to organizational communication identifies an Eastern version of "The Human Relations School." This version provides abundant information about how an emphasis on interpersonal relationships might boost effectiveness, especially through the approach of communication cost.

Inferring from what was discussed above, the Confucian societies and organizations invest heavily in communication through rule learning, long-term interaction, outgroup exclusion, intermediary, personal contact, and education. The investment on these aspects of organizational communication is related to communication cost. "The rule-learning cost" is paid off by the reduced guess work and uncertainty. "The long-term interaction" cost can reduce communication apprehension and increase liking and mutual respect. "The outgroup exclusion cost" may help motivation. "The intermediary" cost can reduce conflict or smooth the conflict-resolution process. "The personal contact cost" is paid back by loyalty and commitment, and, finally, "the education cost" is compensated by the reduced communication gap, misunderstanding and clarification effort. In view of this model (see Table 4), all these costs are in problem prevention rather than in problem solution. This emphasis on employees' satisfaction with the social and interpersonal relationships of peers has been found to influence significantly the organization's productivity (Carey, 1967).

As can be observed from this analysis, in Confucianism-influenced organizations the human aspect of the employee's problem is the focus of attention. This is a feature of high-producing organizations indicated by Likert (1961). Confucianism-influenced organizational communication, therefore, implies positive contributions to lower employee turnover, smaller number of grievances, more easily aroused company morale, and stronger employment commitment. These organizational characteristics are some of the measures of organizational effectiveness (Goldhaber, 1993).

Finally, this analysis identifies a new dimension of communication cost study. Most previous studies on communication costs are from the space perspective emphasizing the relationships between office location and costs maintaining contacts, especially by those employees who are relocated (Goddard, 1975; Pye, 1976; Thorngren, 1970). This study points out a direction toward the human relation aspect of communication cost. It may not be easily quantified from this perspective, but the significance and impact are apparently greater than those of the space perspective.

## Conclusions

In this essay, we delineate Confucianism as the cultural root of the Asian Five Dragons. The impressive economic and social progress has been remarkable over the past three decades in the areas of the Asian Five Dragons. The process of this development is complicated, and many articles and books about the development of the Five Dragons have been published. Although a number of general economic factors are used to interpret the success of the Asian Five Dragons, most scholars agree that cultural influence based on Confucianism is a major factor contributing to the success. Confucius develops a code of ethics that guides the interpersonal relationships of the familistic organizations. The acceptance of Confucian teachings by the Asian Five Dragons shapes a human-oriented workforce. It not only relatively reduces the communication cost, but also generates a greater organizational effectiveness.

The characteristics of Confucianism-influenced organizational communication identified in this study imply several strategies for effective organizational communication. These strategies are basically investing in preventive, as opposed to problem-solving, measures for organizational effectiveness.

First, organizations can facilitate rule-learning of employees by investing more in orientation programs for new employees. These rule-learning programs can be based on the assumption that employees will stay and are encouraged to stay for a relatively long period of time.

Second, socio-emotional communication activities need to be geared toward establishing long term relationships among employees. For example, superficial conversations at cocktail parties can be complemented with group activities that require more personal contacts and interdependent effort. The quality control circle, for instance, is an old but long-neglected tool to this effect. Third, motivational communication efforts can be based on themes that emphasize external competition and promote internal "we" feelings.

Some of these suggestions may not be totally new. Some of them, the quality control circle, for example, have become popular after Japanese success stories in production management were widely recognized. Unfortunately, these programs are not broadly valued in the western organizations. The above strategies may become more evidently

powerful when organizations go international or multicultural such as culturally diversified organizations, multinational corporations, overseas subsidiaries from the West to the East, and vice versa.

As implied in the analysis above, the Confucianism-influenced organizational communication also displays certain weak spots. The in-group/out-group distinction, for example, may make the organization clannish and may reduce the possibility of communicating with the external environments and in turn reinforces the homogeneity and hurts the creativity. Nevertheless, this can hardly emerge as a problem in the Western organizations, given the high mobility, heterogeneity, and individualism in the Western society as a context. It will be interesting for future research to continue this line of research.

## References

Adler, N. (1983). Cross-cultural management research: The ostrich and the trend. *Academy of Management Review, 8,* 226-232.

Bostdorff, D. (1985, November). *Mary Parker Follett.* Paper presented at the annual meeting of the Speech Communication Association, Denver, CO.

Carey, A. (1967). The Hawthorne studies: A radical criticism. *American Sociological Review, 32,* 403-416.

Chan, S. (1990). *East Asian dynamism.* Boulder, CO: Westview.

Chan, W. T. (1952). Basic Chinese philosophical concepts. *Philosophy East and West, 2,* 166-170.

Chen, D. C. (1987). *Confucius thoughts.* Taipei: Cheng Chuong.

Chen, G. M. (1988, November). *A comparative study of value orientations of Chinese and American families: A communication view.* Paper presented at the annual meeting of the Speech Communication Association, New Orleans, Louisiana.

Chen, M. C. (1991). Family culture and management. In G. S. Yang & C. S. Tseng (Eds.), *A Chinese perspective of management* (pp. 189-212). Taipei: Kwei Kwan.

Chiao, C. (1988). A study of Guan Hsi. In K. S. Yang (Ed.), *The psychology of the Chinese people* (pp. 105-122). Taipei: Kwei Kuan.

Child, J. (1981). Culture, contingency and capitalism in the cross-national study of organizations. In L. L. Cummings & B. M. Shaw (Eds.), *Research in organizational behavior* (pp. 303-356). Greenwich, CT: JAI.

Chinese Culture Connection (1987). Chinese values and the search for culture-free dimensions of culture. *Journal of Cross-Cultural Psychology, 18,* 143 – 164.

Chung, J. (1991, April). *Seniority and particularistic ties in a Chinese conflict resolution process.* Paper presented at the annual conference of the Eastern Communication Association, Pittsburgh, Pennsylvania.

Chung, J. (1992, November). *Equilibrium in the Confucianism-influenced superior-subordinate communication system.* Paper presented at the annual meeting of the Speech Communication Association, Chicago, Illinois.

Condon, J. C. (1977). *Interpersonal communication.* New York: Macmillan.

Conrad, C. (1989). *Strategic organizational communication.* Chicago, IL: Holt, Rinehart and Winston.

Eisenberg, E. M., & Goodall, H. L. (1993). Organizational communication: Balancing creativity and constant. New York: St. Martin's.

Goddard, J. (1975). Organizational information flows and the urban system. *Economic Appliquee,* 125 – 164.

Goldhaber, G. (1993). *Organizational communication.* Dubuque, IA: William C. Brown.

Gorden, W. I. (1984, May/June). Organizational imperatives and culture modifiers. *Business Horizons,* 76 – 83.

Hofstede, G. (1980). *Culture's consequences: International differences in work-related values.* Beverly Hills, CA: Sage.

Hofstede, G. & Bond, M. H. (1988). The Confucius connection: From cultural roots to economic growth. *Organizational Dynamics, 16,* 5 – 21.

Hsieh, C. H. & Fang, C. F. (1991). The Confucian idea of management in Analects. In K. S. Yang and S. C. Tseng (Eds.), *A Chinese perspective of management* (pp. 95 – 114). Taipei: Kwei Kuan.

Hwang, K. K. (1988). Renqin and face: The Chinese power game. In K. K. Hwang (Ed.), *The Chinese power game* (pp. 7 – 56). Taipei: Giren.

Hwang, K. K. (1989). Confucian thoughts and modernization: Theory analysis and empirical study. *China Tribune, 319,* 7 – 24.

Jacobs, B. J. (1979). A preliminary model of particularistic ties in Chinese political alliances: Kan-ching and Kuan-hsi in a rural Taiwanese township. *China Quarterly, 78,* 237 – 273.

Kahn, H. (1979). *World economic development: 1979 and beyond.* Boulder, CO: Westview.

Likert, R. (1961). *New patterns of management.* New York: McGraw Hill.

MacFarquhar, R. (1980, February 9). The post-Confucian challenge. *The Economist,* 65 – 72.

Nakane, C. (1970). *Japanese Society.* Berkeley: Center for Japanese and Lorean studies.

Pye, R. (1976). Effect of telecommunication on the location of office employment. *OMEQA,* 289 – 300.

Rehder, R. (1981, April). What American and Japanese managers are learning from each other. *Business Horizons,* 63 – 70.

Shiang, T. C. (1982). *A study of Chinese character.* Taipei: Shang Wu.

Tai, H. C. (1989). The oriental alternative: An hypothesis on culture and economy. In H. C. Tai (Ed.), *Confucianism and economic development: An oriental alternative?* Washington, D.C.: Washington Institute.

Thorngren, B. (1970). How do contact systems affect regional involvement? *Environment and Planning, 2,* 409–427.

Tseng, S. C. (1986). *The Chinese idea of administration.* Taipei: Lien Ching.

Tseng, S. C. (1991). Chinese management: A Confucian perspective. In K. S. Yang & S. C. Tseng (Eds.), *A Chinese perspective of management* (pp. 75 – 94). Taipei: Kwei Kuan.

World Bank (1988). *World development reports.* New York: Oxford.

Wu, R. I. (1988). The distinctive features of Taiwan's development. In P. L. Berger & H. H. M. Hsiao (Eds.), *In search of an East Asian development model* (pp. 179 – 196). New Brunswick: Transaction.

Yum, J. O. (1987). The practice of Uye-Ri in interpersonal relationships. In D. L. Kincaid (Ed.), *Communication theory: Eastern and Western perspectives.* (pp. 87 – 100). New York: Academic.

Yum, J. O. (1988). The impact of Confucianism on interpersonal relationships and communication patterns in East Asia. *Communication Monographs, 55,* 374 – 388.

# The Group: A Japanese Context

DOLORES CATHCART
ROBERT CATHCART

Examining the cultural context of Japanese communication and other social behavior is a process fraught with complexity. Everyone seriously interested in Japan knows that nation as a group culture where individualism is submerged and expression is found in "hidden" ways. Personal honor, reward, prestige, and wealth all depend on one's group affiliation and its position in a larger hierarchy. But, not so easily discerned, is how the Japanese came to be this way. There is no one factor such as hard work or group consensus that can readily account for Japan's highly organized, extremely productive society. Most studies of the Japanese use comparisons with the West, frequently citing examples that present opposing paradigms as if somehow we can understand Japan by thinking of it as a nation completely opposite from our own (see Cleaver, 1976). Perhaps a better way would be to look at Japanese historical development, tracing how the group tradition arose, how it survived major crisis, and how it continues to provide a secure foundation for the inclusion of the modern, the exotic, and even the previously unimagined.

Social context in Japan is circumscribed by numerous historical, social, political, and economic factors. First and foremost, Japan is a tiny nation — a collective of relatively small islands separated from the Asian mainland by the Sea of Japan. This archipelago covers about 377,000 square kilome-

ters (147,000 square miles), an area slightly larger than the size of California and Oregon combined. About 70 percent of the area is mountainous, leaving only 30 percent of the land for farming and urbanization. Japan has less than half the U.S. population but its approximately 124 million people live crowded together in this small area.

Despite Japan's recent prominence as a major world power its home territory is only a small spot on the world globe and its population is far smaller than other world powers. Its isolation, its almost total lack of natural resources, the constant and continual threat of earthquakes and typhoons, along with its small, dense, and homogenous population have fostered attitudes of dependency within the social unit and a sense of separateness from the outside. Japan's geography and its history form an ongoing context apart from which one cannot appreciate or understand the significance of Japanese group culture. We will describe some of this history and analyze its influence in shaping modern Japanese culture. From this basis we will examine the role of the group as the significant context for communication in Japan.

## Historical Developments

### The Japanese Way, *Nihonjin-ron*

Japan's early civilization was based on rice agriculture, a process that demanded cooperation and communal sharing. Rice cultivation is labor intensive, leaving little time for other activities. So demanding was this farming that in the early villages families became extremely interdependent, living so closely together their rooftops often touched. Group values became dominant and the village came to be thought of as an extended family (*ie*). Loyalty to the village group, hard work, and harmony were enshrined as cardinal virtues. With no central source of national power and influence, villages remained insular and established their own codes and rules (Worden, 1992). Any offense could result in ostracism (*mura hichibu*) and for the individual this was the worst of fates since other groups would be unlikely to accept an outsider. The values of the village group were internalized and formalized over

This original essay appeared for the first time in the seventh edition. All rights reserved. Permission to reprint must be obtained from the authors and the publisher. Dolores Cathcart is a freelance writer. Robert Cathcart is Professor Emeritus at Queens College of the City of New York.

time creating what is known as "the Japanese way" (*Nihonjin-ron;* see Taylor, 1983). Through the centuries there has been practically no influx of foreigners into Japan to alter Nihonjin-ron. Imported foreign influences such as Confucianism, Buddhism, and the introduction of Chinese character writing have been blended with the already established Japanese way without changing the group character of society. The Japanese still assimilate foreign ideas, fashions, and designs in this manner. Each is filtered through traditional Japanese concepts of group harmony and loyalty (Irokawa, 1973).

During the "middle ages" of Japanese history strong *shogunates* (ruling families) created a social structure similar in some ways to the feudal societies of Europe but different in function. In Japan, there were no religious or ethnic factions to deal with. There was little wealth to covet beyond the rice stored in granaries. Still, battles to acquire territory and political power were fought. Powerful families secured their large land holdings by building castles, creating samurai armies, and engaging in court intrigues in a constant jostling for power.

The concept of family or ie already included an extended group of villagers, and as strong shoguns gained power they set up *daimyos* in the large villages and demanded that all their serfs pay allegiance to them as head of family. In their own realms the daimyo represented unchallenged authority and held the power of life and death over all subjects. A strict hierarchy was established and elaborate rules requiring conformity, subservience, and the show of humility governed everyone's behavior. A court was established in Edo (now Tokyo) and all daimyos were required to spend part of each year there to keep them from becoming too independent of central authority and to control their powers. Foreigners and foreign influences were kept out except when it served the ruling shogunate's purposes. Foreign trade was severely limited, and travel abroad prohibited (Taylor, 1983, p. 35).

In Edo, power was concentrated and reinforced by establishing a strict hierarchy that demanded a show of deference and humility to those at the top. At court, every nuance of speech, movement, and dress acquired meaning. Every act of communica-

tion became highly dependent on context. The Japanese language itself came to reflect this stratification of society; for example, grammar requires recognition of male superiority, there is an ingroup language and an outgroup one, and there are generational variations. Different disciplines or schools use different language to describe identical things. Important differences also extend beyond the grammatical: "There are differences (in speech) in communicational settings (where and when speech occurs), in topics, in channels (e.g., handwriting etc.)" (Hayashi, 1974). Highly refined ways of nonverbal communication were also given great importance. In negotiation, the nobler the aspiration, the more exquisite and subtle was the expression required, and the greater was the demand on others to interpret. These courtly customs left an indelible mark on the Japanese in as much as Japan's feudalism lasted almost sixteen hundred years (A.D. 300–1868). Its residue continues to influence Japanese social interaction and to shape modern politics (Worden, 1992).

After the demise of the shogunates and the establishment of a central government (the Meiji Restoration period, 1868–1919) there was a drastic reorganization of population and productivity. Japan brought in machinery, created industrial cities, and opened its doors (under pressure from the United States and other powers) to world trade. Despite this upheaval, concepts of extended family, group affiliation, and loyalty not only survived but were reinforced by a national civil code that strengthened Confucian ideas of filial piety and the hierarchical status that had been assimilated in the daimyo period (Long, 1992, p. 104). The Confucian notion of ranking in the family — men and women, father and child — was applied to the new industries and used to create groups of workers dependent on those at the top. In the move from countryside to city there was almost no change toward individual autonomy although some Western ideas of equality were adopted by small numbers of people in the liberalizing atmosphere of the 1920s. Foreign ideas seeped in and in the rapidly developing industrial cities new opportunities arose for small enterprises that were least affected by the traditional codes and rituals. The rise of militarism, however, quickly altered the course of Japan and the old customs were appropriated in the service of a military empire. Powerful generals restored the samurai code and, with fanatic zeal mobilized the nation for war by evoking the traditional loyalty of every group to the larger group, which now was the nation or empire.

## Post–World War II Japan

Japan's defeat in World War II signaled another drastic change in social control. The nation was in complete disarray; people were starving and American atomic and fire bombs had devastated cities and countryside alike. The American occupation (Allied forces) faced the enormous task of organizing a unified work force for rebuilding. American occupational officials looked to heads of important families from prewar Japan, who still commanded much respect. These modern day daimyos were able to use their rank to establish the new hierarchies that became the corporate entities of a newly rebuilt Japan. Again, the traditional social structure was reaffirmed and in the most unlikely circumstances.

The American occupation (1945–1952) brought many changes but it did not radically reform the social order. The constitution guaranteed individual freedoms. The political structure was completely reformed. Yet, half a century later the Japanese continue to live lives centered on group responsibility rather than individual liberty. Nihonjin-ron (the Japanese way) continues alongside constitutional guarantees of individual rights and the people live, somewhat uncomfortably, with the resultant dichotomies. Economically, however, the results have been tremendously successful for the Japanese. Set on a new course with economic development as a priority, the Japanese have used traditional concepts of group effort and hard work to not only rebuild but to catch up with and surpass the West.

Out of this history has evolved a modern nation of diligent workers rewarded by being a part of a greatly successful whole. Japan's most prominent and lasting achievement has been to produce a society that revolves totally around the concept of "group." Long (1992) sees this history as the dominant context for all Japanese social interaction today:

*Creating harmonious relations with others through reciprocity and the fulfillment of social obligations is more significant for most Japanese than an individual's relationship to a transcendent God. Harmony, order, and self-development are three of the most important values that underlie social interaction. . . . Religious practice, too, emphasizes the maintenance of harmonious relations with others (both spiritual beings and other humans) and the fulfillment of social obligations as a member of a family and a community. (p. 93)*

## Women in Japanese Society

We note here that this essay does not address the role of women in Japanese society. The civil code enacted during the Meiji Restoration legally defined women as inferior to men. As Japan became industrialized women were used as workers but were denied access to any advancement in the hierarchy since they were always hired as "temporary" employees. Most women in modern Japan are still denied lifetime employment offered to men despite the fact that the democratic constitution enacted after World War II granted women equal rights. Some observers claim that women's roles are changing (see Iwao, 1976), but within the context of group and the male-dominated hierarchy, women have little direct influence except through the traditional role of "young daughter" (office lady) within the company, and later, wife and mother in the family. Many women accept this as "the way things are." Some Japanese women we know say they would welcome change but most see little possibility of real change, and instead, say they would like to have been born male.

## The Group as Context

Taylor (1983) offers this apt description of modern day Japanese:

*One of Japan's most prominent national characteristics is the individual's sense of the group. At every level of society the Japanese have a very strong sense of who is on the inside [uchi] and who is on the outside [soto]. The group draws firm boundaries between "us" and "them" and, hierarchy, is an essential guidepost to proper behavior. Group ties can be so close that* members feel collective responsibility for each other's actions. Loyalty to the group and willingness to submit to its demands are thus key virtues in Japanese society. It is the values of the group rather than abstract principles, that serve as morality for many Japanese. (p. 67)

This special way of defining "group" exists in contrast to our Western view which holds that each individual has a unique identity, a "self" separate from, though influenced by, other members of the group. There is no counterpart in Japan to the American debate over "what is a group?" or whether committees make better decisions than individuals, and so on. In Japan there is no need to define groups, they simply "are," the "natural" or normal milieu in which human interaction takes place.

*Every Japanese person belongs to a primary group. Even hippies, for instance, or people who from our [Japanese] standards are ruffians, have primary groups of which they are members. There has never in Japan been a stratum of drifters who have been caste out of society and forced to make their own way on their own. The elite have built their own clearly differentiated "islands" as well, and other "islands" can be found everywhere down to the very bottom of society. Everybody has a group he or she is part of. (Nakane 1977, p. 8)*

The individual does not believe it is possible to "go it alone" for each Japanese, at birth, is drawn into this system. A Japanese legal scholar, Takeoyoshi (1967), describes the Japanese way of viewing the individual in the group:

*There is no place for the concepts of the individual as an independent entity equal to other individuals. In (Japanese) culture, the social order consists of social obligations, which are defined not in specific determinate terms, but in diffuse, indeterminate terms. . . . The indeterminateness of social obligations – hence the lack of concepts of equality and independent individual – does not allow the existence of [individual] "right" as the counterpart of social obligations. (p. 274)*

Each person is thought of as a part of a group and each small group as part of a larger one. Within each group individuals are ranked hierarchically according to sex, seniority, and age. In a Japanese group an individual has no problem fitting in or finding a role. A person's place in the group is determined at the time of entrance into the group and remains that ever after. In the family each member is ranked. The youngest daughter in the family remains in that inferior role no matter what occupational or marital status she attains. In the business world the newly hired worker is junior to all those who were there before and senior to all those who follow. This will not change. No bright young member of a group ever leap frogs over those more senior or is assigned a task not commensurate with his or her place in the hierarchy.

An experience we had in Japan exemplifies this. We had spent a long arduous day establishing research procedures for a study of stereotypes with our Japanese and French counterparts. We noticed the Japanese seemed ill at ease, particularly at lunchtime and during our coffee or tea breaks. At dinnertime we were escorted to our places in a restaurant dining room. Our Japanese hosts now appeared very pleased and relaxed. We interpreted this as their pride and pleasure in bringing us to such a fine Tokyo restaurant. This interpretation was proven inaccurate when one of the Japanese researchers whispered that now they were happy because, for the first time in the entire day, we were seated in the correct order. The oldest person and most senior researcher, who happened to be an American, was placed at the head of the group; next in age and status was a Japanese team member, now seated to the left; and so on down the line, everyone arranged, this time, according to age and status. The change in the attitude of the Japanese was amazing. You could hear and feel the difference. They were at ease, comfortable, able to fully participate because the correct order (hierarchy) had been established.

As Taylor (1983) points out, hierarchy is the context for all relationships in Japan:

*All societies establish hierarchies. In few societies, however, are they so widespread or important as in Japan. For the Japanese, rank is so finely determined that equality is rare – everyone and everything are at least slightly above or below the nearest apparent equal.*

*Family members, work mates, schools, companies, even nations and races all have their places. Hierarchy is inseparable from orderliness; a group is not properly organized unless its members are ranked. (p. 42)*

## Group Concepts

This dependency and the interdependency of all members of a group is reinforced by the concept of *on*. A Japanese is expected to feel an indebtedness to those others in the group who provide security, care, and support. This indebtedness creates obligation and when combined with dependency is called *on*. *On* functions as a means of linking all persons in the group in an unending chain because obligation is never satisfied, but continues throughout life. *On* is fostered by a system known as the *oyabun-kobun* relationship (Hall & Beardsley, 1965). Traditionally the *oyabun* is a father, boss, or patron who protects and provides for a son, employee, or student in return for his or her service and loyalty. This is not a one-way dependency. Each boss or group leader recognizes his own dependency on those below. Without their undivided loyalty he or she could not function. Oyabun are also acutely aware of this double dimension because of having had to serve a long period of *kobun* on the way up the hierarchy to the position at the top. All had oyabun who protected and assisted them, much like a father, and now each must do the same for their kobun. Oyabun have one or more kobun whom they look after much as if they were children. The more loyal and devoted the "children" the more successful the "father."

This relationship is useful in modern life where large companies assume the role of superfamily and become involved in every aspect of their workers' lives. Bosses are oyabun and employees are kobun. The company is not viewed as just a place of employment apart from one's life at home. The company or corporation becomes the center of the individual's social and economic life. Off-work hours are spent with one's fellow employees; vacations are taken at the company-owned retreat; health services, insurance, and transportation are provided. In even the most personal situations the company is involved. It isn't unusual for the company to help arrange marriages. In exchange the worker gives the company priority in his or her life. Thus, *on* based on the oyabun-kobun relationship works to promote both company and individual needs and creates a tight bond.

*On* and oyabun-kobun stress dependency and loyalty of superior and inferior in a vertical hierarchy. Without some balance, however, these concepts would produce a highly factional system where each group would have no regard for the interests of the whole. A mutual regard or loyalty to something larger than one's faction or oyabun-kobun link is therefore necessary. It is the concept of *giri* which serves in checking factionalism. Giri controls the horizontal relationships in this vertically organized society.

Giri, a term difficult for Westerners to interpret, is widely used in Japan. Hall and Beardsley (1965) offer the following explanation:

*To some Japanese today, giri is the blanket term for obligation between persons in concrete, actual situations as contrasted with a universalistic ethic of duty. . . . Giri [is the form of] obligations . . . [without] superiority on one side and inferiority on the other [as in the* on *relationship]. . . . Giri connotes obligation and as such sets up the tone of relationship toward specified other persons. (p. 94)*

Giri is well-suited to a society that induces life-long group relationships. These life-long relationships extend obligation horizontally to all the other groups that Japanese are members of or that contain associates from former groups. Japanese spend most of their days in close proximity with the members of their group, and without giri such an intense interaction over such an extended period of time would be impossible to bear. The highly ritualized modes of interpersonal interaction developed to accommodate giri and obligate persons to other group members prevent situations that produce hostility.

## Japanese Decision Making

This uniquely Japanese way of viewing relationships creates a distinctive style of decision making known as *consensus decision*. The Japanese devotion to consensus building seems difficult for most Westerners to grasp but loses some of its mystery when looked at as a solution to representing every member of the group. In a system that operates on oyabun-kobun relationships nothing is decided without concern for how the outcome will affect all. Ideas and plans are circulated up and down the company hierarchy until everyone has had a chance to react. This reactive process is not to exert pressure but to make certain that all matters affecting the particular groups and the company are taken into consideration. Much time is spent assessing the mood of everyone involved and only after all the ramifications of how the decision will affect each group can there be a quiet assent. A group within the company may approve a decision that is not directly in its interest (or even causes it difficulties) because its members know they are not ignored, their feelings have been expressed and they can be assured that what is good for the company will ultimately be good for them. For this reason consensus decisions cannot be hurried along without chancing a slight or oversight that will cause future problems.

The process of consensus building in order to make decisions is a time-consuming one, not only because everyone must be considered, but also because the Japanese avoid verbalizing objections or doubts in order to preserve group harmony. The advice, often found in American group literature, that group communication should be characterized by open and candid statements expressing individual personal feelings, wishes, and dislikes, is the antithesis of the Japanese consensus process. No opposing speeches are made to argue alternate ideas; no conferences are held to debate issues. Instead, the process of assessing the feelings and mood of each work group proceeds slowly until there exists a climate of agreement. This process is possible because of the tight relationships that allow bosses and workers to know each other intimately and to know the group so well that needs and desires are easy to assess. As Kyozaburo (1979) states

*The members of a small, closed society know almost everything about each other, so they do not need too many words to convey meaning. They are accustomed to understanding the other person's feelings through his or her facial expression and attitude. It was considered foolish, even impolite, to explain everything from beginning to end in words. (p. 5)*

The Japanese place a high value on the display of feelings and sensitivity rather than on verbal skill. The first virtue is group harmony; therefore, the free voicing of personal opinions is avoided. Some of our Japanese friends have said they can communicate with persons in their *nakama* (lifelong group) by a kind of telepathy, claiming they do not need words to express their thoughts but depend on an exchange of feelings. A Japanese explains: "It might be said that the culture is primarily visual, not verbal, in orientation, and social decorum provides that silence, not eloquence, is rewarded" (Miyoshi, 1974).

French philosopher Roland Barthes (1982) found the Japanese quite unique:

*[In Japan] it is not the voice (with which we identify the "rights" of the person) which communicates (communicates what? our – necessarily beautiful – soul? our sincerity? our prestige?), but the whole body (eyes, smile, hair, gestures, clothing) which sustains with you a sort of babble that the perfect domination of the codes strips of all regressive, infantile character. To make a date (by gestures, drawings on paper, proper names) may take an hour, but during that hour, for a message which would be abolished in an instant if it were to be spoken (simultaneously quite essential and quite insignificant), it is the other's entire body which has been known, savored, received, and which has displayed (to no real purpose) its own narrative, its own text (p. 10).*

Consensus building is utterly dependent on this sort of communication and dovetails with other values and ideas regarding the individual in society.

One of the consequences of making decisions through consensus is it makes the group and not the individual morally responsible for the decisions. Golden (1982) notes

*Once an opinion is acceptable, it becomes the group's opinion and is no longer associated with its originator.*

*This convention helps keep group unity intact by not singling out any one individual on the basis of performance or initiative. (p. 137)*

When a person commits a transgression it is the group that is embarrassed and, in the final analysis, responsible for the misdeed. It is commonly accepted in Japanese law and practice that the group should make amends and restitution resulting from individual misconduct (Kawashima, 1967). Usually, the person at the head of the particular group offers the necessary apology or makes the restitution expected. Individual Japanese, thus, feel a great deal of pressure and anxiety to always behave appropriately so that the group will not be embarrassed or looked upon with disfavor.

In dealing with such issues as corruption, bribe taking, pollution and price fixing the Japanese government is faced with a new problem because the international news media look to assign blame. It can be very difficult in Japan to investigate groups and assess blame because group members will not talk to outsiders about what happens in their group and they do not express dissatisfaction publicly.

## The Modern Context

The Japanese replicate this ancient model of family hierarchy and process throughout their society. The nuclear family is the first circle in the many circles of groups that dominate life in Japan. Dependency on others is central to this system. It is, therefore, commonly accepted that the Japanese family must teach a child to become a member of society, learning to behave according to the assigned role he or she is born to. "Japanese children learn from their earliest days that human fulfillment comes from close association with others" (Long, 1992). All the intricate rituals and modes of honorific speech are learned within the family in preparation for life in a hierarchical group society. Most importantly, each child learns that personal desire (*ninjo*) must be fulfilled *within the group*. Ninjo is submerged in the opinion and action of the group. This lesson could be hard without the rewards that accrue. Japanese children, at a young age, are extremely indulged and given tender care, learning that comfort and

intimacy are to be found by controlling ninjo and accepting the group as a means of personal fulfillment (Kizaemon, 1954). Japanese psychologist Takeo Doi (1962) describes the dependency that results from such care as *amae* or "the sweet dependency" first experienced through mother love within the family. He contends that throughout life a Japanese participates in close groups in an everlasting quest to duplicate this sweet dependency.

In modern Japan government service or employment with a large important corporation provides the path to success. Children are early groomed to compete for acceptance into that hierarchy. Once that path is entered it is extremely difficult to deviate from; it is rare for a person to withdraw from a group because group affiliation confers identity and security. All through school Japanese children prepare for university entrance exams because their whole future is dependent on scores made during the week of "Exam Hell." The top two universities admit those with the highest scores. The best companies and the government civil service hire graduates from those two universities. All other universities are arranged hierarchically and their graduates are placed in the appropriate business, government, and education hierarchies.

High school students cram for exams and mothers devote themselves to making sure study comes before all else. The goal of gaining admission to a university dominates life; anxiety and work mark these years for both student and mother. Once accepted at a university it is rare for anyone to drop out or leave even temporarily to travel or work. Universities rarely grant readmittance after an absence and credits cannot be transferred. Therefore, everyone who enters the university stays and becomes part of the group hierarchy. Peer groups are formed around those who entered at the same time and are the same age. This has special importance because the connections made while in the university will continue throughout each person's life.

It is commonly reported that Japanese university students do not study hard once they have been admitted to a school. After the grueling competition for admission, students view university life as a time to throw off restraints, to drink, to make love, to protest, or act out against the older established order. Evidence of this seems to abound in the news stories and pictures of youth in Tokyo. These portrayals fail to explain the overnight transformation that occurs when upon graduation day the former student emerges a company man – cutting his hair; dressing in a suit, white shirt, and tie; and adopting a reserved attitude and impeccable manners. This is yet another case of a Japanese trait that seems mysterious until seen in its context. The rigid system that requires constant observance of hierarchy has its safety valves and the period at the university is one of those times when the strict code that controls behavior is relaxed. This time of nonconformity doesn't threaten the whole because it is virtually impossible to deviate from the chosen path that leads to company life. Then too, even though students appear to only be having a good time, they are actually serving the established order by making necessary and important contacts with others that will serve the company later on.

Students at the university form their own *nakamas* (small groups), usually around special interest clubs such as poetry, photography, hiking, or golf. They drink together, confide in one another, and learn to know each other intimately. This is not only practice for joining a company group, it forms links with others who go on to other groups and who will be valuable contacts that help connect company groups. A Japanese company man never actually leaves his university nakama but maintains and nourishes the close contacts with the group by continuing the sport or special interest the group shares as an extension of his business obligations. This interaction provides the necessary connection between groups that maintains the close connections among business, government, and educational institutions. In Japan, groups not only spiral out concentrically from nuclear family to school, to university, to company, to nation but also intersect horizontally on a less hierarchical plane – that is, company to company or agency to agency.

## The Company Man

In this overlapping and connecting of groups, it is always understood that one's loyalty belongs un-

questionably to one's company. This is acknowledged in the ritual and ceremony that surround any transition from one hierarchy to another. Transitions, such as leaving the university to join a company are circumscribed by ceremony and marked as symbolic rights of passage. For example, when a new recruit is welcomed into the company the new worker's parents participate, symbolizing the approval and acknowledgment of the transfer of loyalty from the natural family to the company family. The family metaphor is so pervasive the worker is thought of as being adopted by the company. Still, since one never really leaves a group, the child, the member of a student nakama, and the worker are all roles with continuing obligations. For sociologist Matsumoto (1960), it is this context that circumscribes the role of the individual:

*The individual does not interact as an individual but as a son in a parent-child relationship, as an apprentice in a master-apprentice relationship, or as a worker in an employer-employee relationship. Furthermore, the playing of a role of son, apprentice, student, or worker persists twenty-four hours a day. There is no clear-cut demarcation between work and home life. (p. 60)*

## Nonconformist

While it is nearly impossible for persons enmeshed in corporate hierarchy to make personal decisions to change there is room in modern Japan for nonconformity outside the monolithic government-business enterprises. Not all Japanese, of course, conform to the image of the "company man." Some exceptions to corporate life are the many small entrepreneurs who own bars, beauty shops, noodle stands, imo (hot potato) carts, and so on and the many Japanese who participate in the entertainment world of film, radio, television, photography, and fashion where foreign ideas and techniques are explored safely without threat (presumably) of changing the central group structure.

Throughout Japanese history there have been individuals alienated from traditional groups for one reason or another, producing some interesting and provocative results. Some outsiders have joined the gangster group known as the *yakuzi*. The yakuzi run the gambling, prostitution, bar enterprises, and other rackets in Japan and are tolerated by the establishment until they overstep boundaries somehow understood but never stated. The yakuzi are not only tolerated but it is said that some corporations are known to hire yakuzi to control stockholder meetings and perform other fringe services. Interestingly, the yakuzi have an internal group structure that rivals any other in the nation in its requirements for loyalty and ritual.

## Modern Day Contexts

### Outside Influences

There are, of course, pressures toward change in present day Japan. Japan's goal to catch up with and bypass the West has presented challenges in dealing with other nations. It has become increasingly difficult to protect society from outside influences when businesses must send their employees to foreign countries and when television brings foreign nations to Japan everyday. As the Japanese become aware of how the rest of the world perceives them, their sense of themselves as unique is being challenged and they are seeing outsiders in a different light (see A Report on Television Stereotypes of Three Nations: France, U.S., and Japan, 1968). *Uchi* and *soto* are now harder to define. The necessity to communicate with foreign governments and to do business with foreign companies presents the Japanese with formidable problems. In face-to-face negotiations the Japanese have tried to adapt to the exigencies of dealing with styles of negotiation and decision making totally different from their own.

### *Uchi* and *Soto*

The Japanese view that they are a unique people in a unique nation is, to the outsider, the most frustrating characteristic of the Japanese. It seems to deny what most Americans believe, that there are fundamental beliefs and feelings that unite all people in the modern world. Americans feel strongly that if they just try hard enough they can find that common ground on which to resolve differences with other peoples. Yet, the Japanese we know feel equally strongly that Americans can never really understand "ware, ware, Nihonjin" or "we Japa-

nese" as they so often refer to themselves; the "we" meaning unique or different from anyone else, anywhere. Gould (1972) concurs with his statement that the Japanese have

*an unshakable conviction that no non-Japanese can ever understand the nuances and intuitive perceptions of the Japanese. In many travels over many years in all parts of Japan, I have never met a Japanese who truly believes that the foreign mentality can share the Japanese experience or aspirations. . . . It seems (to be) the Japanese perspective that experiences of Japan are by that fact alone totally different from the rest of the world. (p. 71)*

Most intercultural studies assume there are basic human qualities that are found in every race and people and that by understanding other cultures we can create common goals for humanity. The Japanese do participate in intercultural endeavors but they do not see themselves as "the same" in any way as the soto, or other. Further, their uniqueness is unquestionable to them, though not because of any physiological or psychological difference in nature but because of the extremely intimate and complex group orientation that has been the center of their culture for all its centuries. It is also true that no foreigner in Japan can ever be completely accepted no matter how well the language is spoken or the cultural nuances understood. A foreigner cannot be uchi (inside), and therefore one can never behave or speak in the Japanese way. The Japanese way (ninhonji-ron) has been carefully protected from outside influences and even in these times when the Japanese must deal with outsiders that way is protected. The Japanese are extremely interested in and ready to import foreign ideas, fashions, and trends but only when they are filtered through the traditional system. Japan imports and views more American movies than any other nation. All the French fashion houses have posh showrooms in Tokyo. Coca-Cola and Big Macs thrive on the scene. T-shirts with foreign language logos abound. But, when getting down to business the Japanese insist on maintaining the old ways.

In the international business and political worlds there are tremendous pressures on Japan to change but so far the Japanese have been able to adapt their methods to the exigencies of modern international life. To do business with the outside world, companies and corporations have not only had to admit foreigners to Japan and find ways to negotiate but they have also had to send many of their own employees to other countries. This requires the Japanese to be away from the nakama for months, sometimes years, posing a real threat to maintaining groups in the traditional way. If the Japanese employee in America or Europe adapts too well to his foreign assignment it will be very difficult to return to his nakama or family. The Japanese believe that a person who leaves Japan, even temporarily, chances losing the true Japanese spirit. Persons in foreign positions for any length of time are scrutinized on their return to assess if they have lost their Japaneseness. *Nakama doshi,* or being in one's group, requires diligent and constant participation. When a Japanese has been away from the group it is a hard task to become nakama doshi once again.

To conduct business or diplomatic relations with the Japanese it is often necessary to make the concessions to Japanese style. This is not a stubborn refusal on the part of the Japanese to meet half way, rather it is the real danger to the group that Japanese feel when dealing with soto (outsiders) whose seemingly direct and brash ways disrupt harmony and undermine obligation.

Various styles have evolved but it is very difficult for the Japanese to proceed in any encounter until the relative importance of persons (hierarchical status) they are dealing with is ascertained. Among themselves the Japanese use business cards to accomplish this and they have convinced may foreigners to use business card exchange as a way to begin communication. If the exchange is taking place in Japan the next move is to learn as much as possible about the others they must deal with. This too is done in a traditional Japanese fashion. Foreign businesspeople are entertained in restaurants and bars in an attempt to discover the style and direction the proceedings will take. The Westerner often thinks

of this as becoming friends but friendship is not the purpose. The Japanese are getting a feel for things, assessing the aspirations of the others, and deciding when they feel they know enough to start business. Once negotiations are finally begun matters proceed slowly because everyone in the company must be kept involved (even those not present). If the Japanese decide to stop negotiations or to withdraw it can be very difficult to know this. Nothing happens and only vague and noncommittal responses are offered. There is not a definite "no." There is just a reluctance that must be interpreted. This lack of directness often frustrates foreigners. These behaviors, though, are simply adapted from the normal Japanese way of conducting business. Terasawa (1974) gives this advice:

*When you do business in Japan you must be prepared to take your time, to be alert to indirection. The Japanese businessman is intent on harmony, even if the deal falls through, and he will spend whatever time is necessary to determine his "you to you" approach and he will communicate his own views indirectly and with great sensitivity. . . . This places time in a different perspective. In Japan the Western deadline approach is secondary to a thorough job. Japanese are thorough in their meetings as well as in their production. Thus Americans are often exasperated by the seemingly endless sequences of meetings of many Japanese businessmen. (p. A41)*

## Conclusion

Clearly, the Japanese are now facing demands on them as a prominent power in the world that requires accommodation and new ways of behaving internationally, yet the context for all Japanese behavior remains the group. Group orientation has produced the highly successful blend of big business and government at the top of a hierarchy supported by loyal, hardworking employees and this isn't likely to change in the immediate future.

According to American cultural critic Louis Menand (1992), "Culture isn't something that comes with one's race or sex. It comes only through experience; there isn't any other way to acquire it. And in the end everyone's culture is different because everyone's experience is different." While Menand's statement stands as a justification for American individuality, curiously, the Japanese would find it acceptable as a justification of their view that cultural and racial differences are intractable. They believe that the gulf that separates one people from the next is always, at base, unbridgeable.

## References

Barthes, R. (1982). *Empire of Signs.* (Translated by Richard Howard). New York: Hill & Wang.

Cleaver, C. (1976). *Japanese and Americans: Cultural Parallels and Paradoxes.* Minneapolis: University of Minnesota Press.

Doi, L. T. (1962). "Amae: A Key Concept for Understanding Japanese Culture." In R. J. Smith and R. K. Beardsley (Eds.), *Japanese Culture: Its Developments and Characteristics,* 130–144. New York: Aldine.

Golden, A. S. (1982). "Group Think in Japan, Inc." *The New York Times Magazine,* December 5, pp. 133–140.

Gould, R. (1972). Japan alone. *Japan Quarterly, 19* (1).

Hall, J., and Beardsley, R. (1965). *Twelve Doors to Japan.* NY: McGraw-Hill.

Hayashi, T. (1974). Modernization of the Japanese system of communication. *Language in Society.* April.

Irokawa, D. (1973). "Japan's grass-roots tradition: Current issues in the mirror of history." *Japan Quarterly, 20* (1).

Iwao, S. (1976). "A Full Life for Modern Japanese Women." In *Text of Seminar on "Changing Values in Modern Japan,"* 95–133. Tokyo: Nihonjin Kenkyukai.

Kawashima, T., and Takeoyoshi, K. (1967). "The Status of the Individual in the Notion of Law, Right, and Social Order in Japan." In C. Moore (Ed.), *The Japanese Mind.* Honolulu: University Press of Hawaii.

Kizaemon, A. (1954). The family in Japan. *Marriage and Family Living, 16* (4), 362.

Kyozaburo, D. (1979). Japanese culture. *About Japan 11.* Tokyo: Kinji Kawamura.

Long, S. O. (1992). "The Society and Its Environment." In R. E. Dolan and R. L. Worden (Eds.), *Japan: A Country Study,* 69–128. Washington, D.C.: Library of Congress.

Matsumoto, Y. (1960). Contemporary Japan: The individual and the group. *Transactions of the American Philosophical Society, 50* (1), 60.

Menand, L. (1992). "The Hammer and the Nail." *The New Yorker,* July 20, p. 84.

Miyoshi, M. (1974). *Accomplices of Silence.* Berkeley: University of California Press.

Nakane, C. (1977). Speaking of the Japanese. *About Japan.* Tokyo: Kinji Kawamura.

A Report on Television Stereotypes of Three Nations: France, U.S., and Japan. (1968). International Television Flow Project—Japan. Tokyo: NHK Broadcasting Co.

Taylor, J. (1983). *Shadows of the Rising Sun.* New York: Harcourt Brace Jovanovich.

Terasawa, Y. (1974). "Japanese Style in Decision-Making." *The New York Times.* Sunday, May 12.

Worden. R. L. (1992). "Historical Setting." In R. E. Dolan and R. L. Worden (Eds.), *Japan: A Country Study,* 1–68. Washington, D.C.: Library of Congress.

# Negotiating Cultural Understanding in Health Care Communication

## PATRICIA GEIST

While knowledge and appreciation of cultural diversity is growing in all types of contexts, providers in the health care setting have more to learn about the effects of culture on individuals' perception and expression of their symptoms. The white coat and high-technology image of modern medicine dominating American medicine coincides with what many people see as an excessive medical emphasis on disease and a biological understanding of illness (Littlewood, 1991). The reality of our contemporary society is that it is a culturally diverse community of individuals with many different national, regional, ethnic, racial, socioeconomic, and occupational orientations that influence interactions in health care settings (Kreps, 1992).

This article examines the complex and dynamic features of communication in a health care context challenged by the culturally diverse expectations and behaviors of individuals seeking health care. In the last decade, with increasing numbers of immigrants admitted to the United States, greater attention has been paid to cross-cultural caring, cultural sensitivity, and transcultural care. The article begins with a discussion of the long-standing interest in considering sociocultural backgrounds of patients in health care delivery. What we discover is that the movement to communicate in culturally sensitive ways is constrained by the Western emphasis on the biomedical model and its inherent

progressive ideology. The article continues by presenting specific case examples where providers and patients face difficulties when the culturally specific beliefs and practices of patients are not discussed or considered in diagnosing and determining appropriate treatment. Finally, the article concludes with avenues for overcoming the obstacles revealed in the case examples and for expanding our notions of culture and culturally sensitive health care.

## Linking Culture, Health, and Communication

In 1989 the United States admitted over one million immigrants from all over the world (See Table 1). In fact, California is expected to be the first mainland state with a nonwhite majority in the coming decades (Howe-Murphy, Ross, Tseng, & Hartwig, 1989). With the diversity of individuals entering the United States comes increasing diversity in health care beliefs and practices of persons seeking health care. However, medical education, generally, has failed to integrate intercultural communication training into its curriculum.

Sectors of health care education have long been concerned with cultural influences upon health care delivery. Three decades ago, the field of transcultural nursing was established, and with it an emphasis on culture-specific care, culturally congruent care, and culturally sensitive care (Leininger, 1991). Transcultural nursing, a humanistic and scientific area of formal study and practice, focuses upon differences and similarities among cultures with respect to human care, health (or well-being), and illness based upon the people's cultural values, beliefs, and practices (Leininger, 1991). Operating from this philosophy, nurses work to avoid imposing their cultural beliefs on their patients, and provide them with cultural-specific or culturally congruent care.

Transcultural nursing has been criticized for its limited notion of culture. One criticism is that it views culture as a unified whole with a direct cause and effect relationship upon behavior. Instead, in viewing culture as dynamic, and the experiences of individuals from similar cultures as varied, we begin to focus on the unique requirements of individ-

**Table 1** Immigrants to the United States in 1989

| Country or Region | Number of Immigrants | Percent of Immigrants |
|---|---|---|
| Mexico | 405,660 | 37 |
| Asia | 296,420 | 27 |
| Central America | 101,273 | 9 |
| Europe | 94,338 | 9 |
| Caribbean | 87,597 | 8 |
| South America | 59,812 | 5 |
| Africa | 22,486 | 2 |
| Canada | 18,294 | 2 |
| Oceania* | 4,956 | <1 |

*Includes Australia, Fiji, New Zealand, Tonga, and Western Samoa

uals—their feelings, opinions, and experiences (Mason, 1990). Second, critics believe that transcultural nursing must include more of a global perspective (Lindquist, 1990), one that goes beyond traditional cultural beliefs and practices to the history and political situation in the country from which individuals have immigrated. Finally, culturally sensitive care needs to address the stressful and traumatic experiences of immigrants in adapting to their new home in the United States (Boyle, 1991).

Today, the significant influence of culture on perceptions, treatment, and interaction is being recognized and written about in a wide array of texts, including *Patients and Healers in the Context of Culture* (1980), *Medicine and Culture* (1988), *Culture, Health and Illness* (1990), *Caring for Patients from Different Cultures: Case Studies from American Hospitals* (1991), and *Cross-Cultural Caring* (1991), to name a few. What is clear in just about every examination of health and culture is that "miscommunication, noncompliance, different concepts of the nature of illness and what to do about it, and above all different values and preferences of patients and their physicians limit the potential benefits of both technology and caring" (Payer, 1989, p. 10). Cross-cultural caring considers health care a social process in which professionals and patients

bring a set of beliefs, expectations, and practices to the medical encounter (Waxler-Morrison, Anderson, & Richardson, 1991). The task of negotiating an understanding of the problem, diagnosis, or treatment often is complicated by these cultural differences.

In the United States, the emphasis on technological progress and the biomedical model complicates the task of communicating to negotiate understanding even further. A progressive ideology has produced a society of experts who possess the technical knowledge, not social knowledge, and whose communication to the public places priority on the "body," not the "person" (Hyde, 1990). This progressive ideology places great emphasis on the functioning and malfunctioning of the human machine. One physician points out that this emphasis permeates medical education.

*Disease, we were told [in medical school] was caused by a malfunction of the machine, the body.... The emphasis began and ended with the body.... For this reason the modern medical model is called the molecular theory of disease causation. (Dossey, 1982, pp. 6–8)*

But, as a growing number of providers are discovering, this model does not account for the part of the human psyche that is most centrally involved in the cure of illness, namely varying perceptions of what constitutes health, illness, treatment, and the appropriate interaction between provider and patient (Lowenberg, 1989; Needleman, 1985). In fact, many would argue as Lowenberg (1989) does, that the single, most overriding conflict in the health care system is the polarization between humanistic and technological advances in health care. Fisher (1986) suggests that crosscutting all interactions between providers and patients is an ideology that supports the authority of the medical perspective over the patient's perspective. Consequently, the asymmetry of the medical relationship creates difficulties for patients in raising topics of interest to them and/or providing information they see as relevant (Fisher, 1986; Mishler, 1984).

Negotiating cultural understanding in the health care context necessitates willingness on the part of providers and patients to communicate honestly; to build a supportive, trusting relationship — "a relationship based not on unrealistic certainty, but on honesty in facing the uncertainty in clinical practice" (Inlander, Levin, & Weiner, 1988, p. 206). We need to understand illness and care as embedded in the social and cultural world (Kleinman, 1980). For Kleinman, "medicine is a cultural system, a system of symbolic meanings anchored in particular arrangements of social institutions and patterns of interpersonal interactions" (p. 24). He uses the term *clinical reality* to describe health-related aspects of social reality — especially attitudes and norms concerning sickness and health, clinical relationships, and treatment or healing activities (p. 37).

Increasing immigration of individuals from diverse cultures brings with it an amalgam of modern and traditional beliefs, values, and institutions that often conflict and contradict (Kleinman, 1980). The call to expand our understanding and appreciation of clinical realities implies that we need to acknowledge our ethnocentrism in dictating the proper way to provide care (Leininger, 1991); internationalize our professional education system (Linquist, 1990); consider the sociocultural background of patients (Boyle, 1991; Giger & Davidhizar, 1991); develop our cultural sensitivity (Waxler-Morrison et al., 1991); understand traditional (folk-healing) health care beliefs and incorporate them into care (Krajewski-Jaime, 1991); and generally communicate interculturally, recognizing the problems, competencies, prejudices, and opportunities for adaptation (Barna, 1991; Brislin, 1991; Kim, 1991; Spitzberg, 1991).

## Expanding Cultural Sensitivity in the Health Care Context

A growing crisis in the U.S. health care system is the culture gap between the medical system and the huge number of ethnic minorities it employs and serves (Galanti, 1991). Assessment is a clinical art that combines sensitivity, clinical judgment, and scientific knowledge (Anderson, Waxler-Morrison, Richard, Herbert, & Murphy, 1991). Rather than using phrases like "taking the history," "physical examination," or "case management," health care

providers negotiate a plan that will be acceptable to both themselves and their patients. The following cases reveal the difficulties that providers and patients face negotiating appropriate care. Differences in beliefs about health and illness, perceptions of appropriate treatment, and expectations about interaction in the medical setting complicate the communication process in health care delivery.

## Cultural Differences in Perceptions, Treatment Practices, and Relationships

All cultures have beliefs about health and illness that have been passed down from generation to generation (Galanti, 1991; Krajewski-Jaime, 1991). The difference between the belief system of the Western biomedical model and that of other cultures can result in inappropriate assessment or complications in treatment and communication in the provider-patient relationship. The research investigating the intersection of health and culture abounds with vivid examples of these challenges and the successes and failures in negotiating understandings acceptable to both providers and patients.

One source of misunderstanding in health care delivery stems from the practice of folk-healing medicine. Some practices can result in misdiagnosis; others simply contradict scientific medicine; and still others can result in improper medical treatment (Galanti, 1991). Curanderismo, a Hispanic folk-healing belief system originating in Europe, is the treatment of a variety of ailments with a combination of psychosocial interventions, mild herbs, and religion (Chesney, Thompson, Guevara, Vela, & Schottstaedt, 1980; Comas-Diaz, 1989; Krajewski-Jaime, 1991; Maduro, 1983). The three most common beliefs about the causes of disease are (a) natural and supernatural forces; (b) imbalances of hot and cold; and (c) emotions (Krajewski-Jaime, 1991, p. 161). Three practices central to this belief system are: (a) the role of the social network, particularly kin, in diagnosing and treating illness; (b) the relationship between religion and illness, which includes the use of religious ritual in many healing processes; and (c) consistency (but not uniformity) of beliefs among

Hispanic communities about symptoms and regimens of healing (Krajewski-Jaime, 1991, p. 160).

Knowledge of folk-healing beliefs and practices enables providers to communicate with empathy, sensitivity, and open-mindedness. Social workers, physicians, and nurses who receive special training in interviewing and communication may build trust and mutual sharing of cultural information in their relationships with their patients (Krajewski-Jaime, 1991). When this training has not been part of medical education, differences in health beliefs between predominant-culture providers and minority patients may result in inappropriate assessment. Providers may interpret folk-healing beliefs and practices as ignorance, superstition, abuse, or neglect because patients do not follow prescribed treatments. In the following case, described by Krajewski-Jaime in her research on folk-healing beliefs and practices among Mexican-American families, she reveals how a non-Hispanic caseworker's recommendations could have resulted in the unnecessary removal of a Mexican-American child from his caring and nurturing family.

*The assessment indicated that the child in question was ill and in need of medical care, but the mother had obvious emotional problems and appeared to be irrational: the mother had kept on saying, in broken English, that she could not allow any evil spirits to come near her child and had locked the child in his room; hung from the ceiling a pair of sharp scissors just above his head, and would not allow anyone, including the caseworker and the doctor, to enter the child's room. The caseworker's supervisor, who had some knowledge of the folk-healing practices among some of the agency's Mexican-Americans clients, asked a Mexican-American child protective service worker to reinvestigate the case. The worker visited the mother, who, while upset about the child's illness, welcomed someone who spoke Spanish. The mother explained that she had used several home remedies to help her child's fever go away, but evil spirits had already taken possession of her child and the usual remedies no longer helped. The only thing left to do was to prevent new spirits from entering the child's body. The scissors would immediately cut any spirits that would try to enter the child's body. Since evil spirits could attach to anyone who entered the room, she*

*could not allow anyone to enter the room, thus preventing any further harm to her child. The Mexican-American worker, although familiar with folk-healing practices had not seen this particular cure before. She understood the validity of this belief within the client's cultural context, but to successfully obtain the mother's permission to see the child, to remove the dangerous scissors, and to see that the child received medical attention, she had to validate the mother's beliefs and gain her trust. She told the mother that although she had not seen anyone use this cure before, she had heard her grandmother talk about it. To protect the patient and his or her entire surroundings, however, the grandmother usually nailed the scissors on the room's entrance door. The worker explained that, should the spirits attach themselves to anyone who wished to enter the room, the scissors on the entrance door would immediately prevent them from doing so and thus provided stronger protection to the patient. The Mexican-American worker went on to ask the mother if this made sense to her. She asked the mother if she thought this would be more beneficial since it would allow her child to be seen by the caseworker and the doctor. The mother agreed and emphasized that she wanted only what was best for her child. She changed the location of the scissors and welcomed the caseworker and the doctor to examine the child. (pp. 158–159)*

As Krajewski-Jamie points out, although this is an extreme example because of the dangerousness of the practice, most folk-healing practices are harmless. This case demonstrates how folk-healing, if understood, can become a resource on which to capitalize in building a rapport in relationships with patients or families and negotiating appropriate diagnosis and treatment.

Similar to curanderismo, Chinese folk medicine bases many of its beliefs on maintaining a harmonious balance between the two opposing forces of "hot" and "cold," often substituted for yang and yin (Lai & Yue, 1990). Illness may be seen as an imbalance in hot or cold foods and thus people may seek cures from food substances they associate with their own deficiency.

*For instance, a traditional Chinese may eat animals' brains in order to grow wiser. A diabetic may eat an* animal's pancreas in hope of cure. People thought to be anaemic often eat red foods. These examples illustrate why traditional Chinese may have difficulty in regarding plastic capsules as a cure. (Lai & Yue, p. 80)

These beliefs and practices provide evidence of the Chinese people's great concern about questions of health and health care, more so than Americans (Kleinman, 1980). However, along with this emphasis comes a belief in self-medication that may cause serious health problems.

Three specific examples of health practices reveal the problems that may develop with a patient's self-medication. First, Chinese, embracing the maxim of "all things in moderation," may believe that taking medicine over an extended period of time may weaken their bodies (Li, 1987). As a result, they often feel that:

Western medicine is too potent for them or their small bodies and they may reduce dosages to a quantity they believe suitable. For example, an elderly Chinese with diabetes may reduce his insulin because it is "foreign" and jeopardizes his health. (Lai & Yue, 1990, pp. 83–84)

In fact, Chinese may refuse blood tests, believing that loss of blood will weaken their bodies or that the tests are too invasive (Lai & Yue). Second, dual use of Western medicine and folk medicine is common in the Korean, Bahamian, Haitian, Puerto Rican, Cuban, and Southern U.S. black cultures (Scott, 1974). However, Western prescriptions may contain the same chemical ingredients as herbal prescriptions patients are presently consuming; consequently patients may experience overdose or adverse reactions (Park & Peterson, 1991). Finally, in this third example, we see how the beliefs of a Guatemalan patient's husband led to double dosages of birth control pills:

One couple that came together for family planning counseling returned in only two weeks asking for more pills. The husband responded to all the questions for his wife regarding how she felt, if she was experiencing any irregular bleeding or pain, without consulting her

even though she did understand enough Spanish to know what was being asked. She sat next to him silently as he explained that apparently the woman had taken two pills a day, thinking that they work better if the dosage is doubled. During the initial counseling, the husband also responded to all the questions by the female nurse and translator and stated he understood the procedures required for use of the Pill. However, the subsequent visit indicated that he did not fully understand why he had to take extra precaution during the first few weeks, and thus he had encouraged his wife to double the dosage. (Miralles, 1989, pp. 102–103)

In these three examples, the significance of communication in the provider-patient relationship is pronounced. And it is clear that providers who lack knowledge of health care beliefs and practices must negotiate and construct understanding during their interactions with patients.

The advice to health care providers in communicating with individuals from diverse cultures is to ask specifically about their beliefs and practices concerning herbal medicines or folk-healing practices (Park & Peterson, 1991). Asking these questions directly, rather than waiting for patients to volunteer the information or to ask about such issues, is especially important considering that Chinese and other immigrant groups generally have been taught to respect doctors and not to ask questions (Lai & Yue, 1990). In fact, for many Chinese, agreement and use of the word "yes" help to avoid the embarrassment of saying "no," as the following case illustrates:

Linh Lee, a sixty-four-year-old Chinese woman [was] hospitalized for an acute evolving heart attack. At discharge, her physician suggested that she come back in two weeks for a follow-up examination. She agreed to do so, but never returned. It is likely that she never intended to do so but agreed because he was an authority figure. Chinese are taught to value accommodation. Rather than refuse to the physician's face and cause him dishonor, Mrs. Lee agreed. She simply did not follow through, sparing everyone embarrassment. When Nancy, her Chinese-American nurse, saw her in Chinatown several weeks later, Mrs. Lee was very cordial and said she was feeling fine. (Galanti, 1991, p. 21)

In a case such as this we find that negotiating an agreed upon "yes" cannot be taken at face value. Providers who understand how cultural values can lead patients to communicate in prescribed ways will be sensitive to different communication styles in order to avoid the difficulties created by situations such as the one described above.

One additional factor complicating efforts to construct understanding in the provider-patient relationship is the common problem of patients not possessing English language competence. And although the use of translators can help to mitigate this problem, for a variety of reasons, translators, patients, or family members can complicate and obstruct efforts to negotiate understanding (Fitzgerald, 1988; Galanti, 1991; Hartog & Hartog, 1983; Miralles, 1989).

Miscommunication is a frequent problem with the use of translators (Fitzgerald, 1988; Galanti, 1991; Miralles, 1989). Even with expert translation, problems such as linguistic differences between the terms in English and other languages can present difficulties, especially languages such as Vietnamese which includes diverse dialects.

*[Vietnamese] words that translate "feeling hot" don't mean "fever." What they mean is "I don't feel well" and generalized malaise. And if you should ask your Vietnamese patients, "Have you ever had hepatitis?" the translator [may] translate that into "liver disease," and liver disease in Vietnam means itching. . . . Similarly, the kidney is the center of sexual potency to Indochinese and Vietnamese, and therefore "kidney trouble" may really mean decreased libido or other sexual difficulty. (Fitzgerald, 1988, p. 67)*

In addition, translators sometimes choose not to translate exactly what the patient says for any number of reasons — embarrassment, desire to portray the culture in a certain light, or lack of understanding:

*[Translators] are sometimes reluctant to translate what they think is ignorance or superstition on the part of the patient. So they are sophisticated and tell you what they think rather than what the patient said. [Or the provider may ask] "How do you feel?" The translator then spends five to ten minutes in discussion with*

*the patient and comes back and says, "Fine." (Fitzgerald, 1988, p. 65)*

Linguistic variations, slang, and culturally specific terminology existing within any culture can create communication difficulties even for an excellent translator. In addition, translators often selectively choose what to communicate from the patient's or provider's narratives, giving a synopsis of what the patient says or grossly altering the meaning of the communication (Anderson et al., 1991).

A translator's use of medical jargon and technical vocabulary also may contribute to communication difficulties. In the following case, the provider and patient *appeared* to have negotiated understanding, but unfortunately this was not the case:

*Jackie, an Anglo nurse, was explaining the harmful side effects of the medication [that] Adela Samillan, a Filipino patient, was to take at home after her discharge. Although Mrs. Samillan spoke some English, her husband, who was more fluent, served as interpreter. Throughout Jackie's explanation, the Samillans nodded in agreement and understanding and laughed nervously. When Jackie verbally tested them on the information, however, it was apparent that they understood very little. What had happened? Dignity and self-esteem are extremely important for most Asians. Had the Samillans indicated they did not understand Jackie's instructions, they would have lost their self-esteem for not understanding or they would have caused Jackie to lose hers for not explaining the material well enough. By pretending to understand, Mr. and Mrs. Samillan felt they were preserving everyone's dignity. Jackie's first clue should have been their nervous laughter. Asians usually manifest discomfort and embarrassment by giggling. Once Jackie realized they had not understood the material, she went over it until they were able to explain it back to her. (Galanti, 1991, p. 20)*

This case, as well as other previous cases, demonstrates how important it is not to take smiles and nods of agreement as understanding when communicating with Asian patients. The nurse in this case communicated with the patients in order to assess their understanding and it was only through her continued time, patience, and effort that they were able to negotiate understanding.

And still another complicating factor is the fact that often professional translators are not available in the medical setting and the patient's friends or family members are asked to serve as translators. For a wide variety of reasons, these circumstances can contribute to miscommunication. In the following case, we begin to understand how awkward, embarrassing, or difficult it might be for family members to communicate what they are being asked to translate.

*A Hispanic woman, Graciela Garcia, had to sign an informed consent for a hysterectomy. Her bilingual son served as the interpreter. When he described the procedure to his mother, he appeared to be translating accurately and indicating the appropriate body parts. His mother signed willingly. The next day, however, when she learned that her uterus had been removed and that she could no longer bear children, she became very angry and threatened to sue the hospital. What went wrong? Because it is inappropriate for a Hispanic male to discuss private parts with his mother, the embarrassed son explained that a tumor would be removed from her abdomen and pointed to that general area. When Mrs. Garcia learned that her uterus had been removed, she was quite angry and upset because a Hispanic woman's status is derived in large part from the number of children she produces. (Galanti, 1991, p. 15)*

There are a whole set of issues complicating communications in the health care setting when children serve as translators. In the case above, cultural rules dictate who can discuss what with whom (Galanti, 1991). In other cases, asking a patient's child to interpret can undermine the patient's competence in the eyes of the child, creating tensions in their relationship (Anderson et al., 1991). Once again we find that selection and use of translators is a complex issue that can interfere with providers' and patients' efforts to negotiate cultural understanding. In the final section of this article we discuss avenues for overcoming the obstacles faced in negotiating cultural understanding and for expanding our notions of culturally sensitive health care.

## Culturally Sensitive Health Care

The past ten years have seen a growing body of literature offering advice for increasing cultural sensitivity in health care delivery. Although, many of these suggestions focus on what actions providers should take, it is possible to see the implications these ideas have for anyone's efforts to increase their sensitivity to and understanding of other culture's health care beliefs and practices.

One useful starting point for health professionals is training that assists individuals in examining their own cultural beliefs and values as a basis for understanding and appreciating other cultural beliefs and values (Gorrie, 1989). At the University of Southern California, a course in cross-cultural communication sensitizes physician assistants to their personal biases and prejudices through videotaped mock interviews. Believing that self-awareness of personal discomfort can become a tool for promoting sensitive cross-cultural communication, the curriculum is based on the model, "Differences + Discomforts = Discoveries." Critiquing the interviews, students are encouraged to investigate their own feelings of prejudice and bias and to use their sensitivity to discomfort as "a cue that they are perceiving a difference and to inquire further rather than seek safety in the harbor of fear and prejudice" (Stumpf & Bass, 1992, p. 115).

In a system-wide approach, Howe-Murphy et al. (1989) describe the Multicultural Health Promotion Project, a multidisciplinary, multicultural, and participative model designed to address the need for changes in allied health service delivery to minority populations. Their training efforts are focused on faculty from three allied health departments (Health Science, Nutrition and Food Science, and Occupational Therapy), students preparing for careers in these three professions, and community health care practitioners — all of whom face issues of health promotion in the multicultural environment.

Viewing cultures as dynamic, and not static unified wholes, means that variations exist among individuals of any one culture. Accordingly, health care providers need to assess each patient individually before deciding on a plan of care (Park & Peterson, 1991). Taking a more holistic approach, concentrating on "individual's own experience and understanding of illness" may assist in this assessment (Littlewood, 1991). Providers should acquire a knowledge of the specific language of distress utilized by patients and providers' diagnosis and treatment must make sense to patients, acknowledging patients' experience and interpretation of their own condition (Helman, 1990). Individuals from similar cultural groups often share metaphors (sayings or idioms) that express their perspective on situations, problems, and dilemmas. Providers may use these metaphors in the form of anecdotes, stories, or analogies to build rapport in relationships with patients and to magnify the patient's need to make the changes recommended in treatment plans (Zuniga, 1992).

Listening to the patient's stories (Kreps & Thornton, 1992), soliciting their illness narratives (Kleinman, 1988), and building partnerships (Geist & Dreyer, 1993) will facilitate negotiation of cultural understanding in provider-patient relationships. Since relationships among patients and providers inevitably are shaped by the health care context (Geist & Hardesty, 1992), the complexities and uncertainties of cultural diversity in medical work must continually be negotiated as patients and providers communicate in ways to meet their needs.

## References

Adams, R., Briones, E. H., and Rentfro, A. R. (1992). Cultural considerations: Developing a nursing care delivery system for a Hispanic community. *Nursing Clinics of North America, 27,* 107–117.

Alexander, F. (1965). *Psychosomatic Medicine.* New York: W. W. Norton.

Anderson, J. M., Waxler-Morrison, N., Richardson, E., Herbert, C., and Murphy, M. (1991). "Conclusion: Delivering Culturally Sensitive Health Care." In N. Waxler-Morrison, J. M. Anderson, and E. Richardson (Eds.), *Cross-Cultural Caring: A Handbook for Health Professionals in Western Canada.* Vancouver: University of British Columbia.

Balch, J. F., and Balch, P. A. (1990). *Prescription for Nutritional Healing.* Garden City Park, N.Y.: Avery.

Barna, L. M. (1993). "Stumbling Blocks in Intercultural Communication." In L. A. Samovar and R. E. Porter (Eds.), *Intercultural Communication: A Reader,* 7th ed., 345–353. Belmont, Calif.: Wadsworth.

Boyle, J. S. (1991). Transcultural nursing care of Central American refugees. *Imprint, 38,* 73–79.

Brislin, R. W. (1991). "Prejudice in Intercultural Communication." In L. A. Samovar and R. E. Porter (Eds.), *Intercultural Communication: A Reader,* 6th ed., 366–370. Belmont, Calif.: Wadsworth.

Bulger, R. J. (1989). "The Modern Context for a Healing Profession." In R. J. Bulger (Ed.), *In Search of the Modern Hippocrates,* 3–8. Iowa City: University of Iowa Press.

Chesney, A. P., Thompson, B. L., Guevara, A., Vela, A., and Schottstaedt, M. F. (1980). Mexican-American folk medicine: Implications for the family physician. *The Journal of Family Practice, 11,* 567–574.

Comas-Diaz, L. (1989). "Culturally Relevant Issues and Treatment Implications for Hispanics." In D. R. Kowlow and E. P. Salett (Eds.), *Crossing Cultures in Mental Health,* 31–48. Washington, D.C.: Sietar.

Corea, G. (1985). *The Hidden Malpractice: How American Medicine Mistreats Women.* New York: Harper & Row.

Coward, R. (1989). *The Whole Truth: The Myth of Alternative Health.* Boston: Faber & Faber.

Dossey, L. (1982). *Space, Time, and Medicine.* Boston: New Science.

Fisher, S. (1986). *In the Patient's Best Interest: Women and the Politics of Medical Decisions.* New Brunswick, N.J.: Rutgers University Press.

Fitzgerald, F. T. (1988). How they view you, themselves, and disease. *Consultant, 28,* 65–77.

Galanti, G. (1991). *Caring for patients from different cultures: Case studies from American hospitals.* Philadelphia: University of Pennsylvania Press.

Geist, P., and Dreyer, J. (1993). "Juxtapositioning Accounts: Different Versions of Different Stories in the Health Care Context." In S. Herndon and G. Kreps (Eds.), *Qualitative Research: Applications in Organizational Communication,* 79–105. Cresskill, N.J.: SCA Applied Communication Series/ Hampton Press.

Geist, P., and Hardesty, M. (1992). *Negotiating the Crisis: DRGs and the Transformation of Hospitals.* Hillsdale, N.J.: Lawrence Erlbaum.

Giger, J. N., and Davidhizar, R. E. (1991). *Transcultural Nursing: Assessment and Intervention.* St. Louis: Mosby–Year Book.

Gorrie, M. (1989). Reaching clients through cross cultural education. *Journal of Gerontological Nursing, 15* (10), 29–31.

Gould, R. (1989). Dissident doctoring. *The Times Literary Supplement,* July 7, D 748.

Hartog, J., and Hartog, E. A. (1983). Cultural aspects of health and illness behavior in hospitals. *The Western Journal of Medicine, 139,* 106–112.

Helman, C. G. (1990). *Culture, Health, and Illness: An Introduction for Health Professionals.* Boston: Wright.

Howe-Murphy, R., Ross, H., Tseng, R., and Hartwig, R. (1989). Effecting change in multicultural health promotion: A systems approach. *Journal of Allied Health, 18,* 291–305.

Howze, E. H., Broyden, R. R., and Impara, J. C. (1992). Using informal caregivers to communicate with women about mammography." *Health Communication, 4,* 171–181.

Hyde, M. J. (1990). "Experts, Rhetoric, and the Dilemmas of Medical Technology: Investigating a Problem of Progressive Ideology." In M. J. Medhurst, A. Gonzalez, and T. R. Peterson (Eds.), *Communication and the Culture of Technology,* 115–136. Pullman: Washington State University.

Inlander, C. B., Levin, L. S., and Weiner, E. (1988). *Medicine on Trial: The Appalling Story of Medical Ineptitude and the Arrogance That Overlooks It.* New York: Pantheon.

Jones, J. A., and Phillips, G. M. (1988). *Communicating with Your Doctor.* Carbondale: Southern Illinois University Press.

Kim, Y. Y. (1991). "Communication and Cross-Cultural Adaptation." In L. A. Samovar and R. E. Porter (Eds.), *Intercultural Communication: A Reader,* 6th ed., 401–411, Belmont, Calif.: Wadsworth.

Kleinman, A. (1980). *Patients and Healers in the Context of Culture: An Exploration of the Borderland Between Anthropology, Medicine, and Psychiatry.* Berkeley: University of California Press.

Kleinman, A. (1988). *The Illness Narratives: Suffering, Healing, and the Human Condition.* New York: Basic Books.

Kleinman, A. (1992). Local worlds of suffering: An interpersonal focus for ethnographies of illness experience." *Qualitative Health Research, 2,* 127–134.

Krajewski-Jaime, E. R. (1991). Folk-healing among Mexican-American families as a consideration in the delivery of child welfare and child health care services. *Child Welfare, 70,* 157–167.

Kreps, G. L., and Thornton, B. C. (1992). *Health Communication: Theory and Practice,* 2d ed. New York: Longman.

Lai, M. C., and Yue, K. K. (1990). "The Chinese." In N. Waxler-Morrison, J. A. Anderson, and E. Richardson (Eds.), *Cross-Cultural Caring: A Handbook for Health Professionals in Western Canada,* 69–90. Vancouver: University of British Columbia Press.

Leininger, M. (1991). Transcultural nursing: The study and practice field. *Imprint, 38* (2), 55–66.

Li, K. C. (1987). *The Chinese Perspective Towards Mental Illness and Its Implications in Treatment.* Paper presented at Haughnessy Hospital, Vancouver, February.

Lindquist, G. J. (1990). Integration of international and transcultural content in nursing curricula: A process for change. *Journal of Professional Nursing, 6,* 272–279.

Littlewood, R. (1991). From disease to illness and back again. *The Lancet, 337,* 1013–1015.

Lowenberg, J. S. (1989). *Caring and Responsibility: The Crossroads Between Holistic Practice and Traditional Medicine.* Philadelphia: University of Pennsylvania Press.

Maduro, R. (1983). Curanderismo and Latino view of disease and curing. *The Western Journal of Medicine, 139,* 868–874.

Mason, C. (1990). Women as mothers in Northern Ireland and Jamaica: A critique of the transcultural nursing movement. *International Journal of Nursing Studies, 27,* 367–374.

Miralles, M. A. (1989). *A Matter of Life and Death: Health-Seeking Behavior of Guatemalan Refugees in South Florida.* New York: AMS Press.

Mishler, E. G. (1984). *The Discourse of Medicine: Dialectics of Medical Interviews.* Norwood, N.J.: Ablex.

Needleman, J. (1985). *The Way of the Physician.* San Francisco: Harper & Row.

Northouse, P. G., and Northouse, L. L. (1985). *Health Communication: A Handbook for Health Professionals.* Englewood Cliffs, N.J.: Prentice-Hall.

O'Brien, M. E. (1981). Transcultural nursing research: Alien in an alien land. *Image, 13,* 37–39.

Park, K. Y., and Peterson, L. M. (1991). Beliefs, practices, and experiences of Korean women in relation to childbirth. *Health Care for Women International, 12,* 261–267.

Payer, L. (1989). *Medicine and Culture: Notions of Health and Sickness in Britain, the U.S., France, and West Germany.* London: Victor Gallancz.

Scott, C. (1974). Health and healing practices among five ethnic groups in Miami, Florida. *Public Health Report, 89,* 524–532.

Siegel, B. S. (1986). *Love, Medicine, and Miracles: Lessons Learned About Self-Healing from a Surgeon's Experience with Exceptional Patients.* New York: Harper & Row.

Simon, S. (1992). "A Dose of Their Own Medicine." *Los Angeles Times,* June 25, A1, 9.

Sirott, L., and Waitzkin, H. (1984). "Holism and Self-Care: Can the Individual Succeed Where Society Fails?" In V. W. Sidel and R. Sidel (Eds.), *Reforming Medicine: Lessons from the Last Quarter Century,* 245–264. New York: Pantheon.

Spitzberg, B. H. (1991). "Intercultural Communication Competence." In L. A. Samovar and R. E. Porter (Eds.), *Intercultural Communication: A Reader,* 6th ed., 353–365. Belmont, Calif.: Wadsworth.

Stumpf, S. H., and Bass, K. (1992). Cross cultural communication to help physician assistants provide unbiased health care. *Public Health Records, 107,* 113–115.

U.S. Bureau of the Census. (1991). *Statistical Abstract of the U.S.: 1991,* 11th ed. Washington, D.C.

Wallis, C. (1991). "Why New Age Medicine Is Catching On." *Time,* 68–76.

Waxler-Morrison, N., Anderson, J., and Richardson, E. (1991). *Cross-Cultural Caring: A Handbook for Health Professionals in Western Canada.* Vancouver: University of British Columbia.

Zuniga, M. E. (1992). Using metaphors in therapy: Dichos and Latino clients. *Social Work, 37,* 55–60.

# The Influence of Culture on Classroom Communication

## LISA A. STEFANI

Today, more than ever before, schools in the United States contain a complex mix of students from many cultures. As Chisholm (1994) notes, "National and regional demographic changes and distribution shifts document an increasing minority student population" (p. 44). "The American Association of Colleges for Teacher Education estimates that by 2000 more than one-third of the students in the nation's schools will be members of minority groups" (Nicklin, 1991, p. A16). In California, white school-age children are already a minority at 45 percent of the total public school enrollment (Samovar & Porter, 1991). The many languages, customs, religious affiliations, communication patterns, and cultural values students now bring to the classroom have left educational institutions and instructors scrambling to accommodate this diversity. Leung (1994) echoed much the same idea when she wrote, "The search for an explanation of the role of culture on the achievement patterns of minority students has consumed a great deal of time and effort in the last decade" (p. 96). It is the purpose of this essay to help with that search.

Many of the problems confronting both students and teachers in these culturally diverse classrooms are traceable to culture. In fact, "interactions between teachers and pupils from different cultures are fundamentally problematic and cross-cultural misunderstandings often occur because classroom interaction is an archetypal human phenomenon which is deeply rooted in the culture of a society"

The essay was prepared especially for the eighth edition. All rights reserved. Permission to reprint must be obtained from the publisher and the author. Lisa A. Stefani teaches at San Diego State University.

(Hofstede, 1986, p. 303). Thus, "educators will need to call upon appropriate intercultural communication skills to support the learning process" (Ricard, 1991, p. 13).

It would appear that when students and teachers adapt to one another's cultural values and preferred interaction patterns, shared understanding is achieved and learning is promoted. The purpose of this essay is to explore intercultural communication in the classroom. First, I will discuss the importance of assessing acculturation levels. Next, I will consider cultural variations in learning styles and then examine current problems created by language diversity in the classroom. Finally, I will explore some issues concerning cultural gender expectations and their manifestations in the classroom.

## Assessing Acculturation Levels

Classroom functioning and activities vary from culture to culture. In some cultures classrooms are boisterous and noisy. In other cultures classrooms are quiet. In some cultures classrooms are very active, whereas in other cultures, students sit quietly for most of the day. In one culture the teacher may do all the talking, but in another students and teachers both engage in a great deal of conversation. Written material may be the dominant form of classroom instruction in one culture, while oral communication may be the rule in another. Students become familiar with the classroom patterns and characteristics of their own culture and tend to, at least initially, rely on these classroom "norms" even after arriving in the United States. As Grossman (1995) indicates, "If immigrant students have not been here at least for a few years, you can assume that their classroom functioning will be affected by many of the cultural factors the students or their parents brought with them" (p. 291). For example, the Vietnamese classroom is an environment in which teachers are revered and have a formal relationship with their students. Students are expected to learn individually by listening and memorizing (Nieto, 1992). The influence of these cultural factors will most likely be manifested in the classroom functioning of a recently arrived

Vietnamese immigrant. However, Vietnamese students who have been in the United States educational system for several years may also engage in informal relationships with their teacher, eagerly work in groups, and volunteer to speak in front of the class.

What is true for Vietnamese students who spend time in American classrooms is also true for students in other cultures. This process of learning "new ways to think, feel and behave" so that someone can "coordinate their activities with" members of the new culture is called *acculturation* (Kim, 1994, p. 20). More specifically, acculturation refers to the transformation of a person's identity from foreign to American – it is the melting or fusing process (McLemore, 1994). Non-European American students may adapt to or become acculturated to the American classroom in a variety of ways. Some students may maintain the values, practices, and beliefs of their culture and reject the mainstream culture or engage in cultural resistance. Other students may reject their culture and assimilate into the mainstream culture. Many students become bicultural, accepting both cultural systems. A final adaptation strategy, cultural transmutation, finds students altering both their original culture and the adopted culture, creating a new combination of norms (Grossman, 1995, p. 289; McLemore, 1994, p. 30). Age at immigration, gender, education level, previous intercultural experience, amount of interaction time, amount of support of the original culture, and pressure or encouragement to assimilate are but a few of the issues affecting acculturation.

Because many factors affect the type and level of acculturation students choose, educators have a twofold obligation. First, teachers and administrators should become familiar with the educational structure of the cultural heritage of the students in the class. For example, if Mexican or Hispanic students are in the class, one of the cultural factors the teacher should be aware of is that the Mexican/Hispanic classroom is structured around a present-time (P-time) orientation (Hall, 1983). That is to say, Mexican/Hispanic classrooms are concerned with what is happening at the moment. The next activity is not nearly as important as what is transpiring in the present. Unlike schools in the United States, students do not automatically move from one subject to another simply because the clock tells them it is time to shift topics. Instead, Mexican/Hispanic students continue with the topic at hand until it has been thoroughly discussed, even if the discussion continues through lunch and into what was scheduled as a mathematics lesson. In short, Mexican/Hispanic students are concerned with finishing an assignment before moving on to the next task, regardless of the amount of time required. They also work at a relaxed pace even if it means taking longer to finish (Grossman, 1984).

*For the Hispanic student, this imposition of a rigid chronological regimentation brings unfamiliar confusion and confinement for, at home, he [she] has always been master of his [her] "time" and been allowed to exercise his [her] individuality within the casual rhythm of family life. (Condon, Peters, & Suerio-Ross, 1979, p. 67)*

Thus, an accommodation of cultural diversity requires that teachers educate themselves about the classroom structure, functionings, and preferred interaction patterns of the various cultural heritages contained within the multicultural classroom.

Second, teachers are obligated to assess the acculturation level of each student in the class.

*It is necessary to understand each student as a unique individual, rather than stereotypically. To do so, educators can assess the . . . degree and type of acculturation of non-European students. (Grossman, 1995, p. 20)*

Educators can choose from a wide selection of formal assessment procedures for evaluating students' acculturation level. Instruments such as the Acculturation Scale for Mexican-Americans by Cuellar, Harris, and Jasso (1980), the Acculturation Scale for Mexican-American Children by Franco (1983), and the Asian Self-Identity Acculturation Scale are three such examples. These instruments study the extent to which students are involved in their own and the Anglo-American culture by asking them to reply to a series of questions about their attitudes and values, recreational habits, friendships, interaction patterns, and personal identification. The an-

swers to these and other questions, once analyzed, can tell the teacher the degree of acculturation each student has chosen.

Finally, teachers can determine acculturation levels by observing the students' behavior – which students they socialize with, the language they prefer, how they identify themselves, how they dress, their reaction to ethnic holidays, and the like. Teachers can further interview the student or consult with colleagues who are familiar with the students' background (Grossman, 1995). As a result of these actions, and by implementing assessment instruments, teachers can determine the appropriate cultural response. From observing the teachers' actions, students too will learn acceptable responses and increase their cultural understanding. In this way school communication can help bridge ethnic diversity by educating teachers and students alike to be multicultural (Samovar & Porter, 1995).

## Learning Styles

Once background information about the various cultures represented in the classroom is determined, an examination of student learning styles will further enhance intercultural communication in the classroom. A learning style is a particular way that an individual or individuals receive and process information (Bennett, 1986). Research indicates that culture plays a significant role in the way students approach learning. For example, Stodolsky and Lesser (1971) studied the mental patterns and abilities of Chinese, Jewish, black, and Puerto Rican children. They found that patterns among the mental abilities were different for all four cultural groups and that these patterns remained stable despite social background. "For example, the mental ability patterns of both middle-class and poor Chinese children were strikingly similar" (Nieto, 1992, p. 112). Banks (1988) reviewed several studies and found that ethnicity has a greater influence on cognitive style than does social class. More recently, Hollins, King, and Hayman (1994) found that all types of learning styles are found within all ethnic groups to varying degrees but with a dominant style for each ethnicity. A common thread among these studies is the indication of a strong link between culture and learning.

Culture teaches the student to rely on these consistent patterns of cognition and behavior – learning styles – within the classroom. This discussion of learning styles is divided into three parts. We first discuss communication and relational styles, then various cognitive styles, and finally, motivational styles.

## Communication and Relational Styles

**Direct Versus Indirect Communication.** Culture influences the degree to which communication is direct or indirect. Because the American culture's primary focus is on the individual, communication tends to be direct. That is to say, Americans value people who express themselves in very blunt and frank ways. This level of openness is often shunned by Americans of Asian and Pacific Rim heritage because such behavior violates countless cultural norms in that it causes both the sender and the receiver of the message to lose face.

*American straightforwardness is considered at best impolite if not brutal. In Indochina, one does not come directly to the point. To do so is, for an American, a mark of honesty and forthrightness while a person from Indochina sees it as a lack of intelligence or courtesy. (Nguyen, 1986, p. 6)*

When educators are cognizant of which students are accustomed to direct and indirect communication styles, they can adapt their communication to the individual student, thereby enhancing understanding and learning.

**Formal Versus Informal Communication.** Regardless of the culture, it is a truism that communication is rule-governed. However, the rules offered in each culture reflect the values of that culture. The African American and Anglo-American communication styles tend to be informal (Grossman, 1995). Status differences tend to be deemphasized and the notion of equality for all members of society is often manifested in communication on a first-name basis. In contrast, the communication styles of

Americans of Hispanic, Asian, and Pacific Rim origin are far more formal (Grossman, 1995). For example, Hispanics demonstrate their respect for each other through formal expressions like the use of the formal *Usted,* meaning "you." The informal term for "you" is *tu* (Grossman, 1984).

*In Asian cultures the communication interaction is very structured and predictable. . . . The individual's status in the situation will define the role that he or she is expected to play in communication. These roles are usually defined by tradition and are highly formalized. For communication to proceed smoothly, each participant must behave in the expected manner by using verbal and nonverbal behaviors appropriate to one's role. (Matsuda, 1989, p. 46)*

Formal rules concerning teacher/student interaction can also be seen when we turn to the cultures of Egypt, Turkey, and Iran (Samovar & Porter, 1995, p. 105). Here even teacher/teacher relationships are extremely formal and respectful. There is, for instance, an Egyptian proverb that notes, "Whoever teaches me a letter, I should become a slave to him forever." In these cultures when the teacher enters the room, students are expected to stand. And when they meet their teachers on the street, they are expected to bow. Contrast this with the relaxed, informal atmosphere in the United States, and you can appreciate how different rules regarding formal and informal communication styles between students and teachers can impair learning. However, when teachers and students adapt their communication formality to one another and the situation, learning is enhanced.

**Nonverbal Communication.** Nonverbal communication is a subtle form of culture that can actively impede the learning process. If teachers are not familiar with the nonverbal behaviors associated with their students' cultures, they may often misinterpret them. For example, Puerto Rican students use a nonverbal wrinkling of the nose to indicate "What do you mean?" or "I don't understand." If the teacher assumes that this gesture has no significance, the students' request for clarification or help will go unattended (Nieto, 1992). "If a teacher receives no volunteered answers or head nods from Vietnamese students, he or she may perceive these students as having low intellectual ability" (Samovar & Porter, 1995, p. 256). "In Alaska Native cultures . . . raised eyebrows are often used to signify yes and a wrinkled nose means no" (Nieto, 1992, p. 115). In Jamaica students snap their fingers when they know the answer to a question, but in the United States students raise their hands. In most Asian and Native American cultures direct eye contact with the teacher is perceived as rude, whereas in the United States a lack of direct eye contact is considered rude (Samovar & Porter, 1995). Examples of cultural differences in nonverbal communication abound. A familiarity with the nonverbal behaviors typical of each student's culture will aid in the reduction of miscommunication and improve learning.

**Topic-Centered Communication Versus Topic-Associating Communication.** The manner in which students approach a topic is influenced by the students' culture. For example, European American children tend to be topic-centered. That is, their "accounts were focused on a single topic or closely related topics, were ordered in a linear fashion, and led to a resolution" (Au, 1993, p. 95). Questions are timed so that they do not interfere with the flow of conversation and move from general to specific. In contrast, African American children typically use a topic-associating style. "In the topic-associating style children present a series of episodes linked to some person or theme. These links are implicit in the account and are generally left unstated" (p. 96). When instructors are not familiar with the topic-associating style they may inadvertently mistime their questions or not allow the student to finish their thought because they do not understand how each episode is connected to the other. Awareness of cultural differences in topic approach is an important first step in improving intercultural communication in the classroom.

**Dependent Versus Independent Learning.** Culture influences the degree to which students independently accomplish their assignments and whether they dependently rely upon the support, help, and

opinions of teachers and other adults. "Compared to European American students, many, but not all non–European American students, especially Hispanic Americans, Native Americans, Filipino Americans, and Southeast Asian Americans tend to be more interested in obtaining their teachers' direction and feedback" (Grossman, 1995, p. 265). These students may show little initiative or independence and rarely make decisions without teacher approval. Again, heightened awareness by the educator of the students' desire or lack of desire for support will help develop an effective communication strategy in the classroom.

**Reflectivity Versus Impulsivity.** Culture influences how long students think about things before arriving at conclusions. Often in the United States students are taught to think on their feet and make quick responses or guesses to questions. "Impulsive students respond rapidly to tasks; they are the first ones to raise their hands to answer the teacher's question and the first ones to complete a test" (Gollnick & Chinn, 1994, p. 306). In other cultures students are reflective and seek answers slowly. "In cultures that emphasize reflectivity, if one guesses or errs, it is an admission of not having taken enough time to find the correct answer. This can result in a painful loss of face" (Samovar & Porter, 1995, p. 252). Asian and Native American students are among those who are taught to examine all sides of an issue and all possible implications before answering (Grossman, 1995). Depending on the situation, one type of response may be more suitable to the question being posed than another. For example, impulsivity may be more appropriate on a timed test, whereas reflectivity may be more appropriate when accuracy is the important consideration. Educators who are aware of the impulsive/reflective dichotomy can allow their reflective students sufficient time to answer questions and complete assignments.

**Participatory Versus Passive Learning.** In some cultures students are taught to be active participants in learning, asking questions and discussing ideas as their teacher guides them through the lesson. In other cultures students are taught to be mentally active but physically inactive recipients in the learning process. The teacher holds all information and disseminates it to the students who passively listen and take notes (Grossman, 1995). Often in classrooms in the United States students are expected to actively ask questions, take initiative, and be leaders. There is a long tradition of argumentation and debate in the American school system. However, many Hispanic, Asian, and Pacific Rim cultures expect their students to be passive in the classroom. For example, in Southeast Asian classrooms students are taught to learn by listening, watching (observing), and imitating. Critical thinking and judgmental questioning are emphasized to a lesser degree than in the American school system, and argumentation is not condoned. "If a teacher were to ask a question on the relationship between two concepts, one might see Indochinese students searching through their notes or books for the answers, or they may display reluctance or discomfort" (Kang-Ning, 1981, p. 42). Educators must be cautious not to attribute this passive communication response to shyness or low learning ability. Instead, direct instruction and supervision may encourage a more active role for these students (Grossman, 1995).

**Aural, Visual, and Verbal Learners.** Culture influences whether students are primarily aural, visual, or verbal learners. For example, Native Americans tend to be visual learners. "Native Indian students frequently and effectively use coding with imagery to remember and understand words and concepts. That is, they use mental images to remember or understand, rather than using word association" (More, 1987, p. 26). In contrast, "many students, including African American, Hispanic Americans, Haitian Americans and Hmong Americans tend to be aural learners" (Grossman, 1995, p. 269). "Haitians usually have a highly developed auditory ability as evidenced by the oral traditions and rote learning methods" (Hallman, Etienne, & Fradd, 1982, p. 33). Because the Hmong do not have a written language, they have highly developed aural skills (Grossman, 1995). When instructional techniques are adapted to the students' preference, learning will be more effective. When the classroom contains aural, visual, and verbal learners, a multisensory approach to teaching is often effective.

**Energetic Learning Versus Calm Learning.** Cultural background influences whether students function better in highly active and animated classrooms or calm and placid environments. "African Americans and Hispanic American students are used to more stimulation than students typically experience in school" (Grossman, 1995, p. 270).

*Many African American children are exposed to high-energy, fast-paced home environments, where there is simultaneous variable stimulation (e.g., televisions and music playing simultaneously and people talking and moving in and about the home freely). Hence, low-energy, monolithic environments (as seen in many traditional school environments) are less stimulating. . . . Variety in instruction provides the spirit and enthusiasm for learning. (Franklin, 1992, p. 118–119)*

In most of the schools in Mexico students move around the classroom with great regularity. Because many ages are found in a single class, students are often in constant motion as they move from table to table helping their younger classmates. When educators are aware of which students prefer higher levels of activity and which students prefer calm environments, they can adjust their classroom strategies so that all students can spend at least part of their day working at the activity level they are accustomed to.

## Cognitive Styles

**Field Independence Versus Field Sensitivity.** Cultures differ in the manner in which they perceive their environment and the ideas they confront in that environment. These perceptual differences are reflected in the classroom. That is to say, some classrooms place emphasis on the field (the whole concept) while others stress parts of the field. "Field-sensitive individuals have a more global perspective of their surroundings; they are more sensitive to the social field. Field-independent individuals tend to be more analytical and can more comfortably focus on impersonal, abstract aspects of stimuli in the environment" (Gollnick & Chinn, 1994, p. 306). Low-context, highly industrialized, individualistic societies, such as the United States, are predominantly field-independent, whereas high-context, traditional collectivistic societies like Mexico and Japan tend to be field-sensitive (Samovar & Porter, 1995). Field-independent students can be expected to exhibit certain specific behaviors. For example, they prefer to work independently and are task-oriented. Competition and individual recognition are important. For the field-independent person, details are meaningful, and the parts often have meaning of their own. In contrast, field-sensitive students prefer to work with others in order to achieve a common goal. They seek guidance from the teacher and openly express positive feelings for him or her. Rewards center on strengthened relations with other group members and the teacher. Global aspects of the concept are emphasized and related to personal experiences and interests (Gollnick & Chinn, 1994). Many educators believe that "teachers should begin to function bicognitively in the classroom and teach students to operate bicognitively" as well (p. 307).

**Cooperation Versus Competition.** The degree to which cooperation or competition is emphasized varies from culture to culture. African Americans, Asian and Pacific Rim Americans, Filipino Americans, Hispanic Americans, and Hawaiian Americans tend to raise their children cooperatively. For example, in Hawaiian families, children are brought up by multiple caregivers, particularly older siblings. This behavior is manifested in the classroom by "high rates of peer interaction, frequently offering help to peers or requesting assistance from them" (Hollins, King, & Hayman, 1994, p. 19). As noted earlier, this cooperative attitude is also found in much of Latin America. In contrast, in the United States, teachers often perceive peer helping as a form of cheating and therefore encourage children to work alone. When children do work in groups, they are expected to "carry their own load." This attitude is not found in all cultures.

*Latin cultures typically do not put such requirements on individuals when they are working as part of a group. A group member who does not happen to be working will not be offensive. Those members of the group who best qualify or are most interested in performing the task will probably take it upon themselves to do the bulk of the labor. It is generally understood that each individual has special talents, and he will contribute when these talents are called for. (Jaramillo, 1973, p. 9)*

It is important for teachers to understand which students respond to cooperative learning environments and which students prefer more competitive situations. Many educators recommend the use of both cooperative and individual learning strategies so that students can learn to function effectively in both situations.

**Tolerance Versus Intolerance for Ambiguity.** Some cultures are open-minded about contradictions, differences, and uncertainty. Other cultures prefer a structured predictable environment with little change. The American culture has a low tolerance for ambiguity in the classroom. The American classroom is often highly structured in that topics are covered at a certain time each day. Students move from subject to subject at a designated time. Not all cultures structure their classrooms this way. As noted earlier, the Hispanic classroom is not dictated by the clock, but instead by the completion of the topic. Not only is the classroom structure affected by the culture's tolerance level for ambiguity, but what is taught is also affected. For example, American culture emphasizes right/wrong, correct/incorrect, yes/no answers, while cultures such as that of India have a high tolerance for ambiguity and never regard truth in absolute terms (Samovar & Porter, 1995). Educators who are aware of the level of ambiguity their students are accustomed to can help facilitate a smooth transition to the new structured and predictable environment.

**Trial and Error Versus "Watch, Then Do."** In the United States students learn how to solve problems and reach conclusions by trial and error. They practice over and over, expecting and accepting many mistakes, until they become skilled.

*In other cultures, individuals are expected to continue to watch how something is done as many times and for as long as necessary until they feel they can do it. Only when they are sure they can succeed do they demonstrate their ability to others. (Grossman, 1995, p. 270)*

This "watch, then do" approach is characteristic of many Native American students:

*Native Americans spend much more time watching and listening and less time talking than do Anglos. If they are interested in something they watch how it is done, they inspect the product, they watch the process, they may ask a quiet question or two. Then they may try it for themselves, often out of the public eye. They are their own evaluator to determine whether their effort was successful or needs improvement. When they feel comfortable, they will show what they have done to someone else, usually someone they trust. (Rhodes, 1988, p. 64)*

When educators are aware that some students prefer the "watch, then do" approach they can allow these students time until they are ready to try doing something new (Grossman, 1995).

## Motivation and Student Goals

Motivation is a primary concern in the multicultural classroom, in part because cultures vary in their orientation to school and education. Some cultures place a high value on learning, but in other cultures education is lower on the hierarchy scale. For example, the Mexican culture values family needs above all others; therefore, education generally assumes a position behind the family in importance. But in Japan, "education is a high national priority. The Japanese believe that the best way to ensure their future is to develop their most valued natural resource – their people" (Powell & Andersen, 1994, p. 325). The area of motivation can be problematic for the multicultural teacher who must employ a variety of motivational techniques that coincide with the students' cultural background.

**Intrinsic Versus Extrinsic Motivation.** Whether a student is intrinsically or extrinsically motivated to succeed in school is heavily influenced by culture. European American students are generally motivated to learn for intrinsic reasons. For example, many European American students desire to succeed academically so that they can secure a good position and earn a great deal of money. In contrast, Asian students are often motivated extrinsically. "Asian children are often found to be motivated extrinsically by their parents and relatives. They study hard because they want to please their parents and impress their relatives" (Yao, 1987, p. 84). Native American students are often motivated to learn so that they can please others rather than offend or hurt them (Grossman, 1995; Kleinfeld, 1975). Educators should be aware of whether their students are intrinsically or extrinsically motivated and use appeals appropriate to each type of motivation to encourage students' academic achievement in the classroom.

**Learning on Demand Versus Learning What Is Relevant or Interesting.** "All cultures require children to learn many things whether they want to or not" (Grossman, 1995, p. 273). However, some cultures emphasize learning what is useful and interesting rather than learning information for the sake of learning. The Japanese culture, for example, requires that all students memorize information such as dates, complex sequences, and lengthy formulas in mathematics, science, and social studies. Each student is also required to learn how to play a musical instrument without any regard to musical ability, and instruction often begins in first grade (White, 1987). In contrast, other cultures such as the Hispanic culture and the Native American culture, stress the importance of learning what is relevant and useful. Native American students

*prefer to learn information that is personally interesting to them; therefore, interest is a key factor in their learning. When these students are not interested in a subject, they do not control their attention and orient themselves to learning an uninteresting task. Rather, they allocate their attention to other ideas that are more personally interesting, thus appearing detached from the learning situation. (Walker, Dodd, & Bigelow, 1989, p. 69)*

Hispanic American students are more interested in humanistic concerns than in learning automation and technology – as European Americans do on demand (Grossman, 1995). Given this information, it appears that when multicultural educators establish a relationship between student interests and the lesson material, learning will be enhanced for many students.

**Student Goals.** As noted earlier, motivation can be problematic for the multicultural teacher because students from different cultures vary in their orientation to school and their motivation to learn. We have also suggested that learning can be promoted and motivation increased when a relationship is established between student interest and lesson topics. A final consideration involving motivation is the area of student goals. Motivation can be enhanced when educators are aware of the goals students have set for themselves in the classroom. Whether it be to receive an "A" in the course, to learn new skills, or to please their parents, many students, particularly secondary and university students, have an idea of what they would like to accomplish when they enter the class. It is incumbent on the teacher to find out what goals students bring to the class. This concept maintains that the starting point for learning in the multicultural classroom should be the students themselves. This approach is often referred to as a constructivist approach (Au, 1993). This is not to say that students should set the curricular agenda but, instead, that student goals should be interwoven with the curricular agenda. Teachers may ascertain the goals of their students by asking them directly or having them write about their goals for the class. These goals can usually be incorporated as motivational sources throughout the class.

Motivation should not end with the goals of the student. Since one of the major functions of school is to expand the students' horizons, educators are obligated to help students extend their goals. "Students' own goals are limited by their previous expe-

riences, so part of the teacher's job is to introduce new literacy experiences that may lead students to formulate new goals" (Au, 1993, p. 61). For example, students in a speech class may be focusing on the mechanics of a speech to the degree that topic choice is disregarded. Serious educators might help students find a topic that is interesting and relevant to them. In this way, the students not only master the mechanics of giving a speech, but also learn to speak passionately about a topic of interest.

## Language Diversity

Language holds particular significance both in and out of the classroom. As Samovar and Porter (1995) remind us:

*Language is a system of symbolic substitution that enables us to share our experience and internal states with others. We use words to relate to the past, exercise some control over the present and to form images of the future. (p. 150)*

A common language assumes mutual understanding. It facilitates shared meaning and allows us to communicate on a similar level. However, the National Association of Bilingual Education (1993) indicates that 6.3 million children in the United States report speaking a non-English language at home. As a result, some children come to school barely speaking English, some students are limited in their English usage, and some other students are bilingual. This section will include a discussion of some of the problems faced by Limited English Proficient students, current approaches to language diversity, and some suggestions for improving classroom interaction.

## Problems

Limited English Proficient (LEP) students are faced with several obstacles in the classroom. McKeon (1994) identified four such problems. First, LEP students must be concerned with both cognition and linguistics while their English counterparts need only be concerned with cognition. LEP students "must decipher the many structures and functions of the language before any content will make sense" (p. 46). LEP students must not only grasp the content, but they must also make the new language express what they have learned. This requires LEP students to perform at a much higher cognitive and linguistic level than do their native-speaking peers.

Higher cognitive and linguistic levels are often difficult to attain because of a second problem that plagues LEP students — academic delays. Many students who enter American schools are academically delayed in their first language. As a result, it is virtually impossible for them to function at the prescribed grade levels, much less at higher cognitive and linguistic levels (McKeon, 1994).

Another compounding problem for LEP students is that they enroll in schools in America at various points in their academic career — kindergarten, second grade, eleventh grade, etc. "The higher the grade level, the more limited-English-proficiency is likely to weigh on students because at higher levels of schooling, the cognitive and linguistic loads are heavier" (McKeon, 1994, p. 46).

A final complication for LEP students is that they arrive from countries that may emphasize special curricular sequences, content objectives, and instructional methodologies. For example, Asian students use different rules and formulas for algebra. A deductive instructional approach is generally used in the United States, but Asian cultures use an inductive approach. American schools emphasize written education, whereas African and Middle Eastern schools emphasize oral education. The North American culture values argumentation and debate, while many other cultures emphasize harmony and cooperation. Hence, students from these cultures may not possess argumentative skills that are often found in North American classrooms. Not only does the LEP student carry the burden of a higher linguistic and cognitive load, but he or she must also adjust to new methods of learning.

## Approaches

The language diversity that exists in classrooms in the United States is addressed by three primary instructional approaches: Bilingual Education, English as a Second Language, and Sheltered English.

First, "bilingual education is an instructional approach in which students who do not speak the language of school are taught partly in the language of their homes, and partly in the language of the school" (Fillmore & Valdez, 1986, p. 648). There are three basic educational goals for students of bilingual education: "(1) to attain high levels of proficiency in English, (2) to achieve academically in all content areas to the best of their ability, and (3) to experience positive personal growth" (Hernandez, 1989, p. 86).

There are three programs of instruction under bilingual education: Transitional Bilingual Education (TBE), Maintenance Bilingual Education (MBE), and Immersion Bilingual Education (IBE). First, Transitional Bilingual Education (TBE) begins with content courses in the students' native language and is accompanied by English as a Second Language (ESL) instruction. The goal is to move students to English-only instruction as soon as possible. Ideally the transition should be no more than two or three years. TBE is most closely associated with the ideology of cultural assimilation mentioned earlier (Gollnick & Chinn, 1994; Hernandez, 1989; La Belle & Ward, 1994).

Maintenance Bilingual Education (MBE) also begins with content courses in the students' native language and ESL instruction, but it does not seek to move students to English-only instruction as soon as possible. Instead, MBE is associated with the pluralistic ideology in which both groups' languages and cultures are valued equally. As a result, MBE can last six or more years and seeks proficiency in both cultural languages (Gollnick & Chinn, 1994; Hernandez, 1989; La Belle & Ward, 1994).

Immersion (or enrichment) Bilingual Education (IBE) places students in the new language before they receive academic content in their native language. This approach is usually used for English students who want to speak another language. "English speakers learning French in Quebec are one example" (La Belle & Ward, 1994, p. 175).

English as a Second Language (ESL) is yet another instructional approach to language diversity in the United States. "ESL is the field of teaching English to speakers of other languages" (Alatis,

1976, p. 3). Language development in English is a priority in all ESL programs. "ESL instruction relies exclusively on English for teaching and learning. ESL programs are used extensively in this country as a primary medium to assimilate LEP children into the linguistic mainstream as quickly as possible" (Gollnick & Chinn, 1994, p. 245). "English as a Second Language is an integral component of bilingual education programs, and where these are not feasible, it provides an essential adjunct to instruction in regular classrooms" (Hernandez, 1989, p. 88). ESL programs are predominant in schools with immigrant student populations in which no single group is large enough to need a bilingual program (La Belle & Ward, 1994).

Sheltered English is a third approach to language diversity within the classroom. The factor that distinguishes Sheltered English from the other two approaches is that students are taught the subject matter in a controlled English vocabulary that coincides with their level of English comprehension. "Teachers omit difficult words and forms, explain new vocabulary words, often in students' native languages, and employ as many nonverbal gestures, audiovisual aids, and other materials as possible" (Grossman, 1995, p. 161).

### Suggestions for Improvement

Although much controversy exists within the United States regarding the effectiveness of programs such as Bilingual Education and ESL – and the debate continues over whether or not English should be the primary language of instruction – the fact remains that teachers must face students who are limited in their English proficiency. Not only must teachers instruct these students each day, but they are also responsible for ensuring that these students get the quality education they deserve. Rather than provide a discussion of the debate, therefore, we will offer some suggestions for improving classroom interaction and promoting learning in a classroom with linguistically diverse students.

Hernandez (1989) offers three suggestions for promoting bilingualism and improving interaction in a multilingual classroom. First, she advocates the use of the native language in peer interaction. Because cognitive skills are best acquired through the native language, in situations where there are many different languages represented in the school or classroom, the use of tutoring or peer teaching in each student's language should be encouraged.

Second, teachers should adapt instructional techniques that include modifications in speech and vocabulary. Speaking at a slower rate and defining key terms and concepts before proceeding with the lesson are examples of this adaptation.

Finally, instruction should be accompanied by contextual support. Examples include gestures, facial expressions, pantomime, and paralinguistic clues as well as pictures, charts, graphs, symbols, and diagrams. These additional clues convey meaning and facilitate increased understanding.

### Culture, Gender, and the Classroom

Culture establishes norms regarding what is acceptable behavior for girls and boys and creates expectations based solely on gender. Adherence to rigid gender roles usually depends upon the degree to which the culture accepts and maintains traditional patterns of behavior. Religions often play a large part in gender expectations, particularly when they include masculine and feminine principles as part of their doctrine (Gollnick & Chinn, 1994).

*Because religion defines the ultimate meaning of the universe for a people, the impact may be deep and often emotional rather than intellectual. When male dominance is embodied within religion, it enters the arena that a society considers sacred. This may make it even less open to question and more resistant to change than other social areas. (Stockard & Johnson, 1980, p. 8)*

"Puerto Rican, Mexican American, Appalachian, and Native American families that adhere to traditional religious and cultural patterns are more likely to encourage adherence to rigid gender roles than families that have adopted bicultural patterns" (Gollnick & Chinn, 1994, p. 135).

Additionally, many non-European Americans, including Asian and Pacific Rim Americans, hold the belief that a female's place is in the home (Grossman, 1984). An example of this can be found among the Hmong. "There is also a suspicion among the

Hmong regarding girls who are educated beyond the three or four years required for basic literacy and math skills. . . . the fear is that they will become like western women" (Lewis, Vang, & Cheng, 1989, p. 32).

Having considered the underlying factors in gender roles, namely a culture's traditional and religious patterns, we will now turn to some manifestations of these influences in the classroom. First, in many cultures classes are separated by gender. Native American, Vietnamese, and Arabic students are taught not to interact with members of the opposite sex (Nieto, 1992; Samovar & Porter, 1991). When these children come to the United States they often retain their preference to work in same-sex groups. This of course can produce problems when students find themselves in groups of mixed gender. Educators can minimize this discomfort by allowing some activities to be separated by gender. Research by Kahle and Lakes (1983), Moody and Gifford (1990), and Sadker and Sadker (1994) suggests that female students tend to achieve more in single-sex cooperative learning situations than in mixed-sex situations. In single-sex groups, females are forced to take leadership and responsibility (Moody & Gifford, 1990). Although roles of leadership for females may not be congruent with some cultures' values, if the desired effect is participation and leadership, grouping by gender will accomplish this.

A second manifestation of a culture's gender expectations in the classroom is found in the area of academic success. With the exception of African American females, it appears that European American females, Hispanic females, and several other groups of females are uncomfortable with success in areas traditionally thought to be male domains (American Association of University Women, 1992; George, 1986; McCorquodale, 1983; Sadker & Sadker, 1994). In societies where females are expected to be feminine and collaborative, they may feel less feminine and less popular if they outperform males, particularly in areas considered to be masculine.

A male's success in the classroom is also affected by culture. For example, classrooms containing Hispanic males may be influenced by the Mexican value of machismo. Machismo means that Mexican males try to make their life a living validation that men are stronger, more reliable, and more intelligent than women are (Ready, 1991). Next to devotion to family, the male's manliness outweighs all other aspects of prestige. The concept of male honor requires that the Hispanic male avoid being proven wrong. For example, to take a stand on an issue and then retreat is regarded as degrading. In the classroom this means that males are reluctant to participate for fear of being embarrassed or humiliated. The Hispanic male avoids openly stating an opinion unless he is ready to take a stand by it and defend it. If he were to back down from a stated opinion, he would lose respect in the community.

A third manifestation of culture's effect on gender in the classroom can be found in the area of risk taking. "With many exceptions, girls tend to react less positively than boys to difficult and challenging situations" (Grossman, 1995, p. 279). Ginsberg and Miller (1982) found that girls are less persistent in difficult tasks and less likely to take risks. European American students appear more likely to take risks than Asian and Pacific Rim Americans students (Grossman, 1995). An inability to take risks may inhibit these students from trying new things and from bouncing back from failure. Educators need to encourage these students to engage in new activities and help these students recover from unsuccessful efforts.

## Conclusion

I have attempted to examine some of the prominent issues concerning culture's effects on communication in the classroom. I have suggested that teachers in multicultural classrooms would benefit from a knowledge of the cultural heritages of their students because students tend to rely on functional norms from the classroom of their original culture. Because acculturation level will impact the degree to which these previous cultural norms are acted out in the classroom, I have indicated the importance of assessing each student's acculturation level as a starting point to improve classroom interaction. Because cultures approach learning differently, an awareness of the various learning styles should be considered as a means of determining how best to enhance an individual student's learning. Half of all American teachers will teach a Limited English Proficient student at some time in their career. Thus, I have provided an overview of current approaches to language diversity. I concluded the essay with a brief discussion of culture's impact on gender and classroom communication. In order to provide the quality education that all students deserve, teachers much educate themselves on the many cultural variables that impact today's ethnically diverse classrooms.

## References

Alatis, J. E. (1976). "The Compatibility of TESOL and Bilingual Education." In J. E. Alatis and K. Twaddell (Eds.), *English as a Second Language in Bilingual Education*, 5–14. Washington, D.C.: Teachers of English to Speakers of Other Languages.

American Association of University Women. (1992). *The AAUW Report: How Schools Shortchange Girls*. The Wellesley College Center for Research on Women.

Au, K. H. (1993). *Literacy Instruction in Multicultural Settings*. New York: Harcourt Brace.

Banks, J. A. (1988). Ethnicity, class, cognitive and motivational styles: Research and teaching implications. *Journal of Negro Education, 57,* 452–466.

Bennett, C. I. (1986). *Comprehensive Multicultural Education: Theory and Practice*. Boston: Allyn & Bacon.

Bennett, K. P. (1991). "Doing School in an Urban Appalachian First Grade." In C. E. Sleeter (Ed.), *Empowerment Through Multicultural Education*. Albany: State University of New York Press.

Chisholm, I. (1994). Preparing teachers for multicultural classrooms. *The Journal of Educational Issues of Language Minority Students, 14,* 43–67.

Condon, E. C., Peters, J. Y., and Suerio-Ross, C. (1979). *Special Education and the Hispanic Child: Cultural Perspectives*. Philadelphia: Temple University, Teacher Corps Mid-Atlantic Network.

Cuellar, I., Harris, L. C., and Jasso, R. (1980). An acculturation scale for Mexican American normal and clinical populations. *Hispanic Journal of Behavioral Sciences, 2,* 199–217.

Fillmore, L. W., and Valdez, C. (1986). "Teaching Bilingual Learners." In M. C. Wittrock (Ed.), *Handbook of Research on Teaching*, 3d ed., 648–685. New York: Macmillan.

Franco, J. N. (1983). An acculturation scale for Mexican-American children. *Journal of General Psychology, 108,* 175–181.

Franklin, M. E. (1992). Culturally sensitive instructional practices for African-American learners with disabilities. *Exceptional Children, 59*(2), 115–122.

George, V. D. (1986). Talented adolescent women and the motivation to avoid success. *Journal of Multicultural Counseling and Development, 14*(3), 132–139.

Ginsburg, H. J., and Miller, S. M. (1982). Sex differences in children's risk-taking behavior. *Child Development, 53*(2), 426–428.

Gollnick, D. M., and Chinn, P. C. (1994). *Multicultural Education in a Pluralistic Society,* 4th ed. New York: Macmillan.

Grossman, H. (1984). *Educating Hispanic Students: Cultural Implications for Instruction, Classroom Management, Counseling, and Assessement*. Springfield, Ill.: Charles C. Thomas.

Grossman, H. (1995). *Teaching in a Diverse Society*. Boston: Allyn & Bacon.

Hall, E. T. (1983). *The Dance of Life: Other Dimensions of Time*. New York: Anchor.

Hallman, C. L., Etienne, M. R., and Fradd, S. (1982). *Haitian Value Orientations*. Monograph Number 2. ERIC Document Reproduction Service No. ED 269-532.

Hernandez, H. (1989). *Multicultural Education: A Teacher's Guide to Content and Process*. Columbus, Ohio: Charles E. Merrill.

Hofstede, G. (1986). Cultural differences in teaching and learning. *International Journal of Intercultural Relations, 10,* 301–320.

Hollins, E. R., King, J. E., and Hayman, W. C. (1994). *Teaching Diverse Populations: Formulating a Knowledge Base*. New York: State University of New York Press.

Jaramillo, M. L. (1973). *Cautions When Working with the Culturally Different Child*. ERIC Document Reproduction Service No. ED 115-622.

Kahle, J. B., and Lakes, M. K. (1983). The myth of equality in science classrooms. *Journal of Research in Science Teaching, 20,* 131–140.

Kang-Ning, C. (1981). Education for Chinese and Indochinese. *Theory into Practice, 20*(1), 35–44.

Kim, Y. (1994). "Adapting to a New Culture." In L. A. Samovar and R. E. Porter, (Eds.), *Intercultural Communication: A Reader,* 7th ed., 392–404. Belmont, Calif.: Wadsworth.

Kleinfeld, J. (1975). *Effective Teachers of Indian and Eskimo Students*. Fairbanks: Institute of Social, Economic, and Government Research, University of Alaska.

La Belle, T. J., and Ward, C. R. (1994). *Multiculturalism and Education: Diversity and Its Impact on Schools and Society*. New York: State University of New York Press.

Leung, B. (1994). Culture as a contextual variable in the study of differential minority student achievement.

The Journal of Educational Issues of Language Minority Students, 13, 95–105.

Lewis, J., Vang, L., and Cheng, L. L. (1989). Identifying the language-learning difficulties of Hmong students: Implications of context and culture. Topics in Language Disorders, 9(3), 21–37.

Matsuda, M. (1989). Working with Asian parents: Some communication strategies. Topics in Language Disorders, 9(3), 45–53.

McCorquodale, P. (1983). Social Influences on the Participation of Mexican American Women in Science. (N.I.E. Final Report 6-79-011). Tucson: University of Arizona.

McKeon, D. (1994). When meeting common standards is uncommonly difficult. Educational Leadership, 51, 45–49.

McLemore, D. S. (1994). Racial and Ethnic Relations in America. Boston: Allyn & Bacon.

Moody, J. D., and Gifford, V. D. (1990). The Effect of Grouping by Formal Reasoning Ability, Formal Reasoning Ability Levels, Group Size, and Gender on Achievement in Laboratory Chemistry. ERIC Document Reproduction Services No. ED 326-443.

More, A. J. (1987). Native Indian learning styles: A review for researchers and teachers. Journal of American Indian Education, 27(1), 17–29.

National Association of Bilingual Education. (1993). Census reports sharp increase in number of non-English speaking Americans. NABE News 16(6), 1, 25.

National Clearinghouse for Bilingual Education. (1993). State Profiles Database. Washington, D.C.: NCBE.

Nguyen, L. (1986). "Indochinese Cross-Cultural Adjustment and Communication." In M. Dao and H. Grossman (Eds.), Identifying, Instructing and Rehabilitating Southeast Asian Students with Special Needs and Counseling Their Parents. ERIC Document Reproduction Service No. ED 273-068.

Nicklin, J. L. (1991). "Teacher-Education Programs Face Pressure to Provide Multicultural Training."

The Chronicle of Higher Education, November 27, p. A16.

Nieto, S. (1992). Affirming Diversity: The Sociopolitical Context of Multicultural Education. New York: Longman.

Powell, R. G., and Andersen, J. (1994). "Culture and Classroom Communication." In L. A. Samovar and R. E. Porter, (Eds.), Intercultural Communication: A Reader, 7th ed., 322–333. Belmont, Calif.: Wadsworth.

Ready, T. (1991). Latino Immigrant Youth: Passages from Adolescence to Adulthood. New York: Garland.

Rhodes, R. W. (1988). Holistic teaching/learning for Native American students. Journal of American Indian Education, 27(2), 21–29.

Ricard, V. (1991). How effective intercultural skills can support learning. Adult Learning, February, 13–14.

Sadker, M., and Sadker, D. (1994). Failing at Fairness: How America's Schools Cheat Girls. New York: Charles Scribner's.

Samovar, L. A., and Porter, R. E. (1991). Communication Between Cultures. Belmont, Calif.: Wadsworth.

Samovar, L. A., and Porter, R. E. (1995). Communication Between Cultures, 2d ed. Belmont, Calif.: Wadsworth.

Stockard, J., and Johnson, M. M. (1980). Sex Roles: Sex Inequality and Sex Role Development. Englewood Cliffs, N.J.: Prentice-Hall.

Stodolsky, S. S., and Lesser, G. (1971). "Learning Patterns in the Disadvantaged." In Challenging the Myths: The Schools, the Blacks, and the Poor. Cambridge: Harvard Education Review.

Walker, B. J., Dodd, J., and Bigelow, R. (1989). Learning preferences of capable American Indians of two tribes. Journal of American Indian Education, Special Issue, 63–71.

White, M. (1987). The Japanese Educational Challenge: A Commitment to Children. New York: Free Press.

Yao, E. L. (1987). Asian-immigrant students—Unique problems that hamper learning. NASSP Bulletin, 71(503), 82–88.

## Concepts and Questions for Chapter 6

1. How do Japanese, Mexican, and American workers differ with regard to organizational loyalty, status, and formality?

2. From your own experiences, have you ever observed cultural differences toward work-related attitudes and values?

3. What cultural differences must a manager be concerned about when managing human resources in a multinational organization?

4. As an employee of a U.S. company, you have just been assigned to the international division and will soon take a position as a department manager at a facility in Germany. What differences in the cultural context of the workplace might you expect to encounter? How would you prepare yourself for the new assignment?

5. How do decision-making practices differ among Japanese, Mexican, German, and American managers and/or workers?

6. How do Germans and Americans differ in the area of perceived credibility?

7. Why is it important to understand American negotiation patterns as a starting point for studying international negotiation styles?

8. In what ways do American values carry over into negotiation sessions?

9. What are some cross-cultural considerations in the selection of negotiation team members? How does gender impact the selection process?

10. How do cultural differences regarding risk taking influence cross-cultural negotiations?

11. What is meant by the phrases "direct communication and indirect communication"? How do these two verbal styles impact cross-cultural negotiations?

12. Why is pace an important consideration in the negotiation process?

13. Do you agree with the five hypotheses regarding the relationship between cultural orientations and organizational effects advanced by Chen and Chung? Why? Why not?

14. How would you define the concept of *Jen* discussed by Chen and Chung?

15. What effect does Confucianism have on communication in the organization?

16. How does the Japanese perception of the group differ from those held by Americans?

17. In what manner did the Japanese *shogunates* (ruling families) contribute to the development of the Japanese concept of group?

18. What communication problems might a health care provider working within the Western biomedical health care system encounter when dealing with patients coming from a different medical orientation? What should he or she do to minimize these problems?

19. Why is it important to assess the acculturation level of culturally diverse students in the United States?

20. How might the nine learning styles discussed by Stefani be reflected in the classroom?

21. What are some problems facing students who have English as a second language when they enter schools in the United States?

# Part Four

## Intercultural Communication:
## Seeking Improvement

*Happy are they that hear their detractions and can put them*
*to mending.*
*—Shakespeare*

*Understanding is the beginning of approving.*
*—André Gide*

In a sense, this entire volume has been concerned with the practice of intercultural communication. We have looked at a variety of cultures and a
host of communication variables that operate when people from different
cultures attempt to interact. However, our analysis thus far has been more
theoretical than practical. Previous selections have concentrated primarily
on the issue of understanding intercultural communication. We have not
yet treated the act of practicing intercultural communication.

 We have already pointed out many of the problems that cultural differences introduce into the communication process. And we have shown
how an awareness not only of other cultures but also of one's own culture
can help mediate some of the problems. But intercultural communication
is not exclusively a single-party activity. Like other forms of interpersonal
communication, it requires for its highest and most successful practice the
complementary participation of all parties to the communication event.

 When elevated to its highest level, intercultural communication becomes an act in which participants make simultaneous inferences not only
about their own roles but about the role of the other as well. This act of
mutual role taking must exist before people can achieve a level of communication that results in mutual understanding. In intercultural communication, this means that you must know about your culture and the culture of
the one with whom you are communicating, and that person must also
know about his or her own culture and about your culture as well. Unless
there is mutual acknowledgment of each other's cultures and a willingness
to accept those cultures as a reality governing communicative interactions,
intercultural communication cannot rise to its highest possible level.

 In this final section we have slightly modified our orientation to
discuss the activity of communication. For although the readings in this

portion of the book will increase your understanding, their main purpose is to improve your *behavior* during intercultural communication.

The motivation for this particular section grows out of an important precept found in the study of human communication. It suggests that human interaction is a behavior people engage in for the purpose of changing their environment. Inherent in this notion is the idea that communication is something people *do* — it involves action. Regardless of how much you understand intercultural communication, when you are communicating with someone from another culture you are part of a behavioral situation. You, and your communication counterpart, are doing things that affect each other. This final part of the book deals with that "doing." In addition, it is intended to help your communication become as effective as possible.

As you might well imagine, personal contact and experience are the most desirable methods for improvement. Knowledge and practice seem to work in tandem. The problem, however, is that we cannot write or select readings that substitute for this personal experience. Therefore, our contribution by necessity must focus on the observations of those who have practiced intercultural communication with some degree of success.

# 7

## Communicating Interculturally: Becoming Competent

As we approach the last two chapters of this book, we need to remind you that our primary purpose is to help you become a more effective intercultural communicator. To this end, the readings throughout the text have sought to offer you material that will increase your knowledge about culture in general and also introduce you to a number of specific cultures. In this chapter we continue with these two themes by offering you advice and counsel that applies to all cultures and to specific cultures. That is to say, the essays in Chapter 7 were specifically selected because the suggestions advanced are both universal and specific. Most of the selections discuss problems as well as solutions. Being alert to potential problems is the first step toward understanding. Once problems have been identified, it is easier to seek means of improvement; and it is improvement that is at the heart of this chapter.

The first essay looks at both problems and solutions. In "Stumbling Blocks in Intercultural Communication," LaRay M. Barna deals with some specific reasons why intercultural communication often fails to bring about mutual understanding. She has selected six important causes for communication breakdowns across cultural boundaries: assuming similarity instead of difference, language problems, nonverbal misunderstanding, the presence of preconceptions and stereotypes, the tendency to evaluate, and the high anxiety that often exists in intercultural encounters.

Our second essay moves us from potential problems to possible solutions. In "A Model of Intercultural Communication Competence," Brian W. Spitzberg offers a profile of the effective intercultural communicator. More specifically, he suggests a course of action that is likely to enhance our competence when we are in an intercultural situation. His suggestions take the form of propositions that can be used to guide our actions. We are told that intercultural competence is increased if we (1) are motivated, (2) are knowledgeable, (3) possess interpersonal skills, (4) are credible, (5) meet the expectations of our communication partner, (6) can strike a balance between autonomy needs and intimacy needs, (7) reflect similarities, (8) manifest trust, (9) offer social support, and (10) have access to multiple relationships.

In our next reading, "Managing Intercultural Conflicts Effectively," Stella Ting-Toomey moves us from a general analysis of communication competency to a specific topic associated with intercultural communication: intercultural conflict. The rationale behind this selection is clearly stated in the opening line of the essay: "Conflict is inevitable in all social and personal relationships." To preempt the problems created by interpersonal disharmony, particularly in the intercultural setting, Ting-Toomey maintains that conflict must be defined and managed. To help us improve our capacity to clarify and regulate conflict, the author explains three significant features of intercultural conflict. First, a framework using low-context versus high-context and monochronic and polychronic time is advanced to demonstrate why and how cultures are different and similar. Second, some basic assumptions and factors that contribute to conflict are discussed. Finally, Ting-Toomey offers a series of skills that can help individuals manage conflict when it develops in the intercultural encounter.

The next reading deals with cross-cultural adaptation, a unique and often-overlooked aspect of intercultural communication. Young Yun Kim examines this subject in her essay "Adapting to a New Culture." Because more than a million immigrants come to the United States each year, the issue of adaptation is indeed an important one. For, as Kim notes, "cross-cultural adaptation is achieved mainly through communication." These new arrivals to the United States must learn new ways to think, feel, and behave if they are to coordinate their activities with those of the dominant culture. The process of learning these new modes of communication is called "acculturation." As you would suspect, attempting to learn a new culture, while trying to maintain some behaviors of the original culture, can be very stressful. Understanding the roots of some of these tensions and frustrations and how to overcome them is the central goal of this essay. Our role in the acculturation process is rather clear. Kim tells us that successful adaptation is a joint activity between the "strangers" and members of the dominant culture. By taking on a positive role in that activity, we can help immigrants with the difficult transition they face in their efforts to preserve their original ethnicity while adapting to a new and often-confusing environment.

Our final essay offers some unique suggestions on how to improve intercultural communication. In "Aesthetics as a Bridge to Intercultural Understanding," James Steven Sauceda maintains that we miss an impor-

tant element in intercultural communication when we use only inte̶
devices to understand people from different cultures. It is Sauceda's th̶
that successful interaction needs to include our "viscerally experiencing
the other." According to Sauceda, this new sense of understanding can be
accomplished through the use of aesthetic communication. This means
using artistic performance and artifacts to teach tolerance, empathy, and
acceptance of culturally different groups. Sauceda believes that all forms
of aesthetic communication (including the literary, visual, tactile, musical,
kinesthetic, theatrical) convey the essence of a culture by bringing out "an
immediacy of feeling and the authenticity of another's voice." After establishing the need for greater intercultural understanding, Sauceda offers
specific examples of how performance study, rainbow voices, theater,
painting, and music can be used to gain insight into divergent cultures.

# Blocks
## ural
## ation

## LARAY M. BARNA

Why is it that contact with persons from other cultures so often is frustrating and fraught with misunderstanding? Good intentions, the use of what one considers to be a friendly approach, and even the possibility of mutual benefits don't seem to be sufficient – to many people's surprise. A worse scenario is when rejection occurs just because the group to which a person belongs is "different." It's appropriate at this time of major changes in the international scene to take a hard look at some of the reasons for this. New proximity and new types of relationships are presenting communication challenges that few people are ready to meet.

## The Six Stumbling Blocks

### I. Assumption of Similarities

One answer to the question of why misunderstanding and/or rejection occurs is that many people naively assume there are sufficient similarities among peoples of the world to make communication easy. They expect that simply being human, having common requirements of food, shelter, security, and so on, makes everyone alike. Unfortunately they overlook the fact that the forms of adaptation to these common biological and social needs and the values, beliefs, and attitudes surrounding them are vastly different from culture to

This original essay appeared for the first time in the seventh edition. All rights reserved. Permission to reprint must be obtained from the author and the publisher. Professor Barna is Associate Professor Emerita at Portland State University, Portland, Oregon.

culture. The biological commonalities are not much help when it comes to communication, where we need to exchange ideas and information, find ways to live and work together, or just make the kind of impression we want to make.

Another reason many people are lured into thinking that "people are people" is that it reduces the discomfort of dealing with difference. If someone acts or looks "strange" (different from them), it's then possible to evaluate this as "wrong" and treat everyone ethnocentrically.

The assumption of similarity does not often extend to the expectation of a common verbal language but it does interfere with caution in decoding nonverbal symbols, signs, and signals. No cross-cultural studies have proven the existence of a common nonverbal language except those in support of Darwin's theory that facial expressions are universal.[1] Ekman (1976) found that "the particular visible pattern on the face, the combination of muscles contracted for anger, fear, surprise, sadness, disgust, happiness (and probably also for interest) is the same for all members of our species" (pp. 19–20).

This seems helpful until it is realized that a person's cultural upbringing determines whether or not the emotion will be displayed or suppressed, as well as on which occasions and to what degree (Ekman & Friesen, 1969, p. 1). The situations that bring about the emotional feeling also differ from culture to culture; for example the death of a loved one may be a cause for joy, sorrow, or some other emotion, depending upon the accepted cultural belief.

Since there seem to be no universals or "human nature" that can be used as a basis for automatic understanding, we must treat each encounter as an individual case, searching for whatever perceptions and communication means are held in common and proceed from there. This is summarized by Vinh The Do: "If we realize that we are all culture bound and culturally modified, we will accept the fact that, being unlike, we do not really know what someone else 'is.' This is another way to view the 'people are people' idea. We now have to find a way to sort out the cultural modifiers in each separate encounter to find similarity."[2]

Persons from the United States seem to hold this assumption of similarity more strongly than some other cultures. The Japanese, for example, have the reverse belief that they are distinctively different from the rest of the world. This notion brings intercultural communication problems of its own. Expecting no similarities they work hard to figure out the foreign stranger but do not expect foreigners to be able to understand them. This results in exclusionary attitudes and only passive efforts toward mutual understanding (Tai, 1986, pp. 45–47).

As Western trappings permeate more and more of the world the illusion of similarity increases. A look-alike façade deceives representatives from contrasting cultures when each wears Western dress, speaks English, and uses similar greeting rituals. It is like assuming that New York, Tokyo, and Tehran are all alike because each has the appearance of a modern city. But without being alert to possible underlying differences and the need to learn new rules for functioning, persons going from one city to the other will be in immediate trouble, even when taking on such simple roles as pedestrian or driver. Also, unless a foreigner expects subtle differences it will take a long time of noninsulated living in a new culture (not in an enclave of his or her own kind) before he or she can be jarred into a new perceptual and nonevaluative thinking.

The confidence that comes with the myth of similarity is much stronger than with the assumption of differences, the latter requiring tentative assumptions and behaviors and a willingness to accept the anxiety of "not knowing." Only with the assumption of differences, however, can reactions and interpretations be adjusted to fit "what's happening." Without it someone is likely to misread signs and symbols and judge the scene ethnocentrically.

The stumbling block of assumed similarity is a *troublem,* as one English learner expressed it, not only for the foreigner but for the people in the host country (United States or any other) with whom the international visitor comes into contact. The native inhabitants are likely to be lulled into the expectation that, since the foreign person is dressed appropriately and speaks some of the language, he or she will also have similar nonverbal codes, thoughts, and feelings. In the United States nod-ding, smiling, and affirmative comments from a foreigner will probably be confidently interpreted by straightforward, friendly Americans as meaning that they have informed, helped, and pleased the newcomer. It is likely, however, that the foreigner actually understood very little of the verbal and nonverbal content and was merely indicating polite interest or trying not to embarrass himself or herself or the host with verbalized questions. The conversation may even have confirmed a stereotype that Americans are insensitive and ethnocentric.

In instances like this, parties seldom compare impressions and correct misinterpretations. One place where opportunities for achieving insights does occur is in an intercultural communication classroom. Here, for example, U.S. students often complain that international student members of a discussion or project group seem uncooperative or uninterested. One person who had been thus judged offered the following explanation:[3]

*I was surrounded by Americans with whom I couldn't follow their tempo of discussion half of the time. I have difficulty to listen and speak, but also with the way they handle the group. I felt uncomfortable because sometimes they believe their opinion strongly. I had been very serious about the whole subject but I was afraid I would say something wrong. I had the idea but not the words.*

The classroom is also a good place to test whether one common nonverbal behavior, the smile, is actually the universal sign people assume it to be. The following enlightening comments came from international students newly arrived in the United States.[4]

Japanese student: *On my way to and from school I have received a smile by non-acquaintance American girls several times. I have finally learned they have no interest for me; it means only a kind of greeting to a foreigner. If someone smiles at a stranger in Japan, especially a girl, she can assume he is either a sexual maniac or an impolite person.*

Korean student: *An American visited me in my country for one week. His inference was that people in*

Korea are not very friendly because they didn't smile or want to talk with foreign people. Most Korean people take time to get to be friendly with people. We never talk or smile at strangers.

Arabic student: *When I walked around the campus my first day many people smiled at me. I was very embarrassed and rushed to the men's room to see if I had made a mistake with my clothes. But I could find nothing for them to smile at. Now I am used to all the smiles.*

Vietnamese student: *The reason why certain foreigners may think that Americans are superficial – and they are, some Americans even recognize this – is that they talk and smile too much. For people who come from placid cultures where nonverbal language is more used, and where a silence, a smile, a glance have their own meaning, it is true that Americans speak a lot. The superficiality of Americans can also be detected in their relations with others. Their friendships are, most of the time, so ephemeral compared to the friendships we have at home. Americans make friends very easily and leave their friends almost as quickly, while in my country it takes a long time to find out a possible friend and then she becomes your friend – with a very strong sense of the term.*

Statements from two U.S. students follow.[5] The first comes from someone who has learned to look for differing perceptions and the second, unfortunately, reflects the stumbling block of assumed similarity.

U.S. student: *I was waiting for my husband on a downtown corner when a man with a baby and two young children approached. Judging by small quirks of fashion he had not been in the U.S. long. I have a baby about the same age and in appreciation of his family and obvious involvement as a father I smiled at him. Immediately I realized I did the wrong thing as he stopped, looked me over from head to toe and said, "Are you waiting for me? You meet me later?" Apparently I had acted as a prostitute would in his country.*

U.S. student: *In general it seems to me that foreign people are not necessarily snobs but are very un-*friendly. *Some class members have told me that you shouldn't smile at others while passing them by on the street in their country. To me I can't stop smiling. It's just natural to be smiling and friendly. I can see now why so many foreign people stick together. They are impossible to get to know. It's like the Americans are big bad wolves. How do Americans break this barrier? I want friends from all over the world but how do you start to be friends without offending them or scaring them off – like sheep?"*

The discussion thus far threatens the popular expectation that increased contact with representatives of diverse cultures through travel, student exchange programs, joint business ventures, and so on will automatically result in better understanding and friendship. Indeed, tests of that assumption have been disappointing.[6] For example, research found that Vietnamese immigrants who speak English well and have the best jobs are suffering the most from psychosomatic complaints and mental problems and are less optimistic about the future than their counterparts who remain in ethnic enclaves without attempting to adjust to their new homeland. One explanation given is that these persons, unlike the less acculturated immigrants, "spend considerable time in the mainstream of society, regularly facing the challenges and stresses of dealing with American attitudes" (Horn, 1980, pp. 103–104).

After 24 years of listening to conversations between international and U.S. students and professors and seeing the frustrations of both groups as they try to understand each other, this author, for one, is inclined to agree with Charles Frankel (1965) who says, "Tensions exist within nations and between nations that never would have existed were these nations not in such intensive cultural communication with one another" (p. 1). Recent world events have proven this to be true.

From a communicative perspective it doesn't have to be that way. Just as more opportunities now exist for cross-cultural contact so does more information about how to meet this challenge. There are more orientation and training programs around the country, more courses in intercultural communication in educational institutions, and more published material.[7] Until persons can squarely face the likelihood of meeting up with difference and misunderstanding, however, they will not be motivated to take advantage of these resources.

Many potential travelers who do try to prepare for out-of-country travel (for business conferences, government negotiations, study tours, or whatever) might gather information about the customs of the other country and a smattering of the language. Behaviors and attitudes of its people are sometimes researched, but necessarily from a secondhand source, such as a friend who has "been there." Experts realize that information gained in this fashion is general, seldom sufficient, and may or may not be applicable to the specific situation and area that the traveler visits. Also, knowing "what to expect" often blinds the observer to all but what confirms his or her image. Any contradictory evidence that does filter through the screens of preconception is likely to be treated as an exception and thus discounted.

A better approach is to begin by studying the history, political structure, art, literature, and language of the country if time permits. This provides a framework for on-site observations. Even more important is to develop an investigation, nonjudgmental attitude, and a high tolerance for ambiguity — all of which require lowered defenses. Margaret Mead (1960) suggests sensitizing persons to the kinds of things that need to be taken into account instead of developing behavior and attitude stereotypes. She reasons that there are individual differences in each encounter and that changes occur regularly in cultural patterns, making research information obsolete.

Stewart and Bennett (1991) also warn against providing lists of "do's and don'ts" for travelers for several reasons, mainly that behavior is ambiguous; the same action can have different meanings in different situations and no one can be armed with prescriptions for every contingency. Instead they encourage persons to understand the assumptions and values on which their own behavior rests. This can then be compared with what is found in the other culture, and a "third culture" can be adopted based on expanded cross-cultural understanding (pp. 15 - 16).

## II. Language Differences

The remainder of this article will examine some of the variables of the intercultural communication process itself and point out danger zones therein. The first stumbling block has already been discussed at length, the hazard of *assuming similarity instead of difference*. A second danger will surprise no one: *language difference*. Vocabulary, syntax, idioms, slang, dialects, and so on, all cause difficulty, but the person struggling with a different language is at least aware of being in trouble.

A worse language problem is the tenacity with which someone will cling to just one meaning of a word or phrase in the new language, regardless of connotation or context. The infinite variations possible, especially if inflection and tonal qualities are present, are so difficult to cope with that they are often waved aside. This complacency will stop a search for understanding. The nationwide misinterpretation of Krushchev's statement "We'll bury you" is a classic example. Even "yes" and "no" cause trouble. When a non-native speaker first hears the English phrase, "Won't you have some tea?" he or she listens to the literal meaning of the sentence and answers, "No," meaning that he or she wants some. The U.S. hostess, on the other hand, ignores the double negative because of common usage, and the guest gets no tea. Also, in some cultures, it is polite to refuse the first or second offer of refreshment. Many foreign guests have gone hungry because they never got a third offer. This is another case of where "no" means "yes."

## III. Nonverbal Misinterpretations

Learning the language, which most visitors to foreign countries consider their only barrier to understanding, is actually only the beginning. As Frankel (1965) says, "To enter into a culture is to be able to hear, in Lionel Trilling's phrase, its special 'hum and buzz of implication'" (p. 103). This suggests the third stumbling block, *nonverbal misinterpretations*. People from different cultures inhabit different sensory realities. They see, hear, feel, and smell only that which has some meaning or importance for them. They abstract whatever fits into their personal world of recognition and then interpret it through the frame of reference of their own culture. An example follows:

An Oregon girl in an intercultural communication class asked a young man from Saudi Arabia how he would nonverbally signal that he liked her. His response was to smooth back his hair, which to her was just a common nervous gesture signifying nothing. She repeated her question three times. He smoothed his hair three times. Then, realizing that she was not recognizing this movement as his reply to her question, automatically ducked his head and stuck out his tongue slightly in embarrassment. This behavior *was* noticed by the girl and she expressed astonishment that he would show liking for someone by sticking out his tongue.

The lack of comprehension of nonverbal signs and symbols that are easy to observe – such as gestures, postures, and other body movements – is a definite communication barrier. But it is possible to learn the meanings of these messages, usually in informal rather than formal ways. It is more difficult to note correctly the unspoken codes of the other culture that are less obvious such as the handling of time and spatial relationships and subtle signs of respect or formality.

## IV. Preconceptions and Stereotypes

The fourth stumbling block is the presence of *preconceptions and stereotypes.* If the label "inscrutable" has preceded the Japanese guest, his behaviors (including the constant and seemingly inappropriate smile) will probably be seen as such. The stereotype that Arabs are "inflammable" may cause U.S. students to keep their distance or even alert authorities when an animated and noisy group from the Middle East gathers. A professor who expects everyone from Indonesia, Mexico, and many other countries to "bargain" may unfairly interpret a hesitation or request from an international student as a move to manipulate preferential treatment.

Stereotypes help do what Ernest Becker (1962) asserts the anxiety-prone human race must do – reduce the threat of the unknown by making the world predictable (pp. 84–89). Indeed, this is one of the basic functions of culture: to lay out a predictable world in which the individual is firmly oriented. Stereotypes are overgeneralized, secondhand beliefs that provide conceptual bases from which we "make sense" out of what goes on around us, whether or not they are accurate or fit the circumstance. In a foreign land their use increases our feeling of security and is psychologically necessary to the degree that we cannot tolerate ambiguity or the sense of helplessness resulting from inability to understand and deal with people and situations beyond our comprehension.

Stereotypes are stumbling blocks for communicators because they interfere with objective viewing of stimuli – the sensitive search for cues to guide the imagination toward the other person's reality. They are not easy to overcome in ourselves or to correct in others, even with the presentation of evidence. Stereotypes persist because they are firmly established as myths or truisms by one's own national culture and because they sometimes rationalize prejudices. They are also sustained and fed by the tendency to perceive selectively only those pieces of new information that correspond to the image held. For example, the Asian or African visitor who is accustomed to privation and the values of self-denial and self-help cannot fail to experience American culture as materialistic and wasteful. The stereotype for the visitor becomes a reality.

## V. Tendency to Evaluate

Another deterrent to understanding between persons of differing cultures or ethnic groups is the *tendency to evaluate,* to approve or disapprove, the statements and actions of the other person or group rather than to try to comprehend completely the thoughts and feelings expressed from the world view of the other. Each person's culture or way of life always seems right, proper, and natural. This bias prevents the open-minded attention needed to look at the attitudes and behavior patterns from the other's point of view. A mid-day siesta changes from a "lazy habit" to a "pretty good idea" when someone listens long enough to realize the mid-day temperature in that country is over 115°F.

The author, fresh from a conference in Tokyo where Japanese professors had emphasized the preference of the people of Japan for simple natural settings of rocks, moss, and water and of muted greens and misty ethereal landscapes, visited the Katsura Imperial Gardens in Kyoto. At the appointed time of the tour a young Japanese guide approached the group of 20 waiting U.S. Americans and remarked how fortunate it was that the day was cloudy. This brought hesitant smiles to the group who were less than pleased at the prospect of a shower. The guide's next statement was that the timing of the summer visit was particularly appropriate in that the azalea and rhododendron blossoms were gone and the trees had not yet turned to their brilliant fall colors. The group laughed loudly, now convinced that the young man had a fine sense of humor. I winced at his bewildered expression, realizing that had I come before attending the conference I would have shared the group's inference that he could not be serious.

The communication cutoff caused by immediate evaluation is heightened when feelings and emotions are deeply involved; yet this is just the time when listening with understanding is most needed. As stated by Sherif, Sherif, and Nebergall (1965), "A person's commitment to his religion, politics, values of his family, and his stand on the virtue of his way of life are ingredients in his self-picture – intimately felt and cherished" (p. vi). It takes both the awareness of the tendency to close our minds and the courage to risk changing our own perceptions and values to dare to comprehend why someone thinks and acts differently from us. Religious wars and negotiation deadlocks everywhere are examples of this.

On an interpersonal level there are innumerable illustrations of the tendency to evaluate, resulting in a breach in intercultural relationships. Two follow:[8]

U.S. Student: *A Persian friend got offended because when we got in an argument with a third party, I didn't take his side. He says back home you are supposed to take a friend's or family's side even when they are wrong. When you get home then you can attack the "wrongdoer" but you are never supposed to go against a relative or a friend to a stranger. This I found strange because even if it is my mother and I think she is wrong, I say so.*

Korean student: *When I call on my American friend he said through window, "I am sorry. I have no time because of my study." Then he shut the window. I couldn't understand through my cultural background. House owner should have welcome visitor whether he likes or not and whether he is busy or not. Also the owner never speaks without opening his door.*

The admonition to resist the tendency to immediately evaluate does not intend to suggest that one should not develop one's own sense of right and wrong. The goal is to look and listen emphatically rather than through a thick screen of value judgments that would cause one to fail to achieve a fair and total understanding. Once comprehension is complete it can be determined whether or not there is a clash in values or ideology. If so, some form of adjustment or conflict resolution can be put into place.

## VI. High Anxiety

*High anxiety* or *tension,* also known as *stress,* is common in cross-cultural experiences due to the number of uncertainties present. The two words, "anxiety" and "tension," are linked because one cannot be mentally anxious without also being physically tense. Moderate tension and positive attitudes prepare one to meet challenges with energy. Too much anxiety or tension requires some form of relief which too often comes in the form of defenses, such as the skewing of perceptions, withdrawal, or hostility. That's why it is considered a serious stumbling block. As stated by Kim (1991):

*Stress, indeed, is considered to be inherent in intercultural encounters, disturbing the internal equilibrium of the individual system. Accordingly, to be interculturally competent means to be able to manage such stress, regain internal balance, and carry out the communication process in such a way that contributes to successful interaction outcomes. (p. 267)*

High anxiety or tension, unlike the other five stumbling blocks (assumption of similarity, language, nonverbal misinterpretations, preconceptions and stereotypes, and the practice of immediate evaluation), is not only distinct but often underlies and compounds the other stumbling blocks. The use of stereotypes and evaluations are defense mechanisms in themselves to alleviate the stress of the unknown or the intercultural encounter, as previously explained. If the person was tense or anxious to begin with these would be used even more. Falling prey to the aura of similarity is also a protection from the stress of recognizing and accommodating to differences. Different language and nonverbal patterns are difficult to use or interpret under the best of conditions. The distraction of trying to reduce the feeling of anxiety (sometimes called "internal noise") makes mistakes even more likely. Jack Gibb (1961) remarks:

*Defense arousal prevents the listener from concentrating upon the message. Not only do defensive communicators send off multiple value, motive, and affect cues, but also defensive recipients distort what they receive. As a person becomes more and more defensive, he becomes less and less able to perceive accurately the motives, the values, and the emotions of the sender. (pp. 141 – 148)*

Anxious feelings usually permeate both parties in an intercultural dialogue. The host national is uncomfortable when talking with a foreigner because he or she cannot maintain the normal flow of verbal and nonverbal interaction. There are language and perception barriers; silences are too long or too short; proxemic and other norms may be violated. He or she is also threatened by the other's unknown knowledge, experience, and evaluation — the visitor's potential for scrutiny and rejection of the person and/or the country. The inevitable question "How do you like it here?" which the foreigner abhors, is a quest for reassurance, or at least a "feeler" that reduces the unknown. The reply is usually more polite than honest but this is seldom realized.

The foreign members of dyads are even more threatened. They feel strange and vulnerable, helpless to cope with messages that swamp them. Their own "normal" reactions are inappropriate. Their self-esteem is often intolerably undermined unless they employ such defenses as withdrawal into their own reference group or into themselves, screen out or misperceive stimuli, use rationalization or overcompensation, or become aggressive or hostile. None of these defenses leads to effective communication.

**Culture Shock.** If a person remains in a foreign culture over time the stress of constantly being "on guard" to protect oneself against making "stupid mistakes" takes its toll and he or she will probably be affected by "culture fatigue," usually called *culture shock*. According to Barna (1983):

*. . . the innate physiological makeup of the human animal is such that discomfort of varying degrees occurs in the presence of alien stimuli. Without the normal props of one's own culture there is unpredictability, helplessness, a threat to self-esteem, and a general feeling of "walking on ice" – all of which are stress producing. (pp. 42 – 43)*

The result of several months of this sustained anxiety or tension (or excitation if the high activation is perceived positively) is that reserve energy supplies become depleted, the person's physical capacity is weakened, and a feeling of exhaustion, desperation, or depression may take over (Selye, 1969). He or she, consciously or unconsciously, would then use psychological defenses such as those described previously. If this temptation is resisted, the sojourner suffering from the strain of constant adjustment may find his or her body absorbing the stress in the form of stomach or back aches, insomnia, inability to concentrate, or other stress-related illnesses (Barna, 1983, pp. 29 – 30).

The following account by a sojourner to the United States illustrates the trauma of culture shock:

*Soon after arriving in the U.S. from Peru, I cried almost every day. I was so tense I heard without hearing, and this made me feel foolish. I also escaped into sleeping more than twelve hours at a time and dreamed of my life, family, and friends in Lima. After three months of isolating myself in the house and speaking to no-one, I ventured out. I then began to have severe headaches. Finally I consulted a doctor, but she only gave me a lot of drugs to relieve the pain. Neither my doctor nor my teachers ever mentioned the two magic words that could have changed my life: culture shock! When I learned about this I began to see things from a new point of view and was better able to accept myself and my feelings.*

*I now realize most of the Americans I met in Lima before I came to the U.S. were also in one of the stages of culture shock. They demonstrated a somewhat hostile attitude toward Peru, which the Peruvians sensed and usually moved from an initially friendly attitude to a defensive, aggressive attitude or to avoidance. The Americans mostly stayed within the safe cultural familiarity of the embassy compound. Many seemed to feel that the difficulties they were experiencing in Peru were specially created by Peruvians to create discomfort for "gringos." In other words, they displaced their problem of adjustment and blamed everything on Peru.*[9]

Culture shock is a state of dis-ease, and, like a disease, it has different effects, different degrees of severity, and different time spans for different people. It is the least troublesome to those who learn to accept cultural diversity with interest instead of anxiety and manage normal stress reactions by practicing positive coping mechanisms, such as conscious physical relaxation (Barna 1983, pp. 33–39).

**Physiological Reactions.** Understanding the physiological component of the stumbling block of anxiety/tension helps in the search for ways to lessen its debilitating effects (Selye, 1974, 1976). It is hard to circumvent because, as human animals, our biological system is set so that anything that is perceived as being "not normal" automatically signals an alert (Toffler, 1970, pp. 334–342; Ursin, 1978). Depending on how serious the potential threat seems to be, extra adrenalin and noradrenalin pour into the system; muscles tighten; the heart rate, blood pressure, and breathing rate increase, the digestive process turns off, and other changes occur (Oken, 1974).

This "fight or flight" response was useful, actually a biological gift for survival or effective functioning, when the need was for vigorous action. However, if the "danger" is to one's social self, which is more often the case in today's world, too much anxiety or tension just gets in the way. This is particularly true in an intercultural setting where the need is for understanding, calm deliberation, and empathy in order to untangle misperceptions and enter into smooth relationships.

All is not "doom and gloom" however. As stated by Ursin (1978), "The bodily response to changes in the environment and to threatening stimuli is simply activation" (p. 219). Researchers believe that individuals control their emotional response to that activation by their own cognitions (Brown, 1980; Keating, 1979; Schachter and Singer, 1962). If a person expects something to be exciting rather than frightening, he is more likely to interpret the somatic changes that he feels in his body as excitement. Selye (1978) would label that "the good stress" that does much less harm unless it continues for some time without relief. Feeling "challenged" facilitates functioning as opposed to a person who feels "threatened" (Lazarus, 1979).

People also differ in their stress tolerance. Whatever the reasons, everyone knows people who "fall apart at the least thing" and others who seem unflappable in any crisis. If you are one of the former there are positive ways to handle the stress of intercultural situations, whether these be one-time encounters; frequent dialogues in multicultural settings like a school or workplace, vacation trips; or wherever. For starters, you can find opportunities to become familiar with many types of people so that differences become normal and interesting instead of threatening. And you can practice body awareness so that changes that signify a stress reaction can be identified and counteracted.

## Conclusion

Being aware of the six stumbling blocks is certainly the first stop in avoiding them, but it isn't easy. For most people it takes insight, training, and sometimes an alteration of long-standing habits or thinking patterns before progress can be made. The increasing need for global understanding, however, gives all of us the responsibility for giving it our best effort.

We can study other languages and learn to expect differences in nonverbal forms and other cultural aspects. We can train ourselves to meet intercultural encounters with more attention to situational details. We can use an investigative approach rather than stereotypes and preconceptions. We can gradually expose ourselves to differences so that they become less threatening. We can even learn to lower our tension level when needed to avoid triggering defensive reactions.

The overall goal should be to achieve *intercultural communication competence,* which is defined by Kim (1991) as "the overall internal capability of an individual to manage key challenging features of intercultural communication: namely, cultural differences and unfamiliarity, intergroup posture, and the accompanying experience of stress" (p. 259).

Roger Harrison (1966) adds a final thought:

*. . . the communicator cannot stop at knowing that the people he is working with have different customs, goals, and thought patterns from his own. He must be able to feel his way into intimate contact with these alien values, attitudes, and feelings. He must be able to work with them and within them, neither losing his own values in the confrontation nor protecting himself behind a wall of intellectual detachment. (p. 4)*

## Notes

1. See Charles Darwin, *The Expression of Emotions in Man and Animals* (New York: Appleton, 1872); Irenaus, Eibl-Eibesfeldt, *Ethology: The Biology of Behavior* (New York: Holt, Rinehart & Winston, 1970); Paul Ekman and Wallace V. Friesan, "Constants Across Cultures in the Face and Emotion," *Journal of Personality and Social Psychology,* 17 (1971), pp. 124–129.

2. Personal correspondence. Mr. Do is Multicultural Specialist, Portland Public Schools, Portland, Oregon.

3. Taken from student papers in a course on intercultural communication taught by the author.

4. Ibid.

5. Ibid.

6. See, for example, Bryant Wedge, *Visitors to the United States and How They See Us* (Princeton, N.J.: D. Van Nostrand Company, 1965); and Milton Miller et al., "The Cross-Cultural Student: Lessons in Human Nature," *Bulletin of Menninger Clinic* (March 1971).

7. One good source is the Intercultural Press, Inc., P.O. Box 768, Yarmouth, Maine 04096 U.S.A.

8. Taken from student papers in a course on intercultural communication taught by the author.

9. Personal correspondence.

## References

Barna, L. M. (1983). "The Stress Factor in Intercultural Relations." In D. Landis and R. W. Brislin (Eds.), *Handbook of Intercultural Training,* Vol. II. New York: Pergamon Press.

Becker, E. (1962). *The Birth and Death of Meaning.* New York: Free Press.

Brown, B. B. (1980). "Perspectives on Social Stress." In H. Selye (Ed.), *Selye's Guide to Stress Research,* Vol. 1. New York: Van Nostrand Reinhold.

Ekman, P. (1976). Movements with precise meanings. *Journal of Communication, 26,* Summer.

Ekman, P., and Friesen, W. (1969). The repertoire of nonverbal behavior—Categories, origins, usage and coding. *Semiotica 1.*

Frankel, C. (1965). *The Neglected Aspect of Foreign Affairs.* Washington, D.C.: Brookings Institution.

Gibb, J. R. (1961). Defensive communication. *Journal of Communication 2,* Sept.

Harrison, R. (1966). "The Design of Cross-Cultural Training: An Alternative to the University Model." In *Explorations in Human Relations Training and Research.* Bethesda, Md.: National Training Laboratories. NEA No. 2.

Horn, J. (1980). "Vietnamese Immigrants: Doing Poorly by Doing Well." *Psychology Today,* June.

Keating, J. P. (1979). "Environmental Stressors: Misplaced Emphasis Crowding as Stressor." In I. G. Sarason and C. D. Spielberger (Eds.), *Stress and Anxiety,* Vol. 6. Washington, D.C.: Hemisphere.

Kim, Y. Y. (1991). "Intercultural Communication Competence: A Systems-Theoretic View." In S. Ting-Toomey, and F. Korzenny (Eds.), *Cross-Cultural Interpersonal Communication* (International and Intercultural Communication Annual, Vol. XV). Newbury Park, CA: Sage.

Lazarus, R. S. (1979). "Positive Denial: The Case for Not Facing Reality." *Psychology Today,* Nov.

Mead, M. (1960). "The Cultural Perspective." In Mary Capes (Ed.), *Communication or Conflict.* Associated Press.

Oken, D. (1974). "Stress—Our Friend, Our Foe." In *Blue Print for Health.* Chicago: Blue Cross Association.

Schachter, S., and Singer, J. E. (1962). "Cognitive, Social and Physiological Determinants of Emotional State." *Psychological Review 69.*

Selye, H. (1969). "Stress: It's a G.A.S." *Psychology Today,* Sept.

Selye, H. (1974). *Stress Without Distress.* New York: J. B. Lippincott.

Selye, H. (1976). *The Stress of Life.* New York: McGraw-Hill.

Selye, H. (1978). On the Real Benefits of Eustress. *Psychology Today,* March.

Sherif, C. W., Sherif, W., and Nebergall, R. (1965). *Attitude and Attitude Change.* Philadelphia: W. B. Saunders.

Stewart, E. C., and Bennett, M. J. (1991). *American Cultural Patterns.* Yarmouth, Maine: Intercultural Press.

Tai, E. (1986). Modification of the Western Approach to Intercultural Communication for the Japanese Context. Unpublished master's thesis, Portland State University, Portland, Oregon.

Toffler, A. (1970). *Future Shock.* New York: Bantam.

Ursin, H. (1978). "Activation, Coping and Psychosomatics." In E. Baade, S. Levine, and H. Ursin (Eds.), *Psychobiology of Stress: A Study of Coping Men.* New York: Academic Press.

# $A$ Model of Intercultural Communication Competence

## BRIAN H. SPITZBERG

The world we live in is shrinking. Travel that once took months now takes hours. Business dealings that were once confined primarily to local economies have given way to an extensively integrated world economy. Information that once traveled through error-prone and time-consuming methods now appears in the blink of an eye across a wide range of media. People in virtually all locations of the globe are more mobile than ever, and more likely to traverse into cultures different from their own. Literally and figuratively, the walls that separate us are tumbling down. Though we may not have fully become a "global village," there is no denying that the various cultures of the world are far more accessible than ever before, and that the peoples of these cultures are coming into contact at an ever increasing rate. These contacts ultimately comprise interpersonal encounters. Whether it is the negotiation of an arms treaty, or the settlement of a business contract, or merely a sojourner getting directions from a native, cultures do not interact, people do.

The purpose of this essay is to examine the concept of interactional competence in intercultural contexts. For the purposes of this essay, *intercultural communication competence* is considered very broadly as an impression that behavior is appropriate and effective in a given context. Normally, *competence* is considered an ability or a set of skilled behaviors. However, any given behavior or ability may be judged competent in one context, and incompetent in another. Consequently, competence cannot inhere in the behavior or ability itself. It must instead be viewed as a social evaluation of behavior. This social evaluation is composed of the two primary criteria of appropriateness and effectiveness.

*Appropriateness* means that the valued rules, norms, and expectancies of the relationship are not violated significantly. *Effectiveness* is the accomplishment of valued goals or rewards relative to costs and alternatives. With these dual standards, therefore, communication will be competent in an intercultural context when it accomplishes the objectives of an actor in a manner that is appropriate to the context and relationship.

These two standards obviously bear on the concept of interactional quality. Communication that is *in*appropriate and *in*effective (that is, minimizing) is clearly of low quality. Communication that is appropriate but *in*effective (that is, sufficing) suggests a social chameleon who does nothing objectionable, but also accomplishes no personal objectives through interaction. Finally, communication that is *in*appropriate but effective (that is, maximizing) would include such behaviors as lying, cheating, stealing, bludgeoning, and so forth, messages that are ethically problematic. While there may be instances in which such actions could be considered competent, they are rarely the ideal behaviors to employ in any given circumstance. Only the interactant who is both simultaneously appropriate and effective seems to meet the requirements of the optimal interpersonal communicator. The remainder of this essay examines issues surrounding appropriateness and effectiveness in intercultural interaction.

## A Model of Intercultural Competence

Most existing models of intercultural competence have been fairly fragmented. Typically, the literature is reviewed and a list of skills, abilities, and attitudes is formulated to summarize the literature (Spitzberg & Cupach, 1989). Such lists appear on the surface to reflect useful guidelines for competent interaction and adaptation. For example, Spitzberg's (1989) review of studies, along with

other more recent studies, produces the partial list in Table 1. While each study portrays a reasonable list of abilities or attitudes, there is no sense of integration or coherence across lists. It is impossible to tell which skills are most important in which situations, or even how such skills relate to each other.

A more productive approach would be to develop an integrative model of intercultural competence that is both consistent with the theoretical and empirical literatures, and also provides specific predictions of competent behavior. This approach is reflected in basic form in Figure 1, and is elaborated on by means of the series of propositions that follow. The propositions are broken down into three levels of analysis: (1) the individual system, (2) the episodic system, and (3) the relational system. The *individual system* includes those characteristics an individual may possess that facilitate competent interaction in a normative social sense. The *episodic system* includes those features of a particular Actor that facilitate competence impressions on the part of a specific Coactor in a specific episode of interaction. The *relational system* includes those components that assist a person's competence across the entire span of relationships rather than in just a given episode of interaction. Each successive system level subsumes the logic and predictions of the former. The propositions serve both to provide an outline of a theory of interpersonal competence in intercultural contexts as well as offer practical advice. To the extent that interactants can analyze intercultural situations sufficiently to understand initial conditions, then each proposition suggests a course of action that is likely to enhance their competence in the situation encountered.

The model portrays the process of dyadic interaction as a function of two individuals' *motivation* to communicate, *knowledge* of communication in that context, and *skills* in implementing their motivation and knowledge. Over the course of the interaction both within and across episodes, behavior is matched to expectancies that each interactant has of the other and the interaction process. If expectancies are fulfilled in a rewarding manner, then interactants are likely to perceive both self and

**Table 1** Empirically Derived Factors of Intercultural Competence

| | |
|---|---|
| Ability to adjust to different cultures | Frankness |
| Ability to deal with different societal systems | General competence as teacher (task) |
| Ability to deal with psychological stress | Incompetence |
| Ability to establish interpersonal relationships | Intellectualizing future orientation |
| Ability to facilitate communication | Interaction involvement |
| Ability to understand others | Interpersonal flexibility |
| Adaptiveness | Interpersonal harmony |
| Agency (internal locus and efficacy/optimism) | Interpersonal interest |
| Awareness of self and culture | Interpersonally sensitive maturity |
| Awareness of implications of cultural differences | Managerial ability |
| Cautiousness | Nonethnocentrism |
| Charisma | Nonverbal behaviors |
| Communication apprehension | Personal/Family adjustment |
| Communication competence (ability to communicate) | Opinion leadership |
| Communication efficacy | Rigidity (task persistence) |
| Communicative functions | Task accomplishment |
| Controlling responsibility | Transfer of "software" |
| Conversational management behaviors | Self-actualizing search for identity |
| Cooperation | Self-confidence/Initiative |
| Cultural empathy | Self-consciousness |
| Cultural interaction | Self-disclosure |
| Demand (long-term goal orientation) | Self-reliant conventionality |
| Dependent anxiety | Social adjustment |
| Differentiation | Spouse/Family communication |
| Empathy/Efficacy | Strength of personality |
| Familiarity in interpersonal relations | Verbal behaviors |

other as communicatively competent, and feel relatively satisfied that objectives were accomplished. Interactants may be seen as incompetent because they lack motivation to perform competently, knowledge of the competent lines of action in the context concerned, or the communication skills to carry off a deft interaction. Also, interactants may be viewed as incompetent because their partner has unrealistic expectancies for the person or episode. These and other implications are discussed next.

## Individual System

*1. As communicator motivation increases, communicative competence increases.* Very simply, the more a person wants to make a good impression and communicate effectively, the more likely it is that this person will view self, and be viewed by others, as competent. The question then, becomes what constitutes or leads to high levels of motivation. The following propositions address this question.

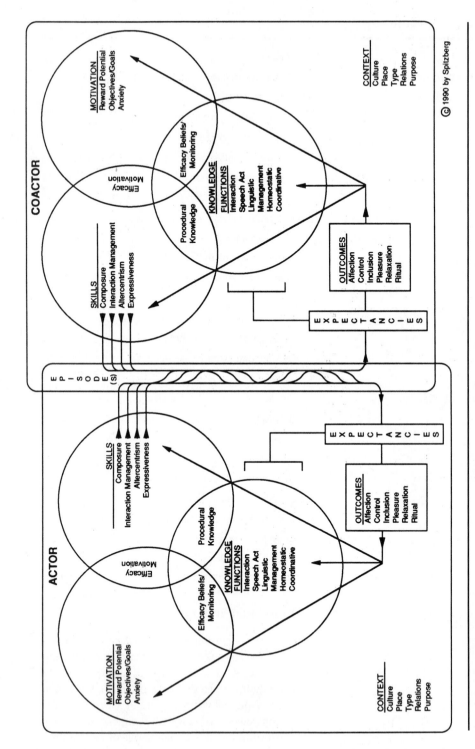

**Figure 1** A Diagrammatic Representation of Relational Competence

© 1990 by Spitzberg

*1a. As communicator confidence increases, communicator motivation increases.* Confidence results from several individual experiences. For example, a person who is nervous meeting strangers is likely to be less confident when encountering a new person from a different culture. Further, the more unfamiliar a person is with a given type of situation, the less confident that person is regarding what to do and how to do it. Finally, some situations carry more significant implications and are more difficult to manage than others. For example, getting directions to a major urban landmark is likely to permit greater confidence than negotiating a multimillion dollar contract for your company. Thus, social anxiety, familiarity with the situation, and the importance or consequences of the encounter all influence an interactant's confidence in a social context.

*1b. As reward-relevant efficacy beliefs increase, communicator motivation increases.* Efficacy beliefs are self-perceptions of ability to perform a given set of behaviors (Bandura, 1982). Basically, the more actors believe that they are able to engage in a set of valued or positive actions, the more prone they are to do so. A professional arbitrator is likely to have much higher efficacy beliefs in negotiating disputes or contracts than the average person. However, this arbitrator might not have any greater confidence than the average person in developing friendships with others in a different culture. Efficacy beliefs are therefore usually task-specific, and correlated to familiarity with the task(s) and context(s).

*1c. As communicator approach dispositions increase, communicator motivation increases.* Approach dispositions refer to personality characteristics that prompt someone to value communicative activity. People who are higher in self-esteem, who consistently seek relatively high levels of sensory stimulation, who believe they have high levels of control over their environment, who are low in social anxiety, and who are generally well-adjusted psychologically, are likely to seek out communication encounters and find them positively reinforcing.

*1d. As the relative cost/benefit ratio of a situation increases, communicator motivation increases.* Very simply, every situation can be viewed as having certain potential costs and benefits. Even in no-win situations (for example, "true" conflicts), the behavior that leads to the least costly or painful outcomes is considered the most preferable or beneficial. Likewise, in a win-win situation the least desirable outcomes are also the most costly. Thus, as the perception of potential benefits increases relative to the potential costs of a course of action, the more motivated a person is to pursue that particular course of action. Obviously, the weighing of costs and benefits must always be done relative to alternatives. Asking directions from someone who does not speak your language may be considered too much effort, but only relative to the alternatives of consulting a map, trial-and-error exploration, seeking someone who speaks your language who might be familiar with the locale, or getting hopelessly lost.

*2. Communicative knowledge increases, communicative competence increases.* A stage actor needs to be motivated to give a good performance to be viewed as a competent actor. However, merely wanting to perform well, and being unhampered by stage fright, are probably insufficient to produce a competent performance. For an actor to give a good performance, it is also important that the actor know the script, the layout of the stage, the type of audience to expect, and so on. So it is with social interaction as well. The more an interactant knows about how to communicate well, the more competent that person is likely to be.

Knowledge of interaction occurs at several microscopic levels (Greene, 1984). As identified in Figure 1, an actor needs to know the interaction function, the basic goals the interaction is to pursue. These interaction behaviors combine to form speech acts, which express content functions such as asking questions, asserting opinions, and so on. To perform speech acts in turn requires knowledge of linguistics — semantics, syntax, and the constituents of a meaningful sentence. Actual performance of these actions requires adaptation of this behavior to the other person. Thus, behaviors need to be adapted to achieve the following functions: management — coherence and continuity of topic, and relatively smooth flow of speaking turns; homeostatic — a relative balance of physiological activity level; and coordinative — individual matching of verbal and nonverbal components. Several predictions help specify the relevance of knowledge to competent interaction.

*2a. As task-relevant procedural knowledge increases, communicator knowledge increases.* Procedural knowledge concerns the "how" of social interaction rather than the "what." For example, knowing the actual content of a joke would be considered the substantive knowledge of the joke. Knowing how to tell it, with all the inflections, the timing, and the actual mannerisms, are all matters of the procedural knowledge of the joke. This knowledge is typically more "mindless" than other forms of knowledge. For example, many skill routines are overlearned to the point that the procedures are virtually forgotten, as in driving a familiar route home and not remembering anything about the drive upon arrival. You "know" how to drive, but you can use such knowledge with virtually no conscious attention to the process. Thus, the more a person actually knows how to perform the mannerisms and behavioral routines of a cultural milieu, the more knowledgeable this person is likely to be in communicating generally with others in this culture. In general, as a person's exposure to a culture increases, his or her stores of relevant subject matters, topics, language forms, and so on, as well as procedural competencies, are likely to increase.

*2b. As mastery of knowledge-acquisition strategies increases, communicator knowledge increases.* A person who does not already know how to behave is not necessarily consigned to incompetence. People have evolved a multitude of means for finding out what to do, and how to do it, in unfamiliar contexts. The metaphor of international espionage illustrates some of the strategies by which people acquire information about others, such as interrogating (asking questions), surveilling (observing others), exchanging information (disclosing information to elicit disclosure from others), posturing (violating some local custom and observing reactions to assess the value of various actions), bluffing (acting as if we know what we are doing and allowing the unfolding action to inform us and define our role), or engaging double agents (using the services of a native or mutual friend as an in-

formant). The more of these types of strategies actors understand, the more capable they are in obtaining the knowledge needed to interact competently in the culture.

*2c. As identity and role diversity increases, communicator knowledge increases.* In general, the more diverse a person's exposure to distinct types of people, roles, and self-images, the more this person is able to comprehend various roles and role behaviors characteristic of a given cultural encounter. Some people live all their lives in a culture within very narrow ranges of contexts and roles. Others experience a wide variety of societal activities (jobs, tasks), roles (parent, worshiper, confidant), and groups (political party, religious affiliation, volunteer organization, cultures and co-cultures). A person who has a highly complex self-image reflecting these social identities (Hoelter, 1985) and who has interacted with a diversity of different types of persons and roles (Havighurst, 1957) is better able to understand the types of actions encountered in another culture.

*2d. As knowledge dispositions increase, communicator knowledge increases.* Many personality characteristics are related to optimal information processing. Specifically, persons high in intelligence, cognitive complexity, self-monitoring, listening skills, empathy, role-taking ability, nonverbal sensitivity, perceptual accuracy, problem-solving ability, and so on are more likely to know how to behave in any given encounter. In short, while mere possession of information may help, a person also needs to know how to analyze and process that information.

*3. As communicator skills increase, communicator competence increases.* Skills are any repeatable, goal-oriented actions or action sequences. An actor who is motivated to perform well, and knows the script well, still may not possess the acting skills required to give a good performance. All of us have probably encountered instances in which we knew what we wanted to say, but just could not seem to say it correctly. Such issues concern the skills of performing our motivation and knowledge. Research indicates that there are four specific types or clusters of interpersonal skills, and one more general type of skill.

Before specifying the skills that facilitate intercultural communication competence, an important qualifier needs to be considered. There are probably no specific behaviors that are universally competent. Even if peoples from all cultures smile, the smile is not always a competent behavior. However, there may be skill modes or clusters that are consistently competent according to standards of appropriate usage within each culture. For example, probably all cultures value the smooth flow of conversation, even though they may differ in the specific behaviors and cues used to accomplish such interaction management. Any skill or ability is constrained by its own culturally and relationally appropriate rules of expression. It is in this sense that the following propositions are developed regarding communication skills.

*3a. As conversational altercentrism increases, communicator skill increases.* Altercentrism ("alter" means other, "centrism" means to focus upon) involves those behaviors that reveal concern for, interest in, and attention to, another person. Behaviors such as eye contact, asking questions, maintenance of others' topics, appropriate body lean and posture, and active listening all indicate a responsiveness to the other person.

*3b. As conversational coordination increases, communicator skill increases.* Conversational coordination involves all those behaviors that assist in the smooth flow of an encounter. Minimizing response latencies, providing for smooth initiation and conclusion of conversational episodes, avoiding disruptive interruptions, providing transitions between themes or activities, and providing informative feedback cues all assist in managing the interaction and maintaining appropriate pacing and punctuation of a conversation.

*3c. As conversational composure increases, communicator skill increases.* To be composed in a conversation is to reflect calmness and confidence in demeanor. Thus, composure consists of avoiding anxiety cues (nervous twitches, adaptors, lack of eye contact, breaking vocal pitch) and displaying such behaviors as a steady volume and pitch, relaxed posture, and well-formulated verbal statements. A composed communicator comes across as assertive, self-assured, and in control.

*3d. As conversational expressiveness increases, communicator skill increases.* Expressiveness concerns those skills that provide vivacity, animation, intensity, and variability in communicative behavior. Specifically, expressiveness is revealed by such behaviors as vocal variety, facial affect, opinion expression, extensive vocabulary usage, and gestures. Expressive communication is closely associated with the ability to display culturally and contextually appropriate effect and energy level through speech and gesture.

*3e. As conversational adaptation increases, communicator skill increases.* Adaptation is a commonly noted attribute of the competent intercultural communicator. It typically suggests several characteristics. First, rather than radical chameleonlike change, adaptation implies subtle variation of self's behavior to the behavioral style of others. Second, it implies certain homeostatic, or consistency-maintaining, regulatory processes. That is, verbal actions are kept relatively consistent with nonverbal actions. Similarly, amount of personal altercentrism, coordination, composure, and expressiveness are kept relatively consistent with personal style tendencies. Third, adaptation suggests accommodation of both the actions of the other person as well as one's own goal(s) in the encounter. Rather than implying completely altercentric or egocentric orientations, adaptation implies altering and balancing self's goals and intentions to those of the other person. Thus, the skill of adaptation implies such behaviors as shifts of vocal style, posture, animation, and topic development as the behaviors of the other person vary and as changes in self's goals change over the course of a conversation.

The propositions in this section have examined three basic components of interculturally competent communication. In general, the more motivated, knowledgeable, and skilled a person is, the more competent this person is likely to be. It is possible that a person can be viewed as highly competent if high in only one or two of these components. For example, a person who is very motivated may compensate for lack of knowledge and skill through perseverance and effort alone. Likewise, someone who is extremely familiar with a given type of encounter may be able to "drift" through ("I've written so many contracts in my life I can negotiate one in my sleep") with minimal motivation and little conscious awareness of the exact procedures involved. Nevertheless, across most encounters, the more of each of these components a person possesses or demonstrates, the more competent this person's interaction is likely to be.

## Episodic System

The first three primary propositions entailed factors that increase the likelihood that an actor will produce behaviors that are normatively competent. As such, the actor producing them, and others generally, will tend to believe that the interactant has behaved competently. However, given that competence is an impression, there is no guarantee that a person who has performed behaviors that normally would be viewed as competent, will be viewed as competent by a particular conversational partner in a particular relational encounter. The propositions in this section address this latter issue. These propositions are episodic in the sense that characteristics of an Actor influence the impressions of the Coactor in a specific episode of interaction. The statements concern those characteristics of an Actor that predict a Coactor's impression of the Actor's competence.

*4. As Actor's communicative status increases, Coactor's impression of Actor's competence increases.* Communicative status is meant here to represent all those factors that enhance this person's positive evaluation. Competence is, after all, an evaluation. Generally, as a person's status goes, so goes his or her competence. There are obvious exceptions, but it is instructive to consider those status characteristics particularly relevant to communicative competence.

*4a. As Actor's motivation, knowledge, and skills increase, Coactor's impression of Actor's competence increases.* The logic of the individual system also applies to the episodic system; the factors that lead a person to behave competently in a normative sense will usually lead to a competent relational performance as well (Imahori & Lanigan, 1989; Spitzberg & Cupach, 1984). This is true in two slightly different senses. In one sense, norms comprise the majority of people's views and behaviors,

so a person who is normatively competent will usually be viewed as competent in any given encounter. In another sense an Actor who is motivated to interact competently with a particular Coactor, knowledgeable about this particular Coactor, and skilled in interacting with this particular Coactor is also more likely to communicate better and be viewed as competent by this Coactor in a given encounter.

Factors that facilitate motivation, knowledge, and skill in a particular episodic system are likely to be logical extensions of the individual system components. For example, motivation is likely to increase as attraction to the Coactor increases and as positive reinforcement history with the Coactor increases. Knowledge of the Coactor is likely to increase with the duration of the relationship, and the depth and breadth of self-disclosure between Actor and Coactor increase. Skill in interacting with the Coactor is likely to increase as adaptation and refinement increase over the lifetime of the relationship.

*4b. As contextual obstruction of Actor's performance increases, Coactor's impression of Actor's competence increases.* When forming an impression of an Actor, a Coactor is left to determine the extent to which the Actor's outcomes are due to the Actor's own abilities and effort, rather than the context or other factors. For example, a physically unattractive Actor who consistently makes friends and has dates is likely to be viewed as more communicatively competent than a person who is physically attractive. The reasoning is that the social context is weighted against the unattractive Actor and in favor of the attractive Actor. Thus, the attractive Actor would achieve the same outcomes due to attractiveness rather than his or her competence, whereas the unattractive Actor must overcome the contextual barriers through competent action. In essence, all other things being equal, an Actor's competence is "discounted" if there are obvious alternative explanations for the Actor's good fortune. Similarly, an Actor's competence is "forgiven" if there are many apparent alternative reasons for his or her failure.

*4c. As Actor's receipt of valued outcomes increases, Coactor's impression of Actor's competence increases.*

While the discounting effect just discussed influences impressions of competence, it is not likely to outweigh other factors entirely. If an Actor is perceived as consistently achieving positive outcomes, a Coactor is likely to assume that the Actor has something to do with this success (Kaplowitz, 1978). The negotiator who consistently presides over significant agreements is likely to be viewed as more communicatively competent as a simple result of the tangible outcomes, almost regardless of extenuating circumstances.

*4d. As Actor's extant-attributed communicative status increases, Coactor's impression of Actor status increases.* An Actor who comes into an encounter with an established high level of status is more likely to be viewed as competent in subsequent interactions. Additionally, an Actor who has established a satisfying relationship with a particular Coactor has, in effect, established a reserve of competence in the Coactor's views. Thus, Desmond Tutu, Boris Yeltsin, or even Lee Iacocca enter any communicative situation with considerable communicative status in tow. In essence then, the impression we initially have of an Actor is likely to be the basis for our later impressions until such time that significant events alter these impressions. Furthermore, certain cultures develop higher regard for other cultures generally. The mutual regard that Americans and Japanese Americans may share is probably quite different than that which South African blacks and whites may share.

*5. Coactor's impression of Actor's competence is a function of Actor's fulfillment of Coactor's expectancies.* Over time, interactants develop expectations regarding how interpersonal interaction is likely to, and should, occur in particular contexts. Not surprisingly, therefore, a person's competence in a given relationship is due partly to expectancy fulfillment and violation. Research indicates that expectancies generally develop along three fundamental dimensions: *evaluation, potency,* and *activity* (commonly referred to as the E-P-A dimensions respectively; see Osgood, May, & Miron, 1975; Spitzberg, 1989). Most contexts are viewed in terms of their valence (good versus bad), power (dominant versus passive), and animation (noisy versus quiet) characteristics. A typical, noncharis-

matic church service is expected to be good, the audience passive and relatively quiet. A typical party, in contrast, is expected to be good, strong, fast and noisy. Upon being fired, an exit interview is expected to be unpleasurable, and the interviewee as weak and relatively passive. The point is that experience with interpersonal encounters produces expectancies and evaluations regarding both anticipated and appropriate behavior. The propositions that follow elaborate on the influence of these cognitions on impressions of competence.

*5a. As Actor's fulfillment of positive Coactor expectancies increases, Coactor's impression of Actor's competence increases.* To the extent that a Coactor expects an encounter with an Actor to be positive, the Actor is likely to be viewed as competent to the extent that he or she fulfills these expectancies. Since the expectancies typically form a consistent system in a Coactor's mind, an Actor needs to fulfill each of the E-P-A dimensions. If an interviewer expects interviews to be good (E), his or her own role to be relatively powerful and the role of the interviewee to be relatively powerless (P), and for the encounter to be generally quiet but quick (A), then the Actor is well-advised to behave according to these expectancies. Since the interviewer has developed these expectancies along all three dimensions, they tend to be "set" in relationship to each other. Thus, part of what makes the interview "good" in the interviewer's opinion is that the interviewer's role is typically powerful, and the interviews tend to go quietly and quickly.

*5b. As Actor's normative violation of Coactor's negative expectancies increases, Coactor's impression of Actor's competence increases.* The logic of the former proposition reverses itself when a Coactor expects an encounter to be negative. Consider the previous interview example from the interviewee's perspective. An interviewee may find interviews highly anxiety-producing, threatening, and difficult. As such, the interview context is expected to be unpleasurable, the interviewee's role as submissive, and the encounter as generally slow and inactive. If the interviewer wants to make a good impression, therefore, he or she needs to violate the interviewee's

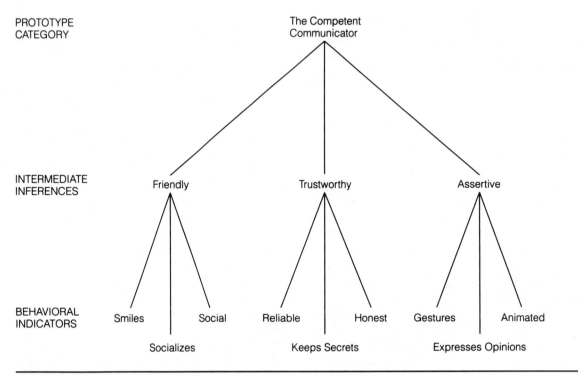

PROTOTYPE CATEGORY

INTERMEDIATE INFERENCES

BEHAVIORAL INDICATORS

**Figure 2** A Simple Cognitive Prototype of a Competent Communicator (Adapted from Pavitt and Haight, 1985)

expectations in an appropriate manner. Such an interviewer might change the setting to a less-formal lunchroom context, dress more casually, tell some stories and initially discuss topics unrelated to the position, and generally spend some time putting the interviewee in a good mood. Such an encounter violates the interviewee's expectancies, but does so in a way that is normatively acceptable and positive.

*5c. As Actor's fulfillment of Coactor's competence prototype expectancies increases, Coactor's impression of Actor's competence increases.* A prototype in this usage is basically a cognitive outline of concepts, analogous to a mental map of the competence territory. The prototype of a competent person is likely to consist of several levels of concepts varying in their abstraction. A simplified and hypothetical example of a prototype for a competent communicator is displayed in Figure 2.

At the highest level is the category label that determines what types of inferences are relevant to a

given set of observed behavior. For example, observing someone changing the oil in a car is not relevant to the category of "competent communicator." At the next level are types of inferences or impressions that collectively make up the label of competent communicator. In this hypothetical example, a competent communicator is someone who is believed to be friendly, trustworthy, and assertive. Each of these inferences, in turn, is based upon certain types of behavior. To the extent that these behaviors are observed, the inferences follow. Observed behaviors are matched or compared to those that over time have come to occupy the position of category indicators. If there is a good match, then the inferences and evaluations that define the label of competent communicator (in this case, friendly, trustworthy, assertive) are attributed to the interactant observed. If only some of the behaviors match, then the inference of competence is diminished proportionately. Certain behaviors in any given encounter may also be weighted in their importance to the impression. When judging whether or not someone is being deceptive, for example, many people would rely most heavily on that person's eye contact, relative to other behaviors, in assessing this person's competence.

*5d. As Actor's normative reciprocity of positive effect and compensation of negative effect increases, Coactor's impression of Actor's competence increases.* Reciprocity implies a matching or similarity of response, whereas compensation suggests an opposite or homeostatic response. Research indicates that across most types of relationships and encounters, interactants are generally considered more competent when they reciprocate positive effect and feel more competent when they compensate for negative effect (Andersen, 1989; Spitzberg, 1989). To the extent that the Coactor expresses positive effect, the Actor's response in kind is likely to produce more positive impressions. When the Coactor expresses negative effect, the Actor is likely to be more competent responding with more neutral or positive effect.

*5e. As Actor's normative compensation of power relations increases, the more Coactor's impression of Actor's competence increases.* Across most types of interpersonal relationships, complementary power relationships tend to produce higher impressions of competence. This is a sweeping statement, and obviously is an overstatement in many ways. For example, optimal negotiation outcomes tend to result when parties begin in fairly competitive, and end up in cooperative, orientations. Still, this principle is useful in most types of relations.

Specifically, dominance is more competently met with passivity, and passivity with dominance. The validity of this proposition is best illustrated by consideration of its alternative. Imagine, for example, what work relationships would be like if every time superiors gave a subordinate orders, the superior was met with orders of refusal. Imagine married couples in which neither person ever actually offered to make a decision. In other words, relationships and encounters tend to work more smoothly and comfortably when dominant moves are responded to with complementary passive moves, and passive moves are met with more directive moves. This does not imply that people should adopt a role

of passivity of dominance, but that on a statement-by-statement basis, most interaction will be viewed as competent to the extent that its power balance is complementary rather than reciprocal.

This section has examined the episodic system of intercultural competence. Specifically, the propositions in this section have involved those characteristics of an Actor that increase the likelihood that the Coactor views the Actor as competent in a given episode of interaction. The following section concerns an abbreviated excursion into the relational system, in which characteristics that facilitate competence across the lifespan of a relationship are considered.

## Relational System

Relationships are not simply sums of episodes over time. Certainly there is likely to be a strong correlation, such that the more competent the average episode of interaction is, the more relationally stable and satisfying the relationship tends to be. Thus, the logic of the individual system and episodic system are also likely to extend to the relational system. However, there are other factors at work, and this section examines some of these features. In this discussion, the phrase "relational competence" refers to the level of communicative quality in an established relationship. It is an index of the mutual adaptation and satisfaction achieved by a relationship.

*6. As mutual fulfillment of autonomy and intimacy needs increases, relational competence increases.* Autonomy and intimacy are two fundamental human needs (McAdams, 1988). Typically, they exist in a form of dialectical tension, in that both "struggle" for dominance over the other at any given time, but both are ever present to some degree. The need for intimacy involves the desire for human contact, connection, belonging, inclusion, camaraderie, communal activity, and nurturance. The need for autonomy, in contrast, is a need for self-control, independence, power, privacy, and solitude. Individuals seem to fluctuate between these two needs over time. And, as with virtually all needs, as each need is fulfilled, it ceases to dominate the individual's behavior. A lonely person continuously thinks about companionship. Once companionship is found, other needs begin to influence this person's thoughts and actions. It follows that if a relationship is competent over the course of its lifespan, the members' need to fulfill the needs of the other as these dialectical needs fluctuates (Spitzberg, 1993).

7. *As mutual attraction increases, relational competence increases.* This highly intuitive proposition simply indicates that as partners grow more and more attracted to each other, the more this is both likely to reflect, and result in, mutually competent interaction over time (Eagly, Ashmore, Makhijani, & Longo, 1991). This proposition gains support from the consistent finding that attraction is closely associated, at least initially, with interpersonal similarity (Feingold, 1988). Highly similar persons provide a world view of similar values and orientations. These in turn are reflected in a reinforcing and self-confirming manner of symbolic expression. In general, we enjoy interacting with those who are similar because they seem to "speak our language." One implication is that initial interactions with culturally dissimilar others should focus upon areas of similarity that can support sufficient motivation and reinforcement for continued interaction. This is not to imply that differences are always negatively reinforcing. However, differences tend to make the *process* of communication more effortful and difficult, and thereby, generally less rewarding.

8. *As mutual trust increases, relational competence increases.* Similar to the above proposition, the more partners trust one another, the more competent interaction is likely to be, and the more competent the relationship is likely to be (Canary & Spitzberg, 1989). Trust provides a context in which interaction can be more honest, spontaneous, direct, and open. Over time, such a trusting climate is likely to be mutually reinforcing, and lead to a productive and satisfying communicative relationship.

9. *As access to social support increases, relational competence increases.* Social support is anything offered by another that assists a person in coping with problematic or stressful situations. Types of support range from tangible (lending money) to informational (offering advice) to emotional (comforting words) forms. Since stresses stimulate personal and often relational crises, anything that diminishes the effects of these stresses is likely to enhance the person's ability to manage the relationship itself. One of the common problems of sojourner couples or families is that the stresses of being in a new culture often cannot be resolved by the social support of a friendship network, since the friendship network has yet to be established in the new culture.

10. *As relational network integration increases, relational competence increases.* When discussing relationships, it is ironically easy to forget that individuals are always simultaneously members of multiple relationships. When two people come together and form a relationship, part of what determines the competence of this relationship is the extent to which each member's personal network integrates with the other person's network of social relationships. Increasingly, as businesses become multinational and move entire management teams to work with labor in other countries, the problems of social network integration will become substantial. The development of common activities and goals that require cooperation or interaction across social networks, and the development of easier access to the network, are likely to facilitate this aspect of intercultural competence.

## Conclusions

Before examining the implications of this essay, an important qualification needs to be considered. Specifically, most of the propositions presented here have what can be considered upper limits. Basically, too much of a good thing can be bad. For example, someone can be *too* motivated, use *too* much expressiveness, or be *too* composed. Virtually any piece of advice, when carried to extremes, tends to lose its functional value. This can be viewed as a curvilinearity principle. In essence, as motivation, knowledge, and skill increase, so do impressions of competence, to a point, after which the relationship reverses, and competence impressions decrease.

Sir Karl Popper, an eminent philosopher of science, has warned that theories are only useful if they are in danger of failing. Theories that tell us what we already know must be true, tell us nothing. The point is that theories are only valuable to the extent they make risky predications that may be proved false. It is in this sense that this essay must be viewed with caution.

The predictions offered in this essay represent statements that in the daily interplay of lives are often in danger of being false. None of the predictions should be considered absolutely true, or as an infallible view of the complex canvas of intercultural relations. Nevertheless, progress in the development of knowledge results from such risky propositions, and this essay has attempted to chart a path to progress. In doing so, I have attempted to paint with very broad brush strokes the outline of a theory of intercultural competence. The lines of this theory are strained by their abstraction to the point of no longer resembling the vibrant landscape they are meant to represent. Thus, like any theory or work of abstract art, the key is that the benefactor will find some significant personal meaning in it, and be ever mindful that the symbol is not the thing to which it refers.

## References

Andersen, P. A. (1989). *A Cognitive Valence Theory of Intimate Communication*. Paper presented at the Iowa Network on Personal Relationships Conference, Iowa City, May.

Bandura, A. (1982). Self-efficacy mechanism in human agency. *American Psychologist, 37,* 122–147.

Canary, D. J., and Spitzberg, B. H. (1989). A model of the perceived competence of conflict strategies. *Human Communication Research, 15,* 630–649.

Eagly, A. H., Ashmore, R. D., Makhijani, M. G., and Longo, L. C. (1991). What is beautiful is good, but . . . : A meta-analytic review of research on the physical attractiveness stereotype. *Psychological Bulletin, 110,* 109–128.

Feingold, A. (1988). Matching for attractiveness in romantic partners and same-sex friends: A meta-analysis and theoretical critique. *Psychological Bulletin, 104,* 226–235.

Greene, J. O. (1984). A cognitive approach to human communication: An action assembly theory. *Communication Monographs, 51,* 289–300.

Havighurst, R. J. (1957). The social competence of middle-aged people. *Genetic Psychology Monographs, 56,* 297–375.

Hoelter, J. W. (1985). A structural theory of personal consistency. *Social Psychology Quarterly, 48,* 118–129.

Kaplowitz, S. A. (1978). Towards a systematic theory of power attribution. *Social Psychology, 41,* 131–148.

Imahori, T. T., and Lanigan, M. L. (1989). Relational model of intercultural communication competence. *International Journal of Intercultural Relations, 13,* 269–286.

McAdams, D. P. (1988). "Personal Needs and Personal Relationships." In S. Duck (Ed.), *Handbook of Personal Relationships: Theory, Research and Interventions,* 7–22. New York: Wiley.

Osgood, C. E., May, W. H., and Miron, S. (1975). *Cross-Cultural Universals of Affective Meaning.* Urbana: University of Illinois Press.

Pavitt, C., and Haight, L. (1985). The "competent communicator" as a cognitive prototype. *Human Communication Research, 12,* 225–241.

Spitzberg, B. H. (1989). Issues in the development of a theory of interpersonal competence in the intercultural context. *International Journal of Intercultural Relations, 13,* 241–268.

Spitzberg, B. H. (1993). The dialectics of (in) competence. *Journal of Social and Personal Relationships, 10,* 137–158.

Spitzberg, B. H., and Cupach, W. R. (1984). *Interpersonal Communication Competence.* Beverly Hills, Calif.: Sage.

Spitzberg, B. H., and Cupach, W. R. (1984). *Handbook of Interpersonal Competence Research.* New York: Springer-Verlag.

Spitzberg, B. H., and Hecht, M. L. (1989). A component model of relational competence. *Human Communication Research, 10,* 575–599.

## ng Intercultural
   Effectively

## STELLA TING-TOOMEY

Conflict is inevitable in all social and personal relationships. The Latin root words for conflict, "com" and "fligere," means "together" and "to strike" or more simply, "to strike together." Conflict connotes a state of dissonance or collision between two forces or systems. This state of dissonance can be expressed either overtly or subtly. In the context of intercultural encounters, *conflict* is defined in this chapter as the perceived and/or actual incompatibility of values, expectations, processes, or outcomes between two or more parties from different cultures over substantive and/or relational issues. Such differences oftentimes, are expressed through different cultural conflict styles. Intercultural conflict typically starts off with miscommunication. Intercultural miscommunication often leads to misinterpretations and pseudoconflict. If the miscommunication goes unmanaged or unclarified, however, it can become actual interpersonal conflict.

This article is developed in three sections: (1) A cultural variability perspective which emphasizes identity construal variations, low-context versus high-context, and monochronic and polychronic time patterns is presented; (2) assumptions and factors leading to conflict induced by violations of expectations are explained; and (3) effective conflict-management skills in managing intercultural conflicts are discussed.

This original essay first appeared in the seventh edition. All rights reserved. Permission to reprint must be obtained from the author and the publisher. Dr. Ting-Toomey is a professor at California State University, Fullerton.

## A Cultural Variability Perspective

To understand differences and similarities in communication across cultures, it is necessary to have a framework to explain why and how cultures are different or similar. A cultural variability perspective refers to how cultures vary on a continuum of variations in accordance with some basic dimensions or core value characteristics. While there are many dimensions in which cultures differ, one that has received consistent attention from both cross-cultural communication researchers and psychologists around the world is individualism-collectivism. Countless cross-cultural studies (Chinese Culture Connection, 1987; Gudykunst & Ting-Toomey, 1988; Hofstede, 1980, 1991; Hui & Triandis, 1986; Schwartz & Bilsky, 1990; Triandis, Brislin, & Hui, 1988; Wheeler, Reis, & Bond, 1989) have provided theoretical and empirical evidence that the value orientations of individualism and collectivism are pervasive in a wide range of cultures. Ting-Toomey and associates (Ting-Toomey, 1988, 1991; Ting-Toomey, Gao, Trubisky, Yang, Kim, Lin, & Nishida, 1991; Trubisky, Ting-Toomey, & Lin, 1991), related individualism-collectivism to conflict styles, providing clear research evidence that the role of cultural variability is critical in influencing cross-cultural conflict negotiation process.

The cultural socialization process influences individuals' basic assumptions and expectations, as well as their process and outcome orientations in different types of conflict situations. The dimension of individualism-collectivism, as existing on a continuum of value tendency differences, can be used as a beginning point to understand some of the basic differences and similarities in individualistic-based or group-based cultures. *Culture* is defined as a system of knowledge, meanings, and symbolic actions that is shared by the majority of the people in a society.

## Individualism-Collectivism
## Value Tendencies

Basically, *individualism* refers to the broad value tendencies of a culture to emphasize the importance of individual identity over group identity, individual rights over group rights, and individual needs over group needs. In contrast, *collectivism* refers to the broad value tendencies of a culture to emphasize the importance of the "we" identity over the "I" identity, group obligations over individual rights, and ingroup-oriented needs over individual wants and desires. An *ingroup* is a group whose values, norms, and rules are deemed as salient to the effective functioning of the group in the society and these norms serve as the guiding criteria for everyday behaviors. On the other hand, an "outgroup" is a group whose values, norms, and rules are viewed as inconsistent with those of the ingroup and these norms are assigned a low priority from the ingroup standard. Macro-level factors such as ecology, affluence, social and geographic mobility, migration, cultural background of parents, socialization, rural or urban environment, mass media exposure, education, and social change have been identified by Triandis (1988, 1990) as some of the underlying factors that contribute to the development of individualist and collectivistic values. High individualistic values have been found in the United States, Australia, Great Britain, Canada, the Netherlands, and New Zealand. High collectivistic values have been uncovered in Indonesia, Colombia, Venezuela, Panama, Equador, and Guatemala (Hofstede, 1991). In intercultural communication research (Gudykunst & Ting-Toomey, 1988), Australia, Canada, and the United States have been identified consistently as cultures high in individualistic value tendencies, while strong empirical evidence has supported that China, Taiwan, Korea, Japan, and Mexico can be identified clearly as collectivistic, group-based cultures. Within each culture, different ethnic communities can also display distinctive individualistic and collectivistic value tendencies. For example, members of first-generation, Asian immigrant cultures in the United States may retain some basic group-oriented value characteristics.

The core building block of individualism-collectivism is its relative emphasis on the importance of the "autonomous self" or the "connected self" orientation. In using the terms "independent construal of self" and "interdependent construal of self" to represent individualist versus group-oriented

identity, Markus and Kitayama (1991) argue that the placement of our sense of self-concept in our culture has a profound influence on our communication with others. They argue that the sense of individuality that accompanies this "independent construal of self" includes a sense of

*oneself as an agent, as a producer of one's actions. One is conscious of being in control over the surrounding situation, and of the need to express one's own thoughts, feelings, and actions of others. Such acts of standing out are often intrinsically rewarding because they elicit pleasant, ego-focused emotions (e.g., pride) and also reduce unpleasant ones (e.g., frustration). Furthermore, the acts of standing out, themselves, form an important basis of self-esteem. (p. 246)*

Conversely, the self-concept that accompanies an "interdependent construal of self" includes an

*attentiveness and responsiveness to others that one either explicitly or implicitly assumes will be reciprocated by these others, as well as the willful management of one's other-focused feelings and desires so as to maintain and further the reciprocal interpersonal relationship. One is conscious of where one belongs with respect to others and assumes a receptive stance toward these others, continually adjusting and accommodating to these others in many aspects of behavior. Such acts of fitting in and accommodating are often intrinsically rewarding, because they give rise to pleasant, other-focused emotions (e.g., feeling of connection), while diminishing unpleasant ones (e.g., shame) and, furthermore, because the self-restraint required in doing so forms an important basis of self-esteem. (p. 246)*

Thus, the cultural variability of independent versus interdependent construal of self frames our existential experience and serves as an anchoring point in terms of how we view ourselves and our communicative actions. For example, if we follow an independent construal of self-orientation, our communicative action will tend to be more self-focused, more ego-based, and more self-expressive. Concurrently, the value we place on particular self-conception also influences the criteria we use to perceive and evaluate others' communicative actions. To illustrate, if we follow an interdependent construal of self-orientation, we will tend to use group norms, group interests, and group responsibilities to interpret and evaluate others' conflict behaviors. Overall, the cultural variability dimension of individualism-collectivism and the independent and interdependent construal of self help us to "make sense" or explain why people in some cultures prefer certain approaches or modes of conflict negotiation than people in other cultures.

## Low Context and High Context

In addition to individualism-collectivism, Edward T. Hall's (1976, 1983) low-context and high-context communication framework helps to enrich our understanding of the role of communication in individualistic and collectivistic cultures. According to Hall (1976), human transaction can be basically divided into low-context and high-context communication systems:

*HC [High Context] transactions featured preprogrammed information that is in the receiver and in the setting, with only minimal information in the transmitted message. LC [Low Context] transactions are the reverse. Most of the information must be in the transmitted message in order to make up what is missing in the context. (p. 101)*

Although no one culture exists exclusively at one extreme of the communication context continuum, in general, low-context communication refers to communication patterns of linear logic interaction approach, direct verbal interaction style, overt intention expressions, and sender-oriented value (Ting-Toomey, 1985). High-context communication refers to communication patterns of spiral logic interaction approach, indirect verbal negotiation mode, subtle nonverbal nuances, responsive intention inference, and interpreter-sensitive value (Ting-Toomey, 1985). Low-context (LC) communication patterns have been typically found in individualistic cultures and high-context (HC) communication patterns have been typically uncovered in collectivistic cultures.

For individualistic, LC communicators, the bargaining resources in conflict typically revolve around individual pride and self-esteem, individual ego-based emotions, and individual sense of autonomy and power. For collectivistic, HC interactants, the negotiation resources in conflict typically revolve around relational "face" maintenance and group harmony, group-oriented status and self-esteem, face-related emotions, and reciprocal sense of favors and obligations. For individualistic, LC negotiators, conflict typically arises because of incompatible personalities, beliefs, or goal orientations. For collectivistic, HC negotiators, conflict typically arises because of incompatible facework or relational management.

The concept of *face* is tied closely to the need people have to a claimed sense of self-respect in any social interactive situations (Ting-Toomey, 1985, 1988, 1994; Ting-Toomey & Cole, 1990). As human beings, we all like to be respected and feel approved in our everyday communicative behaviors. However, how we manage face and how we negotiate "face loss" and "face gain" in a conflict episode differs from one culture to the next. As Cohen (1991) observes:

*Given the importance of face, the members of collectivistic cultures are highly sensitive to the effect of what they say on others. Language is a social instrument – a device for preserving and promoting social interests as much as a means for transmitting information. [Collectivistic], high-context speakers must weigh their words carefully. They know that whatever they say will be scrutinized and taken to heart. Face-to-face conversations contain many emollient expressions of respect and courtesy alongside a substantive element rich in meaning and low in redundancy. Directness and especially contradiction are much disliked. It is hard for speakers in this kind of culture to deliver a blunt "no." (p. 26)*

## M-Time and P-Time

Finally, the concept of time in the conflict-negotiation process also varies in accordance with the individualism-collectivism dimension. Time is reflective of the psychological and the emotional environment in which communication occurs. Time flies when two friends are enjoying themselves and having a good time. Time crawls when two enemies stare at each other and have nothing more to say to one another. Time influences the tempos and pacings of the developmental sequences of a conflict-negotiation session. It also influences the substantive ideas that are being presented in a conflict-bargaining episode.

Hall (1983) distinguished two patterns of time that govern the individualistic and collectivistic cultures: Monochronic Time Schedule (M-time) and Polychronic Time Schedule (P-time). According to Hall (1983):

*P-time stresses involvement of people and completion of transactions rather than adherence to preset schedules. Appointments are not taken as seriously and, as a consequence, are frequently broken. P-time is treated as less tangible than M-time. For polychronic people, time is seldom experienced as "wasted," and is apt to be considered a point rather than a ribbon or a road, but that point is often sacred. (p. 46)*

For Hall (1983), Latin American, Middle Eastern, African, Asian, French, and Greek cultures are representatives of P-time patterns, while Northern European, North American, and German cultures are representatives of M-time patterns. M-time patterns appear to predominate in individualistic, low-context cultures, and P-time patterns appear to predominate in group-based, high-context cultures. People that follow individualistic, M-time patterns usually compartmentalize time schedules to serve individualistic-based needs, and they tend to separate task-oriented time from socioemotional time. In addition, they are more future-conscious of time than centered in the present or the past. People who follow collectivistic, P-time patterns tend to hold more fluid attitudes toward time schedules, and they tend to integrate task-oriented activity with socioemotional activity. In addition, they are more past and present-conscious than future-oriented.

Members of individualistic, M-time cultures tend to view time as something that can be possessed, drained, and wasted, while members of collectivistic, P-time cultures tend to view time as more contextually based and relationally oriented. For individualistic, M-time people, conflict should be contained, controlled, and managed effectively within certain frames or within certain preset schedules. For collectivistic, P-time people, the clock time in resolving conflict is not as important as in taking the time to really know the conflict parties who are involved in the dispute. For P-time individuals, the time spent in synchronizing the implicit interactional rhythms between people is much more important than any preset, objective timetable.

In sum, in individualistic cultures, people typically practice "I" identity-based values, low-context direct interaction, and M-time negotiation schedules. In collectivistic cultures, people typically treasure "we" identity-based values, high-context indirect interaction, and P-time negotiation rhythms.

## Violations of Conflict Expectations

Drawing from the key ideas of the cultural variability perspective, we can now apply these concepts to understanding the specific conflict assumptions, conflict issues and process factors, and the conflict interaction styles that contribute to intercultural miscommunication or intercultural conflict.[1] When individuals from two contrastive cultures meet one another especially for the first time, they typically communicate out of their culturally based assumptions and beliefs, stereotypic images of each other, and habitual communication patterns. These assumptions create expectations for others' conflict behavior.

It is inevitable that we hold anticipations or expectations of how others should or should not behave in any communicative situation. These expectations, however, are grounded in the social norms of the culture and also depend on the symbolic meanings individuals assign to behaviors (Burgoon, 1991). Intercultural miscommunication or intercultural conflict often occurs because of violations of normative expectations in a communication episode. Expectation violations occur frequently, especially if one party comes from an individualistic-based culture and the other party comes from a collectivistic-based culture.

## Cultural Conflict Assumptions

Different cultural value assumptions exist as the metaconflict issues in framing any intercultural conflict episode. Based on the individualism-collectivism dimension, we can delineate several cultural assumptions concerning LC and HC communicators' basic attitudes toward conflict. For individualistic, LC communicators, conflict typically follows a "problem-solving" model: (1) Conflict is viewed as an expressed struggle to air out major differences and problems; (2) conflict can be both dysfunctional and functional; (3) conflict can be dysfunctional when it is repressed and not directly confronted; (4) conflict can be functional when it provides an open opportunity for solving problematic issues; (5) substantive and relational issues in conflict should be handled separately; (6) conflict should be dealt with openly and directly; and (7) effective management of conflict can be viewed as a win-win problem-solving game.

For the collectivistic, HC interactants, their underlying assumptions of conflict follow a "face maintenance" model: (1) Conflict is viewed as damaging to social face and relational harmony and should be avoided as much as possible; (2) conflict is, for the most part, dysfunctional; (3) conflict signals a lack of self-discipline and self-censorship of emotional outbursts, and hence, a sign of emotional immaturity; (4) conflict provides a testing ground for a skillful facework negotiation process; (5) substantive conflict and relational face issues are always intertwined; (6) conflict should be dealt with discreetly and subtly; and (7) effective management of conflict can be viewed as a win-win face negotiation game.

From the conflict as a "problem-solving" model, conflict is viewed as potentially functional, personally liberating, and an open forum for "struggling against" or "struggling with" one another in wrestling with the conflict issues at hand. From the conflict as a "face maintenance" model, conflict is viewed as primarily dysfunctional, interpersonally embarrassing and distressing, and a forum for potential group-related face loss and face humiliation.

These fundamental cultural conflict assumptions influence the mindsets and attitudinal level of the conflict parties in terms of how they should approach an interpersonal conflict episode. Appropriate and inappropriate conflict behaviors, in short, are grounded in the basic value assumptions of the cultural conflict socialization process.

## Conflict Issues and Process Violations

Every conflict entails both substantive and relational issues. Individualistic conflict negotiators typically attend to the objective, substantive issues more than the relational, socioemotional issues. Collectivistic conflict negotiators, in contrast, typically attune to the relational, affective dimension as the key issue in resolving task-related or procedural-related conflict. When collectivistic communicators are in sync with one another and their nonverbal rhythms harmonize with one another, peaceful resolutions can potentially follow. When individualistic communicators are able to rationalize the separation of the people from the problems, and emphasize compartmentalizing affective issues and substantive issues, conflict can be functional.

In reviewing diplomatic negotiation case studies between individualistic, low-context (United States) and collectivistic, high-context (China, Egypt, India, Japan, and Mexico) cultures, Cohen (1991) concludes:

*Individualistic, low-context negotiators can be described as primarily problem oriented and have the definition of the problem and the clarification of alternative solutions uppermost in their thoughts, [collectivistic] high-context negotiators are seen to be predominantly relationship oriented. For them, negotiation is less about solving problems (although, obviously, this aspect cannot be dismissed) than about attending a relationship. For interdependent cultures it is not a conflict that is resolved but a relationship that is mended. . . . In international relations the consequence is concern both with the international relationship and with the personal ties between the interlocutors. (p. 51)*

In individualistic, LC cultures such as Australia and the United States, control of one's autonomy, freedom, territory, and individual boundary is of paramount importance to one's sense of self-respect and ego. In collectivistic, HC cultures such as Japan and Korea, being accepted by one's ingroup members and being approved by one's superiors, peers, and/or family members is critical to the development of one's sense of self-respect. Thus, conflict issues in individualistic cultures typically arise through the violation of autonomous space, privacy, individual power, and sense of individual fairness and equity. In collectivistic cultures, conflict issues typically revolve around the violation of ingroup or outgroup boundaries, norms of group loyalty and commitment, and reciprocal obligations and trust.

In terms of different goal orientations in intercultural conflict, individualists' conflict-management techniques typically emphasize a win-win goal orientation and the importance of a tangible outcome action plan. For collectivists, typically time and energy are invested in negotiating face loss, face gain, and face protection issues throughout the various developmental phases of conflict. While individualists tend to be highly goal or result-oriented in conflict management, collectivists tend to emphasize heavily the relational or facework process of conflict resolution. This collectivistic conflict facework negotiation process can also take place beyond the immediate conflict situation.

Several writers (Cohen, 1991; Leung, 1987, 1988; Ting-Toomey, 1985) indicate that collectivists tend to display a stronger preference for informal third-party conflict mediation procedure than individualists. For example, for the Chinese culture, conflict typically is diffused through the use of third-party intermediaries. However, there exists a key difference in the use of third-party mediation between the individualistic, Western cultures and the collectivistic, Asian cultures. In the Western cultures, conflict parties tend to seek help with an impartial third-party mediator (such as a professional mediator or family therapist). In many Asian cultures, conflict parties typically seek the help of an older (and hence assumed to be wiser) person who is related to both parties. It is presumed that the informal mediator has a richer data base to arbitrate the conflict outcome. Expectations may be violated when an individualistic culture sends an impartial third-party to arbitrate an international conflict with no prior relationship-building sessions. Conflict-process violations also arise if an individualistic culture sends an intermediary that is perceived to be of lower ranking or lower status than the representative negotiators of the collectivistic culture. Conversely, a collectivistic culture tends to violate the individualistic fairness norm when it sends an "insider" or ingroup person to monitor or arbitrate the conflict outcome situation.

The concept of power in a conflict-negotiation situation also varies from an individualistic culture to a collectivistic culture. Power, in the context of individualistic culture, often means tangible resources of rewards and punishments that one conflict party has over another. Power, in the context of collectivistic culture, often refers to intangible resources such as face loss and face gain, losing prestige or gaining reputation, and petty-mindedness versus benevolent generosity as displayed in the conflict anxiety-provoking situation.

Finally, the interpretation of conflict-resolution rhythm also varies along the individualism-collectivism dimension. For individualistic, M-time people, conflict-resolution processes should follow a clear agenda of opening, expressing conflicting interests, negotiating, and closing sequences. For collectivistic, P-time people, conflict facework processes have no clear beginning and no clear end. For M-time individuals, conflict-resolution time should be filled with decision-making activities. For P-time individuals, time is a "being" construct that is governed by the implicit rhythms in the interaction between people. While M-time negotiators tend to emphasize agenda setting, objective criteria, and immediate, future-oriented goals in the conflict-negotiation process, P-time negotiators typically like to take time to engage in small talk, to delve into family or personal affairs, and also to bring in the historical past to shed light on the present conflict situation. As Cohen (1991) observes:

*[North] Americans, then, are mostly concerned with addressing immediate issues and moving on to new challenges, and they display little interest in (and sometimes little knowledge of) history. The idea that*

*something that occurred hundreds of years ago might be relevant to a pressing problem is almost incomprehensible. . . . In marked contrast, the representatives of non-Western societies possess a pervasive sense of the past. . . . This preoccupation with history, deeply rooted in the consciousness of traditional societies, cannot fail to influence diplomacy. Past humiliations for these societies (which are highly sensitive to any slight on their reputations) are not consigned to the archives but continue to nourish present concerns. (p. 29)*

The arbitrary division of clock time or calendar time holds little meaning for collectivistic, P-time people. For them, a deadline, in one sense, is only an arbitrary human construct. For P-time individuals, a deadline is always subject to revision and renegotiation. Graceful handling of time pressure is viewed as much more important than a sense of forceful urgency. In sum, people move with different conflict rhythms in conflict-negotiation sessions. For M-time individuals, a sense of timeline and closure-orientation predominate their mode of conflict resolution. For P-time individuals, a sense of the relational commitment and synchronized relational rhythm signal the beginning stage of a long-term, conflict-bargaining process.

Expectation violations often occur when a person from an individualistic culture engages a person from a collectivistic culture in an interpersonal conflict situation. Different cultural conflict assumptions lead to different attitudes toward how to approach a basic conflict episode. Miscommunication often gives rise to escalatory conflict spirals or prolonged misunderstandings. While common feelings of anxiety, frustration, ambivalence, and a sense of emotional vulnerability typically exist in individuals in any conflict situation, how we go about handling this sense of emotional vulnerability varies from one culture to the next. Individualists and collectivists typically collide over their substantive orientation versus relational face maintenance orientation; goal orientation versus process orientation; formal versus informal third-party consultation process; tangible versus intangible power resources; and different time rhythms that undergird the conflict episode. In addition, the verbal and nonverbal messages they engage in, and the distinctive con-

flict styles they carry with them can severely influence the overall outcome of the conflict dissonance process.

## Cross-Cultural Conflict Interaction Styles

In a conflict situation, individualists typically rely heavily on direct requests, direct verbal justifications, and upfront clarifications to defend one's action or decision. In contrast, collectivist typically use qualifiers ("Perhaps we should meet this deadline together"), tag questions ("Don't you think we might not have enough time"), disclaimers ("I'm probably wrong but . . ."), tangential response ("Let's not worry about that now"), and indirect requests ("If it won't be too much trouble, let's try to finish this report together") to make a point in the subtle, conflict face-threatening situation. From the collectivistic orientation, it is up to the interpreter of the message to pick up the hidden meaning or intention of the message and to respond either indirectly or equivocally. In addition, in an intense conflict situation, many collectivists believe that verbal messages can oftentimes compound the problem. However, by not using verbal means to explain or clarify a decision, collectivists are often viewed as "inscrutable."

Silence is viewed as demanding immense self-discipline in a collectivistic conflict situation. On the other hand, silence can be viewed as an admission of guilt or incompetence in an individualistic culture. In addition, while open emotional expression during a stressful conflict situation oftentimes is viewed as a signal of caring in an individualistic culture, proper emotional composure and emotional self-restraint are viewed as signals of a mature, self-disciplined person in most collectivistic, Asian cultures. In comparing verbal and nonverbal exchange processes in Japan and the United States, Okabe (1983) summarizes:

*The digital is more characteristic of the [North] American mode of communication. . . . The Japanese language is more inclined toward the analogical; its use of ideographic characters . . . and its emphasis on the nonverbal aspect. The excessive dependence of the Japanese on the nonverbal aspect of communication means that Japanese culture tends to view the verbal as only a means of communication, and that the non-verbal and the extra-verbal at times assume greater importance than the verbal dimension of communication. This is in sharp contrast to the view of Western rhetoric and communication that the verbal, especially speech, is the dominant means of expression. (p. 38)*

In short, in the individualistic cultures, the conflict-management process relies heavily on verbal offense and defense to justify one's position, to clarify one's opinion, to build up one's credibility, to articulate one's emotions, and to raise objections if one disagrees with someone else's proposal. In collectivistic conflict situations, ambiguous, indirect verbal messages often are used with the intention of saving mutual face, saving group face, or protecting someone else's face. In addition, subtle nonverbal gestures or nonverbal silence is often used to signal a sense of cautionary restraint toward the conflict situation. The use of deep-level silence can also reflect a sense of resignation and acceptance of the fatalistic aspect of the conflict situation. The higher the person is in positional power in a collectivistic culture, the more likely she or he will use silence as a deliberate, cautionary conflict strategy.

In terms of the relationship between the norm of fairness and cross-cultural conflict interaction style, results from past research (Leung & Bond, 1984; Leung & Iwawaki, 1988) indicate that individualists typically prefer to use the equity norm (self-deservingness norm) in dealing with reward allocation in group conflict interaction. In comparison, collectivists oftentimes prefer to use the equality norm (the equal distribution norm) to deal with ingroup members and thus avoid group disharmony. However, like their individualistic cohorts, collectivists prefer the application of the equity norm (the self-deservingness norm) when competing with members of outgroups, especially when the conflict involves competition for scarce resources in the system.

Findings in many past conflict studies also indicate that individuals do exhibit quite consistent cross-situational styles of conflict negotiation in different cultures. While dispositional, relationship, or conflict salient factors also play a critical part in

conflict-management patterns, culture assumes the primary role of conflict-style socialization process. Based on the theoretical assumptions of the "I" identity and the "we" identity, and the concern of self-face maintenance versus mutual-face maintenance in the two contrastive cultural systems, findings across cultures (China, Japan, Korea, Taiwan, Mexico, and the United States) clearly indicate that individualists tend to use competitive control conflict styles in managing conflict, while collectivists tend to use integrative or compromising conflict styles in dealing with conflict. In addition, collectivists also tend to use more obliging and avoiding conflict styles in task-oriented conflict situations (Chua & Gudykunst, 1987; Leung, 1988; Ting-Toomey et al., 1991; Trubisky, Ting-Toomey, & Lin, 1991).

Different results have also been uncovered concerning ingroup and outgroup conflict in the collectivistic cultures. For example, Cole's (1989) study reveals that Japanese students in the United States tend to use obliging strategies more with members of ingroups than with members of outgroups. They also tend to actually use more competitive strategies with outgroup members than ingroup members. In addition, the status of the ingroup person plays a critical role in the collectivistic conflict process.

Previous research (Ting-Toomey et al., 1991) suggests that status affects the conflict-management styles people use with members of their ingroup. For example, in a collectivistic culture, while a high-status person can challenge the position or opinion of a low-status person, it is a norm violation for a low-status person to directly rebut or question the position or the opinion of the high-status person, especially in the public arena. Again, the issue of face maintenance becomes critical in high–low-status conflict interaction. The low-status person should always learn to "give face" or protect the face of the high-status person in times of stressful situations or crises. In return, the high-status person will enact a reciprocal face-protection system that automatically takes care of the low-status person in different circumstances.

Overall, the preferences for a direct conflict style, for the use of the equity norm, and for the direct settlement of disputes reflect the salience of the "I" identity in individualistic, HC cultures; while preferences for an indirect conflict style, for the use of the equality norm, and for the use of informal mediation procedures reflect the salience of the "we" identity in the collectivistic, HC cultures. In individualistic, LC cultures, a certain degree of conflict in a system is viewed as potentially functional and productive. In collectivistic, HC cultures in which group harmony and consultative decision-making are prized, overt expressions of interpersonal conflict are highly avoided and suppressed. Instead, nonverbal responsiveness, indirect verbal strategies, the use of informal intermediaries, and the use of cautionary silence are some of the typical collectivistic ways of dealing with interpersonal conflict.

## Effective Conflict Management

Effective conflict management requires us to communicate effectively, appropriately, and creatively in different conflict interactive situations. Effective conflict management requires us to be knowledgeable and respectful of different worldviews and ways of dealing with a conflict situation. It requires us to be sensitive to the differences and similarities between low-context and high-context communication patterns and to attune to the implicit negotiation rhythms of monochronic-based and polychronic-based individuals.

Effective conflict management also requires the awareness of the importance of both goal-oriented and process-oriented conflict negotiation pathways, and requires that we pay attention to the close relationship between cultural variability and different conflict communication styles. For both individualists and collectivists, the concept of "mindfulness" can serve as the first effective step in raising our awareness of the differences and similarities in cross-cultural conflict-negotiation processes. Langer's (1989) concept of mindfulness helps individuals to tune-in conscientiously to their habituated mental scripts and expectations. According to Langer, if mindlessness is the "rigid reliance on old categories, mindfulness means the continual creation of new ones. Categorization and recategoriza-

tion, labeling and relabeling as one masters the world are processes natural to children" (p. 63). To engage in a mindfulness state, an individual needs to learn to (a) create new categories, (b) be open to new information, and (c) be aware that multiple perspectives typically exist in viewing a basic event (Langer, 1989, p. 62).

Creating new categories means that one should not be boxed in by one's rigid stereotypic label concerning cultural strangers. One has to learn to draw out commonalties between self and cultural strangers and also learn to appreciate the multifaceted aspects of the individuals to whom the stereotypic label is applied. In order to create new categories, one has to be open to new information. New information relies strongly on responsible sharing and responsive listening behavior.

Some specific suggestions can be made based on differences in individualistic and collectivistic styles of conflict management. These suggestions, however, are not listed in order of importance. *To deal with conflict effectively in the collectivistic culture, individualists need to:*

1. Be mindful of the face-maintenance assumptions of conflict situations that take place in this culture. Conflict competence resides in the strategic skills of managing the delicate interaction balance of humiliation and pride, and shame and honor. The face moves of one-up and one-down in a conflict episode, the use of same status negotiators, and the proprieties and decorum of gracious "face fighting" have to be strategically staged with the larger group audience in mind.

2. Be proactive in dealing with low-grade conflict situations (such as by using informal consultation or the "go between" method) before they escalate into runaway, irrevocable mutual face-loss episodes. Individualists should try to realize that by helping their opponent to save face, they may also enhance their own face. Face is, intrinsically, a bilateral concept in the group-based, collectivistic culture.

3. "Give face" and try not to push their opponent's back against the wall with no room for maneuvering face loss or face recovery. Learn to let their opponent find a gracious way out of the conflict situation if at all possible, without violating the

basic spirit of fundamental human rights. They should also learn self-restraint and try not to humiliate their opponent in the public arena or slight her or his public reputation. For collectivists, the concept of "giving face" typically operates on a long-range, reciprocal interaction system. Bilateral face-giving and face-saving ensures a continuous, interdependent networking process of favor-giving and favor concessions — especially along a long-term, historical time sense.

4. Be sensitive to the importance of quiet, mindful observation. Individualists need to be mindful of the historical past that bears relevance to the present conflict situation. Restrain from asking too many "why" questions. Since collectivistic, LC cultures typically focus on the nonverbal "how" process, individualists need to learn to experience and manage the conflict process on the implicit, nonverbal pacing level. Use deep-level silence, deliberate pauses, and patient conversational turn-taking in conflict interaction processes with collectivists.

5. Practice attentive listening skills and feel the co-presence of the other person. In Chinese characters, hearing or *wun* (聞) means "opening the door to the ears," while the word *listening* or *ting* (聽) means attending to the other person with your "ears, eyes, and heart." Listening means, in the Chinese character, attending to the sounds, movements, and feelings of the other person. Patient and deliberate listening indicates that one person is attending to the other person's needs even if it is an antagonistic conflict situation.

6. Discard the Western-based model of effective communication skills in dealing with conflict situations in the collectivistic, HC cultures. Individualists should learn to use qualifiers, disclaimers, tag questions, and tentative statements to convey their point of view. In refusing a request, learn not to use a blunt "no" as a response because the word "no" is typically perceived as carrying high face-threat value in the collectivistic culture. Use situational or self-effacing accounts ("Perhaps someone else is more qualified than I am in working on this project"), counterquestions ("Don't you feel someone else is more competent to work on this project . . ."),

or conditional statements ("Yes, but . . .") to convey the implicit sense of refusal.

7. Let go of a conflict situation if the conflict party does not want to deal with it directly. A cooling period sometimes may help to mend a broken relationship and the substantive issue may be diluted over a period of time. Individualists should remember that avoidance is part of the integral, conflict style that is commonly used in the collectivistic, LC cultures. Avoidance does not necessarily mean that collectivists do not care to resolve the conflict. In all likelihood, the use of avoidance is strategically used to avoid face-threatening interaction and is meant to maintain face harmony and mutual face dignity.

In sum, individualists need to learn to respect the HC, collectivistic ways of approaching and handling conflicts. They need to continuously monitor their ethnocentric biases on the cognitive, affective, and behavioral reactive levels, and learn to listen attentively, and observe mindfully and reflectively.

Some specific suggestions also can be made for collectivists in handling conflict with individualists. *When encountering a conflict situation in an individualistic, LC culture, collectivists need to:*

1. Be mindful of the problem-solving assumptions. The ability to separate the relationship from the conflict problem is critical to effective conflict negotiation in an individualistic, LC culture. Collectivists need to learn to compartmentalize the task dimension and the socioemotional dimension of conflict.

2. Focus on resolving the substantive issues of the conflict, and learn to openly express opinions or points of view. Collectivists should try not to take the conflict issues to the personal level, and learn to maintain distance between the person and the conflict problem. In addition, try not to be offended by the upfront, individualistic style of managing conflict. Learn to emphasize tangible outcomes and develop concrete action plans in implementing the conflict-decision proposal.

3. Engage in an assertive, leveling style of conflict behavior. Assertive style emphasizes the rights of both individuals to speak up in a conflict situation

and to respect each other's right to defend her or his position. Collectivists need to learn to open a conflict dialogue with an upfront thesis statement, and then develop the key point systematically, with examples, evidence, figures, or a well-planned proposal. In addition, collectivists need to be ready to accept criticisms, counterproposals, and suggestions for modification as part of the ongoing, group dialogue.

4. Own individual responsibility for the conflict decision-making process. Owning responsibility and using "I" statements to describe feelings in an ongoing conflict situation constitute part of effective conflict-management skills in an individualistic, LC culture. Collectivists need to learn to verbally explain a situation more fully and learn not to expect others to infer their points of view. Assume a sender-based approach to resolving conflict; ask more "why" questions and probe for explanations and details.

5. Provide verbal feedback and engage in active listening skills. Active listening skills, in the individualistic, LC culture, means collectivists have to engage in active verbal perception checking and to ensure that the other person is interpreting their points accurately. Collectivists need to use verbal paraphrases, summary statements, and interpretive messages to acknowledge and verify the storyline of the conflict situation. Learn to occasionally self-disclose feelings and emotions; they cannot rely solely on nonverbal, intuitive understanding to "intuit" and evaluate a situation.

6. Use direct, integrative verbal messages that clearly convey their concern over both the relational and substantive issues of a conflict situation. Collectivists should also not wait patiently for clear turn-taking pauses in the conflict interaction, as individualistic conversation typically allows overlap talks, simultaneous messages, and floor-grabbing behavior. Collectivists also may not want to engage in too many deliberate silent moments as individualists will infer that as incompetence or inefficient use of time.

7. Commit to working out the conflict situation with the conflict party. Collectivists should learn to

use task-oriented integrative strategies and try to work out a collaborative, mutual goal dialogue with the conflict party. Work on managing individual defensiveness and learn to build up trust on the one-to-one level of interaction. Finally, confirm the conflict person through explicit relationship reminders and metacommunication talks, while simultaneously working on resolving the conflict substantive issues, responsibly and constructively.

In sum, collectivists need to work on their ethnocentric biases as much as the individualists need to work out their sense of egocentric superiority. Collectivists need to untangle their historical sense of cultural superiority—especially in thinking that their way is the only "civilized" way to appropriately deal with conflict. Both individualists and collectivists need to be mindful of their cognitive, affective, and behavioral blinders that they bring into a conflict-mediation situation. They need to continuously learn new and novel ideas in dealing with the past, present, and the future for the purpose of building a peaceful community that is inclusive in all ethnic and cultural groups.

In being mindful of the potential differences between individualistic, LC and collectivistic, HC conflict styles, the intercultural peacemaking process can begin by affirming and valuing such differences as diverse human options in resolving some fundamental, human communication phenomenon. While it is not necessary that one should completely switch one's basic conflict style in order to adapt to the other person's behavior, mutual attuning and responsive behavior in signalling the willingness to learn about each other's cultural norms and rules may be a first major step toward a peaceful resolution process. In addition, conflicting parties from diverse ethnic or cultural backgrounds can learn to work on collaborative task projects and strive toward reaching a larger-than-self, community goal.

To be a peacemaker in the intercultural arena, one has to be first at peace with one's self and one's style. Thus, the artificial switching of one's style may only bring artificial results. Creative peacemakers must learn first to affirm and respect the diverse values that exist as part of the rich spectrum of the basic human experience. They may then choose to modify their behavior to adapt to the situation at hand. Finally, they may integrate diverse sets of values and behaviors, and be able to move in and out of different relational and cultural conflict boundaries. Creative peacemakers can be at ease and at home with the marginal stranger in their search toward common human peace. *Peace* means, on a universal level, a condition or a state of tranquility — with an absence of oppressed thoughts, feelings, and actions, from one heart to another, and from one nation state to another nation state.

## Notes

I want to thank Bill Gudykunst for his thoughtful suggestions on an earlier version of the manuscript.

1. Many of the ideas in this section are drawn from Ting-Toomey (in press).

## References

Burgoon, J. (1991). "Applying a Comparative Approach to Expectancy Violations Theory." In J. Blumer, J. McCleod, and K. Rosengren (Eds.), *Communication and Culture Across Space and Time*. Newbury Park, CA: Sage.

Chinese Culture Connection. (1987). "Chinese Values and Search for Culture-Free Dimensions of Culture." *Journal of Cross-Cultural Psychology, 18,* 143-164.

Chua, E., and Gudykunst, W. (1987). Conflict Resolution Style in Low- and High-Context Cultures. *Communication Research Reports, 4,* 32-37.

Cohen, R. (1991). *Negotiating Across Cultures: Communication Obstacles in International Diplomacy.* Washington, D.C.: U.S. Institute of Peace.

Cole, M. (May 1989). "Relational Distance and Personality Influence on Conflict Communication Styles." Unpublished master thesis. Arizona State University, Tempe, AZ.

Gudykunst, W., and Ting-Toomey, S. (1988). *Culture and Interpersonal Communication.* Newbury Park, CA: Sage.

Hall, E. T. (1976). *Beyond Culture.* New York: Doubleday.

Hall, E. T. (1983). *The Dance of Life.* New York: Doubleday.

Hofstede, G. (1980). *Culture's Consequences: International Differences in Work-Related Values.* Beverly Hills, CA: Sage.

Hofstede, G. (1991). *Cultures and Organizations: Software of the Mind.* London: McGraw-Hill.

Hui, C., and Triandis, H. (1986). "Individualism-Collectivism: A Study of Cross-Cultural Researchers." *Journal of Cross-Cultural Psychology, 17,* 225-248.

Langer, E. (1989). *Mindfulness.* Reading, MA: Addison-Wesley.

Leung, K. (1987). "Some Determinants of Reactions to Procedural Models for Conflict Resolution: A Cross-National Study." *Journal of Personality and Social Psychology, 53,* 898-908.

Leung, K. (1987). "Some Determinants of Conflict Avoidance." *Journal of Cross-Cultural Psychology, 19,* 125-136.

Leung, K., and Bond, M. (1984). "The Impact of Cultural Collectivism on Reward Allocation." *Journal of Personality and Social Psychology, 47,* 793-804.

Leung, K., and Iwawaki, S. (1988). "Cultural Collectivism and Distributive Behavior." *Journal of Cross-Cultural Psychology, 19,* 35-49.

Markus, H., and Kitayama, S. (1991). "Culture and the Self: Implications for Cognition, Emotion, and Motivation." *Psychological Review, 2,* 224-253.

Okabe, R. (1983). "Cultural Assumptions of East-West: Japan and the United States." In W. Gudykunst (Ed.), *Intercultural Communication Theory.* Beverly Hills, CA: Sage.

Schwartz, S., and Bilsky, W. (1990). "Toward a Theory of the Universal Content and Structure of Values." *Journal of Personality and Social Psychology, 58,* 878-891.

Ting-Toomey, S. (1985). "Toward a Theory of Conflict and Culture." In W. Gudykunst, L. Stewart, and S. Ting-Toomey (Eds.), *Communication Culture, and Organizational Processes* (pp. 71-86), Beverly Hills, CA: Sage.

Ting-Toomey, S. (1986). "Conflict Styles in Black and White Subjective Cultures." In Y. Kim (Ed.), *Current Research in Interethnic Communication.* Beverly Hills, CA: Sage.

Ting-Toomey, S. (1988). "Intercultural Conflict Styles: A Face-Negotiation Theory." In Y. Kim and W. Gudykunst (Eds.), *Theories in Intercultural Communication.* Newbury Park, CA: Sage.

Ting-Toomey, S. (1991). "Intimacy Expressions in Three Cultures: France, Japan, and the United States." *International Journal of Intercultural Relations, 15,* 29-46.

Ting-Toomey, S. (Ed.) (1994). *The Challenge of Facework: Cross-Cultural and Interpersonal Issues.* Albany, NY: State University of New York Press.

Ting-Toomey, S. (in press). *Intercultural Communication Process: Crossing Boundaries.* New York: Guilford.

Ting-Toomey, S., and Cole, M. (1990). "Intergroup Diplomatic Communication: A Face-Negotiation Perspective." In F. Korzenny and S. Ting-Toomey (Eds.), *Communicating for Peace: Diplomacy and Negotiation.* Newbury Park, CA: Sage.

Ting-Toomey, S., Gao, G., Trubisky, P., Yang, Z., Kim, H. S., Lin, S. L., and Nishida, T. (1991). "Culture, Face Maintenance, and Styles of Handling Interpersonal Conflict: A Study in Five Cultures." *The International Journal of Conflict Management, 2,* 275-296.

Triandis, H. (1988). "Collectivism vs. Individualism: A Reconceptualization of a Basic Concept in Cross-Cultural Psychology." In G. Verma and C. Bagley (Eds.), *Cross-Cultural Studies of Personality, Attitudes and Cognition.* London: Macmillan.

Triandis, H. (1990). "Cross-Cultural Studies of Individualism and Collectivism." In J. Berman (Ed.), *Nebraska Symposium on Motivation.* Lincoln: University of Nebraska Press.

Triandis, H., Brislin, R., and Hui, C. H. (1988). "Cross-Cultural Training Across the Individualism-Collectivism Divide." *International Journal of Intercultural Relations, 12,* 269-289.

Trubisky, P., Ting-Toomey, S., and Lin, S. L. (1991). "The Influence of Individualism-Collectivism and Self-Monitoring on Conflict Styles." *International Journal of Intercultural Relations, 15,* 65-84.

Wheeler, L., Reis, H., and Bond, M. (1989). "Collectivism-Individualism in Everyday Social Life: The Middle Kingdom and the Melting Pot." *Journal of Personality and Social Psychology, 57,* 79-86.

# Adapting to a New Culture

## YOUNG YUN KIM

One of the dramatic changes we are witnessing today is the enormous interface of different cultures in human affairs — from politics and economics to the arts and leisure activities. At the forefront of this global reality are the countless people who are on the move across cultural boundaries. Each year, millions of immigrants and refugees change homes. Driven by natural disaster or economic need, or hoping for freedom, security, or social and economic betterment, people uproot themselves from their homes and embark on a new life in an alien and sometimes hostile milieu. In addition, numerous temporary sojourners, such as diplomats, military personnel, and other governmental and intergovernmental agency employees, are on overseas assignments. Peace Corps volunteers have worked in nearly 100 nations since inception of the program in 1960. Researchers, professors, and students visit and study at foreign academic institutions; missionaries carry out religious endeavors. Many business employees are given overseas assignments; and a growing number of accountants, teachers, construction workers, athletes, artists, musicians, and writers find employment in foreign countries.

These individuals and many others like them are, indeed, contemporary pioneers opening new frontiers. They face, at least temporarily, the drastic and all-encompassing challenge of having to construct a new life. This essay presents a brief account of their experiences in confronting the difficult task of adapting to a new cultural and communication system. (For a fuller discussion of this topic, see Kim, 1988, 1995, in press; Kim & Ruben, 1988).

## Stress, Adaptation, and Growth

Individuals move to another country for varied reasons, under differing circumstances, and with differing levels of commitment to the host society. Most immigrants plan the move as permanent in the sense that they now expect the host society to be the primary setting for their life activities. For many short-term sojourners, on the other hand, contacts with new cultures are mostly peripheral, requiring less overall engagement. Foreign students, for example, can limit their adaptation to the bare minimum required to fulfill their role as students and can confine their informal social contact to fellow students from their home country. A similar pattern of self-imposed social isolation is seen among season migrant workers and military personnel and their families in foreign countries. (See Berry, 1990; Brislin, 1981; Dyal & Dyal, 1981; Furnham, 1988; Volkan, 1993, for discussions of various situations of cross-cultural migration.)

Despite such differences in the degree of adaptive demands, most people in a foreign land begin life in the host society as *strangers* (Gudykunst & Kim, in press; Simmel, 1950/1908). Many of their previously held beliefs, taken-for-granted assumptions, and routine behaviors are no longer relevant or appropriate. Faced with things that do not follow their unconscious "cultural script," strangers must cope with a high level of uncertainty and anxiety (Gudykunst, 1995). They are challenged to learn at least some new ways of thinking, feeling, and acting—an activity commonly called *acculturation* (Berry, 1990; Broom & Kitsuse, 1955; Padilla, 1980; Shibutani & Kwan, 1965; Spicer, 1968). At the same time, they go through the process of *deculturation* (Bar-Yosef, 1968; Eisenstadt, 1954), of unlearning some of their previously acquired cultural habits, at least to the extent that new responses are adopted in situations that previously would have evoked old ones.

The experience of acculturation and deculturation inevitably produces *stress* (Barna, 1983; Dyal & Dyal, 1981; Kim, 1988, 1995, in press; Moos, 1976)—in the form of temporary psychic disturbance or even a "breakdown" in some extreme cases. Stress experiences are particularly acute during the initial phase of relocation, when strangers face the severe difficulties and disruptions amply documented in studies of "culture shock" and related issues (Adler, 1975, 1987; Furnham, 1984, 1988; Furnham & Bochner, 1986; Oberg, 1960; Taft, 1977; Torbiorn, 1982). Internally, strangers are temporarily in a state of disequilibrium—undergoing an inner struggle between the desire to retain their original identity and the desire to forge a new identity more in harmony with the changed milieu (Boekestijn, 1988; Chan & Lam, 1987; Ford & Lerner, 1992). Strangers often cope with such a state of flux through various "defense mechanisms," such as selective attention, denial, hostility, cynicism, avoidance, and withdrawal (Lazarus, 1966).

Yet the stress strangers experience also works as the very impetus for their *adaptation*. In time, most strangers manage to achieve a new level of learning and self-adjustment that helps them accommodate to the demands of the host environment and work out new ways of handling their daily activities. In the ongoing relationship with the environment, strangers gradually modify their cognitive, affective, and behavioral habits and acquire increasing proficiency in expressing themselves, understanding new cultural practices, and coordinating their actions with those of the local people. The interplay of stress and adaptation gradually leads to an internal *growth*—a transformation in the direction of increased functional fitness and psychological health vis-à-vis the host environment.

Stress, then, is part and parcel of a stranger's adaptation and growth experiences over time. Together, the three elements—stress, adaptation, and growth—help define the nature of strangers' psychological movement in the direction of an increased chance of success in meeting the demands of the host environment. As shown in Figure 1, the *stress-adaptation-growth dynamic* plays out not in a smooth, arrow-like linear progression, but in a cyclic and continual "draw-back-to-leap" pattern similar to the movement of a wheel. Each stressful experience is responded to with a "draw back" (temporary disintegration and disengagement), which then activates

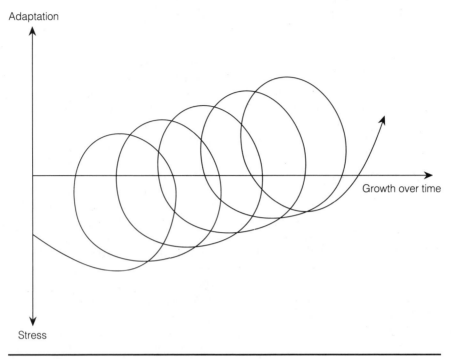

**Figure 1** Stress-adaptation-growth Dynamics of Adaptive Transformation
(Source: Kim, 1988, p. 56)

adaptive energy to help strangers reorganize themselves and "leap forward" (temporary integration or engagement). This internal process reflects a dialectic relationship between new cultural learning (acculturation) and the unlearning of old cultural habits (deculturation). As strangers work through the setbacks, they come out "victorious," with an increased capacity to see others, themselves, and situations in a new light and to face challenges yet to come. Failure to work through this process results in prolonged feelings of inadequacy and frustration.

## The Role of Communication

Given the basic process of cross-cultural adaptation described above, we now turn to the question of differential adaptation rates (speeds at which different strangers adapt). Even though most strangers in alien cultures have demonstrated an impressive capacity to manage cross-cultural challenges successfully without damaging their overall integrity,

some do suffer more intensely and for a longer period due to an extreme inability to find ways to overcome the challenges of the host environment. Some may strongly resist the idea of having to change their old cultural habits, thereby raising psychological barriers that work against adaptation. Others may be ill-equipped to deal with states of panic, causing a prolonged psychological disequilibrium that leads to greater alienation from, and bitterness toward, the natives or even to a decision to return to their home country prematurely.

The fact that individual strangers differ in adaptation rate leads to the question "Why do some strangers adapt faster than others?" or "Given the same length of time, why do some strangers attain a higher level of adaptation?" To explain differential adaptive changes among individual strangers, we need to focus on the process in and through which such changes take place — that is, the communication process. Communication activities of encoding and decoding verbal and nonverbal information lie at the heart of cross-cultural adaptation by serving as the essential mechanism that connects strangers and the host society. Just as natives acquire their capacity to function properly in their society through communicative interactions, strangers come to organize their own and others' activities by learning the significant symbols of the host culture and by participating in various communication activities of the host society.

Strangers' communication activities can be categorized into two basic, inseparable dimensions — personal communication and social communication. According to Ruben (1975), *personal communication* involves "private symbolization" activities — all the internal mental activities that dispose and prepare people to act and react in certain ways in actual social situations. Personal communication is linked to *social communication* when two or more individuals interact with one another, knowingly or not. Ruben (1975) defines social communication as the process underlying "intersubjectivization," a phenomenon that occurs as a consequence of "public symbolization." In Geyer's (1980) terms, the personal communication process can be compared to the "off-line functions" of a computer system, which interfaces with the environment through "on-line functions" involving input-output transactions of messages (p. 32).

## Personal Communication

Personal (or intrapersonal) communication refers to the mental processes by which we organize ourselves in and with our sociocultural milieu, developing ways of seeing, hearing, understanding, and responding to the environment. In Ruben's (1975) words, "Personal communication can be thought of as sensing, making-sense-of, and acting toward the objects and people in one's milieu. It is the process by which the individual informationally fits himself into . . . his environment" (pp. 168–169). In the context of cross-cultural adaptation, then, personal communication can be examined in terms of *host communication competence* — that is, the overall internal capacity of a stranger to decode and encode information in accordance with the communication practices of the host culture. Natives begin to acquire this competence early in life, and it is so internalized in their personal communication system

that, by and large, it operates automatically and unconsciously. For strangers, however, many elements of the same competence must be acquired, often painstakingly, through trial and error. Until strangers have acquired a sufficient level of host communication competence, they are handicapped in their ability to function and relate to the system of host cultural pragmatics. The degree to which a given stranger acquires host communication competence should be reflected in his or her overall ability to fit in the host society, while the lack of such competence manifests itself in various forms of "miscommunication" (Banks, Gao, & Baker, 1991; Gass & Varonis, 1991).

The many elements of host communication competence — from knowledge about the host language and social norms to ability to manage interpersonal relationships and solve impending problems at work — can be grouped into three categories commonly employed in the study of communication competence: cognitive, affective, and operational (or behavioral) (Kim, 1991; Spitzberg & Cupach, 1984). The primary element of *cognitive competence* that strangers must develop is knowledge of the host language and culture, including the knowledge of the history, institutions, laws and regulations, world views, beliefs, norms, and rules of social conduct and interpersonal relationships. Knowledge of the host language means not just linguistic knowledge (such as phonetics, syntax, and vocabulary) but also knowledge about the pragmatic uses of the language in everyday life (such as the many subtle nuances in the way the language is used and interpreted by the natives in various formal and informal social engagements).

Linguistic and cultural knowledge is accompanied by development of cognitive complexity (Kelly, 1955; Schroder, Driver, & Streufert, 1967). Cognitive complexity refers to the structural differentiation and integration in an individual's information-processing capacity. During the initial phase of adaptation, strangers' perceptions of the host environment tend to be overly simplistic and based on gross stereotypes. As strangers learn more about the host language and culture, however, their perceptions become increasingly more refined and complex, enabling them to engage in more effective social interactions.

*Affective competence* facilitates cross-cultural adaptation because it provides the emotional and aesthetic sensibilities that raise communication experiences with the natives from a level that is merely technical to one that is more meaningful and thus more fulfilling. Affective competence allows strangers to empathize with the natives – to share their experiences of joy, excitement, humor, triumph, and beauty, as well as sadness, boredom, sarcasm, despair, and ugliness. The strangers' affective competence thus leads to a sense of belonging and a positive regard for the natives, which, in turn, brings the strangers closer to the local people and their culture. Conversely, strangers who lack affective competence are likely to feel alienated and marginalized, for they cannot show genuine interest in local cultural experiences or in developing close relationships with the natives. In Mansell's (1981) words:

*The concept of aesthetic awareness is linked with ineffable, intuitive feelings of appreciation and celebration. This form of awareness creates a consciousness which transforms individuals' perceptions of the world and imparts a sense of unity between self and surrounding. . . . It is in this transformative mode of experiencing that many people create access to the momentary peaks of fulfillment which makes life meaningful. (p. 99)*

Closely linked with cognitive and affective competence is *operational competence,* or "enactment tendencies" (Buck, 1984, p. vii). This dimension of host communication competence refers to strangers' capacity to express their cognitive and affective experiences outwardly when communicating with others. As strangers try to come up with a mental plan for action, they must base the decision on their current knowledge about the host culture and language; the decision depends also on the degree of sophistication in their information-processing capacity and on their ability and motivation to appreciate the emotional and aesthetic experiences of the natives. Operational competence thus enables strangers to choose the "right" combi-

nation of verbal and nonverbal actions to meet the demands of everyday interactions – managing face-to-face encounters, initiating and maintaining relationships, seeking appropriate information sources, solving various problems they may encounter, and finding ways to succeed in accomplishing their goals.

## Social Communication

Strangers' host communication competence is directly and reciprocally linked to their participation in the social communication activities of the host society. On the one hand, their social communication activities are constrained by their capacity to communicate in the host cultural context. On the other hand, each communication encounter with the host society offers strangers an opportunity to cultivate host communication competence cognitively, affectively, and operationally.

Central to the domain of social communication is *interpersonal communication,* or direct face-to-face interaction in the context of interpersonal relationships with others. As Fogel (1993) argues, individuals develop through their relationships. Interpersonal communication activities help strangers to secure vital information and insight into the mind-sets and behaviors of the local people. In interacting with the natives face to face, strangers also learn about themselves – how they think, express themselves, and respond to others. As a result, strangers' interpersonal communication activities not only enable them to carry out their daily tasks, but also provide them with needed emotional support and points of reference for checking and validating their own thoughts and actions (Adelman, 1988; Kim, 1986, 1987; McPherson, 1991; Pescosolido, 1992; Wellman, 1992).

In addition to interpersonal communication, strangers' participation in the host social communication process occurs as they are exposed to the *mass communication* activities of the host society. These activities involve a wide range of public media, large and small, from radio, television, newspapers, magazines, and movies to art, music, and drama. By engaging in such communication activities, strangers interact with their host milieu without direct involvement with specific individuals;

they expand the scope of their adaptive learning beyond the immediate social context with which they have contact. In transmitting messages that reflect the aspirations, myths, work, and play, as well as the issues and events of the host society, the various mass communication media explicitly or implicitly convey the world views, myths, beliefs, values, mores, and norms of the culture. Of the various forms of mass communication experiences, exposure to information-oriented messages such as those found in newspapers, magazines, television and radio news, and documentaries has been found to be particularly helpful to adaptation, when compared with exposure to more entertainment-oriented media contents (Kim, Lee, & Jeong, 1982; Kim, 1976, 1979b).

The effect of mass communication on adaptation should be particularly significant during the initial phase of resettlement (Kim, Lee, & Jeong, 1982; Kim, 1976, 1979b). During this phase, strangers have not yet developed a level of host communication competence sufficient to forge meaningful interpersonal relationships with local people. Direct communication experiences with the natives can be intensely frustrating or intimidating to many strangers. They may feel awkward and out of place in relating to others, and the immediate negative feedback from another person may be too overwhelming for them to have pleasurable face-to-face encounters with the natives. Under such circumstances, the strangers naturally tend to withdraw from direct contacts and instead prefer mass media as an alternative, pressure-free channel through which elements of the host culture can be experienced (Kim, 1979b; Ryu, 1978; Walker, 1993; Yang, 1988).

## The Role of the Environment

The adaptation function of personal and social (interpersonal and mass) communication cannot be fully understood in isolation from the conditions of the new sociocultural milieu. Societies and communities present different environments for strangers, particularly in three key areas: (1) host receptivity, (2) host conformity pressure, and (3) ethnic group strength. Together, these factors help define the relative degree of "push and pull" that a given stranger is likely to face in a host environment.

## Host Receptivity

The receptivity of a host environment refers to the degree to which the environment is open to, welcomes, or accepts strangers into its social communication networks and offers them various forms of informational, technical, material, and emotional support. The term *host receptivity* incorporates the meaning of other similar terms, such as *interaction potential* (Kim, 1979a) and *acquaintance potential* (Cook, 1962), that have been employed to refer to the access that strangers have to the host social communication processes.

A given environment can be receptive toward certain groups of strangers and unwelcoming toward certain others. For example, Canadian visitors arriving in a small town in the United States are likely to find a largely receptive environment. Yet the same town may show less receptivity toward visitors from lesser known and vastly different cultures such as Turkey or Iran. Such differences in host receptivity toward strangers can be attributed to a number of plausible reasons, including (1) the nature of the relationship, friendly or hostile, between the host country and the stranger's home country, (2) the degree of cultural and ideological difference and incompatibility between the two cultures, (3) the perceived or actual status or power of the stranger's home country and culture, (4) the perceived or actual economic, social, and political standing (or merit) of the stranger's ethnic group within the host society, (5) the perceived or actual economic, social, and political threat to the host society posed by the stranger's ethnic group, and (6) the racial/ethnic prejudice predominantly held by the society against certain groups.

## Host Conformity Pressure

Societies (and communities) also vary in the degree of "conformity pressure" (Zajonc, 1952) they exert — that is, the extent to which the natives exert conscious or unconscious pressure on strangers to change their original patterns of behavior and adopt those of the new culture. Conversely, societies (and communities) differ in the degree to which local people are able or willing to permit, tolerate, accommodate, or appreciate cultural practices that strangers bring with them and to allow strangers to deviate from the hosts' normative expectations. Host conformity pressure should be distinguished from host receptivity in that a society that strongly expects strangers to conform to its cultural life may or may not welcome strangers with distinct cultural and ethnic characteristics.

The conformity pressure of a given host environment is not uniformly applied to all strangers. It is often more acutely felt by those strangers whose livelihood is dependent on communicating well with and being accepted by the natives (De Vos & Suarez-Orozco, 1990, p. 253). Proficiency in the host language and culture is particularly vital to immigrants whose success or failure in pursuing personal goals is dependent on the acceptance and approval of at least the relevant segments of the host population. Even some temporary sojourners, such as employees of multinational companies, Peace Corps volunteers, diplomats, and international students, are subject to some degree of host conformity pressure as they try to carry out their tasks and develop good working relationships with local people. By comparison, other sojourner groups, such as American military personnel stationed overseas, whose daily activities are largely independent of the workings of the host society are subject to only a minimal level of host conformity pressure.

Another factor influencing the degree of host conformity pressure is the ethnic homogeneity or heterogeneity of a given environment. Societies (and communities) that are more pluralistic in ethnic profile and mainstream political ideology (such as metropolitan centers in democratic societies like Australia, Canada, England, and the United States) tend to manifest a greater accommodation of foreign-born individuals as well as native-born ethnic minorities. A stricter imposition of dominant linguistic and cultural patterns on all people can be seen in more traditional societies with authoritarian political systems (such as China, Iran, and Saudi Arabia). In such monolithic societies, foreign-born

visitors or immigrants are likely to be subject to a greater pressure to follow local customs.

## Ethnic Group Strength

Another environmental condition affecting strangers' adaptation is the strength of their ethnic group relative to the host society at large. Ethnic groups differ in their relative status within the host society. A useful insight into ethnic group strength has been provided by sociologists Clarke and Obler (1976), who proposed a three-stage theory of ethnic group development. The first is the stage of the economic adjustment, which begins upon arrival of the group and continues until the group becomes an integral part of the permanent economy. The second stage is community building, which involves the development of community leadership and institutional resources that are used to assert the ethnic group's identity and interests. This stage of ethnic community development corresponds to the concept of "institutional completeness" (Breton, 1964, 1991; Goldenberg & Haines, 1992). The third stage is the period of political growth and aggressive self-assertion, which serves to strengthen the collective ethnic identity and common interests of the group.

The phenomenon of ethnic group strength has been discussed in social psychology in terms of ethnolinguistic vitality (Giles & Johnson, 1987). In research on the influences of the social milieu and the consequences of fluency in a second language, Giles, Bourhis and Taylor (1977) suggested that the influence of ethnolinguistic vitality on individual behavior can be defined in terms of three structural variables: (1) the status of a language in a community, (2) the absolute and relative number of its locuters, and (3) the institutional support (such as governmental services, schools, mass media) for the ethnic language. Ethnolinguistic vitality as an objective environmental condition has been linked to what Giles and his associates (1977) term "subjective ethnolinguistic vitality," or the perceived legitimacy of the position of one's ethnic group. For example, speakers who perceive the subordinate position of their group as legitimate are likely to adjust their communication behaviors to "converge" with those of the dominant outgroup.

The preceding two views on ethnic group strength offer implications for the role of ethnic group strength in a stranger's adaptation to the host society. Integrating these views allows us to describe the strength of an ethnic group in terms of one or more of the following elements: (1) ethnolinguistic vitality, (2) economic status, (3) institutional completeness, and (4) ethnic political activism. Frequently, these community characteristics are closely associated with the size of the ethnic population and the historical "maturity" of the community in the host society. From this perspective, the Cuban Americans in Miami, Florida, for example, have an ethnic community that is stronger than the smaller Russian community in Chicago. Exceptions can be seen in a small ethnic group such as that of the Americans who recently began working and living in the former Czechoslovakia. Despite this group's small size, the fact that it is American gives it political and economic status and prestige that render it a strong ethnic group.

Because a stronger ethnic group provides its members with a stronger subculture and offers many vital services to its members, it is likely to facilitate the cross-cultural adaptation of strangers during the initial phase. In the long run, however, a strong ethnic community tends to discourage the adaptation of strangers to the host society because it encourages ethnolinguistic maintenance. A strong ethnic community is further likely to exert subtle or even explicit pressure to conform to the ethnic community norms; it thereby discourages an active participation in the host social communication activities. Empirical evidence supporting this observation is provided by Rosenthal and Hrynevich (1985), who found that the Greek immigrant community in Australia is more cohesive and organized than is the Italian; they also reported that Greek Australian adolescents placed more emphasis than did Italian Australian adolescents on their ethnic identity and maintenance of their heritage. In addition, according to the investigators, the Greek Australian adolescents placed less emphasis on adapting to the dominant Australian culture. Similar results were reported by Driedger (1976), who found, in Canada, that an ethnic group's status within the host society correlated with its institu-tional completeness; groups high on both status and institutional completeness (the French and Jewish groups) had the strongest sense of ethnic identity.

## The Role of Predisposition

The adaptation of strangers is influenced not only by the conditions of the host environment, but also by the traits that the strangers themselves bring to the adaptive journey. Each stranger begins the adaptation process with a different set of preexisting internal characteristics that help set the parameters for their own subsequent changes. Some begin with enthusiasm and determination, while others find themselves forced into change by unavoidable circumstances. Some may be wide open to new experiences, while others may feel they are too old to make changes in their lifetime habits. The various ways in which strangers differ in their internal conditions can be organized into three categories: (1) preparedness, (2) ethnicity, and (3) personality. Together, these predispositional factors constitute a stranger's "adaptive potential" (Kim, 1979a) or "permeability" (De Vos, 1990) with respect to the host environment.

### Preparedness

Strangers come to their new environment with differing levels of preparedness, or readiness, for dealing with that environment. Specifically, their preparedness is reflected in the level of host communication competence they have acquired prior to moving to the host culture. As previously discussed, host communication competence includes the cognitive, affective, and operational abilities to participate in the social communication activities of the host society — from knowledge of the new language and culture and ability to empathize with the local people's emotional and aesthetic experiences to the capacity to perform appropriately and effectively in various social situations.

Strangers' preparedness is raised when they have realistic expectations and knowledge about the host society, shaped by formal and informal learning (Brabant, Palmer, & Gramling, 1990). Included in such learning activities are schooling and training in, as well as media exposure to, the host language and culture. Education in particular, regardless of its cultural context, helps expand our mental capacity for new learning and for meeting the challenges of life in general. Many cross-cultural training and orientation programs emphasize familiarizing trainees with their host culture (Brislin & Yoshida, 1994; Landis & Bhagat, 1995). For some strangers, an even more effective source of language and culture learning occurs through personal contacts with members of the host society prior to actually entering the host society. Peace Corps volunteers are among the best-prepared sojourners because they go through an intensive screening process and extensive language and cultural training before being given an overseas assignment.

Strangers' preparedness is also influenced by whether their cross-cultural move is voluntary or involuntary and by how long they intend to stay in the host society. Voluntary, long-term immigrants, for example, are likely to enter the host society with greater readiness and willingness to make necessary changes in themselves than are temporary visitors who relocate for reasons (such as wars or natural disasters) other than their own volition.

## Ethnicity

Strangers vary not only in their preparedness but also in their ethnicity (McGuire, McGuire, Child, & Fujioka, 1978). The term *ethnicity* is used here as an inclusive term to refer to various inherited characteristics that strangers have as members of a distinct ethnic group. Japanese sojourners and immigrants, for example, bring to a given host society common physical, linguistic, and cultural features that are different from, say, features of Mexican or French sojourners. Such ethnic characteristics play a crucial role in the cross-cultural adaptation process by affecting the ease or difficulty with which strangers develop communication competence in a given host society and participate in its social communication activities.

The ethnicity of a given stranger influences his or her adaptation process in two interrelated ways. First, each ethnic background presents certain linguistic and cultural barriers for the stranger to overcome before developing host communication competence and being able to participate in host

social communication activities. Second, each individual ethnicity creates a certain psychological barrier (or affinity) in the minds of the natives, which, in turn, affects the natives' receptivity toward the stranger. Strangers embark on their cross-cultural adaptation process with certain advantages (or handicaps) due simply to their ethnic characteristics (Phinney & Rosenthal, 1992, p. 145). Japanese business executives in the United States, for example, are likely to face a greater challenge in overcoming language barriers than are their British counterparts. Their physical features (such as height, skin color, and facial structure) may add to the challenge they face by accentuating the psychological gap between them and their American hosts.

## Personality

Strangers differ from one another not only in ethnicity but also in personality—a set of more or less enduring traits and sensibilities. Each stranger meets the challenges of the new environment within the context of his or her own personal psychological tendencies. Of particular importance are three personality factors—openness, strength, and positivity—that interactively facilitate strangers' adaptation by enabling them to endure stressful challenges and maximize new learning.

*Openness* is defined as an internal posture that is receptive to new information (Gendlin, 1962, 1978). Openness, like a child's innocence, allows strangers to minimize their resistance and to maximize their willingness to attend to the new and changed circumstances. Openness further enables strangers to perceive and interpret various events and situations in the new environment, as they occur, with less rigid, ethnocentric judgments. It is a dimension of personality that encourages strangers to continually seek new cultural learning, to cultivate greater emotional and aesthetic sensitivity, and to expand the range of their behavioral repertoire—all of which are vital to actively participating in and accommodating to the demands of the host milieu. This term incorporates other similar but more specific concepts such as "flexibility," "open-mindedness," and "tolerance for ambiguity."

*Strength* is an additional personality trait that bears significance for cross-cultural adaptation.

Closely related to openness, strength of personality serves as a type of inner resolve that empowers strangers to take on intercultural challenges without losing their basic integrity. Personality strength, unlike stubbornness, includes the quality of flexibility – that is, the ability to "bend," to empathize with others while believing in oneself, and to let go of anxiousness (MacKinnon, 1978). While stubbornness discourages adaptation, strength facilitates creative and effective responses to impending problems. The strength of personality thus represents a personal capacity to cope with various difficulties presented in an alien culture and to find what is best in each potentially problematic situation. It allows strangers to fix their sights and chart a course without depending heavily on, or blaming, external forces because they are equipped with a solid sense of self as the main agent of action and responsibility.

Personality strength, in this sense, is a broad concept that represents a range of interrelated personality attributes such as resilience, risk taking, hardiness, persistence, patience, elasticity, and resourcefulness. It represents all of the inner qualities that help an individual to absorb shocks from the environment and bounce back without being seriously damaged by them. Strangers with a high level of personality strength tend to be stimulated by new challenges and remain effervescent and confident. On the other hand, low levels of personality strength are manifested in tendencies to be shy, fearful, and easily distressed by uncertain or stressful situations.

The open and strong personality tends to be a positive one as well. *Positivity* refers to an affirmative and optimistic outlook and to the capacity to defy negative prediction (Dean & Popp, 1990). Positivity does not mean blind romanticism or far-fetched idealism. It means, instead, the enduring tendency to see the bright side of things while recognizing their dark side. When directed inward, positivity reflects a fundamental confidence in one's ability to overcome obstacles. Positivity helps one to find what is best in each problematic situation and to discover what can be learned from it (Maslow, 1969; Zurcher, 1977).

Positivity, together with openness and strength, helps define the personality predispositions that serve as inner resources. These attributes help strangers "push" themselves in their adaptation process. Strong, open, and positive individuals are less likely to give up easily and more likely to take risks willingly under challenging situations in the host society. They are better equipped to work toward developing host communication competence because they continually seek new learning and new ways to handle their life activities. In doing so, they become better able to make necessary adjustments in themselves. Serious lack of these qualities, on the other hand, weakens an individual's adaptive capacity and works as a self-imposed barrier against adaptive development (Hettema, 1979).

## Summary and Integration

In this essay, I have described the cross-cultural adaptation process as a joint, interactive venture: The strangers and the host environment co-influence the dynamic and fluctuating experiences of stress, adaptation, and growth. The adaptation process is essentially a manifestation of the ever present human capacity to face challenges, learn from them, and arrive at a greater level of self-integration. Few individuals in an alien environment can entirely escape the necessity to adapt. Adaptation occurs naturally and most, if not all, strangers welcome it as long as they are engaged in direct and continual interactions with the host environment.

At the heart of the adaptation process are communication activities that link strangers and the host environment. As strangers undergo continual interaction of push and pull with the new environment, they become more functionally fit and psychologically healthier. These adaptive changes hinge on the psychic movement of the stress-adaptation-growth dynamic strangers experience as they cope with the challenges of the environment. As a result, they acquire new cultural elements (acculturation) and unlearn at least some of their old cultural habits (deculturation). Because of the central role of communication in the adaptation process, the quantity and quality of strangers' interpersonal and mass communication activities contribute critically to, and are facilitated by, the development of their host communication competence. The strangers' host communication competence serves as the internal "engine" that carries them along the adaptive journey, while their participation in host social communication processes serves as the very "fuel" that ignites the engine. Realistically, few strangers can ever adapt completely, no matter how long and how extensive their communication with the host environment. Most of them, nonetheless, do make a workable adaptation given sufficient time and are gradually able to attain a higher level of proficiency in managing their daily affairs.

As strangers participate in various forms of interpersonal and mass communication activities, they are both encouraged and pressured by the host society as well as by their ethnic community. The three environmental conditions – host receptivity, host conformity pressure, and ethnic group strength – help define the "push and pull" dynamics that a receiving society offers strangers. An environment influences stranger adaptation optimally when the native population welcomes and supports the strangers (receptivity), while expecting them to conform to the local norms (host conformity pressure). In facing these environmental forces, the strangers' own predisposition plays an important role. Strangers who are better prepared for the new environment, whose ethnic backgrounds are more similar to the dominant ethnicity of the local people, and whose personality is more open, stronger, and more positive are better able to facilitate their own adaptation process.

Should strangers choose successful adaptation, they must be prepared and willing to face the stressful experiences of coping with the uncertainties and anxieties in the host society. They must concentrate on acquiring new communication habits and putting aside some of the old ones. They must recognize the importance of host communication competence as the fundamental mechanism by which they adapt successfully, and they must work to develop it to the fullest extent possible. They must also take maximum advantage of opportunities to participate in the interpersonal and mass

communication processes of the host society. Finally, they must work toward achieving a greater openness, strength, and positivity in their personal disposition.

However, strangers cannot accomplish their adaptive goals alone. Adaptation is an interactive process involving both strangers and the new environment. Indeed, members of the host society can help facilitate strangers' adaptation by maximizing receptivity toward the strangers – by accepting their original ethnicity and providing them with a supportive interpersonal environment. The host society can actively encourage strangers to adapt through communication training programs. Such programs should facilitate the strangers' acquisition of host communication competence. In addition, the ethnic community can provide a significant adaptive service for the strangers in their early stages of resettlement. Ethnic communities can provide support systems to assist new arrivals in coping with stresses and initial uncertainties and can guide them toward effective adaptation. At the same time, however, strangers must realize that exclusive and prolonged reliance on their ethnic community will delay and eventually limit opportunities for them to adapt to the host milieu.

Ultimately, the adaptation of strangers, particularly long-term immigrants, is of vital interest to the host society as well. Through communication, the host society is able to engender mutual trust and good will among its diverse ethnic and cultural groups (Amir, 1969) and thereby maintain the necessary societal unity and integrity. As long as common channels of communication remain, consensus and patterns of concerted action will persist in the society (Mendelsohn, 1964). Communication, then, makes it possible to merge the incoming new members into a cohesive social organization of commonly shared ideas and values.

## References

Adelman, M. (1988). Cross-cultural adjustment: A theoretical perspective on social support. *International Journal of Intercultural Relations, 12*(3), 183–204.
Adler, P. (1975). The transition experience: An alternative view of culture shock. *Journal of Humanistic Psychology, 15*(4), 13–23.

Adler, P. (1987). "Culture Shock and the Cross-cultural Learning Experience." In L. Luce and E. Smith (Eds.), *Toward Internationalism*, 24–35. Cambridge, Mass.: Newbury.

Amir, Y. (1969). Contact hypothesis in ethnic relations. *Psychological Bulletin, 7*(5), 319–342.

Banks, S., Gao, G., and Baker, J. (1991). "Intercultural Encounters and Miscommunication." In N. Coupland, H. Giles, and J. Wiemann (Eds.), *"Miscommunication" and Problematic Talk*, 103–120. Newbury Park, Calif.: Sage.

Bar-Yosef, R. (1968). Desocialization and resocialization: The adjustment process of immigrants. *International Migration Review, 2*, 27–42.

Barna, L. (1983). "The Stress Factor in Intercultural Relations." In D. Landis and R. Brislin (Eds.), *Handbook for Intercultural Training: Vol. II. Issues in Training Methodology*, 19–49. New York: Pergamon Press.

Berry, J. (1990). "Psychological Acculturation: Understanding Individuals Moving Between Cultures." In R. Brislin (Ed.), *Applied Cross-Cultural Psychology*, 232–253. Newbury Park, Calif.: Sage.

Boekestijn, C. (1988). Intercultural migration and the development of personal identity: The dilemma between identity maintenance and cultural adaptation. *International Journal of Intercultural Relations, 12*(2), 83–105.

Brabant, S., Palmer, C., and Gramling, R. (1990). Returning home: An empirical investigation of cross-cultural reentry. *International Journal of Intercultural Relations, 14*(4), 387–404.

Breton, R. (1964). Institutional completeness of ethnic communities and the personal relations of immigrants. *American Journal of Sociology, 70*, 193–205.

Breton, R. (1991). *The Governance of Ethnic Communities: Political Structures and Processes in Canada*. Westport, Conn.: Greenwood Press.

Brislin, R. (1981). *Cross-Cultural Encounters*. Elmsford, N.Y.: Pergamon Press.

Brislin, R., and Yoshida, T. (1994). *Intercultural Communication Training: An Introduction*. Thousand Oaks, Calif.: Sage.

Broom, L., and Kitsuse, J. (1955). The validation of acculturation: A condition to ethnic assimilation. *American Anthropologist, 62*, 44–48.

Buck, R. (1984). *The Communication of Emotion*. New York: Guilford Press.

Chan, K., and Lam, L. (1987). "Psychological Problems of Chinese Vietnamese Refugees Resettling in Quebec." In K. Chan and D. Indra (Eds.), *Uprooting, Loss and Adaptation: The Resettlement of Indochinese Refugees in Canada*, 27–41. Ottawa: Canadian Public Health Association.

Clarke, S., and Obler, J. (1976). "Ethic Conflict, Community-Building, and the Emergence of Ethnic Political Traditions in the United States." In S. Clarke and J. Obler (Eds.), *Urban Ethnic Conflict: A Comparative Perspective*, 1–34. Chapel Hill, N.C.: University of North Carolina.

Cook, S. (1962). The systematic analysis of socially significant events. *Journal of Social Issues, 18*(2), 66–84.

De Vos, G. (1990). "Self in Society: A Multilevel, Psychocultural Analysis." In G. De Vos and M. Suarez-Orozco (Eds.), *Status Inequality: The Self in Culture*, 17–74. Newbury Park, Calif.: Sage.

De Vos, G., and Suarez-Orozco, M. (1990). "Ethnic Belonging and Status Mobility." In G. De Vos and M. Suarez-Orozco (Eds.), *Status Inequality: The Self in Culture*, 246–264. Newbury Park, Calif.: Sage.

Dean, O., and Popp, G. (1990). Intercultural communication effectiveness as perceived by American managers in Saudi Arabia and French managers in the U.S. *International Journal of Intercultural Relations, 14*(4), 405–424.

Driedger, L. (1976). Ethnic self-identity: A comparison of ingroup evaluations. *Sociometry, 39*, 131–141.

Dyal, J., and Dyal, R. (1981). Acculturation, stress and coping. *International Journal of Intercultural Relations, 5*(4), 301–328.

Eisenstadt, S. (1954). *The Absorption of Immigrants*. London: Routledge & Kegan Paul.

Fogel, A. (1993). *Developing Through Relationships: Origins of Communication, Self, and Culture*. Chicago: University of Chicago Press.

Ford, D., and Lerner, R. (1992). *Developmental Systems Theory: An Integrative Approach*. Newbury Park, Calif.: Sage.

Furnham, A. (1984). Tourism and culture shock. *Annals of Tourism Research, 11*(1), 41–57.

Furnham, A. (1988). "The Adjustment of Sojourners." In Y. Kim and W. Gudykunst (Eds.), *Cross-cultural Adaptation*, 42–61. Newbury Park, Calif.: Sage.

Furnham, A., and Bochner, S. (1986). *Culture Shock: Psychological Reactions to Unfamiliar Environments*. London: Methuen.

Gass, S., and Varonis, E. (1991). "Miscommunication in Nonnative Speaker Discourse." In N. Coupland, H. Giles, and J. Wiemann (Eds.), *"Miscommunication" and Problematic Talk*, 121–145. Newbury Park, Calif.: Sage.

Gendlin, E. (1962). *Experiencing and the Creation of Meaning*. New York: Free Press.

Gendlin, E. (1978). *Focusing*. New York: Everest House.

Geyer, R. (1980). *Alienation Theories: A General Systems Approach*. New York: Pergamon Press.

Giles, H., Bourhis, R., and Taylor, D. (1977). "Towards a Theory of Language in Ethnic Group Relations." In H. Giles (Eds.), *Language, Ethnicity, and Intergroup Relations*, 307–348. London: Academic Press.

Giles, H., and Johnson, P. (1987). Ethnolinguistic identity theory: A social psychological approach to language maintenance. *International Journal of the Sociology of Language, 68,* 69-99.

Goldenberg, S., and Haines, V. (1992). Social networks and institutional completeness: From territory to ties. *Canadian Journal of Sociology, 17*(3), 301-312.

Gudykunst, W. (1995). "Anxiety/Uncertainty Management (AUM) Theory: Current Status." In R. Wiseman (Ed.), *Intercultural Communication Theory,* 8-58. Thousand Oaks, Calif.: Sage.

Gudykunst, W., and Kim, Y. (in press). *Communicating with Strangers: An Approach to Intercultural Communication,* 3d ed. New York: McGraw-Hill.

Hettema, P. (1979). *Personality and Adaptation.* New York: North-Holland.

Kelly, G. (1955). *The Psychology of Personal Constructs: Vol. 1. A Theory of Personality.* New York: W. W. Norton.

Kim, J., Lee, B., and Jeong, W. (1982). *Uses of Mass Media in Acculturation: Dependency, Information Preference, and Gratification.* Paper presented at the annual meeting of the Association for Education in Journalism, Athens, Ohio, May.

Kim, Y. (1976). *Communication Patterns of Foreign Immigrants in the Process of Acculturation: A Survey Among the Korean Population in Chicago.* Unpublished doctoral dissertation, Northwestern University, Evanston, Illinois.

Kim, Y. (1979a). "Toward an Interactive Theory of Communication-Accculturation." In B. Ruben (Ed.), *Communication Yearbook III,* 435-453. New Brunswick, N.J.: Transaction Books.

Kim, Y. (1979b). Mass Media and Acculturation. Paper presented at the annual conference of the Eastern Communication Association, Philadelphia, May.

Kim, Y. (1986). "Understanding of the Social Context of Intergroup Communication: A Personal Network Approach." In W. Gudykunst (Ed.), *Intergroup Communication,* 86-95. London: Edward Arnold.

Kim, Y. (1987). "Facilitating Immigrant Adaptation: The Role of Communication and Interpersonal Ties." In T. Albrecht and M. Adelman (Eds.), *Communicating Social Support,* 192-211. Newbury Park, Calif.: Sage.

Kim, Y. (1988). *Communication and Cross-Cultural Adaptation: An Integrative Theory.* Clevedon, England: Multilingual Matters.

Kim, Y. (1991). "Intercultural Communication Competence: A Systems-Theoretic View." In S. Ting-Toomey and F. Korzenny (Eds.), *Cross-Cultural Interpersonal Communication,* 259-275. Newbury Park, Calif.: Sage.

Kim, Y. (1995). "Cross-Cultural Adaptation: An Integrative Theory." In R. Wiseman (Ed.), *Intercultural Communication Theory,* 170-193. Thousand Oaks, Calif.: Sage.

Kim, Y. (in press). *Becoming Intercultural: An Integrative Theory of Cross-Cultural Adaptation.* Thousand Oaks, Calif.: Sage.

Kim, Y., and Ruben, B. (1988). "Intercultural Transformation." In Y. Kim and W. Gudykunst (Eds.), *Theories in Intercultural Communication,* 299-321. Newbury Park, Calif.: Sage.

Landis, D., and Bhagat, R. (Eds.). (1995). *Handbook of Intercultural Training,* 2d ed. Thousand Oaks, Calif.: Sage.

Lazarus, R. (1966). *Psychological Stress and the Coping Process.* St. Louis: McGraw-Hill.

MacKinnon, D. (1978). *In Search of Human Effectiveness.* Buffalo, N.Y.: Creative Education Foundation.

Mansell, M. (1981). Transcultural experience and expressive response. *Communication Education, 30,* April, 93-108.

Maslow, A. (1969). "A Theory of Metamotivation: The Biological Rooting of the Value-Life." In H. Chiang and A. Maslow (Eds.), *The Healthy Personality,* 35-56. New York: Van Nostrand Reinhold.

McGuire, W., McGuire, C., Child, P., and Fujioka, T. (1978). Salience of ethnicity in the spontaneous self-concepts as a function of one's ethnic distinctiveness in the social environment. *Journal of Personality and Social Psychology, 36,* 511-520.

McPherson, J. (1991). Opportunities for Contact and Network Diversity: Further Explorations of Homophily in Voluntary Organizations. Paper presented at the annual meeting of the International Sunbelt Social Network Conference, Tampa, Florida, February.

Mendelsohn, H. (1964). "Sociological Perspective on the Study of Mass Communication." In L. Dexter and D. White (Eds.), *People, Society, and Mass Communication,* 29-36. New York: Free Press.

Moos, R. (1976). *Human Adaptation: Coping with Life Crisis.* Lexington, Mass.: D. C. Heath.

Oberg, K. (1960). Culture shock: Adjustment to new cultural environments. *Practical Anthropology, 7,* 170-179.

Padilla, A. (Ed.). (1980). *Acculturation: Theory, Models and Some New Findings.* Washington, D.C.: Westview.

Pescosolido, B. (1992). Beyond rational choice: The social dynamics of how people seek help. *American Journal of Sociology, 97*(4), 1096-1138.

Phinney, J., and Rosenthal, M. (1992). "Ethnic Identity in Adolescence." In G. Adams, T. Gullota and R. Montemayor (Eds.), *Adolescent Identity Formation,* 145-172. Newbury Park, Calif.: Sage.

Rosenthal, D., and Hrynevich, C. (1985). Ethnicity and ethnic identity: A comparative study of Greek-, Italian-, and Anglo-Australian working-class adolescents. *Journal of Youth and Adolescence, 12,* 117-135.

Ruben, B. (1975). "Intrapersonal, Interpersonal, and Mass Communication Process in Individual and Multi-Person Systems." In B. Ruben and J. Kim (Eds.), *General Systems Theory and Human Communication,* 164-190. Rochelle Park, N.J. Hayden.

Ryu, J. (1978). *Mass Media's Role in the Assimilation Process: A Study of Korean Immigrants in the Los Angeles Area.* Paper presented at the annual meeting of the International Communication Association, Chicago, May.

Schroder, H., Driver, M., and Streufert, S. (1967). *Human Information Processing: Individuals and Groups Functioning in Complex Social Situations.* New York: Holt, Rinehart and Winston.

Shibutani, T., and Kwan, K. (1965). *Ethnic Stratification: A Comparative Approach.* New York: Macmillan.

Simmel, G. (1950/1908). "The Stranger." In K. Wolff (Ed. and Trans.), *The Sociology of Georg Simmel.* New York: Free Press.

Spicer, E. (1968). "Acculturation." In D. Sills (Ed.), *International Encyclopedia of the Social Sciences,* 21-27. New York: Macmillan & Free Press.

Spitzberg, B., and Cupach, W. (1984). *Interpersonal Communication Competence.* Beverly Hills, Calif.: Sage.

Taft, R. (1977). "Coping with Unfamiliar Cultures." In N. Warren (Ed.), *Studies in Cross-Cultural Psychology: Vol. 1,* 121-153. London: Academic Press.

Torbiorn, I. (1982). *Living Abroad: Personal Adjustment and Personnel Policy in the Overseas Setting.* New York: Wiley.

Volkan, V. (1993). Immigrants and refugees: A psychodynamic perspective. *Mind & Human Interaction,* 4(2), 63-69.

Walker, D. (1993). *The Role of the Mass Media in the Adaptation of Haitian Immigrants in Miami.* Unpublished doctoral dissertation, Indiana University, Indianapolis.

Wellman, B. (1992). Which type of ties and networks provide what kinds of social support? *Advances in Group Processes, 9,* 207-235.

Yang, S. (1988). The Role of Mass Media in Immigrants' Political Socialization: A Study of Korean Immigrants in Northern California. Unpublished doctoral dissertation, Stanford University, Stanford, Calif.

Zajonc, R. (1952). Aggressive attitude of the "stranger" as a function of conformity pressures. *Human Relations, 5,* 205-216.

Zurcher, L. (1977). *The Immutable Self: A Self Concept for Social Change.* Beverly Hills, Calif.: Sage.

# *A*esthetics as a Bridge to Multicultural Understanding

## JAMES STEVEN SAUCEDA

Bicentennial celebrations were taking place throughout Australia, but in Townsville, a remote section of Queensland, a "counter" festival was being staged by aborigines. The people of Townsville were outraged; hostilities ran high. Even *before* opening ceremonies could begin, the local newspaper's banner headline had proclaimed "Festival Fiasco."[1] And the tension continued to escalate as aborigines from all over Australia poured into Townsville. Some tribes, in fact, traveled hundreds of miles on foot to attend, only to be met by suspicion, distrust, and even hatred.

Yet just five days later the headlines gushed: "Wow — What a Festival!"[2] An extra supplement added to the paper featured human interest stories about many of the participants and highlighted the importance of ancient aboriginal art forms such as sand painting. Few of us are likely to realize that the Australian aborigine is said to have the world's oldest continuous tradition of visual art. Westerners, for example, are seldom aware that aboriginal cave paintings date back at least 30,000 years (making them twice as old as those found in France).[3] In one short but remarkable week, the people of Townsville had moved from strident intolerance to open acceptance of and authentic pride in the aborigines. What had happened?

This original essay appears here for the first time. All rights reserved. Permission to reprint must be obtained from the author and the publisher. James Steven Sauceda teaches in the Department of Speech Communication and is Director of the Multicultural Center at California State University, Long Beach.

Television journalist Bill Moyers posed this question to director Peter Sellars, one of the few American eyewitnesses to these extraordinary events. Sellars has a unique vantage point on such issues: His directing of innovative works and his organizing of international extravaganzas and multicultural events give him a deep sensitivity to diversity. So what, then, according to Sellars, had actually happened in Townsville?

*The work itself had transformed the social relation, the work itself was so open, so honest [it] put forward such an intense humanity that [it] could not be denied. The residents of Townsville saw black people in a completely different way. The statement of pride of the aborigines stepping forward and showing who they were and stating it not only for themselves and not only for the people of Townsville, but for their fellow people of the Pacific. It was an occasion that was tremendously moving and filled with honor and hope.*[4]

Put another way, what happened in Townsville was that the voice of "the other" was not only heard but also actually touched (that is, not intellectualized or merely talked about, but *experienced viscerally.*)

The aboriginal arts festival of Townsville may provide us with a significant tool for creating better multicultural understanding right here in America. In this essay, therefore, I posit that an important method of research, crucial for establishing effective intercultural communication and multicultural experience, is the use of aesthetic communication. That is, I propose that artistic performance and artifacts can be a strategy of empowerment and a trigger mechanism for inspiring, first, tolerance, then empathy, and ultimately acceptance of culturally different groups.

All forms of aesthetic communication, whether *literary* (poetry, prose, and drama), *visual* (paintings, graphic art, video images, film, masks), *tactile* (weaving, statuary, and interactive installations), *musical* (all genres), *kinesthetic* (all forms of dance), or *theatrical* (all genres) are perceived as having a unique power to convey culture. In particular, the context of performance adds very important di-

mensions to one's personal experience with other cultures; it brings out an immediacy of feeling and the authenticity of another's "voice."

In order to successfully create a truly multicultural America, we have to do more than merely have passive and monocultural forays into different cultures. Rather, we must individually seek out cross-cultural, interracial and multiethnic experiences where we actively participate and share in another's culture. It is simply not enough, for instance, to go to the library and silently read a work of Chicano poetry in an effort to gain insight into this distinctive culture. It would be much more empowering and helpful to actively listen to Chicano poets *perform* their work and to make the effort to travel *into* the Chicano community itself for the event. Now, I readily admit that this is not easy to do. It requires not only a high level of emotional risk taking but also the energy and effort of planning. Beyond even these prerequisites, you might discover that you are received as an outsider once you arrive. And yet this initial and temporary feeling of being an outsider is precisely *the daily experience* of many ethnic and cultural groups in America. Perhaps, with trust and compassion, the reticence and fear on all sides will fade. Acceptance does have a price, but it is worth the personal investment.

An aesthetic multicultural communication experience adds significantly to the storehouse of our intellectual understanding by offering us *intuitive* knowledge and practical interventions that create a living, interactive, multiethnic context — a context that ignites in us as audience members an experience of immediacy, affect, vulnerability, humor, compassion, and the assumption of emotional risk taking.

## Need for Community

Before we continue our discussion, we need to define the key term *multiculturalism.* Considerable confusion and widely differing opinions exist as to what a multicultural experience involves. The three-part definition originally stated by Meyer Weinberg and adopted in this paper is easy to remember, but difficult to enact:

1. "Multicultural education is teaching and learning about the *equal human worth* of distinctive groups of people."[5]

For me, the crux of a multicultural philosophy is in this commitment to *equal human worth* and in the recognition that we are "distinctive" beyond reasons of our race, ethnicity, or cultural background per se. Other dimensions of our identity and personhood that often play as important a role as race include our religion, age, gender, sexual orientation, and disability. The definition continues:

2. "A multicultural society must, therefore, engage in maximizing equal human worth. Thus, a society simply marked by ethnic or cultural diversity *is not necessarily multicultural*. Socially-patterned denials of equal worth must be countered in order to build a multicultural society."[6]

So, according to this definition, multicultural education must fight not only against racism, but also against *any* and *all* denials of our equal worth: "ableism," sexism, homophobia, anti-Semitism, and so on. It is understandable however, why many people view multicultural education as divisive. For many, multicultural education appears to be a movement that is anti-white or that is meant to address the needs and concerns only of so-called people of color. Sadly, the application of the latter term often encourages the perception of divisiveness — for why isn't white a color? And why are white people often treated by minority groups as if being white means one is automatically racist? Isn't that assumption racist in itself?

I agree. The truth is that there are avowed practitioners of "multiculturalism" who do exclude whites or who so disparage European and American history and culture as to create adversarial relationships. But I hold that such acts of intolerance against whites reflect not multiculturalism, but monoculturalism (and are, indeed, acts of racism.) Our definition states this point another way:

3. "Equal human worth is a *universally valid* principle. Those who deny it for some, while claiming it for themselves, are declaring their own superiority."[7]

For too many years, we in America have lived in a virtual state of denial regarding race relations and our responsibility to truly foster acceptance of the extraordinary cultural diversity of our citizens. Americans have denied the anger, despair, economic stratification, and social disintegration found throughout the nation. This turmoil has usually been experienced most directly by so-called people of color, the non-European Americans, who collectively may be referred to as "the other." Denial, however, produces horrendous repercussions, and eventually a breaking point is reached. We who live in the greater Los Angeles area, for instance, learned this fact in profound and disturbing ways. The Los Angeles "uprising" of April 29 – May 3, 1992, produced the worst urban violence in contemporary U.S. history.[8] But perhaps, in the aftermath, America has been jolted awake by its terrible fury (and by the portent of further and more far-reaching destruction *if* nothing substantially changes).

Add to this volatile situation the findings of the most comprehensive study done on American youth and their views on ethnicity and race relations. *Democracy's Next Generation II* presents "the first fully detailed portrait of the children of the civil rights era."[9] The researchers examined a representative cross section of the 15- to 24-year-old population in the country. At the top of the study's findings was the fact that "young people have a gloomy view of the state of race relations in America today. . . . 50 percent of America's youth . . . describe the state of race relations in our nation as 'generally bad.'"[10]

In "Missing People and Others," Arturo Madrid explores the concept of *the other*. "The Other disturbs, disquiets, discomforts. It provokes distrust and suspicion. The Other frightens, scares."[11] He continues: "In the United States diversity is desirable only as long as it conforms to *my* standards, to *my* mindset, to *my* view of life, to *my* sense of order."[12]

One reason that the other disturbs and frightens is that American ethnic minorities are fast becoming numerical majorities. In 1990, one in four

Americans had already defined themselves as non-white. By the year 2000, the majority of people under 30 in the Southwest will be Latino; by 2020, the number of nonwhite U.S. residents will have more than doubled (while the white population will not have increased at all).[13] This "new" majority will challenge us to forge a truly multicultural democracy (the first in history).

Peter Sellars tells us that now is "the time to notice that we are surrounded by a range of cultures far more ancient, distinguished and profound than our own. My generation may be the first American generation that has had to notice that it's not a white world. Four centuries of intensive disinformation from the British empire notwithstanding, *we* are the minority culture."[14] A healthy view of America, then, is one that sees her as a vibrant, multiethnic society learning to become a multicultural society. Chief among the so-called other groups are American Indians, Latino Americans, African Americans, and Asian Pacific Americans.

Any failure to see America's future as multicultural is a serious error. We cannot, therefore, speak of *the* culture of the United States, for we in America are made up of a plurality of cultures. Sadly, many researchers still equate American only with European American (with all other cultures in America seemingly of little or even no importance). But, as Wong aptly states, "Multiculturalism is not a category of American culture, it is a description of *all* of American culture."[15]

## Creating Community

How, we may well ask, do we create a sense of community from such diversity? As noted recently in the Los Angeles *Times*, "it is a common misperception that last spring's burning, looting, and beatings were purposeless violence dissociated from anything else going on in our culture."[16]

The Los Angeles *Times* elaborated by identifying the important and unique part aesthetic communication can play in dealing with difficult and even violent clashes of class and culture:

*Art has disclosed a deeper truth: that the riots were simply a street version of the disorder that exists at*

*higher levels of society. Artists have attempted to make the truth apparent, not by stating it but instead by creating an environment in which we can discover it for ourselves.*[17]

What is needed for true community building is "the lively interplay of multiple cultural perceptions — a community whose sophistication in traffic management permits it to sustain multiple borders."[18] We will examine a number of aesthetic approaches to creating community.

## Performance Study

One approach to building community may be found in the arena of *performance study*. As the opening anecdote of this essay demonstrates, aesthetic communication can function as a strategy and trigger mechanism for instilling tolerance, empathy, and acceptance of culturally different groups. In short, performance can provide a potent and practical avenue for the building of community on university campuses and in the community at large.

Performance is quickly gaining momentum as an engaging and powerful strategy for building community and fostering the understanding of multicultural experience:

*If we are to forge a new American community from [our] diversity, we will be challenged to accept the new America that we have already become, and to find ways to include within our common cultural ground the vibrant expressions of many different cultural traditions. Because artistic expression is one of the most visible and accessible manifestations of any culture, and because it has the impulse of communication at heart, artists can create a bridge of understanding between different cultures.*[19]

Another key advantage of performance-centered multicultural education is that it can be used in so many areas: in the public and private sector, on campuses — from elementary schools through universities — at churches or local parks, and so forth. Exhibition of art and the performance of domestic multicultural texts thus creates links among diverse local, national, and international communities: "Through these linkages the arts can lead the way to cross-cultural understanding that will be increasingly necessary as we proceed toward a new century."[20]

One of the nation's most influential theater producers and directors is Gordon Davidson of the Los Angeles Music Center complex. What he has said regarding multicultural performance also helps us summarize the need to have *all* of our voices heard:

*We in the theatre use the word "voice" in a peculiar and idiomatic way. In assessing writers, we look for a "voice," by which we mean both an individual style in stagecraft and language and a unique perspective or vision. When an artist has matured, has found his or her style and subject, we often say that they have "found their voice." We sometimes think of the theatre itself as a kind of instrument which can provide a "voice" for, give a "voice" to, a culture and a community. This peculiar theatre diction may reflect a fundamental truth as to how all people engage the world, for many philosophers and psychologists believe that we make sense of our complicated, often overwhelming and incoherent, experience through communicating, through telling stories. Indeed, our experience may not be real to us until we have given "voice" to it. Whether it is a young man who has fallen in love and must tell his friends or a community that has suffered some cataclysm and needs the book or play or movie — perhaps the myth — that tells, explains and completes the event, it is through telling stories that individuals, communities and entire civilizations shape and comprehend their experience and history.[21]*

**Rainbow Voices.** "Rainbow voices" is apt as a metaphor to describe aesthetic communication in general as a bridge to understanding our cultural differences. Envision, if you will, a full spectrum of color, a rainbow, indicative of ethnic and racial diversity. As we will see, this prism of color includes all people. Furthermore, the rainbow signifies our dreams and hopes; it is an image of welcome and promise — invoking the universal principle of "equal human worth."

The term *rainbow voices* is also one that corrects the faulty idea of America as *the great melting pot.* The traditional view of the melting pot posits that, in order to become *truly* American, one's ethnic and cultural heritage must be divested. The alleged result is that one then *melts,* or is assimilated into, a single monochromatic and homogeneous American culture. This fanciful notion masks all the realities of racism. People of color simply have never *melted* — nor could they even if they had wished to do so. In *Strangers from a Distant Shore: A History of Asian Americans,* for instance, Ronald Takaki reveals how, for generations, Asian Americans have been perceived as foreigners in their own land. Takaki's study documents, in excruciating detail, an American history of racism from Japanese internment camps to anti-Asian sentiments on today's college campuses.[22]

Arturo Madrid adds a comment on another aspect of the melting pot concept — the idea that English is the only language of America:

*There [is] a myth, a pervasive myth, to the effect that if we [Latinos and other people of color] only learn to speak English well — and particularly without an accent — we would be welcomed into the American fellowship. . . . the true test is not our speech, but rather our names and our appearance, for we will always have an accent, however perfect our pronunciation, however excellent our enunciation, however divine our diction. That accent is heard in our pigmentation, our physiognomy, our names.[23]*

The words of the Chicano poet Alurista provide many other examples of how, in multicultural America, we must deal with accents and different languages. This California artist is known nationwide for his bold and experimental use of language. One of his most intriguing collections poses a linguistic and cultural confrontation in its title, *Spik in Glyph.*[24] Here is a common example of how the intolerance of multilingualism is expressed. The proclamation "You're in America, speak English!" is, of course, what Alurista is satirizing, yet his clever and deft title also reveals more to us about this complex issue. The clipped diction of ethnic minorities is mirrored – "Spik" for "speak" – as is the alienation of those who live only in monolingual world. For them *any* foreign language is as indecipherable as Egyptian hiero*glyphs*.

But Alurista touches upon yet another important point: how the language of "the insider" gives minorities strength, a unique voice of their own. The Chicano, in this regard, has invented his own hieroglyphs in the form of *placas* – graffiti calligraphy – and in the ideolect known as *calo* – a form of language often called "spinglish" or "spanglish" because it resembles English and Spanish, but is neither.

Multicultural artists, therefore, help us to see and hear another's reality; particularly in performance, the feelings of distance between cultural groups can be lessened. The concept of "voices" in rainbow voices is also compelling. For this reveals how empowerment, performance, and multicultural education are organically linked:

*Education for empowerment demands taking seriously the strengths, experiences, strategies, and goals members of oppressed groups have. It also demands helping them to analyze and understand the social structure that oppresses them and to act in ways that will enable them to reach their own goals successfully.*[25]

Art not only engenders an appreciation of "the other" but can also inspire in us, no matter our ethnic background and cultural heritage, a spirit of social justice, of advocacy, of self-esteem, pride, and dignity. In sum, art gives us permission to discover and promote our own voices. This is what is referred to as "the emancipatory promise of plurality and heterogeneity."[26]

It is to be hoped that the concept of rainbow voices will introduce to us a new and healthy metaphor for multiculturalism. If we begin by seeing ourselves as "voices of the rainbow," then we too learn to accept that all colors, and all cultures, form *one* interrelated chorus – the large and complex American culture. Thus, in place of a melting pot, we discover a dynamic multiethnic orchestra – where one's individual voice is heard, both amplifying and strengthening the aesthetic entirety of the

music. In this way, difference is retained but coexists with the common bonds of a national cultural identity.

In our quest to release and experience rainbow voices, we should avail ourselves of all forms of aesthetic communication. What might surprise you is how much you might learn to like not just the art work, but also the groups of people that they represent. What follows are some highlights, just a few practical suggestions and resources that facilitate our discovery of rainbow voices.

## Theatre

Many universities house special performance troupes that explore issues of ethnicity and culture. The Rainbow Voices at California State University, Long Beach, for example, is one of the few companies that functions as an organic part of a multicultural center.[27] The Catalyst Theatre at Towson State University in Maryland has, since 1988, addressed race relations as well as substance abuse issues under the umbrella of the campus Violence Prevention Center and TSU's theatre department.[28] The Cultural Diversity Players at Shippensburg University in Pennsylvania, by contrast, developed their program under the aegis of the Student Affairs Division.[29]

Another example of studying culture through performance is The Crazy Salad, a company of players that is part of the Interpreters Theatre program in the Department of Communication at Arizona State University.[30] Other troupes dealing with social and campus climate issues can be found at the University of Michigan, the University of Kansas, Duke University, Miami University (Ohio), and Pennsylvania State University.[31]

Another exciting development in multicultural arts education can be found on the professional stage. Recently, at the Public Theatre in New York, for instance, a one-woman show called *Fires in the Mirror* explored the Crown Heights conflict between African Americans and Hasidic Jews that took place in the summer of 1991 in Brooklyn. The performer and playwright, Anna Deavere Smith, portrayed twenty-nine different characters, each based upon her interviews with people involved in the incident.

This work is an excellent example of aesthetic communication as a bridge to multicultural insight and empathy. As one reviewer noted, "In her play and performance, multiple indexes of difference (class, race, ethnicity, religion, gender, language, age, vocal, and bodily mannerisms) refresh and surprise as the story unfolds: people on all sides elude stereotypes."[32]

This work also conscientiously addresses the deep-seated, complex conflicts to be found in multiethnic America. Anna Deavere Smith is unafraid to probe and "enact the volatile, liminal world of cultural boundaries."[33] Part One of *Fires in the Mirror* is instructive on issues of diversity, as it details and broadens our understanding of both "the ideology and language of race."[34] Part Two of *Fires* reveals differing conceptions and perceptions of the Crown Heights incident. The audience is left to deal with the reality of colliding cultures — no simple answers nor any one point of view is offered.

After the uprising in Los Angeles, in April 1992, Gordon Davidson approached Anna Deavere Smith to create another theatrical work. This time, the goal was to probe the complex tensions, fears, and frustrations underlying the multiethnic violence that had recently erupted. The result was *Twilight in Los Angeles, 1992,* which has its world premiere at the Mark Taper Forum on May 23, 1993 — scarcely one year after the Los Angeles rebellion had taken place.[35] As Jack Knoll of *Newsweek* noted, "Smith is an ideal theater artist for the 1990s, as America attempts to synthesize an increasingly diverse culture."[36]

Los Angeles has also become a site where other performances of American ethnic experience originate. The most current is the world premiere production of *The Woman Warrior: A Girlhood Among Ghosts,* which opened February 16, 1995. This full-length play is based on two novels by Maxine Hong Kingston: *The Woman Warrior* and *China Men.*[37]

In the Los Angeles area, as might be expected, there are always a plethora of multicultural theatre events to attend. *Fire in the Treasure House* is an intriguing example of an artistic coalition between different ethnic groups (an approach that is becoming more and more common). In this instance, African Americans and Asian Pacific Americans

have together created a forum for performance and the visual arts. In addition, there are such performance venues as The Inner City Cultural Center, The Los Angeles Theatre Center, and the many smaller theatres in the greater Los Angeles area.

## Dance

When Cambodians first established their community in Long Beach, California, their very first priority was to form a dance company and arts school.[38] The reason dance superseded all other considerations, such as housing and medical services, is that dance, for Cambodians, is the central repository of their cultural history.

This differs from many other cultural traditions, where dance is seen as an art form of beauty and formal precision rather than as the primary method for embodying the history and aspirations of a people. There are also many national touring companies whose work in dance informs us of multicultural diversity; these include the Alvin Ailey Dance Company, the Dance Theatre of Harlem, and the Asian American Dance Company. Various cultural coalitions and collaborations can also be found, such as the Balinese American Dance Company or the choreography of Korean American Trina Nahm-Mijo.

## Painting

Major art museums are now beginning to feature the work of "the other." A case in point was the exhibition "Hispanic Art in the United States." This show recently toured the United States and was the first of its kind to feature thirty contemporary Latino and Latina painters and sculptors. The "Splendor of Mexico" was also a first, an exhibit showcasing thirty centuries of Mexican art. Remember, too, that docent tours, audiocassette tours, guest speakers, and catalogues almost always accompany such major exhibitions.

Look for special installations as well. For example, a fresh take on European art can be quite as enlightening as any exhibition on the so-called minority experience. In July 1995, for example, the J. Paul Getty Museum in Los Angeles housed early

European paintings depicting empowered, nonsexist images of women. Such an exhibition reveals a more complex reality to the social relations of Europe than we would expect.

## Film

Fortunately, for many years films like *To Kill a Mockingbird, In the Heat of the Night,* and *Zoot Suit* have confronted issues of intolerance and racial prejudice. Recently, however, an entire new generation of films addressing race relations has taken center stage. These include virtually all of the works from director, writer, and actor Spike Lee (particularly *Do the Right Thing, Jungle Fever,* and *Malcolm X).* Similarly, the work of director/writer John Singleton offers provocative insights into African American life experiences in *Boyz N the Hood, Poetic Justice,* and *Higher Learning.*

Some very interesting films criss-cross cultures: *Mississippi Masala* brings in Asian Indian concerns vis-à-vis African Americans, whereas *Zebra Head* challenges assumptions about interracial dating. *Stand and Deliver, American Me,* and *Mi Familia* provide insight into the experiences of Latino Americans; *The Joy Luck Club* explores Asian American family histories.

More controversial depictions of modern American multiethnic relationships can be found in Quentin Tarrentino's *Pulp Fiction* – a most remarkable and provocative film. Even such high action fare as *Die Hard – With a Vengeance* contains bold and startling scenes concerning interethnic conflict. Mainstream movies, as well as offbeat films, continue to respond to multicultural issues.

## Music

While music has long been considered a universal language, one transcending cultural borders, there is now a new trend in pop/rock and jazz music that is decidedly multicultural. The "world beat" movement espouses the idea that music benefits from cross-cultural collaboration. The following are some recent examples: Paul Simon's work, particularly *Graceland,* brings South African music to American audiences. For many years, David

Byrne – both as a member of the band Talking Heads and as a solo artist – has created a world beat sound. Mickey Hart's *Planet Drum* is considered to be a veritable atlas of world beat, performed by an ensemble representing the percussion traditions of Africa, Asia, South America, and North America. In addition, Hart has recently produced an album called *The Other Side of This,* featuring the percussion of the Brazilian spiritual healer Airto.

Furthermore, British artists, including Sting and Peter Gabriel, have for many years made enduring contributions to world beat. (The latter founded a record label (WOMAD) specializing in multicultural music.)

The entire catalogue of music performance artist Laurie Anderson forms a massive assault on and postmodern interpretation of American multicultural – and multimedia – relations. Whether heard or seen, her early stage shows (*United States I-V*) and the currently touring *Nerve Bible* (1995) creates deep introspection as well as humor and compassion.

Another fascinating arena of music involves artists producing what may be called "soul quests." This is music reflecting cross-cultural ritual and religious or spiritual incantations. Such artists bring ancient and modern musical traditions together. A contemplative and introspective journey is fostered by such artists as Dead Can Dance, Gabrielle Roth and the Mirrors, Loreena McKennitt, Ruth Barrett, Layne Redmond and the Mob of Angels, Barbara Borden, and Sheilah Glove. All use multicultural composition and instrumentation.

Finally, music often placed under the category of New Age also shows a startling scope of cultural synthesis and spiritual journeying.

## Conclusion

This essay not only serves as an open-ended invitation to seek out aesthetic communication as a vital access route for fostering better multicultural understanding, but also asks readers to accept the challenge of a multicultural society by extending themselves to:

*Learn* that issues of cultural diversity are, more and more, being explored in a variety of art forms

*Locate* and attend a performance or view a work that provides insight into the complex nature of American cultural groups

*Recognize* the need to create cross-cultural, interracial expertise on our campuses and in our communities at large

The truly difficult idea, the really challenging—even frightening—underlying message is one of *personal action;* that is, we must turn into concrete behavior the empowering strategies of aesthetic communication—those of immediacy, compassion, humor, and vulnerability. In short, we must *risk emotionally,* admit our fears, seriously commit to being role models for the tenets of multicultural education by practicing the philosophy of equal human worth.

Cultural diversity is a great gift, with the potential for creating community on our campuses, in our cities, and in our nation. But this promise of plurality requires personal commitment and the willingness to face our fears. Through aesthetic communication, a deeper, more heartfelt experience of American cultural diversity becomes possible. It is not easy. It is easily misunderstood. But without multicultural education, the new America will fail its test of freedom.

## Notes

1. *World of Ideas with Bill Moyers: Peter Sellars Interview, Part One,* prod. Public Affairs TV, New York, PBS, KCET, 1989.

2. *World of Ideas with Bill Moyers: Peter Sellars Interview, Part One,* prod. Public Affairs TV, New York, PBS, KCET, 1989.

3. *The MacNeil-Lehrer News Hour,* PBS, KCET, 1992.

4. *World of Ideas with Bill Moyers: Peter Sellars Interview, Part One,* prod. Public Affairs TV, New York, PBS, KCET, 1989.

5. Meyer Weinberg, "Remedying Historical Injustice" Rededication Reception Keynote Address for the Multicultural Center at California State University, Long Beach, September 23, 1992. The text of Professor Weinberg's address was later published in *Multicultural News,* CSULB's ongoing Multicultural Center Newsletter, under the title "Defining Multicultural Education," December, 1992, Vol. 1, No. 2, p. 2.

6. Weinberg.

7. Weinberg.

8. While the media termed the conflict "riots" we at CSULB's MCC used the word *uprising.* The term *riot* implies vagrant violence for its own sake, or reckless criminality, whereas *uprising* refers to a complex set of oppressive conditions that feed and fuel frustrations that may lead to civil disturbances.

9. *People for the American Way, Democracy's Next Generation II: A Study of American Youth on Race* (Washington, D.C.: People for the American Way, 1992), 8.

10. *People for the American Way, Democracy's Next Generation II: A Study of American Youth on Race* (Washington, D.C.: People for the American Way, 1992), 9–10.

11. Arturo Madrid, Missing people and others: Joining together to expand the circle, *Change, 20* (1988), 56.

12. Arturo Madrid, Diversity and its discontents, *Academe, 76* (1990), 18.

13. "Beyond the Melting Pot," *Time,* April 9, 1990, p. 28.

14. Peter Sellars, Beginning to notice what we are, *The University in Your Future* (Long Beach: California State University, Long Beach, 1990), 62–63.

15. Shawn Wong, The importance of a multicultural education, *Multicultural Publishers Exchange: Catalog of Books by and About People of Color* (Madison: MPE, 1992), 38.

16. Max Benavidez, "The City, the Riots, the Creative Response: Not a Pretty Picture," Los Angeles *Times,* September 6, 1992, Calendar: 7.

17. Max Benavidez, 7.

18. Edgar F. Beckham, Cultural Transactions and the Changing Requirements for Educational Quality, 18th Annual Meeting of the Association of American Colleges, New York, January 11, 1992.

19. The Pew Charitable Trusts Annual Report (Philadelphia: The Pew Charitable Trusts, 1990), 21.

20. The Pew Charitable Trust, 21.

21. Gordon Davidson, From the artistic director/producer, *Woman Warrior Playbill* (CTG/Ahmanson at the UCLA James A. Doolittle Theatre, 1995).

22. Ronald Takaki, *Strangers from a Different Shore: A History of Asian Americans* (New York: Penguin, 1992).

23. Arturo Madrid, Diversity and its discontents, *Academe, 76* (1990), 15.

24. Alurista, *Spik in Glyph* (Revista Chicano-Riquera, 1986).

25. Christine E. Sleeter, Introduction: Multicultural education and empowerment. In Christine E. Sleeter (Ed.), *Empowerment Through Multicultural Education* (New York: State University of New York Press, 1991), 6.

26. Henry A. Giroux, Postmodernism as border pedagogy: Redefining the boundaries of race and ethnicity. In *Postmodernism, Feminism, and Cultural Politics* (New York: State University of New York Press, 1991), 222.

27. The Rainbow Voices performance troupe at CSULB was inaugurated in January 1992 and has spread the message of equal human worth to over 50,000 students, faculty, and staff throughout Southern California (as well as out of state).

28. Dorothy Siegel and Clarinda Harriss Raymond, Catalyst: The theatre for change, *American Association of Higher Education Bulletin* (October 1992), 8.

29. Siegel and Raymond.

30. Frederick C. Corey and Kristin B. Valentine, The interpreters theatre, *Annual Report, Interpreters Theatre* (Tempe: Department of Communication, Arizona State University, 1992), 5.

31. Siegel and Raymond, 6.

32. Kay Ellen Capo, Review/Interview: Anna Deavere Smith — "Fires in the Mirror: Crown Heights, Brooklyn and other Identities," *Text and Performance Quarterly, 14* (1994), 57.

33. Capo, 58.

34. Capo, 58.

35. The Los Angeles uprising, in fact, delayed the opening of *Fires in the Mirror* in New York — the immediacy of the Los Angeles conflict created an atmosphere that was too volatile for the original debut date (which was May 1, 1992) to be kept.

36. Quoted on *Playbill* for *Twilight: Los Angeles 1992.*

37. While Asians, even today, are sometimes considered "foreign" to the American scene, works such as this help us to accept the rich legacy of their American citizenship and their contributions to United States history.

38. *World of Ideas with Bill Moyers: Peter Sellars Interview Part One,* prod. Public Affairs TV, New York, PBS, KCET, 1989.

## Concepts and Questions for Chapter 7

1. If you were going to travel abroad, what preparation would you make to ensure the best possible opportunity for effective intercultural communication?

2. What specific suggestions can you make that could improve your ability to interact with other ethnic or racial groups in your community? How would you go about gaining the knowledge and experience needed to improve intercultural communication?

3. What are the six stumbling blocks in intercultural communication discussed by Barna? How can you learn to avoid them?

4. Can you think of any mannerisms or behaviors that a North American business person might exhibit that could be a detriment to successful intercultural communication?

5. Why is it important to locate similarities between cultures as well as differences?

6. What are some basic differences between cultures that value individualism and those that value collectivism?

7. What does Ting-Toomey mean when she talks about "face loss" and "face gain"?

8. Can you think of examples of conflict situations that include both substantive and relational issues?

9. What are some differences between direct and indirect conflict styles?

10. Can you think of intercultural examples of what Spitzberg refers to as "individual, episodic, and relational" systems?

11. Can you think of specific examples of what Spitzberg calls "appropriate and effective" message behavior?

12. What is acculturation? Why is acculturation often a difficult task for immigrants?

13. What does Kim mean by the phrase "ethnic group strength"?

14. What does Kim mean when she writes "Strangers cannot accomplish their adaptive goals alone"?

15. Can you think of any communication behaviors not mentioned by Kim that would help an immigrant with the acculturation process?

16. Do you agree with Sauceda's premise that aesthetics can be an effective means of understanding another culture?

17. Would Sauceda's aesthetics approach to cultural understanding be an apt substitute for the cognitive and affective approaches to cultural training in organizations that dismay Limaye?

18. Can you think of some specific examples of aesthetic experiences that could be used to teach cultural understanding?

# 8

## Ethical Considerations: Prospects for the Future

The goal of this book is to help you understand intercultural communication and to assist you in appreciating the issues and problems inherent in interactions involving people from cultures that are different from your own — whether those cultures be across the street or across the ocean. To this end, we have presented a series of diverse essays that examine a variety of variables operable during intercultural encounters. In previous chapters we have looked at what is already known about intercultural communication. We now shift our emphasis and focus on issues that are much more speculative and harder to pin down. These are the ethical considerations that are part of every intercultural encounter. In short, this chapter examines some of the questions we all must confront as we interact with cultures that are different from our own. This contact raises both ethical and philosophical issues concerning the question of how people from divergent cultures can live together without destroying themselves and the planet. In short, what sort of interpersonal and intercultural ethic must we develop if we are to improve the art and science of intercultural communication?

To set the tone for this final chapter, we begin with an essay by Harlan Cleveland titled "The Limits to Cultural Diversity." Cleveland eloquently alerts us to some of the problems associated with cultural diversity while offering us guidance for the future. The basic problem brought about by increased cultural contact is clear for Cleveland: "Ethnic and religious diversity is creating painful conflicts around the world." Too often these clashes turn one culture against another in ideological disputes. When this happens, according to Cleveland, "culture is being used as an instrument of repression, exclusion, and extinction." Cleveland fears that when people see the chaos created by alien cultures, they "believe that their best haven of certainty and security is a group based on ethnic similarity, common faith, economic interest, or political like-mindedness." Cleveland rejects this "single culture" hypothesis. What he recommends is a counterforce of wider views, global perspectives, and more universal ideas. This universal view, according to Cleveland, rests in a philosophy that has civilization (universal values, ideas, and practices) as the basic core for all humanity. In this analysis, culture represents the "substance and symbols of the community," while civilization is rooted in compromise and built on "cooperation and compassion." With this orientation, people can deal with each other in ways that respect cultural differences while granting essential overarching values. Cleveland's optimism is clearly stated in his conclusion: "For the twenty-first century, the cheerful acknowledgment of differences is the alternative to a planet-wide spread of ethnic cleansing and religious rivalry."

Our next essay, by Young Yun Kim, is based on one of the central themes of this book — the idea that today's interconnected and fast-changing world demands that we all change our assumptions about culture and our individual places within that culture. Recognizing these changes, Kim advances a philosophical orientation that she calls "intercultural personhood." For Kim, intercultural personhood combines the key attributes of Eastern and Western cultural traditions, and she presents a model using these attributes. This model takes into account basic modes of consciousness, cognitive patterns, personal and social values, and communication behavior. The notion of intercultural personhood also leads us into the concept of the multicultural person, as set forth in the next essay.

Our final selection in this chapter, "Peace as an Ethic for Intercultural Communication," by David W. Kale, offers a number of specific challenges for the future. The future is made real by Kale as he presents us with current examples, ranging from our role in the rain forests of Brazil to events taking place in eastern Europe. Kale begins by acknowledging that most people feel uncomfortable addressing cultural beliefs about what is right and wrong. He reminds us that most of these beliefs are at the very foundation of our lives and our culture. In spite of this uneasiness, increased contact with diverse cultures, combined with the problems that can occur when cultures clash, demand that we examine the issues associated with questions of right and wrong. To assist us in that examination, Kale asks that we begin by looking at five interrelated issues directly associated with any evaluation of intercultural ethics: (1) a definition of communication ethics, (2) cultural relativity versus universal ethic, (3) the concept of spirit as a basis for intercultural ethics, (4) peace as the fundamental value in intercultural ethics, and (5) a universal code of ethics in intercultural communication. Kale amplifies the fifth issue by advancing a specific code, which he urges us to follow, predicated on four principles that should guide the actions of ethical communicators: (1) address people of other cultures with the same respect that you would like to receive yourself, (2) seek to describe the world as you perceive it as accurately as possible, (3) encourage people of other cultures to express themselves in their uniqueness, and (4) strive for identification with people of other cultures.

It might be well to view Kale's contribution and all the other selections in this chapter as only a sampling of the many issues that confront those involved in intercultural communication. The field is relatively new and the challenges are so varied that it is impossible to accurately predict future directions. Our intent in this chapter, therefore, is simply to introduce you to a few of the concepts that await further discussion as we move into the twenty-first century.

One final note: Much of what we offer in this chapter is subjective and, to some, might even appear naive. Neither we nor the authors of the articles apologize for maintaining that in intercultural contacts each person should aim for the ideal. What we introduce here are some suggestions for developing new ways of perceiving oneself and others. In so doing, we can all help make this complex and shrinking planet a more habitable and peaceful place for its more than five and one-half billion residents.

# The Limits to Cultural Diversity

## HARLAN CLEVELAND

I'm engaged just now in an effort to think through the most intellectually interesting, and morally disturbing, issue in my long experience of trying to think hard about hard subjects. I call it The Limits of Cultural Diversity. If that seems obscure, wait a moment.

After the multiple revolutions of 1989, it began to look as if three ideas we have thought were Good Things would be getting in each other's way, which is not a Good Thing. What I have called the "triple dilemma," or "trilemma," is the mutually damaging collision of individual human rights, cultural human diversity, and global human opportunities. Today the damage from that collision is suddenly all around us.

In 1994, in the middle of Africa, ethnicity took over as an exclusive value, resulting in mass murder by machete. In ex-Yugoslavia (and too many other places), gunpowder and rape accomplish the same purpose: trampling on human rights and erasing human futures.

Even on the Internet, where individuals can now join global groups that are not defined by place-names or cordoned off by gender or ethnicity, people are shouting at each other in flaming, capital-letters rhetoric.

Look hard at your home town, at the nearest inner city; scan the world by radio, TV, or newspapers and magazines. What's happened is all too clear: Just when individual human rights have achieved superstar status in political philosophy, just when can-do information technologies promise

From *The Futurist,* March – April, 1995, pp. 23 - 26. Reprinted by permission of the World Future Society. Harlan Cleveland is president of the World Academy of Art and Science.

what the U.N. Charter calls "better in larger freedom," culture and dive a big, ugly boulder in the road calle

"If we cannot end now our differ we can help make the world safe fo was the key sentence in the most in of John F. Kennedy's presidency: his commencement address at American University on June 10, 1963. That speech led directly (among other things) to the first nuclear test ban treaty.

For most of the years since then, we were mesmerized by the threat of strategic nuclear war. But now a big nuclear war has become the least likely eventuality among the major threats to human civilization. And that brings us face to face with the puzzle identified in Kennedy's speech: how to make diversity safe.

But is "cultural diversity" really the new Satan in our firmament? Or does it just seem so because "culture" is being used — as *Kultur* has been used in other times and places — as an instrument of repression, exclusion, and extinction?

## An Excess of Cultural Identity

In today's disordered world, the collision of cultures with global trends is in evidence everywhere. Ethnic nations, fragmented faiths, transnational business, and professional groups find both their inward loyalties and their international contacts leading them to question the political structures by which the world is still, if tenuously, organized. The results are sometimes symbolic caricatures ("In Rome, can a Moslem minaret be built taller than St. Peter's dome?") and sometimes broken mosaics like the human tragedy in what used to be Yugoslavia.

More people moved in 1994 than ever before in world history, driven by fear of guns or desire for more butter and more freedom. (This was true even before a couple of million Rwandans left their homes in terror — and some were floated out of the country as cadavers.) This more-mobile world multiplies the incentives for individuals to develop "multiple personalities," to become "collages" of identities, with plural loyalties to overlapping groups. Many millions of people believe that their best en of certainty and security is a group based on ethnic similarity, common faith, economic interest, or political like-mindedness.

Societies based on fear of outsiders tend toward "totalitarian" governance. Fear pushes the culture beyond normal limits on individuals' behavior. "To say that you're ready to *die* for cultural identity," said one of my colleagues at a workshop of the World Academy of Art and Science in Romania last year, "means that you're also ready to *kill* for cultural identity." Said another: "The ultimate consequence of what's called 'cultural identity' is Hutus and Tutsis murdering each other."

The fear that drives people to cleave to their primordial loyalties makes it harder for them to learn to be tolerant of others who may be guided by different faiths and loyalties. But isolating oneself by clinging to one's tribe is far from a stable condition; these days, the tribe itself is highly unstable. Differences in birth rates and pressures to move will continue to mix populations together. So ethnic purity isn't going to happen, even by forcible "cleansing."

Besides, cultures keep redefining themselves by mixing with other cultures, getting to know people who look, act, and believe differently. In today's more-open electronic world, cultures also expose themselves to new faiths and fashions, new lifestyles, workways, technologies, clothing, and cuisines.

The early stage of every realization of "cultural identity," every assertion of a newfound "right" of differences, *does* create a distinct group marked by ethnic aspect ("black is beautiful"), gender ("women's lib"), religion ("chosen people"), or status as a political minority. But when members of a group insisting on the group's uniqueness do succeed in establishing their own personal right to be different, something very important happens: They begin to be treated *individually* as equals and tend to integrate with more inclusive communities.

Traditions of separateness and discrimination are often persistent, but they are never permanent and immutable. The recent history of South Africa bears witness.

Before the fighting in Yugoslavia, the most-tolerant people in that part of the world were seen by their close neighbors to be the Serbs, Croats, and Moslems living together in Bosnia and Herzegovina, with the city of Sarajevo as a special haven of mutual tolerance.

The problem does not seem to be culture itself, but cultural overenthusiasm. Cultural loyalties, says one European, have the makings of a runaway nuclear reaction. Without the moderating influence of civil society — acting like fuel rods in a nuclear reactor — the explosive potential gets out of hand. What's needed is the counterforce of wider views, global perspectives, and more-universal ideas.

Post-communist societies, says a resident of one of them, have experienced a loss of equilibrium, a culture shock from the clash of traditional cultures, nostalgia for the stability of Soviet culture, and many new influences from outside. What's needed, he thinks, is cultural richness without cultural dominance, but with the moderating effect of intercultural respect.

## Culture and Civilization

We have inherited a fuzzy vocabulary that sometimes treats *culture* as a synonym for *civilization*. At a World Academy workshop, my colleagues and I experimented with an alternative construct.

In this construct, *civilization* is what's universal — values, ideas, and practices that are in general currency everywhere, either because they are viewed as objectively "true" or because they are accepted pragmatically as useful in the existing circumstances. These accepted "truths" offer the promise of weaving together a *civitas* of universal laws and rules, becoming the basis for a global civil society.

What is sometimes called "management culture" appears to be achieving this kind of universal acceptance, hence becoming part of global "civilization." But nobody has to be in charge of practices that are generally accepted. For instance, the international exchange of money — a miracle of information technologies — is remarkably efficient, daily moving more than a trillion dollars' worth of money among countries. Yet, no one is in charge of the system that makes it happen. Recently, the puny efforts of governments to control monetary swings by buying and selling currencies have only demonstrated governments' incapacity to control them.

If civilization is what's universal, *culture* is the substance and symbols of the community. Culture meets the basic human need for a sense of belonging, for participating in the prides and fears that are shared with an in-group.

Both culture and civilization are subject to continuous change. In our time, the most-pervasive changes seem to be brought about by the spread of knowledge, the fallout of information science and information technologies.

Civil society consists of many structures and networks, cutting across cultural fault lines, brought into being by their ability to help people communicate. They are not very dependent on public authority for their charters or their funding, increasingly taking on functions that used to be considered the responsibility of national governments.

Many of these "nongovernments" — such as those concerned, with business and finance, scientific inquiry, the status of women, population policy, and the global environmental commons — have become effective users of modern information technologies. In consequence, they are providing more and more of the policy initiative both inside countries and in world affairs.

Civilization is rooted in compromise — between the idea of a democratic state and a strong state, between a free-market economy and a caring economy, between "open" and "closed" processes, between horizontal and vertical relationships, between active and passive citizenship. The required solvent for civilization is *respect for differences*. Or, as one of my World Academy colleagues puts it, we need to learn *how to be different together*.

Civilization will be built by cooperation and compassion, in a social climate in which people in differing groups can deal with each other in ways that respect their cultural differences. "Wholeness incorporating diversity" is philosopher John W. Gardner's succinct formulation. The slogan on U.S. currency is even shorter, perhaps because it's in Latin: *E pluribus unum* ("from many, one").

## Lessons from American Experience

We Americans have learned, in our short but intensive 200-plus years of history as a nation, a first lesson about diversity: that it cannot be governed by drowning it in "integration."

I came face to face with this truth when, just a quarter century ago, I became president of the University of Hawaii. Everyone who lives in Hawaii, or even visits there, is impressed by its residents' comparative tolerance toward each other. On closer inspection, paradise seems based on paradox: Everybody's a minority. The tolerance is not in spite of the diversity but because of it.

It is not through the disappearance of ethnic distinctions that the people of Hawaii achieved a level of racial peace that has few parallels around our discriminatory globe. Quite the contrary. The glory is that Hawaii's main ethnic groups managed to establish the right to be separate. The group separateness in turn helped establish the rights of individuals in each group to equality with individuals of different racial aspect, different ethnic origin, different cultural heritage.

Hawaii's experience is not so foreign to the transatlantic migrations of the various more-or-less-white Caucasians. On arrival in New York (passing that inscription on the Statue of Liberty, "Send these, the homeless, tempest-tost, to me"), the European immigrants did not melt into the open arms of the white Anglo-Saxon Protestants who preceded them. The reverse was true. The new arrivals stayed close to their own kind, shared religion and language and humor and discriminatory treatment with their soul brothers and sisters, and gravitated at first into occupations that did not too seriously threaten the earlier arrivals.

The waves of new Americans learned to tolerate each other — *first* as groups, only thereafter as individuals. Rubbing up against each other in an urbanizing America, they discovered not just the old Christian lesson that all men are brothers, but the hard, new, multicultural lesson that all brothers are different. Equality is not the product of similarity; it is the cheerful acknowledgment of difference.

What's so special about our experience is the assumption that people of many kinds and colors can together govern themselves *without* deciding in advance which kinds of people (male or female, black, brown, yellow, red, white, or any mix of these) may hold any particular public office in the pantheon of political power.

For the twenty-first century, this "cheerful acknowledgement of difference" is the alternative to a planet wide spread of ethnic cleansing and religious rivalry. The challenge is great, for ethnic cleansing and religious rivalry are traditions as contemporary as Bosnia and Rwanda in the 1990s and as ancient as the Assyrians who, as Byron wrote, "came down like a wolf on the fold" but says the biblical Book of Kings, were prevented by sword-wielding angels from taking Jerusalem.

In too many countries there is still a basic if often unspoken assumption that one kind of people is anointed to be in general charge. Try to imagine a Turkish chancellor of Germany, an Algerian president of France, a Pakistani prime minister of Britain, a Christian president of Egypt, an Arab prime minister of Israel, a Jewish president of Syria, a Tibetan ruler in Beijing, anyone but a Japanese in power in Tokyo.

Yet in the United States during the twentieth century, we have already elected an Irish Catholic as president, chosen several Jewish Supreme Court justices, and racially integrated the armed forces right up to chairman of the Joint Chiefs of Staff. We have not yet adjusted, as voters in India, Britain, and Turkey have done, to having a woman atop the American political heap. But early in the twenty-first century, that too will come. And during that same new century, which will begin with "minorities" as one in every three Americans, there is every prospect that an African American, a Latin American, and an Asian American will be elected president of the United States.

I wouldn't dream of arguing that we Americans have found the Holy Grail of cultural diversity when in fact we're still searching for it. We have to think hard about our growing pluralism. It's useful, I believe, to dissect in the open our thinking about it, to see whether the lessons we are trying to learn might stimulate some useful thinking elsewhere. We do not yet quite know how to create "wholeness incorporating diversity," but we owe it to the world, as well as to ourselves, to keep trying.

# Intercultural Personhood: An Integration of Eastern and Western Perspectives

YOUNG YUN KIM

We live in a time of clashing identities. As the tightly knit communication web has brought all cultures closer than ever before, rigid adherence to the culture of our youth is no longer feasible. Cultural identity in its "pure" form has become more a nostalgic concept than a reality. As Toffler (1980) noted, we find ourselves "[facing] a quantum leap forward. [We face] the deepest social upheaval and creative restructuring of all time. Without clearly recognizing it, we are engaged in building a remarkable new civilization from the ground up" (p. 44). Yet the very idea of cultural identity, coupled with rising nationalism and xenophobic sentiments, looms over much of today's fractious world landscape. Can the desire for some form of collective uniqueness be satisfied without resulting in divisions and conflicts among groups? Can individuals who are committed to one identity render support and confidence to other groups while upholding the communal values and responsibilities that transcend allegiance to their own group?

This essay addresses these issues by proposing the concept of "intercultural personhood" — a way of life in which individuals develop an identity and a definition of self that integrates, rather than separates, humanity. Intercultural personhood projects a kind of human development that is open to growth — growth beyond the perimeters of one's own cultural upbringing.[1] In making a case for the viability of intercultural personhood, we will first survey some of the core elements in the two seemingly incompatible cultural traditions of the East and the West. We will focus on the cultural apriority or "root ideas" that define the respective philosophical perspectives. An argument will be made, built on this comparative analysis, that certain aspects of these two traditions, often considered unbridgeably incompatible, are profoundly complementary and that such complementary elements can be creatively integrated in a ground-level consideration of human conditions. We will then examine how the process of building an intercultural personhood is actually played out in the lives of people whose life experiences span both cultural worlds.

The present discussion of intercultural personhood owes much to the writings of a number of prominent thinkers of this century who have explored ideologies that are larger than national and cultural interests and that embrace all humanity. One such work is Northrop's *The Meeting of East and West* (1966/1946), in which an "international cultural ideal" is presented as a way to provide intellectual and emotional foundations for what he envisioned as "partial world sovereignty." Inspiration has also been drawn from the work of Thompson (1973), who explored the idea of "planetary culture" in which Eastern mysticism is integrated with Western science and rationalism. The primary sources for the present analysis of the Eastern and the Western cultural traditions include Nakamura's *Ways of Thought of Eastern People* (1964), Campbell's *The Power of Myth* (1988), Gulick's *The East and the West* (1963), Oliver's *Communication and Culture in Ancient India and China* (1971), Capra's *The Tao of Physics* (1975), and Hall's *Beyond Culture* (1976) and *The Dance of Life* (1983).

## Eastern and Western Cultural Traditions

Traditional cultures throughout Asian countries, including India, Tibet, Japan, China, Korea, and Southeast Asia, have been profoundly influenced by such religious and philosophical systems as Buddhism, Hinduism, Taoism, and Zen. On the other hand, the Western nations have mainly followed the Greek and the Judeo-Christian traditions. Of course, any attempt to present the cultural assumptions of these two broadly categorized civilizations inevitably sacrifices specific details and the uniqueness of variations within each tradition. No two individuals or groups hold identical beliefs and manifest uniform behaviors, and whatever characterizations we make about one culture or cultural group must be thought of as variable rather than rigidly structured. Nevertheless, there are several key elements that distinguish each perspective clearly from the other. To specify these factors is also to identify the points of connection that tie different nations together to constitute either the Eastern or the Western cultural world.

## Universe and Nature

A fundamental way in which culture shapes human existence is through explicit and implicit teachings about our relationship to the universe and the human and nonhuman realms of the world. Traditional Eastern and Western perspectives diverge significantly with respect to basic premises about these relationships. As Needham (1951) observed in his article "Human Laws and the Laws of Nature in China and the West," people in the West have conceived the universe as having been initially created and, since then, externally controlled by a divine power. As such, the Western world view is characteristically dualistic, materialistic, and lifeless. The Judeo-Christian religious tradition sets "God" apart from this reality; having created it and set it into motion, God is then viewed as apart from "His" creation. The fundamental material of the universe is conceived to be essentially nonliving matter, or elementary particles of matter, that interact with one another in a predictable fashion. It is as though the universe is an inanimate machine wherein humankind occupies a unique and elevated position among the sparse life-forms that exist. Assuming a relatively barren universe, it seems only rational that humans should make use of the lifeless material universe (and the "lesser" life-forms of nature) on behalf of the most intensely living — humankind itself.

On the other hand, the Eastern world view is profoundly holistic, dynamic, and inwardly spiritual. From the Eastern perspective, the entirety of the universe is a vast, multidimensional, living organism consisting of many interdependent parts and forces. The universe is conscious and engaged in a continuous dance of creation: The cosmic pattern is viewed as self-contained and self-organizing. It unfolds itself because of its own inner necessity and not because it is "ordered" by any external volitional power. Whatever exists in the universe is a manifestation of a divine life force. Beneath the surface appearance of things, an "ultimate reality" is continuously creating, sustaining, and infusing our worldly experience. The all-sustaining life force that creates our manifest universe is not apart from humans and their worldly existence. Rather, it is viewed as continuously creating and intimately infusing every aspect of the cosmos — from its most minute details to its grandest features.

The traditional Eastern worldview, then, reveres the common source out of which all things arise. As Campbell (1990) noted, people in the Eastern cultures — whether they are Indians, Japanese, or Tibetans — tend to think that

*the real mystery is in yourself. . . . Finding the divine not only within you, but within all things . . . And what the Orient brings is a realization of the inward way. When you sit in meditation with your hands in your lap, with your head looking down, that means you've gone in and you're coming not just to a soul that is disengaged from God: you're coming to that divine mystery right there in yourself. (p. 89)*

The Eastern perspective further recognizes that everything in this dynamic world is fluid, ever changing, and impermanent. In Hinduism, all static forms are called "maya," that is, existing only as illusory concepts. This idea of the impermanence of all forms is the starting point of Buddhism. Buddhism teaches that "all compounded things are impermanent" and that all suffering in the world arises from our trying to cling to fixed forms — objects, people, or ideas — instead of accepting the world as it moves. This notion of the impermanence

of all forms and the appreciation of the vitality of the universe in the Eastern world view contrasts strongly with the Western emphasis on the visible forms of physical reality and their improvement through social and material/technological progress.

## Knowledge

Because the East and the West have different views of the cosmic pattern, we can expect them to have different approaches to knowledge. In the East, the universe is seen as a harmonious organism; there is a corresponding lack of any dualism in epistemological patterns. The Eastern view emphasizes perceiving and knowing things and events holistically and synthetically rather than analytically. Further, the ultimate purpose of knowledge is to transcend the apparent contrasts and "see" the interconnectedness of all things and the underlying unity among them. When the Eastern mystics tell us that they experience all things and events as manifestations of a basic oneness, they do not mean that they pronounce all things to be equal. Instead, they recognize that all differences and contrasts are relative within an all-encompassing unity while recognizing the individuality of things. The awareness that all opposites are polar and thus unified, is seen as one of the highest aims of knowledge. As Suzuki (1968) writes, "The fundamental idea of Buddhism is to pass beyond the world of opposites, a world built up by intellectual distinctions and emotional defilements, and to realize the spiritual world of non-distinction, which involves achieving an absolute point of view" (p. 18).

Because all opposites are interdependent, their conflict can never result in the total victory of one side but will always be a manifestation of the interplay between the two sides. In the East, therefore, a virtuous person is not one who undertakes the impossible task of striving for the "good" and eliminating the "bad," but rather one who is able to maintain a dynamic balance between the two. Transcending the opposites, one becomes aware of the relativity and polar relationship of all opposites. One realizes that good and bad, pleasure and pain, life and death, winning and losing, light and dark, are not absolute experiences belonging to different categories, but are merely two sides of the same reality — extreme parts of a single continuum. This point has been emphasized most extensively by the Chinese sages in their symbolism of the archetypal poles yin and yang. And that opposites cease to be opposites is the very essence of Tao. To know the Tao, the illustrious way of the universe, is the ultimate purpose of human learning.

This holistic approach to knowledge in the East is pursued by means of "concepts by intuition," a sense of the aesthetic components of things. A concept by intuition is something immediately experienced, apprehended, and contemplated. Northrop (1966/1946) described this way of knowing as the "differentiated aesthetic continuum," within which there is no distinction between subjective and objective. The aesthetic continuum is a single all-embracing continuity. The aesthetic part of the self is also an essential part of the aesthetic object, whether the object is a person or a flower. With respect to immediately apprehended aesthetic nature, the person is identical with the aesthetic object.

In this orientation, Taoism pursues the all-embracing, immediately experienced, emotionally moving aesthetic continuum as it is manifested in the differentiated, sensed aesthetic qualities in nature. Confucianism pursues the all-embracing aesthetic continuum as it is manifested in human nature and is concerned with its moral implications for human society. The Taoist claim is that only if we accept the aesthetic continuum in its all-embracingness as ultimate and irreducible, will we properly understand the meaning of the universe and nature. The Confucian claim is similar: Only if we take the same standpoint, recognizing the all-embracing aesthetic continuum as an ultimate and irreducible part of human nature, will we have compassion for human beings other than ourselves.

The ultimate, irreducible, and undifferentiated aesthetic continuum is the Eastern philosopher's conception of the constituted world. The differentiations within it, such as particular scenes, events, or persons, are not irreducible atomic identities, but merely arise out of the undifferentiated ground-level reality of the aesthetic continuum. Sooner or later, they fade back into it again. They are transitory and impermanent. Thus, when Eastern sages insist that one must become self-less, they assume

that the self consists of two components: One is a differentiated, unique element that distinguishes one person from any other person, whereas the other is the all-embracing, aesthetically immediate, emotionally moving, compassionate, undifferentiated component. The former is temporary and transitory, and the cherishing of it, the desire for its immortality, is a source of suffering and selfishness. The part of the self that is not transitory and immortal is the aesthetic component of the self, and it is identical not merely in all persons but also in all aesthetic objects throughout the universe.

While the East has concentrated its mental processes upon the all-embracing, holistic, intuitive, aesthetic continuum, the Western pursuit of knowledge has been based on a doctrinally formulated dualistic world view. Since, in this view, the world and its various components came into existence through the individual creative acts of a god, the fundamental question is, How can I reach out to the external inanimated world or to other people? In this question, there is a basic dichotomy between the knower and the things to be known. Accompanying this epistemological dualism is the Western emphasis on rationality in the pursuit of knowledge. Since the Greek philosopher Plato "discovered" reason, virtually all subsequent Western thought — the themes, the questions, and the terms — relies on an essential rational basis (Wei, 1980). Even Aristotle, the great hero of all anti-Platonists, was not an exception. Although Aristotle did not propose, as Plato did, a realm of eternal essences that are "really real" to justify the primacy of reason, he was by no means inclined to deny this primacy. This means that, while the East has tended to emphasize the direct experience of oneness via intuitive concepts and contemplation, the West has viewed the faculty of the intellect as the primary instrument of worldly mastery. While Eastern thought tends to result in more or less vague, imprecise statements, consistent with its emphasis on existential flexibility, Western thought emphasizes clear and distinct ideas, categorization, and the linear, analytic logic of syllogism. While the Eastern view expresses its drive for growth in terms of spiritual attainment of oneness with the universe, the Western view expresses its drive for growth in terms of material progress and social change.

## Time

Closely parallel to differences regarding the nature of knowledge are differences in the perception and experience of time between the two cultural traditions. Along with the immediate, undifferentiated experiencing of the here and now, the Eastern time orientation can be portrayed as placid, silent pool within which ripples come and go. Historically, the East has tended to view material existence as cyclical and has often depicted worldly existence using metaphors of movement such as a wheel or an ocean: The "wheel of existence" or the "ocean of waves" appears to be in continual movement but is "not really going anywhere." Although individuals living in the world may experience a rise or fall in their personal fortunes, the lot of the whole is felt to be fundamentally unchanging. As Northrop (1966/1946) noted, "the aesthetic continuum is the great mother of creation, giving birth to the ineffable beauty of the golden yellows on the mountain landscape as the sun drops low in the late afternoon, only a moment later to receive that differentiation back into itself and to put another in its place without any effort" (p. 343).

Because worldly time is not experienced as going anywhere and because in spiritual time there is nowhere to go but the eternity within the now, the future is expected to be virtually the same as the past. Recurrence in both cosmic and psychological realms is very much a part of Eastern thought. Thus, the individual's aim is not to escape from the circular movement into linear and profane time, but to become a part of the eternal through the aesthetic experience of the here and now and the conscious evolution of spirituality to "know" the all-embracing, undifferentiated wholeness. Whereas the East traditionally perceives time as a dynamic wheel with circular movements and the "now" as a reflection of the eternal, the West has represented time either with an arrow or as a moving river that comes out of a distant place and past (which are not here and now) and that goes into an equally distant place and future (which are also not here

and now). In this linear view of time, history has been conceived of as goal-directed and gradually progressing in a certain direction (toward universal salvation and the second coming of Christ or, in secular terms, toward an ideal state such as boundless freedom or a classless society).

Closely corresponding to the preceding comparison of Eastern and Western time orientation is the recent characterization by Hall (1976, 1983) of Asian cultures as "polychronic" and Western cultures as "monochronic" in their respective time orientations. Hall explains that individuals in a polychronic system are less inclined to adhere rigidly to time as a tangible, discrete, and linear entity; instead, they emphasize completion of transactions in the here and now, often carrying out more than one activity simultaneously. In contrast, a monochronic system emphasizes schedules, segmentation, promptness, and standardization of human activities. We might say that the traditional Eastern orientation to time is dependent on the synchronization of human behavior with the rhythms of nature. On the other hand, the Western orientation to time depends on the synchronization of human behavior with the rhythms of the clock or machine.

## Communication

The historical ideologies examined so far have shaped the empirical content of Eastern and Western traditions. The respective Eastern and Western perspectives on the universe, nature, knowledge, and time are reflected in many of the specific activities of individuals as they relate themselves to fellow human beings — how they view "self" and the group and how they use verbal and nonverbal symbols in communication.

First, the view of self and identity cultivated in the Eastern view of reality is that of an individual embedded within an immutable social order. People tend to acquire their sense of identity from an affiliation with, and participation in, a virtually unchanging social order. As has been pointed out in many of the contemporary anthropological studies, the sense of "self" that emerges from this social context is not the strongly differentiated "existential ego" of the West, but a less distinct and relatively unchanging "social ego." Thus, individual members of the family tend to be more willing to surrender their own self-interest for the good of the family. Individuals and families are often expected to subordinate their views to those of the community or the state.

The Eastern tradition also accepts hierarchy in social order. In a hierarchical structure, individuals are viewed as differing in status, although all are considered to be equally essential to the total system and its processes. A natural result of this orientation is the emphasis on authority — the authority of parents over children; of grandparents over their descendants; of the official head of the community, the clan, and the state over all its members. Authoritarianism is an outstanding feature of Eastern life, not only in government, business, and family, but also in education and in beliefs. The more ancient a tradition, the greater its authority. The Eastern view further asserts that who "we" are is not limited to our physical existence. Consciousness is viewed as the bridge between the finite and differentiated (our sense of uniqueness) and the infinite and undifferentiated (the experience of wholeness and eternity). With sufficient training, each person can discover that who "he" or "she" is, is correlated with nature and the "divine." All are one and the same in the sense that the divine, undifferentiated, aesthetic continuum of the universe is manifested in us and in nature. Through this aesthetic connection, we and nature are no other than the Tao, the ultimate reality, the divine life force, Nirvana, God.

Comparatively, the Western view (in which God, nature, and humans are distinctly differentiated) fosters the development of autonomous individuals with strong ego identification. The dualistic world view is manifested in an individual's view of his or her relationship to other persons and to nature. Interpersonal relationships are essentially egalitarian — cooperative arrangements between two equal "partners" in which the personal needs and interests of each part are more or less equally respected, negotiated, or resolved by compromise. While the East emphasizes submission (or conformity) of the individual to the group, the West encourages individuality and individual needs to override the group. If the group no longer serves the individual's needs, it (not the individual) must be changed. The meaning of an interpersonal relationship is decided upon primarily by the functions which each party performs in satisfying the needs of the other. A relationship is regarded as healthy to the extent that it serves the expected function for all parties involved. As extensively documented in anthropology and cross-cultural psychology (for example, Hsu, 1981; Kluckhohn & Strodtbeck, 1960; Triandis, 1995), individualism is the central theme of the Western personality, distinguishing the Western world from the collectivistic non-Western world.

This pragmatic interpersonal orientation of the West can be contrasted with the Eastern tradition, in which group membership is taken as "given," and therefore unchallenged, and in which individuals must conform to the group in case of conflicting interest. Members of the group are encouraged to maintain harmony and minimize competition. Individuality is discouraged, while moderation, modesty, and "bending" of one's ego are praised. In some cases, both individual and group achievement (in a material sense) must be forsaken so as to maintain group harmony. In this milieu, the primary source of interpersonal understanding is the unwritten and often unspoken norms, values, and ritualized mannerisms pertinent to a particular context. Rather than relying heavily on verbalized, logical expressions, the Eastern communicator "grasps" the aesthetic "essence" of the communication dynamic by observing subtleties in nonverbal and circumstantial cues. Intuition, rather than logical reasoning, plays a central role in the understanding of how one talks: how one addresses the other and why, under what circumstances, on what topic, in which of various styles, with what intent, and with what effect.

These implicit communication patterns are reflected in the Eastern fondness for verbal hesitance and ambiguity — out of fear of disturbing or offending others (Cathcart & Cathcart, 1982; Doi, 1982; Kincaid, 1987). Silence is often preferred to eloquent verbalization, even in expressing strong compliments or affection. Easterners are often suspicious of the genuineness of excessive verbal praises or compliments since, in the Eastern view, the truest feelings are intuitively apparent and, therefore, do not need to be, and cannot be, articulated. As a result, the burden of communicating effectively is shared by both the speaker and the listener, who is expected, through attentiveness and good "listening" to "hear" the implicit, contextual messages. In contrast, the Western communicative mode is primarily direct, explicit, and verbal, relying heavily on logical and rational perception, thinking, and articulation. Participants in communication are viewed as distinctly different individuals, and the expression of their individuality has to be made through clear and accurate verbal articulation. Inner feelings are not to be intuitively "grasped" and understood, but to be honestly, clearly, and assertively verbalized and discussed. In this sense, the burden of communicating effectively in the Western mode lies primarily with the speaker.

The preceding characterization of communication patterns in Eastern and Western traditions is largely consistent with observations by other scholars such as Kincaid (1987), Yum (1994), and Hall (1976, 1983). Hall, in particular, has characterized Asian cultures as "high-context," as compared to the "low-context" cultures of the West, based on his ethnographic studies of various cultures. The focal point of Hall's cross-cultural comparison is "contexting" behavior — that is, the act of taking into account information that is either embedded in physical context (which includes nonverbal behaviors) or internalized in the communicator. In this scheme, low-context communication, more prevalent in the West than in the East, is observed when the majority of interpersonal information is expressed via the explicit, verbalized codes.

## Beyond Cultural Differences

As has been pointed out, many of the specific cultural differences that we observe today between Eastern and Western societies hinge upon the respective culture premises about the reality of the universe, nature, time, and communication. Based on an organic, holistic, and cyclic perspective, the East developed an epistemology that emphasized direct, immediate, and aesthetic components in the human experience of the world. The ultimate aim

of human learning was to transcend the immediate, differentiated self and to develop an integrative perception of the undifferentiated universe. In other words, the goal is to be spiritually one with the universe and to find the eternal within the present moment. The present moment, in this view, is a reflection of the eternal, or, alternatively, the eternal resides in the present moment. The Western tradition, in contrast, has been founded on the cosmology of dualism, determinism, and materialism. It engenders an outlook that is rational, analytic, and indirect. History is viewed as a linear progression from the past into the future. The pursuit of knowledge is not so much a pursuit of spiritual enhancement as it is a quest to improve the human condition.

These different world views, in turn, have been reflected in the individual's conception of the self, the other, and the group. While the East has stressed the primacy of the group over the individual, the West has stressed the primacy of the individual over the group. Interpersonally, the East conceptualizes the self as less differentiated from others and more deeply merged in the "group ego," while the West encourages distinct and autonomous individuality. Explicit, clear, and logical verbalization has been the most salient feature in the Western communication system, as compared to the emphasis on implicit, intuitive, and nonverbal messages in the Eastern tradition.

The cultural premises of the East and the West that we have examined are suggestive of the areas of vitality, as well as areas of weakness, characteristic of each civilization. The Western mechanistic and dualistic world view has helped to advance scientific efforts to systematically describe and explain physical phenomena, leading to extremely successful technological advancements. The West has also learned, however, that the mechanistic world view and its corresponding communication patterns may not be adequate for understanding the rich and complex phenomena of human relationships and that this lack of understanding can cause alienation from self and from others. The West has also learned that its dualistic distinction between humanity and nature has brought about alienation from the natural world. The analytical mind of the West has led to modern science and technology, but it has also resulted in knowledge that is compartmentalized, specialized, fragmented, and detached from the fuller totality of reality.

In comparison, the East has not experienced the level of alienation that the West has been experiencing in recent centuries. However, the East has not developed as much science or technology, for its view of the world does not promote material and social development. It has not encouraged the attitudes of civic-mindedness, global activism, humanitarianism, and volunteerism that flourish in the West, nor has it promoted the rights of individuals to assert their views and take public action to improve human conditions, both social and material. Instead of building greater "ego strength," which supports self-determining behaviors, the Eastern view tends to encourage "ego dependency," or passivity, as people conceive of themselves as being more or less locked into an unchanging social order.

It should be stressed at this point that the Western emphasis on logical, theoretical, dualistic, and analytical thinking does not mean that it has been devoid of an intuitive, direct, purely empirical, aesthetic element. Conversely, emphasizing the Western contributions of worldly dynamism and sociomaterial development is not meant to suggest that the East has been devoid of learning in these areas. The differences that have been pointed out do not represent diametric opposition but rather differences in emphasis that are, nonetheless, significant and observable. Clearly, the sophistication of Western contributions to the sociomaterial domain far exceeds that of contributions from the East. However, the aesthetic and holistic view and emphasis on self-mastery of the East has offered a system of life philosophy that profoundly touches upon the depth of human experience vis-à-vis other humans, the natural world, and the universe.

What the preceding considerations suggest is that many Eastern and Western philosophical premises offer views of reality that are not competitive, but complementary. Of course, the cultural values, norms, and institutions of the West cannot, and should not, be substituted for their Eastern counterparts, and vice versa. The West should no more adopt the world view of the East than the East should adopt the world view of the West. What is being advocated here, therefore, is not that one view be exchanged for another (thereby perpetuating the excesses of the other), but that elements of both be integrated when doing so would help enrich the lives of people, wherever they may be. In doing this, our task is to reach for the unity in human experiences and simultaneously to express diversity. A general synthesis of East and West is probably not possible, not is it desirable, because the purpose of evolution is not to create a homogeneous mass but to continuously unfold an ever diverse and yet organic whole. Yet, in the context of the human evolutionary process, knowledge of differing cultural traditions can help each society move toward greater collective self-understanding – especially by revealing "blind spots" that can be illuminated only by adopting a vastly different way of "seeing."

Indeed, increasing realization of limitations in the Western world view has been expressed by many. Using the term "extension transference," for instance, Hall (1976) points out the danger of a common intellectual maneuver in which extensional systems, including language, logic, technology, institutions, and scheduling, are confused with or take the place of the process extended. We observe the tendency in the West to assume that the remedy for problems arising from technology should be sought not in an attempt to rely upon an ideal minimum of technology, but in the development of even more technology. Burke (1974) calls this tendency of extension transference "technologism": "[There] lie the developments whereby 'technologism' confronts its inner contradictions, a whole new realm in which the heights of human rationality, as expressed in industrialism, readily become "solutions" that are but the source of new and aggravated problems" (p. 148).

Self-criticism in the West has also been directed at rigid scientific dogmatism that insists on the discovery of "truth" based on mechanistic, linear causality and "objectivity." In this regard, Thayer (1983) comments:

*What the scientistic mentality attempts to emulate, mainly, is the presumed method of laboratory science.*

*But laboratory science predicts nothing that it does not control or that is not otherwise fully determined. . . . One cannot successfully study relatively open systems with methods that are appropriate only for closed systems. Is it possible that this is the kind of mentality that precludes its own success? (p. 88)*

Similarly, Hall (1976) points out that the Western emphasis on logical conclusions as synonymous with the "truth" denies that part of the human self that integrates. Hall sees that logical thinking represents only a small fraction of our mental capability and that there are many different and legitimate ways of thinking that have tended to be less emphasized in Western cultures (p. 9).

The criticisms raised by these and other critics of so-called "scientific" epistemology do not deny the value of rational, inferential knowledge. Rather, they refer to the error of traditional Western philosophy in regarding concepts that do not adhere to its mode as less valid. They refer to the arrogance and overconfidence of believing that scientific knowledge is the only way to discover "truth," when, in reality, the very process of scientific study requires an immediate, aesthetic experience of the phenomenon under investigation. Without the immediately apprehended component, the theoretical hypotheses proposed could not be tested empirically with respect to their truth or falsity and would lack relevance to the corresponding reality. As Einstein once commented:

*Science is the attempt to make the chaotic diversity of our sense-experience correspond to a logically uniform system of thought. In this system single experiences must be correlated with the theoretic structure in such a way that the resulting coordination is complete and convincing. (Quoted in Northrop, 1966/1946, p. 443)*

In this description of science, Einstein is careful to indicate that the relationship between the theoretically postulated component and the immediately experienced aesthetic component is one of correspondence. Indeed, the wide spectrum of our everyday life activities demands both scientific and aesthetic modes of apprehension: critical analysis as well as perception of wholes; doubt and skepticism as well as unconditional appreciation; abstraction as well as concreteness; perception of the general and regular as well as the individual and unique; the literalism of technical terms as well as the power and richness of poetic language, silence, and art; relationships with casual acquaintances as well as intimate personal engagement. If we limit ourselves to the dominant Western scientific mode of apprehension and if we do not value the Eastern aesthetic mode, we would be making the error of limiting the essential human to only a part of the full span of life activities.

One potential benefit of incorporating the Eastern aesthetic orientation into Western life is a heightened sense of freedom. As discussed earlier, the aesthetic component of human nature is, in part, indeterminate. It is this aesthetic component in us that is the basis of our freedom. We might also transcend clock-bound worldly time to find the "Eternal Now," the "timeless moment" that is embedded within the center of each moment. By withdrawing into the indeterminate, aesthetic component of our nature, away from determinate, transitory circumstances, we could overcome the pressures of everyday events — at least in part — and creatively integrate them into a basis for renewal of our life spirit. The traditional Eastern practice of meditation is designed primarily for the purpose of moving one's consciousness from the determinate to the indeterminate, freer state.

Second, incorporation of the Eastern view could bring the West to a heightened awareness of the vitality of the universe we inhabit. The universe is engaged in a continuous dance of creation at each instant of time. Everything is intensely alive — brimming with a silent, clear energy that creates, sustains, and infuses all that exists. With an expanded perspective on time, we would increase our sensitivity to the rhythms of nature — such as the seasons and the cycles of birth and decay. This holistic world view is one that pacifies us. Because of its all-embracing oneness and unity, the indeterminate aesthetic continuum also tends to make us compassionate and flexible human beings with intuitive sensitivity — not only for other humans, but for all of nature's creatures. In this regard, Maslow (1971) refs to Taoistic receptivity or "let-be" as an important attribute of "self-actualizing" persons:

*We may speak of this respectful attention to the matter-in-paradigm as a kind of courtesy or deference (without intrusion of the controlling will) which is akin to "taking it seriously." This amounts to treating it as an end, something per se, with its own right to be, rather than as a means to some end other than itself; i.e., as a tool for some extrinsic purpose. (p. 68)*

Such aesthetic perception is an instrument of intimate human meeting, a way to bridge the gap between individuals and groups. In dealing with each other aesthetically, we do not subject ourselves to a rigid scheme but do our best in each new situation, listening to the silence as well as the words of the other and experiencing the other person or group as a whole living entity without being biased by our own egocentric and ethnocentric demands. A similar attitude can be developed toward the physical world around us; this will strengthen our determination to achieve maximum ecological integrity.

Each cultural tradition can be viewed as playing a necessary part in the continuing evolution of humanity, out of which another birth, a higher integration of human consciousness, may arise. Indeed, we recognize that a combination of rational and intuitive modes of experiencing life leads to a human life that is most real and most meaningful. We realize that both Eastern and Western cultures have given expression to things that are, in part, true. Thus, the two seemingly incompatible perspectives can be related and reconciled, without contradictions, in an intercultural metaperspective—one that moves us closer to a fuller understanding of truth.

## Emergence of Intercultural Personhood

The task of synthesizing elements of Eastern and Western cultural traditions is undertaken not merely to satisfy an esoteric academic curiosity, but is of keen relevance to the everyday realities of numerous individuals whose life experiences extend beyond their primary cultural world. Through extensive and prolonged experience in interfacing with other cultures, they have embarked on a personal evolution, creating a new culture of their own, fusing diverse cultural elements into a single "personality." As Toffler (1980) noted, they have created a new personal culture that is "oriented to change and growing diversity" and that attempts "to integrate the new view of nature, of evolution and progress, the new, richer conceptions of time and space, and the fusion of reductionism and wholism, with a new causality" (p. 309).

## Identity Transformation

The emergence of intercultural personhood is a direct function of dramatically increasing direct intercultural communication activities—from the personal observations and experiences of diverse people and events through face-to-face encounters to interactions in classrooms where cultural issues are taught, discussed, and debated. In addition to such direct intercultural encounters are pervasive, indirect, technologically assisted interactions via various communication media—books, magazines, letters, faxes, telegrams, television programs, audio- and videotapes, movies, magazines, art museums, electronic mail, and telephone calls.

Communicating across cultural identity boundaries is often full of challenges as it provokes questions about our taken-for-granted cultural premises and habits, as well as about our inevitable "intergroup posturing," the "us-and-them" psychological orientation (Kim, 1991). Yet it is precisely such challenges that offer us openings for new cultural learning, self-awareness, and personal growth (Adler, 1982; Kim, 1988, 1995, in press). The greater the severity of intercultural challenges, the greater the potential for reinvention of an inner self that goes beyond the boundaries of our original cultural conditioning. In this process, our identity is transformed, gradually and imperceptibly, from an "ascribed" or "assigned" identity to an "achieved" or "adopted" identity—an emergent intercultural personhood at a higher level of integration (Grotevant, 1993). Such an identity transformation takes place in a progression of stages. In each stage, some new concepts, attitudes, and behaviors are incorporated into an individual's psychological makeup. As previously unknown life patterns are etched into our nervous systems, they become part of our new psyches.

As noted previously, the evolution of identity from cultural to intercultural is far from smooth or easy. Moments of intense stress can reverse the process at any time, as individuals "regress" toward reidentifying with their origins, having found the alienation and malaise involved in maintaining a new identity to be too much of a strain (De Vos & Suarez-Orozco, 1990). Such strain may take various forms of an "identity crisis" (Erickson, 1968) or be expressed as "cultural marginality" (Stonequist, 1964; Taft, 1977). Yet the stress experience also challenges individuals to accommodate to different cultural practices so as to become more capable of making deliberate and appropriate choices about action as situations demand.

The emerging intercultural personhood, then, is a special kind of mind-set that promises greater fitness in our increasingly intercultural world (Kim, 1995, in press; Kim & Ruben, 1988). It represents a continuous struggle of searching for the authenticity in self and others within and across cultural groups. It is a way of existence that transcends the perimeters of a particular culture and one that is capable of embracing and incorporating seemingly divergent cultural elements into one's own unique world view. The process of becoming intercultural affirms the creative courage and resourcefulness of humans so they can discover new symbols and new patterns of life on which to build a new identity at a higher level of integration. This creative process of identity development speaks to a uniquely human plasticity, "our relative freedom from programmed reflexive patterns . . . the very capacity to use culture to construct our identities" (Slavin & Kriegman, 1992, p. 6). It is the expression of normal, ordinary people in the act of "stretching" themselves out of their habitual perceptual and social categories. In Adler's (1982) words, the development of an intercultural identity places strangers in the position of continually "negotiating ever new formations of reality" (p. 391).

This kind of human development echoes one of the highest aims for humans in the spiritual traditions of the Eastern cultures. Suzuki (1968) writes, "The fundamental idea of Buddhism is to pass be-

yond the world of opposites, a world built up by intellectual distinctions and emotional defilements, and to realize the spiritual world of non-distinction, which involves achieving an absolute point of view" (p. 18). A virtuous person in this philosophical tradition is not one who undertakes the impossible task of striving for the good and eliminating the bad, but rather one who is able to maintain a dynamic balance between good and bad. This Eastern notion of dynamic balance is reflected in the symbolic use by Chinese sages of the archetypal poles of yin and yang. These sages call the unity lying beyond yin and yang the Tao and see it as a process that brings about the interplay of the two poles. Yoshikawa (1988) describes this development as a stage of "double-swing" or "transcendence of binary opposites" (p. 146). With this transcendental understanding, intercultural persons are better able to creatively conciliate and reconciliate seemingly contradictory elements and transform them into complementary, interacting parts of a single whole.

## An Illustration

Indeed, many people have been able to incorporate experiential territories seldom thought possible, attainable, or even desirable. In doing so, they have redrawn the lines of their original cultural identity boundary to accommodate new life patterns; they remind us of the fact that we humans are active, if not always successful, strategists of our own development in a world of competing and overlapping interests. Although few theories or empirical studies have directly examined the phenomenon of identity development, many firsthand accounts are available that bear witness to the reality of intercultural personhood in many individuals' experiences of crossing cultures. Such accounts have appeared in case studies, memoirs, biographical stories, and essays of self-reflection and self-analysis (see, for instance, Ainslie, 1994; Copelman, 1993; Keene, 1994; O'Halloran, 1994) and present vivid insights into the emotional ebb and flow of the progress toward and eventual realization of intercultural transformation.

One example of a personal fusion of Eastern and Western cultural elements can be seen in the canvases of the artist C. Meng. Meng, since leaving

Shanghai in 1986, has earned a master of fine arts degree in the United States and has been teaching at a university in Texas. In response to Meng's recent exhibit in Dallas, an art critic and reporter, C. Mitchell, characterized Meng's painting as masterful expressions of "the contrast between Eastern and Western modes of thought" and noted the unique synthesis of the two sensibilities in Meng's method, which uses both Chinese calligraphy and Western-style abstraction techniques (*The Dallas Morning News*, June 15, 1992, p. C6).

An illustrative case of intercultural synthesis is also offered by Duane Elgin, who was born and raised in the United States as a Christian and studied Buddhism in Tibet and Japan for many years. In his book *Voluntary Simplicity* (1981), Elgin integrates the philosophical ideas of Eastern and Western world views into his concept of "voluntary simplicity." He presents this idea as "global common sense" and as a practical lifestyle that reconciles the willful, rational approach to life of the West and the holistic, spiritual orientation of the East. Examining historical trends, cycles of civilizations, and related ecological concerns, the author proposes voluntary simplicity as a goal for all of humanity. The main issue Elgin addresses is how humans can find ways to remove, as much as possible, the nonessential "clutters" of life. The author suggests, for example, that one own or buy things based only on real need and consider the impact of one's consumption patterns on other people and on the earth. Before purchasing nonessential items, one should ask oneself if these items promote or compromise the quality of one's nonmaterial life. One could also consciously simplify communications by making them clearer, more direct, and more honest, eliminating idle, wasteful, and manipulative speech. One should also respect the value of silence and nonverbal actions.

Perhaps one of the most succinct testimonials to the present conception of identity transformation is offered by Muneo Yoshikawa (1978). Yoshikawa was born in Japan and has been teaching at a university in the United States for many years. Yoshikawa's observation on his psychic development captures the essence of what it means to be an intercultural person:

*I am now able to look at both cultures with objectivity as well as subjectivity; I am able to move in both cultures, back and forth without any apparent conflict. . . . I think that something beyond the sum of each [cultural] identification took place, and that it became something akin to the concept of "synergy" – when one adds 1 and 1, one gets three, or a little more. This something extra is not culture-specific but something unique of its own, probably the emergence of a new attribute or a new self-awareness, born out of an awareness of the relative nature of values and of the universal aspect of human nature. . . . I really am not concerned whether others take me as a Japanese or an [North] American; I can accept myself as I am. I feel I am much freer than ever before, not only in the cognitive domain (perception, thoughts, etc.), but also in the affective (feeling, attitudes, etc.) and behavioral domains. (p. 220)*

From these and other personal case histories emerge a number of common patterns associated with the development of intercultural personhood. Among them is a mind-set that is less ethnocentric and parochial and more open to different perspectives. Such an outlook cultivates a "third-culture" orientation, overcoming the "paradigmatic barrier" (Bennett, 1976) between divergent philosophical perspectives. Development of an intercultural identity and personhood leads to a "cultural relativistic insight" (Roosens, 1989) or "moral inclusiveness" (Opotow, 1990) that is based on an understanding of the profound similarities in human conditions as well as on recognition of the important differences between and among human groups. In becoming intercultural, then, we can rise above the hidden "grips" of our childhood culture and discover that there are many ways to be "good," "true," and "beautiful." In this process, we attain *a wider circle of identification*, approaching the limits of many cultures and, ultimately, of humanity itself. This process is not unlike climbing a mountain. As we reach the mountaintop, we see that all paths below ultimately lead to the same summit and that each path offers unique scenery. Likewise, the process of becoming intercultural leads to an awareness of ourselves as being part of a larger, more inclusive whole and gives us a greater empathic capacity to "step into and imaginatively participate in the other's world view" (Bennett, 1976, p. 49).

Such developments, in turn, endow us with a special kind of *freedom and creativity* – with the ability to make deliberate choices about action in specific situations rather than to have these choices simply be dictated by habitual conventions of thought and action. This psychic evolution presents the potential for achieving what Harris (1979) defined as "optimal communication competence." As we achieve a significant level of intercultural transformation, we are able to make more deliberate and thoughtful choices of action in accordance with specific situational constraints. An optimally competent communicator, according to Harris, has a sophisticated "meta system" for critiquing his/her own managing system and interpersonal system. The very existence of the meta system makes the difference between the optimal level and the other two levels of competence a qualitative one (p. 31).

In the end, it is people like Meng, Elgin, and Yoshikawa who serve as the sustaining core or "cross-links" of our intercultural world. They provide an infrastructure of moral cement that helps hold together the human and planetary community, discouraging excessive identity claims to the exclusion of other identities. They are the ones who can best meet the enormous challenge that confronts us all – that is, "to give not only yourself but your culture to the planetary view" (Campbell, 1990, p. 114).

## Note

1. The term *intercultural personhood* represents other similar terms such as "multicultural man" (Adler, 1982), "universal man," (Tagore, 1961; Walsh, 1973), "international man" (Lutzker, 1960), and "species identity" (Boulding, 1990), as well as "meta-identity" and "transcultural identity."

## References

Adler, P. (1982). "Beyond Cultural Identity: Reflections on Cultural and Mulicultural Man." In L. Samovar and R. Porter (Eds.), *Intercultural Communication: A Reader,* 3d ed., 389–408. Belmont, Calif.: Wadsworth.

Ainslie, R. (1994). Notes on the psychodynamics of acculturation: A Mexican-American experience. *Mind and Human Interaction, 5*(2), 60–67.

Bennett, J. (1976). *The Ecological Transition: Cultural Anthropology and Human Adaptation.* New York: Pergamon Press.

Boulding, E. (1990). *Building a Global Civic Culture.* Syracuse, N.Y.: Syracuse University Press.

Burke, K. (1974). Communication and the human condition. *Communication, 1,* 135–152.

Campbell, J. (1988). *The Power of Myth* (with B. Moyers). New York: Doubleday.

Campbell, J. (1990). *An Open Life* (in conversation with M. Toms). New York: Harper & Row.

Capra, F. (1975). *The Tao of Physics.* Boulder, Colo.: Shambhala.

Cathcart, D., and Cathcart, R. (1982). "Japanese Social Experience and Concept of Groups." In L. Samovar and R. Porter (Eds.), *Intercultural Communication: A Reader,* 3d ed., 120–127. Belmont, Calif.: Wadsworth.

Copelman, D. (1993). The immigrant experience: Margin notes. *Mind and Human Interaction, 4*(2), 76–82.

De Vos, G., and Suarez-Orozco, M. (1990). *Status Inequality: The Self in Culture.* Newbury Park, Calif.: Sage.

Doi, T. (1982). "The Japanese Patterns of Communication and the Concept of Amae." In L. Samovar and R. Porter (Eds.), *Intercultural Communication: A Reader,* 3d ed., 218–222. Belmont, Calif.: Wadsworth.

Elgin, D. (1981). *Voluntary Simplicity.* New York: Bantam.

Erickson, E. (1968). *Identity, Youth, and Crisis.* New York: W. W. Norton.

Grotevant, H. (1993). "The Integrative Nature of Identity: Bridging the Soloists to Sing in the Choir." In J. Kroger (Ed.), *Discussions on Ego Identity,* 121–146. Hillsdale, N.J.: Lawrence Erlbaum.

Gulick, S. (1963). *The East and the West.* Rutland, Vt.: Charles E. Tuttle.

Hall, E. (1976). *Beyond Culture.* Garden City, N.Y.: Anchor.

Hall, E. (1983). *The Dance of Life: The Other Dimension of Time.* Garden City, N.Y.: Anchor.

Harris, L. (1979). *Communication Competence: An Argument for a Systemic View.* Paper presented at the annual meeting of the International Communication Association, Philadelphia, May.

Hsu, F. (1981). *The Challenges of the American Dream.* Belmont, Calif.: Wadsworth.

Keene, D. (1994). *On Familiar Terms: A Journey Across Cultures.* New York: Kodansha International.

Kim, Y. (1988). *Communication and Cross-Cultural Adaptation: An Integrative Theory.* Clevedon, England: Multilingual Matters.

Kim, Y. (1991). "Intercultural Communication Competence." In S. Ting-Toomey and F. Korzenny (Eds.), *Cross-Cultural Interpersonal Communication,* 259–275. Newbury Park, Calif.: Sage.

Kim, Y. (1995). "Cross-Cultural Adaptation: An Integrative Theory." In R. Wiseman (Ed.), *Intercultural Communication Theory,* 170–193. Thousand Oaks, Calif.: Sage.

Kim, Y. (in press). *Becoming Intercultural: An Integrative Theory of Communication and Cross-Cultural Adaptation.* Thousand Oaks, Calif.: Sage.

Kim, Y., and Ruben, B. (1988). "Intercultural Transformation." In Y. Kim and W. Gudykunst (Eds.), *Theories in Intercultural Communication,* 299–321. Newbury Park, Calif.: Sage.

Kincaid, L. (1987). "Communication East and West: Points of Departure." In L. Kincaid (Ed.), *Communication Theory: Eastern and Western Perspectives,* 331–340. San Diego: Academic Press.

Kluckhohn, F., and Strodtbeck, F. (1960). *Variations in Value Orientations.* New York: Row, Peterson.

Lutzker, D. (1960). Internationalism as a predictor of cooperative behavior. *Journal of Conflict Resolution, 4,* 426–430.

Maslow, A. (1971). *The Farther Reaches of Human Nature.* New York: Viking Press.

Nakamura, H. (1964). *Ways of Thought of Eastern Peoples.* Honolulu: University Press of Hawaii.

Needham, J. (1951). Human laws and laws of nature in China and the West. *Journal of the History of Ideas, XII.*

Northrop, F. (1966/1946). *The Meeting of the East and the West.* New York: Collier Books.

O'Halloran, M. (1994). *Pure Heart, Enlightened Mind.* Boston: Charles E. Tuttle.

Oliver, R. (1971). *Communication and Culture in Ancient India and China.* New York: Syracuse University Press.

Opotow, S. (1990). Moral exclusion and inclusion. *Journal of Social Issues, 46*(1), 1–20.

Roosens, E. (1989). *Creating Ethnicity: The Process of Ethnogenesis.* Newbury Park, Calif.: Sage.

Slavin, M., and Kriegman, D. (1992). *The Adaptive Design of the Human Psyche.* New York: Guilford Press.

Stonequist, E. (1964). "The Marginal Man: A Study in Personality and Culture Conflict." In E. Burgess and D. Bogue (Eds.), *Contributions to Urban Sociology,* 327–345. Chicago: University of Chicago Press.

Suzuki, D. (1968). *The Essence of Buddhism.* Kyoto: Hozokan.

Taft, R. (1977). "Coping with Unfamiliar Culture." In N. Warren (Ed.), *Studies in Cross-cultural Psychology.* Vol. 2, 121–153. London: Academic Press.

Tagore, R. (1961). *Toward Universal Man.* New York: Asia Publishing House.

Thayer, L. (1983). On "doing" research and "explaining" things. *Journal of Communication, 33*(3), 80–91.

Thompson, W. (1973). *Passages About Earth: An Exploration of the New Planetary Culture.* New York: Harper & Row.

Toffler, A. (1980). *The Third Wave.* New York: Bantam.

Triandis, H. (1995). *Individualism and Collectivism.* Boulder, Colo.: Westview.

Walsh, J. (1973). *Intercultural Education in the Community of Man.* Honolulu: University Press of Hawaii.

Wei, A. (1980). *Cultural Variations in Perception.* Paper presented at the 6th Annual Third World Conference, Chicago, March.

Yoshikawa, M. (1978). "Some Japanese and American Cultural Characteristics." In M. Prossor (Ed.), *The Cultural Dialogue: An Introduction to Intercultural Communication,* 220–239. Boston: Houghton Mifflin.

Yoshikawa, M. (1988). "Cross-Cultural Adaptation and Perceptual Development." In Y. Kim and W. Gudykunst (Eds.), *Cross-Cultural Adaptation: Current Approaches,* 140–148. Newbury Park, Calif.: Sage.

Yum, J. (1994). "The Impact of Confucianism on Interpersonal Relationships and Communication Patterns in East Asia." In L. Samovar and R. Porter (Eds.), *Intercultural Communication: A Reader,* 7th ed., 75–86. Belmont, Calif.: Wadsworth.

# Peace as an Ethic for Intercultural Communication

## DAVID W. KALE

A Ford Foundation executive with over twenty years experience in overseas travel has been quoted as saying that "most problems in cross-cultural projects come from different ideas about right and wrong" (Howell, 1981, p. 3). This executive's statement refers to two problem areas that have caused a great deal of difficulty in intercultural communication. First, many people have been in the uncomfortable position of doing something completely acceptable in their own country, while unknowingly offending the people of the culture they were visiting. This problem arose when I took a group of university students to Guyana in South America. In that warm climate, our students wore the same shorts they would have worn at home, but the Guyanese were offended by what they considered to be skimpy clothing, particularly when worn by the women. A second problem that arises in intercultural situations results when we try to get the rest of the world to live according to our culture's ideas about right and wrong. Interestingly, we get rather upset when people of another culture tell us how to behave. We like to believe that the way our culture chooses to do things is the right way and we do not appreciate people of other cultures telling us we are wrong.

Both of these problems have a bearing on ethics in intercultural communication. Discussing this topic causes stress to people of all cultures. Bon-

hoeffer suggests this is because we get the feeling that the basic issues of life are being addressed. When that happens, some of our most cherished beliefs may be challenged. When our cultural beliefs about right and wrong are being threatened, we feel the very foundation of our lives may be under attack (Bonhoeffer, 1965, pp. 267 - 268).

While such a discussion may be threatening, it must be undertaken nonetheless. With contact among people of various cultures rapidly on the rise, an increase in the number of conflicts over matters of right and wrong is inevitable. This essay addresses the ethics of intercultural communication by developing the following points: (1) a definition of communication ethics, (2) cultural relativity versus universal ethics, (3) the concept of spirit as a basis for intercultural ethics, (4) peace as the fundamental value in intercultural ethics, and (5) a code of ethics in intercultural communication.

## A Definition of Communication Ethics

Richard Johannesen (1978, pp. 11 - 12) has said that we are dealing with an ethical issue in human communication when

1. People voluntarily choose a communication strategy.
2. The communication strategy is based on a value judgment.
3. The value judgment is about right and wrong in human conduct.
4. The strategy chosen could positively or negatively affect someone else.

It is important to note in this definition that values are the basis for communication ethics. For example, we place a value on the truth and therefore it is unethical to tell a lie to another person. Without this basis in values, we have no ethical system whatsoever.

We face a major problem in our society because some people think they can decide right and wrong for themselves with no regard for what others think. Such a mind-set shows that these people really don't understand ethics at all. If they did they would know that ethics are based on values, and values are determined by culture. Thus, there can be no such thing as a totally individual system of ethics. Such an approach would eventually result in the total destruction of human society (Weaver, 1971, p. 2; Hauerwas, 1983, p. 3).

Within a culture there is a continual dialogue about the things that are the most meaningful and important to the people of that culture. As a result, cultures are continually in a state of change. When cultures change, so do the values that culture holds. Thus, we must acknowledge that there is no fixed order of values that exists within a culture (Brummett, 1981, p. 293). This does not mean, however, that we are free to determine right and wrong for ourselves. It is much more accurate to say that we are shaped by the values of our culture than to say that we shape the values of our culture (Hauerwas, 1983, p. 3).

## Cultural Relativism Versus Universal Ethics

Because the values on which our ethics are built are generated by dialogue within a culture, the question must then be asked whether a person of one culture can question the conduct of a person in another culture. The concept of *cultural relativity* would suggest that the answer to this question is generally "No." Cultural relativity suggests that a culture will develop the values it deems best for the people of that culture. These values are dependent on the context in which the people of that culture go to work, raise their children, and run their societies. As such, those who are from a different context will develop a different set of cultural values and therefore have no basis on which to judge the conduct of people in any culture other than their own.

However, few would be willing to strictly follow the concept of cultural relativity. To do so would suggest that it was all right for Hitler to murder six million innocent people since the German people did nothing to stop it (Jaska and Pritchard, 1988, p. 10). At the same time, however, few are willing to support the idea that people of all cultures must abide by the same code of ethics. We know cultures develop different value systems and thus must have different ethical codes.

Both Brummett (p. 294) and Hauerwas (p. 9) have argued that because values are derived through dialogue, there is nothing wrong with attempting to persuade people of other cultures to accept our values. Before we do that, however, we must be convinced that our values are worthy and not based on limited self-interest. We must also be willing to work for genuine dialogue; too often these discussions tend to be monologues. We are generally far more willing to present the case for our own value system than we are to carefully consider the arguments for those of other cultures.

At the time of this writing, for example, people of many cultures are attempting to get the people of Brazil to stop cutting down their rain forests. As long as these persuasive efforts are based on a genuine concern for the negative effect cutting these trees is having on the global climate, there is nothing unethical about them. We must, however, also be willing to understand what is motivating the Brazilians' behavior and accept some responsibility in helping them to solve the serious economic problems their country is facing.

## Spirit as the Basis for Ethical Universals

To develop the next point, how we are to make ethical decisions in intercultural communication, let me suggest that there is a concept on which we can base a universal code of ethics: the human spirit (Eubanks, 1980, p. 307). In the words of Eliseo Vivas,

*The person deserves unqualified respect because he (or she) is not merely psyche but also spirit, and spirit is, as far as we know, the highest form of being. It is through the human spirit that the world is able to achieve cognizance of its status as creature, to perceive its character as valuable, and through human efforts to fulfill a destiny which it freely accepts. (p. 235)*

It is this human spirit which people of all cultures have in common that serves as a basis of belief that there are some universal values on which we can build a universal code of ethics in intercultural communication.

We have watched dramatic changes take place in the world as people in Eastern Europe and the

Commonwealth of Independent States (the former Soviet Union) have attempted to improve the quality of life for themselves and their offspring. We identify with their efforts because we share a human spirit that is the same regardless of cultural background. It is this spirit that makes us people who *value* in the first place. It is from this spirit that the human derives the ability to make decisions about right and wrong, to decide what makes life worth living, and then make life the best it can possibly be. Therefore, the guiding principle of any universal code of intercultural communication should be to protect the worth and dignity of the human spirit.

## Peace as the Fundamental Human Value

There is a strong temptation for those of us in Western democracies to identify freedom of choice as the fundamental human value. Hauerwas (pp. 9–12) has convincingly argued that freedom of choice is an unachievable goal for human endeavor. He notes that it is not possible for everyone to have freedom of choice. At the time of this writing, some people in Czechoslovakia want to have the country stay together as a whole while others want it to divide into two separate countries, with each being the home of a different ethnic group. It cannot be that both parties will have their choice.

A goal that is possible to achieve, however, is to direct our efforts toward creating a world where people of all cultures are living at peace with one another. This goal consists of three different levels: minimal peace, moderate peace, and optimal peace.

*Minimal peace* is defined as merely the absence of conflict. Two parties in conflict with each other are at minimal peace when they would be involved in violent conflict if they felt free to act out their hostile feelings. Perhaps there are U.N. peacekeeping forces restraining the two sides from fighting. Perhaps both sides know that continual fighting will bring condemnation from the rest of the world community. Whatever the reason, the peace is only superficial.

*Moderate peace* results when two conflicting parties are willing to compromise on the goals they want to achieve. In this case, each party has major concessions it is willing to make to reach agreement, but considerable irritation still exists with the opposing party in the conflict. Each party considers its own goals as worthy and justifiable and any of the other party's goals that conflict with its own are clearly unacceptable.

Moderate peace describes the situation that exists today between Israel and its Arab neighbors. Negotiations are proceeding in Washington between Israel and countries such as Syria, Jordan, and Egypt. The fact that these countries are at least willing to sit down at the same table and negotiate indicates that their relationship has developed beyond that of minimal peace. If those negotiations break off and hostile feelings intensify, they could be back to a relationship of minimal peace in a very short period of time.

*Optimal peace* exists when two parties consider each other's goals as seriously as they do their own. This does not mean that their goals do not ever conflict. The United States and Canada have a relationship that could be considered as optimal peace, yet there is considerable disagreement over the issue of whether acid rain from U.S. factories is destroying Canadian woodlands. Each side pursues its own goals in negotiations, but considers the other party's goals as worthy and deserving of serious consideration.

At the current time the Soviet republics of Armenia and Azerbaijan are locked in a bitter ethnic conflict over a territory within the republic of Azerbaijan that is populated mostly by Armenians. Because the territory is in their republic, the people of Azerbaijan say they should control it; because it is populated largely by Armenians, the Armenians say they should control it. Both groups cannot have freedom of choice in this situation, but they can live in peace if they are willing to submit to reasonable dialogue on their differences.

The concept of peace applies not only to relations between cultures and countries, but to the right of all people to live at peace with themselves and their surroundings. As such it is unethical to communicate with people in a way that does violence to their concept of themselves or to the dignity and worth of their human spirit.

## A Universal Code of Ethics in Intercultural Communication

Before launching into the code itself, a "preamble" should first be presented based on William Howell's suggestion that the first step to being ethical in any culture is the intent to do what one knows is right (1982, p. 6). All societies set out rules of ethical conduct for people to follow based on cultural values. The foundation of ethical behavior is that people intend to do what they know is right. To choose to do something that you know to be wrong is unethical in any culture.

*Principle #1* Ethical communicators address people of other cultures with the same respect that they would like to receive themselves.

It is based on this principle that I find ethnic jokes to be unethical. Some people may argue that ethnic jokes are harmless in that they are "just in fun," but no one wants to be on the receiving end of a joke in which their own culture is demeaned by people of another culture (LaFave and Mannell, 1978). Verbal and psychological abuse can damage the human spirit in the same way that physical abuse does damage to the body. Verbal and psychological violence against another person, or that person's culture, is just as unacceptable as physical violence. People of all cultures are entitled to live at peace with themselves and the cultural heritage which has had a part in shaping them. It is, therefore, unethical to use our verbal and/or nonverbal communication to demean or belittle the cultural identity of others.

*Principle #2* Ethical communicators seek to describe the world as they perceive it as accurately as possible.

While in our culture we might call this telling the truth, what is perceived to be the truth can vary greatly from one culture to another. We know that reality is not something that is objectively the same for people of all cultures. Reality is socially constructed for us by our culture; we live in different perceptual worlds (Kale, 1983, pp. 31-32).

The point of this principle is that ethical communicators do not deliberately set out to deceive or mislead, especially since deception is very damaging to the ability of people of various cultures to trust each other. It is only when people of the world are able to trust one another that we will be able to live in peace. That trust is only possible when the communication that occurs between those cultures is devoid of deliberate attempts to mislead and deceive (Hauerwas, 1983, p. 15; Bok, 1978, pp. 18-33).

*Principle #3* Ethical communicators encourage people of other cultures to express themselves in their uniqueness.

This principle is reflected in Article 19 of the Universal Declaration of Human Rights as adopted by the United Nations. It states:

*Everyone has the right to freedom of opinion and expression; this right includes the freedom to hold opinions without interferences and to seek, receive and impart information and ideas through any media and regardless of frontiers. (Babbili, 9)*

In his book, *I and Thou*, Martin Buber cogently discusses the need for us to allow the uniqueness of the other to emerge if genuine dialogue is to take place. Frequently, we place demands on people of other cultures to adopt our beliefs or values before we accept them as full partners in our dialogue.

Is it the right of the U.S. government to demand that Nicaragua elect a non-communist government before that country is granted full partnership in the intercultural dialogue of this hemisphere? It is certainly possible that the people of that country will elect a communist government, and if they do, they are still entitled to equal status with the other governments of Central America. At the same time, we celebrate the fact that in central Europe people of several countries are finally being allowed to express themselves by throwing off the stranglehold of communist ideology imposed on them by forces outside their culture. Ethical communicators place a high value on the right of cultures to be full partners in the international dialogue, regardless of how popular or unpopular their political ideas may be. It is the height of ethnocentrism, and also unethical, to accord people of another culture equal status in the international arena only if they choose to express themselves in the same way we do.

*Principle #4* Ethical communicators strive for identification with people of other cultures.

Identification is achieved when people share some principles in common, which they can do while still retaining the uniqueness of their cultural identities (Burke, 1969, p. 21). This principle suggests that ethical communicators encourage people of all cultures to understand each other, striving for unity of spirit. They do this by emphasizing the commonalities among cultural beliefs and values, rather than their differences.

At the present time we are, unfortunately, seeing an increasing number of racial incidents occurring on our college and university campuses. Many times these take the form of racist slogans appearing on the walls of campus buildings. The purpose of these actions is often to stir up racial animosity, creating wider divisions among ethnic groups. Such behavior is unethical according to this principle in that it is far more likely to lead to conflict than it is to peace.

## Note

The author wishes to thank Angela Latham-Jones for her critical comments of an earlier version of this essay.

## References

Babbili, A. S. (1983). The Problem of International Discourse: Search for Cultural, Moral and Ethical Imperatives. Paper presented at the convention of the Association for Education in Journalism and Mass Communication, Corvales, Oregon.

Bok, S. (1978). *Lying: Moral Choice in Public and Private Life*. New York: Random House.

Bonhoeffer, D. (1965). *Ethics*. Eberhard Bethge, ed. New York: Macmillan.

Brummett, B. (1981). A defense of ethical relativism as rhetorically grounded. *Western Journal of Speech Communication, 45*(4), 286-298.

Buber, M. (1965). *I and Thou*. New York: Peter Smith.

Burke, K. (1969). *A Rhetoric of Motives*. Berkeley: University of California Press.

Eubanks, R. (1980). Reflections on the moral dimension of communication. *Southern Speech Communication Journal, 45*(3), 240-248.

Hauerwas, S. (1983). *The Peaceable Kingdom*. South Bend, Ind.: University of Notre Dame.

Howell, W. (1981). Ethics of Intercultural Communication. Paper presented at the 67th convention of the Speech Communication Association. Anaheim, California.

Howell, W. (1982). Carrying Ethical Concepts Across Cultural Boundaries. Paper presented at the 68th convention of the Speech Communication Association, Louisville, Kentucky.

Jaska, J., and Pritchard, M. (1988). *Communication Ethics: Methods of Analysis*. Belmont, Calif.: Wadsworth.

Johannesen, R. (1978). *Ethics in Human Communication*. Wayne, N.J.: Avery.

Kale, D. (1983). In defense of two ethical universals in intercultural communication. *Religious Communication Today*. Vol. 6, Sept., 28-33.

LaFave, L., and Mannell, R. (1978). Does ethnic humor serve prejudice? *Journal of Communication*, Summer, 116-124.

Vivas, E. (1963). *The Moral Life and the Ethical Life*. Chicago: Henry Regnery.

Weaver, R. (1971). *Ideas Have Consequences*. Chicago: University of Chicago Press.

## Concepts and Questions for Chapter 8

1. Why does Cleveland believe that "culture and diversity have formed a big, ugly boulder in the road called Future"?

2. Explain what Cleveland means when he writes, "The problem does not seem to be culture itself, but cultural overenthusiasm."

3. Do you agree with Cleveland's argument that "civilization is what's universal, culture is the substance and symbols of the community"?

4. Is Cleveland's view of respect for differences a realistic solution to the problems created by cultural diversity?

5. Explain Cleveland's idea that "equality is not the product of similarity; it is the cheerful acknowledgment of difference."

6. What does Kim mean when she refers to a holistic approach to knowledge in the East, and how does this approach differ from the Western tradition?

7. Explain how Kim views Eastern and Western views of reality as complementary rather than competitive.

8. What does Kim mean by "intercultural personhood"?

9. Do you believe that Kim's approach to "intercultural personhood" is realistic and/or possible?

10. What are the important ethical questions that communicators must ask themselves as they engage in intercultural communication?

11. Do you see a future where people of different cultures come closer together or a future where they become increasingly isolated from each other? Why?

12. Why does Kale believe that ethnocentric behavior is such a serious problem in intercultural communication?

13. Should we persuade people to accept our values if we believe they are not based on self-interest? Can there be persuasion without self-interest?

14. Can you offer an ethical position that goes beyond the ones offered in this chapter?

15. Is it possible in this age of international contact to have a philosophy based on "live and let live"?

# Epilogue

We introduced the topic of intercultural communication by pointing out both its boundaries and its territory. By looking at what intercultural communication is and is not, we were able to establish some guidelines for our investigation. In general terms, we suggested that intercultural communication occurs whenever a message sender is a member of one culture and a message receiver is of another culture. Once this broad definition was presented, we were able to survey some specific refinements. We noted that culture is the sum total of the learned behaviors of a particular group and that these behaviors (attitudes, values, language, artifacts, and so forth) are transmitted from generation to generation. Differences among international, interracial, and cross-cultural communication also were examined.

Following our general introduction to intercultural communication, we focused on the concept of cultural history, a central motif in this book. This concept suggests that to understand the intricacies of intercultural communication one must realize the impact and influence of past experience. Anyone who has observed human interaction will have little trouble accepting the notion that where people come from — their cultural history — is crucial to communication. Your prior experiences, structured by your culture, help to determine what you value, what you see, and how you behave. In short, what your culture has taught you, in both conscious and unconscious ways, will be manifested during intercultural communication. Navajo Indians, for example, believe that the universe is full of dangers and that illness is a price to be paid for disorder and disharmony. These particular views are bound to be reflected in Navajo intercultural interactions. In another example, people from some cultures deem men more important then women. The behavior of these people toward each sex will be influenced by this orientation. One's background even colors what one perceives. Judgment of beauty is an example. In the United States, the slim, statuesque female represents the cultural stereotype of beauty. Yet in many Eastern European countries, a heavier, stockier body reflects the ideal. These examples — and there are countless others — point out that your culture provides the framework for your experiences and values. They, in turn, define your view of the world and dictate how you interact within the world.

Because people share cultural experiences in a symbolic manner, we explored the two most common symbol systems — verbal and nonverbal. Representing ideas and feelings by symbols is a complex and complicated procedure at best. When the dimension of culture is added to the encoding and decoding process, however, the act of sharing internal states becomes even more intricate. To help you understand this act, we sought to demonstrate the relationship between three closely related axioms: (1) language helps shape thoughts and perceptions (Sapir-Whorf hypothesis), (2) diverse cultures have *different* words with *similar* meanings (foreign languages), and (3) cultures can use the same words with vastly different meanings (co-cultural use of vernacular and argot). We noted that the problems of coding systems plague actions as well as words. Even a simple hand motion can convey a host of unrelated meanings and interpretations. The hand gesture used by a hitchhiker in the United States is apt to produce a punch in the nose in Ghana. In short, the symbols used to share cultural experiences may often be subject to confusion and ambiguity.

Because communication takes place within a social context, we next explored how context affects communication and how communication differs according to the context. By considering the issue of cultural diversity, we were able to demonstrate that not only the expected forms and patterns of communication change from context to context, but also the expectations within a particular context change from culture to culture.

Next, we examined ideas and techniques that contribute to successful intercultural communication. We proceeded on the assumption that intercultural communication is, by its very definition and nature, an action and an overt activity. Intercultural communication is, in short, something people do to and with each other. Because of advances in technology, such as improved transportation and communication systems, virtually everyone seems to be communicating with people from other cultures. In addition to increased communication among nations, there is communication among the communities within the boundaries of the United States. Co-cultures such as African Americans, the urban poor, the disabled, women, gays and lesbians, the elderly, youth, Latinos, and Asians want and demand contact and dialogue with the main culture. Consequently, all Americans are engaging in intercultural communication at an accelerating rate.

If this interaction is to be significant, and if intercultural communication is to foster increased understanding and cooperation, then potential problems must be avoided.

Finally, we extended our analysis toward the future, where most intercultural interactions and meetings lie. Although the success of your communication experiences may well depend on your philosophy and attitude toward intercultural communication, it will more importantly be influenced by the beliefs and attitudes you hold about members of other cultures and co-cultures. These attitudes and behaviors are deeply ingrained and influenced by racist and ethnocentric values. By this, we mean that as each person acquires a culture, that person is, in both obvious and subtle ways, being taught a corresponding subjective and normative value system used to evaluate others. Many people are taught that their cultural group, whatever it may be, is superior to all others. This is one of the negative aspects of culture; it can also teach us whom we must grow to hate. Richard Rogers and Oscar Hammerstein II aptly demonstrated this in their 1949 musical *South Pacific*. The lyrics of their song "You've Got to Be Carefully Taught" tell us a great deal about this cultural mechanism for creating hate:

*You've got to be taught to hate and fear . . . you've got to be taught to be afraid of people whose eyes are oddly made and people whose skin is a different shade . . . you've got to be taught before it's too late, before you are six or seven or eight, to hate all the people your relatives hate; you've got to be carefully taught.*

Everyone, therefore, grows up to judge other cultures and co-cultures by his or her own learned standards. We frequently observe this when we hear people make such value expressive statements as "Our way is the right way" or when we hear people refer to members of another culture or co-culture as "them" or as "those people."

The danger of such positions should be self-evident. It is indeed difficult to achieve mutual understanding if one's culture is placed in a central position of priority or worth. How foolish to assume that because one culture prays on Saturday while another worships on Sunday, one is superior to the other. Or take, for example, the cultural values of competition and winning. Because they are important values to North Americans, many assume that all cultures ought to strive to win and to be first. There are numerous cultures, however, where competition and winning are unimportant. On the contrary, cooperation and sharing are valued highly. To be guilty of racism or ethnocentrism is to doom intercultural communication to failure.

Yes, each person is capable of change, but change is not simple. If intercultural exchanges are to be considered worthy of time and energy, each person must begin to realize that such change is possible and begin to accept others as equals.

Intercultural communicative behavior should not only be void of racism and ethnocentrism but also ought to reflect an attitude of mutual respect, trust, and worth. We emphasize that intercultural communication will not be successful if, by actions or words, the communicators act in a superior or condescending manner. Every individual and every culture wants to believe it is as worthy as any other. Actions that manifest the opposite will stifle meaningful interaction.

The changes required are not easy. They require that we all possess a willingness to communicate, have empathy toward foreign and alien cultures, be tolerant of views that differ from our own, and develop a universalistic, relativistic approach to the universe. If we have the resolve to adopt these behaviors and attitudes and the desire to overcome racism and ethnocentrism and feelings of superiority, we can begin to know the feelings of exhilaration that come when we have made contact with someone far removed from our own sphere of experience. Intercultural communication offers the arena for this interpersonal contact. It is our ability to change, to make adjustments in our communication habits, that gives us the potential tools to make that contact successful.

# Index

Acceptance, 149
Accommodation theory, 177-178
Acculturation, 350-351
Acuff, F. L., 309, 312-313
Adaptation. *See* Cross-cultural adaptation
African American communication
  background of, 147
  effectiveness of, 148
  improvement strategies for, 151-153
  intergroup issues in, 149-151
  intragroup issues in, 148-149
  by males, 227-233
  personal space and, 273-274
  underlying assumptions of, 147-148
Age, personal space and, 268-269
Almaney, A. J., 13, 99
al-Otaiba, Mani Said, 99
Alurista, 421-422
Alwan, A. J., 13, 99
Al-Zafer, Mohammed, 100
Amae, 40-41
Ambiguity
  classroom communication and, 355
  tolerance for, 31, 192-193, 252, 316
Americans
  cultural diversity and, 433-434
  individualism of, 78-79, 86-87
  language use by Finns and, 221-226
  managers and business culture of, 297-305
  negotiation styles of, 309-315

speaking rules of, 225-226
use of superlatives by, 223-224
Americans with Disabilities Act (ADA), 155, 156
Andersen, J. F., 247-248
Andersen, P. A., 242, 244, 247-248
Anderson, Janice Walker, 76, 98
Anderson, Laurie, 424
Anxiety, 375-377
Arabic language, 98-99
Arabs
  business conducted by, 310-311, 315
  indirect communication by, 314
  orientation toward discourse in, 98-99
  rhetorical strategies of, 100-106
Argumentation
  Arab orientation toward, 98-99
  negotiation through, 308
Aristotle, 437
*Artha,* 92, 93
Ascription, 40, 41
Assertiveness
  as aspect of conflict management, 401-402
  to improve communication, 151
Athelstan, G., 156
Attitudes, 16
Attribution, 9
Australia, 417-418
Authenticity, 150
Avoidance, in conversation, 151
Avowal, 40, 41

Baldwin, John R., 136, 147
Barker, Roger, 51-52
Barna, LaRay M., 367, 376
Barnlund, Dean C., 3-4, 27
Barthes, Roland, 334
Barton, Richard, 98
Basho, 27
Bateson, G., 217
Beardsley, R., 333
Bedouins, 98
Behavioral residue, 9
Behavioral source, 10
Being orientation, 238
Beliefs
  description of, 16
  similarities in systems of, 31-32
Bellah, R. N., 248
Benedict, Ruth, 35
Bernstein, Basil, 48
*Besprechung,* 300-302
Bigelow, R., 357
Bilingual education, 357-359
Binstock, R. H., 175
Bipolar language, 192
Birren, Faber, 49
Bochner, S., 268
Body language, Japanese use of, 258
Bond, M. H., 249
Borker, Ruth, 167
Bounded cultures, 56
*Brahman,* 91, 92
Braithwaite, Charles A., 136, 154
Braithwaite, Dawn O., 136, 154

Broome, Benjamin J., 76, 116
Brown, R., 208
Buber, Martin, 451
Buddhism, 436, 444
Burke, Kenneth, 101
Business. *See also* Managers;
    Negotiation
  Confucian influence on Asian,
    317 - 327
  in East Asia, 82 - 83
  German and American culture
    and, 297 - 305
  growth in international, 285 - 286,
    307 - 308, 317 - 318
  Japanese view of, 336, 338
  training for international,
    305 - 306
Business cards, Japanese, 260
Butts, H. F., 235
Byrd, M. L., 139
Byrne, David, 424
Byrne, Donn, 31

Campa, A. L., 235
Campbell, J., 436
Canada, 66
Canter, D., 268
Cantril, H., 73
Carbaugh, Donal, 41, 189, 221
Caste system
  in India, 95 - 96, 142
  nondominant groups and,
    142 - 144
Cathcart, Dolores, 288, 329
Cathcart, Robert, 288, 329
Catholicism, 128 - 129
Centered pluralism, 68 - 69
Channels, 11
Chen, Guo-Ming, 287, 317
Children
  communication between
    grandparents and grand-,
    178 - 179
  gender socialization of, 167 - 168
  value placed on, 110
China, 5
Chinese
  folk medicine practices of,
    343 - 344
  risk taking by, 312
  U.S. university instructors vs.
    instructors in, 204 - 205
  use of time by, 315
Chinese immigrants, 210 - 211

Chinese language
  context and, 48, 253
  cultural study of, 209 - 211
Chisolm, I., 349
Chodorow, Nancy, 167
Chronemics. *See* Time
Chung, Jensen, 287, 317, 325
Classroom communication. *See also*
    Education
  acculturation level assessment
    and, 350 - 351
  cognitive styles and, 354 - 356
  cultural diversity and, 349 - 350
  gender issues and, 359 - 360
  language diversity and, 357 - 359
  learning styles and, 351 - 357, 361
  motivation and, 356 - 357
  relational styles and, 352 - 354
  student goals and, 357
Claudi, U., 112, 113
Cleveland, Harlan, 428 - 429, 431
Co-cultures
  background of, 135
  elderly as, 175 - 180
  problems in dealing with, 7
Code switching, 151
Cogdell, R. T., 138, 139
Cognitive styles
  classroom communication and,
    354 - 356
  problem solving and, 196, 197
  types of, 192 - 193
Cohen, R., 394, 396 - 398
Coleman, L. M., 156 - 157
Collectivism
  conflict and, 393, 397, 398, 401,
    402
  description of, 78 - 79, 393
  high-context communication and,
    193, 194
  Japanese concept of, 257, 260
  in Mexican American proverbs,
    236 - 237
  negotiation and, 312
  in various cultures, 248 - 250
Collier, Mary Jane, 4, 36, 42, 55, 60
Communication. *See also*
    Intercultural communication;
    Intracultural communication;
    Nonverbal communication;
    Verbal communication
  aesthetic, 418 - 425
  characteristics of, 11 - 12
  classroom, 349 - 361. *See also*
    Classroom communication

context and, 23 - 24, 185 - 186
direct vs. indirect, 85 - 86, 352
Eastern vs. Western patterns in,
  439 - 440
effective, 148
ethnocentrism and, 15
ethnography of, 208 - 209
formal vs. informal, 352
ingredients of, 10 - 11
link between culture and, 20, 185,
  246
process vs. outcome-oriented, 83
receiver vs. sender centeredness
  in, 86
social perception as aspect of, 15
topic-centered vs. topic-associated,
  353
underlying assumptions of,
  147 - 148
understanding and defining, 8 - 10
Communication patterns
  impact of Confucianism on,
    83 - 86
  roots of, 78
Communication rules, 23 - 24
Communication technology
  barriers removed by, 78
  developments in, 5 - 6, 256
Communicative styles
  mastery of, 35
  similarities in, 32
Community, 420 - 425
Competition
  classroom communication and,
    355
  in Greek culture, 122 - 123
  negotiation as, 309
Condon, E. C., 351
Condon, J. C., 98, 249, 272
Conflict
  cross-cultural interaction styles
    and, 398 - 400
  cultural value assumptions and,
    396
  culture-based views of, 116,
    392 - 395
  description of, 392
  effective management of,
    400 - 403
  Greek culture and interpersonal,
    117 - 118
  implications for research on,
    123 - 124
  ingroup behavior and, 119 - 120
  ingroup-outgroup distinctions
    and, 118 - 119

process violations and, 396–397
in social transactions, 120–123
violations in expectations of,
395–396
Conformity, 409–410
Confrontation, 152
Confucianism
communication patterns and,
83–86
description of, 79–80, 318–319,
436
family system in, 320–321
impact on organizational
communication of,
322–327
interpersonal relationship patterns
and, 80–83, 87, 313
principles of, 319–320
role of education in, 322
role of *Jen* in, 321–322
Confucius, 79, 80, 207, 318–319
Connotative meaning, 185
Conrad, C., 322
Contact cultures, 247
Context
communication and, 23–24
external, 49–50
meaning and, 47–49
nonverbal cues and, 252–254
research in, 51–53
role of, 45–47
Conversation
Greek style of, 121–122
in Ireland, 126, 128–132
in Japan, 261
places for, 130–132
prayer as, 128–129
Core symbols, 41, 59
Crewe, N., 156
Crime, in Japan, 336–337
Cross-cultural adaptation
elements of, 413–414
overview of, 404–405
role of communication in,
406–409
role of environment in, 409–411
role of predisposition in, 411–413
stress as element of, 405–406
Cultural calamity, 14
Cultural cognition, 196–197
Cultural competence, 43
Cultural diversity
appreciation for, 75
classroom communication and,
349–350
problems associated with, 431–434

Cultural identity
affective, cognitive, and behavioral
components of, 42–43
communication competence and,
43–44
from communication perspective,
39–40
creation of, 55
description of, 39, 147
forms of, 42
properties of, 40–42
Cultural norms, 35
Cultural unconscious, 35
Cultural values, 16
Culture
characteristics of, 13–15
civilization and, 432–433
definition of, 12–13, 36–37,
174–175, 208
functions of, 12, 29, 45
high- and low-context, 24, 47–49,
193–194
history of, 108
ingredients of, 13
link between communication and,
20, 185, 246
perception and, 108
types of, 37–39
understanding international,
75–76
Culture shock, 23
Cupach, W. R., 43
Curanderismo, 342

Dance, 423
Davidson, Gordon, 421, 423
Death, 112
Decision-making process
cultural variation in, 314–315
Japanese, 261, 333–335
Decoding, 11
Delany, M., 130
Denotative meaning, 184–185
DePaulo, B. M., 157
*Dharma*, 92–95
Diffusion, 14
Direct communication
indirect vs., 85–86, 352
negotiation and, 313–314
Disabled individuals
communication challenges for,
156–157
cultural communication and,
155–156
cultural groups formed by, 39

experiences of, 154–155
guidelines for communication
with, 162–163
redefinition issues related to,
158–162
research on, 158
Discourse. *See* Conversation
Do, Vinh The, 370
Dodd, J., 357
Dolphin, Carol Zinner, 243, 266
Dossey, L., 341
Double/multiple description,
217–218
Doumanis, M., 123
Dylan, Bob, 5

East Asia. *See also specific countries*
communication perspectives in,
78, 79
dominant culture of, 318–322
growth of business in, 317–318
impact of Confucianism on, 79,
80, 322–326
indirect communication in,
85–86, 352
interpersonal relationship patterns
in, 80–83
linguistic codes in, 83–84
receiver centeredness of
communication in, 86
Economy, globalization of, 6–7
Education. *See also* Classroom
communication
bilingual, 357–359
Confucian emphasis on, 322, 325
gender issues in, 359–360
in Germany, 304
in Japan, 335–336, 356
multicultural, 419–425
in United States, 303
Einstein, Albert, 442
Eisely, Loren, 48–49
Elderly individuals
co-culture of, 175–180
personal space and, 268–269
social status of, 110
stereotyping of, 176–178
Elgin, Duane, 445
Ellison, Ralph, 142
El-Messiri, Abdel-Wahab, 98, 101
Emerson, Ralph Waldo, 73
Empathy, 258
Encoding, 10
Enculturation, 13

English language
  linguistic codes in, 84
  as second language, 189, 214, 215,
    357-361
  as used in Ireland, 126-128
Environment
  cross-cultural adaptation and,
    409-411
  personal space and, 270-272
Ethics
  cultural relativism vs. universal,
    449
  description of communication,
    448
  universal code of, 449-452
Ethnic groups
  adaptation and strength of,
    410-411
  collectivism vs. individualism in,
    248-249
  description of, 38
  paradigms of relations between,
    63-69
Ethnic nationalism, 66
Ethnicity
  adaptation and, 412
  description of, 147
  personal space and, 272-274
  race vs., 55-56
Ethnocentrism
  culture and, 15
  institutionalization of, 8
Ethnographic research, 208-209,
    211-212
European Americans
  intragroup communication in, 148
  study of compliment interactions
    in, 210-211
Expressiveness
  cultural variations in, 247-248
  in intergroup communication,
    149-150
Eye contact
  Japanese use of, 258-259
  as nonverbal communication, 19,
    245

Families, 17
Family values, 238-239
Fanon, Frantz, 142
Fatalism, 237-238
Feedback, 11
Females. See also Gender
  in Japanese society, 258, 331
  as negotiators, 310-311

Field-dependent cognitive style
  classroom communication and,
    354-355
  description of, 192, 193
Field-independent cognitive style
  classroom communication and,
    354-355
  description of, 192, 193
Figians, 194
Finnish linguistic patterns, 221-226
Fitzgerald, F. T., 345
Folb, Edith A., 57, 136, 138
Folk-healing beliefs, 342-344
Fong, Mary, 188, 207, 209
Forston, R., 267
Foster, D. A., 309, 310, 312, 313
Frankel, Charles, 372, 373
Frankenburg, Ruth, 57, 58
Frankl, Viktor, 8
Franklin, M. E., 354
Freud, Sigmund, 34
Friday, Robert A., 287, 297
Friedl, Ernestine, 117, 121
Friendship
  among elderly, 175
  friendliness vs., 224-225

Gabriel, Peter, 424
Gaelic, 126-128
Gage, Nicholas, 117
Galanti, G., 344, 346
Gallagher, Charles A., 58
Gannon, Martin J., 76-77, 125
Gays, 42
Geertz, C., 246
Geist, Patricia, 288, 340
Gender. See also Females; Males
  classroom issues related to,
    359-360
  communication cultures and, 166
  communication styles and,
    168-171
  description of, 165-166
  impact of, 164-165
  of negotiators, 310-311
  nonverbal behavior and, 250-251
  social-symbolic construction of,
    165-166
Gender cultures
  categories of, 38
  effective communication between,
    171-173
  socialization and, 167-168
Genuineness, 152
Geopolitics, 144-145

Germans, 297-305
Gibb, Jack, 376
Gide, André, 365
Global village
  attainment of, 27-28
  events leading to development
    of, 5
Globalism, 66-68
Goal-oriented talk, 215-217
Golden, A. S., 334-335
Gould, R., 337
Grandparents, 178-179
Greece
  approach to conflict in, 117-118
  implications for future research
    on, 123-124
  ingroup behavior in, 119-120
  ingroup-outgroup distinctions in,
    118-119
  interpersonal struggle in,
    120-123
Griffin, C., 194
Grossman, H., 350, 351, 356
Groups. See Ingroup-outgroup
    distinctions
Gudykunst, W., 98, 101, 300

Hall, Edward T., 4, 24, 45, 107-108,
    193, 243, 253, 266-275, 277,
    303, 394, 395, 440-442
Hall, J., 333
Hammerstein, Oscar, 456
Hamod, H. Samuel, 98
Hardiman, Rita, 60, 61
Harrison, Roger, 378
Hart, Mickey, 424
Haskins, J., 235
Hastorf, A. H., 73
Hauerwas, S., 450
Health care
  background of, 340-342
  cultural differences impacting,
    342-346
  cultural sensitivity in, 342,
    346-347
Hecht, Michael L., 136, 147
Heine, B., 112, 113
Hellweg, Susan A., 287, 307
Helms, Janet, 59
Hemisphericity
  educational systems and, 197-198
  learning styles and, 196, 197
Higgins, P. C., 156
High-context communication
  collectivism and, 193, 194
  description of, 47, 253

High-context cultures
  conflict and, 394, 396, 401
  description of, 24, 355
  examples of, 247
  indirect communication of, 314
  nature of, 52
  nonverbal communication and,
    253-254
Hinduism. *See also* India
  aims of human life in, 92-93
  caste system in, 95-96
  description of, 89
  *dharma* in, 92-95
  *karma* in, 91-92
  paths to salvation in, 93-94
  reincarnation in, 91
  spirit of tolerance in, 96-97
  world view of, 89-91
Hobbes, Thomas, 139
Hofstede, Geert, 132, 205, 249-251,
    311, 318
Holden, D., 117, 122, 123
Homosexuals, 42
Hospitality, 129-130
Host receptivity, 409
Howell, William, 451
Hubbell, Lorenzo, 277
Human Relations School, 326
Hymes, D., 208, 212

Identity. *See also* Cultural identity;
    White identity
  communication perspective of,
    54-55
  development of, 60
  power and, 56-57
Idioms
  high- and low-context cultures
    and, 219-220
  method for intercultural
    understanding of, 215-219
  problems in intercultural
    communication created by,
    213-215
Immediacy behavior
  description of, 246-247
  variations in, 247-248
Immigration
  changes in patterns of, 7
  melting pot paradigm and, 64-66
India. *See also* Hinduism
  caste system in, 95-96, 142
  cultural patterns in, 89
  religious tolerance in, 89, 96-97
  world view in, 89-90

Indirect communication
  description of, 85
  in East Asia, 85-86
  learning style and, 352
  negotiation and, 313-314
Individual unconscious, 34
Individualism
  conflict and, 393, 397, 398, 401,
    402
  description of, 78, 79, 392-393
  low-context communication and,
    193, 194
  negotiation and, 312
  social relationships vs., 78-79,
    86-87
  in various cultures, 248-250
Ingroup-outgroup distinctions
  in business relationships, 325, 327
  in East Asian countries, 82, 325
  in Greece, 118-120, 123
Intercultural communication
  changes resulting in increase in,
    1-2
  cultural identity and, 36-44
  definition of, 8
  with disabled individuals,
    155-156. *See also* Disabled
    individuals
  model of, 21-23
  nature of, 2, 20
  study of, 1
  stumbling blocks in, 370-378
Intercultural competence
  description of, 43, 379-380,
    390-391
  episodic system of, 386-389
  factors of, 381
  individual system of, 381,
    383-386
  model of, 380-381
  relational system of, 382,
    389-390
Intercultural personhood
  cultural differences and, 440-443
  description of, 429, 434-435
  Eastern and Western traditions
    and, 435-440
  emergence of, 443-444
  illustration of, 444-446
Intermediaries, 82
Interpersonal equation, 32
Interpersonal relationships
  impact of Confucianism on
    patterns of, 80-83

individualism vs., 78-79, 86-87
  negotiation and, 312-313
Interpersonal understanding, 31
Intracultural communication
  concept of, 138-139
  frame of reference for, 139-141
  geopolitics and, 144-145
  issues in, 148-149
  nondominance and, 141-144
Invention, 14
Ireland
  background of, 125-126
  style of conversation in, 128-132
  use of Gaelic and English in,
    126-128

Jain, Nemi C., 76, 89
Jainism, 87, 97
Janzen, Rod, 4, 63
Japan
  crime in, 336-337
  developments in modern,
    335-336
  historical developments in,
    329-331
  outside influences on, 337-338
  role of education in, 335-336, 356
Japanese
  brain function in, 196-197
  business relationships among,
    324, 325, 336
  cultural context of, 329, 331-332
  cultural themes of, 257-258, 262
  decision making process of, 261,
    333-335
  group concepts of, 333
  indirect communication by, 314
  Maquiladora industry and,
    289-295
  nonverbal communication used
    by, 258-263, 272
  role of "face" to, 85
  use of time by, 260-261,
    294-295, 315
Japanese language, 84
Jaramillo, M. L., 355
*Jen,* 80, 81, 321-322
Jews, 64
Johannesen, Richard, 448
Johnson, M. M., 359
Johnstone, J., 113
Joyce, James, 126-127

Kale, David W., 429-430, 448
*Kama,* 92, 93
Kantrowitz, Nathan, 138
Kaplan, R., 195
*Karma,* 91-92
Keesing, Felix M., 15
Kelly, George, 30
Kenya. *See also* Maasai
   background of, 108
   family planning in, 110
   role of Maasai in, 109
Kim, Young Yun, 98, 101, 300, 368,
      375, 378, 404, 429, 434
Kinesic behavior
   in collectivist cultures, 249
   intercultural variances in, 245
   Japanese, 258
   Maasai, 114
Kingston, Maxine Hong, 423
Kitayama, S., 393
Kleinman, A., 342
Knoll, Jack, 423
Koester, J., 249
Koller, J. M., 91
Korea, 82
Korean language, 84
Kpelles, 194
Krajewski-Jaime, E. R., 343
Krizek, Robert, 56, 59
Kussman, Ellen D., 76, 89

Labels
   description of, 41
   identity and, 59-60
Labov, William, 166
Lai, M. C., 344
Land, Edwin, 49
Language. *See also* Conversation
   description of, 18
   differentiation of codes between,
      83-84
   function of, 112
   as stumbling block to
      communication, 373
Language translation
   in health care settings, 345
   human element in, 45-46
   symbols and, 188
Laughter, 261
Learning styles
   classroom communication and,
      351-352
   cognitive, 354-356

cultural differences in, 191
   German vs. American, 303-304
   hemisphericity and, 196-198
   motivational, 356-357
   relational, 352-354
Lee, D., 120
Lee, Spike, 424
Lee, Wen-Shu, 188, 213
Left-hemisphere skills
   educational systems and, 197-198
   learning styles and, 196, 197
Lesbians, 42
Leung, B., 349
Lewis, Paul, 99
Lieberman, Devorah A., 187-188,
   191
Lieberman, M., 266
Limited English Proficiency (LEP)
   students, 357-358
Linguistic research, 208-209
Listening
   as aspect of conflict management,
      401
   Confucianism and role of,
      321-322
Low-context communication
   conflict and, 394, 396-397
   description of, 47, 253
   individualism and, 193, 194
   nature of, 52
Low-context cultures
   description of, 24, 355
   examples of, 247
Lustig, M. W., 247-249

M theory, 323
Maasai
   background of, 108
   history of, 108-109
   metaphors used by, 112-113
   nonverbal processes used by,
      114-115
   proverbs used by, 113-114
   values of, 110-111
   verbal processes used by, 112
   world view of, 111-112
Madrid, Arturo, 419, 421
Males, 227-233. *See also* Gender
Maltz, Daniel, 167
Managers, 297-305
Maquiladora industry
   description of, 286, 289
   study of, 289-295
March, R. M., 314

Markus, H., 393
Martin, Judith N., 4, 55
Masculine cultures, 250-251
Maslow, A., 442-443
Matsuda, M., 352
Matsumoto, D., 249
Matsumoto, Y., 336
McClelland, D. C., 298-299, 304
McDaniel, Edwin R., 242, 256, 286,
      289
McIntosh, Peggy, 57-58
McKay, Valerie C., 137, 174
McLuhan, Marshall, 5
Mead, Margaret, 35, 300-301, 373
Meaning
   sources of, 29-30
   transmitted through culture, 37
Melting pot
   immigration and, 64-66
   Planet Earth, 66-67
Meng, C., 444-445
Messages
   description of, 10-11
   high- vs. low-context, 45, 47-48
Messek, A. O., 113
Mestenhauser, J., 192
Metaphors, 112-113
Metatalk, 215-217
Mexican Americans
   diversity of, 189
   intragroup communication in, 148
   proverbs of, 236-239
   role of friendship to, 42
Mexicans
   decision-making process of, 315
   Maquiladora industry and,
      289-295
Minimal peace, 450
Miralles, M. A., 344
Mobil Oil Corporation
   advertisement
   conclusions regarding, 105-106
   historical context of, 99-100
   rhetorical strategies of, 100-105
Moderate peace, 450
*Moksha,* 92-94
Monochronic time schedule
   (M-time), 395, 397
Moore, T., 127
Motivation
   in business, 302-303
   classroom communication and,
      356-357
M-time, 395, 397
Multicultural Health Promotion
   Project, 346

Multiculturalism, 418–419
Music, 424

Nakamura, H., 435
Nakane, C., 325, 332
Nakayama, Tom, 56, 59
Nationalism, 66
Nationality
  sharing of, 38
  whiteness and, 57
Native Americans
  learning styles and, 354, 356–357
  problem solving of, 194
Nature
  as aspect of world view, 111
  perspectives on, 435–436
Needham, J., 435
Negative stereotyping, 149, 177. *See also* Stereotyping
Negotiation
  American styles of, 309–310
  decision-making variations and, 314–315
  role of values and cultural knowledge in, 311–314
  selection of individuals for, 310–311
  suggestions for improvements in cross-cultural, 315–316
Nehru, Jawaharlal, 183
Nguyen, L., 352
Nixon, Richard, 28, 29
Nondominant groups
  description of, 141–142
  geopolitics and, 144–145
  nature of, 142–144
Nonverbal communication. *See also specific forms of nonverbal communication*
  codes of, 18–20, 245–246, 257, 258
  context and, 252–254
  gender and, 250–251
  immediacy and expressiveness as, 246–248
  individualism and, 248–250
  learning style and, 352–353
  misinterpretation of, 373–374
  overview of, 241–242
  power distance and, 251–252
  uncertainty and, 252
Nonverbal processes
  description of, 18–20
  of Maasai, 114–115
Normative values, 16

Norms
  cultural identity formed by, 41
  description of, 37
  of Hinduism, 91
  of whites, 59
Northrop, F., 435

O'Brien, Flann, 127
Oculesics. *See* Eye contact
Okabe, R., 398–399
Olfactics
  Japanese use of, 261
  as nonverbal code, 246
Openness, 412
Optimal peace, 450
Orbe, Mark P., 189, 227
Organizational communication, 322–327
Organizations, 38–39
Outgroup members. *See* Ingroup-outgroup distinctions

Painting, 423–424
Paralanguage
  of Japanese, 261
  of Maasai, 114
  as nonverbal code, 246
Particularistic relationships, 80
Patterson, M. L., 247
Peace, 450
Pennebaken, J. W., 247
Perception
  culture and, 108
  description of, 15
  life experiences and, 59
  role of beliefs, values and attitudes on, 16–17
  social, 15–16
Perceptual orientation
  description of, 31, 32
  mastery of, 35
Peres, Shimon, 8
Personal space
  age, sex, and, 268–270
  culture and, 266–268
  ethnicity and, 272–274
  Japanese use of, 259, 260, 294
  Maasai use of, 115
  relationship, environment and, 270–272
  research suggestions on, 274–275
  varying concepts of, 19–20, 245, 294, 295
Personality, 412–413

Persuasion, 98
Peters, J. Y., 351
Phenomenology, 228
*Philotimo,* 119–120
Physical abilities, 39
Physical appearance
  Japanese and, 260
  as nonverbal code, 245
Physical surroundings, 12
Plato, 437
Pluralism, centered, 68–69
Poetry, 99
Polanyi, Michael, 46
Political activity, 175
Polychronic time schedule (P-time), 395, 397
Pomo Native Americans, 194
Porter, Richard E., 5, 108, 138, 142, 357
Positivity, 413
Posture, of Maasai, 114
Power
  dynamics of, 150–151
  identity and, 56–57
  social status and, 140–141
Power distance, 251–252
Prayer, 128–129. *See also* Religion
Preparedness, 411–412
Present-time orientation, 238
Problem solving
  cognitive styles and, 192–193, 196, 197
  culture-based approaches to, 191–192
  hemisphericity and, 197–198
  illustrations of, 194–195
  in mainstream cultures, 195–196
  teaching styles and, 198–204
Professionals, 38
Proverbs
  culture and, 235–236
  Maasai, 113–114
  Mexican American, 236–239
Proxemics. *See* Personal space
P-time, 395, 397

Quran, 99

Race, ethnicity vs., 55–56
Racism
  institutionalization of, 8
  traditional Eurocentric, 63–64
Rainbow voices, 421–422

Reality
  levels of, 90 – 91
  normative dimension of, 91
  ultimate, 90
Reciprocity, 81
Redefinition
  description of, 158
  of disability, 160 – 162
  disabled culture and, 158 – 160
Reeve, Christopher, 155, 160
Reincarnation, 91
Reischauer, Edwin, 28
Relationships, personal space and, 270 – 272
Religion
  as aspect of world view, 111 – 112
  in Ireland, 128 – 129
Residue, behavioral, 9
Responders, 11
Response, 11
Rhodes, R. W., 356
Ribeau, Sidney A., 55, 136, 147
Rigby, P., 115
Right-hemisphere skills
  educational systems and, 197 – 198
  learning styles and, 196, 197
Risk taking, 311 – 312
Rogers, Richard, 456
Rokeach, Milton, 33
Roosevelt, Franklin D., 143
Ruch, William V., 309

Saint-Exupery, Antoine, 207
Sakkaf, Omar, 100
Salvation, Hindu paths to, 93 – 94
Samovar, Larry A., 5, 76, 107, 108, 138, 142, 189, 235, 286 – 289, 307, 357
Sampson, Anthony, 99
Sapir, Edward, 208, 244
Sapir-Whorf hypothesis, 188, 207 – 208
Sarbaugh, L. E., 139
Sato, Premier, 28, 29
Sauceda, James Steven, 368 – 369, 417
Scarf, Maggie, 281
Schmertz, Herbert, 99
Schmitt, Madeline, 267
School, as social organization, 17
Second language. See English language, as second language
Self-esteem, use of space and, 259
Self-orientation, 78

Self-presentation, 151
Sellars, Peter, 418, 420
Sellers, J. M., 236
Selye, H., 377
Sex
  description of, 165
  gender vs., 166
  personal space and, 268 – 270
Sherzer, J., 208 – 209
Shimanoff, S. B., 210
Shuter, R., 270
Sidai, J. O., 113
Silence, 261
Similarities
  assumptions of, 370 – 373
  in communicative styles, 32
  in systems of beliefs, 31 – 32
Simon, Paul, 424
Simpson, O. J., 58 – 59
Singing
  collectivism and, 250
  intercultural studies of, 246
Sitaram, K. S., 138, 139
Skow, Lisa, 76, 107
Smell. See Olfactics
Smile, Japanese use of, 259
Smith, Anna Deavere, 422, 423
SNAP! culture, 230
Social context, 12
Social obligations, 222 – 223
Social organization, 17
Social perceptions, 15 – 16
Social status
  of elderly individuals, 110
  hierarchy of, 140 – 141
  in Japan, 293, 294
  in Mexico, 293, 294
  of negotiators, 310
  nondominant groups and, 142, 143
Space. See Personal space
Spitzberg, Brian H., 43, 367, 379, 380
Stefani, Lisa A., 287, 288, 307, 349
Stereotyping
  of disabled individuals, 157
  of elderly, 176 – 178
  negative, 149
  as stumbling block to communication, 374
Sting, 424
Stockard, J., 359
Stress, 405 – 406
Suerio-Ross, C., 351
Sullivan, H. S., 47

Superlatives, 223 – 224
Suzuki, D., 436, 444
Symbols
  core, 41, 59
  description of, 37
  language as set of, 184
  verbal, 184 – 185

Tai, H. C., 322
Tannen, Deborah, 171
Tanno, Dolores, 60
Tanzania, 108. See also Maasai
Tarrentino, Quentin, 424
Taylor, J., 331 – 333
Teaching styles
  case studies of, 198 – 204
  hemisphericity and, 197 – 198
Terasawa, Y., 338
Thayer, L., 441 – 442
Theater, 422 – 423
Thought patterns
  description of, 18
  in varying cultures, 195, 196
Thurber, James, 1
Time
  conflict and, 394 – 395, 397 – 398
  Eastern vs. Western orientation to, 438
  Japanese use of, 260 – 261, 294 – 295, 315
  Maasai concepts of, 115
  monochronic vs. polychronic, 278 – 283
  negotiation process and, 309, 315
  varying concepts of, 19, 245, 277 – 278
Ting-Toomey, Stella, 368, 392
Tocqueville, Alexis de, 79
Toffler, A., 434
Tolerance
  for ambiguity, 31, 192 – 193, 252, 316, 355
  as aspect of Hinduism, 96 – 97
Touch
  intercultural variances in, 245, 247
  Japanese use of, 259, 260
  as nonverbal communication, 19
  teacher-initiated, 201
  used by Maasai, 114 – 115
Translation. See Language translation
Transportation technology, 5
Triandis, H. C., 117, 118, 120, 121, 193
Trilling, Lionel, 373
Trobriands, 194 – 195

Tseng, S. C., 323
Tzu-lu, 79

Uncertainty, 252
Unconscious
   cultural, 35
   existence of individual, 34
   individual, 34
Understanding, 150
University instructors, 204–205
Ursin, H., 377

Values
   description of, 16, 311
   negotiation and, 311
Verbal communication. *See also*
        Communication
   context and, 185–186
   description of, 17–18
   meaning and, 183–185

Verbal symbols
   connotative, 185
   denotative, 184–185
Vocalics
   description of, 246
   of Japanese, 261
   power distance and, 252

Walker, B. J., 357
Weber, Max, 79
White identity
   core symbols, norms, and labels,
        59–60
   development of, 60–62
   dimensions of, 57
   meaning of, 56
   perceptions and, 58–59
   structural privilege and, 57–58

Whorf, Benjamin Lee, 46, 208
Wilson, S., 59
Wood, Julia T., 137, 164
World view
   description of, 17, 75
   of Hindus, 89–91
   of Maasai, 111–112
*Wu Lun,* 319, 324

*Yoga,* 93–94
Yoshikawa, Muneo, 444
Yousef, F., 98, 249, 272
Yue, K. K., 344
Yum, June Ock, 75–76, 78

Zormeier, Shelly M., 189, 235